THE ROUTLEDGE COMPANION TO IDENTITY AND CONSUMPTION

"Tell me what you eat, I'll tell you who you are," said Anthelme Brillat-Savarin. Today, "You are what you consume" is more apt. Barbara Krueger's ironic twist of Descartes – "I shop therefore I am" – has lost its irony. Such phrases have become commonplace descriptions of our identity in the contemporary world. In our materialistic world it seems as if there is no debate that our consumption behavior is fused with our self-identity – shaping it, changing it and often challenging it.

The Routledge Companion to Identity and Consumption introduces the reader to state-of-the-art research, written by the world's leading scholars, regarding the interplay between identity and consumption. The book addresses the diverse issues regarding the ways identity affects our consumption behavior and vice versa, and in doing so presents a broad perspective on the dynamics of self-identity and consumption.

With chapters discussing the theory, research and practical implications of these dynamics, including the way they change across our life span and their expression within different social, cultural and religious contexts, this book will be a valuable reference source for students and academics from a variety of disciplines.

Ayalla A. Ruvio is Assistant Professor of Marketing at the Fox School of Business at Temple University, USA. Her research focuses on issues such as consumers' self-identity, materialism and consumers' need for uniqueness. Her published work has received extensive media attention worldwide, including the TODAY show, Good Morning America, *Time* magazine, *The New York Times*, *The Atlantic*, CNN, and *The Daily Telegraph*.

Russell W. Belk is Kraft Foods Canada Chair in Marketing at the Schulich School of Business, York University, Canada. He is past President of the International Association of Marketing and Development and is a Fellow, past President and Film Festival co-founder of the Association for Consumer Research. He also co-initiated the Consumer Behavior Odyssey and the Consumer Culture Theory Conference. He has received the Paul D. Converse Award and the Sheth Foundation/*Journal of Consumer Research* Award for Long-Term Contribution to Consumer Research. His research involves the meanings of possessions, collecting, gift-giving, materialism, sharing and global consumer culture.

Routledge Companions in Business, Management and Accounting

Routledge Companions in Business, Management and Accounting are similar to what some publishers call 'handbooks' – i.e. prestige reference works providing an overview of a whole subject area or sub-discipline, and which survey the state of the discipline including emerging and cutting-edge areas. These books provide a comprehensive, up-to-date, definitive work of reference which can be cited as an authoritative source on the subject.

One of the key aspects of the Routledge Companions in Business, Management and Accounting series is their international scope and relevance. Edited by an array of well-regarded scholars, these volumes also benefit from teams of contributors that reflect an international range of perspectives.

Individually, Routledge Companions in Business, Management and Accounting provide an impactful one-stop-shop resource for each theme covered, whilst collectively they represent a comprehensive learning and research resource for researchers, postgraduates and practitioners.

Published titles in this series include:

The Routledge Companion to Fair Value and Financial Reporting
Edited by Peter Walton

The Routledge Companion to Nonprofit Marketing
Edited by Adrian Sargeant and Walter Wymer, Jr

The Routledge Companion to Accounting History
Edited by John Richard Edwards and Stephen P. Walker

The Routledge Companion to Creativity
Edited by Tudor Rickards, Mark A. Runco and Susan Moger

The Routledge Companion to Strategic Human Resource Management
Edited by John Storey, Patrick M. Wright and David Ulrich

The Routledge Companion to International Business Coaching
Edited by Michel Moral and Geoffrey Abbott

The Routledge Companion to Organizational Change
Edited by David M. Boje, Bernard Burnes and John Hassard

The Routledge Companion to Cost Management
Edited by Falconer Mitchell, Hanne Nørreklit and Morten Jakobsen

The Routledge Companion to Digital Consumption
Edited by Russell W. Belk and Rosa Llamas

The Routledge Companion to Identity and Consumption
Edited by Ayalla A. Ruvio and Russell W. Belk

THE ROUTLEDGE COMPANION TO IDENTITY AND CONSUMPTION

Edited by

Ayalla A. Ruvio and Russell W. Belk

Routledge
Taylor & Francis Group
LONDON AND NEW YORK

First published 2013
by Routledge
2 Park Square, Milton Park, Abingdon, Oxon OX14 4RN

Simultaneously published in the USA and Canada
by Routledge
711 Third Avenue, New York, NY 10017

Routledge is an imprint of the Taylor & Francis Group, an informa business

British Library Cataloguing in Publication Data
A catalogue record for this book is available from the British Library

Library of Congress Cataloging in Publication Data
The Routledge companion to identity and consumption / edited by Ayalla Ruvio and Russell W. Belk.
p. cm. – (Routledge companions in business, management, and accounting)
Includes bibliographical references and index.
1. Consumer behavior. 2. Identity (Psychology) 3. Consumption (Economics) I. Ruvio, Ayalla. II. Belk, Russell W.
HF5415.32.R68 2012
658.8'342–dc23
2012021223

ISBN: 978-0-415-78306-4 (hbk)
ISBN: 978-0-203-10533-7 (ebk)

Typeset in Bembo
by Taylor & Francis Books

Printed and Bound in the United States of America
by Edwards Brothers Malloy

CONTENTS

ILLUSTRATIONS

Figures

Tables

Boxes

CONTRIBUTORS

Justin W. Angle is Assistant Professor of Marketing at the School of Business Administration at the University of Montana, USA. His research focuses on identity and implicit social cognition.

Yun Mi Antorini is Assistant Professor at the Department of Language and Business Communications at Aarhus University, Denmark. She has a Master's degree and a PhD from Copenhagen Business School. Prior to the PhD she worked as a Strategic Planner in the advertising industry and as a Senior Director of Global Brand Strategies at the LEGO Group. Her research and teaching focuses on consumer behavior involving topics such as user innovation and brand community.

Søren Askegaard is Professor of Marketing at the University of Southern Denmark, Odense. His research is currently oriented toward globalization processes of consumer culture. He serves as an associate editor of the *Journal of Consumer Research*.

Richard P. Bagozzi is Dwight F. Benton Professor of Behavioral Science in Management, Ross School of Business, and Professor of Clinical, Social and Administrative Sciences, College of Pharmacy, University of Michigan, USA. He conducts basic research in human emotions, social identity, the theory of action, plural subject theory and structural equation models and measurement. His applied research is in consumer behavior, sales force behavior, managerial action, organizational dynamics, health behaviors and multivariate statistics. He earned his PhD at Northwestern University, USA, and has been awarded honorary doctorates from the University of Lausanne, Switzerland, and Antwerp University, Belgium. He has received the O'Dell and Maynard best article awards and has been appointed fellow by the Association for Consumer Research and the Association for Psychological Science. He received the Irwin Distinguished Educator Award, the Churchill Lifetime Achievement Award, the Outstanding Marketing Educator of Award and the Converse Award (twice).

Shalini Bahl is Co-Founder of The Mindfulness Connection and is a researcher and mindfulness consultant interested in studying and creating programs in self-awareness and mindfulness for corporations, academia and healthcare institutions. Her research using dialogical self theory and mindfulness has been published in top marketing journals. She also teaches social media for the

MBA program at the Isenberg School of Business, University of Massachusetts Amherst, USA. themindfulnessconnection.com.

Russell W. Belk is Kraft Foods Canada Chair in Marketing at the Schulich School of Business at York University, Canada. He is past president of the International Association of Marketing and Development, and is a fellow and past president in the Association for Consumer Research. He has received the Paul D. Converse Award, the Sheth Foundation/*Journal of Consumer Research* Award for Long-Term Contribution to Consumer Research, two Fulbright Fellowships, and honorary professorships on four continents. He initiated the Consumer Behavior Odyssey, the Association for Consumer Research Film Festival, and the Consumer Culture Theory Conference. He has over 500 publications, involving the meanings of possessions, collecting, extended self, sharing, materialism, and global consumer culture. His work is often cultural, visual, and interpretive.

Mariam Beruchashvili is Assistant Professor in the Department of Marketing, California State University, Northridge, USA. Her research focuses on social construction of emotion, overweight identity, and consumer goals.

James R. Bettman is Burlington Industries Professor at the Fuqua School of Business at Duke University, USA. His research focuses on constructive preferences, adaptive decision making, emotion, integrating conscious and non-conscious processing and identity. He was co-editor of the *Journal of Consumer Research* and president of the Association for Consumer Research.

Lauren G. Block is Lippert Professor of Marketing at the Zicklin School of Business, Baruch College, City University of New York, USA. Her work is primarily in areas of consumer persuasion, goal achievement, self-control and food well-being.

James E. Burroughs is Professor of Commerce at the McIntire School of Commerce, University of Virginia, USA. His research interests are in the areas of consumer creativity, consumer culture, materialism and transformative consumer research. He has published in the *Journal of Marketing*, *Journal of Public Policy & Marketing*, *Journal of Consumer Research* and the *Journal of Consumer Psychology*, among others. He currently serves as an Associate Editor of the *Journal of Consumer Research* and is on the Editorial Review board of the *Journal of Public Policy & Marketing*.

Marylouise Caldwell is Associate Professor at the University of Sydney, Australia, and has a strong interest in how disadvantaged consumers deal with public health and social policy issues. In this respect, she has published research papers and coproduced two international award-winning films: *Right to Life: Reducing Maternal Death and Morbidity in Pakistan*, and *Walk the Talk: How HIV+ Consumers Become Embodied Health Activists in Botswana.*

Benedetta Cappellini is Lecturer in Marketing at Royal Holloway University of London, UK. Her research interests include food consumption, material culture and market discourses. Her approach to research is ethnographic and interpretive.

Stephanie M. Carpenter is a doctoral student in Marketing at the University of Michigan, Ross School of Business, USA. She holds a BA and MS in Psychology from the University of Oregon. Her research examines decision making across the adult lifespan.

Lan Nguyen Chaplin is Assistant Professor of Marketing at Villanova University, USA. Her research focuses on children's consumer behavior and has published in top marketing journals such as *Journal of Consumer Research* and *Journal of Consumer Psychology*.

Nicole Verrochi Coleman is Assistant Professor of Marketing at the Katz Graduate School of Business at the University of Pittsburgh, USA. Her research examines how consumers' regulation and experience of emotions and social identities impacts persuasion and consumption.

Paul M. Connell is Senior Lecturer at Cass Business School at City University, London, UK. His current research interests include self and identity, attitudes and persuasion, and child/adolescent consumers. His research has appeared in *Journal of Consumer Psychology* and *Journal of Public Policy & Marketing*.

Keisha M. Cutright is Assistant Professor of Marketing at The Wharton School, University of Pennsylvania, USA. She studies the role of personal belief systems in individuals' consumption decisions. In particular, her research focuses on how consumption and certain belief systems provide interchangeable sources of order, certainty and value.

Darren W. Dahl is Fred H. Siller Professor in Applied Marketing Research at the Sauder School of Business, University of British Columbia, Canada. His research interests focus on creativity, social influence, new product adoption and emotions. His published work has appeared in a number of top-tier journals.

Deirdre Duffy is Programme Director of Fashion Buying at the Dublin Institute of Technology (DIT), Ireland. She lectures in the areas of consumer behavior and marketing. Research interests include consumer culture, masculinity studies, Gaelic sport and fashion consumption.

Lea Dunn is a PhD student in Marketing at the Sauder School of Business, University of British Columbia, Canada. Her research interests focus on social media applications, social influence and complaining behavior.

Jennifer Edson Escalas is Associate Professor at the Owen Graduate School of Management at Vanderbilt University, USA. She obtained her PhD from Duke University, USA, and her research examines consumers' self-brand connections and narrative processing of advertising. Jennifer is also an associate editor for the *Journal of Consumer Research*.

Gavan J. Fitzsimons is the R. David Thomas Professor of Marketing and Psychology and the F.M. Kirby Research Fellow at the Fuqua School of Business, Duke University, USA. He focuses on understanding the psychology of consumers, particularly as it relates to understanding how consumers may be influenced without their conscious knowledge or awareness by marketers and marketing researchers.

Mark R. Forehand is Pigott Family Professor of Marketing at the Foster School of Business, University of Washington, USA. His research on the implicit self-concept has appeared in the *Journal of Consumer Research*, *Journal of Marketing Research* and *Journal of Consumer Psychology*.

Adam D. Galinsky is Kaplan Professor of Ethics and Decision in Management at the Kellogg School of Management, Northwestern University, USA. He studies how hierarchy shapes thinking and behavior, counterfactual thinking and reasoning, and auction and negotiation behavior.

Güliz Ger is Professor of Marketing at Bilkent University, Turkey. Her research interests involve the sociocultural and global dimensions of consumption and markets, particularly in transitional contexts. Her current work includes consumption among immigrants, cultural products, and historical foundations of consumption.

Hillary Greer is an undergraduate student in the College of Media at the University of Illinois at Urbana-Champaign, USA. Passionate about new media and literacy, she hopes to pursue a career in library science and youth literature.

Elizabeth C. Hirschman is Professor of Marketing at Rutgers Business School, USA. She has published over 200 journal articles and academic papers in marketing, consumer behavior, sociology, psychology, and semiotics. She is past president of the Association for Consumer Research and American Marketing Association-Academic Division. She was named one of the Most Cited Researchers in Economics and Business by the Institute for Scientific Information in 2009.

Margaret K. Hogg is Fulgoni Chair of Consumer Behaviour and Marketing in the Marketing Department at Lancaster University Management School, UK. Her work has appeared in the *Journal of Advertising*, *Journal of Business Research*, *Journal of Services Marketing*, and *European Journal of Marketing*. She edited six volumes on consumer behavior in the Sage Major Works series.

Junko Kimura is Professor of Marketing at the Faculty of Business Administration, Hosei University, Japan. Her research focuses on Consumer Culture Theory, mother-daughter relationships and identity formulation. She will be a Visiting Professor at University of Venezia, Italy from September 2012 for two years, researching Italian family consumption.

Shinobu Kitayama is Robert B. Zajonc Collegiate Professor of Psychology, and Director of both the Culture and Cognition Program and the Center for Culture, Mind, and the Brain, at the University of Michigan, USA. Currently he is the editor-in-chief of *Personality and Social Psychology Bulletin*. His research revolves around cultural influences in cognition, emotion, and motivation.

Dannie Kjeldgaard is Professor of Marketing at the University of Southern Denmark. Dannie is Head of the Consumption Studies research group at the Department of Marketing at the University of Southern Denmark as well as Director for the International Master of Science program in Marketing, Globalization and Communication, and a member of the study board for the PhD School at the Faculty of Social Sciences. Before joining academia he worked for four years in a London-based PR consultancy. Published in numerous international journals and books, Dannie's work analyzes change processes of market-based globalization in domains such as place branding, branding, media and identity construction, global consumer segments, body culture, ethnicity and qualitative methodology. His research is published in the *Journal of Consumer Research*, *Journal of Consumer Behaviour*, *Consumption, Markets and Culture*, *Marketing Theory*, *Journal of Macromarketing* and in several anthologies.

Ingeborg Astrid Kleppe is Associate Professor at the Norwegian School of Economics, Norway. Her research focuses on the voice of consumers in social media and public health marketing. She has also extensive experience in politics, public health activism and working with monitoring poverty in sub-Saharan Africa for the World Bank.

John L. Lastovicka is Professor of Marketing at Arizona State University's W.P. Carey School of Business, USA. Earlier in his career, his quantitative research on consumer trait and state motivations appeared in the *Journal of the American Statistical Association*, *Psychometrika* and *Journal of Marketing Research*. His more recent research relies more on qualitative data and examines the emotive meanings that consumers project onto their possessions; this more recent work appears in the *Journal of Consumer Research* and *Consumption, Markets & Culture*.

Jaehoon Lee is Assistant Professor of Marketing at the University of Houston–Clear Lake, USA. He earned his PhD in Marketing from the University of Texas at San Antonio, USA. His current research interests focus on the effects of self-threats on consumer behavior.

Rosa Llamas is Associate Professor of Marketing at the University of León, Spain. Her research interests include the meaning of luxury, transformative consumer research and global consumer culture. Her work is visual, qualitative and interpretive, and has been conducted in different cultural settings.

Katherine E. Loveland is Assistant Professor of Marketing at HEC Montréal, Canada. She can be reached at: kate.loveland@hec.ca.

Naomi Mandel is State Farm Professor of Marketing at the W.P. Carey School of Business, Arizona State University, USA. She can be reached at: Naomi.Mandel@asu.edu.

Daniele Mathras is a doctoral student of Marketing at the W.P. Carey School of Business, Arizona State University, USA. She can be reached at: daniele.mathras@asu.edu.

Risto Moisio is Assistant Professor in the Marketing Department, California State University, Long Beach, USA. His research interests include pro-social behavior, gender identity, and consumer well-being.

Alokparna (Sonia) Basu Monga is Associate Professor of Marketing at the University of South Carolina, USA. Her research interests are at the intersection of branding and consumer behavior. Her publications have appeared in the *Journal of Marketing Research*, *Journal of Consumer Research*, *Journal of Consumer Psychology*, and *Journal of Marketing*, among others.

Andrea Morales is Associate Professor of Marketing and Dean's Council of 100 Distinguished Scholar at the W.P. Carey School of Business at Arizona State University, USA. Her research interests include the role of emotions in a consumer context, and consumer responses to retail and service environments.

James A. Mourey is a doctoral candidate in Marketing at the Ross School of Business at the University of Michigan, USA. Studying culture, consumption and non-conscious processing, Jim explores the implicit influence contextual cues exert in decision making, particularly when consumers are conflicted.

Albert M. Muñiz, Jr is Associate Professor of Marketing at DePaul University, USA. His research interests are in the sociological aspects of consumer behavior and branding, including consumer-generated content and online communities. His teaching interests include consumer behavior, consumer culture and brand management. He received his BS, MS and PhD from the University of Illinois, Urbana-Champaign, USA.

Jacob Östberg is Associate Professor at the Center for Fashion Studies and Deputy Director at the Center for Consumer Culture Theory, Stockholm University, Sweden. He holds a PhD in marketing from Lund University, Sweden.

Jiyoung Park is a postdoctoral fellow in the department of psychology at the University of Michigan. She received her PhD at the same university in 2012. Her research interests include cultural neuroscience, with a focus on health and well-being.

Elizabeth Parsons is Reader in Marketing at Keele Management School, UK. Her research interests include consumer culture, critical marketing, and gender, identity and subjectivity at work. Recent co-edited texts include *Branded Lives: The Production and Consumption of Meaning at Work* (Edward Elgar), and *Key Concepts in Critical Management Studies* (Sage). She is co-editor of the journal *Marketing Theory*.

Linda L. Price is Department Head and Professor of Marketing, Soldwedel Family Faculty Fellow in the Eller College of Management, University of Arizona, USA. Much of Linda's recent theory and research addresses collective, family and global identity and is published in *Journal of Marketing*, *Journal of Consumer Research*, and *International Journal of Research in Marketing*.

Americus Reed, II is Whitney M. Young Jr Associate Professor of Marketing at the Wharton School, University of Pennsylvania, USA. He is an identity theorist whose work has won honorable mention in the 2005 Robert Ferber Award and the 2009 Best Paper Award, both given out by the *Journal of Consumer Research*.

Aric Rindfleisch is Head of the Business Administration Department and John M. Jones Professor of Marketing at the University of Illinois at Urbana-Champaign, USA, and Research Professor at Korea University, South Korea. He has also served as a faculty member at the University of Wisconsin-Madison, University of Arizona, Tilburg University and Korea University. His research focuses on understanding interorganizational relationships, consumption values and new product development.

Deborah Roedder John is Professor and Curtis L. Carlson Chair in Marketing at the University of Minnesota, USA. She is recognized as one of the most prolific authors in top marketing journals and publishes in the areas of branding and children's consumer behavior.

Derek D. Rucker is Associate Professor of Marketing at the Kellogg School of Management, Northwestern University, USA. His research focuses broadly on attitudes, persuasion and cognition with emphasis on how psychological mindsets tied to confidence, power and emotion affect consumer behavior.

Ayalla A. Ruvio is Assistant Professor of Marketing at the Fox School of Business at Temple University, USA. She is a consumer behavior researcher who focuses on issues such as consumers' self-identity, possessions as an extension of the self, materialism, consumers' need for uniqueness, and cross-cultural consumer behavior. Her published work has received extensive media attention worldwide, including the TODAY show, Good Morning America, *Time* magazine, *The New York Times*, *The Atlantic*, CNN, and *The Daily Telegraph*.

Mototaka Sakashita is Associate Professor of Marketing at the Graduate School of Business Administration, Keio University, Japan. He studies how brand knowledge, brand commitment and interpersonal relationships affect consumer behavior such as information acquisition, repeat purchase and self-development.

Adriana Samper is Assistant Professor of Marketing at the W.P. Carey School of Business, Arizona State University, USA. She studies the influence of self and identity goals on consumption decisions and subsequent behaviors. She focuses particularly on the effect of product choice and use on self-concept and behavior.

Özlem Sandıkcı is Assistant Professor of Marketing at Bilkent University, Turkey. Her research focuses on the relationship between globalization, marketing and culture. She is currently working on branding stories and histories in emerging markets and the Islamic marketplace.

Shay Sayre is Professor Emeritus at California State University, Fullerton, USA, where she taught entertainment marketing. The author of five textbooks, she has published in academic journals and has presented at conferences internationally. She divides her time between Montana and California.

Hope Jensen Schau is Associate Professor of Marketing and Gary M. Munsinger Chair in Entrepreneurship and Innovation at the Eller College of Management, University of Arizona, USA. She has published in the *Journal of Consumer Research*, *Journal of Marketing*, *Journal of Retailing* and *Journal of Advertising*.

L.J. Shrum is Professor and Department Chair of Marketing at the University of Texas at San Antonio, USA. He has published widely on the effects of media consumption on values, attitudes and beliefs, and he is author of the edited volume *The Psychology of Entertainment Media* (2nd edn, Routledge). His current research focuses on the self and consumer behavior. He is past president of the Society for Consumer Psychology.

Nancy J. Sirianni is Assistant Professor of Marketing at the Neeley School of Business, Texas Christian University, USA. Her research focuses on creating meaningful connections with consumers through the emotional design of brands, products and services. Her research appears in the *Journal of Consumer Research*.

Ian Skurnik is Associate Professor at the David Eccles School of Business, University of Utah, USA, and he received his PhD in social psychology from Princeton University, USA. He previously taught at the Darden Graduate School of Business, University of Virginia, and the Rotman School of Management, University of Toronto, Canada.

Vanitha Swaminathan is Associate Professor of Business Administration and Robert W. Murphy Faculty Fellow in Marketing at the University of Pittsburgh, USA. Her research interests are in branding strategy and consumer-brand relationships. Her publications have appeared in the *Journal of Marketing Research*, *Journal of Consumer Research* and *Journal of Marketing*, among others.

Siok Kuan Tambyah is Senior Lecturer at the NUS Business School, National University of Singapore. She has published articles in a number of journals, including, the *Journal of Marketing Theory and Practice* and the *Journal of Consumer Research*. She can be reached at: biztsk @nus.edu.sg.

Craig J. Thompson is Churchill Professor of Marketing at the University of Wisconsin-Madison, USA. He has published articles in the *Journal of Consumer Research*, *Journal of Public Policy & Marketing* and *Advances in Consumer Research*. He serves on the editorial boards of the *Journal of Consumer Research* and the *Journal of Public Policy & Marketing*. He can be reached at: cthompson@bus.wisc.edu.

Patrick T. Vargas is Associate Professor of Advertising at the University of Illinois at Urbana-Champaign, USA. He earned his PhD in Social Psychology, with a minor in Quantitative Psychology, at the Ohio State University, USA. He likes his cat and his dog; however, they do not like each other.

Kathleen D. Vohs is McKnight Presidential Fellow, Land O' Lakes Professor of Excellence in Marketing and Professor of Marketing at the Carlson School of Management, University of Minnesota, USA.

Katherine White is Associate Professor at the Sauder School of Business, University of British Columbia, Canada. Her research interests focus on social influence and sustainability marketing. Her published work has appeared in top-tier journals including *Journal of Marketing*, *Journal of Consumer Research* and *Journal of Marketing Research*.

Keith Wilcox is Assistant Professor of Marketing at the Columbia Business School at Columbia University, USA. His research focuses on consumer self-control in health and money decisions. He has published articles in the *Journal of Marketing Research* and the *Journal of Consumer Research*. Additionally, his research has been featured in *The New York Times*, *Time* magazine and *Psychology Today*.

Patti Williams is Ira A. Lipman Associate Professor of Marketing at the Wharton School at the University of Pennsylvania, USA. Her research focuses on the role of discrete and mixed emotions on consumption.

Phoebe W.S. Wong is Lecturer in Marketing and Public Relations at PolyU SPEED, Hong Kong. Her work has appeared in the *Journal of Marketing Management* and in proceedings from US and European meetings of the Association for Consumer Research (ACR), Consumer Culture Theory Conference (CCT), and Society for Consumer Psychology (SCP) at the American Psychiatric Association (APA) Annual Convention.

David B. Wooten is the Alfred L. Edwards Associate Professor of Marketing at the Ross School of Business at the University of Michigan, USA. He uses qualitative and experimental research methods to examine consumer culture, self-presentation and social influences on consumption.

Eugenia Wu is Assistant Professor of Marketing at the Johnson Graduate School of Management at Cornell University, USA. Her research focuses on how emotions and motivations affect the way consumers behave, with a particular interest in mixed emotions and disgust.

Carolyn Yoon is Associate Professor at the Stephen M. Ross School of Business, University of Michigan, USA. Her research interests are focused on understanding psychological and neural mechanisms underlying judgment and decision processes across the lifespan in sociocultural and consumer-related contexts.

Yinlong Zhang is Associate Professor of Marketing at the University of Texas at San Antonio, USA. He earned his PhD in Marketing from the University of Pittsburgh, USA. His research has been published in the *Journal of Consumer Research*, *Journal of Marketing Research* and *Personality and Social Psychology Bulletin* on the topics of consumer psychology of cross-cultural and globalization issues.

PREFACE

As Bagozzi (Chapter 26) observes, "It might be said that consumption begins and ends with the self." The interface of identity and consumption involves a vitally important set of concerns that cut across a range of fields. In the consumer cultures in which we live, consumption – for better or worse – is an increasingly dominant part of our identity. At a verbal level, we are still prone to position people by their answer to the question, "What do you do?" However, at a non-verbal level we are more apt to form an impression of people based on their home, vehicle, clothing, and visible accessories. There are several reasons why we rely so strongly on these visible consumption cues. One is that it would be rude to ask or tell someone about our wealth or taste in possessions, but it is perfectly acceptable to encode and decode silent messages about self through such consumption. Furthermore, with social media sites, blogs, and photo and video sharing sites, the rules have changed and we can create personal profiles that show photos of our consumption activities (e.g. vacation travel, restaurant meals), list our preferences (e.g. favorite music and films), and celebrate our identifications (e.g. favorite celebrities, sports teams) – all things that are not as readily disclosed in brief, face-to-face encounters (Belk, Chapter 8; Cutright, Samper, and Fitzsimons, Chapter 9). Thus a second reason why we rely on consumption cues to try to learn about someone is that there are many more such cues than ever before, while a third reason is that in largely anonymous urban societies, most of those we encounter in everyday life are strangers whose implicit and explicit visible status claims are unlikely to be contradicted by a priori knowledge of their occupations, families, friends, neighbors, or cultural capital. For those whom we encounter casually each day, they are what they consume. There is even evidence that we continue to associate people with their possessions after they have died (Hirschman, Ruvio, and Belk, Chapter 32).

It is not just other people who define us through our consumption. We are also apt to present ourselves to ourselves in this manner. Cutright, Samper, and Fitzsimons (Chapter 9) explore the impact of our possessions in altering our self-identities. The extent of this effect is not limited to our tangible possessions. As Blascovich and Bailenson summarize, even our digital avatars in online worlds affect our sense of self:

> dozens of psychological experiments have shown that people change after spending even small amounts of time wearing an avatar. A taller avatar increases

> people's confidence, and this boost persists later in the physical world. Similarly, a more attractive avatar makes people act warm and social, an older avatar raises people's concern about saving money, and a physically fit avatar makes people exercise more.
>
> *(Blascovich and Bailenson 2011: 4)*

As Lastovicka and Sirianni (Chapter 5) suggest, in such cases the boundary between person and beloved object may be a blurry one. However, as Wooten and Mourey (Chapter 17) observe with regard to cool, there is also a certain performance that a consumption object may demand of us if we are to successfully incorporate the object into our self-presentation. Furthermore, performance of identity is not just a matter of displaying durable goods and brands, but may also involve consumable goods such as foods and the rituals through which they are consumed (Tambyah and Thompson, Chapter 33).

The self is not necessarily the singular entity that we commonly take it to be (Bahl, Chapter 3). We may well harbor different selves that are called to the fore by differing situations and cues (Angle, Forehand, and Reed, Chapter 38). Nor is the individualistic construal of self something that is universal across times and cultures (see Kitayama and Park (Chapter 1), Wong and Hogg (Chapter 10), Shrum and Zhang (Chapter 24), Askegaard and Kjeldgaard (Chapter 34), and Swaminathan and Monga (Chapter 36). Within a given culture and era there are also individual variations in construing self in an independent and personal manner versus an interdependent and collective manner (see Kitayama and Park, Chapter 1, and Bagozzi, Chapter 26). However, in broad historical perspective the self as well as the role of consumption in constituting or representing this self has not always been quite the same as we observe today. As Katayama and Park (Chapter 1) and Nisbett (2003) observe, there are beginnings of the individual self in ancient Greece and China. In the contemporary era in the West, the Reformation and Enlightenment are credited with supporting the emergence of the autonomous self (Wiley 1994). In order for purchased consumer goods to become expressive signs of the self (either individual or collective), profound changes had to take place economically, politically, psychologically, and sociologically (Stearns 2001; Trentmann 2006). In Europe, Campbell (1987) characterizes these changes as culminating in the rise of contemporary imaginative hedonism. Other changes had to occur as well, such as a transformation of malicious envy into a more benign form of envy in which emulation rather than hatred resulted from seeing others' "superior" consumption (Belk 2011).

The result is the "sovereign individual" (Abercrombie *et al.* 1986) who sees him- or herself as free, self-motivated, responsible, and able to make choices about how to earn and spend money as well as where and how to live. Such perceived consumer freedom doesn't necessarily mean that consumers are able to self-actualize through consumption and achieve their ideal selves. Even if this is not a mythical goal (Askegaard and Kjeldgaard, Chapter 34), there are the constraints due to monetary resources (Vohs, Chapter 25), our bodies (Beruchashvili and Moisio, Chapter 6; Ruvio and Belk, Chapter 14; Sayre, Chapter 16; Rindfleisch and Burroughs, Chapter 20), our age (Yoon, Skurnik, and Carpenter, Chapter 19; Mathras, Loveland and Mandel, Chapter 39), our health (Kleppe and Caldwell, Chapter 15), our will power (Block and Wilcox, Chapter 23; Shrum and Zhang, Chapter 24), and our culture (Morales and Wu, Chapter 7; Sandıkcı and Ger, Chapter 11; Kleppe and Caldwell, Chapter 15; Ruvio and Belk, Chapter 14). When the conflicts between our ideal selves and our experienced selves are great, we may experience powerful negative emotions (Coleman and Williams, Chapter 4; Kleppe and Caldwell, Chapter 15; Bagozzi, Chapter 26; Askegaard and Kjeldgaard, Chapter 34; Escalas and Bettman, Chapter 37). Emotions may also be positive, of course, especially in cases where the object is not seen as a means to self-completion as much as an end in itself (Lastovicka and Sirianni, Chapter 5). Control may be a factor in the emotions experienced, in that some stigmas impose themselves on us (e.g. Ruvio and Belk, Chapter 14; Kleppe and Caldwell, Chapter 15), while in other cases we choose stigmatizing consumption practices (Sandıkcı and Ger, Chapter 11). When there is a threat to our self-esteem or existential security we also experience negative emotions and often try to compensate through consumption (Rindfleisch and Burroughs, Chapter 20; Rucker and Galinsky, Chapter 21; Lee and Shrum, Chapter 22; Angle, Forehand, and Reed, Chapter 38). We may also attempt to dissociate ourselves from undesired consumption identities (Dunn, White, and Dahl, Chapter 28) or attempt more radical consumption exercises like cosmetic surgery (Sayre, Chapter 16). We may also deploy consumer goods strategically as part of a therapeutic effort to heal and complete the self (Askegaard and Kjeldgaard, Chapter 34; Lears 1983). Among the most fraught areas of self-presentation are the arenas of identity during childhood and adolescence (Wooten and Mourey, Chapter 17; John and Chaplin, Chapter 18), and gender identity (Östberg, Chapter 13; Ruvio and Belk, Chapter 14; Duffy, Chapter 35; Vargas and Greer, Chapter 40).

However, the self is never isolated from others. Others influence our consumption and identity in several ways. They make social judgments that help define our identity and influence our sense of self (e.g. Wooten and Mourey, Chapter 17). They are objects of social comparison and reference groups against whom we judge our own self-presentation (Bagozzi, Chapter 26; Swaminathan and Monga, Chapter 36; Mathras, Loveland and Mandel, Chapter 39). They help make up our aggregate selves (Belk, Chapter 8; Belk and Llamas, Chapter 27) at various levels, including those of family (Kimura and Sakashita, Chapter 30; Price, Chapter 31), ethnic group (Tambyah and Thompson, Chapter 33), nation, and brand community (Bagozzi, Chapter 26; Antorini and Muñiz, Chapter 29). The way that we incorporate others in our sense of self can also depend upon the ways in which we regard these others (Connell and Schau, Chapter 2; Wong and Hogg, Chapter 10). The extent to which others can even come to take priority in our choices is vividly seen in the sacrifices of motherhood (Cappellini and Parsons, Chapter 12).

In the majority of our self-relevant consumption choices in the consumer cultures within which we are embedded, the choice of the self or selves we pursue is often parallel to our choice of brands (Dunn, White, and Dahl, Chapter 28; Swaminathan and Monga, Chapter 36; Escalas and Bettman, Chapter 37). In the extreme, brands are cathected as a part of self and excuses are made for brand failures much as we might seek to excuse a misbehaving family pet (Escalas and Bettman, Chapter 37). Rather than brands as pets, brands as significant others may be a more apt analogy, however (Swaminathan and Monga, Chapter 36). Images crafted by mass media, new media, social media, and advertising offer an enticing menu of selves being proffered directly or indirectly (Belk, Chapter 8; Sayre, Chapter 16; Duffy, Chapter 35; Mathras, Loveland and Mandel, Chapter 39; Vargas and Greer, Chapter 40). It is not quite as easy as shopping in a "cultural supermarket" of identities (Mathews 2000), but we face the same hyper-abundance of choices that we do in a contemporary supermarket containing tens of thousands of branded items.

Fortunately for the reader, the chapters of this volume do not present a similar explosion of theoretical perspectives. They cluster around a meaningful set of themes, which we have grouped into four sections: I What is the self in the context of consumption?; II The dynamic self; III Social and cultural aspects of self and consumption; and IV Marketing and the self. We are extremely pleased with this set of papers, not least because they represent both qualitative consumer culture theory approaches and quantitative psychological approaches to the topic of identity and consumption. It is our great hope that both sets of researchers will read across these sets of papers. For there is no better proof of the ability of these perspectives to inform one another than to read each other's work. We hope that this volume is a stimulus for doing so.

Russell Belk
Ayalla Ruvio

References

Abercrombie, Nicholas, Hill, Stephen, and Turner, Bryan S. (1986) *Sovereign Individuals of Capitalism.* London: Allen and Unwin.

Belk, Russell (2011) "Benign Envy." *Academy of Marketing Science Review* 1 (December): 117–34.

Blascovich, Jim and Bailenson, Jeremy (2011) *Infinite Reality: Avatars, Eternal Life, New Worlds, and the Dawn of the Virtual Revolution.* New York: HarperCollins ebooks.

Campbell, Colin (1987) *The Romantic Ethic and the Spirit of Modern Consumerism.* Oxford: Blackwell.

Lears, T.J. Jackson (1983) "From Salvation to Self-Realization: Advertising and the Therapeutic Roots of the Consumer Culture, 1880–1930." In Richard W. Fox and T.J. Jackson Lears (eds), *The Culture of Consumption: Critical Essays in American History, 1880–1980.* New York: Pantheon, pp. 1–38.

Mathews, Gordon (2000) *Global Culture/Individual Identity: Searching for Home in the Cultural Supermarket.* London: Routledge.

Nisbett, Richard E. (2003) *The Geography of Thought: How Asians and Westerners Think Differently … and Why.* New York: The Free Press.

Stearns, Peter N. (2001) *Consumerism in World History: The Global Transformation of Desire.* London: Routledge.

Trentmann, Frank (2006) "The Modern Genealogy of the Consumer: Meanings, Identities, and Political Synapses." In John Brewer and Frank Trentman (eds), *Consuming Cultures: Global Perspectives: Historical Trajectories, Transnational Exchanges.* Oxford: Berg, pp. 19–69.

Wiley, Norbert (1994) "History of the Self: From Primates to Present." *Sociological Perspectives* 37(4): 527–45.

I

What is the self in the context of consumption?

1.1

Conceptions of the self within consumption

1

CULTURE AND THE SELF

Implications for consumer behavior

Shinobu Kitayama and Jiyoung Park

Introduction

Over the last two decades, substantial progress has been made on cultural differences and similarities in a variety of psychological processes (Kitayama and Uskul 2011; Markus and Kitayama 1991, 2010). We now know that many aspects of cognition (e.g. Nisbett *et al.* 2001), emotion (e.g. Mesquita and Leu 2007; Tsai 2007), and motivation (e.g. Heine and Hamamura 2007) show considerable variations across cultures. This is the case especially when comparisons are drawn globally between Western cultures (North American middle-class cultures in particular) and Eastern cultures (East Asian cultures in particular). Initially, much of this work focused on student populations at relatively elite universities in North America and East Asia.

More recent work, however, has validated conclusions from this work with non-student adult populations (e.g. Kitayama *et al.* 2010b; Kitayama *et al.* 2012; Park *et al.* 2012). Furthermore, researchers have begun to illuminate some significant within-culture variations by examining social structural or ecological factors including social class and educational attainment (Stephens *et al.* 2007), residential mobility (Oishi 2010), relational stability (Yuki *et al.* 2005), historical risk of parasite infection (Fincher *et al.* 2008), and voluntary settlement (Kitayama *et al.* 2006a). Further, the dimension of tightness (vs. looseness) of cultural rules and norms has been suggested as correlated with and, yet, distinct from individualism vs. collectivism or independence vs. interdependence – the dimensions that have been used typically to understand the existing cultural variations in psychological processes (Gelfand *et al.* 2011). This emerging literature is reviewed elsewhere (Kitayama and Uskul 2011).

The aim of the present chapter is to provide an updated review of empirical evidence on the cultural variations in cognitive, emotional, and motivational processes. In so doing, our intent is to situate the empirical evidence within a broader theoretical framework of culture and the self (e.g. Markus and Kitayama 1991), with a sharpened focus placed on implications for consumer psychology and consumer behavior.

Theoretical framework: self, situational affordances, and psychological processes

Our theoretical framework is illustrated in Figure 1.1. In Western cultures, particularly European-American middle-class culture, there is a strong emphasis on independence of the self from others. This

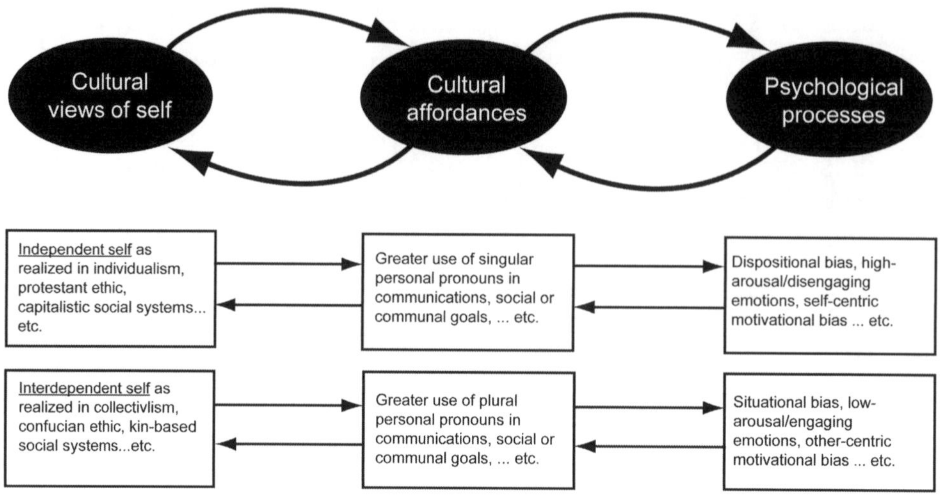

Figure 1.1 Theoretical framework linking cultural views of self, cultural affordances, and cross-culturally variable psychological processes

view of the self as independent has many historical roots, including Greek emphasis on analytic thought and debate as a means for conflict resolution (Nisbett 2003), Protestantism (Sanchez-Burks 2005; Weber 1904/1930), and Enlightenment conceptions of freedom, self-interest, and social contract (e.g. Smith 1759). These ideas have historically been used to generate various practices, conventions, and more domain-specific lay theories, resulting in individualistic ethos and cultural systems. As a consequence, various elements of cultural contexts of Western societies today appear to have the potential to induce behaviors that are matched to or congruous with the very notion of independence.

In North American middle-class culture, for example, there is a strong emphasis on personal self in communicative practices. In particular, singular, first-person pronouns such as "I," "my," "me" and "mine" are frequently used (Kashima and Kashima 1998). Likewise, linguistic practices of North America emphasize personal goal pursuit (e.g. "What do you want?" "Which wine would you like?" "Be all you can be!"). The potential of cultural practices to induce certain psychological responses have been called cultural or situational affordances (Kitayama *et al.* 1997). Western cultural contexts in general and North American middle-class contexts in particular are expected to carry a number of affordances for independence.

Individuals who are born in the environment characterized by these affordances are likely to develop corresponding independent psychological tendencies, including cognition, emotion, and motivation. They may, for example, become more focused in attention *vis-à-vis* their personal, current goals and desires. Or they may acquire conceptions of good life, well-being, and happiness that are primarily personal rather than social or interpersonal. Moreover, their motivations may be anchored in their own personal goals. These psychological tendencies are acquired through repeatedly performing cultural practices based on the model of the self as independent. Such tendencies are therefore likely to become more or less automatic and, thus, often occur unconsciously or subconsciously without any awareness, although they are likely to be highly sensitive to various contextual cues at the same time. Kitayama *et al.* (2009) called these psychological tendencies *implicit independence*.

In contrast, Asian cultures tend to have a contrasting view of the self as interdependent. Because the self is embedded in significant relationships or social groups, it is made meaningful in reference to such relations and groups. This view of the self as interdependent also has some notable historical roots, such as Buddhist cosmology that unites man and its surrounding and Confucianism with its emphasis on social hierarchy. These ideas are at the heart of traditional, feudalistic social order wherein kin or quasi-kin relations are regarded as central. Altogether, there emerge collectivistic cultural ethos and social systems. As a consequence, various elements of cultural contexts of Asian societies today have the potential of inducing behaviors that are congruous with the notion of interdependence. For example, plural first-person pronounces such as "we," "our," "us" and "ours" are likely to be used much more frequently than their singular counterparts (Kashima and Kashima 1998). Or, group goals or relational goals are emphasized in daily discourses. Asian cultural contexts, in other words, are expected to carry a number of situational affordances for interdependence.

By repeatedly engaging in and performing various cultural practices that afford interdependence though socialization, Asians are likely to acquire correspondingly interdependent cognitive, emotional, and motivational tendencies that are largely automatic and subconscious or, in other words, implicit. They may, for example, become more holistic in attention *vis-à-vis* many socially relevant stimuli in the environment including other people. Or they may acquire conceptions of good life, well-being, and happiness that are much more social or interpersonal – the one that is anchored in social harmony. Moreover, their motivations may also be closely tied to social expectations. Social expectations are likely to be internalized to such an extent that one's own goals and desires are finely coordinated or in large part concordant with the expectations held by significant others.

Our theoretical framework emphasizes that cultural differences in psychological processes are mutually interdependent with cultural affordances that are realized in the practices, conventions, as well as other scripted behavioral patterns of the culture at issue. These behavioral patterns or practices are in turn linked historically to the ideologies and philosophical thoughts that are available in the respective societies and cultures. According to this conceptualization, psychological processes that are formed through repeated engagement in a given set of cultural practices may be expected to be most likely to be recruited again when these practices are in fact available in a given situation. We may therefore expect that European Americans may be most likely to be independent in their thinking, feeling, and acting (i.e. cognition, emotion, and motivation, respectively) when the relevant cultural affordances are activated and reinstated in any given situation and, conversely, Asians may be most likely to be interdependent in their psychological tendencies when the corresponding cultural affordances are reinstated. As we shall see, recent work on situation sampling as well as cultural priming has provided substantial evidence for this possibility.

Evidence for our theoretical framework comes from many different sources. Given space limitation, however, we will focus on three relatively specific domains – i.e. analytic vs. holistic cognition, engaging vs. disengaging emotion, and self-centric motivation. In each case, we will summarize overall East–West cultural differences that have been identified. In so doing, we will emphasize both behavioral and neural evidence, illustrating the profound degree to which culturally shaped implicit psychological tendencies are inscribed into brain processes. We will then discuss the nature of situational affordances that have been empirically linked to these differences. Finally, there will be a discussion on what the current evidence on cultural variation in specific psychological processes might imply with respect to consumer psychology and consumer behavior.

Analytic and holistic cognition

Attention

The culturally shared views of the self have been suggested to have profound influences on basic attention processes. In Western cultures, individuals are encouraged to discover their internal attributes such as desires and personal goals, and therefore they may be expected to focus their attention on events that are relevant to such desires and goals. As a result, their attention may become focused. This cognitive style, which is anchored in a focal object in lieu of its context, has been called *analytic* (Nisbett *et al.* 2001). In contrast, in Eastern cultures individuals are more attuned to various aspects of ever-important social relations and, as a consequence, they may be expected to attend more broadly to a focal object as well as to its surrounding context, drawing inferences about the relationship between the object and its context. This mode of cognition has been called *holistic* (Nisbett *et al.* 2001). These predictions have been borne out. For example, when presented with an animated vignette of an underwater scene and subsequently asked to remember what they saw, European Americans were more likely to recall focal objects, whereas Japanese were more likely to refer to contextual information as well as relationships between the focal objects (Masuda and Nisbett 2001).

Similar cultural variations are also evident even when the stimuli are completely non-social. In one study, participants were shown a line drawn within a square frame. Immediately afterward, they were presented with another square of different size and asked to draw a line in this new square frame (Kitayama *et al.* 2003). In one condition, participants were asked to draw a line that was identical in absolute length to the first line (i.e. absolute task). To perform this task well, they have to ignore the square frames. In another condition, however, participants were asked to draw a line that is proportional to the height of the respective square frames (i.e. relative task). To perform this task well, they have to incorporate the size of the respective squares into account. Consistent with the hypothesis that attention is narrowly focused on an immediate object for European Americans, performance of European Americans was significantly better in the absolute task than in the relative task. Also in support of the hypothesis that attention is holistically allocated to both a target and its context for Asians, performance of Asians was significantly better in the relative task than in the absolute task.

Dispositional bias

In social perception, it is a social actor that often constitutes the focal figure of a scene. Given the attention difference across cultures summarized above, European Americans may be expected to focus their attention on the target person, thereby making inferences on the person's internal and dispositional attributes. In contrast, Asians may be more holistic, allocating more attention to the situation in which the target person is embedded. In line with this reasoning, people from Western cultures have been found to show a strong dispositional bias or the fundamental attribution error (FAE) (Ross 1977) – the tendency to explain another person's behavior based on the person's disposition even in the presence of obvious situational constraints. As may be predicted, however, it has been found that Asians are much less susceptible to this bias, due to their holistic cognitive tendencies. For example, European Americans have been shown to make dispositional inferences about a target person even when the situational constraint on the behavior of the target person is made salient (Gilbert *et al.* 1988). In sharp contrast, under comparable conditions, Asians – both Koreans (Choi and Nisbett 1998) and Japanese (Masuda and Kitayama 2004) – show little or no dispositional inference.

More recent work finds that this cultural difference is likely to occur very early on in the sequence of information processing at the stage where dispositions are automatically inferred from behaviors. Na and Kitayama (2011) had European and Asian American participants memorize a large number of pairings of a face and a behavior that implies a certain trait (e.g. "Judy checks a fire alarm before going to bed," which implies "cautiousness"). A sample stimulus is shown in Figure 1.2. If the dispositional inference is truly automatic, next time when they are shown the

Figure 1.2 A sample stimulus used in the Na and Kitayama (2011) study

face of the same person, it may be this personality trait ("cautious") that automatically occurs to their mind.

To determine the extent to which the trait is automatically activated upon exposure to the face, the researchers asked participants to perform a lexical judgment task in which they were to judge if different strings of alphabets were a legitimate English word or not. Right before the presentation of a letter string, the face was briefly presented as a fixation. Trials of interest concerned those on which the word presented was either the trait corresponding to the behavior paired with the face (called target trait) or another trait that was unrelated to the trait (called unrelated trait). If the face indeed activates the target trait, the lexical judgment ought to be easier for the target trait than for the unrelated trait. Analysis of response time in the lexical judgment task showed that European Americans did find the task significantly easier for the target traits than for the unrelated traits, thereby providing evidence for trait inference during the memorization phase of the study. Because there was no requirement for trait inference during that phase of the study, the trait inference must have been spontaneous, thereby providing strong evidence for *spontaneous trait inference effect* for European Americans (Uleman *et al.* 2008). Importantly, however, this effect was completely eliminated for Asian Americans (Na and Kitayama 2011).

Na and Kitayama conceptually replicated the behavioral evidence (i.e. response time) with an event-related brain potential (ERP) measure. They monitored participants' electroencephalogram (EEG) while participants performed the lexical judgment task, during which the target traits (congruent trials), antonyms of the target traits (incongruent trials), and non-word stimuli were randomly presented following a presentation of a face. For European Americans, an ERP marker for the detection of semantic incongruity (N400) was reliably greater for incongruent trials than for congruent trials. However, this effect completely vanished for Asian Americans. Both the behavioral and neural evidence suggest that dispositional inference, which is highly spontaneous for European Americans, is quite optional, neither spontaneous nor automatic, for Asian Americans.

Situational affordances

The notion that analytic vs. holistic cognition is fostered by independent vs. interdependent views of the self has received substantial evidence from an increasing body of research on priming of independence (vs. interdependence). For example, participants are asked to read a brief paragraph describing a tour of a city that includes either a number of singular first-person pronouns (I, my, me) or plural first person pronouns (we, our, us) (Brewer and Gardner 1996). In another procedure, participants are asked to read a paragraph about a king in a foreign kingdom who promoted his generals on the basis of either merit or kinship (Trafimow *et al.* 1991). These priming procedures are known to induce a more analytic (vs. holistic) cognitive style (Oyserman and Lee 2008).

The priming of this sort can come even from physical environment. As compared to street scenes typical in American cities, those typical in Japanese cities are more complex and less systematic, with blurred boundaries between various objects that constitute the scenes. That is, even physical scenes appear to be more interdependent in Japan than in the USA. Miyamoto and colleagues (Miyamoto *et al.* 2006) found that exposure to the holistic scenes in fact predisposes both Asians and European Americans to become more holistic in cognitive style.

Implications for consumer behavior

The analytic vs. holistic cognitive style can offer far-reaching implications for consumer choice. Any commodities are defined by multiple attributes, but exactly which commodities are attractive would depend on how widely their attributes are attended and considered carefully. Whereas analytic thinkers may be attracted by a very small number of highly attractive attributes, holistic thinkers may weigh more evenly such attributes and other attributes that might otherwise be missed. Moreover, this cultural difference might be especially pronounced when people carefully think about their choice and when they are held accountable for their choices. These predictions have received empirical support (Briley *et al.* 2000).

Engaging and disengaging emotions

Disengagement vs. engagement

Emotions differ on various dimensions, but one dimension that seems especially important in cultural analysis concerns the notion of social engagement vs. disengagement (Kitayama *et al.* 2006b). Some positive emotions such as pride and feelings of self-confidence are likely to result from success in tasks of independence such as accomplishment of personal goals. These emotions, therefore, are likely to disengage the self from the surrounding, highlighting it as a separate entity with its own distinct attributes. Likewise, some negative emotions such as anger and frustration result when a pursuit of one's independent goals is interfered with. These emotions therefore motivate the person to restore the state of independence. Regardless of the valence, then, these emotions tend to disengage the self from the social surrounding and, thus, they lend themselves to one's independence. Kitayama and colleagues have called these emotions *socially disengaging*.

In contrast, some positive emotions such as respect and feelings of connectedness result from success in tasks of interdependence such as maintaining harmonious relationships with others.

Likewise, some negative emotions such as guilt and feelings of indebtedness are likely to result from one's failure in the tasks of interdependence. These emotions will subsequently motivate the person to restore the state of interdependence. For example, someone feeling guilty because of his or her failure to live up to group expectations may be motivated to work hard to compensate for the failure by doing something else for the group. These emotions, both positive and negative, are therefore likely to engage the self with the pertinent social relations and help the person to achieve or reestablish the state of interdependence. As such, these emotions have been called the *socially engaging* emotions. It should not come as any surprise, then, that Asians experience engaging emotions relatively more strongly than disengaging emotions, whereas the reverse is true for European Americans (Kitayama *et al.* 2006b; Kitayama *et al.* 2009).

Moreover, the dimension of social engagement and disengagement has proved to be crucial in understanding cross-cultural variations in the nature of happiness. Whereas Western happiness is based on personal achievement and realization of one's independence, happiness for Asians relies much more on social harmony and one's interdependence with others. In a recent study, Uchida and Kitayama (2009) demonstrated this cultural difference by asking American and Japanese participants to list "features and characteristics of happiness." All the generated features were then compiled and printed on different index cards, which were then handed down to a different group of both Japanese and American participants, who sorted the features by similarity. A multi-dimensional scaling analysis performed on the similarity judgment identified several categories, three of which were common across cultures: personal achievement (e.g. "creative," "becoming wealthy"), social harmony (e.g. "caring attitude," "being tolerant of others"), and general positive affect (e.g. "elation," "calm feelings"). Importantly, among Americans general positive affect as a proxy of happiness was linked much more closely to personal achievement than to social harmony, but as predicted, among Japanese general positive affect was linked more closely to social harmony than to personal achievement.

Note that socially disengaging emotions are likely to be relatively high in arousal because disengagement and independence often entail high dominance and power, whereas socially engaging emotions are likely to be relatively low in arousal because engagement and interdependence often come with a tendency to adjust the self to expectations of others in the pertinent relations. Hence the body of research focusing on engagement vs. disengagement of emotions is consistent with a recent proposal by Tsai and colleagues (Tsai *et al.* 2006) that Eastern and Western cultures value low vs. high arousal emotions, respectively.

Emotion regulation

The cultural value for low arousal emotions such as calmness and serenity is historically related to Confucian traditions, which have regarded emotions – particularly strong, socially disengaged ones such as anger and frustration – as a hindrance against ever-important social harmony and social order (Kitayama *et al.* 2006b). Moreover, recent work has suggested that emotion control (Mauss and Butler 2010), especially control of emotional expression by suppression (Matsumoto *et al.* 2008), is strongly valued in Asia. These emotion-related values and attitudes are in stark contrast to those in European American culture wherein emotional expression is more valued and, correspondingly, expressive suppression is often considered as undesirable and unhealthy (Kim and Markus 1999; Mauss and Gross 2004), with various negative psychological consequences (Butler *et al.* 2007).

On the basis of these considerations, Murata *et al.* (2012) hypothesized that Asians are likely to learn, through the socialization process, to attenuate emotional processing when they are required to suppress their emotional expression (Mauss and Butler 2010). In contrast, European

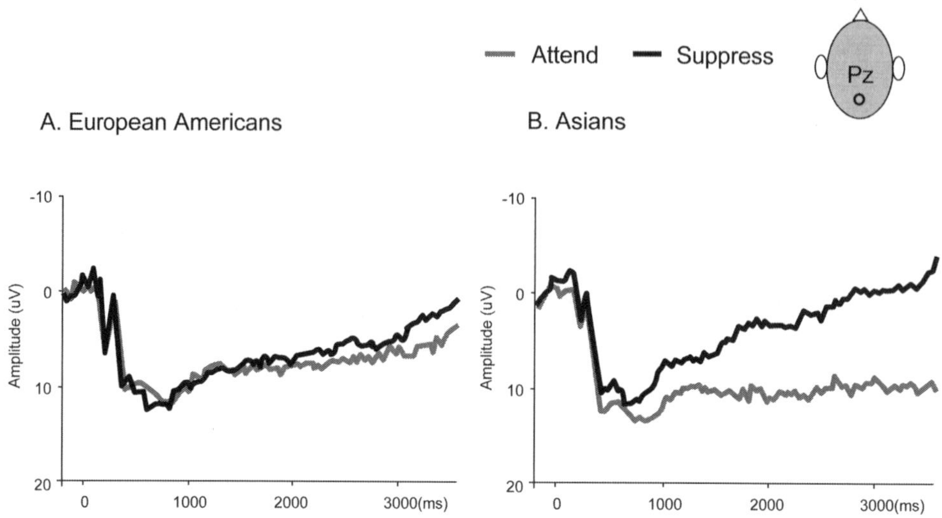

Figure 1.3 Late positive potential from the central parietal site for European Americans and Asian participants when they merely attended emotionally evocative negative pictures (black line) and when they sought to suppress their emotional responses (grey line)

Americans value the inner experience of emotion so much that they may rarely down-regulate emotional processing even though it could be quite advantageous for them to do so for the purpose of suppressing emotional expression. As an objective measure of emotional processing, Murata *et al.* used a parietal late positive potential (LPP) event-related brain potential component. Previous work showed that this ERP component reflects categorization and further cognitive elaboration on an impinging emotional stimulus that is instigated by subcortical emotional arousal the stimulus instigates (Schupp *et al.* 2000). Both Asians and European Americans were exposed to either aversive or neutral pictures while instructed to either attend or suppress expression of emotions. As can be seen in Figure 1.3A and Figure 1.3B, both groups showed an equally pronounced parietal positivity approximately 600 milliseconds post-stimulus. As predicted, however, Asians subsequently showed a significant decrease of the parietal LPP in the suppression (vs. attend) condition (Figure 1.3B). The initial positivity completely disappeared 2,000 ms post-stimulus in the suppression condition. In contrast, for European Americans the parietal LPP suppression effect was completely absent (Figure 1.3A).

Situational affordances

The cultural differences in emotional experience are likely to be contingent on available cultural affordances. Several studies now suggest that when mundane social situations are sampled from European American vs. Asian cultural contexts, the situations sampled from European American contexts lend themselves much more to feelings of pride, self-confidence and self-esteem compared to the situations sampled from Asian contexts (Kitayama *et al.* 1997; Morling *et al.* 2002; Savani *et al.* 2011). Whether the same might be true with respect to socially engaging emotions remains to be tested.

Another important consideration comes from recent work on regional variation in the value placed on uniqueness. Disengaging emotions are based on a unique configuration of internal attributes of the self such as personal goals, idiosyncratic desires, and agendas. Values for self-uniqueness may then be at the core of situational affordances for disengaging emotions. We now know that commercial advertisements that appear in popular magazines emphasize personal uniqueness in the USA to a far larger extent as compared to South Korea (Kim and Markus 1999). Varnum and Kitayama (2011) have extended this work by examining within-cultural variation in the USA. They observed that the cultural emphasis on uniqueness is revealed in the frequency of unconventional baby names. The relative frequency of unconventional names increases as a function of cultural regions' settlement history. For example, Figure 1.4 illustrates the relative frequency of highly popular (and thus conventional) names for baby boys (a) and girls (b). As can be seen, conventional names are much more common and, by implication, more unique names are less common, in the East coast. Relatively speaking, babies tend to receive more unique names in western states of the USA. This supports the hypothesis that settlers in the frontier and their descendants tend to be more independent and, thus, in favor of uniqueness as compared to

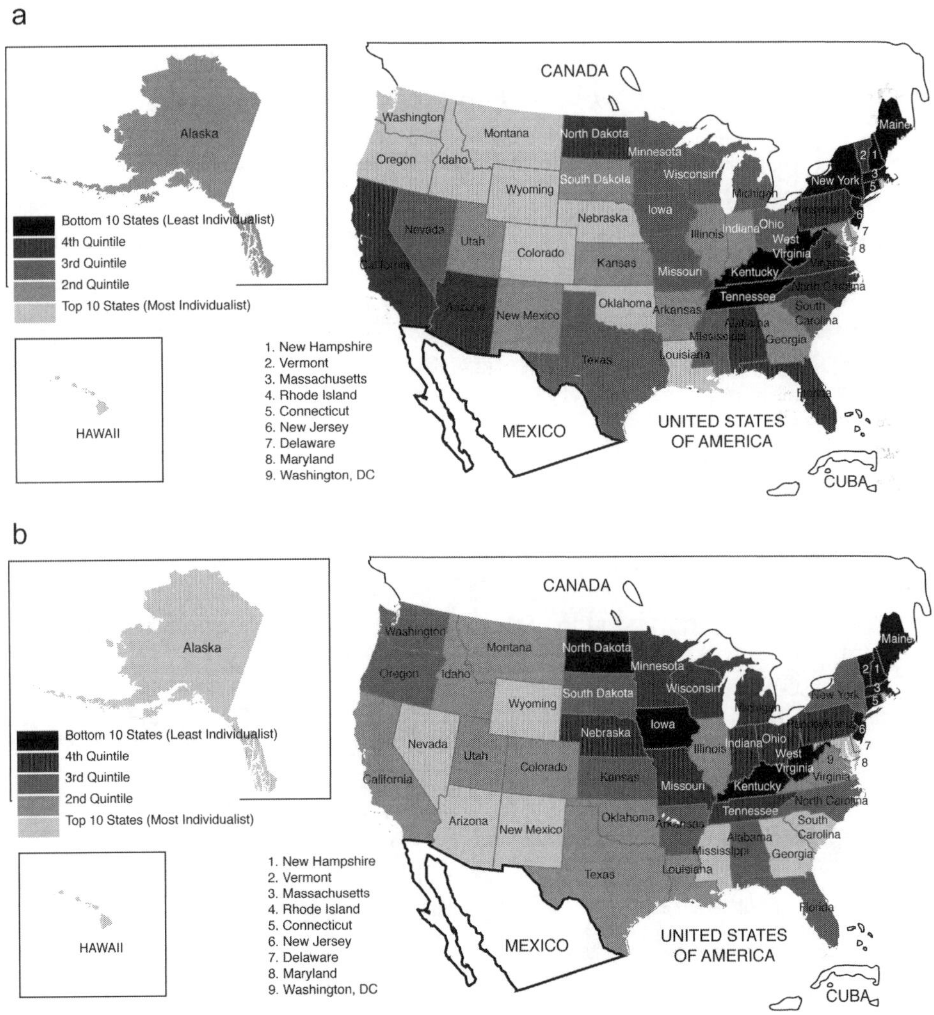

Figure 1.4 Relative frequency of conventional names in the USA for baby boys (a) and girls (b)

residents of more traditional regions. Further analysis showed that uniqueness is valued more in North America or Australia than in their European counterparts (e.g. the United Kingdom) (see Kitayama *et al.* 2010a, for reviews; Kitayama *et al.* in press).

Implications for consumer behavior

Given the centrality of emotions in decision making, it may be expected that emotional appeals to independence vs. interdependence will have differential impacts on European American vs. Asian or Asian American consumers. Whereas European Americans are more likely to be persuaded by messages that speak to one's positive, disengaging emotions, Asians may be more likely to be persuaded by messages that highlight one's positive, engaging emotions. Available evidence is consistent with this proposition. A study by Han and Shavitt (1994) showed that individualistic messages are more effective in European American cultures, but collectivistic messages are more effective in Asian cultures. It is likely that these messages have persuasive impacts by appealing to the corresponding emotions such as pride for European Americans and feelings of connectedness for Asians. This point, however, has yet to be fully explored.

Self-centric motivation

Cognitive dissonance

For a long time in Western philosophies and social theories, it has been strongly believed that self-interest is a fundamental human motive (Bentham 1789; Campbell 1975; Greenwald 1980; Hobbes 1651). These views suggest that individuals can not only be self-centric, but also be so righteously. This assumption, however, may be a cultural construction that is grounded in the view of the self as independent. With views of the self as interdependent in place, a much greater emphasis may be placed on the welfare of others in a significant relationship.

A series of studies conducted by Hoshino-Browne and colleagues (Hoshino-Browne *et al.* 2005) are consistent with this analysis. The researchers had participants make a choice between two equally attractive items and tested whether they would justify their choice by increasing the liking of the chosen item and decreasing the liking of the rejected item. Theoretically, the effect like this, called choice justification, occurs because the choice entails accepting unwanted features of the chosen item while giving up wanted features of the rejected item and, as a consequence, this process produces cognitive dissonance. Individuals are considered to justify the choice so as to defray this dissonance. As proposed by Festinger (1957) in his original formulation, however, this effect may be expected to occur only when the choice is perceived as sufficiently important.

Seen from this vantage point, the results of the Hoshino-Browne *et al.* (2005) studies were quite revealing. To begin, European Canadian participants showed the choice justification effect when they made a choice for themselves, but not when they made a choice for their friend. Evidently, the choice was much more important when made for the self than when made for the friend. In sharp contrast, Asians and Asian Canadians showed the choice justification effect only when they made a choice for their friend. Notably, these participants exhibited little justification effect when they made a choice for themselves. Evidently, the choice was less important when made for the self (see also Kitayama *et al.* 2004).

Self-serving bias

Another phenomenon where a substantial cultural variation in self-interest is observed is self-serving bias. People are motivated to maintain positive views of the self in many different ways

(Dunning *et al.* 1989; Langer 1975; Miller and Ross 1975). For example, they take credit for their success while blaming external factors for their failure (Miller and Ross 1975). People are also likely to have unrealistically optimistic views of themselves and their future (Taylor and Brown 1988). Although self-serving bias is often regarded as universal, numerous cross-cultural investigations have shown that European Americans, who are strongly encouraged to develop the positivity of the self that is distinguished from others, show stronger self-serving bias than Asians, who are strongly expected to fit in to significant relations and social expectations (Heine *et al.* 1999).

A recent study by Kitayama and Park (2012) revealed a neural basis of the foregoing cultural differences in self-serving effects. Participants performed a computer task to increase reward points either for themselves or for their close friend, while their brain responses were monitored using EEG. In particular, they were shown a set of gift items that can be exchanged with earned points. In some blocks, they performed the task to earn points for the self whereas in the remaining blocks, they did so to earn points for their same-sex friend. As they performed the task, their brain responses to error commission were assessed with error-related negativity (ERN), a neurophysiological marker of error detection (Falkenstein *et al.* 1991; Gehring *et al.* 1993). Previous work shows that the size of the ERN increases as a function of motivational significance of errors (Hajcak *et al.* 2005; Pailing and Segalowitz 2004). People are likely to become more motivated when performing a task that is high in personal importance. Therefore, performing well in the self-condition should be more important than performing well in the friend-condition, especially for those who are high in self-centric motivation. Confirming this prediction, Kitayama and Park found that European Americans, who are likely to be high in self-centric motivation, showed larger ERN in the self-condition than in the friend-condition. Importantly, Asians, who are likely to be lower in self-centric motivation, did not differ in their ERN amplitude across the two conditions.

In this study the researchers also measured each subject's interdependent self-construal. In line with the hypothesis that self-centric motivation is grounded in the personal self that is detached from others and, conversely, is antithetical to interdependence, Kitayama and Park expected that the self-centric effect in ERN would decrease as a function of interdependent self-construal. The relevant data are shown in Figure 1.5. As predicted, as interdependent self-construal becomes higher, the relative enhancement of the ERN amplitude in the self-condition (relative to the friend-condition) becomes weaker.

Situational affordances

The relative importance of the self vs. friend may vary as a function of situational affordances and, correspondingly, even European Americans may justify a choice they make for their friend as long as they are exposed to subtle situational cues that enhance their interdependent tendencies toward affiliation and social harmony. In a recent series of studies, Kimel *et al.* (2012) tested this idea by subliminally activating affiliation-related concepts right before European American participants made a choice either for the self or for their friend. The choice items were toys that were pretested to be quite popular among college students. Without this affiliation priming, Kimel *et al.* (2012) replicated the aforementioned studies by Hoshino-Browne *et al.* (2005), observing a significantly stronger choice justification when the choice was made for the self than when it was made for the friend. However, after the affiliation priming, the pattern was completely reversed, with the choice justified more when it was made for the friend than for the self, even for European Americans. It remains to be tested whether priming independent tendencies would lead Asians to justify a choice they make for the self but not a choice they make for their friend.

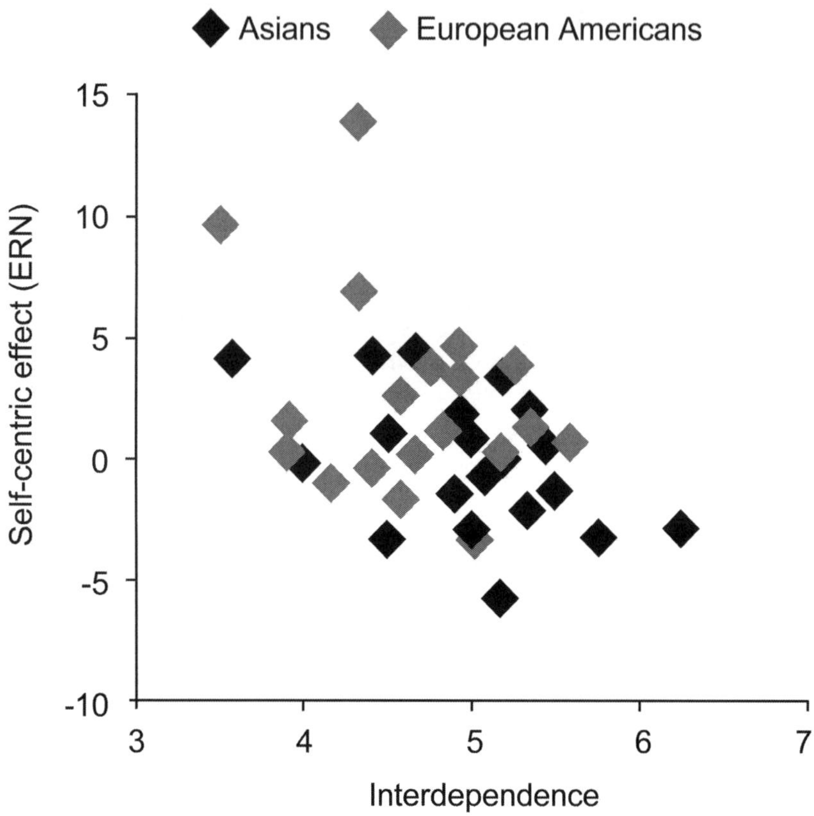

Figure 1.5 Scatterplot illustrating the negative correlation between interdependent self-construal and the self-centric effect in ERN

Implications for consumer behavior

As the holiday season approaches every year, people are busy choosing their gifts for their loved ones. The research summarized here suggests that specific psychological mechanisms underlying gift-giving behavior are likely to depend on the specific state of the mind of the consumer. If affiliation orientation is high, the consumers may be very much motivated to purchase what would be truly good for their loved ones. They may take into more careful consideration the preferences of the loved ones before buying their gifts. In contrast, if the affiliation orientation is relatively low, the consumers may not care as much, not taking into account preferences of the loved ones. It may then be expected that people may end up spending much more, especially 1, if their affiliation orientation is either chronically high or, if not, temporarily enhanced by some situational affordances; and 2, if commodities that appear to fit well to the preferences of the loved ones are made cognitively salient. Future work should test this and other related predictions and spell out specific mechanisms underlying consumer behaviors at the core of gift-giving.

Conclusion and future directions

The goal of the present chapter was to provide a brief overview of the advancements of cultural psychology of the self over the last two decades, with a focus on implications of this work for consumer psychology and consumer behavior. The cultural views of the self as independent and interdependent are likely to shape cognitive styles, salient emotions, as well as predominant motivational tendencies. This body of work further illustrates how these different forms of the self can influence consumer choice, effectiveness of different types of magazine advertisements, and motives underlying gift shopping. The different views of the self are most commonly associated with broad geographic cultural regions of West (particularly European American cultures) and East (particularly Asian cultures). Although this cultural variation is often sizable and, in fact, can discriminate among different groups of people especially when multiple measures are used (Kitayama *et al.* 2009), there do exist substantial individual differences as well. Some of such individual differences can be highly systematic, as illustrated in the type of correlation reported in Figure 1.5. Moreover, these cultural differences are not purely psychological. They appear to be constantly afforded by social contexts that by themselves do show systematic cultural variations. As one example, we highlighted regional variation in naming conventions in the USA (Figure 1.4).

Future work should extend this literature to various immigrants and sojourners as well as various international populations. As the economy is globalizing, this kind of work will be indispensable to draw implications for consumer psychology and consumer behavior. Another important issue is to investigate both malleability and stability of culturally shaped psychological traits. While priming effects do exist and, in fact, can be substantial, it is also clear that certain psychological traits, once acquired early in life, can be very hard to change. Language acquisition is a case in point. Future work must address the questions of both when cultural effects can be stable and when easily they can be overridden.

It is very clear that the self is a central element in social cognition and social behavior. If the self is different, the form of social cognition and social behavior can change accordingly. This principle has received ample evidence with a focus on cultural variations in social cognition and behavior, as shown in the present review. Following up on this may prove to be a highly profitable avenue to take in investigating processes and mechanisms underlying consumer psychology and consumer behavior.

Further reading

Kitayama, S., Conway, L.G., Pietromonaco, P., Park, H., and Plaut, V. (2010) "Ethos of Independence Across Regions of the US: The Production-adoption Model of Cultural Change." *American Psychologist* 65: 559–74.

Kitayama, S., and Uskul, A.K. (2011) "Culture, Mind, and the Brain: Current Evidence and Future." *Annual Review of Psychology* 62: 419–49.

Markus, H.R. and Kitayama, S. (1991) "Culture and the Self: Implications for Cognition, Emotion, and Motivation." *Psychological Review* 98: 224–53.

Nisbett, R.E. (2003) *The Geography of Thought: How Asians and Westerners Think Differently … and Why*. New York: The Free Press.

References

Bentham, J. (1789) *An Introduction to the Principles of Morals and Legislation*. Oxford: Clarendon Press.

Brewer, M.B. and Gardner, W. (1996) "Who is the 'We'? Levels of Collective Identity and Self-representations." *Journal of Personality and Social Psychology* 71: 83–93.

Briley, D.A., Morris, M., and Simonson, I. (2000) "Reasons as Carriers of Culture: Dynamic vs. Dispositional Models of Cultural Influence on Decision Making." *Journal of Consumer Research* 27: 157–78.

Butler, E.A., Lee, T.L., and Gross, J.J. (2007) "Emotion Regulation and Culture: Are the Social Consequences of Emotion Suppression Culture-specific?" *Emotion* 7: 30–48.

Campbell, D.T. (1975) "On the Conflicts Between Biological and Social Evolution and Between Psychology and Moral Tradition." *American Anthropologist* 30: 1130–26.

Choi, I. and Nisbett, R.E. (1998) "Situational Salience and Cultural Differences in the Correspondence Bias and in the Actor-observer Bias." *Personality and Social Psychology Bulletin* 24: 949–60.

Dunning, D., Meyerowitz, J.A., and Holzberg, A. (1989) "Ambiguity and Self-evaluation: The Role of Idiosyncratic Trait Definitions in Self-serving Assessments of Ability." *Journal of Personality and Social Psychology* 57: 1082–90.

Falkenstein, M., Hohnsbein, J., Hoormann, J., and Blanke, L. (1991) "Effects of Crossmodal Divided Attention on Late ERP Components. II. Error Processing in Choice Reaction Tasks." *Electroencephalography and Clinical Neurophysiology* 78: 447–55.

Festinger, L. (1957) *A Theory of Cognitive Dissonance*. Stanford, CA: Stanford University Press.

Fincher, C.L., Thornhill, R., Murray, D.R., and Schaller, M. (2008) "Pathogen Prevalence Predicts Human Cross-cultural Variability in Individualism/Collectivism." *Proceedings of the Royal Society* 275: 1279–85.

Gehring, W.J., Goss, B., Coles, M.G.H., Meyer, D.E., and Donchin, E. (1993) "A Neural System for Error Detection and Compensation." *Psychological Science* 4: 385–90.

Gelfand, M.J., Raver, J.L., Nishii, L., Leslie, L.M., Lun, J., Lim, B.C., Duan, L., Almaliach, A., Ang, S., Arnadottir, J., Aycan, Z., Boehnke, K., Boski, P., Cabecinhas, R., Chan, D., Chhokar, J., D'Amato, A., Ferrer, M., Fischlmayr, I.C., Fischer, R., Fülöp, M., Georgas, J., Kashima, E.S., Kashima, Y., Kim, K., Lempereur, A., Marquez, P., Othman, R., Overlaet, B., Panagiotopoulou, P., Peltzer, K., Perez-Florizno, L.R., Ponomarenko, L., Realo, A., Schei, V., Schmitt, M., Smith, P.B., Soomro, N., Szabo, E., Taveesin, N., Toyama, M., Van de Vliert, E., Vohra, N., Ward, C., Yamaguchi, S. (2011) "Differences Between Tight and Loose Cultures: A 33-nation Study." *Science* 332 (6033): 1100–4.

Gilbert, D.T., Pelham, B.W., and Krull, D.S. (1988) "On Cognitive Business: When Person Perceivers Meet Persons Perceived." *Journal of Personality and Social Psychology* 54: 733–40.

Greenwald, A.G. (1980) "The Totalitarian Ego: Fabrication and Revision of Personal History." *American Psychologist* 35: 603–18.

Hajcak, G., Moser, J.S., Yeung, N., and Simons, R.F. (2005) "On the ERN and the Significance of Errors." *Psychophysiology* 42: 151–60.

Han, S. and Shavitt, S. (1994) "Persuasion and Culture: Advertising Appeals in Individualistic and Collectivistic Societies." *Journal of Experimental Social Psychology* 30: 326–50.

Heine, S.J. and Hamamura, T. (2007) "In Search of East Asian Self-enhancement." *Personality and Social Psychology Review* 11: 4–27.

Heine, S.J., Lehman, D.R., Markus, H.R., and Kitayama, S. (1999) "Is There a Universal Need for Positive Self-regard?" *Psychological Review* 106: 766–94.

Hobbes, T. (1651) *Leviathan*. London: Dent & Son.

Hoshino-Browne, E., Zanna, A.S., Spencer, S.J., Zanna, M.P., Kitayama, S., and Lackenbauer, S. (2005) "On the Cultural Guises of Cognitive Dissonance: The Case of Easterners and Westerners." *Journal of Personality and Social Psychology* 89: 294–310.

Kashima, E.S. and Kashima, Y. (1998) "Culture and Language: The Case of Cultural Dimensions and Personal Pronoun Use." *Journal of Cross-Cultural Psychology* 29: 461–86.

Kim, H. and Markus, H.R. (1999) "Deviance or Uniqueness, Harmony or Conformity?: A Cultural Analysis." *Journal of Personality and Social Psychology* 77: 785–800.

Kimel, S.Y., Grossman, I., and Kitayama, S. (2012) "When Gift-giving Produces Dissonance: Effects of Subliminal Affiliation Priming on Choices for One's Self Versus Close Others." *Journal of Experimental Social Psychology* 48(5): 1221–24.

Kitayama, S., Conway, J.G., Pietromonaco, P.B., Park, H., and Plaut, V.C. (2010a) "Ethos of Independence Across Regions of the United States: The Production-adoption Model of Cultural Change." *American Psychologist* 65: 559–74.

Kitayama, S., Duffy, S., Kawamura, T., and Larson, J.T. (2003) "Perceiving an Object and its Context in Different Cultures: A Cultural Look at New Look." *Psychological Science* 14: 201–6.

Kitayama, S., Ishii, K., Imada, T., Takemura, K., and Ramaswamy, J. (2006a) "Voluntary Settlement and the Spirit of Independence: Evidence from Japan's 'Northern Frontier'." *Journal of Personality and Social Psychology* 91(3): 369–84.

Kitayama, S., Karasawa, M., Curhan, K., Markus, H.R., and Ryff, C.D. (2010b) "Independence and Interdependence Predict Health and Wellbeing: Divergent Patterns in the United States and Japan." *Frontiers in Cultural Psychology* 1: 1–10.

Kitayama, S., Karasawa, M., Matsubara, M., Grossmann, I., Na, J., Varnum, M.E.W., and Nisbett, R.W. (2012) *East-West Differences in Cognitive Style and Social Orientation: Do they Hold for Non-college Populations?* Ann Arbor, MI: University of Michigan.

Kitayama, S., Markus, H.R., Matsumoto, H., and Noraskkunit, V. (1997) "Individual and Collective Processes in the Construction of Self: Self-enhancement in the United States and Self-criticism in Japan." *Journal of Personality and Social Psychology* 72: 1245–67.

Kitayama, S., Mesquita, B., and Karasawa, M. (2006b) "The Emotional Basis of Independent and Interdependent Selves: Socially Disengaging and Engaging Emotions in the US and Japan." *Journal of Personality and Social Psychology* 91: 890–903.

Kitayama, S., Park, H., Sevincer, A.T., and Karasawa, M. (2009) "A Cultural Task of Analysis of Implicit Independence: Comparing North America, Western Europe, and East Asia." *Journal of Personality and Social Psychology* 97: 236–55.

Kitayama, S. and Park, J. (2012) *Error Related Brain Activity Reveals Self-centric Motivation: Culture Matters.* Ann Arbor, MI: University of Michigan.

Kitayama, S., Snibbe, A.C., Markus, H.R., and Suzuki, T. (2004) "Is There Any 'Free' Choice? Self and Dissonance in Two Cultures." *Psychological Science* 15: 527–33.

Kitayama, S. and Uskul, A.K. (2011) "Culture, Mind, and the Brain: Current Evidence and Future." *Annual Review of Psychology* 62: 419–49.

Kitayama, S., Varnum, M.E.W., and Sevincer, A.T. (in press) "The Frontier: Voluntary Settlement and Cultural Change." In A. Cohen (ed.), *New Directions in the Psychology of Culture.* Washington, DC: American Psychological Association – APA Books.

Langer, E. (1975) "The Illusion of Control." *Journal of Personality and Social Psychology* 32: 311–28.

Markus, H.R. and Kitayama, S. (1991) "Culture and the Self: Implications for Cognition, Emotion, and Motivation." *Psychological Review* 98: 224–53.

——(2010) "Cultures and Selves: A Cycle of Mutual Constitution." *Perspectives on Psychological Science* 5: 420–30.

Masuda, T. and Kitayama, S. (2004) "Perceiver-induced Constraint and Attitude Attribution in Japan and in the US: A Case for the Cultural Dependence of the Correspondence Bias." *Journal of Experimental Social Psychology* 40: 409–16.

Masuda, T. and Nisbett, R.E. (2001) "Attending Holistically vs. Analytically: Comparing the Context Sensitivity of Japanese and Americans." *Journal of Personality and Social Psychology* 81: 922–34.

Matsumoto, D., Yoo, S.H., Nakagawa, S., Alexandre, J., Altarriba, J., Anguas-Wong, A.M., Arriola, M., Bauer, L.M., *et al.* (2008) "Culture, Emotion Regulation, and Adjustment." *Journal of Personality and Social Psychology* 94(6): 925–37.

Mauss, I.B. and Butler, E.A. (2010) "Cultural Context Moderates the Relationship Between Emotion Control Values and Cardiovascular Challenge Versus Threat Responses." *Biological Psychology* 84: 521–30.

Mauss, I.B. and Gross, J.J. (2004) "Emotion Suppression and Cardiovascular Disease: Is Hiding your Feelings Bad for your Heart?" In L.R. Temoshok, A. Vingerhoets and I. Nyklicek (eds), *The Expression of Emotion and Health.* London: Brunner-Routledge, pp. 62–81.

Mesquita, B. and Leu, J. (2007) "The Cultural Psychology of Emotion." In S. Kitayama and D. Cohen (eds), *The Handbook of Cultural Psychology.* New York: Guilford Press.

Miller, D. and Ross, M. (1975) "Self-serving Biases in Attribution of Causality: Fact or Fiction?" *Psychological Bulletin* 82: 213–25.

Miyamoto, Y., Nisbett, R.E., and Masuda, T. (2006) "Culture and Physical Environment: Holistic Versus Analytic Perceptual Affordances." *Psychological Science* 17: 113–19.

Morling, B., Kitayama, S., and Miyamoto, Y. (2002) "Cultural Practices Emphasize Influence in the US and Adjustment in Japan." *Personality and Social Psychology Bulletin* 28: 311–23.

Murata, A., Moser, J.S., and Kitayama, S. (2012) "Culture Shapes Electrocortical Responses During Emotion Suppression." *Social Cognitive and Affective Neuroscience.* doi: 10.1093/scan/nss036.

Na, J. and Kitayama, S. (2011) "Trait-based Person Perception is Culture-specific: Behavioral and Neural Evidence." *Psychological Science* 22(8): 1025–32.

Nisbett, R.E. (2003) *The Geography of Thought: How Asians and Westerners Think Differently … and Why.* New York: The Free Press.

Nisbett, R.E., Peng, K., Choi, I., and Norenzayan, A. (2001) "Culture and Systems of Thought: Holistic vs. Analytic Cognition." *Psychological Review* 108: 291–310.

Oishi, S. (2010) "The Psychology of Residential Mobility: Implications for the Self, Social Relationships, and Well-being." *Perspectives on Psychological Science* 5: 5–21.

Oyserman, D. and Lee, S.W.S. (2008) "Does Culture Influence What and How We Think? Effects of Priming Individualism and Collectivism." *Psychological Bulletin* 134: 311–42.

Pailing, P.E. and Segalowitz, S.J. (2004) "The Error-related Negativity as a State and Trait Measure: Motivation, Personality, and ERPs in Response to Errors." *Psychophysiology* 40: 84–95.

Park, J., Kitayama, S., Karasawa, M., Curhan, K., Markus, H.R., Kawakami, N., Ryff, C. (2012) "Clarifying the Links Between Social Support and Health: Culture, Stress, and Neuroticism Matter." *Journal of Health Psychology*. doi: 10.1177/1359105312439731.

Ross, L. (1977) "The Intuitive Psychologist and his Shortcomings." In L. Berkowitz (ed.), *Advances in Experimental Social Psychology*. New York: Academic Press, vol. 10, pp. 173–220.

Sanchez-Burks, J. (2005) "Protestant Relational Ideology: The Cognitive Underpinnings and Organizational Implications of an American Anomaly." In B. Staw and R. Kramer (eds), *Research in Organizational Behavior*. New York: Elsevier, vol. 26, pp. 267–308.

Savani, K., Morris, M.W., Naidu, N.V.R., S., K., and Berlia, N. (2011) "Cultural Conditioning: Understanding Interpersonal Accommodation in India and the US in Terms of the Modal Characteristics of Interpersonal Influence Situations." *Journal of Personality and Social Psychology* 100: 84–102.

Schupp, H.T., Cuthbert, B.N., Bradley, M.M., Cacioppo, J.T., Ito, T.A., and Lang, P.J. (2000) "Affective Picture Processing: The Late Positive Potential is Modulated as a Function of Motivational Relevance." *Psychophysiology* 37: 257–61.

Smith, A. (1759) *The Theory of Moral Sentiments*. Indianapolis, IN: Liberty Fund.

Stephens, N.M., Markus, H.R., and Townsend, S.S.M. (2007) "Choice as an Act of Meaning: The Case of Social Class." *Journal of Personality and Social Psychology* (98): 814–30.

Taylor, S.E. and Brown, J.D. (1988) "Illusion and Well-being: A Social Psychological Perspective on Mental Health." *Psychological Bulletin* 103: 193–210.

Trafimow, D., Triandis, H.C., and Goto, S.G. (1991) "Some Tests of the Distinction Between the Private Self and the Collective Self." *Journal of Personality and Social Psychology* 60: 649–55.

Tsai, J.L. (2007) "Ideal Affect: Cultural Causes and Behavioral Consequences." *Perspectives on Psychological Science* 2: 242–59.

Tsai, J.L., Knutson, B., and Fung, H.H. (2006) "Cultural Variation in Affect Valuation." *Journal of Personality and Social Psychology* 90: 288–307.

Uchida, Y. and Kitayama, S. (2009) "Happiness and Unhappiness in East and West: Themes and Variations." *Emotion* 9: 441–56.

Uleman, J.S., Saribay, S.A., and Gonzalez, C. (2008) "Spontaneous Inferences, Implicit Impressions, and Implicit Theories." *Annual Review of Psychology* 59: 329–60.

Varnum, M. and Kitayama, S. (2011) "What's in a Name? Popular Names are Less Common on Frontiers." *Psychological Science* 22: 176–83.

Weber, M. (1904/1930) *Protestant Ethic and the Spirit of Capitalism*. Winchester, MA: Allen & Unwin.

Yuki, M., Maddux, W.W., Brewer, M.B., and Takemura, K. (2005) "Cultural Differences in Relationship- and Group-based Trust." *Personality and Social Psychology Bulletin* 31: 48–62.

2

THE SYMBIOSIS MODEL OF IDENTITY AUGMENTATION

Self-expansion and self-extension as distinct strategies

Paul M. Connell and Hope Jensen Schau

Prior research demonstrates that people are identity seekers and makers (Markus and Nurius 1986), and individuals are thought to have a fundamental motive to enlarge their personal identities beyond their immediate selves (Aron *et al.* 1991; Aron *et al.* 1992; Belk 1988). Previous consumer research has found that individuals use the symbolic meaning of consumption in order to construct the identities of their multiple selves (Aaker 1999; Belk 1988; Levy 1959; Schouten 1991). Consumer research has explored the fact that people use consumption to engage in attempts to grow their identities beyond their corporeal selves (Ahuvia 2005; Belk 1988; Reimann and Aron 2009; Schau and Gilly 2003; Strahilevitz and Loewenstein 1998). However, the different strategies that people employ when pursuing identity beyond their immediate selves have not been systematically analyzed. We provide a framework for how and under what conditions people use different strategies when engaging in creating, building, and maintaining identity.

We argue that two frequently used terms, self-expansion and self-extension, are used interchangeably when they are actually distinct strategies for broadening the self. We offer the term *identity augmentation* to capture the general concept of identity broadening beyond the corporeal self, and suggest that self-expansion and self-extension be used to mark specific identity-augmenting strategies. We argue that people use strategies that either extend identity outward by casting consumption aspects of themselves onto others (Belk 1988), or seek to envelop aspects of another into their own selves (Aron *et al.* 1991; Aron *et al.* 1992).

We argue that neither Aron and his colleagues nor Belk are being cited for the entire merit of their work. Rather, the depth of these theoretical frameworks and the nuances between them has been lost as the citation counts of these papers continue to multiply. The Belk framework has come to be known as a theory for incorporating possessions into the self, and the Aron framework has come to be known as a theory for incorporating close others into the self. Thus, the different strategies individuals can take when augmenting identity, whether it be with objects or with other humans, has taken a back seat to the contexts of the theories.

Nuance between the theories is lost even when these works are cross-cited. In his seminal paper, Belk (1988) described objects as creating a person-object-person bridge. Nevertheless, when Belk's framework is cited in the psychology literature, it is typically to note that people incorporate objects into their self-concepts (e.g. Beggan 1992; Dittmar *et al.* 1995, 1996; Huang *et al.* 2009; Sedikides and Skrowronski 1997; Van Boven and Gilovich 2003). Use of this theory in the context of interpersonal relationships and extension of identity into other people is conspicuously absent. We were unable to find exception to this citation pattern of Belk's (1988) work in the psychology literature.

Some consumer researchers have used Aron and his colleagues' (Aron *et al.* 1991) framework to demonstrate that individuals incorporate other human beings into their own identities (Lastovicka and Fernandez 2005; LeRouge and Warlop 2006; Small and Simonsohn 2007), or feel love for brands or objects (Ahuvia 2005; Fournier and Mick 1999). Other consumer researchers have primarily used Aron and his colleagues' (Aron *et al.* 1992) inclusion of other in the self (IOS) scale for methodological reasons as a measure for connectedness or identification with others (e.g. Hung and Wyer 2009; Liu and Gal 2011; Shang *et al.* 2008). While we agree that these are all useful and valid uses of the Aron framework, they have not utilized it as a conceptual background for augmenting identity by enveloping objects of consumption into one's self-concept.

We argue that the full potential of both frameworks has not yet been realized, and that the nuances between these two motivationally different frameworks have not been previously recognized. Understanding the different strategies that individuals take in augmenting identity beyond the corporeal self, whether it be via interpersonal relationships or through consumption, will give greater insights into the motivations behind augmenting identity. In this chapter, we first theoretically parse out self-expansion and self-extension as distinct strategies for identity augmentation. We then provide a symbiosis model of identity augmentation, which provides a framework for how individual, relational and collective identities (Brewer and Gardner 1996; Epp and Price 2008) interplay when dyads or networks of people utilize different combinations of self-expansion and self-extension strategies for identity augmentation. We conclude with a discussion of the implications of our framework.

Distinctions between self-expansion and self-extension

Belk's (1988) "Possessions and the Extended Self," published in the *Journal of Consumer Research*, explains how individuals regard their possessions as part of themselves. In this theory of self-extension, individuals cathect objects with meaning and extend their identities from themselves into objects and other people (see Figure 2.1). As of February 2009, this paper had 514 citations in the Social Sciences Citation Index (SSCI), making it a foundational classic of consumer research. Analysis of these citations reveals that 75% of them appear in business-related journals, whereas 13% appear in psychology journals and the remaining 11% in various other journals. Because the paper was written primarily in the context of possessions and appeared in the *Journal of Consumer Research*, this citation pattern is not surprising.

Two articles published by Aron and his colleagues (1991, 1992) in the *Journal of Personality and Social Psychology* describe a fundamental human motive to absorb aspects of close others into the self (Aron *et al.* 1991) and develop a scale (using Venn diagrams) used to measure the motive that they called self-expansion (Aron *et al.* 1992). In this theory, individuals treat a close other's resources, perspectives, and identities as if these were their own (see Figure 2.2). Analysis of the combined 595 SSCI citations of the 1991 and 1992 papers reveal that 88% of them appear in psychology-related journals, whereas 5% appear in business-related journals and 6% in various other journals. Again, self-expansion theory could indeed apply to consumer behavior, but because the theory devised by Aron and his colleagues was written in the context of personal relationships, the citation pattern is not surprising in this instance, either.

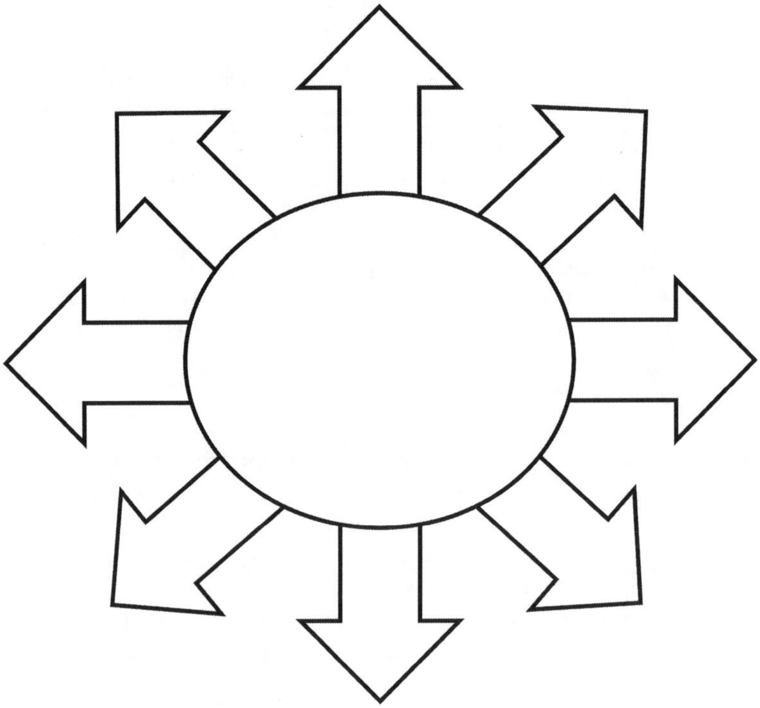

Figure 2.1 Self-extension in the Belk (1988) model

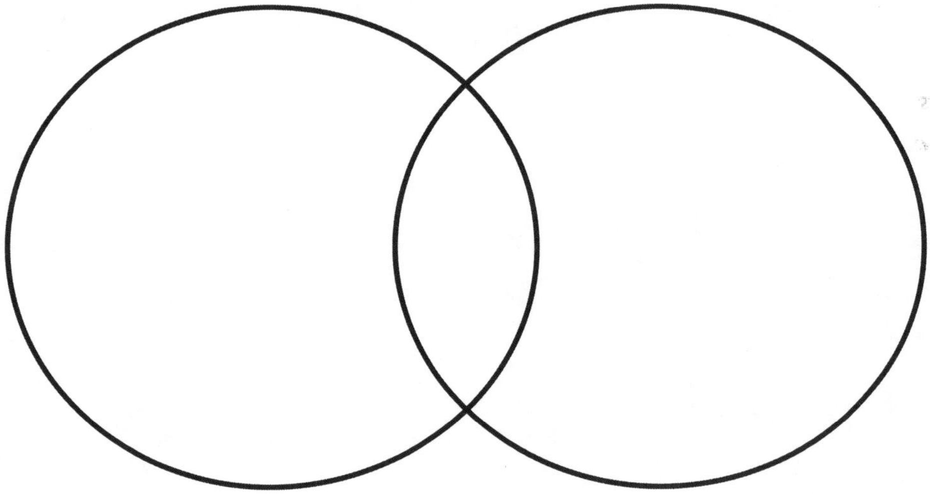

Figure 2.2 Self-expansion in the Aron *et al.* (1991), Aron *et al.* (1992) model

Reimann and Aron (2009) have, however, recently applied self-expansion theory to the realm of consumption. Similarly, they suggest that people treat their possessions' resources, perspectives, and identities as their own. Independently, consumer researchers have begun to embrace the IOS scale in a number of recent studies (e.g. Hung and Wyer 2009; Liu and Gal 2011; Shang *et al.* 2008). As the IOS scale is used more and more frequently within the consumer research domain and with the potential for increased influence of the Aron framework within the consumer research domain, it is possible that it could be confused with the Belk (1988) framework, or that authors will cite both Aron and Belk when writing about consumer identity augmentation without considering the nuances between the two theories.

We argue that neither theory is superior in explaining individuals' attempts to augment identity either through consumption or through close relationships with others. Rather, we argue that both theories explain different strategies for implementing an identity augmentation project. Indeed, we believe that the two perspectives offer two sides of the same coin: both expanders and extenders are requisite for identity augmentation to be successful. When both exist, both parties mutually benefit in a symbiotic relationship. In the section that follows, we provide a framework for a symbiosis model of identity augmentation.

The symbiosis model of identity augmentation

In order to illustrate the requirement of both an active extender and an active expander for symbiotic identity augmentation, we offer a biological analogy by describing each identity project as if it were a living organism that acts according to its whims and reacts to the actions of other identity projects. This single, independent, personal identity project can, however, exist and thrive on its own. When the organism exists in this form, it is analogous to an individual identity project, which is focused on promoting a single individual's personal identity development (Brewer and Gardner 1996; Epp and Price 2008).

However, as previously mentioned, people appear to have a fundamental motive to enlarge the self (Aron *et al.* 1991; Aron *et al.* 1992; Belk 1988). In order to accomplish this, the identity project requires the ability to both expand and extend. Thus, it needs the proper organs to facilitate these actions. Furthermore, the identity project needs multiple sets of organs to accommodate identity augmentation not just with one other individual identity project, but also with many individuals (see Figure 2.3). Because self-extension more closely resembles a projective or penetrative aspect of inserting aspects of one's identity into someone else, we call

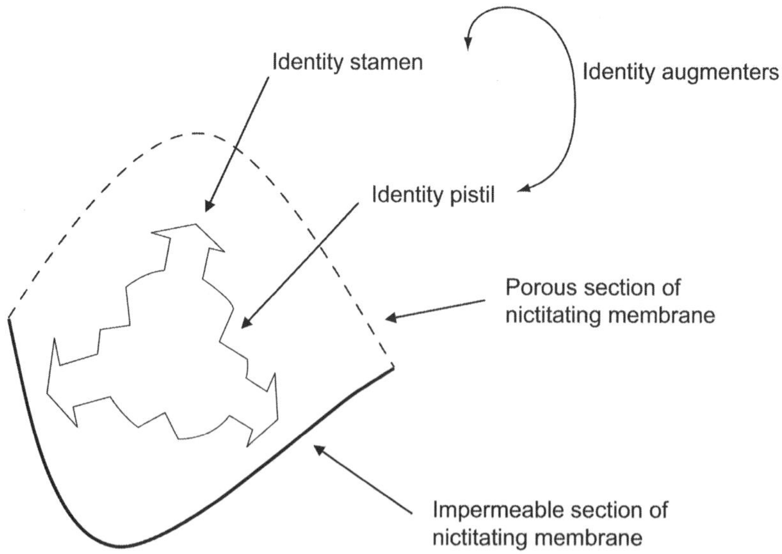

Figure 2.3 The identity project as a dichogamous organism

the extension organs of the identity project its stamens, referring to the male reproductive parts of a flower. Because self-expansion more closely resembles a process of envaginating aspects of the other into the self, we call the expansion organs of the identity project its pistils, referring to the female reproductive parts of a flower. Not all identity projects will have an equivalent will to both expand and extend, however. Therefore, the organism needs to be able to change its organs from stamens (extenders) to pistils (expansions) at will. Thus, each organ in the identity project is dichogamous, meaning that it can switch genders (i.e. identity augmentation strategies) at will.

When two identity projects meet and join, they fuse into a relational identity project, which is then focused on the connections and social relationships with the significant other (Brewer and Gardner 1996; Epp and Price 2008). The organ of the identity project facilitates its actions in relation to the other when one wishes to extend and the other wishes to expand in a communal, symbiotic identity project. However, because the organism also reacts to the expansion and extension attempts of other identity projects, it also needs a shield that can be brought down to welcome desired identity augmentation projects but can be put up to protect it from unwanted identity augmentation attempts. The analogy for this function is demonstrated by a nictitating membrane (referring to a third, translucent eyelid extant in many animals for the purposes of protection). This membrane surrounds the organism, and can be made porous or impermeable at will. When the identity project aims to expand or extend, it retracts the impermeable portion of its nictitating membrane and expands its porous portion so that the other identity project is allowed to comingle. When the identity project resists expansion or extension attempts from others' identity projects, it raises the impermeable portion of its membrane and retracts the porous portion (possibly completely shut) in order to reject the other's unwanted advance.

It is possible, however, that an individual identity project organism can have a symbiotic relationship with more than one other identity project. For example, it could act as a self-extender for one and a self-expander for the other. The other two organisms, however, may not be aware of each other or may not desire to connect. In this case, the original organism shares two separate relational identities with more than two separate organisms. In turn, these two organisms may join with still more identity project organisms, which may or may not join with the original organism. In this case, the identity project becomes collective in nature and begins to resemble something like a coral reef. Thus, a collective identity community is born (Muñiz and O'Guinn 2001; Muñiz and Schau 2005; McAlexander *et al.* 2002; Schouten and McAlexander 1995), which is focused on aspects of building a "we" identity that are consistent among the group members (Brewer and Gardner 1996; Epp and Price 2008).

Symbiotic consumer identity augmentation

When two or more identity projects meet, and when both willing expanders and extenders are extant, then symbiosis occurs (see Figure 2.4). The organisms live in harmony with one another and mutually benefit from the relationship. Nevertheless, it is not realistic to expect that all identity augmentation projects that are important to the extender will be met with similar enthusiasm by the targeted expander. When such conflicts occur, the politics of identity occurs. That is, the definition of the "we" must be negotiated between individual projects or it will fail. In the section that follows, we examine how a passionate extender, the augmentation attempt of which is indeed central to identity, copes with rejection from a potential expander.

Resolution imperative

When an extension attempt is met with resistance by a potential expander, there are conflicting aims of the expander and extender, resulting in a conflict that we call melee (see Figure 2.5).

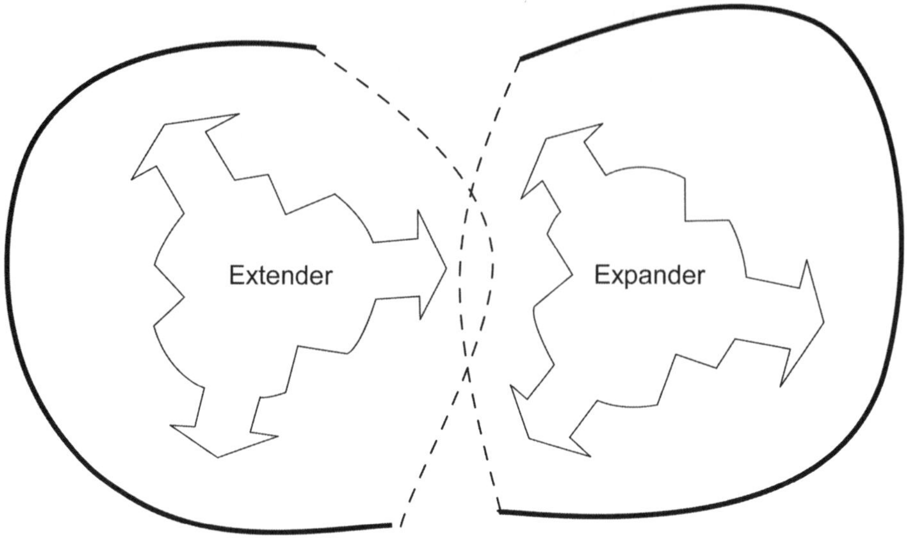

Figure 2.4 Consumer identity augmentation in symbiosis

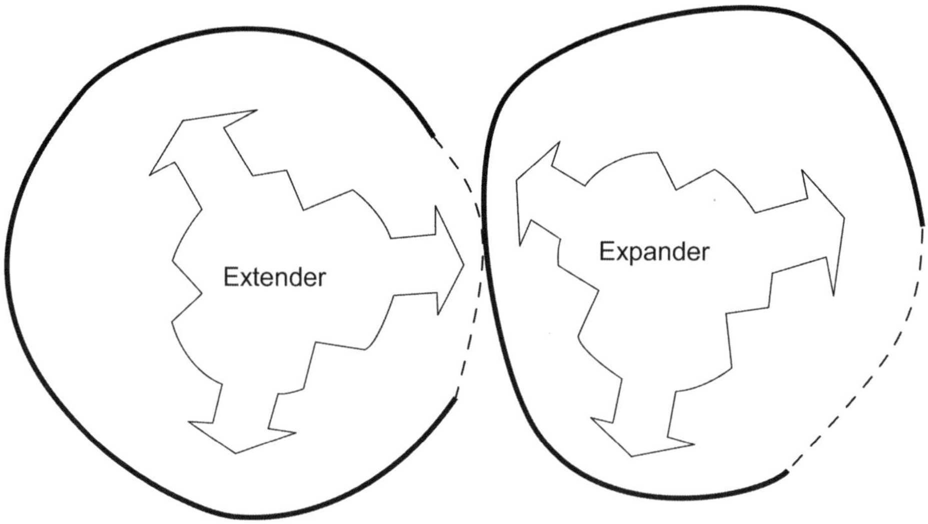

Figure 2.5 Consumer identity augmentation in melee

Using our biological analogy, the identity project attempting to extend via one of its stamens is unable to penetrate the pistils of the expander target because it has expanded the impermeable portion and has retracted the porous portion of its nictitating membrane. When the extender is passionate about the identity augmentation attempt, melee can result in open and ongoing conflict as the extender continues to make attempts to augment identity that are continually rejected by the potential expander. This situation, which we call resolution imperative, calls for the problem to be addressed.

We suggest that the ability to abstract identity projects to a higher level might be the most effective means of dealing with resolution imperatives. If the extender truly wants to achieve symbiosis with the chosen target, then common ground must be found. Otherwise, conflict will continue until the extender finally gives up or the expander pays lip service to accepting the identity augmentation attempt but does not truly accept it. Nevertheless, expanders can have just as much difficulty in engaging in symbiotic identity augmentation as extenders. We delve into how expanders cope with unsuccessful identity augmentation attempts in the next section.

Resolution capitulation

When an expansion attempt is met with indifference by a targeted extender, the expander tends to be ignored by the extender, resulting in a different kind of conflict in aims that we call vacuum (see Figure 2.6). Using our biological analogy, the identity project attempting to expand via one of its pistils is unable to envelop the stamen of the extender target because it has expanded the impermeable portion and has retracted the porous portion of its nictitating membrane. When the expander longs to self-expand by enveloping aspects of a extender target's identity into their own to no avail, a vacuum results. This situation, which we call resolution capitulation, calls for the expander eventually to give up trying to envelop a nonresponsive target.

In some cases, a self-extender and self-expander become so entrenched in identity-augmenting consumption that others are left behind, leading to a state of resolution capitulation. That is, a coalition forms within the collective where some members engage in mutually beneficial identity augmentation but exclude others (Connell *et al.* 2011). When this occurs, it is possible that the rejected members could experience feelings of rejection and perhaps even bitterness about being left out. Just as extenders might need to abstract their identity augmentation attempts to a higher level to get buy-in from expansion targets, either the coalitional members or the rejected expander(s) might need to make conscious efforts to prompt the coalition members to make these abstractions so that the expander is not left behind.

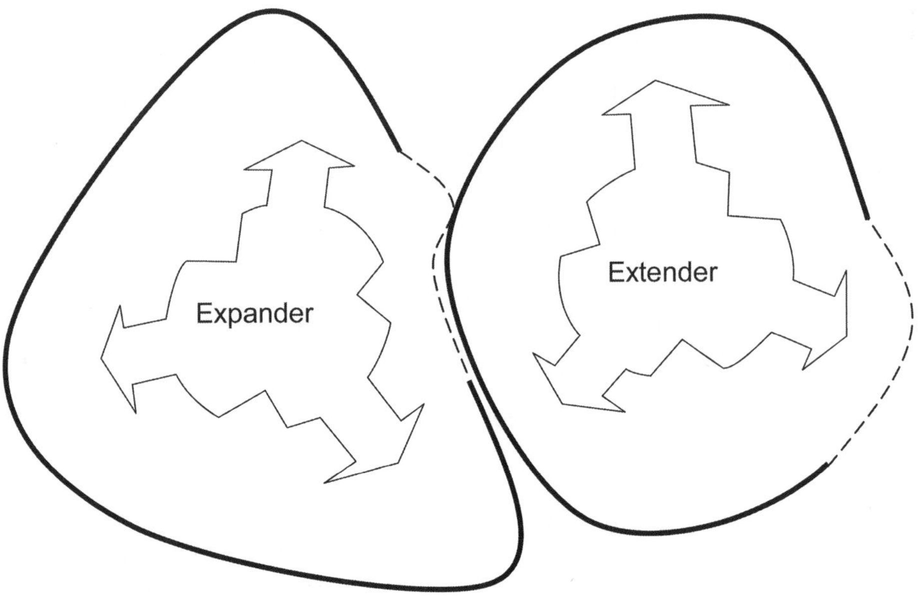

Figure 2.6 Consumer identity augmentation in vacuum

Summary of the identity symbiosis model

In our framework, we demonstrate that not only are self-expansion and self-extension distinct strategies for engaging in identity augmentation, but that they are both prerequisites for it. That is, at least one party needs to be willing and able to share a part of oneself with another, and at least one other party has to be willing and able to accept this part of the other. When both of these conditions are satisfied, symbiosis occurs. In the event that two parties are engaged in symbiotic identity augmentation, relational identities emerge. When more than two parties engage in symbiotic identity augmentation, collective identity communities coalesce.

However, there are instances when these conditions are not met. When extenders are unable to find purchase for their identity seed, then melee between the parties can occur. Melees could create an uncomfortable state of conflict, where there is a resolution imperative to address the conflict. When expanders are ignored or met with indifference by extenders, then a vacuum occurs. In a vacuum, the expander must eventually give up trying to envelop the extender(s). Vacuums could create feelings of isolation and ostracism, particularly when the expander is trying to join a collective.

We believe that a productive means of dealing with melees or vacuums involves abstracting the identity project to a higher level. That is, identity augmentation attempts could focus on what the important aspects of the identity project are for all parties involved. After doing so, then it is far more likely that the parties will be able to find a common ground and achieve symbiosis.

Discussion

In this chapter, we seek to clarify distinctions between two different identity-augmenting strategies. We suggest that people use strategies that are consistent both by extending identity outward by influencing the consumption of others (Belk 1988), and also by enveloping aspects of others' consumption inward into their own identities (Aron *et al.* 1991; Aron *et al.* 1992). Indeed, we believe that both self-extenders and self-expanders are necessary for successful identity augmentation to take place, and offer a symbiosis model of identity augmentation, using biological analogies to identity projects.

Identity projects can be marked by points of conflict, internal contradictions, and ambivalence (Arnould and Thompson 2005). Consistent with this finding, we believe that disconnects between the aims of an identity extender and the person he or she hopes to influence can result in tension. This tension can be alleviated by abstracting the conduit of identity augmentation to a broader level where both parties are able to engage in identity augmentation in a way that is satisfying to all involved. However, there may be times when an extender's identity is very specified and exact. In this case, when the person whom the extender wishes to influence rejects their identity augmentation attempt, the extender can feel threatened, as the attempt to augment the self is thwarted. When the extender is unwilling or unable to redefine identity augmentation in a way that is agreeable to the other, then conflict or tension between the individuals can develop, possibly leading to long-term damage to their relationship.

Similarly, attempts to engage in self-expansion by enveloping parts of another's consumption into one's own identity can also fail. This does not necessarily occur from rejection of an expansion attempt. Rather, it appears that the potential extender has an inability or lack of motivation to conceive of the consumption in terms that allows for the expander to incorporate those elements into his or her identity. When strategies to self-expand fail, individuals might have feelings of isolation, ostracism, or rejection, which also could lead to long-term damage to relationships.

Our model has implications for both consumer and personal relationships research. We find that the nuances between Aron's and Belk's frameworks have not been previously revealed. Previous literature has not focused on the differences between ways in which people augment identity and the underlying motives as well as consequences of employing these two distinct identity augmentation strategies. Rather, it has treated both frameworks as essentially the same theory in two different contexts: Aron's in close personal relationships and Belk's in consumption. Thus, neither Aron nor Belk is being cited for the entire merit of their work due to the intricacies and depth of their theories being lost in translation. This occurs even when Aron's work is cross-cited in consumer research and Belk's work is cross-cited in psychology. As a consequence, we believe that the full potential of understanding identity augmentation has not yet been realized, and represents a potentially vast and rich stream of research.

Our model is also potentially useful for consumer research and personal relationships research in the context of family dynamics and friendships, particularly in the context of intergenerational transfers (Connell *et al.* 2011; Moore *et al.* 2002). We believe that attempts to extend identity to close others can be positive for both parties when the intended extension target also seeks to expand identity by enveloping aspects of the extender's identity. However, in many cases the extender and expander have to negotiate what aspects of identity are most important to them by abstracting consumption relationships to higher levels. Instead of being set in one's ways about extending a particular aspect of one's self to one's children (e.g. Disney princesses), one could consider which aspects of that relationship are most important to one's identity (e.g. family-oriented entertainment). Otherwise, attempts to extend could fail, and could potentially result in intense conflict along the way, due to the unacceptability of the identity augmentation attempt to the potential expander.

We believe that the most harmonious and constructive identity augmentation projects in fact occur when two or more parties engage in both extension and expansion strategies simultaneously. That is, the extender reaches out to a potential expander, negotiates the extension by considering the other's needs and desires (essentially engaging in a form of expansion), and moves forward with identity augmentation projects that are satisfactory for both parties. Similarly, expanders that are assertive but constructive in which parts of identity they are willing to envelop from extenders engage in a form of extension themselves by injecting their own preferences, wants, and needs into the identity augmentation project. In addition, we believe that dyads or groups engaged in intense identity augmentation may need to carefully consider the needs of others in the relationship network so that they, too, are able to expand identity if they so wish. Otherwise, coalitions between the involved parties develop and outsider attempts to augment identity with the coalition via self-expansion are likely to fail, potentially leading to feelings of isolation and resentment.

References

Aaker, Jennifer L. (1999) "The Malleable Self: The Role of Self-Expression in Persuasion." *Journal of Marketing Research* 36: 45–57.

Ahuvia, Aaron C. (2005) "Beyond the Extended Self: Loved Objects and Consumers' Identity Narratives." *Journal of Consumer Research* 32(1): 171–84.

Arnould, Eric J. and Thompson, Craig J. (2005) "Consumer Culture Theory: Twenty Years of Research." *Journal of Consumer Research* 31(4): 868–82.

Aron, Arthur, Aron, Elaine N. and Smollan, Danny (1992) "Inclusion of Other in the Self Scale and the Structure of Interpersonal Closeness." *Journal of Personality and Social Psychology* 63(4): 596–612.

Aron, Arthur, Aron, Elaine N., Tudor, Michael and Nelson, Greg (1991) "Close Relationships as Including Other in the Self." *Journal of Personality and Social Psychology* 60: 241–53.

Beggan, James K. (1992) "On the Social Nature of Nonsocial Perception: The Mere Ownership Effect." *Journal of Personality and Social Psychology* 62(2): 229–37.

Belk, Russell (1988) "Possessions and the Extended Self." *Journal of Consumer Research* 15(2): 139–68.

Brewer, Marilynn B. and Gardner, Wendi (1996) "Who is This 'We'? Levels of Collective Identity and Self Representations." *Journal of Personality and Social Psychology* 71(1): 83–93.

Connell, Paul M., Schau, Hope Jensen and Price, Linda L. (2011) "Intergenerational Transfer of Consumption Practices within Families." In Rohini Ahlwalia, Tanya L. Chartrand and Rebecca K. Ratner (eds), *Advances in Consumer Research*, forthcoming.

Dittmar, Helga, Beattie, Jane and Friese, Susanne (1995) "Gender Identity and Material Symbols: Objects and Decision Considerations in Impulse Purchases." *Journal of Economic Psychology* 16(3): 491–511.

——(1996) "Objects, Decision Considerations and Self-image in Men's and Women's Impulse Purchases." *Acta Psychologica* 93(1–3): 187–206.

Epp, Amber M. and Price, Linda L. (2008) "Family Identity: A Framework of Identity Interplay in Consumption Practices." *Journal of Consumer Research* 35(1): 50–70.

Fournier, Susan and Mick, David Glen (1999) "Rediscovering Satisfaction." *Journal of Marketing* 63(4): 5–23.

Huang, Yunhui, Wang, Lei and Shi, Junqi (2009) "When Do Objects Become More Attractive? The Individual and Interactive Effects of Choice and Ownership on Object Evaluation." *Personality and Social Psychology Bulletin* 35(6): 713–22.

Hung, Iris and Wyer, Robert S. (2009) "Differences in Perspective and the Influence of Charitable Appeals: When Imagining Oneself as the Victim is Not Beneficial." *Journal of Marketing Research* 46(3): 421–34.

Lastovicka, John L. and Fernandez, Karen V. (2005) "Three Paths to Disposition: The Movement of Meaningful Possessions to Strangers." *Journal of Consumer Research* 31(4): 813–23.

LeRouge, Davy and Warlop, Luk (2006) "Why is it So Hard to Predict Our Partners' Product Preferences: The Effect of Target Familiarity on Prediction Accuracy." *Journal of Consumer Research* 33(3): 393–402.

Levy, Sidney (1959) "Symbols for Sale." *Harvard Business Review* 37: 117–24.

Liu, Wendy and Gal, David (2011) "Bringing Us Together or Driving Us Apart: The Effect of Soliciting Consumer Input on Consumers' Propensity to Transact with an Organization." *Journal of Consumer Research* 38(2): 242–59.

McAlexander, James H., Schouten, John W., and Koenig, Harold F. (2002) "Building Brand Community." *Journal of Marketing* 66(1): 38–54.

Markus, Hazel and Nurius, Paula (1986) "Possible Selves." *American Psychologist* 41: 954–69.

Moore, Elizabeth, Wilkie, William and Lutz, Richard (2002) "Passing the Torch: Intergenerational Influences as a Source of Brand Equity." *Journal of Marketing* 66(2): 17–37.

Muñiz, Albert M., Jr and O'Guinn, Thomas C. (2001) "Brand Community." *Journal of Consumer Research* 27(4): 412–32.

Muñiz, Albert M., Jr and Schau, Hope Jensen (2005) "Religiosity in the Abandoned Apple Newton Brand Community." *Journal of Consumer Research* 31(4): 737–47.

Reimann, Martin and Aron, Arthur (2009) "Self-expansion Motivation and Inclusion of Brands in Self: Toward a Theory of Brand Relationships." In Deborah J. Macinnis, C. Whan Park, and Joseph W. Priester (eds), *Handbook of Brand Relationships*. Armonk, NY: Sharpe, pp.65–81.

Schau, Hope Jensen and Gilly, Mary C. (2003) "We Are What We Post? Self-Presentation in Personal Webspace." *Journal of Consumer Research* 30(1): 385–404.

Schouten, John W. (1991) "Selves in Transition: Symbolic Consumption in Personal Rites of Passage and Identity Reconstruction." *Journal of Consumer Research* 17(1): 412–25.

Schouten, John W. and McAlexander, James H. (1995) "Subcultures of Consumption: An Ethnography of the New Bikers." *Journal of Consumer Research* 22(1): 43–61.

Sedikides, Constantine and Skrowronski, John J. (1997) "The Symbolic Self in Evolutionary Context." *Personality and Social Psychology Review* 1(1): 80–102.

Shang, Jen, Reed, Americus, II, and Croson, Rachel (2008) "Identity Congruency Effects on Donations." *Journal of Marketing Research* 45(3): 351–61.

Small, Deborah A. and Simonsohn, Uri (2007) "Friends of Victims: Personal Experience and Prosocial Behavior." *Journal of Consumer Research* 35(3): 532–42.

Strahilevitz, Michal A. and Loewenstein, George (1998) "The Effect of Ownership History on the Valuation of Objects." *Journal of Consumer Research* 25(3): 276–89.

Van Boven, Leaf and Gilovich, Thomas (2003) "To Do or to Have? That is the Question." *Journal of Personality and Social Psychology* 85(6): 1193–202.

Warde, Alan (2005) "Consumption and Theories of Practice." *Journal of Consumer Culture* 5(2): 131–53.

3

THE DIALOGICAL CONSUMER SELF

Shalini Bahl

CLIENT: Sometimes I feel like I have multiple personalities.
THERAPIST: I see, for instance?
CLIENT: Well there's the Shy me, and the No-Nonsense me, Spiky me, Fierce me, Kitten me, the Man-eater me …

The above dialog taken from a 2010 TV commercial for DSW shoes takes place between a therapist and a client. Both characters are depicted as animated shoes. As the client speaks about her different personalities, her appearance and her voice change to match the corresponding shoe type. The ad ends with the caption, "Shoes let you be you. All of you," and there is a voiceover that says, "Multiple choices, one more reason to love DSW." This ad encapsulates a fairly prevalent idea that consumers today have a plethora of marketplace choices to create, maintain, and augment their multiple identities (e.g. Ahuvia 2005; Fournier 1998; Schouten 1991; Thompson 1997; Tian and Belk 2005). Having multiple identities can be liberating in that consumers can choose who they want to be in different situations (Askegaard *et al.* 2005; Firat and Venkatesh 1995), but it can also be a source of conflict if consumers lack the resources to satisfy the inconsistent preferences of different identities (Üstüner and Holt 2007). In the midst of multiple and sometimes conflicting identities, how do consumers make sense of who they are and their consumption decisions?

This chapter uses dialogical self theory (DST) to explore a relatively new way of understanding how consumers make meaning and consumption choices in the marketplace (Bahl and Milne 2010). DST attends to people's internal dialogs that render to an ongoing process of meaning making and shaping preferences. Further, the DST framework recognizes the self at three levels – the meta-position, I-positions, and *Me's*. As such, multiple subject positions exist within an individual, which allows multiple narratives to be authored and co-authored at the different I-positions. This theory provides researchers a new lens to understand consumers at their different I-positions and the dialog between I-positions to make meaning and navigate inconsistencies within the self. The understanding of meta-position has been successfully used in psychotherapy and offers much promise in consumer and marketing contexts as well.

The chapter is organized in the following manner. First, I describe dialogical self theory and its potential use in consumer behavior. Next, I briefly describe a methodology that can be used to study consumers' dialogical selves. Following this, I discuss how the key characteristics of dialogical self inform our understanding of consumers' navigation of inconsistent choices. I conclude with a discussion on new insights that DST offers in the context of consumer identities, dialog, and consumption choices with suggestions for future research.

Dialogical self theory in consumer research

Consumer researchers have explored the multidimensional and dynamic nature of self using different self-conceptualizations including the extended self (Belk 1988), malleable self (e.g. Aaker 1999; Schouten 1991), situational self (e.g. Hogg and Savolainen 1998; Schenk and Holman 1980), fragmented self (Firat and Venkatesh 1995), narrative identities (e.g. Ahuvia 2005; Fournier 1998; Thompson 1997), and so forth. Dialogical self theory is relatively new to consumer behavior (Bahl and Milne 2010) and can add to this discussion of consumer identities by attending to the inner dialogs between multiple I-positions in consumers. Narrative approaches commonly used in consumer behavior embrace the Jamesian distinction between I and Me. The I refers to the self as knower and Me is the self as known and comprises everything and everyone with which the self identifies. DST extends the narrative framework by acknowledging multiple I-positions in the consumer. The I can move from one spatial position to another and imaginatively endow each self-position with a voice so that dialogical relations between positions can emerge (Hermans and Kempen 1993). Consumers make meaning and negotiate consumption preferences as a result of this ongoing exchange between different I-positions (Bahl and Milne 2010). Consumer researchers and marketers studying consumers' processes of meaning and decision making in the marketplace can gain new insights by attending to this array of back and forth conversations between different I-positions.

The dialogical self is defined by inter- and intra-subjective exchange and social domination (Hermans and Kempen 1993). Not only are consumers' identities shaped by relevant others and marketplace exchanges but also by the dialog among different I-positions. Further, an intrinsic aspect of dialog is turn taking in which one voice gains temporary dominance to speak while the listening voices recede in the background. As such, the notion of dominance is not necessarily negative in the dialogical self (Hermans and Kempen 1993).

The dialogical self can be thought of as a society involving oppositions, conflicts, negotiations, cooperation, and coalition among positions (Hermans 1996). Consumer researchers have studied identity conflicts in consumers and the role of possessions and specific brands in creating a coherent sense of self (e.g. Ahuvia 2005; Fournier 1998; Schouten 1991; Thompson 1997; Tian and Belk 2005). Resolution between conflicting identities is seen as an ongoing process of choosing consumption objects and experiences to create a coherent sense of self. Western culture in particular, partly due to the influence of Aristotelian logic, finds it hard to accept and assimilate contradictions (Williams and Aaker 2002). DST, on the other hand, recognizes the potential in internal tensions and conflicts as a "fertile basis for the innovation of the self in particular and for creativity in general" (Hermans and Hermans-Konopka 2010: 151). This perspective offers to consumers and consumer researchers a new way to approach internal inconsistencies whereby dialog offers possibility of new meanings and solutions that would be improbable at any one position (Hermans and Kempen 1993).

Postmodern research in consumer behavior acknowledges the fragmented subject with multiple narratives reflecting multiple realities and even celebrates the liberating aspect of the fragmented self (Askegaard *et al.* 2005; Firat and Venkatesh 1995; Üstüner and Holt 2007). A big focus of postmodern studies in consumer research has been on the fluidity between conflicting cultural identities and the different ways that consumers deal with acculturation issues. Attending to dialog provides a new approach to exploring consumers' negotiation of the dominant cultural influences and loyalty to the minority ideologies. Moreover, the DST framework extends the exploration of the fluid nature of consumers' selves beyond cultural fragmentation to multiple I-positions shaped by consumers' attachments to people, life events, body orientation, possessions and consumption experiences relevant to them.

One other contribution of DST to consumer behavior is the introduction of the meta-position. Given the multiplicity of I-positions and dominance in relationships, Hermans and Kempen (1993) describe the organization among these positions by recognizing the role of a meta-position. The meta-position reflects the ability of the self to observe the different positions from a distance and see how they relate with each other. It provides an overview and evaluation of the different positions, their linkages, and their accessibility, which allows the individual to have a broader perspective in decision making (Hermans and Hermans-Konopka 2010). The meta-position is different from notions of core self or an agency that guarantees a coherent sense of self. Rather, "the meta-position is typically influenced by one or more internal or external positions that are actualized at the moment of self-examination" (Hermans and Hermans-Konopka 2010: 148). Moreover, it is important to see meta-position as an ongoing process of synthesizing the centrifugal and centripetal nature of I-positions (Hermans and Kempen 1993). The centrifugal forces refer to I-positions' needs to retain autonomy and pursue their own strivings. The centripetal forces manage the I-positions so they can live like a harmonious community.

Methodology

In this section I briefly describe the integrated mixed methods approach used by Bahl and Milne (2007, 2010) to discern different voices in informants and their inner dialogs. They employed a combination of narratives, clustering – quantitative and qualitative, and metaphors in a study conducted over four stages. Mixed methods render to "divergent interpretations" (Thompson *et al.* 1998) that are consistent with the idea of multiple narrative voices in dialogical self and therefore a useful methodology to study consumers' dialogical selves.

The first two stages in the mentioned study were adapted from Raggatt's (2000, 2002) personality web protocol in order to discern important I-positions in the informants. The subsequent stages used metaphors as a way to get informants to speak about their feelings and perspectives at different I-positions. The nature of the study dictated an in-depth study of a small sample size of six participants. See Table 3.1 for informants' description and I-positions. The relationships among the I-positions in the six informants with respect to six different consumption experiences resulted in 90 possible relationships between I-positions and 216 self-consumption dyads (Bahl and Milne 2010). However, future studies exploring the dialogical nature of consumers could adapt the above combination of methods for larger sample sizes.

Table 3.1 Participants' information and I-positions

	Informant	*Age*	*Profession*	*I-positions*
1	Ari	40	Musician/teacher	Sensitive, artist and teacher, striver, survivor, helpless
2	Beth	54	Activist	Quilt maker, teacher, activist, spiritual, mother and grandmother, lover of nature
3	Brad	26	Realtor	Athletic, closed, open, spiritual, experience with women, critical
4	Dee	37	Project manager	Strong, competitive, giving, low self-esteem, insecure
5	Jessica	21	Student	Irish, social, concerned with appearance, realistic, goal-oriented, politically aware
6	Sam	57	Artist	Connected with world, spiritual, enjoying life, healing, expressive

Narratives

Dialogical self theory is rooted in narrative psychology. As per the narrative approach, people make sense of who they are through the psychosocial construction of life stories (Escalas and Bettman 2000; Harré and Gillett 1994; Hermans *et al.* 1992; McAdams 1996; Raggatt 2002). Dialogical self theory extends this view by acknowledging multiple narrative voices within any life story (Raggatt 2002). Narrative voices in participants can be discerned, as in the first stage of Bahl and Milne's (2007, 2010) study, by attending to participants' most important symbolic valuations or attachments in the social (people), temporal (events), bodily, physical (objects and places) and moral (beliefs) spheres (Harré and Gillett 1994; Raggatt 2002).

Quantitative and qualitative clustering

The second stage of the Bahl and Milne (2007, 2010) study involved participants thinking about relationships among their attachments using qualitative and quantitative methods. Informants' narratives provided important attachments that were used as input for multidimensional scaling (MDS) and cluster analysis in this stage. The qualitative clustering task invited participants to group their attachments into self-relevant clusters that reflected their different I-positions and to provide a name for each I-position cluster. The resulting MDS and cluster solutions were analyzed in combination with the informants' narratives and qualitative clusters in order to discern I-positions relevant to the informants at the time. A more detailed description of the use of MDS and cluster analysis in this stage can be read in Bahl and Milne's (2007) contribution.

Metaphors

Pictures effectively elicit respondents' subconscious thought processes (Belk *et al.* 1989; Collier and Collier 1986; Zaltman 1997). Further, as emphasized by Zaltman (1997), metaphors can elicit cognitive processes and important mental states that are not easily accessible to the conscious mind of participants. The third stage in the study used metaphor analysis to get a deeper understanding of the I-positions and their dialogical relationships. Informants brought in three-to-five images that represented their feelings and thoughts about their I-positions discerned in the previous stages. After describing the metaphorical meanings for each I-position, the informants created a montage that provided an overview from the meta-position of how the different I-positions relate with each other. In addition, the informants described dialogues that are typical between their I-positions.

In the fourth stage, metaphors were used to understand the meaning of consumption at different levels of the self and dialogical relations between them in the context of consumption choices. Informants were asked to bring three-to-five metaphorical pictures for each of their three most positive and three most negative consumption experiences with respect to products, brands, and/or services. After describing each consumption experience from the meta-position, informants were invited to describe the experience from the perspective of each I-position, providing examples from real situations involving different I-positions and possible or actual dialogue between different positions with respect to the consumption experience.

Looking at consumption through the lens of dialogical self

Consumers' preferences and narratives are not the same at a meta-position and their different I-positions (Bahl and Milne 2010). The importance and feelings pertaining to consumption objects and activities differ across the I-positions with some overlap across positions and some unique perspectives, which point to the specific needs and concerns at the different I-positions. If consumption narratives at different I-positions involve inconsistent feelings, how do consumers make decisions? In this section, I discuss specific characteristics of the dialogical self – dominance reversal, innovative solutions, and meta-position – that explain how consumers navigate inconsistent consumption preferences across their I-positions.

Dominance reversal: fluidity, compartmentalization, and negotiations

Dominance reversal: Dominance is a normal aspect of any dialogue. It is natural that in a dialogue between two I-positions the speaking voice gains dominance while other voices recede. DST also speaks of dominance reversal suggesting that different I-positions take turns in being dominant (Hermans and Kempen 1993). As such, consumption decisions and experiences are driven by the I-position that is dominant in that situation.

To illustrate dominance reversal, let's study the example of Ari (Bahl and Milne 2010), an artist and teacher whose metaphors to depict his feelings for Doritos (a brand of packaged food) at the meta-position conveyed mixed feelings including "wearing food," needing "damage control," "love them [Doritos] but can kill me," "unhealthy but appealing," and "seductive." Ari's voice, meaning, and feelings related to Doritos change depending upon which I-position is describing the experience. For the *spiritual* I-position, it is a "tasty treat" and he can see the "humor" in it. From this position eating Doritos is a "joyous experience" and there is no "guilt." He is satisfied after eating a few chips. The survivor I-position is in more "control" so he will either "not eat the Doritos" or "control" what he does eat. For the survivor I-position Doritos is a "reward" for exercising. The *helpless* I-position views them as being "more seductive" and "a crutch." When he is in pain he uses Doritos as a "distraction" and finds that he gives into the seduction more easily. From his *helpless* I-position Ari can eat "a whole bag of Doritos" because he is feeling "weak and helpless." The decision to eat and how much along with the experience and meanings for Doritos changes and is determined by the I-position that is dominant at the time.

Fluidity: What allows consumers to move easily between different I-positions is the notion of fluidity. The ease with which informants moved between their I-positions is noted by one of the informants, Brad: "Sometimes I indulge one or the other [I-position], in fact, I guess I always do" (Bahl and Milne 2010: 188). The celebratory nature of the fragmented self (Firat and Venkatesh 1995) and the protean self (Lifton 1993) speak to the freedom postmodern consumers have in moving between different I-positions without any conflict.

Compartmentalization: Dominance reversal naturally renders to the ability in people to compartmentalize consumption activities to specific I-positions (Bahl and Milne 2010). Compartmentalization enables people to engage in negative or seemingly contradictory consumption behaviors because they are able to isolate those behaviors to specific I-positions for which such behaviors are acceptable. For example, Jessica continues to enjoy smoking in company even though all her other voices are against smoking because she can compartmentalize her smoking to her *social* I-position:

> When I'm here [at school], [I] don't view [myself] as like a smoker, it's just when I go out, people see me smoking, but I associate that more with like a different part of my lifestyle. When I'm here it's like I'm not a smoker and I'm goal oriented ambitious Jessica, not the smoker Jessica.
>
> *(Bahl and Milne 2010: 188)*

Negotiations: The ability to move between different I-positions allows for negotiations between I-positions in order to justify their choices (Bahl and Milne 2010). This aspect of the dialogical self adds to the current research on intra-self negotiations, which have been examined in specific contexts such as time styles' preferences (Cotte *et al.* 2004) and the use of rituals, brands, and possessions to negotiate identities (Ahuvia 2005; Bonsu and Belk 2003; Fournier 1998; Holt 2002; Kjeldgaard and Askegaard 2006; Schau and Gilly 2003; Tian and Belk 2005).

Consumer researchers have studied the liberatory aspect of moving between I-positions in the context of cultural identities (Askegaard *et al.* 2005; Üstüner and Holt 2007). The notion of dominance reversal, which is an important aspect of DST, offers the three vehicles of fluidity, compartmentalization, and negotiation that help consumers navigate inconsistent identities and choices in the marketplace. However, Hermans and Hermans-Konopka (2010) warn against trends in consumerism promoted by the choices available that can result in consumers lacking the depth of experience and a leveling of enjoyment. This is an important area of investigation that needs further exploration in consumer research.

Innovative solutions: coalitions and conciliations

Dialogue between I-positions initiates possibilities for innovative solutions that wouldn't have been possible in the absence of dialogue. Two distinct types of dialogical relationships that offer innovative outcomes are coalition and conciliation (Bahl and Milne 2010; Hermans and Hermans-Konopka 2010).

Coalition: Coalition involves two or more I-positions working together to come up with a win-win solution that caters to the needs of both I-positions (Ahuvia 2005; Bahl and Milne 2010). For example, the *quilt maker* and the *activist* I-positions in Beth have been in conflict over how her time should be spent, but this dialogue allows her to see a new way of meeting the needs of both her I-positions:

> I can't really be a *quilt maker* when I'm spending time as an *activist*. I don't have enough time really to do both. Well, I'm making a choice. I'm looking at my life and finding choices that reflect who I am now and I might give up a certain amount of the activism so I can have this other life. Otherwise I'm gonna miss out on having a life that I would really like.
>
> I guess there's another way to look at it in that my making quilts and giving them away to children in orphanages is also being an activist it's a different kind of activism. My activism is gonna take a different turn now. It has to somehow incorporate the quilting thing, so that I can be an activist in a way of giving something lovely to someone. I might not be an activist standing on a street corner trying to change what's happening. I'll be an activist by offering my love to children.
>
> *(Bahl and Milne 2010: 189)*

Conciliation: Conciliation involves the creation of a new position that resolves the conflict between the earlier positions (Hermans and Hermans-Konopka 2010). For example, Beth's *spiritual* and *activist* I-positions have conflicted because she doesn't see spirituality and activism as compatible. She creates a new position defined by the Native American approach to spirituality that allows her to pursue activism in a spiritual way:

> there's a lot of people who are spiritual who meditate a lot and they aren't activists. I can't do that. It's like if I care about something, I have to be out there, if it's a tree being killed, find out why and do something about it. To me spirituality, especially

> eco-spirituality, ecological spirituality is caring about the planet, caring about the land. I guess it's more of a Native American approach to spirituality – I have to be out there and saying, doing something.
>
> *(Beth, Interview 4, from transcripts made for Bahl and Milne 2010)*

Meta-position: balance and compassion

The meta-position has the important quality of seeing multiple I-positions and the ability to juxtapose different perspectives so that they can be compared. The ability to view the world from the perspective of a meta-position instead of the narrow lens of a particular I-position offers many advantages to consumers including bringing balance and compassion in situations involving conflict (Bahl and Milne 2010). The balancing quality is reflected in Jessica's *realistic* I-position, which has the ability to see multiple points of view. From this I-position she approaches junk food in a balanced way even though she initially picked it as a negative consumption experience: "I guess the realistic part of me knows how to balance the two [indulging with friends and concerned about weight]" (Jessica, Interview 4, from transcripts made for Bahl and Milne 2010).

Research in psychology has noted the importance of self-compassion as an important coping mechanism to deal with negative or unpleasant situations (e.g. Adams and Leary 2007; Crocker and Canevello 2008; Neff 2003). In the context of consumer research, compassionate dialogs can help deal with inconsistent I-positions and choices by offering a non-judgmental acceptance of the values and preferences at different I-positions (Bahl and Milne 2010). In an example exemplifying compassion, Sam's different voices are angry when Sam gives in to eating sugar products when he is depressed. Sam's *spiritual* voice speaking from a meta-position is compassionate as it can see the pattern in other voices related to overconsumption of sugar products:

> *The spiritual* I-position: "okay, you [his healing I-position] aren't doing something very smart here but I'm not gonna get down on you for doing it. Because you have a lot of patterns of doing something stupid, which get reinforced because there's a part of you that is dying to feel stupid and this is the way to feel stupid and so you keep on doing the stupid thing." If you're gonna do any bad habits whatsoever, less you can feel about it the better. Because it's feeling bad will make you do it more in association with a behavior that reinforces it.
>
> *(Bahl and Milne 2010: 187)*

By being compassionate towards other voices, the *spiritual* I-position helps Sam in dealing with sugar addiction. These findings are consistent with the work on self-compassion in psychology. The positive impact that the meta-position can have on consumer decision making makes it a viable topic for further research in consumer behavior.

Discussion and future research

Dialogical self theory introduced the study of dialogical relationships between I-positions in consumer research (Bahl and Milne 2010). Attending to the dialogical self offers new insights into how consumers navigate the sea of inconsistent identities and consumption preferences. In this section I conclude with three key insights using DST in consumer research with related questions for future research.

The innovative potential of dialog

Many consumer studies suggest that consumers strive to avoid conflicts and create a coherent and unified sense of self (e.g. Ahuvia 2005). DST, on the other hand, argues that conflicts and contradictions are not necessarily negative as they offer the potential for innovations in the self. Dialog between I-positions invites creative exchanges like coalition and conciliation that bring win-win solutions for the concerned I-positions or the creation of new I-positions that embrace the goals of conflicting I-positions in innovative ways.

Further, DST suggests that that consumers are not always looking to resolve internal inconsistencies among I-positions because of their ability to compartmentalize (Bahl and Milne 2010). As seen in Jessica's case, she is able to smoke despite all her I-positions disliking smoking because of her ability to compartmentalize smoking to her *social* I-position. People's ability to move between I-positions and engage in innovative exchanges allows them to embrace seemingly inconsistent consumption preferences. Some other questions related to the innovative nature of dialog that still need to be addressed are:

- Under what conditions do consumers seek to resolve internal inconsistencies and when do they find it useful to compartmentalize?
- What are other innovative dialogical relations between I-positions besides coalition, conciliation, and compartmentalization?
- How do post-consumption outcomes such as customer satisfaction, evaluation, and well-being vary as a result of different dialogical relationships, including compassion, coalition, conciliation, compartmentalization, and domination?

Compassion, conflicts, and self-control

Compassion is a fairly new concept within consumer research that offers much potential for future research. Bahl and Milne (2010) found compassion to be a kind of dialog that helps to avoid conflict between I-positions with different preferences. Their findings corroborate research in psychology that self-compassion is an effective mechanism to deal with addictions and negative behaviors. These initial findings beg more research in consumer behavior:

- What is the difference between self-control and self-compassion in dealing with negative consumption behaviors?
- How do self-compassion and self-control compare in bringing long-term changes in lifestyles and habits? Do some personality types and situations call for one intervention rather than the other?
- Can self-compassion be taught to people to bring positive changes in their consumption habits?

Meta-position and mindful choices

The meta-position is another valuable contribution of DST. Even though a meta-position may be drawn to some positions more than others, it offers an overarching view of different I-positions and their relationships with each other (Hermans and Hermans-Konopka 2010). The findings in the Bahl and Milne (2010) study suggest that the ability to see different positions with non-judgmental acceptance assists in overcoming overconsumption and addiction problems (e.g. Ari and Sam eat fewer unhealthy foods when they are compassionate toward other I-positions addicted to such foods). The meta-position as a process of synthesizing multiple perspectives also creates possibility of bringing balance by alternating unhealthy consumption with healthier choices. For example, Jessica's *realistic* position allows her *social* I-position to enjoy eating with her friends, knowing that she can go the gym the next day to make up for any overeating. Future research can further explore the role of a meta-position in consumers:

- Are consumers' decisions different when made from a meta-position versus other I-positions?
- Can activating a meta-position provide a more holistic view of a consumption decision and provoke more mindful choices than decisions made at specific I-positions? If so, such research would be valuable in getting people to make choices that are healthy and sustainable for them and the environment.
- How can consumers be taught to activate their meta-position in the marketplace?

DST offers a useful framework to study consumer behavior as it facilitates studying consumers at different levels of the dialogical self. Especially, as interest in transformative consumer research grows (Mick 2006), researchers are going to need innovative theoretical frameworks to explore identity formations and negotiations in a fragmented postmodern world. DST provides such a framework to consumer researchers by introducing important concepts including dialogical relationships, dominance reversal, meta-position, and compassion. DST opens new doors for transformative consumer researchers to engage in cross-disciplinary work with direct impact on consumer well-being.

References

Aaker, Jennifer (1999) "The Malleable Self: The Role of Self-Expression in Persuasion." *Journal of Marketing Research* 36 (February): 45–57.

Adams, C. E. and Leary, M.R. (2007) "Promoting Self-compassionate Attitudes Toward Eating Among Restrictive and Guilty Eaters." *Journal of Social and Clinical Psychology* 26: 1120–44.

Ahuvia, A. C. (2005) "Beyond the Extended Self: Loved Objects and Consumers' Identity Narratives." *Journal of Consumer Research* 32: 171–84.

Askegaard, S., Arnould, E.J., and Kjeldgaard, D. (2005) "Postassimilationist Ethnic Consumer Research: Qualifications and Extensions." *Journal of Consumer Research* 32: 160–70.

Bahl, S. and Milne, G.R. (2007) "Mixed Methods in Interpretive Research: An Application to the Study of Self-Concept." In R.W. Belk (ed.), *Handbook of Qualitative Marketing Research*. London: Edward Elgar.

——(2010) "Talking to Ourselves: A Dialogical Exploration of Consumption." *Journal of Consumer Research* 37: 176–95.

Belk, R.W. (1988) "Possessions and the extended self." *Journal of Consumer Research* 15: 139–67.

Belk, R.W., Wallendorf, M., and Sherry, J.F., Jr (1989) "The Sacred and the Profane in Consumer Behavior: Theodicy on the Odyssey." *Journal of Consumer Research* 16: 1–38.

Bonsu, S.K. and Belk, R.W. (2003) "Do Not Go Cheaply into That Good Night: Death Ritual Consumption in Asante Ghana." *Journal of Consumer Research* 30 (June): 41–55.

Collier, John, Jr, and Collier, Malcolm (1986) "Visual Anthropology: Photography as a Research Method." Revised and expanded edition. Albuquerque: University of New Mexico Press.

Cotte, J., Ratneshwar, S., and Mick, D.G. (2004) "The Times of Their Lives: A Phenomenological Inquiry on the Nature and Role of Consumers' Timestyles." *Journal of Consumer Research* 31 (September): 333–45.

Crocker, J. and Canevello, A. (2008) "Creating and Undermining Social Support in Communal Relationships: The Role of Compassionate and Self-image Goals." *Journal of Personality and Social Psychology* 95: 555–75.

Escalas, J.E. and Bettman, J. (2000) "Using Narratives to Discern Self-Identity Related Goals and Motivations." In S. Ratneshwar, D.G. Mick, and C. Huffman (eds), *The Why of Consumption: Contemporary Perspectives on Consumer Motives, Goals, and Desires*. London: Routledge.

Firat, F.A. and Venkatesh, A. (1995) "Liberatory Postmodernism and the Reenchantment of Consumption." *Journal of Consumer Research* 22: 239–67.

Fournier, S. (1998) "Consumers and Their Brands: Developing Relationship Theory in Consumer Research." *Journal of Consumer Research* 24: 343.

Harré, R. and Gillett, G. (1994) *The Discursive Mind*. London: Sage.

Hermans, H.J.M (1996) "Voicing the Self: From Information Processing to Dialogical Interchange." *Psychological Bulletin* 119: 31–50.

——(2001) "The Construction of a Personal Position Repertoire: Method and Practice." *Culture & Psychology* 7: 323–65.

Hermans, H.J.M. and Hermans-Konopka, A. (2010) *Dialogical Self Theory: Positioning and Counter-Positioning in a Globalizing Society*. Cambridge: Cambridge University Press.

Hermans, H.J.M. and Kempen, H.J.G. (1993) *The Dialogical Self: Meaning as Movement*. New York: Academic Press.

Hermans, H.J.M., Kempen, H.J.G., and Van Loon, R.J.P. (1992) "The Dialogical Self: Beyond Individualism and Rationalism." *American Psychologist* 47: 23–33.

Hogg, Margaret K. and Savolainen, Maria H. (1998) "Symbolic Consumption and the Situational Self." *European Advances in Consumer Research* Vol. 3: 11–16.

Holt, Douglas B. (2002) "Why Do Brands Cause Trouble? A Dialectical Theory of Consumer Culture and Branding." *Journal of Consumer Research* 29 (June): 70–90.

Kjeldgaard, D. and Askegaard, S. (2006) "The Glocalization of Youth Culture: The Global Youth Segment as Structures of Common Difference." *Journal of Consumer Research* 22 (September): 231–47.

Lifton, R.J. (1993) *The Protean Self: Human Resilience in an Age of Fragmentation*. New York: Basic Books.

McAdams, D.P. (1996) "Personality, Modernity, and the Storied Self: A Contemporary Framework for Studying Persons." *Psychological Inquiry* 7(4): 295–321.

Mick, D.G. (2006) "Presidential Address: Meaning and Mattering Through Transformative Consumer Research." *Advances in Consumer Research* 33: 1–4.

Neff, K.D. (2003) "Self-compassion: An Alternative Conceptualization of a Healthy Attitude Toward Oneself." *Self and Identity* 2: 85–102.

Raggatt, P.T.F. (2000) "Mapping the Dialogical Self: Towards a Rationale and Method of Assessment." *European Journal of Personality* 14: 65–90.

——(2002) "The Landscape of Narrative and the Plural Self: Exploring Identity Using the Personality Web Protocol." *Narrative Inquiry* 12: 290–318.

Schau, Hope Jensen and Gilly, Mary C. (2003) "We Are What We Post? Self-Presentation in Personal Web Space." *Journal of Consumer Research* Vol.30: 385–414.

Schenk, T.C. and Holman, R.H. (1980) "A Sociological Approach to Brand Choice: The Concept of Situational Self Image." *Advances in Consumer Research* Vol. 7: 610–14.

Schouten, J.W. (1991) "Selves in Transition: Symbolic Consumption in Personal Rites of Passage and Identity Reconstruction." *Journal of Consumer Research* 17: 412–25.

Thompson, C.J. (1997) "Interpreting Consumers: A Hermeneutical Framework for Deriving Marketing Insights from the Texts of Consumers' Consumption Stories." *Journal of Marketing Research* 34: 438–55.

Thompson, Craig J., Stern, Barbara, and Arnould, Eric (1998) "Writing the Differences: Poststructural Pluralism, Retextualization, and the Construction of Reflexive Ethnographic Narratives in Consumer Research." *Consumption, Markets, and Culture* 2 (September): 105–60.

Tian, K. and Belk, R.W. (2005) "Extended Self and Possessions in the Workplace." *Journal of Consumer Research* 32: 297–310.

Üstüner, T. and Holt, D.B. (2007) "Dominated Consumer Acculturation: The Social Construction of Poor Migrant Women's Consumer Identity Projects in a Turkish Squatter." *Journal of Consumer Research* 34: 41–56.

Williams, P. and Aaker, J.L. (2002) "Can Mixed Emotions Peacefully Coexist?" *Journal of Consumer Research* 28: 636–49.

Zaltman, G. (1997) "Rethinking Market Research: Putting People Back In." *Journal of Marketing Research* 34: 424–37.

I.II

Emotions and the self

4
THE EMOTIONAL SELF

Nicole Verrochi Coleman and Patti Williams

Historically, the self has been described as possessing a unique duality: it is both an experiencer and doer, on the one hand, and an object of evaluation and affective responses, on the other (Greenwald and Pratkanis 1984). Affect, or emotion, as understood in this literature, has typically focused on the self as an object of evaluation leading to emotional outcomes associated with self-esteem. In contrast, contemporary emotion literature focuses on the self as an experiencer or interpreter of situations: stimuli gain emotional impact as they reward or punish the individual (Carver and White 1994). The self is considered so crucial to emotion experience that "it is impossible to define effective emotional stimuli independent of the subject" (Frijda 1986: 268). The self is a set of concerns that may be implicated in a conscious or non-conscious assessment, or appraisal, of situations; relevance to the self imbues situations with meaning and emotional impact (Frijda 1986). Emotions function to set priorities among the many goals and stimuli that impinge upon individuals at any given moment (Simon 1967). In this view, the self-structure is the basis of emotional response, an experiencer that relies upon emotions to guide behavioral tendencies.

In this chapter, we extend this view of emotions to the social identity literature. We review literature on identity and emotions, presenting a new perspective in which emotions are components of an identity's knowledge structure, supporting identity enactment and realization. We argue that discrete emotions, along with cognitions, values and beliefs, are integral to social identities. Specific emotions may help individuals engage in successful identity enactment, helping to set priorities, achieve important goals, and facilitate the experience of living that identity.

Emotions and social identity theory

Social identities are organizing constructs allowing individuals to understand and unify their everyday actions (Kleine *et al.* 1993; Reed 2004; White and Dahl 2007). Individuals possess a constellation of individual identities varying in salience and centrality, through which the global self can be deconstructed (Tajfel 1982). Attitudes, behaviors, and brands that assist in performing a specific identity become associated with it, subsumed into its knowledge structure, providing "what-to-do" information when expressing the identity (Kleine *et al.* 1993). The more important an identity, and the more representative a behavior, attitude, or brand is of that identity, the greater the likelihood of association.

Individuals rely on their social identities to provide social categorization, self-definition, and behavioral guidance (Markus and Wulf 1987), avoiding activities and objects inconsistent with the held identity (White and Dahl 2007), and approaching those that are consistent (Reed 2004). Recent work has emphasized the effect of identity on advertising effectiveness (Forehand and Deshpandé 2001), preference formation, and consumption (Reed 2004; White and Dahl 2007). While this literature has examined attitudes, behaviors and beliefs associated with social identities, it has largely neglected discussion of potential social identity and emotion associations, and whether such links might also influence consumption.

Emotions as identity feedback

Emotions have previously been implicated in the social identity literature through feedback processes; individuals examine and evaluate their identity performance, resulting in emotional outcomes such as pride (success) or shame (failure) (Laverie *et al.* 2002) prompting corrective identity enactment. In this view, emotions arise because of appraisals of the self as an attitude object (Greenwald and Pratkanis 1984).

The symbolic interactionist literature, from which the concept of social identity arose, has long considered emotions relating to identities, via self-reflection or self-evaluation. Starting with Cooley (1902), sociologists have seen emotions as originating in evaluations of whether the self presented to the world is seen as the presenter desires. Cooley described various "sentiments" occurring to support or re-calibrate the self in society: pride, honor, and self-respect are feelings of social approval, while resentment, shame, and mortification arise from social disapproval. Similarly, Shott (1979) suggested that self-conscious emotions such as guilt, shame, and embarrassment promote conformity to social norms, encouraging reparation of one's self-concept or self-presentation. Similar ideas have been explored in Higgins's self-discrepancy theory, where discrepancies between "actual," "ought," and "ideal" selves give rise to specific emotional reactions (e.g. disappointment, shame) (Higgins 1987). Recently, Burke and Stets (2009) suggested a perceptual control model, whereby a discrepancy between identity standards and perceived performance leads to negative emotions, which motivate the individual to self-regulate and relieve the discrepancy. Thus, in the domain of social identity, emotions have largely been considered as part of a feedback process arising from an evaluation of identity performance, rather than as part of identity enactment itself.

Emotions associated with identities

In contrast, we propose that emotions are not merely evaluations of the self (self as object), but rather an intrinsic part of performing identities (self as experiencer), such that specific emotions are connected to the knowledge structures of particular social identities. We propose a process whereby individuals experience and regulate emotions during identity performance in order to better enact those identities. Just as different attitudes, values, beliefs, and products are associated with distinct identities and their enactment (Kleine *et al.* 1993), we argue that there are also distinct emotions associated with different social identities.

Emotions may become associated with social identities in several ways. First, there may be identity "prototypes" affiliated with specific emotions (e.g. Mike Tyson is an athlete and is always angry); second, discrete emotions imply action tendencies (Frijda 1986) that may correspond to the characteristics and objectives of that identity. Emotions arise when an individual attends to a situation and sees it as relevant to his or her goals, leading to goal-related action tendencies. Thus, specific emotions may be uniquely linked to identity-relevant action readiness. For instance, anger leads to the desire to overcome obstacles and punish others – qualities that may aid athletes during competition. In this way, emotions can provide instrumental benefits (Tamir 2009) where the action tendencies align with the identity's goals.

Both explanations suggest that specific emotions may be useful in the expression of an identity, leading to a set of emotional prescriptions or emotion profiles associated with distinct social identities. For instance, a mother should be warm and caring, but that same woman in the boardroom is expected to be coolly professional and possibly even aggressive. Conforming to the emotion profile enhances identity enactment – a woman who is warm is more "motherly" than one who is aggressive (Simpson and Stroh 2004). We propose the term emotion "profile" to suggest that there is a *set* of emotions that may be associated with each identity, rather than the one-to-one emotion-identity relationship implied in terms such as "feeling rule" or "emotion norm." Two research domains, organizational behavior and cross-cultural psychology, allude to associations between identities and emotions, providing support for our perspective.

In organizational behavior, "emotion labor" literature proposed that certain emotions are associated with specific jobs (e.g. flight attendants are happy and excited) (Hochschild 1983). Importantly, for some occupations, displaying the correct emotion actually becomes part of job training and execution. Hochschild (1983) found that much on-the-job stress originates from a discrepancy, termed "emotional dissonance," between the individual's actual emotional state and the emotion required to uphold the job's "feeling rules," such as a flight attendant forcing a happy demeanor when dealing with a rude passenger, despite actually feeling anger. This emotional dissonance creates feelings of personal inauthenticity, and thus, job dissatisfaction, poorer service outcomes, and a more stressful workplace (Simpson and Stroh 2004). Although occupations are not necessarily identities, they can be, and thus the emotion labor literature suggests specific emotions may be associated with self-knowledge structures. However, while the work on emotional labor has focused on the discrepancy between felt and expressed emotion, we instead suggest that when individuals conform to the emotions associated with their active identity, they will experience enhanced authenticity in its enactment.

Cross-cultural psychology has also examined emotions as they relate to the self, with an emphasis on how cultural differences in self-construals shape emotional experiences. Markus and Kitayama (1991) argued that the emotion-relevant appraisals of situations are constrained by, and largely derived from, distinct self-construals. Thus, emotional experience, including which emotions are expressed and experienced, should vary with different self-definitions. An independent self-construal views the self as the source of action and motivation, based on an internal set of traits, attributes, values and goals. Ego-focused emotions (e.g. pride, anger) arising from the independent self-construal, are associated with an individual's internal state or attributes and are consistent with the need for individual awareness, experience and expression (Aaker and Williams 1998). In contrast, an interdependent self-construal views the self as inherently connected with others, making relationship partners an important source for individual actions and motivations. Other-focused emotions (empathy, shame) are associated with others in a social context and are consistent with the need for unity, harmony and the alignment of one's actions with those of others (Aaker and Williams 1998). For example, among those with independent self-construals, happiness arises from personal and internal aspects and is seen as caused by personal achievement, while for those with interdependent self-construals happiness is associated with harmonious social relationships (Uchida and Kitayama 2009).

These literatures suggest that emotion profiles are acquired through learned norms (Hochschild 1983), are uniquely associated with self-structures (Markus and Kitayama 1991) and that conforming to them can enhance the enactment of key roles (Simpson and Stroh 2004). They support our contention that emotions can be more than evaluations of identity performance;

specific emotions may be associated with specific social identities, giving rise to emotion profiles that constrain the set of emotions consistent with that identity.

We present two studies examining the associations between specific identities and discrete emotions. If identities are associated with emotions, activating a particular identity should impact the range of emotion experience. This experience is generally described as a system beginning with appraisals, leading to reactions and expressions, the activation of motivation through action readiness, and ultimately, regulation (Frijda 1986). Appraisals are the origination point of emotions; individuals must attend to stimuli and assess their relevance and valence. Emotion expressions facilitate communication of information: when a friend is happy we know something good has happened. Experiencing an emotion often prompts motivations for individuals to act or exert effort in a specific direction. The final dimension of emotion experience is regulation – the management of ongoing emotional experiences, influencing the course of the emotion process (Gross 1998).

Recent work by Coleman and Williams (2012) demonstrates the impact of social identity emotion profiles on motivation, persuasion and emotion regulation. In a series of studies, they identify and examine three identity-emotion associations widely held by undergraduates (athlete-anger, volunteer-sadness, environmentalist-disgust). In one study, participants primed with an athlete (volunteer) identity worked harder on an effortful task when they listened to angry (sad) music, than when listening to sad (angry) music. In others, participants were more persuaded by emotional appeals that were consistent (versus inconsistent) with their active identity, and participants consumed more of a product positioned as helping regulate their emotions in an emotion profile-consistent manner. We extend these earlier findings, predicting that activation of a social identity and its corresponding emotion profile will impact emotional contagion and product preferences; an individual will only "catch" identity-consistent emotions and will prefer products that support the experience of identity-consistent emotions.

Experiment 1: emotion profiles and contagion

Emotions can serve information functions – particularly through the facial display of emotion, which reveals the emotional state of a person to other individuals (Frijda 1986; Ekman 1992). Emotional expression can also produce emotional convergence between the expresser and observers: an event known as emotional contagion (Hatfield *et al.* 1993). Importantly, the likelihood of contagion varies with the group membership and relevance shared by the observer and expresser (Chartrand and Dalton 2009).

If relevance is critical for contagion, emotion contagion should intensify if the expresser's emotional state is consistent with the emotion profile of the receiver's identity. Thus, individuals should be more likely to catch expressions consistent with their active identity, while proving resistant to inconsistent expressions.

Participants and procedure

Students and staff (N = 169; average age 24, range 18–66; 56% female) participated in this study. Participants completed a writing task to prime a specific, common, social identity (athlete, volunteer, control), spending five minutes describing a time when they performed well as either an athlete or volunteer (control participants wrote about their day) (Reed 2004). Then, participants moved to a second study ostensibly examining reactions to pictures of unknown people. A photograph showing either an angry or sad facial expression was presented for 20 seconds (Beaupré and Hess 2005). After viewing the photograph, participants rated their emotional state on 13 items (happy, sad, angry, calm, bored, warm, frustrated, touched, depressed, agitated, anxious, cheerful, and dejected, using a nine-point scale where 1 = not at all, to 9 = extremely) (Small and Verrochi 2009).

Results

Two emotion indices were created: anger (angry, frustrated, agitated; $\alpha = 0.835$), and sadness (sad, depressed, dejected; $\alpha = 0.774$). There were no effects of identity or expression on the remaining filler items.

Anger ratings were analyzed with a two-way ANOVA (ANalysis Of VAriance in a between-groups design) using emotion expression (anger or sadness) and identity (volunteer, athlete, control) as predictors. A main effect of emotion emerged, such that participants experienced greater levels of anger when they viewed a photograph expressing anger (4.13) versus a photograph expressing sadness (3.20), $p = 0.002$. However, this is qualified by the predicted interaction between identity and emotion ($F(2, 163) = 32.123$, $p < 0.001$) shown in Figure 4.1. Contrasts show that athletes who viewed an angry photograph experienced more anger (5.25) than either volunteers (2.18, $p < 0.001$) or control participants (4.12, $p < 0.001$). Participants with an active volunteer identity experienced little emotional contagion from angry photos; their experienced anger was significantly lower than that of control participants (2.18 vs. 4.12, $p < 0.001$). This

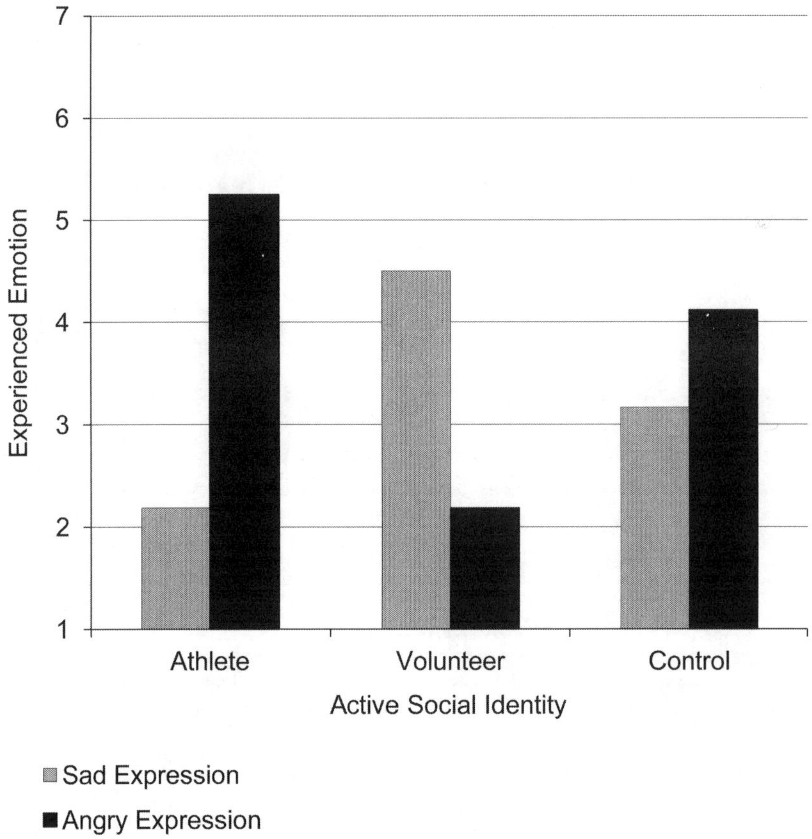

Figure 4.1 Emotion profiles and emotion contagion

suggests that individuals with an active athlete identity, for which anger is in the emotion profile, responded to an angry expression with a high degree of emotional contagion. Volunteers, for whom anger is identity inconsistent, rejected emotional contagion of anger.

Sadness ratings were analyzed similarly with emotion expression and identity as predictors. Again, the predicted interaction between identity and emotion emerged ($F(2, 163) = 28.799$, $p < 0.001$); ratings of experienced sadness were higher for volunteers (4.51) than either athletes (2.19, $p < 0.001$) or control participants (3.17, $p < 0.001$). Athletes showed significantly lessened contagion of the emotion profile-inconsistent stimuli, with lower levels of sadness as compared to control, $p < 0.001$.

Discussion

This study tested whether emotion profiles would influence emotional contagion. Supporting this, athletes experienced emotional contagion when presented with an angry expression, and volunteers experienced contagion when presented with a sad expression. In both cases, the intensity of the caught identity-consistent emotion was greater than the control condition: athletes experienced more anger than control when viewing an angry expression, and volunteers experienced more sadness than control when viewing a sad expression. While able to correctly recognize the emotion expression in the picture, participants resisted those expressions that would have violated their active emotion profile.

What happens, though, when an athlete is experiencing sadness, or a volunteer anger? How might an individual change her emotions in order to better conform to her active identity? The second study presents individuals with an emotion-regulating product, and tests whether individuals will prefer products that help achieve emotion profile consistency.

Experiment 2: emotion profiles and regulation

This study has a 3 (identity: athlete, volunteer, control) × 2 (emotion: anger, sadness) × 2 (product positioning: enhance, reduce emotions) between-subjects design, where emotion is induced incidentally and product positioning is done via advertisements (Williams and Drolet 2005). We expect that athletes will prefer products that reduce emotion when experiencing sadness, but not anger, and volunteers will prefer products that decrease anger, but not sadness. Theories such as mood repair (Labroo and Mukhopadhyay 2009) and emotion regulation (Gross 1998) predict preferences for emotion-regulating products should not differ based on either the identity or the emotion: all participants are in negative states, thus all should want to decrease their emotions. Our unique prediction highlights the contribution of the proposed theory; consistency with identity-specific emotion profiles is a driver of emotion experience and regulation.

Participants and procedure

Participants ($N = 224$; average age 24, age range 18–59; 59% female) completed two studies. First, they were primed with either the athlete, volunteer, or control identity, as before. Next, they completed a "divided attention" study, in which they performed two tasks simultaneously. This study contained both the emotion manipulation and the product evaluation.

Emotions were induced through a facial and bodily feedback procedure. Participants were asked to position their faces and bodies into specific orientations corresponding to either anger or sadness (Duclos *et al.* 1989), and told to maintain the position throughout the study. These types of emotion manipulations induce mild-to-moderate levels of the target emotion (e.g. anger position induces anger, not general negativity) (Duclos *et al.* 1989).

Participants then saw a product to test and evaluate. They watched one of two advertisements about a fictional product, AudioClear White Noise Headphones, positioned as either enhancing or reducing emotions. In the enhance emotions condition, participants read that the product would intensify emotional experiences, "tightening the connection between their mind and body." The reduce emotions advertisement stated that the product would reduce emotions, "making their minds calm and rational." During the video, white noise played through participants' headphones as a simulated product sample. Following the advertisement, participants evaluated the brand on multiple measures.

Results

Two measures – attitude toward the product (1 = dislike, to 9 = like intensely) and purchase intention (1 = definitely would not, to 9 = definitely would buy) – were combined to form a single index of brand attitude ($\alpha = 0.878$) and analyzed via a three-way ANOVA, with identity, emotion and product positioning as between-subjects factors. A main effect of identity was found, where participants with an active volunteer identity had significantly higher attitudes toward the headphones (4.69) than participants in the control condition (3.72), $p < 0.05$. No other contrasts were significant.

This was qualified by the predicted three-way interaction between identity, emotion, and product positioning (F (2, 212) = 8.432, $p < 0.001$). As predicted, participants with an active athlete identity experiencing sadness significantly preferred the reducing headphones (5.21) to the enhancing ones (3.25), $p < 0.01$. Participants with an active athlete identity experiencing anger had no preference for the reducing headphones (4.03) versus the enhancing ones (4.63), $p > 0.30$. However, participants with active athlete identities experiencing an inconsistent emotion (sadness) preferred a product that promised to reduce the inconsistent emotions.

Participants with active volunteer identities experiencing anger had significantly higher attitudes toward the product positioned as reducing (5.04) versus enhancing (3.71) emotions, $p < 0.05$. When participants with an active volunteer identity experienced the emotion profile-consistent emotion of sadness, however, they had significantly higher attitudes toward the product positioned as enhancing emotion (5.74) versus reducing it (4.30), $p < 0.05$. These participants were attempting to increase their experience of sadness, further boosting their emotion profile-consistency. Control condition participants showed no preference differences for either product, regardless of emotion experienced, all $p > 0.50$.

Discussion

This experiment further supports the proposed theory: individuals engage in emotion regulation to enhance emotions that are consistent with the identity's emotion profile, or to decrease emotions that are inconsistent with the emotion profile. Using a different type of emotion manipulation, this study finds that participants with active athlete identities attempt to eliminate sadness, while those with active volunteer identities try to reduce anger. Importantly, participants regulated their emotions with a product, explicitly connecting the theorized process to consumer choices.

Conclusion

Social identity has a rich research tradition both in and out of the consumer behavior literature (e.g. Cooley 1902; Reed 2004), but has typically taken a more cognitive approach or only treated affect as an attitudinal evaluation of identities. Starting with the earliest conceptualizations of the self as a social mirror, emotions have been interpreted as feedback mechanisms, informing the individual about his conformity to or invalidation of important identity characteristics (Cooley 1902; Burke and Stets 2009). In contrast to these self-as-attitude-object views, we present a new perspective on the self-as-experiencer: discrete emotions are associated with specific social identities, and are an important component of identity enactment. The studies presented here provide two implications of emotion profiles: stronger contagion of emotion profile-consistent emotions and preference for products that enhance emotion profile-consistency.

However, these results merely scratch the surface of emotion-self connections. Burgeoning research investigates how emotions are experienced at the group level (Smith *et al.* 2007; Swann *et al.* 2010). Intergroup emotions theory research (IET) (Smith *et al.* 2007) shows that emotions can be felt at the group level, and greater overlap between group and individual emotions tightens bonds between the social identity and the individual (Swann *et al.* 2010). Thus, emotions can function not only to support the individual's identity, but his sense of connectedness with those groups with which he identifies. Our work suggests that groups may share identity-consistent emotions and perhaps engage in group-level regulatory processes to enhance these emotions (and reduce identity-inconsistent emotions) at a social level. For example, athletes may strive to experience anger individually, with their teammates, and perhaps their fans.

Ultimately, we ask: how does the self influence and incorporate emotion? Research on the self describes the various attitudes, behaviors, and belief structures that comprise identities, which then combine into a global self-concept (Tajfel 1982). As research on the self has investigated the behaviors that lead to identity expression and support of the self-concept, emotions have begun to enter the self-concept discussion. This chapter describes two research streams relating emotions to the self: emotions as feedback mechanisms supporting identity expression and emotions as components of the actual identities. We believe this new link between emotions and identity enactment provides rich opportunities for exploration, particularly regarding how these emotional-self connections influence consumption patterns and identity expression in the marketplace.

Further reading

Burke, P.J. and Stets, J.E. (2009) *Identity Theory*. Oxford: Oxford University Press. (A recent review of the symbolic interactionist view of self.)

Hochschild, A.R. (1983) *The Managed Heart: Commercialization of Human Feeling*. Los Angeles, CA: University of California Press. (The classic text connecting emotions with job performance and satisfaction.)

Kleine, S.S., Kleine, R.E., III, and Kernan, J.B. (1993) "Mundane Consumption and the Self: A Social Identity Perspective." *Journal of Consumer Psychology* 2(3): 209–35. (One of the first papers linking the self to consumption.)

Markus, H.R. and Kitayama, S. (1991) "Culture and the Self: Implications for Cognition, Emotion and Motivation." *Journal of Personality and Social Psychology* 98(2): 224–53. (A foundational paper in cross-cultural psychology.)

References

Aaker, J.L. and Williams, P. (1998) "Empathy Versus Pride: The Influence of Emotional Appeals Across Cultures." *Journal of Consumer Research* 25(3): 241–61.

Beaupré, M.G. and Hess, U. (2005) "Cross-cultural Emotion Recognition Among Canadian Ethnic Groups." *Journal of Cross-Cultural Psychology* 36(3): 355–70.

Burke, P.J. and Stets, J.E. (2009) *Identity Theory*. Oxford: Oxford University Press.

Carver, C.S. and White, T.L. (1994) "Behavioral Inhibition, Behavioral Activation, and Affective Responses to Impending Reward and Punishment: The BIS/BAS Scales." *Journal of Personality and Social Psychology* 67(2): 319–33.

Chartrand, T.L. and Dalton, A.N. (2009) "Mimicry: Its Ubiquity, Importance, and Functionality." In E. Morsella, J.A. Bargh, and P.M. Gollwitzer (eds), *Oxford Handbook of Human Action*. New York: Oxford University Press, pp. 458–83.

Coleman, N.V. and Williams, P. (2012) *Feeling Like My Self: Emotion Profiles and Social Identity*. Working Paper: University of Pittsburgh.

Cooley, C.H. (1902) *Human Nature and the Social Order*. New Brunswick: Transaction Publishers.

Duclos, S.E., Laird, J.D., Schneider, E., Sexter, M., Stern, L. and Van Lighten, O. (1989) "Emotion-specific Effects of Facial Expressions and Postures on Emotional Experience." *Journal of Personality and Social Psychology* 57(1): 100–8.

Ekman, P. (1992) "Facial Expressions of Emotion: New Findings, New Questions." *Psychological Science* 3 (January): 34–8.

Forehand, M.R. and Deshpandé, R. (2001) "What We See Makes Us Who We Are: Priming Ethnic Self-awareness and Advertising Response." *Journal of Marketing Research* 38 (August): 336–48.

Frijda, N.H. (1986) *The Emotions*. New York: Cambridge University Press.

Greenwald, A.G. and Pratkanis, A.R. (1984) "The Self." In R.S. Wyer and T.K. Srull (eds), *Handbook of Social Cognition*. Hillsdale, MI: Erlbaum, pp. 129–78.

Gross, J.J. (1998) "The Emerging Field of Emotion Regulation: An Integrative Review." *Review of General Psychology* 2(3): 271–99.

Hatfield, E., Cacioppo, J.T. and Rapson, R.L. (1993) "Emotional Contagion." *Current Directions in Psychological Science* 2(3): 96–9.

Higgins, E.T. (1987) "Self-Discrepancy: A Theory Relating Self and Affect." *Psychological Review* 94(3): 319–40.

Hochschild, A.R. (1983) *The Managed Heart: Commercialization of Human Feeling*. Los Angeles, CA: University of California Press.

Kleine, S.S., Kleine, R.E., III, and Kernan, J.B. (1993) "Mundane Consumption and the Self: A Social Identity Perspective." *Journal of Consumer Psychology* 2(3): 209–35.

Labroo, A.A. and Mukhopadhyay, A. (2009) "Lay Theories of Emotion Transience and the Search for Happiness: A Fresh Perspective on Affect Regulation." *Journal of Consumer Research* 36(2): 242–54.

Laverie, D.A., Kleine, R.E., III, and Kleine, S.S. (2002) "Reexamination and Extension of Kleine, Kleine & Kernan's Social Identity Model of Mundane Consumption: The Mediating Role of the Appraisal Process." *Journal of Consumer Research* 28(4): 659–69.

Markus, H.R. and Wulf, E. (1987) "The Dynamic Self-concept: A Social Psychological Perspective." *Annual Review of Psychology* 38: 299–37.

Markus, H.R. and Kitayama, S. (1991) "Culture and the Self: Implications for Cognition, Emotion and Motivation." *Journal of Personality and Social Psychology* 98(2): 224–53.

Reed, A., II (2004) "Activating the Self-importance of Consumer Selves: Exploring Identity Salience Effects on Judgments." *Journal of Consumer Research* 31(2): 286–95.

Shott, S. (1979) "Emotion and Social Life: A Symbolic Interactionist Analysis." *American Journal of Sociology* 84(6): 1317–34.

Simon, H.A. (1967) "Motivational and Emotional Controls of Cognition." *Psychological Review* 74(1): 29–39.

Simpson, P.A. and Stroh, L.K. (2004) "Gender Differences: Emotional Expression and Feelings of Personal Inauthenticity." *Journal of Applied Psychology* 89(4): 715–21.

Small, D.A. and Verrochi, N.M. (2009) "The Face of Need: Facial Emotion Expression on Charity Advertisements." *Journal of Marketing Research* 46 (December): 777–87.

Smith, E.R., Seger, C.R. and Mackie, D.M. (2007) "Can Emotions Be Truly Group Level? Evidence Regarding Four Conceptual Criteria." *Journal of Personality and Social Psychology* 93(3): 431–46.

Swann, W.B., Jr, Gómez, Á., Huici, C., Morales, J.F., and Hixon, J.G. (2010) "Identity Fusion and Self-sacrifice: Arousal as a Catalyst of Pro-group Fighting, Dying, and Helping Behavior." *Journal of Personality and Social Psychology* 99(5): 824–41.

Tajfel, H. (1982) "Social Psychology of Intergroup Relations." *Annual Review of Psychology* 33(1): 1–39.

Tamir, M. (2009) "What Do People Want to Feel and Why? Pleasure and Utility in Emotion Regulation." *Current Directions in Psychological Science* 18(2): 101–5.

Uchida, Y. and Kitayama, S. (2009) "Happiness and Unhappiness in East and West: Themes and Variations." *Emotion* 9(4): 441–56.

White, K. and Dahl, D.W. (2007) "Are All Out-groups Created Equal? Consumer Identity and Dissociative Influence." *Journal of Consumer Research* 34(4): 525–36.

Williams, P. and Drolet, A. (2005) "Age-related Differences in Responses to Emotional Advertisements." *Journal of Consumer Research* 32(3): 343–54.

5

BELOVED MATERIAL POSSESSIONS

Ends or means?

John L. Lastovicka and Nancy J. Sirianni

> The car smelled like rotten milk and Cheerios ... But I absolutely, unconditionally and devotedly loved that car ... it finally hit me that my attachment to the car was that ... I was ... a mom. That was my mom car. And I loved it. And everybody in the neighborhood knew it was me, you know. And they would all wave ... when I [would] drive by.
>
> A reporter recalls a car she lost in an accident (Schulte 2011a, 2011b)

> She [my mother] said, "I've never heard anyone describe their car as a dating relationship." I said, "What else would you call it?" You might as well call it [my car] a girlfriend.
>
> A young man recalls a conversation about his car (Lastovicka and Sirianni 2011: 327)

Love for a material object refers to the nature and degree of consumers' emotional attachment to specific material objects – and not brands (Lastovicka and Sirianni 2011). Our epigraph presents introspections from two different consumers who both love their cars. These introspections illustrate two different metaphors used by consumer researchers in understanding consumer love for specific material objects.

The first consumer's attachment to her car reflects her "mom" identity. This is consistent with Ahuvia's (2005) portrayal of consumers' beloved possessions acting as anchors in identity construction. This is rooted in both Belk's (1988) perspective of considering meaningful possessions as extensions of self, as well as Aron *et al.*'s (1991) contention that love involves a fusion of identities, where beloved others are part of a sense of self. Thus this identity metaphor treats the possession of a beloved consumer product as a *means* for forming and communicating identity both to the owner and to others. The "mom car" illustrates that "possessions are an important component of sense of self" (Belk 1988: 139).

With the second consumer, the appropriateness of the identity metaphor is less clear. In the second case, the car appears less as a *means* to some intended end (such as an identity of being masculine or financially prosperous) and more as a relational *end* in itself. This consumer has consciously blurred the person-object distinction and his relationship with his car appears to be an end in itself. Thus this second metaphor is relational. Rooted in Belk's (1987) semiotic perspective, this second view recognizes that any given consumption object's meaning is polysemous (or multiple) and idiosyncratic. Thus depending upon the private meanings of a possession to a given consumer, a possession may serve either as a means of identity construction or, alternatively, as the young man's introspection illustrates, as an end in itself as an emotional partner in a consumer-object relationship (Belk 1987).

Whereas the first metaphor (of beloved possession as a means of identity construction) has received considerable application in consumer research, we will refine and further explicate the relatively less explored relational metaphor (of beloved material object as an end in a consumer-possession relationship). Thus our chapter is organized in three sections. First we review our conceptual foundations and consider a fundamental consumption phenomenon where the relational metaphor informs what the identity metaphor does not. Next we demonstrate an empirical benefit of the relational metaphor. Finally, we discuss the implications of this work for consumer research. In particular, we note how the relational metaphor informs our understanding of smitten consumers' identities.

Conceptual foundations

The identity metaphor and possessions as means to identity construction

As reviewed elsewhere (Arnould and Thompson 2005), Belk's (1988) conceptualization of the extended self has frequently been used as a theoretical basis for understanding how consumers use market-generated and consumer-co-created symbolic resources to forge self-identities. This perspective treats the possession of a beloved consumer product as a potential *means* for forming and communicating identity. Because of the prominence of this often-used and well-known perspective in the consumer research literature – which is considered in other chapters in this volume (Belk 2012) – we choose to begin with an examination of the less well-employed perspective in which a beloved possession is viewed as a relational *end* in itself.

The relational metaphor and beloved possessions as relational ends

With the exception of Lastovicka and Sirianni's (2011) research on consumers' loving relationships with their cars, computers, bicycles and firearms, the majority of prior work that has explored possessions as relational ends has focused on consumers' connections with their pets (Ahuvia 2008; Belk 1996; Hill *et al.* 2008; Holbrook *et al.* 2001; Holbrook and Woodside 2008). This line of inquiry provides evidence that some consumers consider their household animals as close companions – namely as friends and family members like siblings, children and grandchildren (Hirschman 1994), and as such, include their pets in family events such as holidays and group portraits (Belk 1996). While the animals' status is not typically equal to other human family members such as human children (Belk 1996), their treatment as relationship partners – and not just as objects that exist to meet consumers' needs – is justified by their inherent value (Ahuvia 2008; Beverland, Farrelly and Lim 2007). Following Holbrook *et al.* (2001: 11), what pet owners "share in common is a deep awareness that their relationship with one or more animal companions is an end in itself and definitely not a means to some other end such as the admiration of others, an excuse to get exercise, or a creature to protect the house against intruders." In sum, this stream of research finds that consumers purchase their pets to satisfy social needs often resulting in close, intimate ties akin to those with human relationship partners. That is, consumers' relationships with their animal companions are considered ends in themselves, and not means to achieve other goals such as forming and communicating identity.

Limits of the identity metaphor

Due to the prominence of the extended self in the consumer research literature, it is possible that the identity metaphor has become the default foundation for understanding possession love (Ahuvia 2005), brand love (Carroll and Ahuvia 2006), or attachment (Park *et al.* 2010). This very useful metaphor, however, is like all metaphors in that it has limitations. In particular, it does not directly consider the acquisition of beloved objects. How, for example, does infatuation begin? What sparks such love at first sight? This is important as research on this form of object love, consumer infatuation, is largely absent (Lastovicka and Sirianni 2011).

When it is said that "possessions are an important component of sense of self" (Belk 1988: 139), this clearly assumes possession, and, therefore, acquisition is a *fait accompli.* Those beloved objects studied empirically with the identity metaphor are typically already owned objects that, in many cases, have histories with consumers that are well beyond an initial infatuation. For example, consider Ahuvia's (2005) deconstruction of an urban consumer's beloved antique furniture. The furniture had been owned and used on her family's ranch for decades and, as such, reflected her rancher identity. Moreover, due to the renewed fashionable nature of Mission-styled antiques, her heirlooms also solidified a sophisticated urbane identity. Ahuvia (2005) used this case to illustrate how a beloved possession resolved an identity conflict (such as between an urban versus rural identity). However, the example also illustrates that the lens of the extended self and the identity metaphor most readily informs possessing, owning and having – as opposed to acquiring a beloved object and the infatuation leading to such acquisition.

As we subsequently demonstrate, in contrast, the relationship metaphor does offer insights for addressing the questions we have posed. The deep-seated and innate motivating attachment systems described by Bowlby (1969) offer templates for early-in-life and later-in-life interpersonal relationships (Hazan and Shaver 1987; Shaver and Mikulincer 2006). As Lastovicka and Sirianni (2011) contend, some consumer-object relationships are metaphorically enacted within these interpersonal templates. Moreover, the questions we have posed – which consider infatuation and the nascent stages of consumers' loves for material objects – have largely been ignored by prior work on consumer love.

An aesthetically beautiful material object can touch the human heart and can lead consumers to experience the emotion of love (Norman 2005). One look at an attractive product, and comparable to gazing at a beautiful person (Sternberg 1986, 2006), some consumers may experience infatuation or a love-at-first-sight response. Such infatuation may capture consumer interest and may feed an immediate and powerful desire for sensory proximity, interaction and acquisition. However, what happens if consumers who are already in love with their own material possession are confronted with a comparable and attractive alternative product? Are they interested in the other? Or do they resist? Do such consumers surrender to temptation?

Aesthetics and infatuation in interpersonal relations

Prior research has addressed comparable questions in interpersonal relationships. Much of this work is rooted in the Darwinian concept of intersexual selection – namely, organisms develop alluring physical and behavioral characteristics to attract potential mates. Such characteristics are thought to signal reproductive fitness (Sugiyama 2005). In research on human relationships, Walster *et al.* (1966) report that physical attractiveness is the best predictor of whether a heterosexual pair will see each other beyond a first date and initiate a relationship. Passion is the quickest component of love to ignite and it is typically sparked by physical attractiveness (Sternberg 1986, 2006). Thus a physically attractive quality sparks passion and the motivational drive in passion leads to infatuation or love at first sight and a desire to be proximate to the beloved. The peacock's tail feathers are the standard Darwinian example of physical attractiveness. In research on humans, several human body-aesthetic properties – including symmetry and golden-ratio proportions – are found attractive (Schmid *et al.* 2008). Moreover, consistent with the Darwinian perspective of attractiveness signaling fitness, human body symmetry has been found empirically correlated with general intelligence (Prokosch *et al.* 2005) and athletic ability (Manning and Pickup 1998).

In human relationships, the lure of attractiveness is moderated by current relationship status. In particular, those involved in loving interpersonal relationships, relative to those who are not in such relationships, tend to devalue – and pay less attention to – attractive potential partners (Johnson and Rusbult 1989; Maner *et al.* 2007). Evolutionary psychologists view such devaluation of attractive others as an innate mechanism facilitating the maintenance of long-term loving relationships (Maner *et al.* 2007).

Aesthetics and infatuation in consumer-object relations

Lastovicka and Sirianni (2011) speculate that many loving consumer-object relationships are born in an infatuation, in which a consumer's initial encounter with an object's sensory experience (i.e. its look, motion, feel, scent, taste and sound) elicits a captivating aesthetic response. Lastovicka and Sirianni (2011) view infatuation as a nascent form of love characterized by passion, but without the intimacy and commitment found in other established forms of consumption love.

A material object that becomes the focus of a consumer's infatuation relies on what industrial design theorist Donald Norman (2005) calls visceral design. Norman contends that successful product designs viscerally do what nature does, with both succeeding in eliciting biologically pre-wired emotive reactions to attractive forms. One attractive form found both in-nature and in the man-made world is the golden ratio.

Euclid's φ, or the golden ratio, is the ratio obtained when a line through the sequential points A, B and C is cut such that the ratios of the line segments AC/AB = AB/BC = φ = 1: which is an irrational number approximately equal to 1.618. The mathematics of the Fibonacci sequence, logarithmic spirals and φ are intimately connected (Livio 2002). This ratio is a natural phenomenon, appearing ubiquitously in nature, including the spiral of DNA molecules, leaf arrangements of plants and unperturbed gestational growth (Thompson 1992; Cook 1978). In the man-made environment, some analyses of major ancient architectural achievements show evidence of φ – e.g. the Parthenon's façade and the blocks used to construct the Great Pyramids (Livio 2002). Moreover, plastic surgeons rely on φ when planning facial reconstructions (Bashour 2006).

Consumer researchers have investigated φ with two-dimensional objects and find preferences for product labels (Raghubir and Greenleaf 2006) and brand logotypes (Pittard *et al.* 2007) with φ-rectangle properties: a φ rectangle's longer side (L) and shorter side (S) have the ratios [S+L]/L = L/S = φ. Consumer research, however, has yet to consider the aesthetic appeal of φ in three-dimensional material objects where, for example, a profile view of the object's major horizontal line includes a φ proportion. As an example of this, Norman (2005) points to the E-type Jaguar sports car – which is in the design collection of the Museum of Modern Art in New York – as a prototype of visceral design; the ratio of the Jaguar's total length relative to distance between the windshield and the rear of the car is nearly φ.

Thus sports cars with φ-proportioned profiles may well be attractive to consumers. However, what happens if consumers with a passion-charged relationship with their own car are confronted with such an attractive car? Does it capture their interest? Would they want to drive it?

Or do they resist? If, as Lastovicka and Sirianni (2011) suggest, consumer-object relationships are metaphorically enacted within the deep-seated interpersonal templates we have discussed, then consumers in an existing passionate relationship with a beloved possession should not be interested in an attractive and comparable alternative and, consequently, a new infatuation would not be sparked. Alternatively, among the less restricted, who are not in an existing passionate relationship, then infatuation with an attractive new object may occur. We now proceed to empirically examine these ideas in an experiment.

A relationship-based experiment

Participants

A total of 350 automobile-owning undergraduate students at Arizona State University participated in our laboratory experiment in exchange for course credit in an introductory business school course. Their median age was 21 years, with a mean age of 22.3 years.

Procedure

Upon arriving in the behavioral laboratory, participants were told they were assisting with an "advertising planning study" where they would both view and rate a television program in which TV spots might be run, as well as view and rate props being considered for use in the background of a television advertisement. In addition, they were told that they would be asked to provide some background information about themselves.

Each participant was seated in their own carrel, which was equipped with a laptop computer running data collection and stimuli presentation software/hardware. Participants then viewed and rated the short video excerpt and subsequently viewed and rated slides of two different automobiles (described as potential props for use in the background of an advertisement). One of the automobiles was a filler automobile and, by random assignment, the second automobile viewed was either: 1 the image of an automobile with the φ property, or 2 an image of the same automobile digitally altered to degrade the φ property. The figures below portray the automobile-stimuli manipulation. The φ-property automobile in Figure 5.1 was an unbranded concept car image, digitally created to have a horizontal proportion like that found in the

Figure 5.1 Unbranded concept car with golden-ratio property

Figure 5.2 Unbranded altered concept car without golden-ratio property

E-type Jaguar sports car; in contrast, the proportion of the car in Figure 5.2 was digitally altered to be greater than φ.

After exposure to an automobile image for seven seconds, participants were asked how interesting they found the car on a semantic-differential (boring-interesting) scale. Response latencies (at the time of loading the screen asking of their interest and at the time of their response) were recorded. Participants were also asked if they wanted to drive the cars they were shown. Subsequently, after viewing and rating the stimuli, participants completed a set of background questions, including Lastovicka and Sirianni's (2011) material possession love battery; responses to this battery allowed classification of those above and below average with respect to the passion they had for their own car.

Results

To examine if, 1 the φ property of a car's design, and 2 being in a passionate relationship with their own car influenced the interest in the cars viewed in the experiment, we conducted a series of 2 (φ property of car: present vs. absent) × 2 (passionate relationship with own car: above average vs. below average) between-subjects analysis of variances. Using participants' interest (1 = boring – 7 = interesting) as the dependent variable, analysis showed that the φ-proportioned car was more interesting ($M = 6.42$) than the non-φ-proportioned version ($M = 6.19$) of the same car (F 1,346 = 4.59, $p < 0.05$).

The degree of interest in the more attractive, φ-proportioned car, however, was moderated by whether or not consumers professed a passionate relationship with their own car (F 1,346 = 4.39, $p < 0.05$). This interaction is portrayed in Figure 5.3. Those without a passionate relationship with their own car were more attracted to φ-based proportionality ($t = 3.28$ $p < 0.05$), with the φ version more interesting ($M = 6.63$) than the non-φ car ($M = 6.18$). In contrast, among those already in a passionate relationship with their own car ($t = 0.028$ $p > 0.05$), the φ-proportioned car was just as interesting ($M = 6.21$) as the other car ($M = 6.20$).

These results are consistent with the relational metaphor where a beloved possession is treated as a relationship partner. An image of a man-made object with a property found attractive in the natural and interpersonal environment – that is φ proportionality – was overall found more interesting by consumers. However, interest in an attractively styled car occurred largely only among those who were less restricted and who were without a loving relationship with their own car. If already in a relationship with some possession, then the attractive alternative was not seen as more interesting. As found in comparable work in interpersonal relationships (Johnson

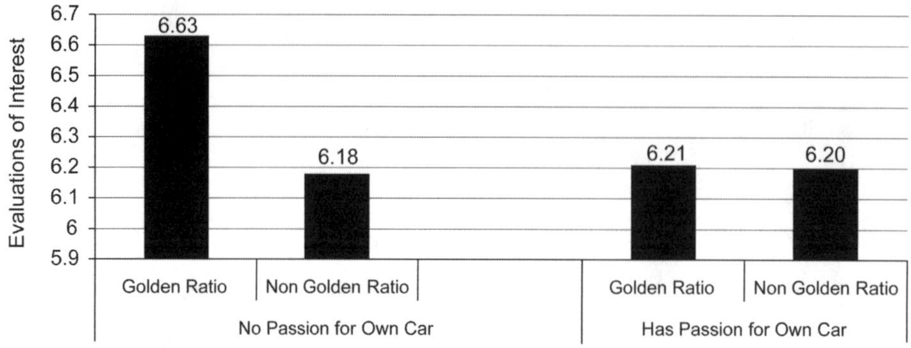

Figure 5.3 Evaluations of interest

and Rusbult 1989; Maner *et al.* 2007), those already in a relationship with a comparable object devalued a more attractive alternative.

Response latency was assessed by differencing, 1 the loading time of the screen asking the interest question, and 2 the time of the mouse click reporting degree of interest. The difference between these two times (in milliseconds) reflects the amount of time used to compose and report interest in the car viewed. Analyses showed that response latency was explained only by an interactive effect of the φ property of the stimuli with the relationship status of the consumer (F 1,346, $p < 0.05$). This interaction is portrayed in Figure 5.4. Consumers in a passionate relationship who were exposed to the φ car (M = 3,151) were slower, and did take about one half-second more time ($t = 2.49$, $p < 0.05$) in reporting their degree of interest than all other consumers ($M = 2{,}566$).

This second finding suggests that those in a passionate relationship with their own car engaged in more mental processing when articulating their interest in a car with the φ property. Whereas the prior set of results showed those with extant relationships did not evaluate the more attractive care as more interesting, this current result implies that consumers already in a passionate relationship apparently thought about the attractive alternative more. When interpreted with a relationship metaphor, this suggests (that among those in a relationship) that while a temptation to stray to the more attractive may occur, it appears that such temptation is resisted.

Participants were also asked if they wanted to drive the stimuli car (1 = do not want to drive it – 7 = really want to drive it). Analyses of wanting to be proximate to, and interact with,

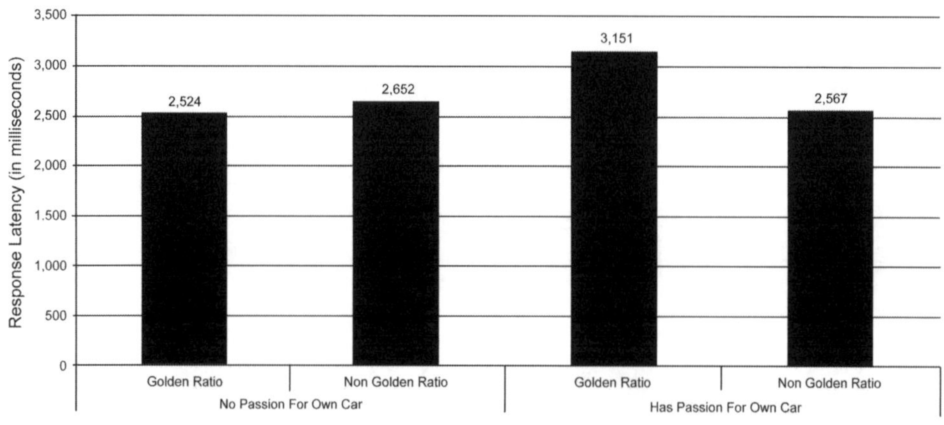

Figure 5.4 Response latency

the car revealed the same patterns found as with the analyses of the interest variable. Those consumers not in a relationship wanted to drive the φ-proportioned car ($M = 6.24$) more ($t = 3.21$ $p < 0.05$) than the less attractive alternative ($M = 5.51$). In contrast, among those already in a relationship with their own car, wanting to drive the more attractive φ car ($M = 5.81$), was equivalent ($t = 0.029$ $p > 0.05$) to wanting to drive the non-φ car ($M = 5.80$).

Discussion

A beloved possession is not necessarily only a means for constructing or maintaining self-identity; a beloved possession can also be an end in itself as an emotional partner in a consumer-object relationship. Indeed, those consumers in our experiment who were already in a relationship devalued the attractive alternative; this is comparable to that found with interpersonal relationships. It is recognized that consumers form relationships with brands (Fournier 1998) and so it should be no surprise that consumers metaphorically enact relationships with particular consumption objects.

Belk (1987: 162) speculated that depending upon the meanings held by consumers then "[an] automobile may change from being a sexual extension of self to a sex object (end rather than means)." Whether an object is a means and the identity metaphor is most appropriate, or an end when the relational metaphor is most appropriate, depends upon the life trajectory and goals of the consumer involved, but ultimately upon the meaning of the object to the consumer.

The degree to which consumers anthropomorphize (Aggarwal and McGill 2007) – or attribute human qualities to some material object – is a critical dimension of such object meaning. Commensurate with his principle of autonomy, Kant asserted that humans should be treated as ends rather than means. Kant (1959: 23) argued, "rational beings are called persons inasmuch as their nature already marks them out as ends in themselves … [and] every rational being exists as an end in himself and not merely as a means to be arbitrarily used … " Once a material object is anthropomorphized and approaches being viewed in Kantian terms as autonomous and having a mind of its own, this facilitates consumers having a relationship with it. Thus we urge future research to examine how object meanings are influenced by consumers' trait-like predispositions to anthropomorphize (Waytz *et al.* 2010), as well as the situational circumstances which encourage anthropomorphizing (Chandler and Schwarz 2010). For example, it is likely that the relational phenomena we observed in our experiment are most pronounced among consumers who are most prone to anthropomorphize. Moreover, other individual difference variables may prove fruitful for understanding which metaphor is most operant. In particular, loneliness has been found associated with a tendency to anthropomorphize (Waytz *et al.* 2010), as well as having a loving relationship with a possession (Lastovicka and Sirianni 2011).

Although we have treated the two metaphors as distinct, we urge future research to examine how the relational metaphor and the identity metaphor are intertwined. We suspect that a consumer's choice to treat a beloved possession as an emotive partner in a consumer-object relationship has implications for the inadvertent and unwitting construction of an unfavorable identity in the eyes of other consumers. In particular, an all-consuming love for a possession may create social isolation, with the result of a dearth of friendships or romantic partners (Lastovicka and Sirianni 2011). Consider the following recollection from the young man, whom we quoted in the opening epigraph, who consciously blurred the distinction between human- and object-relationships.

> You know, my sister came out with her friends [while I was working on the car outside] and I was talking to Maybellene [his pet name for his car]. And my sister was like: "Don't pay any attention to the idiot talking to the car." … My sister's girl friends

> actually laughed … But I was talking to her, I was telling her that I was going to shine up her new tires, get everything ready so that she could go out.
>
> *(interview as part of Lastovicka and Sirianni 2011)*

Given the Kantian social norm that persons should be treated as ends, and objects as means, then the sister and her friends likely have constructed an unfavorable identity of the young man for themselves. The construction of such a stigmatized self (Sandikci and Ger 2009, 2012) is a likely inadvertent result of the young man's pursuit of a consuming, but one-sided and controllable, relationship with a material object. We encourage future work to simultaneously consider both metaphors and to consider how intentional enactment of one metaphor may have inevitable consequences for the other.

The preliminary empirical work we have presented in this chapter is a first step in developing an understanding of an unexamined form of material possession love – namely, infatuation or love at first sight. Prior work on material possession love has studied owners of beloved possessions who have typically owned their beloved for years; such smitten consumers are most often in more established forms of love like romantic or enduring romantic love (Lastovicka and Sirianni 2011). In contrast, in this empirical work we examined non-owners of our sports car stimuli, who although perhaps driven by a passion to have a hands-on interaction with the cars portrayed in our experiment's visual stimuli, were without first-hand intimacy or any period of committed ownership found in more established forms of love. Consumer infatuation is thought to be driven by the consumer's captivating aesthetic response to initial encounters with an object's total sensory experience (Norman 2005), that is its look, motion, feel, scent, taste and sound (Peck and Childers 2008).

Evolutionary psychology contends that humans are hardwired for rapid-fire emotive responses to particular sets of circumstances and stimuli (Nesse and Ellsworth 2009). For example, one look at that beautiful someone across the room and – unencumbered by the thought process – many will experience infatuation or a love-at-first-sight response (Sternberg 1986, 2006). Consequently, what evolutionary psychology has learned about what humans find physically attractive should be more fully considered by consumer researchers in their pursuit of identifying object characteristics that spark consumer infatuation (Sugiyama 2005). While our empirical work was limited to examining the φ property of an object's visual representation, we have neglected the more complete sensory experience to which consumers are exposed outside of the laboratory. Thus we encourage researchers to go beyond this one visual property and to consider the broader palette of characteristics found attractive by evolutionary psychologists. In particular, given some of our experimental participants' desire to drive and have a hands-on experience with attractive cars (Peck and Childers 2003; Peck and Wiggins 2006), then the haptic properties of initial encounters with real, three-dimensional material objects – and not just merely two-dimensional images (Klatzky and Lederman 1992, 1993) – should be a priority for future research.

Further reading

American Psychologist (2009) 64 (2). (The entire issue of the February–March 2009 issue of *American Psychologist* is devoted to the emergence of evolutionary psychology and the evolutionizing of more traditional disciplines such as social psychology, cognitive psychology and personality psychology.)

Banks, M.R., Willoughby, L.M., and Banks, W.A. (2008) "Animal-assisted Therapy and Loneliness in Nursing Homes: Use of Robotic Versus Living Dogs." *Journal of the American Medical Directors Association* 9(3): 173–77. (This article offers a poignant portrayal of close relationships between consumers and man-made objects.)

Krishna, A. (ed.) (2010) *Sensory Marketing: Research on the Sensuality of Products*. New York: Routledge. (This edited volume presents 22 chapters on single and multi-sensory consumption, building connections between the senses, psychology, neuroscience and neuropsychology to explore consumers' sensorial longings and subsequent behavior.)

Livio, M. (2002) *The Golden Ratio*. New York: Broadway Books. (Mario Livio is Head of Science for the Hubble telescope. His book presents a readable treatment of both the science and mythology of the Golden Ratio.)

References

Aggarwal, P. and McGill, A. (2007) "Is That Car Smiling at Me? Schema Congruity as a Basis for Evaluating Anthropomorphized Products." *Journal of Consumer Research* 34(4): 468–79.

Ahuvia, A.C. (2005) "Beyond the Extended Self: Loved Objects and Consumers' Identity Narratives." *Journal of Consumer Research* 32(1): 171–84.

——(2008) "Commentary on Exploring the Dark Side of Pet Ownership: Status- and Control-based Pet Consumption. A Reinterpretation of the Data." *Journal of Business Research* 61(5): 497–9.

Arnould, E.J. and Thompson, C.J. (2005) "Consumer Culture Theory (CCT): Twenty Years of Research." *Journal of Consumer Research* 31(4): 868–82.

Aron, A., Aron, E.N., Tudor, M., and Nelson, G. (1991) "Close Relationships as Including Other in Self." *Journal of Personality and Social Psychology* 60(2): 241–53.

Bashour, M. (2006) "An Objective Measuring System for Facial Attractiveness." *Plastic Reconstructive Surgery* 118(3): 757–74.

Belk, R.W. (1987) "Identity & the Relevance of Market & Personal Objects." In J. Umiker-Sebeok (ed.), *Marketing & Semiotics*. Berlin: Mouton de Gruyter, pp. 151–64.

——(1988) "Possessions and the Extended Self." *Journal of Consumer Research* 15(2): 139–68.

——(1996) "Metaphoric Relationships With Pets." *Society and Animals* 4(2): 121–45.

——(2012) "Extended Self." In R. Belk and A. Ruvio (eds), *Identity and Consumption*, London: Routledge Publishing.

Beverland, M.B., Farrelly, F., and Lim, E. (2008) "Exploring the Dark Side of Pet Ownership: Status- and Control-based Pet Consumption." *Journal of Business Research* 61(5): 490–6.

Bowlby, J. (1969) *Attachment and Loss: Volume 1*. New York: Basic Books.

Carroll, B.A. and Ahuvia, A.C. (2006) "Some Antecedents and Outcomes of Brand Love." *Marketing Letters* 17(2): 79–89.

Chandler, J. and Schwarz, N. (2010) "Use Does Not Wear Ragged the Fabric of Friendship: Thinking of Objects as Alive Makes People Less Willing to Replace Them." *Journal of Consumer Psychology* 20(2): 138–45.

Cook, T.A. (1978) *The Curves of Life*. New York: Dover Publications.

Fournier, S. (1998) "Consumers and Their Brands: Developing Relationship Theory in Consumer Research." *Journal of Consumer Research* 24(4): 343–53.

Hazan, C. and Shaver, P.R. (1987) "Romantic Love Conceptualized as an Attachment Process." *Journal of Personality and Social Psychology* 52(3): 511–24.

Hill, R.P., Gaines, J. and Wilson, R.M. (2008) "Animal Companions, Consumption Experiences, and the Marketing of Pets: Transcending Boundaries in the Animal-human Distinction." *Journal of Business Research* 61(5): 377–81.

Hirschman, E.C. (1994) "Consumers and Their Animal Companions." *Journal of Consumer Research* 20 (March): 616–32.

Holbrook, M.B., Stephens, D.L., Day, E., Holbrook, S.M., and George, S. (2001) "A Collective Stereographic Photo Essay on Key Aspects of Animal Companionship: The Truth About Dogs and Cats." *Acad Mark Sci Rev*, www.amsreview.org/Amsrev/theory/holbrook01-01.html (accessed 26 September 2011).

Holbrook, M.B. and Woodside, A.G. (2008) "Consumer Behavior, Extended-self, and Sacred Consumption: An Alternative Perspective from our Animal Companions." *Journal of Business Research* 61(5): 553–62.

Johnson, D.J. and Rusbult, C.E. (1989) "Resisting Temptation: Devaluation of Alternative Partners as a Means of Maintaining Commitment in Close Relationships." *Journal of Personality and Social Psychology* 57(6): 967–80.

Kant, I. (1959) *Foundations of the Metaphysics of Morals*. (L.W. Beck, trans. from the 1786 original). New York: Macmillan.

Klatzky, R.L. and Lederman, S.J. (1992) "Stages of Manual Exploration in Haptic Object Identification." *Perception & Psychophysics* 52(6): 661–70.

——(1993) "Toward a Computational Model of Constraint-driven Exploration and Haptic Object Identification." *Perception* 52: 597–621.

Lastovicka, J.L. and Sirianni, N.J. (2011) "Truly, Madly, Deeply: Consumers in the Throes of Material Possession Love." *Journal of Consumer Research* 37(2): 323–42.

Livio, M. (2002) *The Golden Ratio*. New York: Broadway Books.

Maner, J.K., Gailliot, M.T., Rouby, D.A., and Miller, S.L. (2007) "Can't Take My Eyes Off You: Attentional Adhesion to Mates and Rivals." *Journal of Personality and Social Psychology* 93(3): 389–401.

Manning, J.T. and Pickup, L.J. (1998) "Symmetry and Performance in Middle Distance Runners." *International Journal of Sports Medicine* 19(3): 205–9.

Nesse, R.M. and Ellsworth, P.C. (2009) "Evolution, Emotions, and Emotional Disorders." *American Psychologist* 64(2): 129–39.

Norman, D. (2005) *Emotional Design: Why We Love (or Hate) Everyday Things*. New York: Basic Books.

Park, C.W., MacInnis, D.J., Priester, J., Eisingerich, A.B., and Iacobucci, D. (2010) "Brand Attachment and Brand Attitude Strength: Conceptual and Empirical Differentiation of Two Critical Brand Equity Drivers." *Journal of Marketing* 74(6): 1–17.

Peck, J. and Childers, T.L. (2003) "To Have and to Hold: The Influence of Haptic Information on Product Judgments." *Journal of Marketing* 67(2): 35–48.

——(2008) "Effects of Sensory Factors on Consumer Behavior: If it Tastes, Smells, Sounds, and Feels Like a Duck, Then it Must be a …" In C.P. Haugtvedt, P.M. Herr, and F.R. Kardes (eds), *Handbook of Consumer Psychology*. New York: Lawrence Erlbaum Associates, pp. 193–219.

Peck, J. and Wiggins, J. (2006) "It Just Feels Good: Customers' Affective Response to Touch and its Influence on Persuasion." *Journal of Marketing* 70(4): 56–69.

Pittard, N., Ewing, M., and Jevons, C. (2007) "Aesthetic Theory and Logo Design: Examining Consumer Response to Proportion Across Cultures." *International Marketing Review* 24(4): 457–73.

Prokosch, M.D., Yeo, R.A., Miller, G.F. (2005) "Intelligence Tests With Higher G-loadings Show Higher Correlations with Body Symmetry: Evidence for a General Fitness Factor Mediated by Developmental Stability." *Intelligence* 33(2): 203–13.

Raghubir, P. and Greenleaf, E.A. (2006) "Ratios in Proportion: What Should the Shape of the Package Be?" *Journal of Marketing* 70(2): 95–107.

Sandikci, O. and Ger, G. (2009) "Veiling in Style: How Does a Stigmatized Practice Become Fashionable?" *Journal of Consumer Research* 37(1): 15–26.

——(2012) "Stigmatized Self." In R. Belk and A. Ruvio (eds), *Identity and Consumption*. London: Routledge Publishing.

Schmid, S.E., Marx, D., and Samal, A. (2008) "Computation of Face Attractiveness Index Based on Neoclassical Canons, Symmetry, and Golden Ratios." *Pattern Recognition* 41(8): 2710–17.

Schulte, B. (2011a) "Crash and Yearn." *The Washington Post Magazine*, www.washingtonpost.com/lifestyle/magazine/crash-and-yearn/2011/06/17/gIQAPbXiGI_story.html (accessed 17 July 2011).

——(2011b) "Kicking Love into Gear: A Journalist and her Car." On *Tell Me More,* interviewed by Michel Martin (radio) National Public Radio, 20 July 2011.

Shaver, P.R. and Mikulincer, M. (2006) "A Behavioral Systems Approach to Romantic Love Relationships: Attachment, Caregiving, and Sex." In R.J. Sternberg and K. Weis (eds), *The Psychology of Love*, 2nd edn. New Haven: Yale University Press, pp. 35–64.

Sternberg, R.J. (1986) "A Triangular Theory of Love." *Psychological Review* 93(2): 119–35.

——(2006) "A Duplex Theory of Love." In R.J. Sternberg and K. Weis (eds), *The Psychology of Love*, 2nd edn. New Haven, CT: Yale University Press, pp.184–99.

Sugiyama, L.S. (2005) "Physical Attractiveness in Adaptationist Perspective." In D.M. Buss (ed.), *The Handbook of Evolutionary Psychology*. Hoboken, NJ: John Wiley & Sons Inc, pp. 292–343.

Thompson, D.A.W. (1992) *On Growth and Form*. New York: Dover Publications.

Walster, E., Aronson, V., Abrahams, D., and Rottman, L. (1966) "Importance of Physical Attractiveness in Dating." *Journal of Personality and Social Psychology* 4(5): 508–16.

Waytz, A., Cacioppo, J., and Epley, N. (2010) "Who Sees Human? The Stability and Importance of Individual Differences in Anthropomorphism." *Perspectives on Psychological Science* 5(3): 219–32.

6

OVERWEIGHT AND EMOTIONAL IDENTITY PROJECTS

Mariam Beruchashvili and Risto Moisio

This chapter seeks to elucidate the link between consumers' identities and emotions. While consumer culture theory (CCT) scholarship has long examined how consumers define, perceive, and enact their identities though consumption (e.g. Belk and Costa 1998; Kates 2002; Luedicke *et al.* 2010), research remains silent on the emotional dimension of consumers' identities. It is only marginally noted that consumers' identity pursuits are emotion-laden, whether it is pride of being a Harley rider (Schouten and McAlexander 1995), ambivalence of being a bride (Otnes *et al.* 1997), guilt of being a working mother (Thompson 1996), or envy that consumers feel toward others' consumption (Belk 2011). It is the purpose of this chapter to address this oversight. Building on the sociology of emotions tradition, we propose that rather than being a fleeting state, emotions are central to consumers' identity projects. In so doing, our chapter develops a framework of emotional identity projects.

Consumer identity projects

Numerous studies examining how consumers define, shape, express, and enact their identities posit that they are entrenched in socio-historic and cultural structures (e.g. Luedicke *et al.* 2010; Thompson and Tian 2008). Consumption of products and services aids identity work linked to gender, race, nation state, family or community. Importantly, these identities are socially shared pursuits construed in light of cultural ideologies (Arnould and Thompson 2005). For instance, the pursuit of physical beauty and youth integral to many consumers' identity projects animates consumption of plastic surgery (Schouten 1991) or other self-change-related products such as weight-loss supplements or dieting services (Thompson and Hirschman 1995). There is also work suggesting that the self is plural rather than singular and that consumers pursue not just one identity project, but several (e.g. Ahuvia 2005; Bahl and Milne 2010).

Emotions as social constructions

In contrast to the psychological view that examines emotions as predominantly intrapsychic phenomena (e.g. Bagozzi *et al.* 1999), sociologists treat emotions as largely conditioned and espoused by the socio-cultural factors (Thoits 1989). From the sociological perspective, emotions represent "socially constructed patterns of sensations, expressive gestures, and cultural meanings organized around a relationship to a social object, usually another person … or group" (Gordon 1981: 566–7). This view argues that "cultural ideologies, beliefs, and norms as they impinge on social structures define what emotions are to be experienced and how these culturally defined emotions are to be expressed" (Turner and Stets 2005: 2). Consequently, what individuals feel is conditioned by socialization into a culture and by participation in social structures that supply blueprints in the form of vocabularies, beliefs, and expression norms governing the feeling of a specific emotion (Gordon 1989).

The sociology of emotions tradition elucidates ways in which identities and emotions are interlinked. Cultural meaning systems and social structures not only shape our identities, but they also influence feelings associated with these identities. Hochschild (1983) demonstrates how flight attendants try to feel or at least express cheer instead of anger in order to enact an identity of a nurturing and helpful service worker. Role identities inscribed within gender ideologies operating in a specific socio-historic time dictate whether and how husbands and wives feel and express love and anger in marriage (Cancian and Gordon 1988). The identity transition of becoming a parent prescribes the feeling of joy even if burdens of parenthood instigate depression in some women (Thoits 1991). When disabled identity becomes salient to wheelchair users who need assistance from able "walkers" in public spaces, they counter the embarrassment by emotional reservation and poise (Cahill and Eggleston 1994). Thus, emotions are governed by similar structures that guide identity projects more broadly.

Framework of emotional identity projects

Our review of literature on overweight consumers and emotion, which follows, is limited to consumers, especially female consumers, who perceive themselves as overweight, and resort to consumption of dieting products and services that they believe will aid their pursuit of slimming down. We do not focus on consumers with eating disorders, such as bulimia or anorexia, whose emotional identity projects may differ significantly from the framework developed here. From our reading of prior literature on overweight consumers, we have identified four distinct emotion-based identity projects and identity work associated with each, represented in Figure 6.1

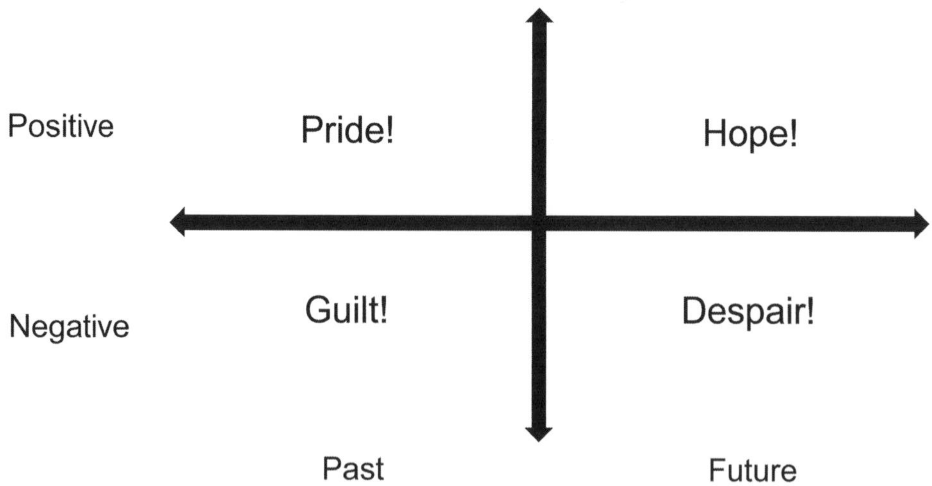

Figure 6.1 Framework of emotional identity projects

along two continua: valence (positive-negative) and time-orientation (past-future). Negative emotions captured by our analysis encompass despair and guilt, while the positive emotions include hope and pride. Pride and guilt are past-oriented, whereas hope and despair are present- or future-oriented. The four discrete emotions can be thought of as self-feelings or feelings "that the self directs toward itself" (Scheff 1988: 398) made salient by the respective socio-cultural milieu.

Overweight and despair

Despair

Overweight identity is connected to the emotion of despair. Despair represents an emotional state of hopelessness, which functions as "a feeling of ... discouragement; a thought process that expects nothing; and a behavioral process in which the person attempts little or takes inappropriate action" (Farran *et al.* 1995: 25). It should be noted that the despair discussed here in connection to overweight identity is conceived as an emotion that can be transient, different from the despair as a trait (i.e. chronic despair), manifested as extreme helplessness characteristic of individuals suffering from clinical depression (e.g. Farran *et al.* 1995; Seligman 1992). The emotion of despair usually signals that something is wrong – goals have not been met or life or situation has become difficult or unbearable. As a de-energizing force, consumers who are in the state of despair cannot imagine that there is a solution to the problem or that anyone can help them, and consequently they expect little of others or themselves. Often despair leads to the inability to act because individuals feel entrapped by the situation (Farran *et al.* 1995). Despair, thus, can be detrimental to overweight consumers' identity projects.

Obesity research implicates the social nature of despair primarily stemming from social and cultural sanctioning of being overweight as possessing a Goffmanian "spoiled identity" (DeJong and Kleck 1986). In a culture where identity is intimately linked to one's physical appearance, with slenderness being the dominant standard (Bordo 1993), overweight consumers are more likely to feel socially deviant. The well-documented discrimination bias against overweight/obese individuals is one prominent source contributing to the sense of desperation. Overweight individuals are more likely to be discriminated against in academic settings such as high school and college, as well as in work environment in terms of hiring, wages, promotions, and employment termination (Puhl and Brownell 2001). Academics or professional employment are individual achievement arenas that directly influence our sense of self-worth, and discriminatory experiences in these life areas undermine overweight consumers' selfhood. Even in healthcare provision, medical professionals manifest prejudice in attitude and treatment of overweight or obese patients (Puhl and Brownell 2001), some openly holding them responsible for being lazy and weak in self-discipline, further undermining overweight consumers' sense of self. Weight discrimination also tends to be gendered, as women are more at risk for discrimination.

Identity work linked to despair

Thus, despair over being "fat" is an aversive state of self-awareness from which consumers attempt to escape (Heatherton and Baumeister 1991). Women who are perceived and/or perceive themselves as overweight are especially bound to invoke the cultural tale that excess weight makes them less attractive, less feminine, and less desirable as sexual partners (Regan 1996). Feeling physically and sexually unappealing exacerbates negative body image, body dissatisfaction, and self-esteem, which increase psychological distress and lead to depression (Ross 1994). One way to escape from overweight self-awareness is avoidance, whereby consumers avoid situations in which being fat is problematic. For instance, consumers in an aversive state brought about by despair are more likely to avoid seeing their reflection in a mirror, standing on a scale, standing next to others in public spaces, or visiting venues and using services where they cannot fit into chairs (Degher and Hughes 1999). Overweight consumers experiencing despair are also prone to avoid going to a buffet with company (Maykovich 1978), and avoid shopping for clothes (Sobal 1999). Despair may result in compliance, whereby overweight consumers either accept to comply to a socially accepted stereotype of a fat person by, for instance, enduring jokes about fatness, or they may agree to diet to silence others without actual commitment to lose weight (Degher and Hughes 1999). Desperation over being overweight can also lead to compensatory identity pursuits in other identity-related domains, such as higher involvement in school or community organizations (Degher and Hughes 1999).

Overweight and guilt

Guilt

Guilt is an emotion evoked in response to appraisals of responsibility and self-accountability (Smith and Lazarus 1993). One of the prominent sources for experiencing guilt is the assignment of personal responsibility for being overweight. A few important cultural influencers, such as the medical profession, emerging fads in nutrition, and the growing weight-loss industry, help proliferate the view that overweight persons are solely to blame for their bodily condition, and thus inadvertently underscoring that it is entirely within consumers' agentic power to implement self-change (Stearns 2002). For instance, the early modeling of obesity in American medical textbooks held individuals accountable for their overweight condition, suggesting that excess weight was the result of individual choices (Chang and Christakis 2002). Moralization of body shape and size further contributed to casting blame toward the overweight. As the slim body developed into the symbol of the person's character and moral values (Bordo 1993; Jutel 2005), corpulence came to be associated with the lack of those virtues. In contemporary culture dominated by the ideology of self-control (Thompson and Hirschman 1995), overweight consumers are cast as blameworthy for the absence of self-discipline.

Identity work linked to guilt

Overweight people, especially women, experience guilt for being large, and for being unable to inhibit behaviors, primarily eating, that presumably lead to being overweight (Heatherton and Vohs 1998). Guilt over their moral transgressions often results in overweight consumers generating "fat stories," in which they try to explain away why they became fat (Degher and Hughes 1999). "Fat stories" represent the equivalent of "excuses" or accounts (Scott and Lyman 1968), in which consumers admit the wrongdoing such as bingeing (Wilk 2004) but deny full responsibility for it. For instance, overweight consumers are likely to hold other circumstances such as the "fat gene" (Braziel and LeBesco 2001) responsible for their excess weight. Other guilt-alleviating excuses that aid restoration of self-view may include hormones, getting married, or giving birth (Beruchashvili *et al.* n.d.). Guilt also motivates generation of "eating stories," in which consumers seek excuses for the inability to control eating. In excuses, overweight consumers assume responsibility, but attempt to justify the behavior as situationally appropriate (Degher and Hughes 1999).

Beyond generating "fat stories" and "eating stories" to construct their identity narratives, guilt propels search for moral correctives. To alleviate the characterological moral shortcoming associated with guilt (DeJong and Kleck 1986), overweight consumers take on dieting as a moral corrective, reinforced by the cultural belief that losing weight and taking control of their bodies is possible with expansion of effort. In dieting, one avenue to alleviate the burden of guilt is confessional, practiced either in private or public forums (Foucault 1978). Such confessionals are likely to occur in weight-loss support group settings, granting consumers albeit temporary relief from guilt (Moisio and Beruchashvili 2010). Compounding guilt further, dietary lapses are usually attributed to the lack of personal control and self-discipline, and along with confessionals, overweight consumers choose to succumb to the public surveillance of weight-loss support groups to help overcome moralized dietary failures.

Overweight consumers and hope

Hope

Hope, "a positively valenced emotion evoked in response to an uncertain but possible goal-congruent outcome" (MacInnis and de Mello 2005: 2) is an emotion that also animates overweight consumers' identity projects. It is evoked in response to an unsatisfactory life circumstance, and for many overweight consumers, body fat represents such a circumstance that prompts their yearning for slimming down. Hope for weight loss is potent given that weight reduction is intimately woven with central aspects of many female consumers' gender identities. Overweight consumers cherish identity goals such as improved self-esteem, self-confidence, physical attractiveness, sexual appeal, and the sense of control (Beruchashvili *et al.* n.d.). Such goals mediate overweight consumers' hope for a thinner body.

Identity work linked to hope

Uniquely, hope is an identity-rejuvenating emotion. Because weight loss represents such a powerful and instantly visible means of self-change, overweight consumers are thought to be in a perpetual state of hope such that some have even designated this state as *false hope syndrome* (Polivy and Herman 2002). According to this view, consumers experiencing hope are more prone to continue weight loss even in the face of previous histories of failure. Although supported by research on dieting as an inefficient method of achieving self-change (Heatherton *et al.* 1997), the term "false hope syndrome" misses out on deeper experiential content that colors overweight consumers' yearning for a slim body. As mentioned earlier, consumers experiencing hope yearn for weight loss because it is viewed as a passkey to achieving other important life goals such as health, beauty, social success, and personal happiness (Seid 1994).

Overweight consumers experiencing hope are prone to attach greater importance to products that promise removal of excess body weight. Because of its positive valence and reenergizing nature, consumers tend to be protective of hope to the extent that they are more likely to reason away counter-evidence if the product is not delivering the coveted result, and engage in selective search of product-favorable information (de Mello *et al.* 2007). Thus, when consumers who purchase a weight-loss supplement or enroll in a weight-loss program experience setbacks in achieving the hoped-for outcome of shedding pounds, hope may propel them to seek reasons rather than casting doubt over the product or the service itself. Hope is also a communal emotion that is cultivated through supportive communications and interactions among overweight individuals (Moisio and Beruchashvili 2010), or simply through the presence of others (Farran *et al.* 1995). Hope, therefore, may propel overweight consumers to seek a community of the like-minded others.

Overweight consumers and pride

Pride

Fat-acceptance scholarship suggests that the emotion of pride distinctly shapes overweight consumers' identities. Pride is an emotion stemming from the perception of a competent identity that stands well with others, leading to identity confirmation and identity importance (Laverie *et al.* 2002). Traditionally, fat-acceptance research shares the pathos with gay scholarship, focusing on elucidating the social processes of acceptance (LeBesco 2001). Similar to the social movement for acceptance of alternative lifestyles that prominently promote pride among gay and lesbian consumers (e.g. Kates and Belk 2001), various fat acceptance movements strive to instill pride in consumers who perceive their overweight condition more as a source of shame. The National Association to Aid Fat Americans or NAAFA, later renamed the National Association for the Advancement of Fat Acceptance, aims not only to redefine societal values and practices about body weight, but also to provide social support to its members (Saguy and Riley 2005), one form of which is taking pride in overweight identity. Although the fat-acceptance movement may fuel pride in overweight identity, pride is also associated with successful, and especially publicized dramatic weight losses.

Identity work linked to pride

Pride as an aspect of overweight consumers' identity work inspires public identity work. In particular, overweight consumers experiencing pride are particularly prone to deploy fashion as a cultural resource in identity construction to glamorize overweight. Overweight consumers, especially females, readily embrace participation in fashion that furnishes opportunities for exposure of a large body and feeling proud about it. Examples include television shows such as *Mo'Nique's Fat Chance* or *Big Sexy*, glossy magazines such as *Big Beautiful Woman* or *Mode* for full-figured women or *Dimensions* for men who are fat admirers (Sobal 1999). Proliferation of these cultural forums indicates that overweight consumers are willing to "come out" and affirm that overweight bodies should be admired rather than be hidden (Klein 2001). Overweight consumers are also more freely participating in other domains of consumer culture. For instance, the self-help book market targeting large-bodied customers has surged, with wide-ranging publications on fitness, healthcare, fashion, and beauty (Sobal 1999). In the area of personal relationships, dating services such as the Fat Admirers club provide a public venue for large people to meet freely and find a partner (Millman 1981). Overweight consumers' uninhibited engagement in consumer culture as its full-fledged participants supplies myriad opportunities for pride-espousing identity work.

An emotional look at consumers' identity projects

In this chapter, we highlight consumer identity projects' emotional dimension. Specifically, focusing on overweight consumers, we propose the emotional identity projects framework (Figure 6.1), identifying four discrete emotions that permeate overweight consumers' identity projects: despair, guilt, hope, and pride. Despair and guilt are negatively valenced emotions, which may not provide a motivational surge necessary to seek resolution to the aspects of the identity inducing these negative feelings. Positively valenced hope provides a motivational impetus for much of consumption focused on identity betterment (e.g. MacInnis *et al.* 2004). Identity work can also involve espousing pride through engagement in consumer culture such as consumption of fashion or fitness.

Our framework suggests directions for future research into the intersections between consumer identity projects and emotion. Most importantly, there is a need to investigate the relationships between identity work and specific emotions outside the context of overweight. No specific research has examined in detail how identities come to possess an emotional style of valence, and particularly, whether marketplace structures influence the emotional styles toward which consumers gravitate.

Another area for future inquiry would be to examine how consumers shift from one emotional identity to another (e.g. from guilt to pride, or from pride to guilt). This shift can potentially occur in consumers' pursuit of identity goals that are directly related to self-change. For instance, consumers who materialize the possible "thin" identity through weight loss may experience "identity interruption" when self-change outcomes do not match social feedback they receive, and thus, the new identity is not socially validated (Granberg 2006). In such cases, consumers are destined to revise their identity narratives and in doing so, may oscillate between conflicting emotional states. Consumers are likely to undergo similar identity-related changes (e.g. post-plastic surgery) that are emotional experiences, and emotions can serve as authenticating proxies for identity changes. Understanding how consumption communities orchestrate emotional states offers a richer insight into consumers' identity projects.

Another avenue for exploration is the relationship between emotions and multiple identities (Ahuvia 2005; Bahl and Milne 2010; Laverie *et al.* 2002). The experience of multiple identity projects can sometimes be a complicated process invoking emotional conflicts. For instance, consumers juggle to combine identities tied to workplace and home (Tian and Belk 2005), renegotiating their relationships and trying to cope with emotional conflict that such juggling evokes. Emotions may inhibit or facilitate identity renegotiation and coping, and the understanding of how these processes unfold in detail will further add to theorizing on identity and emotions. We hope our framework offers inroads for novel conceptualizations of the interactions among marketplace structures, emotion, and consumers' identity projects.

Further reading

Brumberg, J. (1997) *The Body Project: An Intimate History of American Girls*. New York: Random House. (An in-depth socio-cultural analysis into the emotionally intimate project of caring for the female body.)

Chernin, K. (1986) *The Hungry Self: Women, Eating, and Identity*. New York: Harper & Row. (A compelling feminist scrutiny of culturally valorized slenderness ideal on women's identity construction.)

Gimlin, D. (2001) *Body Work: Beauty and Self-Image in American Culture*. Berkeley, CA: University of California Press. (An in-depth ethnographic study into the emotional and intellectual complex of overweight women to redefine their identities through participation in the body work.)

LeBesco, K. (2001) *Revolting Bodies? The Struggle to Redefine Fat Identity*. Amherst, MA: University of Massachusetts Press. (A powerful reading on identity politics surrounding construction and reconstruction of fatness and beauty.)

References

Ahuvia, A. (2005) "Beyond the Extended Self: Loved Objects and Consumers' Identity Narratives." *Journal of Consumer Research* 32: 171–84.

Arnould, E. and Thompson, C. (2005) "Consumer Culture Theory (CCT): Twenty Years of Research." *Journal of Consumer Research* 31: 868–82.

Bagozzi, R., Gopinath, M., and Nyer, P. (1999) "The Role of Emotions in Marketing." *Journal of the Academy of Marketing Science* 27: 184–206.

Bahl, S. and Milne, G. (2010) "Talking to Ourselves: A Dialogical Exploration of Consumption Experiences." *Journal of Consumer Research* 37: 176–95.

Belk, R. (2011) "Benign Envy." *Academy of Marketing Science Review* 1.

Belk, R. and Costa, J. (1998) "The Mountain Man Myth: A Contemporary Consuming Fantasy." *Journal of Consumer Research* 25: 218–40.

Beruchashvili, M., Moisio, R., and Gentry, J. (n.d.) "The Sacralization of Hope." *Working Paper.*

Bordo, S. (1993) *Unbearable Weight: Feminism, Western Culture, and the Body*. Berkeley, CA: University of California Press.

Braziel, J. and LeBesco, K. (2001) *Bodies Out of Control: Fatness and Transgression*. Berkeley, CA: University of California Press.

Cahill, S. and Eggelston, R. (1994) "Managing Emotions in Public: The Case of Wheelchair Users." *Social Psychology Quarterly* 57: 300–12.

Cancian, F. and Gordon, S. (1988) "Changing Emotion Norms in Marriage: Love and Anger in U.S. Women's Magazines Since 1900." *Gender and Society* 2: 308–42.

Chang, V. and Christakis, N. (2002) "Medical Modelling of Obesity: A Transition from Action to Experience in a 20th Century American Medical Textbook." *Sociology of Health & Illness* 24: 151–77.

Degher, D. and Hughes, G. (1999) "The Adoption and Management of 'Fat' Identity." In J. Sobal and D. Maurer (eds), *Interpreting Weight: The Social Management of Fatness and Thinness*. New York: Aldine, pp.11–27.

DeJong, W. and Kleck, R. (1986) "The Social Psychological Effects of Overweight." In C. Herman, M. Zanna, and T. Higgins (eds), *Physical Appearance, Stigma, and Social Behavior: The Ontario Symposium*, vol. 3. Hillsdale, NJ: Erlbaum, pp. 65–89.

de Mello, G., MacInnis, D., and Stewart, D. (2007) "Threats to Hope: Effects on Reasoning About Product Information." *Journal of Consumer Research* 34: 153–61.

Farran, C., Herth, K., and Popovich, J. (1995) *Hope and Hopelessness: Critical Clinical Constructs*. Thousand Oaks, CA: Sage.

Foucault, M. (1978) *The History of Sexuality: An Introduction*. New York: Pantheon Books.

Gordon, S. (1981) "The Sociology of Sentiments and Emotion." In M. Rosenberg and R. Turner (eds), *Social Psychology: Sociological Perspectives*. New York: Basic Books, pp. 562–92.

——(1989) "The Socialization of Children's Emotions: Emotional Culture, Competence, and Exposure." In C. Saarni and P. Harris (eds), *Children's Understanding of Emotion*. Cambridge: Cambridge University Press, pp. 319–49.

Granberg, E. (2006) "'Is That All There Is?' Possible Selves, Self-Change, and Weight Loss." *Social Psychology Quarterly* 69: 109–26.

Heatherton, T. and Baumeister, R. (1991) "Binge Eating as Escape from Self-Awareness." *Psychological Bulletin* 110: 86–108.

Heatherton, T., Mahamedi, F., Striepe, M., Field, A., and Keel, P. (1997) "A 10-Year Longitudinal Study of Body Weight, Dieting, and Eating Disorder Symptoms." *Journal of Abnormal Psychology* 106: 117–25.

Heatherton, T. and Vohs, K. (1998) "Why is it So Difficult to Inhibit Behavior?" *Psychological Bulletin* 9: 212–15.

Hochschild, A. (1983) *The Managed Heart: The Commercialization of Human Feeling*. Berkeley, CA: University of California Press.

Jutel, A. (2005) "Weighing Health: The Moral Burden of Obesity." *Social Semiotics* 15: 113–25.

Kates, S. (2002) "The Protean Quality of Subcultural Consumption: An Ethnographic Account of Gay Consumers." *Journal of Consumer Research* 29: 383–99.

Kates, S. and Belk, R. (2001) "The Meanings of Lesbian and Gay Pride Day: Resistance through Consumption and Resistance to Consumption." *Journal of Contemporary Ethnography* 30: 392–429.

Klein, R. (2001) "Fat Beauty." In J. Braziel and K. LeBesco (eds), *Bodies Out of Bound: Fatness and Transgression*. Berkeley, CA: University of California Press, pp. 19–38.

Laverie, D., Kleine, R., and Kleine, S. (2002) "Reexamination and Extension of Kleine, Kleine, and Kernan's Social Identity Model of Mundane Consumption: The Mediating Role of the Appraisal Process." *Journal of Consumer Research* 28: 659–69.

LeBesco, K. (2001) "Queering Fat Bodies/Politics." In J. Braziel and K. LeBesco (eds), *Bodies Out of Bounds: Fatness and Transgression*. Berkeley, CA: University of California Press, pp. 74–87.

Luedicke, M., Thompson, C., and Giesler, M. (2010) "Consumer Identity Work as Moral Protagonism: How Myth and Ideology Animate a Brand-Mediated Moral Conflict." *Journal of Consumer Research* 36: 1016–32.

MacInnis, D. and de Mello, G. (2005) "The Concept of Hope and Its Relevance to Product Evaluation and Choice." *Journal of Marketing* 69: 1–14.

MacInnis, D., de Mello, G., and Patrick, V. (2004) "Consumer Hopefulness: Construct, Relevance to Internet Marketing, Antecedents and Consequences." *International Journal of Internet Marketing and Advertising* 1: 174–95.

Maykovich, M. (1978) "Social Constraints in Eating Patterns Among the Obese and Overweight." *Social Problems* 25: 453–60.

Millman, M. (1981) *Such a Pretty Face: Being Fat in America.* New York: Berkley Books.

Moisio, R. and Beruchashvili, M. (2010) "Questing for Well-Being at Weight Watchers: The Role of the Spiritual-Therapeutic Model in a Support Group." *Journal of Consumer Research* 36: 857–75.

Otnes, C., Lowrey, T., and Shrum, L.J. (1997) "Toward an Understanding of Consumer Ambivalence." *Journal of Consumer Research* 24: 80–93.

Polivy, J. and Herman, C. (2002) "If At First You Don't Succeed: False Hopes of Self-Change." *American Psychologist* 57: 677–89.

Puhl, R. and Brownell, K. (2001) "Bias, Discrimination, and Obesity." *Obesity Research* 9: 788–805.

Regan, P. (1996) "Sexual Outcasts: The Perceived Impact of Body Weight and Gender on Sexuality." *Journal of Applied Social Psychology* 26: 1803–13.

Ross, C. (1994) "Overweight and Depression." *Journal of Health and Social Behavior* 35: 63–79.

Saguy, A. and Riley, K. (2005) "Weighing Both Sides: Morality, Mortality, and Framing Contests over Obesity." *Journal of Health Politics, Policy and Law* 30: 869–922.

Scheff, T. (1988) "Shame and Conformity: The Deference-Emotion System." *American Sociological Review* 53: 395–406.

Schouten, J. (1991) "Selves in Transition: Symbolic Consumption in Personal Rites of Passage and Identity Reconstruction." *Journal of Consumer Research* 17(4): 412–25.

Schouten, J. and McAlexander, J. (1995) "Subcultures of Consumption: An Ethnography of the New Bikers." *Journal of Consumer Research* 22: 43–61.

Scott, M. and Lyman, S. (1968) "Accounts." *American Sociological Review* 33: 42–62.

Seid, R. (1994) "Too 'Close to the Bone': The Historical Context for Women's Obsession with Slenderness." In P. Fallon, M. Katzman, and S. Wooley (eds), *Feminist Perspectives on Eating Disorders.* New York: Guilford, pp. 3–16.

Seligman, M. (1992) *Helplessness: On Depression, Development, and Death.* New York: W.H. Freeman.

Smith, C. and Lazarus, R. (1993) "Appraisal Components, Core Relational Themes, and the Emotions." *Cognition and Emotion* 4: 3233–69.

Sobal, J. (1999) "The Size Acceptance Movement and the Social Construction of Body Weight." In J. Sobal and D. Maurer (eds), *Weighty Issues: Fatness and Thinness as Social Problems.* New York: Aldine, pp. 231–50.

Stearns, P. (2002) *Fat History: Bodies and Beauty in Modern West.* New York: NYU Press.

Thoits, P. (1989) "The Sociology of Emotions." *Annual Review of Sociology* 15: 317–43.

——(1991) "Gender Differences in Coping with Emotional Distress." In J. Eckenrode (ed.), *The Social Context of Coping.* New York: Plenum, pp. 107–38.

Thompson, C. (1996) "Caring Consumers: Gendered Consumption Meanings and the Juggling Lifestyle." *Journal of Consumer Research* 22: 388–407.

Thompson, C. and Hirschman, E. (1995) "Understanding the Socialized Body: A Poststructuralist Analysis of Consumers' Self-Conceptions, Body Images, and Self-Care Practices." *Journal of Consumer Research* 22: 139–53.

Thompson, C. and Tian, K. (2008) "Reconstructing the South: How Commercial Myths Compete for Identity Values Through the Ideological Shaping of Popular Memories and Countermemories." *Journal of Consumer Research* 34: 595–613.

Tian, K. and Belk, R. (2005) "Extended Self and Possessions in the Workplace." *Journal of Consumer Research* 32: 297–310.

Turner, J. and Stets, J. (2005) *The Sociology of Emotions.* Cambridge: Cambridge University Press.

Wilk, R. (2004) "The Binge in the Food Economy of Nineteenth-Century Belize." In P. Lysaght (ed.), *Changing Tastes: Food Culture and the Processes of Industrialization.* Basel: Verlag, pp. 110–20.

7
DISGUST AND IDENTITY

Andrea Morales and Eugenia Wu

Who we are defines what we like – what we like to do, what we like to eat, what we like to wear – and what we like, in turn, defines who we are. Indeed, the primary motivation for this book is to examine the relationship between self-identity and consumption behavior. In this chapter we take the reverse approach and argue that an equally critical issue in defining who we are is what we do not like, and even more so, what repels us. Specifically, we suggest that self-identity and disgust each shape the other, and that the reciprocal relationship between the two can significantly influence how we consume.

In what follows, we survey current research in psychology and marketing to examine the relationship between self-identity and disgust. In doing so, we propose a novel framework that connects the two literatures while also providing new insights into established work and offering suggestions for future research. In considering the many ways in which identity and disgust might be related, we contend that there are two main questions to address: 1 how might the identity of the person *experiencing* disgust impact disgust responses?; and, 2 how might the identity of the source *causing* the disgust impact disgust responses? In this chapter we examine each of these questions in the context of the two types of disgust – physical and moral – before considering their implications for consumption behavior.

Physical disgust and identity

Disgust is characterized as a basic and primal emotion (Olatunji *et al.* 2008). It is experienced uniquely and independently from other emotional states (Rozin *et al.* 2000) and results in distinct physiological responses: an increased tightening in the throat, a decreased heart rate, and activation of the *levator labii* muscle region of the face, characteristic of an oral-nasal rejection response (Chapman *et al.* 2009). Disgust often leads to responses that can be characterized as "distancing from some object, event, or situation" (Rozin *et al.* 2000: 638), be it physical or psychological (Sheikh and Janoff-Bukman 2010). Indeed, the way our bodies respond physiologically with closed nostrils, an open mouth (Ekman and Friesen 1975; Izard 1971), nausea, and revulsion, is consistent with the idea of people trying to distance themselves from sources of disgust. Consequently, disgust is associated with a rejection appraisal (Lerner and Keltner 2001), triggering a "shut out and get away" response (Smith and Ellsworth 1985: 833).

Although reactions to disgust are consistent across people and cultures, there is high variability in the sources that *cause* people to experience disgust (Angyal 1941; Rozin and Fallon 1981). The 32-item disgust-sensitivity scale developed by Haidt *et al.* (2002) explores this idea, measuring disgust responses for seven domains of disgust (food, animals, body products, sex, body envelope violations, death, and hygiene). It finds that disgust sensitivity is correlated positively with fear of death and neuroticism, and negatively with sensation-seeking and psychoticism. Moreover, females have been shown to be more sensitive to disgust than men, and two of the big five factors, agreeableness and conscientiousness, are positively correlated with disgust sensitivity (Haidt *et al.* 2002; Druschel and Sherman 1999).

Although how one responds to different disgust elicitors need not define an individual, in certain cases it is possible that disgust sensitivity could significantly influence an individual's life and identity. In an interesting study examining phobias, Tolin *et al.* (1998), found that phobic participants (e.g. blood-injection-injury phobics and spider phobics) reacted to medical stimuli and spiders with disgust in addition to, or even instead of, fear. Based on this finding, the authors suggest that disgust, rather than overwhelming fear, may play a key role in defining the emotional underpinnings of specific life-impacting phobias. Consistent with this, Olatunji *et al.* (2008) also suggest that individuals' disgust responses may contribute to different clinical conditions. More generally, individuals' disgust tolerances may play an important role in shaping who they are by influencing what they avoid. For example, an individual who is readily disgusted by animal cruelty or raw meat may become a vegetarian, and an individual who is easily disgusted by blood may avoid professions that potentially involve contact with bodily fluids, like being a doctor, butcher or soldier.

Moving into the consumer domain, the prevalence of feelings of disgust in many typical consumer situations (e.g. Morales and Fitzsimons 2007; Argo *et al.* 2006) suggests that what causes consumers to feel disgusted can significantly influence how they consume. Indeed, the idea that individuals respond differently to specific disgust elicitors is illustrated clearly by differences in food preferences across cultures; what some consumers find disgusting, others consider a rare delicacy. While this may seem obvious for more extreme food examples (e.g. the Filipino delicacy Balut, a soft-boiled, fertilized duck embryo), what is somewhat less obvious is that distinct heterogeneity in disgust responses also exists for commonly purchased household products.

In a survey of 140 consumers, Morales and Fitzsimons (2007) found that many of the top supermarket sellers (as defined by the Food Institute's *Food Industry Review 2004*) such as cat litter, mayonnaise, cigarettes, and feminine napkins each elicit moderate feelings of disgust with a mean disgust rating of 5 or higher on a 10-point scale. Although this may seem to suggest convergence with regard to what North American consumers find disgusting, responses to two products (cigarettes and tobacco) were distinctly bi-modal in distribution, and responses to several other product categories (e.g. mayonnaise, cat litter) also seemed to indicate clear differences, with some consumers reporting very high and others reporting very low levels of disgust. The question is what determines these different disgust responses?

Although empirically untested, we propose that differences in individual disgust responses may be explained by self-identity. For example, though smokers are generally not disgusted by cigarettes, non-smokers often rate cigarettes as one of the most disgusting product categories (Morales and Fitzsimons 2007). Presumably, the same argument holds for responses to cat litter: cat owners are generally less disgusted by kitty litter than those without cats. This explanation is consistent with prior work indicating that repeated close contact with a disgusting item can weaken the disgust response by the process of extinction or adaptation (cannibalism in the Andes, in Read 1974; concentration camps, in DesPres 1976). In the case of smokers/cigarettes as well as cat owners/cat litter, then, individuals who have more contact with the product find it less disgusting.

However, the literature also suggests that increased contact alone is not sufficient to lower disgust reactions. For example, research on product contagion, where a disgust-inducing product (e.g. feminine napkins) lowers evaluations of an otherwise appealing product (e.g. cookies) through physical contact with it, finds no evidence of gender effects. Despite having more contact with the disgust-inducing product, women were as likely to rate the cookies as less attractive when they were touching the feminine napkins as men (Morales and Fitzsimons 2007), suggesting that what people find disgusting is based on more than just their familiarity with potential sources of disgust.

Speaking to the complexity of what evokes disgust, work in consumer contamination has demonstrated that when people think (but do not actually see) that another shopper has touched an item that they are considering for purchase, their evaluations of the item decrease significantly (Argo *et al.* 2006). Because they are so disgusted by the thought of another shopper having had physical contact with the item of interest, they choose not to buy the item, even though the item itself is not physically dirty. That is, feelings of disgust were shown to mediate evaluations and purchase intent for the touched item, whereas ratings of the item's dirtiness did not.

Interestingly, this process does not always occur when consumers actually see the specific individual who has touched the item of interest. When a male (female) consumer sees an attractive female (male), respectively, coming out of a dressing room after trying on a target item, rather than causing a disgust response as was the case when the person touching the item was anonymous, the physical contact with the attractive shopper actually makes the item more appealing. When the shopper and observing consumer are the same gender, however, the physical contact again elicits disgust and lowers target item evaluations. Thus, in this situation, the identities of the two individuals are critical in determining whether or not disgust is evoked. Rather than being the exception, we propose that identity plays a key, and as of yet overlooked, role in determining disgust responses in many consumer contexts.

If our assertion is true and identity changes the degree to which consumers experience disgust, the potential implications are numerous, as identity could influence responses through either the person who is *experiencing* disgust or the source who is *causing* disgust, or both. In the consumer contamination shopping scenario described above, it was the interaction between the identity (i.e. gender) of the observing consumer (i.e. the person potentially experiencing disgust) and the other shopper (i.e. the person potentially causing disgust) that moderated responses, but we argue that it is also possible for identity to influence disgust reactions through either path independently. For example, a man who is on active duty as a soldier may have different disgust reactions to wounded soldiers on the battlefield than he would when he is on leave at home in his role as a father and his son is injured on the playground. In such cases, we argue that disgust responses vary as a function of the *identity of the person* experiencing disgust (e.g. soldier vs. father). Similarly, the same man, when his identity of soldier is salient, may have very different responses to witnessing severely injured soldiers than he would to severely injured young children; here, we predict that disgust responses vary as a function of the *identity of the source* of disgust (e.g. soldiers vs. children).

By priming a specific identity and examining disgust responses, Verrochi and Williams (2011) provide direct empirical evidence that disgust responses change as a function of the person's salient social identity. As discussed earlier in Chapter 4, on "the emotional self," their work demonstrates that certain identities make specific emotions more likely to be experienced because consumers hold *emotion profiles* that suggest which emotional experiences are most appropriate (and useful) for individuals enacting a particular identity. Though this work does not focus on disgust specifically, their results show that when an "environmentalist" identity is primed, people are more inclined to experience disgust.

Taken together, prior research demonstrates convincingly that the identity of the person *experiencing* disgust can change disgust responses by making individuals more likely to feel disgusted. However, empirical work has not yet examined the possibility that certain identities might also make individuals less likely to feel disgusted. Going back to the soldier example, although he may not experience disgust readily on the battlefield in order to stay focused on completing his mission, that same man may be more easily disgusted when other identities are salient. Thus, in this case, rather than heightening a disgust response, it seems possible that identity might actually serve to mitigate it. The degree to which identity can both bolster and block disgust responses, and how this process develops over time, would be an interesting area for future research.

The reverse of this, the extent to which the identity of the source *causing* disgust might heighten and dampen disgust responses, would be another intriguing avenue for future research. Although the literature has provided support for how the identity of the person experiencing disgust can change disgust responses, apart from the consumer contamination papers that show a difference in product evaluations depending on the attractiveness and anonymity of the shopper touching a product (Argo *et al.* 2006, 2008), little work has considered how the identity of the disgust-causing source might also change responses. As explored previously in the soldier example, however, we speculate that the identity of the disgust-eliciting source may have significant implications for the degree to which the disgust response is evoked, and that this may interact with the identity of the individual experiencing disgust to shape overall behavior.

Beyond influencing which products consumers may choose to avoid, the extent to which identity influences whether feelings of disgust are felt or not can influence other aspects of consumption behavior. For example, Diehl *et al.* (2011) show that because disgust activates rejection and distancing appraisals, shopping for a disgust-inducing product reduces the degree to which consumers search in the store, increasing the average prices paid for other products purchased on the same shopping trip. Notably, one of the disgust-evoking products used in this research is anti-diarrheal medicine. If mothers by matter of increased contact with dirty diapers have a higher disgust tolerance, we would argue that a woman would be less subject to the reduction in search or the increase in prices paid when she shops for anti-diarrheal medicine in her "mother" identity than in her "lawyer" or "professor" identity. Although previous work discussed earlier in this chapter found that increased contact alone does not lower disgust reactions (Morales and Fitzsimons 2007), these studies did not prime specific identities, which could account for the null results. Additional research is needed to investigate these and related issues more deeply.

Similarly, the extent to which identity amplifies or dampens feelings of disgust has important implications for consumer compliance with persuasion appeals. In recent work, Morales *et al.* (2011) found that the addition of a disgust-eliciting element to a fear-evoking appeal results in heightened consumer compliance relative to an appeal that elicits fear only, and they trace this boost in persuasion to disgust's strong and immediate avoidance reaction. Again, since it is the disgust response that leads to the change in behavior and because specific identities are associated with varying levels of disgust responses, the efficacy of disgusting fear appeals will be at least partially dependent on the identity with which individuals view the appeal. Moreover, fear appeals that make identities with lower disgust responses more salient should also not see the benefit from evoking disgust. In fact, given that persuasion appeals have been identified as a primary way in which social identities can be activated and made salient (Forehand and Deshpandé 2001), the interaction between identity and disgust is particularly important in this domain and warrants a more nuanced examination.

In sum, we suggest that physical disgust can shape identity by influencing what consumers choose to avoid, but that identity can also shape disgust by determining what repels consumers.

Next, we shift from examining the interaction between physical disgust and identity to focusing on the interplay between self-identity and moral disgust.

Moral disgust and identity

Although disgust is commonly understood as an emotion that evolved to keep us safe from harmful physical substances and disease (Rozin *et al.* 2000), recent research has also linked feelings of disgust to non-physical or moral issues such as racism, abuse and greed (Haidt *et al.* 1997). Physiologically, the two types of disgust – physical and moral – are similar. FMRI (functional magnetic resonance imaging) scans show that both activate the lateral and medial orbitofrontal cortex (Moll *et al.* 2005), and that both result in the same physiological reactions – an increased tightening in the throat and a decreased heart rate (Sherman *et al.* 2009), and similar facial expressions (Rozin *et al.* 1994). Where physical and moral disgust differ is in the aspects of the human experience that trigger them (Haidt 2003); whereas physical disgust is associated with physical objects such as insects or bodily fluids, moral disgust is linked to social violations such as incest or abuse. Research suggests that disgust connects to morality in two ways: feelings of disgust can arise from the moral violations themselves (e.g. Rozin *et al.* 1999) or incidental feelings of disgust can carry over and increase the severity of moral judgments (e.g. Wheatley and Haidt 2005; Schnall *et al.* 2008).

In this chapter, we argue that self-identity and moral disgust each shape the other. First, we suggest that moral disgust can influence identity. Essentially this is the idea that what causes you to be morally outraged can also influence who you are. For example, individuals who are morally outraged by pollution and wasteful practices are likely to be environmentalists, those who find sexist, chauvinistic behavior appalling are likely to be feminists, and those who reject people of other racial backgrounds are likely to be racists. Though the suffix "-ist" commonly refers to an individual who performs a certain action (e.g. pianist) or adheres to a certain philosophy (e.g. hedonist), in cases like the ones mentioned above, we argue it can also refer to individuals who are defined by the specific actions, beliefs, or groups they avoid and reject – that is, individuals whose disgust defines them. Second, we suggest that identity can significantly shape moral disgust responses. For example, Inbar *et al.* (2009) show that people holding more conservative political attitudes ("conservatives") have a higher predisposition to feel disgust than their more liberal counterparts ("liberals"), especially when it comes to purity-related issues like abortion and gay marriage. Providing additional support for the relationship between conservatism and disgust, Terrizzi *et al.* (2010) found a positive correlation between socially conservative values and disgust sensitivity, arguing that such propensity to experience disgust can result in conservatives holding prejudicial attitudes toward out-groups. Although both of these papers measured (vs. manipulated) individuals' self-reported level of conservatism and disgust sensitivity, their findings are consistent with the assertion that one's identity can shape moral disgust responses.

Building on this, we propose that identity can also influence moral disgust responses through either the identity of the person committing the moral transgression or through the identity of the moral transgression victim. For example, although murdering children is clearly abhorrent regardless of the identity of the killer, the American public's responses to cases where a mother is accused of killing her own children (e.g. Andrea Yates drowned her five young children in their bathtub in 2001; Spinelli 2004) suggest that the same murderous act is perceived as even more disgusting and unforgivable in these instances than when the killer holds a different identity. This suggests that it may not be simply the act or crime itself that influences moral disgust responses, but that the identity of the transgressor (e.g. mother vs. serial criminal) as well as the identity of the victim (e.g. own child vs. unrelated adult) play a key role in determining how individuals respond.

Indeed, the identity of both the transgressor and his victims seemed to be at the core of the Bernie Madoff investment scandal. As the trusted financial advisor of many prominent executives and organizations, his deception and fraud was perceived as even more egregious than it perhaps would have been had he held the identity of a less reputable professional (e.g. used-car salesman). In addition, another aspect of his crimes that seemed particularly offensive was that he used his own Jewish identity to make himself seem more trustworthy to Jewish clientele. He "worked the so-called 'Jewish circuit' of well-heeled Jews he met at country clubs on Long Island and in Palm Beach," reported the *New York Post* (n.a. 2008), and they "trusted him because he is Jewish," wrote the Associated Press (n.a. 2009). Such targeted deception that preys upon members of specific religious or ethnic communities is classified as affinity fraud and is similar to a hate crime, or a bias-motivated crime, which occurs when a perpetrator chooses a victim because of his or her perceived identity in a particular social group. Given that the legal penalties for hate crimes are often steeper than those for the same acts not targeting specific groups, the identities of the victims clearly matter in both the perceptions and consequences of moral transgressions.

A related question that links moral disgust and identity is whether individuals who share the same social identity as a perpetrator might have different moral disgust responses to a transgression than those who do not. In other words, if I am also a mother or a financial advisor, am I even more disgusted by Andrea Yates and Bernie Madoff's crimes, respectively, than others would be because I feel they have violated key tenets of what it means to hold that identity? Or is it that because I share a social identity and am therefore affiliated with the perpetrators, I am potentially less morally disgusted? Future work should examine how sharing a basis for social identification operates in the domain of moral disgust responses.

Finally, the extent to which identity shapes moral disgust reactions has implications for downstream behavior. For example, Winterich *et al.* (2011) find that feelings of disgust lead to rejection and dehumanization, and by extension, moral disengagement. Across several studies, they link feelings of incidental disgust to increased moral disengagement and cheating behavior, and find stronger effects for men than women. To the extent that different identities, like gender, can heighten or dampen the moral disgust response, we speculate that the degree to which disgusted individuals will become morally disengaged is highly dependent on the identities that are salient at that time.

Conclusion

Although the majority of identity research in consumer behavior has looked at the relationship between self-identity and consumers' attraction to and preferences for products, services, charities, and people, we have argued in this chapter that identity also significantly impacts what consumers avoid and reject, and that what consumers avoid and reject in turn shapes their identity. Across the physical and moral disgust domains, we have proposed a novel framework that considers the reciprocal and dynamic relationship between identity and disgust, examines its implications for overall consumer behavior and offers suggestions for future research. In doing so, we hope that despite the strong rejection tendencies associated with disgust, our discussion serves to raise interest in further exploring the complex relationship between disgust and identity.

Further reading

Haidt, J., McCauley, C. and Rozin, P. (2002) "Individual Differences in Sensitivity to Disgust: A Scale Sampling Seven Domains of Disgust Elicitors." *Personality and Individual Differences* 16(5): 701–13. (An introduction to individual differences in disgust sensitivity.)

Rozin, P., Haidt, J. and McCauley, C. (2000) "Disgust." In M. Lewis and J.M. Haviland (eds), *Handbook of Emotions*. New York: Guilford, pp. 637–53. (A good overview of disgust and its properties.)

Rozin, P., Lowery, L., Imada, S. and Haidt, J. (1999) "The CAD Triad Hypothesis: A Mapping Between Three Moral Emotions (Contempt, Anger, Disgust) and Three Moral Codes (Community, Autonomy, Divinity)." *Journal of Personality and Social Psychology* 76(4): 574–86. (An early paper that examines how emotions (including disgust) relate to morality.)

References

Angyal, A. (1941) "Disgust and Related Aversions." *Journal of Abnormal and Social Psychology* 36: 393–412.

Argo, J.J., Dahl, D.W. and Morales, A.C. (2006) "Consumer Contamination: How Consumers React to Products Touched by Others." *Journal of Marketing* 70 (April): 81–94.

——(2008) "Positive Consumer Contamination: Responses to Attractive Others in a Retail Context." *Journal of Marketing Research* 45(6): 690–701.

Chapman, H.A., Kim, D.A., Susskind, J.M. and Anderson, A.K. (2009) "In Bad Taste: Evidence for the Oral Origins of Moral Disgust." *Science* 323: 1222–26.

DesPres, T. (1976) *The Survivor*. Oxford: Oxford University Press.

Diehl, K., Morales, A.C., Fitzsimons, G.J. and Simester, D. (2011) "Shopping Interdependencies: How Emotions Affect Consumer Search and Shopping Behavior." Under review at *Journal of Marketing Research*.

Druschel, B.A. and Sherman, M.F. (1999) "Disgust Sensitivity as a Function of the Big Five and Gender." *Personality and Individual Differences* 26(4): 739–48.

Ekman, P. and Friesen, W.V. (1975) *Unmasking the Face*. Englewood Cliffs, NJ: Prentice-Hall.

The Food Institute (2004) "The Food Institute's Food Industry Review 2004." Elmwood Park, NJ.

Forehand, M.R. and Deshpandé, R. (2001) "What We See Makes Us Who We Are: Priming Ethnic Self-Awareness and Advertising Response." *Journal of Marketing Research* 38(3): 336–48.

Haidt, J. (2003) "The Moral Emotions." In Richard J. Davidson, Klaus R. Scherer, and Goldsmith H. Hill (eds), *Handbook of Affective Sciences*. London: Oxford University Press, pp. 852–70.

Haidt, J., McCauley, C. and Rozin, P. (2002) "Individual Differences in Sensitivity to Disgust: A Scale Sampling Seven Domains of Disgust Elicitors." *Personality and Individual Differences* 16(5): 701–13.

Haidt, J., Rozin, P., McCauley, C. and Imada, S. (1997) "Body, Psyche, and Culture: The Relationship between Disgust and Morality." *Psychology and Developing Societies* 9: 107–31.

Inbar, Y., Pizarro, D. and Bloom, P. (2009) "Conservatives are More Easily Disgusted than Liberals." *Cognition and Emotion* 23(4): 714–25.

Izard, C.E. (1971) *The Face of Emotion*. New York: Appleton-Century-Crofts.

Lerner, J.S. and Keltner, D. (2001) "Fear, Anger, and Risk." *Journal of Personality and Social Psychology* 81: 146–59.

Moll, J., de Oliveira-Souza, R., Moll, F.T., Ignácio, F.A., Bramati, I.E., Caparelli-Dáquer, E.M. and Eslinger, P.J. (2005) "The Moral Affiliations of Disgust: A Functional MRI Study." *Cognitive and Behavioral Neurology* 18(1): 68–78.

Morales, A.C. and Fitzsimons, G. (2007) "Product Contagion: Changing Consumer Evaluations Through Physical Contact with 'Disgusting' Products." *Journal of Marketing Research* 44: 272–83.

Morales, A.C., Wu, E. and Fitzsimons, G. (2011) "That's so Disgusting – I'll Take Two! How Disgust Enhances the Effectiveness of Fear Appeals." Under review at *Journal of Marketing Research*.

n.a. (2008) "Investor Furor over '50B Scam'." *New York Post*. 14 December, m.nypost.com/ms/p/nyp/nyp/view.m?id=23907&storyid=143966 (accessed 17 December 2008).

n.a. (2009) "Tough Task Ahead to Find Madoff Money, Co-schemers." Associated Press. 13 March 13, www.google.com/hostednews/ap/article/ALeqM5hnkPe640MG8WMCAvAwv5GqtqxsOAD96T6K8G0 (accessed 13 March 2009).

Olatunji, B.O., Haidt, J., McKay, D. and David, B. (2008) "Core, Animal Reminder, and Contamination Disgust: Three Kinds of Disgust with Distinct Personality, Behavioral, Physiological, and Clinical Correlates." *Journal of Research in Personality* 42(5): 1243–59.

Read, P.P. (1974) *Alive*. Hillsdale, NJ: Erlbaum.

Rozin, Paul and Fallon, A.E. (1981) "The Acquisition of Likes and Dislikes for Foods." In J. Solms and R.L. Hall (eds), *Criteria of Food Acceptance: How Man Chooses What He Eats. A Symposium*. Zurich: Forster, pp. 35–48.

Rozin, P., Haidt, J. and McCauley, C. (2000) "Disgust." In M. Lewis and J.M. Haviland (eds), *Handbook of Emotions*. New York: Guilford, pp. 637–53.

Rozin, P., Lowery, L. and Ebert, R. (1994) "Varieties of Disgust Faces and the Structure of Disgust." *Journal of Personality and Social Psychology* 66(5): 870–81.

Rozin, P., Lowery, L., Imada, S. and Haidt, J. (1999) "The CAD Triad Hypothesis: A Mapping between Three Moral Emotions (Contempt, Anger, Disgust) and Three Moral Codes (Community, Autonomy, Divinity)." *Journal of Personality and Social Psychology* 76(4): 574–86.

Schnall, S., Haidt, J., Clore, G.L. and Jordan, A.H. (2008) "Disgust as Embodied Moral Judgment." *Personality and Social Psychology Bulletin* 34(8): 1096–109.

Sheikh, S. and Janoff-Bukman, R. (2010) "Tracing the Self-Regulatory Bases of Moral Emotions." *Emotion Review* 2: 386–96.

Sherman, G.D., Haidt, J. and Coan, J.A. (2009) "Viewing Cute Images Increases Behavioral Carefulness." *Emotion* 9(2): 282–6.

Smith, C.A. and Ellsworth, P.C. (1985) "Patterns of Cognitive Appraisal in Emotion." *Journal of Personality and Social Psychology* 48: 813–38.

Spinelli, Margaret G. (2004) "Maternal Infanticide Associated With Mental Illness: Prevention and the Promise of Saved Lives." *American Journal of Psychiatry* 161(9): 1548–57.

Terrizzi J.A., Jr, Shook, N.J. and Ventis, W.L. (2010) "Disgust: A Predictor of Social Conservatism and Prejudicial Attitudes Toward Homosexuals." *Personality and Individual Differences* 49(6): 587–92.

Tolin, D.F., Lohr, J.M., Sawchuk, C.N. and Lee, T.C. (1998) "Disgust and Disgust Sensitivity in Blood-Injection-Injury and Spider Phobia." *Behavior Research and Therapy* 35(10): 949–53.

Verrochi, N.M. and Williams, P. (2011) "Feeling Like My Self: Emotion Profiles and Social Identity." Under review at *Journal of Consumer Research*.

Wheatley, T. and Haidt, J. (2005) "Hypnotic Disgust Makes Moral Judgments More Severe." *Psychological Science* 16(10): 780–4.

Winterich, K.P., Morales, A.C. and Mittal, V. (2011) "No Harm, No Foul: Cheating is OK When I'm Dirty and Disengaged." Under review at *Organizational Behavior and Human Decision Processes*.

I.III

Extending the self into possessions

8
EXTENDED SELF IN A DIGITAL AGE

Russell W. Belk

When I first wrote about the extended self (Belk 1987, 1988), cellular phones, MP3 players, the Internet, and most of the other digital technologies that we take for granted today did not exist. By the time Kelly Tian and I looked at extended self in the workplace (Tian and Belk 2005), it was clear that thanks especially to digital technologies consumers have multiple selves, that the work self and family self are no longer tethered to specific and distinct times and places, that we have begun to outsource portions of our memories to digital devices like computers, and that we sometimes use personal digital devices not only to connect with other people but also to carve out areas of privacy within ostensibly public spaces. However, a more comprehensive treatment of the extended self in a digital world is still missing. This chapter outlines some of the changing avenues for digitally enabled self-extension at the current point in time and some of the changes taking place in consumer identity management.

Changing notions of self

Although Shakespeare said "All the world's a stage" (*As You Like It*, act II, scene VII) and Goffman (1959) described how we perform different selves with different audiences and in different settings using various costumes, ensemble teams, and props, the postmodern sensibility insists that the self has become decentered, unstable, fragmented, liquid, malleable, and multiple (e.g. Bauman 2000; Best and Kellner 2001; Clarke 2003; Firat and Dholakia 1998). Although this view has not gone unchallenged (e.g. Hammer 2005), it would be difficult to find a better demonstration of these arguments than the multiple identities that we are able to maintain online. As Turkle observes:

> Traditional ideas about identity have been tied to a notion of authenticity that such virtual experiences actively subvert. When each player can create many characters and participate in many games, the self is not only de-centered but multiplied without limit.
>
> *(Turkle 1997: 185)*

There are many types of digital interfaces and they vary considerably in the extent to which they allow or encourage us to present different selves to others. There is considerable variation in the potential for self-presentation on social media sites, Internet dating sites, e-mail, multiple-user online games like World of Warcraft, virtual worlds like Second Life, chatrooms, forums, brand and fan community sites, video sites like YouTube, photo sharing sites like Flickr, hospitality sharing sites like Couchsurfing.org, mobile phones, SMS messages, websites, sites for feedback and reviews of online sellers and their products or services, and other interactive digital devices, programs, sites, games, and social media vehicles for digitally presenting ourselves to others. It is also important to recognize that besides extending ourselves through different objects as well as virtual objects and representations, we also extend ourselves through other people and places. With their potential for fostering virtual communities and creating webs of friends, followers, and fans, the Internet and our digital devices also allow for much more expansive networks of extended social self than were feasible in pre-digital days. Although it is true that many of these connections involve the sort of weak ties of which Granovetter (1973) wrote, the fact that it is easy to connect, interact, and keep these ties alive through participation via messages, postings, tweets, tags, comments, likes, pokes, missions, location coordinates, and activity updates, means that these networks can be much more active than with face-to-face contact alone.

A further possible change in our notions of self is our virtualization. Although earlier technologies allowed us to virtually interact via "snail mail," disembodied voices on the telephone, messages delivered via telegraph (which Standage (1998) called the Victorian Internet), and via the exchange of *cartes de visite* (which we might regard as the Victorian Facebook) and photographs, it has never been so easy to instantaneously communicate and represent ourselves to a broad range of others as it is today. What is more, we can often represent ourselves in digital media via avatars, we can digitally manipulate our photographic portraits, and we can assume pseudonyms, change genders, and appear to become animals, vegetables, or minerals if we wish. However, even though the possibilities for self-representation are expanded in digital media, it was also true that we previously constructed imagined communities and aggregate senses of self via earlier media (Anderson 1983). We should also make a distinction between identity and self. What digital technologies affect most directly is our identity – who we appear to be, our "identifiers," our nominal affiliations, and our representations – but these things are not the same as our sense of self. Thus, we may worry about identity theft in using digital media, but we don't worry about someone stealing our self. Even though identity theft may suggest a rough analogy to the Devil stealing our soul, we don't really see our disembodied digital representations as being the essential "us." Furthermore, the sort of virtual memory that digital storage and access allow also had earlier analogues in books (Manguel 1996). This is not to say that our notions of self are not being changed by digital media; they are. It is just that some of these changes may be less radical than they first appear to be.

Changing self-extensions

Virtual self-extension

Following on from the preceding discussion of digital self-representation, let us first consider the self-extension that takes place via what Tian and Belk (2005) called the prosthetic self. We were not referring to artificial limbs, pacemakers, and implanted insulin pumps, although these aspects of the posthuman cyborg have also been enhanced or made possible by digital technologies (e.g. Giesler and Venkatesh 2005; Haraway 1991; Hemetsberger 2005; Venkatesh *et al.* 2002). Rather, we were referring to things like storing contact information on our phones and computers, archiving our e-mail, articles, photos, videos, and other digital artifacts in digital storage, and doing online searches for information we previously had to remember or look up in books and journals that existed in physical form on a shelf somewhere. An extreme example of this is the personal project of Microsoft engineer Gordon Bell (Bell and Gemmell 2009). Bell attempted to digitally record as much or his life as possible including photos, e-mails, documents, memorabilia, tweets, phone calls, GPS coordinates of his movements, instant messages, appointment calendars, daily activities, and much more. He wore a motion-sensitive automatic camera around his neck that started recording whenever it detected activity in his environment. All this is searchable and readily accessible. Theoretically someone in the future could use this archive to understand Gordon Bell's life much more thoroughly and accurately than any autobiography. This approach has its detractors and critics like Mayer-Schönberger (2009), who worries, for example, that with devices and Internet trails that remember everything, we will lose the ability to forgive and forget, be burdened by the dead weight of the past, and be embarrassed by compromising photos, outdated information, and information taken out of context. Facebook faux pas, for example, have led to job loss and job denial as the everlasting memory of the Internet trail we leave reaches audiences we never intended. Carr (2008, 2010) worries that in outsourcing our memory to Google, we will become stupid and know much less despite our greater access to information. To put this in perspective, though, this is very similar to an argument between Plato and Socrates when we began outsourcing our knowledge to books (Manguel 1996). Issues of privacy from Internet sites, web browsers, governments, and other entities are also a concern as more and more about us is stored online and increasingly capable technologies like facial recognition software and database matching become possible in real time (e.g. Nissenbaum 2010).

Nevertheless, there are others who look at the permanent presence of our digital artifacts as a good thing. Carroll and Romano (2011), for example, regard our future heirlooms as being increasingly digital and suggest that these digital possessions must be managed and perpetuated so that we may continue to "live" on online even after we die. They suggest that we should actively control and preserve our photos, movies, personal letters, and other documents, while trying to erase our pornography, junk e-mail, and other embarrassing or unflattering traces. The fact that we have a digital estate and that our digital presence remains active to some degree when we are no longer here, is something most people have not yet thought about. There may be a certain amount of hubris in striving to make ourselves digitally immortal with post-mortem self-presentations, but we don't have to be professional artists, composers, filmmakers, or novelists to worry about our digital legacy and passing along our digital possessions to others. After all, we who are academics may occasionally wonder whether any of our scholarly work will outlive us.

A now obvious set of digital self-extensions involves our web pages (Schau and Gilly (2003), blogs (Kretz and de Valck 2010), creations on YouTube and other video archives (Hediger 2010), and postings on Facebook and other social media sites (Gilpin 2011; Veer 2011). Unlike physical possessions, these digital creations are not static. They are both changing and, to varying degrees, interactive. Even discussion forums are more than ephemeral as threads are archived and presumably available indefinitely (Schwob and de Valk 2010). All of these and most other digital representations are clearly self-extensions, and because of the greater flexibility and creative possibilities of digital possessions they may allow a projection of something closer to our ideal selves (Schau and Gilly 2003). Furthermore, because they allow the use of text as well as images, these self-representations can create self-narratives, self-disclosure, and displays of competence, expertise, and artistic abilities much more readily than physical possessions alone.

Even the ringtone, applications, contact list, music playlists, favorite websites, and other customizable configurations of our smartphones make them much more personal and identifiable than earlier with much more standardized landline telephones. There was a time in the 1950s through the 1970s when computers were large mainframe objects owned by huge corporations, governments, and militaries for the avowed purpose of prediction and control. We received bills in the mail on pre-punched computer cards with instructions not to bend, fold, staple, or mutilate these proofs that we were simply a number in some vast, impersonal database. However, this began to change in the 1980s, when the computer became personal, laptops emerged, and we began to feel that we were the ones in control. Computers began to be fun and by the 1990s, when e-mail became common, they also became social instruments for contacting others (Streeter 2011). If you think our computers are not personal, think about how comfortable you would feel giving a stranger access to your hard drive, playlists, and e-mails. We have come to feel that not only are these things ours, but they are a part of us; a part of our identity; an important element of who we are. With a number of websites devoted to certain brands, bands, films, television shows, sports teams, or other foci of our devoted and loyal interest, we may feel we are joint devotees of a cult or tribe (Belk and Tumbat 2005; Cova *et al.* 2007; Jenkins 2006; Kozinets 1999, 2001, 2002; Watson 1997). This is potentially a doubly extended self-focusing both on the object of interest and on the community of fellow believers. These are what Baym (2010) terms "shared identities."

Besides digital "possessions," even seemingly ephemeral activity online can come to form part of our extended self. For example, Turkle describes:

> Roger … a fifty-year-old businessman who seeks out video games to achieve a state of mind that he gets into when he skis. He plays a game until that point where "the strategies are part of you," where he feels like an extension of the game or the game is an extension of him.
>
> *(Turkle 1984: 85)*

Zwick and Dholakia (2006) call such consumer-object relations "epistemic consumption objects," by which they mean changing and materially elusive objects of knowledge that reveal themselves progressively. Roger and his video games is an example of a relationship between a single person and an epistemic consumption object, but such objects could also involve interactions with joint others as in massively multiplayer online role-playing games (MMORPGs) like World of Warcraft (WoW). In January 2010 WoW had more than 11.5 million players who had invested the cumulative equivalent 5.93 million years playing the game, with each player averaging 17–22 hours a week in WoW (McGonigal 2011). Consumers who devote this much time as well as money to any activity are likely to invest much of their identity in it (Gee 2007).

Those who actively participate in role-playing games like WoW and virtual worlds like Second Life (SL) also identify with the avatars they have created. As Turkle (2011) finds, our Avatars in WoW and SL are not so much veridical representations of our selves as they are ideal projections of the selves we would like to be:

> Online, the plain represented themselves as glamorous, the old as young, the young as older. Those of modest means wore elaborate virtual jewelry. In virtual space, the crippled walked without crutches, and the shy improved their chances as seducers.
>
> *(Turkle 2011: 158)*

Moreover, there is also some evidence that online selves provide confidence to carry some of these ideal traits with us into the real world as well (e.g. Boellstorff 2008; Turkle 2011). This is not to say that all players strictly identify with a single avatar and many also keep "alts" on reserve because sticking to a single avatar can be too constraining (Boellstorff 2008; Ducheneaut and Moore 2004; Miller 2011). Thus, it appears that virtual worlds and games not only allow us to take on more diverse identities, but also multiple selves.

Self and others

As noted above, besides extending self through things and places – virtual or real – we also extend our selves through other people whom we feel are a part of our aggregate self. As Belk (1988; Belk *et al.* 2003) observes, object relations are also never just person-thing, but always person-thing-person, such that other people's regard for our objects or the objects that we desire determine the meanings of these objects for our sense of self. In addition to the more personal expression that takes place through our digital possessions and creations, there are also affiliative communities centered around brands, political candidates, social movements, celebrities, and numerous other interests (Kozinets 2001; Kozinets and Handelman 2004; Muñiz and O'Guinn 2000; Muñiz and Schau 2005). Although online communities may be imagined to a greater degree than face-to-face communities (Anderson 1983), the give and take on the forums, discussion groups, blogs, and websites of such groups still allows ample opportunity to express ourselves, demonstrate expertise, and develop reputations (Kozinets 1999; Kozinets *et al.* 2010). Most notably, this sort of Internet content along with web pages, social media, photo and video sharing sites, blogs, and forums is *our* content generated actively and voluntarily by many contributors rather than top-down passive content as has been dominant for many decades of broadcast content (Weinberger 2007). This together with our ability to create or select sites of particular interest to us, means that we are likely to feel that this content is more a part of us since we may well have had a hand in creating it. Even for an online retail site like Amazon, the fact that we can contribute reviews, rate products and non-Amazon merchants, and participate in collaborative filtering to obtain the preferences of other "people like us," means that we are co-producing part of the content of the site, even if we must give up some privacy to do so (Humphreys 2006).

Social networking sites (SNS) and online dating sites provide opportunities to create an identity vis-à-vis others through digital objects like photos, videos, and self-descriptions, as well as by the friends we have (both their number and attractiveness), the values and tastes we display in our music, film, book, and other preferences, the sorts of offline activities and interests we depict ourselves pursuing or claim to enjoy, our online activity including posts about us or on our wall, our vocabulary and grammar, and the clothes and other possessions we display in our photos or links (Baym 2010). These possessions and presentations of self have a real impact on online popularity on SNS, leading to more "friends," leading to more social capital, potentially leading to further popularity (Bourdieu 1984; Ellison *et al.* 2011; Liu 2007). All this is perceived as dynamic and tentative, however, so that sometimes we may seemingly addictively add to SNS pages and tweets in order to seem to be continually active and interesting (Larose *et al.* 2011). It might appear that there would be a temptation to exaggerate and engage in deceptive self-presentation given these SNS pressures, but there is generally greater honesty on SNS sites than in other online sites such as dating sites (Toma *et al.* 2008). An explanation that has been offered is that because of the larger number of viewers and the fact that they may also know us offline, SNS sites are less amenable to successful deception (Donath 2007; Ellison *et al.* 2011).

In online dating sites, by contrast, there is a greater degree of anonymity, at least until partners meet face-to-face. However, the sorts of deceptions found in Internet dating sites are not blatant and generally involve people describing themselves as taller, thinner, and with other exaggerated qualities, such as being a non-smoker when they do in fact smoke (Ellison *et al.* 2006). Some also use photos from when they were younger and omit mentioning the details that they have children or are married (Lawson and Leck forthcoming). Males tend to present themselves as having good and well-paying jobs and females present themselves as being young and attractive. In this respect these patterns are not much different from pre-Internet personal advertisements.

The difference is instead in the ease of connection and the mediated relationship provided by eHarmony™ or other dating sites (Humphreys 2007; Lawson and Leck forthcoming).

Conclusion

There is more to the impact of digital technologies on the extended self than I have been able to cover here. For example, the aggregate self resulting from sharing online is something that is better addressed in Chapter 27 of this volume, with Rosa Llamas. There are also further impacts of virtual reality technologies on the dissolution of the Cartesian ego (Bolter and Grusin 2000; Novak 1991). Clearly, too, this is an area that continues to change. Turkle's (2011) discussion of marrying robots is one example. The point to emphasize for now is that digital technologies are dramatically changing our notions of self, possessions, and extended self. This is an area that is ripe for future research.

Acknowledgement

I would like to thank Risto Moisio and Mariam Beruchashvili for their helpful comments on an earlier version of this chapter.

References

Anderson, Benedict (1983) *Imagined Communities*. London: Verso.

Bauman, Zygmunt (2000) *Liquid Modernity*. Cambridge: Polity.

Baym, Nancy (2010) *Personal Connections in the Digital Age*. Cambridge: Polity.

Belk, Russell (1987) "Identity and the Relevance of Market, Personal, and Community Objects." In Jean Sebeok (ed.), *Marketing and Semiotics: New Directions in the Study of Signs for Sale*. Berlin: Mouton de Gruyter, pp.151–64.

——(1988) "Possessions and the Extended Self." *Journal of Consumer Research* 5(2) (September): 139–68.

Belk, Russell, Ger, Güliz, and Askegaard, Søren (2003) "The Fire of Desire: A Multi-Sited Inquiry into Consumer Passion." *Journal of Consumer Research* 30 (December): 311–25.

Belk, Russell and Tumbat, Gülnur (2005) "The Cult of Macintosh." *Consumption, Markets and Culture* 8 (September): 205–18.

Bell, Gordon and Gemmell, Jim (2009) *Total Recall: How the E-Memory Revolution Will Change Everything*. New York: Dutton.

Best, Steven and Kellner, Douglas (2001) *The Postmodern Adventure: Science, Technology, and Cultural Studies at the Third Millennium*. New York: Guilford Press.

Boellstorff, Tom (2008) *Coming of Age in Second Life: An Anthropologist Explores the Virtually Human*. Princeton, NJ: Princeton University Press.

Bolter, Jay David and Grusin, Richard (2000) *Remediation: Understanding New Media*. Cambridge, MA: MIT Press.

Bourdieu, Pierre (1984) *Distinction: A Social Critique of the Judgement of Taste*. London: Routledge and Kegan Paul.

Carr, Nicholas (2008) "Is Google Making Us Stupid?" *Atlantic Monthly* 302(1) (July/August): 56–62.

——(2010) *The Shallows: What the Internet is Doing to Our Brains*. New York: W.W. Norton.

Carroll, Evan and Romano, John (2011) *Your Digital Afterlife: When Facebook, Flickr and Twitter Are Your Estate, What's Your Legacy?* Berkeley, CA: New Riders.

Clarke, David B. (2003) *The Consumer Society and the Postmodern City*. London: Routledge.

Cova, Bernard, Kozinets, Robert, and Shankar, Avi (2007) *Consumer Tribes*. Oxford: Butterworth-Heinemann.

Donath, Judith (2007) "Signals in Social Supernets." *Journal of Computer-Mediated Communication* 13 (October): 231–51.

Ducheneaut, Nicolas and Moore, Robert (2004) "Let Me Get My Alt: Digital Identiti(es) in Multiplayer Games." Position paper for the CSCW2004 workshop on Representation of Digital Identities. 6 November 2004. Chicago, IL. www2.parc.com/csl/members/nicolas/documents/CSCW2004-Digital_identity.pdf.

Ellison, Nicole, Heino, Rebecca, and Gibbs, Jennifer (2006) "Managing Impressions Online: Self-Presentation Processes in the Online Dating Environment." *Journal of Computer-Mediated Communication* 11 (January): 415–41.

Ellison, Nicole B., Lampe, Cliff, Steinfield, Charles, and Vitak, Jessica (2011) "With a Little Help From My Friends: How Social Network Sites Affect Social Capital Processes." In Zizi Papacharissi (ed.), *A Networked Self: Identity, Community, and Culture on Social Network Sites*. New York: Routledge, pp. 124–45.

Firat, A. Fuat and Dholakia, Nikhilesh (1998) *Consuming People: From Political Economy to Theaters of Consumption*. London: Routledge.

Gee, James P. (2007) "Learning by Design: Good Video Games as Learning Machines." In Paul Messaris and Lee Humphreys (eds), *Digital Media: Transformations in Human Communication*. New York: Peter Lang, pp. 173–86.

Giesler, Markus and Venkatesh, Alladi (2005) "Reframing the Embodied Consumer as Cyborg: A Posthumanist Epistemology of Consumption." *Advances in Consumer Research* 32: 661–69.

Gilpin, Dawn R. (2011) "Working the Twittersphere: Microblogging as Professional Identity Construction." In Zizi Papacharissi (ed.), *A Networked Self: Identity, Community, and Culture on Social Network Sites*. New York: Routledge, pp. 232–50.

Goffman, Erving (1959) *The Presentation of Self in Everyday Life*. Garden City, NY: Anchor Books.

Granovetter, Mark (1973) "The Strength of Weak Ties." *American Journal of Sociology* 78(6): 1360–80.

Hammer, Anita (2005) "Weaving Trickster: Myth and Tribal Encounters on the World Wide Web." In Eric Rothenbuhler and Mihai Coman (eds), *Media Anthropology*. Thousand Oaks, CA: Sage, pp. 260–8.

Haraway, Donna (1991) *Simians, Cyborgs, and Women: The Reinvention of Nature*. New York: Routledge.

Hediger, Vinzenz (2010) "YouTube and the Aesthetics of Political Accountability." In Pelle Snickars and Patrick Vonderau (eds), *The YouTube Reader*. Stockholm: National Library of Sweden, pp. 252–65.

Hemetsberger, Andrea (2005) "Creative Cyborgs: How Consumers Use the Internet for Self-Realization." *Advances in Consumer Research* 32: 653–60.

Humphreys, A. (2006) "The Consumer as Foucauldian 'Object of Knowledge'." *Social Science Computer Review* 24(3): 296–309.

Humphreys, Lee (2007) "Photographs and the Presentation of Self through Online Dating Services." In Paul Messaris and Lee Humphreys (eds), *Digital Media: Transformations in Human Communication*. New York: Peter Lang, pp. 39–50.

Jenkins, Henry (2006) *Fans, Bloggers, and Gamers: Exploring Participatory Culture*. New York: NYU Press.

Kozinets, Robert (1999) "E-Tribalized Marketing?: The Strategic Implications of Virtual Communities on Consumption." *European Management Journal* Vol.17 (June): 252–64.

——(2001) "Utopian Enterprise: Articulating the Meanings of *Star Trek*'s Culture of Consumption." *Journal of Consumer Research* 28 (June): 67–88.

——(2002) "Can Consumers Escape the Market? Emancipatory Illuminations from Burning Man." *Journal of Consumer Research* 29 (June): 20–38.

Kozinets, Robert and Handelman, Jay (2004) "Adversaries of Consumption: Consumer Movements, Activism, and Ideology." *Journal of Consumer Research* 30 (December): 691–704.

Kozinets, Robert, de Valck, Kristine, Wojnicki, Andrea, and Wilner, Sarah (2010) "Networked Narratives: Understanding Word-of-mouth Marketing in Online Communities." *Journal of Marketing* 74 (March): 71–89.

Kretz, Gachoucha and de Valck, Kristine (2010) "'Pixelize Me!': Digital Storytelling and the Creation of Archetypal Myths Through Explicit and Implicit Self-Brand Association in Fashion and Luxury Blogs." In Russell Belk (ed.), *Research in Consumer Behavior*. Bingley: Emerald, pp. 313–29.

Larose, Robert, Kim, Junghyun, and Peng Wei (2011) "Social Networking: Addictive, Compulsive, Problematic, or Just Another Media Habit?" In Zizi Papacharissi (ed.), *A Networked Self: Identity, Community, and Culture on Social Network Sites*. New York: Routledge, pp. 59–81.

Lawson, Helene and Leck, Kira (forthcoming) "Dating on the Internet." In Russell Belk and Rosa Llamas (eds), *The Digital Consumer*. London: Routledge.

Liu, Hugo (2007) "Social Network Profiles as Taste Performances." *Journal of Computer-Mediated Communication* 13(1), jcmc.indiana.edu/vol13/issue1/liu.html.

McGonigal, Jane (2011) *Reality is Broken: Why Games Make Us Better and How they Can Change the World*. New York: Penguin Press.

Manguel, Alberto (1996) *A History of Reading*. Toronto: Alfred A. Knopf.

Mayer-Schönberger, Viktor (2009) *Delete: The Virtue of Forgetting in the Digital Age*. Princeton, NJ: Princeton University Press.

Miller, Vincent (2011) *Understanding Digital Culture*. London: Sage.
Muñiz, Albert, Jr and O'Guinn, Thomas C. (2000) "Brand Community." *Journal of Consumer Research* 27 (March): 412–32.
Muñiz, Albert, Jr and Schau, Hope Jensen (2005) "Religiosity in the Abandoned Apple Newton Brand Community." *Journal of Consumer Research* 31 (March): 737–47.
Nissenbaum, Helen (2010) *Privacy in Context: Technology, Policy, and the Integrity of Social Life*. Stanford, CA: Stanford University Press.
Novak, Marcos (1991) "Liquid Architectures in Cyberspace." In Michael Benedikt (ed.), *Cyberspace: First Steps*, Cambridge, MA: MIT Press, pp. 225–54.
Schau, Hope Jensen and Gilly, Mary C. (2003) "We Are What We Post? Self-Presentation and Personal Web Space." *Journal of Consumer Research* 30 (December): 385–404.
Schwob, Alexandre and de Valck, Kristine (2010) "Better Understanding Construction of the Self in Daily Contingencies: An Investigation of the Materiality of Consumption Experiences in Online Discussion Forums." In Russell Belk (ed.), *Research in Consumer Behavior*. Bingley: Emerald, vol.12, pp. 287–312.
Standage, Tom (1998) *The Victorian Internet: The Remarkable Story of the Telegraph and the Nineteenth Century's On-Line Pioneers*. New York: Walker and Company.
Streeter, Thomas (2011) *The Net Effect: Romanticism, Capitalism, and the Internet*. New York: New York University Press.
Tian, Kelly and Belk, Russell W. (2005) "Extended Self and Possessions in the Workplace." *Journal of Consumer Research* 32 (September): 297–310.
Toma, Catalina L., Hancock, Jeffrey T., and Ellison, Nicole B. (2008) "Separating Fact from Fiction: An Examination of Deceptive Self-Presentation in Online Dating Profiles." *Personality and Social Psychology Bulletin* 34(8): 1023–36.
Turkle, Sherry (1984) *The Second Self: Computers and the Human Spirit*. New York: Simon & Schuster.
——(1997) *Life On Screen: Identity in the Age of the Internet*. New York: Touchstone.
——(2011) *Alone Together: Why We Expect More from Technology and Less from Each Other*. New York: Basic Books.
Veer, Ekant (2011) "Staring: How Facebook Facilitates the Breaking of Social Norms." In Russell Belk, Kent Grayson, Albert Muñiz, Jr, and Hope Jensen Schau (eds), *Research in Consumer Behavior*. Bingley, UK: Emerald, vol. 13.
Venkatesh, Alladi, Karababa, Eminigul, and Ger, Güliz (2002) "The Emergence of the Posthuman Consumer and the Fusion of the Virtual and the Real: A Critical Analysis of Sony's Ad for Memory Stick™." *Advances in Consumer Research* 29: 446–52.
Watson, Nessim (1997) "Why We Argue About Virtual Community: A Case Study of the Phish.Net Fan Community." In Steven G. Jones (ed.), *Virtual Culture: Identity and Communication in Cybersociety*. London: Sage, pp. 102–32.
Weinberger, David (2007) *Everything is Miscellaneous: The Power of the New Digital Disorder*. New York: Holt.
Zwick, Detlef and Dholakia, Nikhilesh (2006) "Bringing the Market to Life: Screen Aesthetics and the Epistemic Consumption Object." *Marketing Theory* 6(1): 41–62.

9

WE ARE WHAT WE BUY?

Keisha M. Cutright, Adriana Samper and Gavan J. Fitzsimons

In the 2008 Beijing Olympic Games, American swimmer Michael Phelps astounded viewers around the world by winning a record-breaking eight gold medals. To stay warm before each race, Phelps wore a "swim parka" with the Speedo brand prominently featured. Speedo was subsequently flooded with requests from swimmers around the world hoping to don a Phelps parka of their very own (Walker 2008). One can argue that this is a straightforward example of people wanting to signal that they are similar to another impressive individual. However, could something even more intriguing be going on? Might the Michael Phelps swim parka actually make one a better swimmer? More broadly, can using certain brands actually change who we are? If so, can we strategically select brands with aspirational qualities to self-improve? It might seem silly to believe a consumer will actually become a faster swimmer by wearing the same parka Phelps wore, but we will present evidence that suggests that this trend is precisely what might happen over time, largely outside of consumers' conscious awareness.

In what follows, we will explore how our identities and consumption choices interact in two ways. First, we will briefly highlight interesting new findings that complement the well-established literature suggesting that identity and self-expression goals impact consumption choices. We will then focus on the provocative and under-explored question of how our consumption choices may change who we are.

How does who we are impact what we buy?

As illustrated by the Michael Phelps example, "who we are," or the set of identities that we use to define ourselves, has a significant influence on what we buy (e.g. Belk 1988; Escalas and Bettman 2005; Kleine *et al.* 1993; Berger and Heath 2007). A great deal of research suggests that this is possible largely because of the symbols (Levy 1959), personalities (Aaker 1997), communities (Muñiz and O'Guinn 2001), and other traits associated with products (Belk *et al.* 1982) that provide opportunities to assert who we are. In particular, researchers have found that products often allow consumers to reflect, restore and create new aspects of the self.

Reflect

Consumers' desires to reflect the self, or communicate something about who they are today, motivate many choices. Such choices often communicate one's identity as an individual (Aaker

1999), but may also reflect one's identity as a member of a group (e.g. Kleine *et al.* 1993). It is important to note, however, that individuals are complex and often have many different aspects of the self that are important to them (Turner 1985; Markus and Kunda 1986). Researchers have learned that the identity that is most salient at a particular time is the one that is most likely to be reflected in a given choice (e.g. Reed 2004; LeBoeuf *et al.* 2010).

The general notion that the desire to reflect a salient identity strongly impacts consumer behavior has been explored across a variety of domains. For example, researchers have found that individuals make consumption decisions that reflect or involve aspects of their identity such as gender (e.g. Griskevicius *et al.* 2007; Puntoni *et al.* 2011), culture (e.g. Briley and Aaker 2006; Kacen and Lee 2002; Mandel 2003; Wu *et al.* 2011; Winterich and Barone forthcoming), religion (e.g. Shachar *et al.* 2011; Rindfleisch *et al.* 2010), preferred social affiliations (e.g. Berger and Ward 2010; Escalas and Bettman 2005; Muñiz and O'Guinn 2001), and skills (e.g. Burson 2007). In addition, consumers are often motivated by more than just reflecting on a current state of affairs; they may also be on a mission to restore and defend the self.

Restore

A growing body of research has shown that when consumers experience threats to "who they are," they often choose products that allow them to restore their perceived identity or defend themselves against the threat. For example, Gao *et al.* (2009) demonstrate that when people feel doubtful about an important self-view, they use consumption to bolster the self. In one study, individuals primed to feel less confident about their intelligence were more likely to choose a product that reaffirmed their intelligence (a pen) over another well-liked option (candy). Similar compensatory behaviors have been revealed when individuals experience threats to their sense of self-worth (Pettit and Sivanathan 2010; White and Argo 2009), power (Rucker and Galinsky 2008), belongingness (Mead *et al.* 2011), and order (Cutright *et al.* 2011; Cutright forthcoming).

Create

Of course, individuals may have goals beyond reflecting or restoring aspects of their current self in their consumption choices. People may choose products to attain or communicate identities that they wish to have in the future (Wicklund and Gollwitzer 1981). Samper (2011) finds that the further individuals feel from an identity goal, the more likely they are to believe that using an identity-relevant product will improve their performance in that domain.

In sum, it seems clear that "who we are" plays an important role in our consumption decisions. Whether the goal is to reflect, restore, or create an identity, individuals find ample opportunities to communicate their desired identities through their choices. In what follows, we explore the downstream consequences of these choices.

How does what we buy shape who we are?

Only recently has a focus emerged on how the products we buy actually influence different dimensions of "who we are": how we feel about ourselves, how we view the world around us, and how we behave. This approach begins to look at the traits and expectations associated with specific products that we buy (e.g. swim speed for Speedo; creativity for Apple computers; business prowess for a leather briefcase), and investigates how and whether these traits are passed on to consumers. Do products associated with desired traits help transform us into our ideals? Or, do they have unintended consequences for who we may become? We first briefly review prior work that has called for this investigation and then examine how aspects associated with product use (exposure to or consumption of a product) may influence our self-concept and behavior.

Prior insights regarding the importance of the role of product use

Belk (1988) was the first to explicitly describe how objects can extend the self – physically, such as when a tool allows us to do things we would otherwise be incapable of, and symbolically, as when a uniform or trophy allows us to convince ourselves (and perhaps others) that we can be a different person with it than we would have been without it. In this sense, the meaning evoked by the products we buy may influence how we feel about ourselves, and even, as Belk states, "our capabilities for doing and being" (Belk 1988: 145). This dovetails with work by Solomon (1983), who first called for products to be treated as social stimuli that can define our social reality. To date, however, research in this area has been limited. In what follows, we review work that investigates how product use may influence how we feel about ourselves, how we perceive others and, finally, how we behave.

Self-perceptions

The notion that products may be imbued with a certain symbolism and that exposure to such symbolism can shape self-concept and behavior is consistent with research in priming, yet much of the priming literature focuses on the influences of human traits and social constructs (e.g. Bargh *et al.* 1996; Wheeler *et al.* 2007). Recent work, however, demonstrates that nonhuman objects associated with humanlike characteristics (e.g. pets) may affect perceivers' behavior in the same fashion as significant others and members of social groups (Chartrand *et al.* 2008). This research has facilitated the examination of how consumer products associated with specific characteristics shape who we are. We discuss such work next, separating the effects into those of assimilation and contrast.

Assimilation

Examining the role of brands on self-perceptions, Park and Roedder-John (2010) recently investigated whether using a brand with an appealing personality caused the brand's personality to "rub off" on consumers. In other words, do people assimilate their attitudes about themselves to the products to which they are exposed? The authors found that this depends on one's implicit self-theory (Dweck and Leggett 1988). Specifically, entity theorists, or individuals who view their personal qualities as fixed and not improvable through their own direct efforts, do change their self-perceptions following brand use, while incremental theorists, or those who view their personalities as malleable and improvable through their own efforts, do not. Following an hour of carrying around a Victoria's Secret shopping bag (vs. a plain pink bag), only entity theorists felt better looking, more feminine and glamorous. Thus, the symbolism associated with specific products can lead certain individuals to assimilate their self-perceptions to that meaning.

These effects have also been observed in products that are imbued by others with meanings of luck or good fortune. Damisch *et al.* (2010) found that products activated superstitious beliefs such that using a "lucky" golf ball led to increased self-efficacy and performance accuracy in an upcoming putting task.

Most recently, Cutright *et al.* (2011b) investigated how brands influence a person's religiosity. Participants who were exposed to branded (vs. generic) products through choice tasks reported lower levels of religiosity. In other words, individuals who were able to assimilate and identify themselves with brands reduced their need to identify themselves by religion.

Contrast

Other recent research on the influence of counterfeit and identity-relevant products on self-perceptions has demonstrated that contrast may occur when individuals feel "different" from the product they are using. In the context of counterfeit products, which often reflect a desire to be something one is not (e.g. wealthier), Gino *et al.* (2010) found that individuals who were randomly assigned to wear counterfeit (vs. real) sunglasses were more likely to feel inauthentic and self-alienated (Wood *et al.* 2008) relative to non-counterfeit-wearing individuals. In this sense, the use of products that consumers do not believe reflect themselves could lead to contrasts in self-perceptions.

As previously described, Samper (2011) looked at this phenomenon using products that were symbolic of a given identity domain (e.g. designer bags in a fashion domain). She found that individuals who felt more discrepant from their fashion identity goals and who used a high-end designer bag (vs. no product) actually felt less fashionable. Thus, to feel more similar to the aspired identity, it was optimal for these discrepant individuals to avoid using a symbolic product.

How we view others

In addition to changing how we feel about ourselves, products may also affect who we are by influencing how we view others. Kay *et al.* (2004) found that participants exposed to business-related products (e.g. a briefcase on a table instead of a backpack on a table) were more likely to perceive an ambiguous passage as adversarial (vs. friendly). Similarly, Gino *et al.*'s (2010) study of counterfeit goods revealed that wearing a pair of counterfeit (vs. real) sunglasses was more likely to cause participants to interpret others' behavior as dishonest and unethical.

Behavior and performance

Recent studies across multiple domains suggest that, beyond affecting perceptions of ourselves and others, exposure to products and product use may influence who we are by affecting our behavior. We briefly discuss the results below.

Cooperation/giving: Previously described as affecting the construal of a situation, Kay *et al.*'s (2004) work on material priming also found that exposure to business-related products led to more selfish behaviors on Ultimatum and Prisoner's Dilemma games. Importantly, this occurred only when the goals of the game and situation were ambiguous. When the norms of the games were more clearly cued toward sharing, the effects of product exposure on selfishness disappeared.

Creativity and honesty: Other work examining the effects of brands on behavior demonstrates that exposure to brand primes can increase performance in relevant domains. Fitzsimons *et al.* (2008) subliminally presented participants with Apple vs. IBM logos and found that creativity increased for those exposed to Apple logos. On a subsequent task, a similar effect was found in the honesty domain for Disney vs. E!-primed individuals. In this sense, product meanings may evoke reminders of our ideal selves, resulting in assimilation to this ideal.

Cheating: Cheating behaviors can also be impacted by product use. Gino *et al.*'s (2010) paper on the consequences of counterfeit product use demonstrated that individuals using counterfeit products were more likely to cheat. This behavior was mediated by feelings of perceived authenticity (or self-alienation) described above.

Effort on goal-relevant tasks: In the context of perceived identity self-discrepancies, product use has led to ironic effects. In the research previously mentioned, Samper (2011) found that participants who felt more discrepant, or further from their identity goals, and who used higher-end products (e.g. leather padfolio vs. spiral notebook) reduced their performance on subsequent effort tasks versus those who used lower-end products, or no product at all. Individuals who felt more proximate to their goals were not affected by high-end identity product use, presumably because the product meaning was less discrepant from their self-perceptions.

Placebo-related performance: Research on the placebo effect constitutes another area where product-associated meanings can shape our behavior. While this phenomenon has been well documented in the medical literature (see de Craen *et al.* 1999 for a review), it has only recently been examined in marketing contexts. Waber *et al.* (2008) demonstrated that the therapeutic effects of medication – in this case, the extent to which individuals felt pain – were affected by price. When informed about a purported new analgesic (really a placebo pill) costing either $2.50 per pill or having been discounted to $0.10 per pill, more individuals (85.4%) presented with the higher price experienced a pain reduction relative to the discounted price group (61%). In another examination of price, Shiv *et al.* (2005) found that participants performed better on puzzles after consuming an ostensibly regular-priced (vs. discounted) energy drink. This was shown to stem from the activation of expectancies of the product (which appears to be a non-conscious process).

Irmak *et al.* (2005) replicated this result and also presented evidence suggesting that this effect was strongly driven by motivation. Like Shiv and colleagues (Shiv *et al.* 2005), Irmak *et al.* (2005) used energy drinks and found a placebo effect of price on performance, but they also found that this was pronounced for highly motivated individuals, or consumers who strongly desired the arousing effects of the energy drink. This motivation was also shown to influence placebo effects on significant physiological measures (e.g. blood pressure, arousal and alertness).

Also in the placebo domain, Amar *et al.* (2011) designed contexts that were less motivationally driven and found a consistent set of branding effects: 1 branded teas increased performance in a concentration task; 2 branded noise-canceling headphones increased the ability to identify words correctly; and 3 branded sunglasses improved an individual's ability to read a text under glare. Such studies support the notion that product use can change actual performance based on the meanings associated with the product.

Discussion

We have briefly described how consumers' desires to reflect, restore, and create identities have significant implications for their consumption behavior, and we have focused largely on emerging research demonstrating how the products we buy impact who we are. This focus on how products shape who we are underscores the notion that product choice is not the research endpoint, but rather an important beginning that should generate increased examination.

In looking at these more downstream consequences, we have begun to answer the question of whether consumers "get what they pay for." As evidenced by work on branding and self-perceptions, if you are an entity theorist, splurging on a luxurious brand may positively affect your self-perceptions. Along similar lines, the placebo effects research suggests that consumers do in fact get what they pay for, receiving performance benefits with perceived higher price. When incorporating work on counterfeit goods and self-discrepancy, however, using a product that may not reflect the real "you" may actually lead to negative consequences for self-concept and behavior (e.g. greater cheating with counterfeit goods; reduced effort on goal-relevant tasks for discrepant individuals using high-end designer goods). As such, unanticipated consequences can emerge from purchasing the very products that we so desire. Future work could greatly benefit consumer welfare by examining how we can encourage consumers to both desire and consume in their own best interests.

Additional research might also look at greater nuance in product use. For example, how do products received as gifts change our behavior from those willingly purchased and paid for? When do we assimilate versus contrast our self-perceptions toward the products that we choose? Important moderators, such as religion or power/status, may also play a role in how products ultimately shape our self-concept and notion of who we are. For example, one might anticipate that highly devout individuals would receive less of a performance boost from branded or higher-priced products.

Returning to our opening example, is the consumer who purchased that Michael Phelps swim parka likely to change and become a faster swimmer? The answer, of course, is that it depends. A novice swimmer may find that the jacket makes him feel even more inexperienced or slower. An expert swimmer may feel a bit silly expecting to swim faster as he wears his new jacket. However, after a few mornings with the jacket on, he may forget what drove him to purchase the jacket in the first place. Still, outside of his conscious awareness, this consumer will think about Michael Phelps and all those gold medals. This might just give him the added burst of speed he needs to push beyond his personal limits. In other words, the brand he purchases might indeed change who he is.

Further reading

Belk, R.W. (1988) "Possessions and the Extended Self." *Journal of Consumer Research* 15(2): 139–68. (A classic introduction to the power of consumption in reflecting consumers' identities.)

Fitzsimons, G.M., Chartrand, T.L., and Fitzsimons, G.J. (2008) "Automatic Effects of Brand Exposure on Motivated Behavior: How Apple Makes You 'Think Different'." *Journal of Consumer Research* 35(1): 21–35. (An example of how brands impact who we are.)

Gao, L., Wheeler, C.S., and Shiv, B. (2009) "The 'Shaken Self': Product Choices as a Means of Restoring Self-View Confidence." *Journal of Consumer Research* 36(1): 29–38. (An example of how who we are and who we want to be impacts what we buy.)

References

Aaker, J.L. (1997) "Dimensions of Brand Personality." *Journal of Marketing Research* 34(3): 347–56.

——(1999) "The Malleable Self: The Role of Self-Expression in Persuasion." *Journal of Marketing Research* 36(1): 45–57.

Amar, M., Ariely, D., Bar-Hillel, M., Carmon, Z., and Ofir, C. (2011) *Brand Names Act Like Marketing Placebos*. Jerusalem, Israel: Center for Rationality and Interactive Decision Theory, Hebrew University.

Bargh, J.A., Chen, M., and Burrows, L. (1996) "Automaticity of Social Behavior: Direct Effects of Trait Construct and Stereotype Activation on Action." *Journal of Personality and Social Psychology* 71(2): 230–44.

Belk, R.W. (1988) "Possessions and the Extended Self." *Journal of Consumer Research* 15(2): 139–68.

Belk, R.W., Bahn, K.D., and Mayer, R.N. (1982) "Developmental Recognition of Consumption Symbolism." *Journal of Consumer Research* 9(1): 4–17.

Berger, J. and Heath, C. (2007) "Where Consumers Diverge from Others: Identity-Signaling and Product Domains." *Journal of Consumer Research* 34(2): 121–34.

Berger, J. and Ward, M. (2010) "Subtle Signals of Inconspicuous Consumption." *Journal of Consumer Research* 37(4): 555–69.

Briley, D.A. and Aaker, J.L. (2006) "When Does Culture Matter? Effects of Personal Knowledge on the Correction of Culture-Based Judgments." *Journal of Marketing Research* 43(3): 395–408.

Burson, K.A. (2007) "Consumer-Product Skill Matching: The Effects of Difficulty on Relative Self-Assessment and Choice." *Journal of Consumer Research* 34(1): 104–10.

Chartrand, T.L., Fitzsimons, G.M. and Fitzsimons, G.J. (2008) "Automatic Effects of Anthropomorphized Objects on Behavior." *Social Cognition* 26(2): 198–209.

Cutright, K.M. (forthcoming) "The Beauty of Boundaries: When and Why We Seek Structure in Consumption." *Journal of Consumer Research.*

Cutright, K.M., Wu, E.C., Banfield, J.C., Aaron, K.C., and Fitzsimons, G.J. (2011a) "When Your World Must Be Defended: Choosing Products to Justify the System." *Journal of Consumer Research* 38(1): 62–77.

Cutright, K.M., Shachar, R., Erdem, T., and Fitzsimons, G. (2011b) "Finding Brands and Losing Your Religion?" Working paper.

Damisch, L., Stoberock, B., and Mussweiler, T. (2010) "Keep Your Fingers Crossed!" *Psychological Science* 21(7): 1014–20.

de Craen, A.J., Kaptchuk, T.J., Tijssen, J.G., and Kleijnen, J. (1999) "Placebos and Placebo Effects in Medicine: Historical Overview." *Journal of the Royal Society of Medicine* 92(10): 511–15.

Dweck, C.S. and Leggett, E.L. (1988) "A Social-Cognitive Approach to Motivation and Personality." *Psychological Review* 95(2): 256–73.

Escalas, J.E. and Bettman, J.R. (2005) "Self-Construal, Reference Groups, and Brand Meaning." *Journal of Consumer Research* 32(3): 378–89.

Fitzsimons, G.M., Chartrand, T.L., and Fitzsimons, G.J. (2008) "Automatic Effects of Brand Exposure on Motivated Behavior: How Apple Makes You 'Think Different'." *Journal of Consumer Research* 35(1): 21–35.

Gao, L., Wheeler, C.S., and Shiv, B. (2009) "The 'Shaken Self': Product Choices as a Means of Restoring Self-View Confidence." *Journal of Consumer Research* 36(1): 29–38.

Gino, F., Norton, M.I., and Ariely, D. (2010) "The Counterfeit Self." *Psychological Science* 21(5): 712–20.

Griskevicius, V., Tybur, J.M., Sundie, J.M., Cialdini, R.B., Miller, G.F., and Kenrick, D.T. (2007) "Blatant Benevolence and Conspicuous Consumption: When Romantic Motives Elicit Strategic Costly Signals." *Journal of Personality and Social Psychology* 93(1): 85–102.

Irmak, C., Block, L.G., and Fitzsimons, G.J. (2005) "The Placebo Effect in Marketing: Sometimes You Just Have to Want It to Work." *Journal of Marketing Research* 42(4): 406–9.

Kacen, J.J. and Lee, J.A. (2002) "The Influence of Culture on Consumer Impulsive Buying Behavior." *Journal of Consumer Psychology* 12(2): 163–76.

Kay, A.C., Wheeler, C.S., Bargh, J.A., and Ross, L. (2004) "Material Priming: The Influence of Mundane Physical Objects on Situational Construal and Competitive Behavioral Choice." *Organizational Behavior and Human Decision Processes* 95(1): 83–96.

Kleine, R.E., III, Kleine, S.S., and Kernan, J.B. (1993) "Mundane Consumption and the Self: A Social-Identity Perspective." *Journal of Consumer Psychology* 2(3): 209–35.

LeBoeuf, R.A., Shafir, E., and Bayuk, J.B. (2010) "The Conflicting Choices of Alternating Selves." *Organizational Behavior and Human Decision Processes* 111(1): 48–61.

Levy, S.J. (1959) "Symbols for Sale." *Harvard Business Review* 37 (July/August): 117–24.

Mandel, N. (2003) "Shifting Selves and Decision Making: The Effects of Self-Construal Priming on Consumer Risk-Taking." *Journal of Consumer Research* 30(1): 30–40.

Markus, H. and Kunda, Z. (1986) "Stability and Malleability of the Self-Concept." *Journal of Personality and Social Psychology* 51(4): 858–66.

Mead, N.L., Baumeister, R.F., Stillman, T.F., Rawn, C.D., and Vohs, K.D. (2011) "Social Exclusion Causes People to Spend and Consume Strategically in the Service of Affiliation." *Journal of Consumer Research* 37(5) (February): 902–19.

Muñiz, A.M., Jr and O'Guinn, T.C. (2001) "Brand Community." *Journal of Consumer Research* 27(4): 412–32.

Park, J. and Roedder-John, D. (2010) "Got to Get You into My Life: Do Brand Personalities Rub Off on Consumers?" *Journal of Consumer Research* 37(4): 655–69.

Pettit, N. and Sivanathan, N.C. (2010) "Protecting the Self Through Consumption: Status Goods as Affirmational Commodities." *Journal of Experimental Social Psychology* 46(3): 564–70.

Puntoni, S., Sweldens, S., and Tavassoli, N.T. (2011) "Gender Identity Salience and Perceived Vulnerability to Breast Cancer." *Journal of Marketing Research* 48(3): 413–24.

Reed, A. (2004) "Activating the Self-Importance of Consumer Selves: Exploring Identity Salience Effects on Judgments." *Journal of Consumer Research* 31(2): 286–95.

Rindfleisch, A., Wong, N., and Burroughs, J.E. (2010) "God and Mammon: The Influence of Religiosity on Brand Connections." In S. Wuyts, M.G. Dekimpe, E. Gijsbrechts, and R. Pieters (eds), *The Connected Customer: The Changing Nature of Consumer and Business Markets.* Taylor and Francis Group, pp. 163–99.

Rucker, D.D. and Galinsky, A.D. (2008) "Desire to Acquire: Powerlessness and Compensatory Consumption." *Journal of Consumer Research* 35(2): 257–67.

Samper, A. (2011) *Do the Clothes Make the Man? How Gaps Between Current and Ideal Self Shape Product-Related Perceptions and Behavior.* Durham, NC: Duke University.

Shachar, R., Erdem, T., Cutright, K.M., and Fitzsimons, G.J. (2011) "Brands: The Opiate of the Nonreligious Masses?" *Marketing Science* 30(1): 92–110.

Shiv, B., Carmon, Z., and Ariely, D. (2005) "Placebo Effects of Marketing Actions: Consumers May Get What They Pay For." *Journal of Marketing Research* 42(4): 383–93.

Sivanathan, N. and Pettit, N.C. (2010) "Protecting the Self Through Consumption: Status Goods as Affirmational Commodities." *Journal of Experimental Social Psychology* 46(3): 564–70.

Solomon, M.R. (1983) "The Role of Products as Social Stimuli: A Symbolic Interactionism Perspective." *Journal of Consumer Research* 10(3): 319–29.

Stapel, D.A. and Koomen, W. (2001) "I, We, and the Effects of Others on Me: How Self-Construal Level Moderates Social Comparison Effects." *Journal of Personality and Social Psychology* 80(5): 766–81.

Turner, J.C. (1985) "Social Categorization and the Self-concept: A Social Cognitive Theory of Group Behavior." *Advances in Group Processes* 2: 77–121.

Waber, R.L., Shiv, B., Carmon, Z., and Ariely, D. (2008) "Commercial Features of Placebo and Therapeutic Efficacy." *The Journal of the American Medical Association* 299(9): 1016–17.

Walker, R. (2008) "Subconscious Warm Up: Team Speedo USA Parka." *The New York Times Magazine.*

Wheeler, C.S., DeMarree, K.G., and Petty, R.E. (2007) "Understanding the Role of the Self in Prime-to-Behavior Effects: The Active-Self Account." *Personality and Social Psychology Review* 11(3): 234–61.

White, K. and Argo, J.J. (2009) "Social Identity Threat and Consumer Preferences." *Journal of Consumer Psychology* 19(3): 313–25.

Wicklund, R.A. and Gollwitzer, P.M. (1981) "Symbolic Self-Completion, Attempted Influence, and Self-Deprecation." *Basic & Applied Social Psychology* 2(2): 89–114.

Winterich, K.P. and Barone, M.J. (forthcoming) "Warm Glow or Cold, Hard Cash? Social Identity Effects on Consumer Choice for Donation versus Discount Promotions." *Journal of Marketing Research.*

Wood, A.M., Linley, A.P., Maltby, J., Baliousis, M., and Joseph, S. (2008) "The Authentic Personality: A Theoretical and Empirical Conceptualization and the Development of the Authenticity Scale." *Journal of Counseling Psychology* 55(3): 385–99.

Wu, E.C., Cutright, K.M., and Fitzsimons, G.J. (2011) "How Asking 'Who Am I?' Affects What Consumers Buy: The Influence of Self-Discovery on Consumption." *Journal of Marketing Research* 48(2): 296–307.

10
EXPLORING CULTURAL DIFFERENCES IN THE EXTENDED SELF

Phoebe W.S. Wong and Margaret K. Hogg

Introduction

The potential importance of different cultural interpretations of the concepts of self and possessions was recognized by consumer researchers as early as the 1980s (Belk 1984). Culture plays a significant role in shaping individuals' behaviors, values and attitudes and also provides an important context within which to understand the self, and the meaning of possessions (Kitayama and Cohen 2007). However, much of the work that followed from Belk's (1988) seminal paper concentrated on the Western self, and on how Western consumers' identity projects evolved in relation to material objects and possessions. There were a few exceptions. Some researchers moved beyond the rather narrow conceptualizations of the self (e.g. focus on the individual independent and personal self) traditionally adopted for studies undertaken in Western contexts to examine more closely the concept of self and possessions in different cultural contexts. For example, Mehta and Belk (1991) studied how Indians who immigrated to America used social and cultural symbols of possessions to negotiate their sense of self and identity during this period of transition. Wallendorf and Arnould (1988) conducted a cross-cultural inquiry comparing American families and Nigerian families in terms of their favorite objects. They found that American families tended to focus on the personal memories linked to their favorite objects whereas Nigerian families highlighted the social status of their favorite objects. These studies pointed to the advantages of using different cultural contexts not just as a source of richer empirical findings for understanding the relationship between the extended self and possessions, but also for conceptual and theoretical insights into the interrelationships between different aspects of the extended self and possessions (Bih 1992; Piron 2006).

Possessions and the extended self

Consumers often use possessions and consumption goods as symbols to form their identity, to connect with significant others, and to take part in a larger group in a society (Banister and Hogg 2004; Solomon 1988). Possessions, things or objects have been studied for being "important" (Csikszentmihalyi and Rochberg-Halton 1981; Dittmar 1994), "special" (Price *et al.* 2000; Richins 1994; Bih 1992), "cherished" (Curasi *et al.* 2004), "favorite" (Wallendorf and Arnould 1988; Schultz *et al.* 1989; Piron 2006; Mehta and Belk 1991), and "treasured" (Kamptner 1995). Although

Richins's (1994) classification of possession meanings has been widely used in consumer research, Eckhardt and Houston (2001) argued that Richins's classification has its limitations in terms of explaining the findings from their research into the nature of possessions in China. Eckhardt and Houston (2001) used the Chinese cultural context to explore possessions and the extended self, and concluded that Chinese have a broader sense of the nature of possessions, ranging from tangible possessions used mainly to maintain and enhance social ties, to intangible possessions (e.g. love of the family and friendship), to desired objects (e.g. objects they do not have at present but wish to have in the future). Eckhardt and Houston's (2001: 256) findings suggested that Chinese people might have "a broader and more holistic idea of what possession is," and suggested that the definition of possession is quite different from that used in studies of Western possessions (e.g. Richins 1994).

In this chapter, in order to contribute to current debates (Belk 1988; Richins 1994; Dittmar 1989) concerning the relationship between the extended self, possessions and consumption in different cultural contexts, we report the findings from a study of Hong Kong Chinese consumers. We sought to answer the question: how do Hong Kong Chinese consumers construct their sense of self in relation to the meanings of possessions? Chinese values and cultural influences, i.e. Buddhism, Taoism and Confucianism, play important roles in shaping the Chinese sense of self (Aaker and Schmitt 2001) and in gift-giving behavior (Joy 2001), even in a Westernized city like Hong Kong. This study is positioned within the first research program of consumer culture theory (CCT) (Arnould and Thompson 2005), i.e. *consumer identity projects* and aligns with Kleine *et al.*'s (1993; Kleine *et al.* 2005) studies of consumption and the self.

Self-construal and the trichotomization of the self

We begin by showing how the literature on self-construal can be usefully employed to distinguish between the independent (Western-oriented) and interdependent (Eastern-oriented) sense of self, and how combining Markus and Kitayama's (1991) important work on self-construal with work on the trichotomization (i.e. personal, relational and collective dimensions) of the self (Brewer and Gardner 1996) provides a valuable way to distinguish the extended self across cultural contexts.

Studies on the self and possessions in consumer research often draw on the disciplines of cultural psychology and social psychology. First, from cultural psychology, Markus and Kitayama (1991) proposed independent and interdependent self-construals or individual and collective selves (Triandis 1989) to explain people's construction of the self. People with an independent self-construal tend to focus on their autonomy, differentiation from others and inner attributes, whereas people with an interdependent self-construal seem to focus on harmony, connectedness and togetherness in terms of their relationships with significant others or groups. In addition, recent research has proposed that people can hold onto both these different self-construals at the same time (Singelis 1994; Kashima *et al.* 1995; Brewer and Roccas 2001). Second, from social psychology, Brewer and Gardner (1996) developed Markus and Kitayama's concept of self-construals further by suggesting a trichotomization of the self – the personal, relational and collective dimensions of the self. The personal dimension of the self focuses on individualistic characteristics, traits, personal development and achievement. The relational self is defined by the interpersonal dyadic relationship between an individual and significant others via bonds of attachment (e.g. relationships of husband-wife, parent-child, siblings, friends, romantic partners, teacher-student, etc.) (Aron *et al.* 1991; Sedikides and Brewer 2001; Markus and Kitayama 1991). In contrast to the relational dimension of the self, the collective dimension of the self refers to an individual's depersonalized relationships with others who share membership in different groups (e.g. religious groups, political groups, ethnic groups, etc.). Brewer and Gardner (1996) also suggested that these three dimensions of the self coexist within every individual.

Consumer researchers have acknowledged the co-existence of the trichotomization of the self in every individual (Aaker and Lee 2001; Aaker and Schmitt 2001; Escalas and Bettman 2005; Ng and Houston 2006; Jain *et al.* 2007), but they have tended to neglect the potential implications of the coexistence and interrelationship among these three dimensions for the extended self in consumer research. As Higgins and May (2001: 48) argued, "Although most theories of the self allow for the possibility that all three types of self-representation exist within the same person, the question of how they coexist remains."

So far, no studies have explored how consumers construct and reveal the concept of self in the light of the trichotomization of the self and how different configurations of these three dimensions of the self potentially coexist within individual consumers in relation to possessions. The question then becomes: how do these different parts of the self (personal, relational and collective) relate to possessions? We examine this question via our study of Hong Kong Chinese consumers, a cosmopolitan city of China where both traditional Chinese cultural values and Western cultural influences play significant roles in shaping people's sense of self.

Hong Kong Chinese consumers' narratives

This study investigated how people from a Chinese cultural background constructed their sense of self on the personal, relational and collective dimensions through their possession stories. Narratives of life stories and life themes (i.e. life events) are common concepts that are often used in CCT analyses (Mick and Buhl 1992; Schau *et al.* 2009). We elicited 115 stories using Wagner and Wodak's (2006) method of narrative interview. The 20 informants (10 men, 10 women) were aged between 29 and 42, either single, married or divorced (see Table 10.1). It should be

Table 10.1 Demographic information of informants

Number of informants	*Name*	*Gender*	*Age*	*Occupation*	*Marital status*
1	Edward	M	37	Music director	Married
2	Alan	M	35	Lecturer	Married
3	Sam	M	30	Doctor	Single
4	Jake	M	39	Accountant	Married
5	Peter	M	36	Engineer	Married
6	Rico	M	34	News reporter	Single
7	Paul	M	32	Business development manager	Married
8	Mark	M	36	Business development manager	Single
9	Andrew	M	35	Theology student	Married
10	Winston	M	35	Customs officer	Married
11	Fiona	F	36	Product manager	Single
12	Ada	F	29	Law student	Single
13	Danni	F	34	Social worker	Married
14	Ann	F	42	Matured student	Divorced
15	Renay	F	35	Behavioral analyst	Married
16	Iris	F	32	Cinema manager	Single
17	Kate	F	39	Boutique owner	Divorced
18	Lucy	F	33	Music teacher	Married
19	May	F	38	Service officer	Married
20	Shirley	F	34	Flight attendant	Married

noted that it was a middle-class sample with a limited age range which leaves considerable scope for further research in terms of socioeconomic status and age bands.

We applied Brewer and Gardner's (1996) analytical framework of the personal, relational and collective dimensions of the self deductively to our dataset in order to examine and conceptualize how informants make sense of themselves reflecting the trichotomization of the self through their possession stories (Wong 2010: 131–245, 361–452), and uncovered several themes associated with the nature and meanings of important possessions.

These possessions represented different stages in informants' lives in their consumer identity projects. Each story about an important possession was linked to a life event that composed part of the life story of the informant. Stories about possessions helped informants to make sense of who they were in the past, who they are at present and who they possibly will be in the future (Ahuvia 2005). Hong Kong Chinese consumers' views of personal, relational and collective aspects of the self differed markedly in the weightings assigned to the importance of each of these three aspects of the self in contrast to many consumers from Western societies who often prioritize the individual (personal) over the social aspects (relational and collective) of the self. Based on the findings, Chinese consumers seem to view the boundary between their self and the familial relational self as blurred and flexible so that these two selves are blended together and become a "great self" (*da wo*) (Bedford and Hwang 2003). As Yang (1995: 22) noted, "in Chinese society, it is the family, rather than the individual, that is the basic structural and functional unit."

Boundaries between different aspects of the self and possession

First of all, our findings reveal that informants seem to have a broader interpretation of the boundary between the extended self and possessions. Our research shows that most of the informants narrated stories about important possessions that actually belonged to their partners, not themselves (e.g. Alan's gift to his wife) as among their own important possessions, i.e. the *extended possessions* (Wong *et al.* forthcoming) and thus part of their selves. Rudmin (1994) argues that people are ready to extend the concept of ownership beyond its tangible and factual bounds and argues that the traditional definitions of ownership do not capture the essence of the concept. Psychological ownership is recognized by individuals who have feelings of ownership over an object. This means that psychological ownership can occur in the absence of factual or legal ownership where individuals do not actually own an object (see Wilpert 1991; Etzioni 1991; Peck and Shu 2009). Chinese consumers seem to use *extended possessions* for the purpose of maintaining and enhancing their interpersonal relationships, as Eckhardt and Houston (2001: 253) commented: "The meaning of possession in China is almost wholly social in nature."

Self-configurations: personal, relational and collective

Second, we conceptualized different patterns or specific self-configurations of how different aspects of the extended self (personal, relational and collective) are related to consumers' personal stories via their narratives about their possessions in which they disclose different time-linked phases of the self (past, present and future) (Wong 2010: 131–245, 361–452). While a few of the informants focused on the personal aspect of extended self, most of the informants emphasized the relational aspect of the extended self when narrating their stories about important possessions. From the empirical findings we identified five patterns or specific self-configurations of the personal, relational and collective selves (see Figure 10.1: elements 1–5): complete relational self-configuration (element 1.1); relationally led self-configuration (element 1.2); personal-relational equilibrium self-configuration (element 1.3); personally led self-configuration (element 1.4);

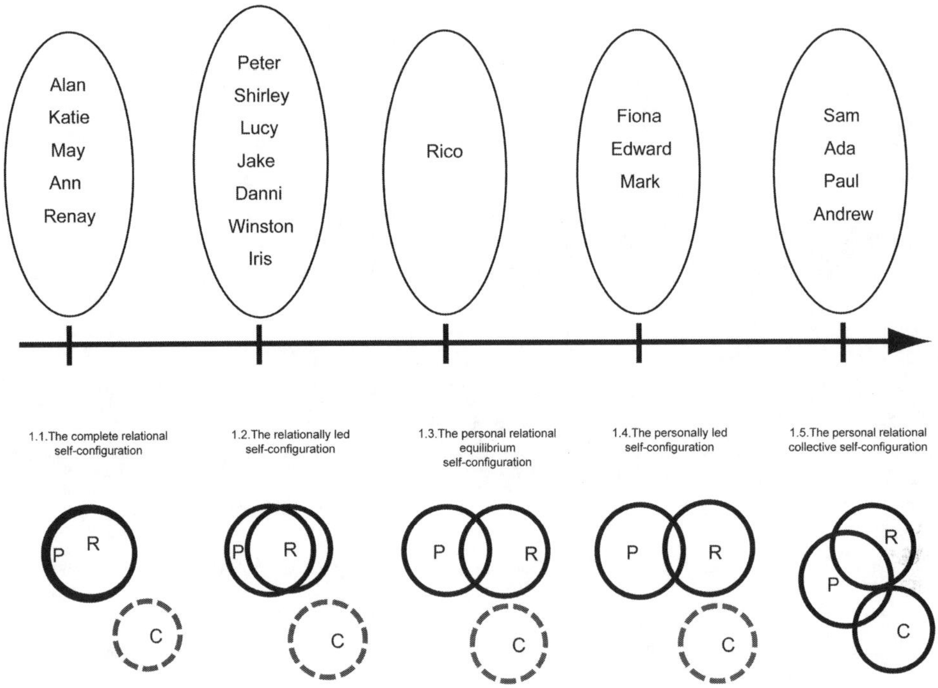

Figure 10.1 Five patterns of specific self-configurations (P = personal self, R = relational self, C = collective self)

personal-relational-collective self-configuration (element 1.5). Detailed descriptions of each pattern are presented in Figure 10.2.

Proposing a generic continuum of self-configurations across cultures

Here we move beyond theory building based solely on the Hong Kong empirical data (Figure 10.1 and Figure 10.2) to propose an extended more generic continuum of self-configurations (Figure 10.3), which we suggest might have applicability across cultures. To illustrate what we are trying to argue here, we might draw an analogy with the periodic table, which in its earliest constructions had gaps which scientists sensed could be filled by matter that remained undiscovered in the universe at that point. We know that people from different cultures place different emphasis on constructions of their self-construals (Markus and Kitayama 1991). "The self is a dynamic cultural creation; individuals' self views, emotions, and motivations take shape and form within a framework provided by cultural values, ideals, structures, and practices" (Cross and Madson 1997: 6). We would conjecture that there could be consumers in different cultural or societal contexts who would potentially represent additional and different patterns of self-configurations that might fit somewhere either side of the five specific patterns of self-configurations characterized from our dataset and represented by Configuration 2 in the extended continuum (Figure 10.3). For example, people from individualistic societies who tend to place more emphasis on the personal dimension of their self might form relatively different patterns of self-configurations. Different patterns of self-configurations possibly exist in other contexts that could be explored in future research. The extended theoretical framework of a

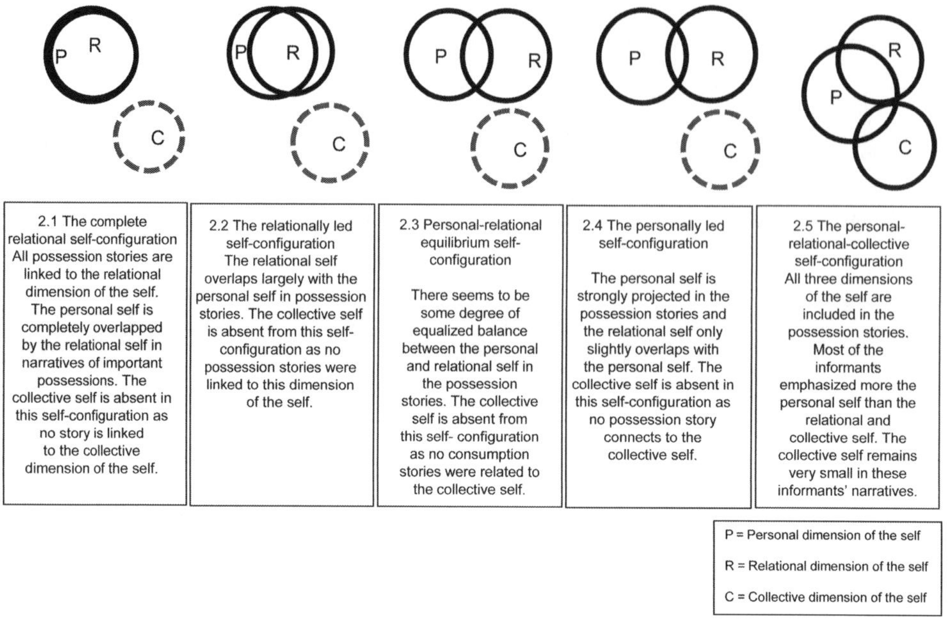

Figure 10.2 Possessions and the extended self (personal, relational and collective) mapped via five specific self-configurations

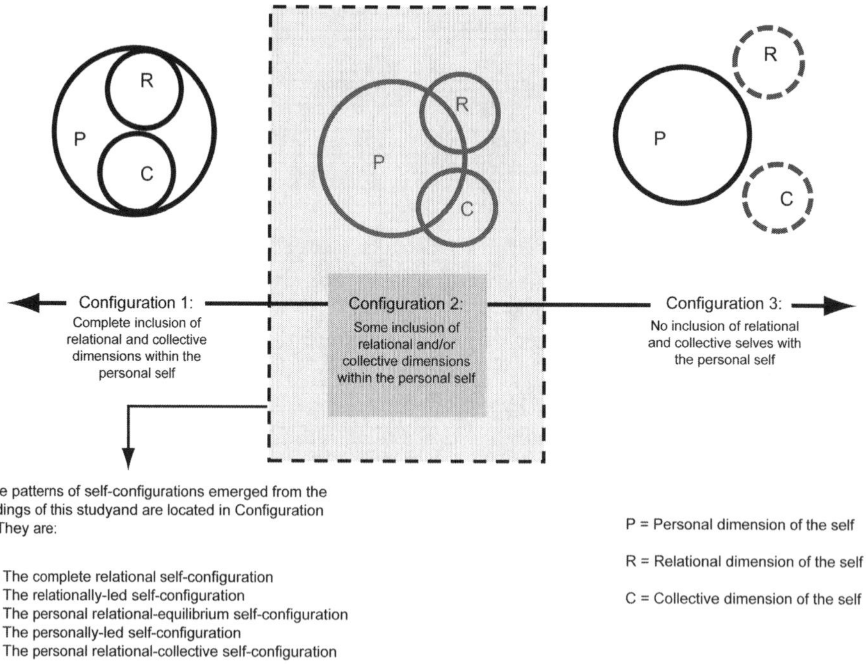

Figure 10.3 Generic continuum of patterns of self-configurations across cultures

generic continuum of self-configurations potentially provides an addition to earlier literature (Markus and Kitayama 1991; Brewer and Gardner 1996; Aaker and Lee 2001; Escalas and Bettman 2005) and allows researchers to examine various configuration patterns of people's personal, relational and collective dimensions of the self in different cultural contexts in future research.

In Figure 10.3 Configuration 1 is located at one end of the continuum representing the complete inclusion of others (the relational dimension of the self) and in-groups (the collective dimension of the self) in the self (hence little evidence of the personal dimension of the self). It is conjectured that people in Configuration 1 would reveal both the relational and collective dimensions of the self in their possession stories and would offer no stories linked to their personal dimension of the self. As a result, their personal self would be completely embraced by the relational and collective dimensions of the self. We would expect stories about possessions from people in Configuration 1 to tend to describe consumption and possessions that reveal and emphasize the relational dimension of their self (e.g. strengthening romantic relationships or affirming familial relationships) and the collective dimension of their self (e.g. in-group recognition, social status) in their *consumer identity projects*.

In contrast, Configuration 3 is situated at the other end of the continuum indicating that there is no inclusion of others (the relational dimension of the self) and in-groups (the collective dimension of the self) in the personal self at all. The relational and collective circles are absent in this configuration as marked by the dotted lines. Drawing on Kleine and Kleine's (2000) material, it would be possible to suggest that people in Configuration 3 might define their sense of the self only through consumption and possessions that are linked to their own individualistic qualities (e.g. achievement, personal growth, or history) in their *consumer identity projects*.

Configuration 2 shows that the self, to a certain extent, includes others (the relational dimension of the self) and/or in-groups (the collective dimension of the self). Different patterns of inclusions in the personal dimension of the self are formed depending on how individuals reveal their sense of self in relation to possessions and consumption in their *consumer identity projects* in Configuration 2. It should be noted that based on the empirical data, five patterns of specific self-configurations were identified in this study as characterizing Configuration 2 (see Figure 10.3).

Conclusion

In future research, it would be interesting to see how far these findings and patterns of self-configuration exist and/or differ cross-culturally. For example, future research may explore how self-configurations work at different stages in relationships (e.g. dating, married, divorced or even remarried), or in different stages of the family life cycle (e.g. married with no children, parents with children, single parents with children or empty-nest family), and how self-configurations form during different life stages (e.g. young people, working adults or retired people). Inter-generational comparison in relation to self-configurations would be another interesting topic for future research. In addition, inter-cultural marriages are commonly found nowadays. It would be worthwhile exploring how people raised in inter-cultural families (e.g. American-Chinese mixed families) construct their self-configurations.

This chapter contributes to current debates concerning the relationship between the self, possessions and consumption, and tries to provide a richer explanation extending previous work on possessions and the extended self (Belk 1988; Richins 1994; Dittmar 1989). Categorizations such as the Western self versus Eastern self, although a useful shorthand way of highlighting potential differences, are labels that themselves subsume a variety of different cultural contexts within which the identity projects in relation to consumption occur and where different aspects of the self emerge and evolve in a series of different interrelationships. In this chapter we used the example of Hong Kong Chinese consumers' narratives to show how the concept of the self, far from being homogeneous, is itself heterogeneous and constructed via a variety of different interrelationships between personal, relational and collective selves. We thus showed the importance of recognizing the nuanced nature of the construction of the relationship between the extended self and possessions within cultures as well as across cultures.

Further reading

Brewer, M.B. and Chen, Y.R. (2007) "Where (Who) are Collectives in Collectivism? Toward Conceptual Clarification of Individualism and Collectivism." *Psychological Review* 114: 133–51. (This paper enhances our understanding of collectivism by suggesting concepts of relational-based collectivism and group-based collectivism.)

Joy, A., Hui, M., Chan, T. S. and Cui, G. (2006) "Metaphors of Self and Self-Gifts in Interdependent Cultures: Narratives from Hong Kong." In R.W. Belk (ed.), *Research in Consumer Behavior*. Boston, MA: JAI Press, pp. 99–126. (This chapter provides insightful interpretations of the meanings of self-gift using a non-Western dataset.)

Mathews, G. (1997) "On the Past, Present, and Future of Hong Kong Identity." *The Bulletin of Concerned Asian Scholars* 29: 3–13. (This paper examines Hong Kong identity from the historical perspective.)

References

Aaker, J.L. and Lee, A.Y. (2001) "'I' Seek Pleasures and 'We' Avoid Pains: The Role of Self-Regulatory Goals in Information Processing and Persuasion." *Journal of Consumer Research* 28: 33–49.

Aaker, J.L. and Schmitt, B. (2001) "Culture-Dependent Assimilation and Differentiation of the Self: Preferences for Consumption Symbols in the United States and China." *Journal of Cross-Cultural Psychology* 32: 561–76.

Ahuvia, A.C. (2005) "Beyond the Extended Self: Loved Objects and Consumers' Identity Narratives." *Journal of Consumer Research* 32: 171–84.

Arnould, E.J. and Thompson, C.J. (2005) "Consumer Culture Theory (CCT): Twenty Years of Research." *Journal of Consumer Research* 31: 868–82.

Aron, A., Aron, E.N., Tudor, M., and Nelson, G. (1991) "Close Relationships as Including Other in the Self." *Journal of Personality and Social Psychology* 60: 241–53.

Banister, E.N. and Hogg, M.K. (2004) "Negative Symbolic Consumption and Consumers' Drive for Self-Esteem." *European Journal of Marketing* 38: 850–68.

Bedford, O. and Hwang, K.K. (2003) "Guilt and Shame in Chinese Culture: A Cross-cultural Framework from the Perspective of Morality and Identity." *Journal for the Theory of Social Behaviour* 33: 127–44.

Belk, R.W. (1984) "Cultural and Historical Differences in Concepts of Self and their Effects on Attitudes Toward Having and Giving." In T.C. Kinnear (ed.), *Advances in Consumer Research*. Provo, UT: Association for Consumer Research, pp. 754–63.

——(1988) "Possessions and the Extended Self." *Journal of Consumer Research* 15: 139–68.

Bih, H.-D. (1992) "The Meaning of Objects in Environmental Transitions: Experiences of Chinese Students in the United States." *Journal of Environmental Psychology* 12: 135–47.

Brewer, M.B. and Gardner, W. (1996) "Who is this 'We'? Levels of Collective Identity and Self Representations." *Journal of Personality and Social Psychology* 71: 83–93.

Brewer, M.B. and Roccas, S. (2001) "Individual Values, Social Identity, and Optimal Distinctiveness." In C. Sedikides and M.B. Brewer (eds), *Individual Self, Relational Self, Collective Self*. Hove: Taylor & Francis.

Cross, S.E. and Madson, L. (1997) "Models of the Self: Self-Construals and Gender." *Psychological Bulletin* 122: 5–37.

Csikszentmihalyi, M. and Rochberg-Halton, E. (1981) *The Meaning of Things: Domestic Symbols and the Self*. Cambridge: Cambridge University Press.

Curasi, C.F., Price, L.L. and Arnould, E.J. (2004) "How Individuals' Cherished Possessions Become Families' Inalienable Wealth." *Journal of Consumer Research* 31: 609–22.

Dittmar, H. (1989) "Gender Identity-related Meanings of Personal Possessions." *British Journal of Social Psychology* 28: 159–71.

——(1994) "Material Possessions as Stereotypes: Material Images of Different Socio-economic Groups." *Journal of Economic Psychology* 15: 561–85.

Eckhardt, G.M. and Houston, M.J. (2001) "To Own Your Grandfather's Spirit: The Nature of Possessions and Their Meaning in China." In P.M. Tidwell and T.E. Muller (eds), *Asia Pacific Advances in Consumer Research*. Provo, UT: Association for Consumer Research, pp. 251–57.

Escalas, J.E. and Bettman, J.R. (2005) "Self-Construal, Reference Groups, and Brand Meaning." *Journal of Consumer Research* 32: 378–89.

Etzioni, A. (1991) "The Socio-Economics of Property." *Journal of Social Behavior and Personality* 6: 465–68.

Higgins, E.T. and May, D. (2001) "Individual Self-Regulatory Functions: It's Not 'We' Regulation, but It's Still Social." In C. Sedikides and M.B. Brewer (eds), *Individual Self, Relational Self, Collective Self.* Philadelphia, PA: Psychology Press.

Jain, S.P., Desai, K.K. and Mao, H. (2007) "The Influence of Chronic and Situational Self-Construal on Categorization." *Journal of Consumer Research* 34: 66–76.

Joy, A. (2001) "Gift Giving in Hong Kong and the Continuum of Social Ties." *Journal of Consumer Research* 28: 239–56.

Kamptner, N.L. (1995) "Treasured Possessions and Their Meanings in Adolescent Males and Females." *Adolescence* 30: 301–18.

Kashima, Y., Yamaguchi, S., Kim, U., Choi, S.-C., Gelfand, M.J. and Yuki, M. (1995) "Culture, Gender, and Self: A Perspective from Individualism-Collectivism Research." *Journal of Personality and Social Psychology* 69: 925–37.

Kitayama, S. and Cohen, D. (2007) "Preface." In S. Kitayama and D. Cohen (eds), *Handbook of Cultural Psychology*. New York: Guildford.

Kleine, R.E. and Kleine, S.S. (2000) "Consumption and Self-Schema Changes Throughout the Identity Project Life Cycle." In S.J. Hoch and R.J. Meyer (eds), *Advances in Consumer Research*. Provo, UT: Association for Consumer Research, pp. 279–85.

Kleine, R.E., Kleine, S.S., and Kernan, J.B. (1993) "Mundane Consumption and the Self: A Social Identity Perspective." *Journal of Consumer Psychology* 2: 209–35.

Kleine, S.S., Kleine, R.E., III, and Laverie, D.A. (2005) "Exploring How Role-Identity Development Stage Moderates Person-Possession Relations." *Research in Consumer Behavior* 10: 66–78.

Markus, H.R. and Kitayama, S. (1991) "Culture and the Self: Implications for Cognition, Emotion, and Motivation." *Psychological Review* 98: 224–53.

Mehta, R. and Belk, R.W. (1991) "Artifacts, Identity, and Transition: Favourite Possessions of Indians and Indian Immigrants to the US." *Journal of Consumer Research* 17: 398–411.

Mick, D.G. and Buhl, C. (1992) "A Meaning Based Model of Advertising Experiences." *Journal of Consumer Research* 19: 317–38.

Ng, S. and Houston, M.J. (2006) "Exemplars or Beliefs? The Impact of Self-View on the Nature and Relative Influence of Brand Associations." *Journal of Consumer Research* 32: 519–29.

Peck, J. and Shu, S.B. (2009) "The Effect of Mere Touch on Perceived Ownership." *Journal of Consumer Research* 36(3): 434–47.

Piron, F. (2006) "China's Changing Culture: Rural and Urban Consumers' Favorite Things." *Journal of Consumer Marketing* 23: 327–34.

Price, L.L., Arnould, E.J. and Curasi, C.F. (2000) "Older Consumers' Disposition of Special Possessions." *Journal of Consumer Research* 27: 179–201.

Richins, M.L. (1994) "Special Possessions and the Expression of Material Values." *Journal of Consumer Research* 21: 522–33.

Rudmin, F.W. (1994) "Gender Differences in the Semantics of Ownership: a Quantitative Phenomenological Survey Study." *Journal of Economic Psychology* 15: 487–510.

Schau, H.J., Gilly, M.C. and Wolfinbarger, M.F. (2009) "Consumer Identity Renaissance: The Resurgence of Identity-inspired Consumption in Retirement." *Journal of Consumer Research* 38: 255–76.

Schultz, S.E., Kleine, R.E., and Kernan, J.B. (1989) "'These are a Few of my Favorite Things': Toward an Explication of Attachment as a Consumer Behavior Construct." *Advances in Consumer Research* 16: 359–66.

Sedikides, C. and Brewer, M.B. (2001) "Individual Self, Relational Self, and Collective Self: Partners, Opponents, or Strangers?" In C. Sedikides and M.B. Brewer (eds), *Individual Self, Relational Self, Collective Self.* Sussex: Taylor & Francis.

Singelis, T.M. (1994) "The Measurement of Independent and Interdependent Self-Construals." *Personality and Social Psychology Bulletin* 20: 580–91.

Solomon, M.R. (1988) "Mapping Product Constellations: A Social Categorization Approach to Symbolic Consumption." *Psychology & Marketing* 5: 233–58.

Triandis, H.C. (1989) "The Self and Social Behavior in Differing Cultural Contexts." *Psychological Review* 96: 506–20.

Wagner, I. and Wodak, R. (2006) "Performing Success: Identifying Strategies of Self-presentation in Women's Biographical Narratives." *Discourse and Society* 17: 385–411.

Wallendorf, M. and Arnould, E.J. (1988) "'My Favorite Things': A Cross-Cultural Inquiry into Object Attachment, Possessiveness, and Social Linkage." *Journal of Consumer Research* 14: 531–47.

Wilpert, B. (1991) "Property, Ownership, and Participation: On the Growing Contradictions Between Legal and Psychological Concepts." In R. Russell and V. Rus (eds), *International Handbook of Participation in Organizations: For the Study of Organizational Democracy, Co-operation, and Self-management*. New York: Oxford University Press.

Wong, P. (2010) *Exploring and Conceptualising the Interrelationships Between Self and Possessions Through Hong Kong Chinese Consumers' Narratives*. PhD, Lancaster University.

Wong, P., Hogg, M.K. and Vanharanta, M. (forthcoming) "Consumption Narratives of Extended Possessions and the Extended Self." *Journal of Marketing Management*.

Yang, K.S. (1995) "Chinese Social Orientation: An Integrative Analysis." In T.Y. Lin, W.S. Tseng and E.K. Yeh (eds), *Chinese Societies and Mental Health*. Hong Kong: Oxford University Press.

I.IV

Stigma, sacrifice, and self

11
STIGMA, IDENTITY, AND CONSUMPTION

Özlem Sandıkcı and Güliz Ger

Despite all the 21st-century rhetoric of diversity, most people expect and desire some normalcy – however that is defined by their milieu. If a person is to deviate from what is considered to be "normal" at a particular point in time and place, s/he is likely to face some consequences. Then, if consumption is fundamentally linked to identity, how identities are received and assessed by others will have wide-reaching implications for the ways individuals consume. Identity is not simply a personal thing; it is valorized differentially by various collectivities and refracts back to the practices of the individual. An individual will consume in a manner that will serve to shift the experienced socio-cultural valorization, to make it more positive, accepted, appropriate, or normal, at least among a particular collectivity, or consume in a manner to protest the particular valorization, or both. As consumption serves to objectify relationships (Miller 1987), it helps navigate the distance to particular associative and dissociative groups. Thus, if and when a person is stigmatized, and thus treated with prejudice and discrimination, that person's experience of stigmatization has important ramifications for the manner in which she engages with life in general and consumption in particular. Moreover, the self is always a social self: persons cannot be individuated outside of their social relationships with other individuals, collectivities, and societies. Thus, identity is always (social) self-constructed in relationship to the others, including things as well as the others who think that an act, a characteristic, or a manner of consumption is not "normal."

The others' gaze and reactions are not always positive. People can be stigmatized for reasons as diverse as race (Dovidio *et al.* 2001), gender (Brown and Pinel 2003), sexual orientation (Herek 2004), weight (Crocker *et al.* 1993), physical disabilities (Hebl and Kleck 2000), mental disabilities (Corrigan 2000), and socioeconomic status (Twenge and Campbell 2002). Moreover, individuals can experience stigmatization due to their particular consumption patterns. Consider, for example, getting tattoos and piercings, dressing too flashily, putting on too much jewelry, too much make-up, too skimpy clothes, too coquettish attire, or too sissy attire; they can all be stigmatized at different times and places. In some cases the stigmatization fades away – jeans are no longer associated with motorcycle gangs (Davis 1989) or tattoos with intimidating ex-convicts (DeMello 2000); in others it does not.

We view stigmatization as a socially embedded process and stigma a social construction. Stigma emerges as people interact with in- and out-groups and as these groups evaluate differences negatively and stereotypically. As (sub)cultures classify and group people, the us–them distinction emerges. The us–them difference is usually much more than a simple difference: it also entails an inherent evaluation of the in- and the out-groups. Consider, for example, categorizations like gay or straight. Such categorizations are culturally created and rest on oversimplifications, yet they come to positively or negatively differentiate and label individuals. However, the socially constructed nature of stigma also suggests that what is seen as different is not fixed but time- and context-dependent. In- and out-groups interact with each other and with other collectivities and other actors, and over time the stigmatization processes and consequences can change under certain conditions. We discuss how a stigmatized self faces the identity tension of similarity and difference as anyone else, and how this tension shapes her consumption actions and practices. First, though, we review how existing scholarship conceptualizes stigma and stigmatization.

Stigma and stigmatization

In his classic work, *Stigma: Notes on Management of a Spoiled Identity*, Goffman defined stigma as "an attribute that is deeply discrediting" and proposed that stigma reduces the bearer "from a whole and usual person to a tainted, discounted one" (Goffman 1963: 3). Goffman differentiated between three forms of stigma: physical deformations, such as scars; character blemishes, such as mental illnesses and addictions; and tribal traits, such as ethnic or religious associations. He argued that stigmatized individuals are seen by society as possessing "an undesirable difference" which set them apart from "normals" (ibid.). Goffman's conceptualization emphasized stigma as a process of social construction of identity and highlighted that stigma is embedded in a "language of relationships" (ibid.). That is, stigma is not a fixed attribute located in the individual but a socially constructed "gap" between what is seen as accepted and undesirable in a society at a given time.

Since the publication of Goffman's book, the concept of stigma has received significant research attention within the social sciences (for reviews, Dovidio *et al.* 2000; Major and O'Brien 2005). Studies investigated the nature, causes, and consequences of stigma in numerous domains. Stigmatized individuals were reported to suffer from serious consequences, such as poor mental health, poverty, academic underachievement, physical illness, and reduced access to housing, education, and jobs (Crocker *et al.* 1998; Jones *et al.* 1984; Link and Phelan 2001). As stigma often leads to prejudice and discrimination, researchers also focused on understanding how people cope with the negative effects of being stigmatized (Compas *et al.* 2001; Miller and Kaiser 2001). Various strategies were identified. These include concealment (Elliott *et al.* 1982), deviance disavowal (Davis 1961), secrecy, rationalization and manipulation of the physical setting (Clinard and Meier 1985), withdrawal (Sutton and Callahan 1987), and confrontation (Miller and Kaiser 2001).

Crocker *et al.* (1998) argued that the visibility and perceived controllability of the stigmatized condition shape coping strategies. Observable conditions such as physical disabilities can act as primary marks to define individuals and make them more vulnerable to social rejection. Moreover, when people are stigmatized because of characteristics perceived to be controllable, they tend to blame themselves. Yet stigma does not always translate into despair (Shih 2004). While some stigmatized people suffer from various negative effects (Stangor and Crandall 2000), many others successfully utilize coping strategies and do not experience a low self-esteem (Compas *et al.* 2001; Crocker and Major 1989).

In recent years, the dominant socio-cognitive perspective, which treats stigma as a characteristic of an individual, has come under criticism (Link and Phelan 2001; Parker and Aggleton 2003). Scholars drew attention to the institutional forces that shape stigmatization and the social and cultural processes that create stigma in the lived experiences of the stigmatized. For example, in their model Link and Phelan (2001) conceptualize stigmatization as a process involving several interrelated components: distinguishing and labeling differences; associating differences with negative attributes or stereotyping; separating "us" from "them"; and status loss and discrimination. Link and Phelan stress the structural nature of discrimination and argue that stigmatization happens only when differential access to social, economic, and political power allows for the interrelated components to occur. The emphasis on the processual and structural nature of stigma opens the door for exploring the ways power contributes and perpetuates stigma within a social milieu.

Overall, conceptualizations of stigma have gradually progressed from an individualistic focus to an understanding of stigma as a socio-cultural process embedded in power relations. Scholars acknowledge that stigma is not only an interpersonal attribution but also a dynamic and social process related with the construction of difference. Stigmatized people certainly suffer from individual effects, but stigmatization also produces societal consequences – it contributes to the production and maintenance of social hierarchies and the boundaries between "us" and "them."

Stigma in consumer behavior literature

Stigma is present in different domains of consumer life. Consumers who are members of certain age groups, race, social class, sexual orientation, ethnicity or religion can become targets of stigmatization. Some products, such as those that are environmentally unfriendly or sexually provocative, might become associated with stigma. Consumers who engage in consumption activities, such as smoking cigarettes or gambling, may experience negative social evaluation and feel stigmatized. However, despite its prevalence in the marketplace, the concept of stigma has received limited attention within the marketing literature.

Emergent research on the relationship between stigma and consumption has some parallels with the literature reviewed above. Much of the existing work adopts a socio-cognitive approach and seeks to understand how consumers cope with stigmatization. In these studies, the focus is typically on "deviant" subcultures or consumer groups such as heavy metal music followers (Henry and Caldwell 2006), Star Trek fans (Kozinets 2001), Apple Newton brand community members (Muñiz and Schau 2005), gay consumers (Kates 2002), Mexican immigrants (Penaloza 1994), and low literacy consumers (Adkins and Ozanne 2005). For example, Adkins and Ozanne (2005) identify a set of personal, situational, and social coping strategies low literacy consumers use to get their needs met in the marketplace. They find that low literate consumers can engage with stigma actively or passively, and can accept, negotiate or reject stigma. In a similar vein, in his study of Star Trek fans, Kozinets (2001) discusses how these consumers negotiate the tensions between their devotion to the Star Trek community and the social stigma attached to being a "Trekkie." Some fans fear that their identities will be spoiled if they are identified as a Trekkie and choose to conceal their identity in public. More devoted fans proudly embrace their Trekker identities and accept the associated social stigma as a means to attain greater self-acceptance. In line with the extant literature, the focus of these studies has been on stigma management – that is, identification of coping strategies that consumers use in order to deal with prejudice and discrimination.

A few other studies examine stigma in the context of marketplace behaviors, such as coupon redemption (Argo and Main 2008), discount usage (Tepper 1994) or labeling (Ellen and Bone 2008). Instead of subcultural affiliations, the focus of these studies lies in marketing practices that are associated with stigma. For example, research reveals that stigma-related concerns are one driver of the low coupon redemption rates (Ashworth *et al.* 2005) and that many consumers choose not to redeem coupons to avoid stigmatization. Furthermore, Argo and Main (2008) report that even non-coupon-redeeming shoppers may experience stigma by association. That is, coupon redemption by one consumer in a retail setting may result in a non-coupon-redeeming shopper being stigmatized as a cheap person. Ellen and Bone (2008) show that package labeling can stigmatize a product. When a food product is labeled as containing genetically modified ingredients it triggers negative associations, increases perceived risk and renders the product undesirable in the minds of consumers.

Finally, Sandıkcı and Ger (2010) look at stigma in the context of Islamic veiling. Shifting the focus from individual coping strategies to socio-cultural processes of stigmatization, they discuss how certain consumption practices become stigmatized, why consumers voluntarily engage in stigmatized practices, and how stigmatized practices can over time become regarded as normal and even desirable. Adopting a view of stigma as a socio-cultural process embedded in power relations, Sandıkcı and Ger's study draws attention to the complex relationship between stigma and consumer choice and the role of market in stigmatization and destigmatization processes. Thus, it focuses on the implications of engaging in stigmatized consumption practices for consumers' identity projects and the role of consumption in the construction and deconstruction of stigma. Drawing upon Sandıkcı and Ger's work, we next offer a closer look at the relationship between stigma, identity and consumption. Unless another reference is given, all of the following refer to Sandıkcı and Ger (2001, 2005, and 2010).

Choosing a stigmatized identity – the case of Islamic veiling

Miller argues that the "whole system of things, with their internal order, make us the people we are" (Miller 2010: 53). In other words, objects help us "learn how to act appropriately" (ibid.). Then consumption can help us be received and accepted as "normal." Let's consider the case of veiling. From a Western, secular perspective, veiling has been historically seen as a symbol of oppression and backwardness of Muslim people. As Göle (2003) argues, as a bodily sign and practice through which difference and exclusion are carried out, the veil typifies what Goffman discussed as stigma. In secular Turkey, veiling had been a similarly stigmatized practice, mostly associated with the peasant, the poor and the elderly, since the renunciation of the veil in the 1920s. However, in the early 1980s, young, urban, middle-class, educated women, whose mothers were uncovered, began to veil – albeit in a totally new style. Adapting a new form of veiling did not simply indicate a heightened religious sensitivity, but a collective expression of the commitment to Islamism as an emergent global social and political movement (Brenner 1996; Göle 2003). In the middle-class, urban, secular social milieu in Turkey, where dress is an important marker of modern, "normal" lifestyles, the new form of veiling, with its connections to global political Islam, was read as a profound threat to the secular regime, and became even more stigmatized.

Despite the stigmatization, driven by different combinations of religious and socio-political reasons, many women have taken on the new veil. Having voluntarily chosen to adopt a stigma symbol, these women sought to be perceived to be "normal" in various ways. One was to be associated with a new collectivity and dress in a manner deemed appropriate by that small collectivity rather than the society at large. However, being a member of a new community was not enough: they also wanted to receive fewer frowns on the streets. Initially, the women who adopted the new form of veiling covered in a rather uniform manner – loose, long, dull overcoats and large headscarves. This style eventually came to be regarded as "uncomfortable," both materially and psychologically. Not only the bulkiness of clothes made walking, driving, and working physically harder for these women but the clothes' perceived lack of fashionable aesthetic exacerbated the symbolic distance between veiled women and the "normal," uncovered women. Enabled by a growing Islamic fashion market, covered women developed a more "comfortable" style, "soft veiling" – tighter jackets and pants and smaller and more colorful headscarves. Veiled women worked at both shopping and forming an urban, modern, fashionable look in an attempt to prevent being taken to be a "backward," radical Islamist.

While these women clearly differentiate themselves from the uncovered women, they also want to be respected and accepted by the covered women. They mimic the fashions and styles of the uncovered women; they mimic the aesthetics of the uncovered women of the world they see in the media. In their attempt to avoid being perceived as "strange," they want to be similar to the uncovered women in terms of being modern individuals with their own fashion preferences, their own individual choices. Such a woman has to juggle and navigate numerous tensions simultaneously. She attempts to craft a personal style that at once distinguishes her as an individual yet affiliates with the new Muslim community, distinguishes her from the uncovered women and yet begs for acceptance by them too. One informant poignantly commented that "when they [uncovered women] see that the clothes they wear are also worn by a covered woman, they might think 'the covered aren't abnormal people; they dress like us'." So she attempts to construct a personal style that is at once somewhat similar to that of the members of her religious community as well as the urban, modern, secular women.

The newly emergent urban, middle-class veiled women differentiate themselves from each other as well as all of the following: uncovered urban women (associated with the indecency of "open" ways of life); rural women who wear a headscarf out of habit; the Islamic newly rich flaunting their Hermès scarves and Versace clothes; more radical/orthodox Islamists wearing the black chador; and the older generation of covered women. In that pursuit, similarities as well as differences become significant. This attempt at distinction is materialized in the colors, designs, and the brands of clothes and scarves that they choose, the particular ways of tying the headscarf and the accessories used, and the combination of different items of clothing.

Rethinking stigma, identity and consumption

The experiences of Turkish, urban, covered women illustrate that identity is not solely about difference and social distinction; it is also about sameness (Simmel 1904), mimicry (Taussig 1993), and mimesis (Girard 1977). Consider also how all teenagers want the same model and brand of jeans or sports shoes. Yet the consumption literature has typically treated identity as a (re)construction of a difference. The ideology of individualism perhaps made us focus more on differences than anything else. Yet, in addition Girard, Simmel, and Taussig's works, Bourdieu's notions of habitus and social capital also suggest that we need to go beyond difference per se.

Our habitus tells us what feels comfortable. As Wilk (2009: 194) also points out, consumption "is embodied through … the daily habitus which tells us what tastes and feels right. This is why we feel ridiculous wearing the wrong colors and uncomfortable eating a food at the wrong time of day." We consume things as much for other people as for ourselves. In daily practice, consumers seek to fit in with familiar groups and to do what is socially acceptable or considered normal by the collectivities to which they want to belong or with which they want to affiliate. At least as much as they seek difference and individuation. Consumers buy and use things and experiences in order to build and maintain relationships with others (Miller 1987; Belk *et al.* 2003), particularly the desirable others. Involvement and participation in a network of relations serves not only sociability but, potentially, also enhancement of social capital. Hence, identity is woven within the consumer's social relations, networks within which she acts and navigates, and the social capital she accumulates and relies upon, in her daily habitus.

Turkish women's voluntary adoption of a stigma symbol and their socio-culturally, economically and politically embedded and enabled negotiation of what constitutes "normal" at a given social milieu illustrate the equally important role of difference and similarity in identity construction and negotiation. At a fundamental level, veiling can constitute a religious experience. One can argue that if a woman believes that covering is God's command, she accepts discrimination for the believed spiritual reward. However, any choice, be it framed as a religious command or an act of free will, involves making several subsequent choices. Women who adopt veiling do not only choose to cover; they also choose to cover themselves in particular styles. Going well beyond a religious act, veiling is a practice of consumption, and in the context of Turkey, a political one as well, replete with multiple possibilities as well as tensions. In other words, veiling acts as a space where socially embedded personal negotiations of faith and fashion, ethics and aesthetics, the modern and the traditional, the normal and the deviant take place.

In the negotiation of sameness and difference, the "me–others" as well as "us–them" tensions and comparisons are critical for individual and social identity. When we consider the us–them interplay, we notice that the boundaries and impositions of the in- and out-groups can make identity construction difficult and painful, especially when social exclusion mechanisms are strong, as often in the case of stigmatized collectivities. The us-versus-them comparison can be painful, even when it is chosen. Despite having personally chosen a particular life path, the Star Trekkies or the Gothic youth with piercings face discrimination or ridicule. The consequences of stigmatization are heavier for persons who have not voluntarily chosen their race or ethnicity or physical appearance. Then the sameness and difference negotiations will be much more intense, emotional, and significant. The intensity of such negotiations implies that identity (re)construction is not always a happy (postmodernist) pick-and-choose process, but rather a burdensome and contingent work. As the experiences of covered women reveal, adopting, constructing, negotiating their identities as veiled women and achieving sameness – as modern, urban woman – while maintaining difference is a socially embedded process, informed by particular compositions of power relations prevailing in a society at a given time.

In sum, we suggest that approaching identity from the perspective of not only difference but also sameness will enable us to understand how stigmatized consumers negotiate their identity in relation to others through their choices and perform a comfortable "normal" through their practices. Thus, future research that examines consumption contexts associated with stigma and tries to understand how consumers cope with the negative consequences of stigmatization needs to focus on the dynamics of sameness and difference. Furthermore, we also need research that uncovers socio-cultural processes that relate to stigmatization and destigmatization of certain consumption practices. Understanding these helps reveal both the dynamics and ramifications of stigmatization/destigmatization as socio-culturally embedded processes and the role of consumption in maintaining, creating and reconstructing social hierarchies. In doing so, again, the notion of normality and the dynamics of sameness-difference will be useful. Ultimately, unpacking stigma and stigmatization will provide new insights into consumers' search for legitimacy in the marketplace and the role of consumption in realizing it.

Further reading

Reckwitz, A. (2002) "Toward a Theory of Social Practices: A Development in Culturalist Theorizing." *European Journal of Social Theory* 5(2): 243–63.

Steele, C.M., Spencer, S.J., and Aronson, J. (2002) "Contending with Group Image: The Psychology of Stereotype and Social Identity Threat." *Advances in Experimental Social Psychology* 34: 379–440.

Yang, L.H., Kleinman, A., Link, B.G., Phelan, J.C., Lee, S, and Good, B. (2007) "Culture and Stigma: Adding Moral Experience to Stigma Theory." *Social Science and Medicine* 64: 1524–35.

References

Adkins, N.R. and Ozanne, J.L. (2005) "The Low Literate Consumer." *Journal of Consumer Research* 32(1): 93–106.

Argo, J.J. and Main, K.J. (2008) "Stigma by Association in Coupon Redemption: Looking Cheap Because of Others." *Journal of Consumer Research* 35(4): 559–72.

Ashworth, L., Darke, P.R. and Schaller, M. (2005) "No One Wants to Look Cheap: Trade-Offs between Social Disincentives and the Economic and Psychological Incentives to Redeem Coupons." *Journal of Consumer Psychology* 15(4): 295–306.

Belk, R.W., Ger, G., and Askegaard, S. (2003) "The Fire of Desire: A Multisited Inquiry into Consumer Passion." *Journal of Consumer Research* 30 (December): 326–52.

Brenner, S. (1996) "Reconstructing Self and Society: Javanese Muslim Women and 'The Veil'." *American Ethnologist* 23 (November): 673–97.

Brown, R.P. and Pinel, E.C. (2003) "Stigma on my Mind: Individual Differences in the Experience of Stereotype Threat." *Journal of Experimental Social Psychology* 39(6): 626–33.

Clinard, M.B. and Meier, R.E. (1985) *Sociology and Deviant Behavior.* New York: Holt, Rinehart, and Winston.

Compas, B.E., Connor-Smith, J.K., Saltzman, H., Thomsen, A.H., and Wadsworth, M.E. (2001) "Coping with Stress during Childhood and Adolescence: Problems, Progress and Potential in Theory and Research." *Psychological Bulletin* 127: 87–127.

Corrigan, P.W. (2000) "Mental Health Stigma as Social Attribution: Implications for Research Methods and Attitude Change." *Clinical Psychology: Science and Practice* 7: 48–67.

Crocker, J., Cornwell, B. and Major, B. (1993) "The Stigma of Overweight: Affective Consequences of Attributional Ambiguity." *Journal of Personality and Social Psychology* 64(1): 60–70.

Crocker, J. and Major, B. (1989) "Social Stigma and Self-Esteem: The Self-Protective Properties of Stigma." *Psychological Review* 96: 608–30.

Crocker, J., Major, B. and Steele, C. (1998) "Social Stigma." In S. Fiske, D. Gilbert and G. Lindzey (eds), *Handbook of Social Psychology*. Boston, MA: McGraw-Hill, vol. 2, 504–53.

Davis, F. (1961) "Deviance Disavowal: The Management of Strained Interaction by the Visibly Handicapped." *Social Problems* 9: 120–32.

——(1989) "Of Maids' Uniforms and Blue Jeans: The Drama of Status Ambivalences in Clothing and Fashion." *Qualitative Sociology* 12(4): 337–55.

DeMello, M. (2000) *Bodies of Inscription: A Cultural History of the Modern Tattoo Community*. Durham, NC: Duke University Press.

Dovidio, J.F., Gaertner, S.L., Niemann, Y.F., Snider, K.F. (2001) "Racial, Ethnic, and Cultural Differences in Responding to Distinctiveness and Discrimination on Campus: Stigma and Common Group Identity." *Journal of Social Issues* 57(1): 167–88.

Dovidio, J.F., Major, B., and Crocker, J. (2000) "Stigma: Introduction and Overview." In T.F. Heatherton, R.E. Kleck, M.R. Hebl, and J.G. Hull (eds), *The Social Psychology of Stigma*. New York: Guilford Press, 1–29.

Ellen, P.S. and Bone, P.F. (2008) "Stained by the Label? Stigma and the Case of Genetically Modified Foods." *Journal of Public Policy & Marketing* 27(1): 69–82.

Elliott, G.C., Ziegler, H.L., Altman, B.M. and Scott, D.R. (1982) "Understanding Stigma: Dimensions of Deviance and Coping." In Clifton D. Bryant (eds), *Deviant Behavior.* New York: Hemisphere, 423–43.

Girard, R. (1977) *Violence and the Sacred.* Baltimore, MD: Johns Hopkins University Press.

Goffman, E. (1963) *Stigma: Notes on the Management of Spoiled Identity.* New York: Prentice-Hall.

Göle, N. (2003) "The Voluntary Adoption of Islamic Stigma Symbols." *Social Research* 70 (Fall): 809–27.

Hebl, M.R. and Kleck, R.E. (2000) "The Social Consequences of Physical Disability." In R.E. Kleck, T.F. Heatherton, M.R. Hebl, and J. Hull (eds), *Stigma: Social Psychological Perspectives.* New York: Guilford.

Henry, P.C. and Caldwell, M.L. (2006) "Self-Empowerment and Consumption: Consumer Remedies for Prolonged Stigmatization." *European Journal of Marketing* 40(9/10): 1031–48.

Herek, G.M. (2004) "Beyond 'Homophobia': Thinking about Sexual Prejudice and Stigma in the Twenty-First Century." *Sexuality Research and Social Policy* 1(2): 6–24.

Jones, E.A., Farina, A., Hastorf, A., Markus, H., Miller, D.T., and Scott, R. (1984) *Social Stigma: The Psychology of Marked Relationships.* New York: Freeman.

Kates, S.M. (2002) "The Protean Quality of Subcultural Consumption: An Ethnographic Account of Gay Consumers." *Journal of Consumer Research* 29 (December): 383–99.

Kozinets, R.V. (2001) "Utopian Enterprise: Articulating the Meaning of *Star Trek*'s Culture of Consumption." *Journal of Consumer Research* 28 (June): 67–89.

Link, B.G. and Phelan, J.C. (2001) "Conceptualizing Stigma." *Annual Review of Sociology* 27: 363–85.
Major, B. and O'Brien, L.T. (2005) "The Social Psychology of Stigma." *Annual Review of Psychology* 56: 393–421.
Miller, D. (1987) *Material Culture and Mass Consumption*. Oxford: Blackwell.
——(2010) *Stuff*. Cambridge: Polity.
Miller, C.T. and Kaiser, C.R. (2001) "A Theoretical Perspective on Coping with Stigma." *Journal of Social Issues* 57(1): 73–92.
Muñiz, A. and Schau, H. (2005) "Religiosity in the Abandoned Apple Newton Brand Community." *Journal of Consumer Research* 31 (March): 737–47.
Parker, R. and Aggleton, P. (2003) "HIV and AIDS-related Stigma and Discrimination: A Conceptual Framework and Implications for Action." *Social Science & Medicine* 57: 13–24.
Penaloza, L. (1994) "*Atravesando Fronteras*/Border Crossings: A Critical Ethnographic Exploration of the Consumer Acculturation of Mexican Immigrants." *Journal of Consumer Research* 21(1): 32–45.
Sandıkcı, O. and Ger, G. (2001) "Fundamental Fashions: The Cultural Politics of the Turban and the Levi's." In J. Meyers-Levy and M. Gilly (eds), *Advances in Consumer Research*. Provo, UT: Association for Consumer Research, vol. 28, pp.146–50.
——(2005) "Aesthetics, Ethics and the Politics of the Turkish Headscarf." In S. Kuechler and D. Miller (eds), *Clothing as Material Culture*. Oxford: Berg, pp. 61–82.
——(2010) "Veiling in Style: How Does a Stigmatized Practice Become Fashionable?" *Journal of Consumer Research* 37 (June): 15–36.
Shih, M. (2004) "Positive Stigma: Examining Resilience and Empowerment in Overcoming Stigma." *Annals of the American Academy of Political and Social Sciences* 591: 175–84.
Simmel, G. (1904) "Fashion." *International Quarterly* 10 (October): 130–55.
Stangor, C. and Crandall, C.S. (2000) "Threat and Social Construction of Stigma." In T.F. Heatherton, R.E. Kleck, M.R. Hebl, and J.G. Hull (eds), *The Social Psychology of Stigma*. New York: The Guilford Press, pp. 62–87.
Sutton, R.I. and Callahan, A.L. (1987) "The Stigma of Bankruptcy: Spoiled Organizational Image and its Management." *Academy of Management Journal* 30(3): 405–36.
Taussig, M. (1993) *Mimesis and Alterity: A Particular History of the Senses*. New York: Routledge.
Tepper, K. (1994) "The Role of Labeling Processes in Elderly Consumers' Responses to Age Segmentation Cues." *Journal of Consumer Research* 20 (March): 503–19.
Twenge, J.M. and Campbell, W.K. (2002) "Self-Esteem and Socioeconomic Status: A Meta-Analytic Review." *Personality and Social Psychology Review* 6(1): 59–71.
Wilk, R. (2009) "Difference on the Menu: Neophilia, Neophobia and Globalization." In D. Inglis and D. Gimlin (eds), *The Globalization of Food*. Oxford: Berg, pp. 185–95.

12

(RE)ENACTING MOTHERHOOD

Self-sacrifice and abnegation in the kitchen

Benedetta Cappellini and Elizabeth Parsons

Introduction

My mother never liked fried anchovies. She found them disgusting to clean, smelly to keep in the fridge and too salty to eat. Nevertheless she has cooked them once a week, every Wednesday, for the past 20 years. It was my father's and my favorite dish. She stopped cooking it when my father passed away, but when I go back home she makes sure she cooks it at least a couple of times. She still pulls the same disgusting face in serving this dish and she can't help commenting that it is a meal more appropriate for our dog. A couple of weeks ago I asked her why she punishes herself in serving a dish she detests. She replied: "Once you have a child you will find out."

The first author's mother, a 70-year-old Italian woman from a small Tuscan town, has a sense of care toward her family which is not very different from that of her female neighbors, friends and relatives and from the participants of our study, a group of young, middle-class and well-educated British women living in the Midlands, UK. Indeed, they all demonstrate the same devotion and self-sacrifice toward their family, and their children in particular. In this chapter we seek to understand our participants' self-sacrifice through looking at the practices of planning, cooking and serving an ordinary meal to the family.

Looking at sacred elements in everyday consumption practices, such as sacrifice, is not a new research direction in consumer research. There is a long history of studies looking at consumption as "a vehicle of transcendent experience," and at consumer behavior as a display of "certain aspects of the sacred" (Belk *et al.* 1989: 2). Following Belk *et al.*'s (1989) seminal work defining the elements of sacred consumption experiences, empirical works have shown how such elements can be found in extraordinary practices including sharing Thanksgiving meals with the family (Wallendorf and Arnould 1991), but also ordinary practices such as enacting self-sacrifice in shopping in supermarkets (Miller 1998). We took inspiration from the latter set of studies here and we look at the mother's self-sacrifice in cooking and serving an everyday meal to the family. We do so by presenting an interdisciplinary discussion on sacrifice and motherhood borrowing insights from consumer research, anthropology and sociology. We then use the story of mealtimes in Tracey's household (one of our study participants) to explore what she gives up and to whom, as well as what she receives in return. Our study departs from previous work on sacrifice within the family in two key senses: first we explore the whole range of practices surrounding mealtimes including planning, cooking and serving the meal; and second we explore the reciprocal practices of other family members in recognition of this motherly sacrifice. In doing so we explore how the perpetuation of a family identity is a shared endeavor amongst family members as opposed to the preserve of mothers. In closing we return to the question of what Tracey receives in return for her sacrifice, observing that on one level she gains a level of satisfaction that comes from self-sacrifice for others but through this sacrifice she is also performing identity work that shores up her sense of self as a devotional mother. For future research we suggest that the practices of familial sharing (Belk 2010) during mealtime practices require fuller attention in order to understand how family identity is collectively performed, maintained and contested in everyday family life.

Sacrifice in everyday life

Consumer research studies have shown how sacrifice is widely present in "various areas of human activity … when something of value is surrendered in the expectation or hope of greater gain" (Bourdillon 1980: 11). Borrowing theoretical underpinnings from anthropology and sociology, consumer studies have highlighted different, and often contradictory, aspects of sacrifice, such as its sacred dimensions (Belk *et al.* 1989), self-abnegation and gift giving (Cappellini 2009; Cappellini and Parsons forthcoming 2012, 2013; Miller 1998), and getting rid of surplus and purification (Cherrier 2009).

In studies of motherhood self-abnegation seems to dominate debates. Indeed, studies that directly or indirectly refer to sacrifice, conceptualize "being a mum" as a process of self-abnegation characterized by giving up her own desires for the benefits of the family, which is her object of devotion (Miller 1998; de Vault 1991). These accounts of motherhood seem to come from a specific notion of sacrifice, which the anthropologist Bourdillon calls "calculated sacrifice":

> When a person gives up the economic rewards of a promising career for the benefit of his family or of a political cause, his vision of what makes life meaningful and worthwhile is dramatized and communicated. Such a sacrifice may be central to a person's beliefs and values, and it certainly expresses them. Although it does not necessarily involve the prescribed use of conventional symbols, … a significant material sacrifice for a cause highlights a theme that ritual sacrifice can express, namely, the subordination of lesser goods to an overriding ideal. The idea that sacrifice involves giving up some material good for the sake of an ideal has a parallel usage (possibly its origin) in Christian religious contexts, when voluntary ascetical practices (like giving up sweets for Lent) are referred to as sacrifices.
>
> *(Bourdillon 1980: 12)*

This notion of sacrifice as giving up something precious and donating it to a deity in the hope of communicating with such a deity, is central to Hubert and Mauss's (1964) work which has been widely used in consumer research. As Milbank (1995) and Marcel (2003) underline, the key elements of Hubert and Mauss's sacrifice are self-abnegation, the communication between the profane (humanity) and sacred (gods), and the legitimation of wider social forces.

Sacrifice follows the logic *do ut des*, and therefore self-abnegation is connected to self-interest. As Hubert and Mauss observe, "fundamentally there is perhaps no sacrifice that has not some contractual element. The two parties present exchange their services and each gets his due" (Hubert and Mauss 1964: 100). In fact, individuals donate to God their best resources, and thus "slaves are put to death, precious oil burnt, copper objects cast into the sea, and even the houses of princes set on fire" (Mauss 1990, cited in Marcel 2003: 143). In return for these offerings the deity is asked to provide a defined benefit (for instance health or a safe journey). In such exchange the sacred and profane communicate with each other through the donation of a victim (objects or persons) which during the sacrifice is consecrated, passing "from the common into the religious domain" (Hubert and Mauss 1964: 9). The humans' self-abnegation – the renunciation of precious objects to be donated to God – expresses moral values and sustains social forces. Hubert and Mauss highlight that "the act of abnegation implicit in every sacrifice, by recalling frequently to the consciousness of the individual the presence of collective forces, in fact sustains their ideal existence" (Hubert and Mauss 1964: 102). Thus through the sacrifice humanity constantly re-creates their deities and communicates with them. As they point out, "if nothing were set aside from the harvest, the god of the corn would die; in order that Dionysus may be reborn, Dionysius' goat must be sacrificed at the grape-harvest" (Hubert and Mauss 1964: 100).

The everyday sacrifice of being a mum

Interpretive consumer studies looking at everyday food consumption practices and family relations emphasize how food consumption in the household is not driven by self-satisfaction, but rather by love for family members (Miller 1998; Thompson 1996). Love is not understood as "an element of romanticism," but rather as a "simply devotional duty" (Miller 1998: 117) which takes the form of wives' and mothers' anxiety to satisfy their loved ones' desires through various consumption practices.

Indeed, these studies show how women make visible their love through shopping (Miller 1998), cooking (Bugge and Almås 2006; Carrigan and Szmigin 2006), and all the other practices surrounding the work of feeding the family (de Vault 1991). Despite their juggling lifestyles (Thompson 1996), mothers perceive the family meal as an important occasion for reinforcing family identity and their position in the family (Bugge and Almås 2006; Carrigan and Szmigin 2006). Conversely, Bugge and Almås (2006) highlight how opting for convenience foods is a source of guilt in women because it (re)defines their role within the family in a negative sense. Others (Carrigan and Szmigin 2006) highlight how adopting convenience foods is perceived by some mothers as a solution accommodating juggling lifestyles and family care, as well as resolving problems of a lack of culinary skills and conflicts around other family members' food choice.

In her work on family food consumption, de Vault (1991) shows how the restless work of feeding the family is perceived by her female participants as an essential and "natural" abnegation embedded in their gendered roles of being good mothers and wives. Ruskola (2005) explains this abnegation in terms of gift exchange. Like other gift exchanges based on reciprocity and equivalence, family resources are allocated through a *do ut des* system, which perpetuates kinship and love between members. In simpler terms, women's housework and caring are gifts reciprocated by their husbands' salary (Ruskola 2005). Miller (1998) highlights that the gift giving between women and their husbands and children is an unbalanced and non-reciprocal exchange, wherein wives and mothers donate more than they receive in return. He explains such an unbalanced relation through the process of sacrifice. Taking inspiration from the work of Hubert and Mauss (1964), Miller (1998) highlights that the modern form of this sacrifice is practiced by women (as mothers and wives) who, through their everyday thrifty shopping, save extra value to be invested in extraordinary consumption occasions wherein women's objects of devotion (their children) are celebrated.

Taking inspiration from Miller's work, we try to extend his notion of sacrifice to other consumption practices, such as serving the everyday meal. In doing so we try to show how the mother's sacrifice is not simply directed towards saving money during everyday shopping in order to spend what has been saved on special occasions. We explore how the mother's sacrifice extends beyond the supermarket into the kitchen. These sacrifices include the many taken-for-granted practices of self-abnegating her own desires and prioritizing others' preferences and requests.

Getting into Tracey's kitchen

This study of motherly sacrifice is taken from a wider study looking at discourses and practices surrounding the everyday meal. Fieldwork consisted of observations of meal times of 20 households and semi-structured interviews of the person in the family responsible for the food provision. Interviews covered themes such as the organization of everyday meals, practices surrounding the process of having a meal, the division of work in the household, but also the ideas, emotions and life goals associated with domestic food consumption. Participants were recruited through convenience sampling accompanied by a snowball sampling technique (Silverman 2006). Both authors iterated the data analysis and as such a "triangulation across co-authors led to new insights and resolved differences in interpretation" (Askegaard *et al.* 2005: 163). Interpretation of the data involved continual movement between data and theoretical frameworks until an agreed interpretation was reached (Silverman 2006). We also passed this chapter to Tracey herself for her feedback and for respondent validation of our interpretations. Tracey was happy with our analysis and in fact mentioned to us that it revealed to her elements of her everyday practices that she hadn't really reflected on before.

In this section we present the story of Tracey's household mealtimes. We chose her amongst our participants because we think that her story best illustrates everyday motherly sacrifice. While all participants were different, Tracey's practices and experiences are reflective of our wider sample and nearly all participants displayed at least some experiences in common with her. Therefore, rather than present fragments of different lives we present a single story that allows us to explore in more depth the everyday dynamics of sacrifice. In presenting Tracey's story and her process of sacrifice we organize our interpretation following some of the central questions of sacrifice (Beattie 1980) – i.e. Who is giving up something? What is given up? To whom? What does s/he receive in return? We think that these questions can help us to understand the story of Tracey and how her sacrifice is displayed every evening at dinner time. Tracey's story is constructed from two in-depth interviews with the first author and her participant observation of dinner time at Tracey's house with Tracey, two of her sons and her husband.

Who is giving up something?

Tracey is in her forties, she is married to Paul and they have three teenage sons together. Having worked in industry for 15 years she decided to undertake an MA in history. She describes this career change as a "family revolution," since she now takes care of the housework and her husband has returned to full-time work after having been a stay-at-home dad for 10 years. However, even when Tracey worked full time, she carried the responsibility of planning the meals for the family. As she observes, her husband used to "execute" her meal plan, which she recorded in a diary on a weekly basis. The diary is still in use and she fills it in every Thursday morning before going to the local supermarket. Tracey talks about her weekly shopping in a manner similar to the devotional mothers whom Miller (1998) met in London more than 10 years ago. She never forgets treats for her children, such as their favorite crisps for their lunchboxes and a few bottles of red wine to share with her husband. However, Tracey's devotion does not start and finish in the supermarket, but is "dramatized and communicated" (Bourdillon

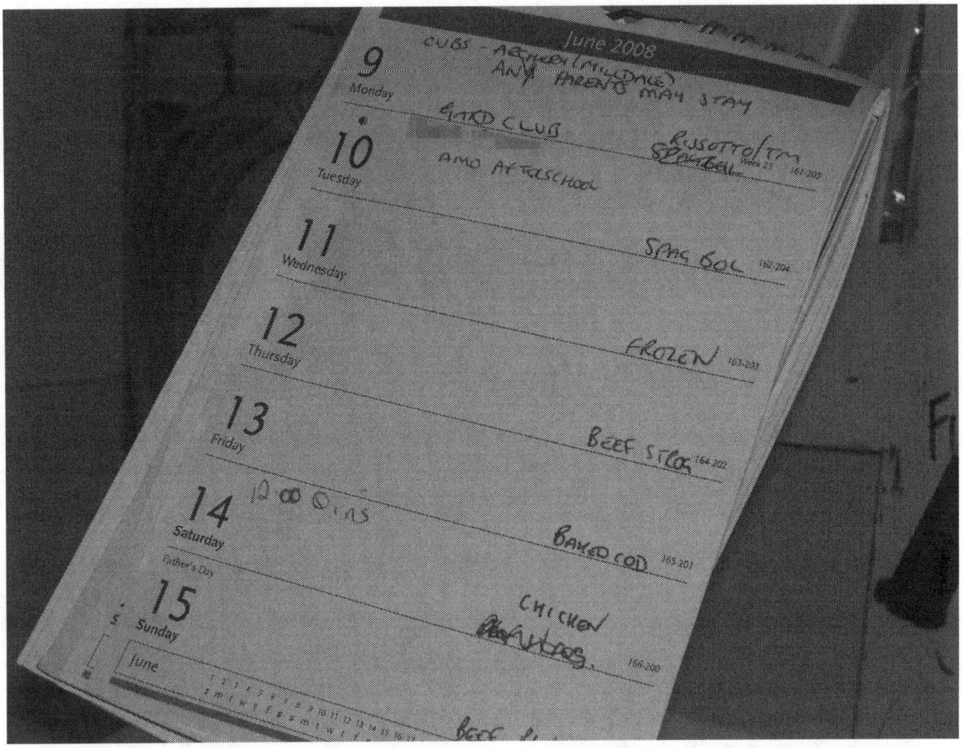

Figure 12.1 Tracey's diary

1980: 12) in a whole range of practices surrounding the work of feeding her family. As de Vault (1991) points out, feeding the family is not simply cooking; rather it consists of all the practices that make cooking possible and also the dedication needed to provide "good" food for the family. Providing good food implies considering every member of the family's needs and desires in everyday food consumption practices.

Tracey defines herself as a "strict mum," but the interviews and the observation did not always confirm this. Rather while she was strict in her planning of meals she demonstrated flexibility in the pains she took to consider the needs of her family and did not try and force them to eat things they were not keen on. In planning dinners she avoids any "clashes" with her children's school meals. She plans dinners on a weekly basis and records them in a diary next to the fridge on which she posts her children's school canteen menus (Figure 12.1 and Figure 12.2). Her planning depends upon her children's school menu, their sporting activities and their changing requests. As she says:

> I look at what the children have at school and then I plan the meals for the week … so I make sure that the meal is not clashing with the school meal and I have to check because on Monday they have some sport so … I try to cook meals that I don't think are too heavy.
>
> The kids may have sausages in rolls for breakfast … they usually want something for three or four weeks and then they change their mind and they want something else. They went through a phase of breakfast cereals but they don't like them anymore … then they wanted toast … yogurt has been the last one … now it is sausages in rolls.

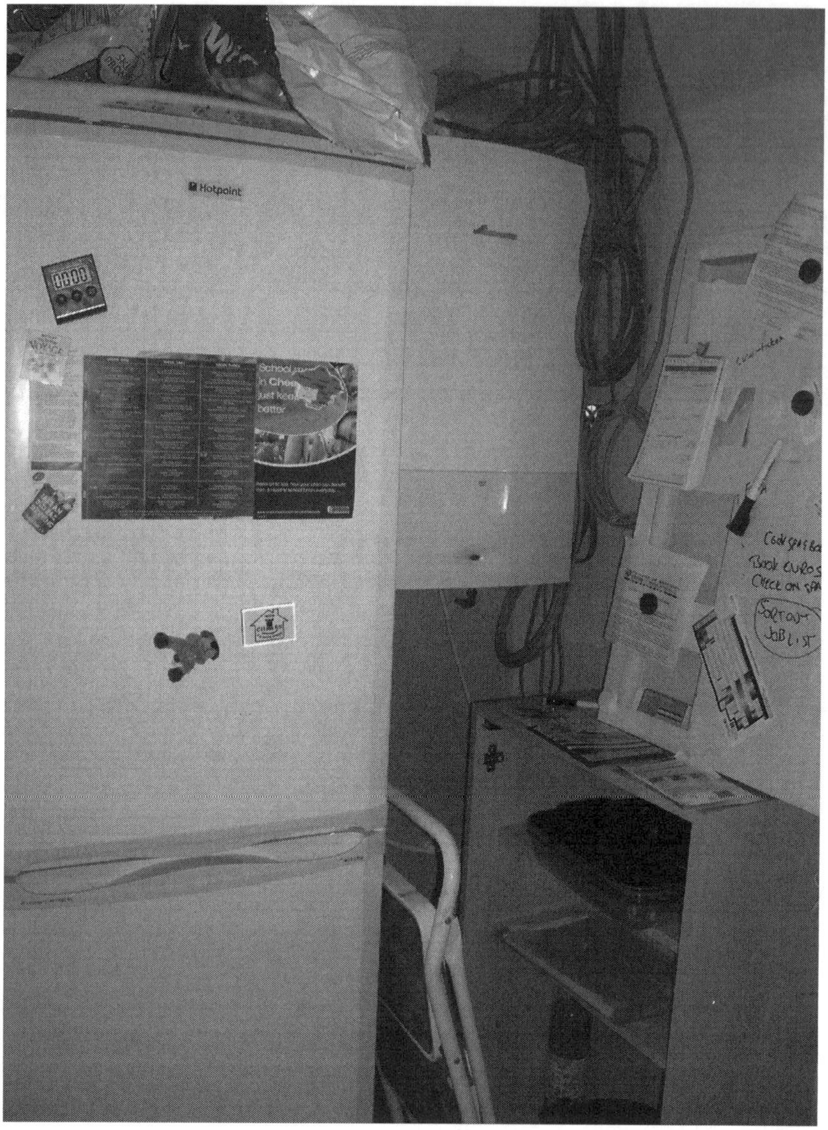

Figure 12.2 Children's school canteen menus

The diary is reserved for weekly evening dinners and Sunday lunch, the only meals that the family eats together. The meals that are not written down in the diary are the weekly lunches that Tracey eats on her own. Here it is clear that she considers others family members' desires and preferences over her own. After having prepared her children's lunchboxes in the morning with treats and the *requested* food, her lunch consists of "whatever is left." Indeed, her lunch does not involve any complex planning, rather simply reheating leftovers from the previous evening's dinner or making some sandwiches with "what is left in the fridge." In her account of the family meal routine Tracey is the one who saves up something to be donated to her family. Indeed, she does not shop for herself but she fills the trolley with treats and with food that she thinks will satisfy the changing requests of her children. When planning breakfasts and dinners she does not appear to consider what is more convenient for her, but rather what is more appropriate for, and likely to be appreciated by, her children. Finally, when she eats her lunches on her own she eats leftovers so that she can save her energy for the preparation of the coming family dinner.

What does Tracey give up? To whom?

Despite describing herself as a "foodie," Tracey's household food organization reveals that she prioritizes her children's tastes over her own desires. Such abnegation guides all of her practices surrounding the feeding of the family, but it reaches its climax in the serving of the meal. This practice might be said to be the climax of Tracey's self-sacrifice because this is where her prior efforts are displayed to the rest of the family. In this respect the practice of serving the meal involves a series of noteworthy symbolic presences and absences.

The night that Tracey invited me for dinner she cooked a different meal for one of her children, and she left out the onions from the bolognese sauce because her husband does not like the taste of onion.

> I tend to cook the same dish for everyone, but sometimes I need to cook different dishes, like tonight Mark (her son) doesn't like bolognese sauce … I make another pasta for him.
>
> I have to leave out onion because my husband doesn't like it … I like onion but … it is easier just not using it!

In making a bolognese sauce without any onion she creates a gift for her husband. The extra pasta dish that she made for her son is also a gift. These gifts that Tracey plates up individually on the kitchen worktop (Figure 12.3), symbolize her devotion to each member of her family. This plating up of meals represents Tracey's individual attention to each family member in providing

Figure 12.3 Tracey serving the meal

them with a customized dish. Indeed, she does not simply cook dinner for her family; rather she *feeds* her family by serving to each of them a meal that she hopes will satisfy their desires.

Although pleasing her family implies more work and planning (i.e. cooking more than one dish) and abnegating her own desire to add onion to the bolognese sauce, Tracey describes this as an easy task. In affirming that it is "easy" to leave out the onion from the bolognese sauce, to change the breakfast menu, and to prepare an extra dish for her son, she highlights that she does not view these tasks as work. Indeed, this work goes entirely unacknowledged by Tracey. As we discuss later, this work is rather seen by her as "essentialized within" the role of a caring mother. In making these everyday mealtime gifts for her family Tracey both performs and communicates her devotion and self-sacrifice, which includes practices as diverse as filling in her food diary, doing the shopping and eating leftovers for lunch. This sacrifice is also made visible through a series of presences and absences – the absence of onion in the bolognese sauce and the presence of a dish especially made for her son symbolize what Tracey donates to her family (her tireless work and care), and what she gives up for her family (her own desires).

What does Tracey receive in return?

If Tracey is the one who sacrifices herself in making a dinner that pleases her sons and husband, they in turn reciprocate her gift in some ways. In listening to a conversation that Tracey had with her sons on the non-negotiable importance of finishing all the food that has been put on their plates, I remember my sense of duty in finishing up the fried anchovies that my mother had made especially for me. Similarly to my mother, Tracey reminds her sons of their duty to reciprocate her sacrifice by playing the role of devotional sons, eating up the food made especially for them. Other mothers similarly asked their families to reciprocate through "sitting down and talking" at dinnertime, or "eating up what was on the plate." Tracey asked her children to set the dining table (Figure 12.4) and load the dishwasher after dinner. Her husband takes the dog for a walk

Figure 12.4 Tracey's son setting the dining table

before and after dinner. She describes these requests as "little helps" in preparing the family meal, which she views as otherwise entirely her responsibility.

These "little helps" are not the only things that she gets back from her family. What she gets back is an everyday confirmation of her maternal identity which is embedded in her sense of sacrificing herself for her family. As she says:

> This [planning different dishes] is not a big deal. I guess it is what mums do. If they [the family] are happy and they like the food, I am happy too.

Sharing a meal, which makes everyone "happy," is not simply a compromise between different preferences, but rather is a manifestation of having accomplished her duty, and doing what "mums do." Her description of self-sacrifice reminds us of what Bourdillon (in his observations on Hubert and Mauss's theory of sacrifice), points out:

> Even when a religious sacrifice is performed privately and for private ends, it reflects community values, including a common assessment of what can legitimately be given up for the end required.
>
> *(Bourdillon 1980: 15)*

Tracey's everyday sacrifice perpetuates her maternal identity because through this sacrifice she makes visible her ideals of motherhood. In cooking a bolognese sauce without onion and serving her son a dish made only for him, Tracey does not simply donate the results of her tireless work to her family. She also accomplishes her own perceived "duty as a mother," which she also sees as based on – to use Bourdillon's words – "a common assessment of what can legitimately be given up," thus reflecting a universally held set of ideals of motherhood. As Tracey observes, it is "what Mums do."

Conclusion

In telling Tracey's story, we have attempted to illustrate how her self-sacrifice, embedded in maternal identity, is performed daily at dinner time. As our brief excursion into the literature shows, sacrifice, understood as a self-abnegation, is a way of communicating with a deity through the logic of gift-giving. Here, the profane world can connect with the sacred through the symbolic mediation of a gift. This is what happens every night in Tracey's kitchen, where the climax of her sacrifice takes place in the serving of a dinner to her family. The dinner she serves symbolizes her donation of time and work to her children and husband, as well as her prioritizing of their desires over hers. This constant self-abnegation made visible through the dishes she makes every night, is a means of communicating with the sacred. As Miller (1998) points out, the object of devotion consists of family members who are the recipients of the mothers' gift. Similarly to Miller's participants, Tracey's devotional love is addressed to her family, but in her case she also receives something back from the sacred and profane world. In satisfying the desires of her deities, Tracey communicates with them, and thus she perpetuates and reinforces her identity of a "devotional mother." The profane world reciprocates Tracey with "little helps" from her children and her husband. These "little helps" are noteworthy of future attention. They testify that Tracey is not the only actor on the stage of sacrifice and thus their voices should be heard. As Epp and Price (2008) suggest, consumer research needs to consider the family as a collective rather than merely the sum of single identities. Dinner time seems an interesting place to start because the family contributes, albeit to different degrees, to the meal. The meal can be studied not only as the mother's gift but also as an example of sharing (see Belk 2010) amongst family members. Indeed, sharing a meal would be a useful future focus in understanding how a collective family identity is both perpetuated and made manifest.

Further reading

de Vault, M.L. (1991) *Feeding the Family: the Social Organization of Caring as Gendered Work*. Chicago, IL: University of Chicago Press. (A seminal text exploring the materiality of maternal love.)

Miller, D. (1998) *A Theory of Shopping*. New York: Cornell University Press. (A key work offering significant insights into shopping as sacrifice.)

References

Askegaard, S., Arnould, E.J., and Kjeldgaard, D. (2005) "Postassimilationist Ethnic Consumer Research: Qualifications and Extensions." *Journal of Consumer Research* 32: 160–70.

Beattie, J.H.M (1980) "On Understanding Sacrifice." In M.F.C. Bourdillon and M. Fortes (eds), *Sacrifice*. London: Academic Press, pp. 29–44.

Belk, R.W. (2010) "Sharing." *Journal of Consumer Research* 36: 715–34.

Belk, R.W., Wallendorf, M., and Sherry, J.F. (1989) "The Sacred and Profane in Consumer Behavior: Theodicy on the Odyssey." *Journal of Consumer Research* 16: 1–38.

Bourdillon, M.F.C. (1980) "Introduction." In M.F.C. Bourdillon and M. Fortes (eds), *Sacrifice*. London: Academic Press, pp. 1–28.

Bugge, B.A. and Almås, R. (2006) "Domestic Dinner: Representations and Practices of a Proper Meal Among Young Suburban Mothers." *Journal of Consumer Culture* 6: 203–28.

Cappellini, B. (2009) "The Sacrifice of the Re-use: The Travels of Leftovers and Family Relations." *Journal of Consumer Behaviour* 8: 365–75.

Cappellini, B. and Parsons, E. (forthcoming 2012) "Sharing the Meal: Food Conumption and Family Identity," in *Research in Consumer Behaviour* 14.

——(forthcoming 2013) "Practising Thrift at Dinnertime: Mealtime Leftovers, Sacrifice and Family Membership." *The Sociological Review*.

Carrigan, M. and Szmigin, I. (2006) "'Mothers of Invention': Maternal Empowerment and Convenience Consumption." *European Journal of Marketing* 40: 1122–42.

Cherrier, H. (2009) "Disposal and Simple Living: Exploring the Circulation of Goods and the Development of Sacred Consumption." *Journal of Consumer Behavior* 8: 327–39.

de Vault, M.L. (1991) *Feeding the Family: The Social Organization of Caring as Gendered Work*. Chicago, IL: University of Chicago Press.

Epp, M.A. and Price, L. (2008) "Family Identity: A Framework of Identity Interplay in Consumption Practices." *Journal of Consumer Research* 35: 50–70.

Hubert, H. and Mauss, M. (1964 [1899]) *Sacrifice: Its Nature and Functions*. Chicago, IL: University of Chicago Press.

Marcel, J.C. (2003) "Bataille and Mauss: A Dialogue of the Deaf?" *Economy and Society* 32: 141–52.

Milbank, J. (1995) "Stories of Sacrifice: From Wellhausen to Girard." *Theory, Culture and Society* 12: 15–46.

Miller, D. (1998) *A Theory of Shopping*. New York: Cornell University Press.

Ruskola, T. (2005) "Home Economics: What is the Difference Between a Family and a Corporation?" In M.M. Ertman, J.C. Williams (eds), *Rethinking Commodification: Cases and Readings in Law and Culture*. New York: New York University Press, pp. 324–44.

Silverman, D. (2006) *Interpreting Qualitative Data: Methods for Analysing Talk, Text and Interaction*. London: Sage.

Thompson, C.J. (1996) "Caring Consumers: Gendered Consumption Meanings and the Juggling Lifestyle." *Journal of Consumer Research* 22: 388–407.

Wallendorf, M. and Arnould, E.J. (1991) "'We Gather Together': Consumption and Rituals of Thanksgiving Day." *Journal of Consumer Research* 18: 13–31.

13

MASCULINE SELF-PRESENTATION

Jacob Östberg

> Guys need an exclusive space to hang out in their homes – a refuge where they can enjoy what they love, whether it's a soundproofed basement used as a rock 'n' roll lounge and adorned with limited edition guitars; a room where diehard ski fans can chill out with a roaring fireplace and alpine atmosphere; or a lush golf-lover's paradise, featuring a state-of-the-art virtual reality driving range, media center and top-notch equipment storage space. Because DIY Network understands there's an environment for every guy that makes him feel fulfilled …

The quote above, taken from the description of the TV show *Man Caves* (DIY Network 2011), illustrates the popular idea that consumer society is launching an assault on men. Being a *real man* used to be easy, or so the contemporary fantasy goes: as long as one had a family and brought home the bacon one was fine. Then consumer society happened, however, along with other charges on manhood typically connected to feminism – power relations between the sexes many times being construed as a zero-sum game, in which increased power for women leads to decreased power for men (LaFollette 1992) – and things became a whole lot more complicated. Consequently, men need a *refuge* where they can be *real* men, where they can find the *fulfillment* that they will not find in the other spheres of their lives now that their roles as heads of families and breadwinners are challenged. As an added benefit, the DIY project of building a *man cave* is itself the perfect masculine identity project where men can take control and *produce* a personalized space for themselves rather than merely consuming what consumer society has to offer. A further illustration of the supposed hardships of being a man is the opening of a new IKEA store in Melbourne in the fall of 2011, where a feature named *The Mänland* was introduced as "basically a crèche for husbands and boyfriends with short retail attention spans" (news.com.au 2011). The event captures stereotypical views of masculine and feminine consumer roles. A journalist covering the event noted that "while some men may pretend to enjoy the shopping experience, we all know they prefer to be playing an X-box or watching the footie over pushing a trolley any day." Again, the idea that men somehow need a refuge from consumer society is given and it is assumed that men will not really enjoy shopping, homemaking or other such activities related to traditional female consumer roles. On the contrary, real men are those who publicly express distaste for shopping (Campbell 1997).

In mainstream media, as well as in much research both in the social sciences more broadly and in consumer research, it is a popular, yet contested belief that there has been a crisis in contemporary masculinities making men insecure in their role as men. This crisis has led to the belief that a "New Man" has seen the light of day (Mort 1996) and that traditional men need to compensate through overtly masculine consumption practices (for a critical discussion, see Holt and Thompson 2004). In this chapter I will discuss the construction of masculinity in consumer society. I will start by looking at the social categories of men and women and how these social categories are connected to certain traits, and ways of being a consumer, that are typically described as masculine and feminine. Then I will look at some emblematic ways in which men's consumption is described, before I turn to the specific case of masculinity and appearance. Finally, I discuss how masculinity is represented in consumer culture.

Consuming men?

Traditionally, most research on gender and consumption has started with the assumption that men and women are fundamentally different and that this is mirrored in consumption. Being a man is always defined in relation to what men are not. Most notably men are defined in opposition to women, who are seen as the antithesis of men, but men are also defined vis-à-vis other relevant categories, such as boys and elders. Furthermore, heterosexual men, which is the hegemonic masculine identity position, are also defined in opposition to homosexual men (Connell 1996: 163). The difference between men and women is typically portrayed through a number of binary oppositions (see e.g. Stevens and Ostberg 2012). In general terms, masculinity is associated with the mind and logic, and men were thus traditionally regarded as being naturally more rational than women, and thus they had the ability to transcend their bodily urges; women, however, were not perceived as being able to do this, and were envisaged as being at the mercy of their bodily wants and desires (Joy and Venkatesh 1994).

Recent scholarship influenced by post-structural thinking has begun to challenge this dichotomous worldview. While the social categories of female and male have been, and are, fundamental to the organization of society – as illustrated by, for example, most countries' legislation for who is allowed to marry another person and virtually our entire world's canon of romance literature, poetry and song lyrics – the stability of these categories is increasingly challenged. For example, the University of Texas at Austin recently declared that gender-neutral restrooms should be available throughout campus to cater to persons with "non-normative gender identities" (Pagan 2011), and the Australian government announced that their passports should henceforth have a third gender option – indeterminate – to "counter discrimination against intersex people" (*The Guardian* 2011). The idea that gender categories are not as unambiguous as we might have previously assumed is just now starting to creep into mainstream consciousness, but the fundamental questions of the relationships between biological sex, gender, and gender identity have been discussed by post-structuralist gender theories for a couple of decades (Butler 1993) and have also influenced marketing thought (Borgerson 2005; Kacen 2000). Essentially, the designation of individuals to the two categories is made through the application of socially agreed-upon biological criteria: whether you possess recognizable male or female genitalia (Butler 1993; West and Zimmerman 1987). The designation to these categories is so fundamental that it is typically the first social event that occurs in an infant's life. This might seem straightforward, bordering on the self-evident, which is exactly the point of the post-structuralist theorists who question whether these social categories – and the obligations and expectations connected to them – need play such a large role in society. They suggest that there are those who have vested interests in keeping these categories appear self-evident, most notably the so-called patriarchy. Rather than taking this as the natural order, Butler (1993) theorizes that these body parts are not simply *there*, but that one's sex is performatively constituted when one's body is first categorized. In the words of Borgerson (2005: 68): "[t]he subject takes form from language and gestures – produced with body positions, speech acts, reflective processes, and other performative behavior, including consumption and production itself – given, or normatively imposed, as limits that at the same time offer and foreclose." The language that appears to be merely describing the subjects thereby actually constitutes them. From birth and onwards various authorities continuously reiterate, and have subjects act according to, these categories in ways that give a naturalized effect of the categories being stable and self-evident.

The implication of this for masculine self presentation is that by taking a post-structural perspective we cannot rest in the notion that men consume in certain ways because they are men. Rather, they *become* men through performing certain actions. Even though post-structural gender theorists question the naturalness of gender categories, they do not deny that males and females are important social categories, nor do they deny that there are stereotypical consumption behaviors connected to these roles. Rather they reinforce that these categories are social constructions, which is not to say that they do not have very real consequences for how we organize society. On the contrary, the identity project of being a man is of high importance in consumer society, especially since it supposedly should come naturally to those belonging to the category male.

Consuming masculinity

Gender research for a long time dealt with the degrees to which gender identity functioned to determine preferences for certain types of products, brands, types of advertising, service encounters, shopping behaviors, and leisure activities (see Palan 2001; Patterson and Hogg 2004 for overviews). This research used to focus mostly on femininity, to highlight the many times absent voices of female consumers. Masculinity was oftentimes not studied per se, but as an implicit norm. Following an overall influence of feminist thought in the social sciences, critical ideas were introduced to marketing in the early 1990s; these exposed the ways in which the entire marketing field was infused with a taken-for-granted male logic privileging certain ways of understanding, typically described as masculine (Bristor and Fischer 1993; Joy and Venkatesh 1994). Consumption has historically been connected to femininity whereas masculinity has been connected to production. Men were seen as rational customers who ultimately purchased products and services, and women were seen as the emotional consumers who were targeted by advertisers (Stevens and Maclaran 2007). This gendered division reflected distinct and different gendered roles and responsibilities in Western society, and furthermore these differences have a long history. Men used to be the ones who engaged in paid productive labor outside of the household, while women engaged in unpaid productive labor inside the household, which therefore was conceptualized as consumption. These are not merely neutral designators, since production is seen as something that adds value and consumption as something that devours value. It is because of these historical connections between consumption and femininity that men are so anxious not to be seen as mere consumers.

Instead, men typically strive to frame their consumption in such a way that it is distinguished from the stereotypically feminine consumption. Gender theorist Connell (1996) argues that independence is a core feature of hegemonic masculinity and many of the studies looking at males' consumption show that they frame their consumption as independent from market forces. Males seem to eschew the consumer role of "the dupe" being charmed by the alluring market offerings and giving into instinct, passions and desire – character traits typically connected to femininity. Gill *et al.* (2005), for example, in looking at males' body practice found a recurrent theme where the informants portrayed themselves as independent, or even rebellious, and that their choice to engage in various consumption practices that could be regarded as rather uncontroversial, such as joining/not joining a gym or buying/not buying particular branded goods, were justified by their unique and independent conviction.

As mentioned above, both mainstream depictions of masculinity and scientific studies many times make the assumption that contemporary masculinities are under assault and that there is a crisis of masculinity. When men's traditional role as breadwinner is challenged they react by finding refuges where they can orchestrate an archaic form of masculinity through compensatory consumption. Belk and Costa (1998) show how modern mountain men enact a shared fantasy in which they jointly create a socially constructed unreality where they seek refuge from their ordinary work lives in order to (re-)connect with what they perceive to be a truer way of life. Similarly, Schouten and McAlexander (1995) show how "New Bikers," i.e. mainstream Harley Davidson riders, construe their consumption of the motorcycles as rebellious acts whereby they distance themselves from their less rewarding nine-to-five jobs. Holt and Thompson (2004) are critical of this dichotomous view of the two masculine roles of breadwinners and rebels, partly because the rebellious acts seem to occupy such a small subset of men's consumption activities. Based on a study of males' everyday consumption as well as a discourse analysis of the media, marketing, and popular culture, they suggest that these two roles must be complemented by a third one, the man-of-action hero who manages to negotiate between the rebel and the breadwinner. While this depiction of masculine consumption is perhaps less thrilling than the accounts of rebellious compensatory consumption, the man-of-action hero role is rather useful in understanding how men negotiate the different roles. In essence, the authors show how men reconfigure everyday consumption activities as to encompass traditional masculine traits such as competition and independence. They thereby manage to change focus from *what* consumption activities are engaged in, to *how* these consumption activities are undertaken.

One consumption behavior that is traditionally tied very closely to femininity is childrearing. Harrison and Gentry (2007), in a study of single fathers, identified transitions that single fathers needed to undertake to become truly involved parents. These men voiced concern that they needed to accept a modified masculine self-identity in order to become a caring parent. A traditional masculine role was simply incongruous with the role of being the main caregiver. The authors show how the informants' redefinitions of their masculinities was made more problematic by advertising messages that seemingly embedded the status quo in terms of traditional gender norms. Coskuner-Balli (2008) found similar tendencies in her study of stay-at-home dads, where she showed how they used market resources to negotiate a new social identity at odds with mainstream masculinity.

Masculinity and appearance

All the above studies in different ways relate to the tensions between the traditional role of men as breadwinners and various roles focusing more on consumption. Another important but not well-theorized tension resides between the more traditionally masculine consumer roles that focus on rationality and usability, and the more feminized consumer roles that focus on appearance. Contemporary male consumers, especially in the younger age groups, must negotiate these seemingly contradictory roles in their everyday consumption to construct an appropriately well-groomed male consumer identity. Tuncay (2005) theorizes that contemporary heterosexual male consumers need to find a balance between conforming to gender roles while still expressing individuality, and between caring too much about appearance and thus running the risk of appearing homosexual and expressing sufficient levels of heterosexuality. Rinallo (2007) puts forth a similar argument and shows that in between the polar opposites of effeminacy and sloppiness, there is a "safe zone" where heterosexual men can safely experiment with consumption activities and objects. On either side of this "safe zone" lies a "danger zone." If a man shows no care of self he will suffer negative social consequences, and if a man is too careful with his appearance he will be viewed as effeminate. Ostberg (2012) has illustrated how men, in their consumption of fashion, many times try to offset the possibility of coming across as effeminate by foregrounding traditionally masculine traits such as knowledge and rationality; real men do not just dress to look pretty, but instead gather knowledge and become style experts, referencing authorities in distant locations and times.

This insecurity among male consumers is connected to an increasingly popular conception that something has happened to the traditional masculine consumer role. Ever since the great masculine renunciation, the idea that men are naturally disinterested in appearance has been dominant, and attempts to overturn this hegemony viewed with skepticism (McNeil and Karaminas 2009). In the last couple of decades, however, we have repeatedly heard rallying cries about some "new masculinity" overtaking some older, primitive or perhaps even natural masculinity (Edwards 2006). This discussion has been especially true in the realms of clothing and fashion. In the 1980s men's lifestyle magazines wrote about, and companies tried to sell products and services to, the "New Man" (Mort 1996), then the "New Lad" in the 1990s (MacKinnon 2003), and subsequently to the so-called "Metrosexual" in the first years of the new millennium (Simpson 2002). One should be careful, however, to take the outcries about new masculinities at face value and think that there has been some substantial change to masculinity in the last couple of decades. Rather, it is more feasible to regard these new conceptualizations as co-productions of a media and marketing system in which there is constant pressure to define new target groups in order to sell both advertising space and new products (Mort 1996).

Research on masculinity and consumption has given attention to the degree to which men feel urged to comply with certain standards of idealized bodies or images (e.g. Elliott and Elliott 2005; Patterson and Elliott 2002). There is some idea of a normative masculinity, or rather a set of contrasting normative masculinities, with which men compare and contrast (Connell 1996). Gill *et al.* (2005) show that while the body has become an identity project in late modernity (Featherstone 1991), the body projects of individual men are "fraught with difficulties," as young men must simultaneously work on and discipline their bodies while disavowing any (inappropriate) interest in their own appearance. The authors also suggest that the body in consumer society has become a source of symbolic capital in Bourdieu's terms, less because of what the body is able to do than because of how it looks. While looks might be important, those looks still typically need a functional excuse; bodies need to signal that they are functional as evidenced by the type of discursive repertoires used in talking about their appearances (Gill *et al.* 2005: 43).

Representing masculinity

Representations of masculinity in media and advertising provide us with visual repertoires of how life should be orchestrated (cf. Elliott and Wattanasuwan 1998). Schroeder and Zwick (2004: 33) even suggest that advertising has replaced fine art as the taste-maker *par excellence* in that it provides powerful cultural discourses that appear to merely represent the consumer lifestyles that it actually constructs. In discussing masculine self-presentation it is therefore important to look at how representations of men in advertising have shifted to encompass a broader, yet still limited, array of masculinities. Some claim that gender today has become a "pastiche of possibilities" and that "traditional notions of femininity and masculinity come across as antiquated and illusory" (Kacen 2000: 345). Still, most available images of men and women in advertising stick to a fairly traditional standard of representation. There has, however, been an increase in the amount of portrayals of men as objects in advertising, media, and popular culture (Ostberg 2010). It has been suggested that as a result, men today are being taught (or allowed) to gaze at other men either for pleasure or for anxiety-evoking contrast, and that changing representations of the male body make men increasingly aware of, and dissatisfied with, bodies that do not meet various cultural ideals (Elliott and Elliott 2005; Gill *et al.* 2005; Kacen 2000; Mort 1996; Patterson and Elliott 2002).

In contrast to females, males have not traditionally been represented in eroticized ways, but rather as doers, men of action (Goffman 1979). In his classic study of gender in advertisements, Goffman (1979) found that women are typically represented as cradling or caressing an object but not grasping, holding or manipulating it in a utilitarian way. This legacy was unchallenged up to the 1970s. During the 1980s this slowly changed as men started appearing alone, passive, and in close-up. During the 1990s, men's role as homemakers/breadwinners was further diminished and contempt for stereotypically unpleasant male behaviors – such as uncleanliness and poor household skills – became a staple of advertising. This open ridicule of masculinity paved the way for an increased eroticization of the male body (MacKinnon 2003). Consequently, during the 1990s men were increasingly portrayed "to-be-looked-at" (Mulvey 1989) without the protective shelter of humor, degradation or ridicule.

Patterson and Elliott (2002) show how the increasing visualization of male bodies in advertising and the media makes the negotiation and renegotiation of male identities all the more possible, and suggest that the male gaze has been inverted. This position is questioned by Schroeder and Zwick (2004), who instead suggest an expansion of the male gaze and suggest that the intersection of consumption and several marketing discourses such as advertising, market segmentation, and visual communication provide opportunities for multiple, potentially subversive readings. There are thus changes in how men are represented in advertising, and subversion and gender bending is no longer merely a subcultural phenomena. Still, as Gentry and Harrison (2010) show, advertising representations of men, and particularly fathers, are still very much steeped in a traditional form.

Directions for future research

While there has been an increased amount of research looking at masculinity, identity and consumption, there is still need for more research – partly because masculinity never has been well understood and partly because we are living in a time when traditional norms of how to be a man are undergoing changes. Even though masculinity has never been as homogeneous as was once imagined, changing gender ideologies are paving new ground for the identity positions available. Continued research inspired by post-structuralism, where masculinity is seen less as a biological fact and more as a dynamic meaning position, will likely yield more insights. Connell (1996) has suggested that we need to look at masculinities rather than masculinity to adhere to the notion that masculinity projects are likely to look very different depending on other societal structuring devices such as ethnicity and class. Researchers in marketing and consumer culture who follow this lead are likely to yield interesting results. Kates (2002), for example, has looked at gay men's masculinity projects, but there are other marginalized, as well as dominant, masculinities that are worth exploring. Also, an increased focus on everyday masculinity projects, such as being a father (cf. Gentry and Harrison 2010) or a husband trying to live up to ideals of equality between the sexes, are likely to provide a needed adjustment to the studies that have hitherto focused on special events whereby masculinity comes to the fore.

Further reading

Bordo, S. (1999) *The Male Body: A New Look at Men in Public and in Private*. New York: Farrar, Straus and Giroux. (A personal yet richly theoretically informed account on male embodiment in consumer society.)

Connell, R. (1995) *Masculinities*. Berkeley, CA: University of California Press. (A classic study of hegemonic masculinities overturning many of the taken-for-granted notions of what "real men" are.)

Holt, D.B. and Thompson, C.J. (2004) "Man-of-Action Heroes: The Pursuit of Heroic Masculinity in Everyday Consumption." *Journal of Consumer Research* 31 (September): 425–40. (An influential article looking at male consumers' everyday consumption practices as well as dominant discourses of masculine consumption styles.)

References

Belk, R.W. (1988) "Possessions and the Extended Self." *Journal of Consumer Research* vol.15 (September): 139–68.

Belk, R.W. and Costa, J.A. (1998) "The Mountain Man Myth: A Contemporary Consuming Fantasy." *Journal of Consumer Research* 25 (December): 218–40.

Bordo, S. (1997) "Reading the Male Body." In P. Moore (ed.), *Building Bodies*. New York: Routledge, pp.31–73.

Borgerson, J.L. (2005) "Judith Butler: On Organizing Subjectivities." *The Sociological Review* 53 (October): 63–79.

Bristor, J.M. and Fischer, E. (1993) "Feminist Thought: Implications for Consumer Research." *Journal of Consumer Research* 19 (March): 518–36.

Butler, J. (1993) *Bodies That Matter: On the Discursive Limits of "Sex."* New York: Routledge.

Campbell, C. (1997) "Shopping, Pleasure and the Sex War." In P. Falk and C. Campbell (eds), *The Shopping Experience*. Thousand Oaks, CA: Sage, pp. 166–76.

Connell, R.W. (1996) *Maskuliniteter*. Göteborg, Sweden: Daidalos.

Coskuner-Balli, G. (2008) *The Emerging Lifestyle of Stay-at-home Dads: Creating and Legitimating a New Social Identity in the Marketplace*. Madison, WI: The University of Wisconsin-Madison.

DIY Network (2011) *DIY Man Caves: About This Show*. www.diynetwork.com/man-caves/show/index.html (accessed 22 September 2011).

Edwards, T. (2006) *Cultures of Masculinity*. Florence, KY: Psychology Press.

Elliott, R. and Elliott, C. (2005) "Idealized Images of the Male Body in Advertising: A Reader-response Exploration." *Journal of Marketing Communications* 11(1): 3–19.

Elliott, R. and Wattanasuwan, K. (1998) "Brands as Symbolic Resources for the Construction of Identity." *International Journal of Advertising* 17(2): 131–44.

Featherstone, M. (1991) *Consumer Culture & Postmodernism*. London: Sage.

Gentry, J. and Harrison, R. (2010) "Is Advertising a Barrier to Male Movement Toward Gender Change?" *Marketing Theory* 10(1): 74.

Gill, R., Henwood, K. and McLean, C. (2005) "Body Projects and the Regulation of Normative Masculinity." *Body & Society* 11(1): 37–62.

Goffman, E. (1979) *Gender Advertisements*. New York: Harper & Row.

The Guardian (2011) "Australian Passports to Have Third Gender Option." *The Guardian*. 15 September. www.guardian.co.uk/world/2011/sep/15/australian-passports-third-gender-option/print (accessed 19 September 2011).

Harrison, R. and Gentry, J.W. (2007) 'Vulnerability of Single Fathers in the Transition to Their New Parental Role.' Paper presented at the European Association for Consumer Research Conference, Milan, June.

Holt, D.B. and Thompson, C.J. (2004) "Man-of-Action Heroes: The Pursuit of Heroic Masculinity in Everyday Consumption." *Journal of Consumer Research* 31 (September): 425–40.

Joy, A. and Venkatesh, A. (1994) "Postmodernism, Feminism and the Body: The Visible and the Invisible in Consumer Research." *International Journal of Research in Marketing* 11(4): 333–57.

Kacen, J.J. (2000) "Girrrl Power and Boyyy Nature: The Past, Present, and Paradisal Future of Consumer Gender Identity." *Marketing Intelligence & Planning* 18(6/7): 345–55.

Kates, S.M. (2002) "The Protean Quality of Subcultural Consumption: An Ethnographic Account of Gay Consumers." *Journal of Consumer Research* 29 (December): 383–99.

LaFollette, H. (1992) "Real Men." In L. May and R. Strikwerda (eds), *Rethinking Masculinity: Philosophical Explorations in Light of Feminism*. Lanham, MD: Rowman & Littlefield Publishers, pp. 59–74.

MacKinnon, K. (2003) *Representing Men: Maleness and Masculinity in the Media*. New York: Bloomsbury Publishing.

McNeil, P. and Karaminas, V. (2009) "Introduction: The Field of Men's Fashion." In P. McNeil and V. Karaminas (eds), *The Men's Fashion Reader*. Oxford: Berg, pp. 1–14.

Mort, F. (1996) *Cultures of Consumption: Masculinities and Social Space in Late Twentieth-century Britain*. London and New York: Routledge.

Mulvey, L. (1989) *Visual and Other Pleasures*. Basingstoke: Macmillan.

news.com.au (2011) *IKEA Introduces MANLAND, the Crèche for Retail-weary Men*. 1 September. www.news.com.au/entertainment/celebrity/ikea-introduces-manland-the-creche-for-retail-weary-men/story-fn9ql3sf-1226127519690#ixzz1YUOwwEnI (accessed 21 September 2011).

Ostberg, J. (2010) "Thou Shalt Sport a Banana in Thy Pocket: Gendered Body Size Ideals in Advertising and Popular Culture." *Marketing Theory* 10(1): 45–73.

——(2012) "Masculinity and Fashion." In Cele Otnes and Linda Tuncay Zayer (eds), *Gender, Culture, and Consumer Behavior*. London and New York: Routledge, pp. 253–81.

Pagan, V. (2011) "Gender-neutral Restrooms to be Phased in to Broader Use on Campus." *The Daily Texan*. 24 July. www.dailytexanonline.com/news/2011/07/24/gender-neutral-restrooms-be-phased-broader-use-campus (accessed 19 September 2011).

Palan, K.M. (2001) "Gender Identity in Consumer Behavior Research: A Literature and Research Agenda." *Academy of Marketing Science Review* 10(1).

Patterson, M. and Elliott, R. (2002) "Negotiating Masculinities: Advertising and the Inversion of the Male Gaze." *Consumption, Markets and Culture* 5(3): 231–46.

Patterson, C. and Hogg, M.K. (2004) "Gender Identity, Gender Salience and Symbolic Consumption." In L.M. Scott and C.J. Thompson (eds), *Proceedings from the Gender and Consumer Behavior Conference*. Duluth, MN: Association for Consumer Research.

Rinallo, D. (2007) "Metro/Fashion/Tribes of Men: Negotiating the Boundaries of Men's Legitimate Consumption." In B. Cova, R.V. Kozinets and A. Shankar (eds), *Consumer Tribes*. Oxford: Elsevier/Butterworth-Heinemann, pp. 76–92.

Schouten, J.W. and McAlexander, J.H. (1995) "Subcultures of Consumption: An Ethnography of the New Bikers." *Journal of Consumer Research* 22 (June): 43–61.

Schroeder, J.E. and Borgerson, J.L. (1998) "Marketing Images of Gender: A Visual Analysis." *Consumption, Markets and Culture* 2(2): 161–201.

Schroeder, J.E. and Zwick, D. (2004) "Mirrors of Masculinity: Representation and Identity in Advertising Images." *Consumption, Markets and Culture* 7(1): 21–52.

Simpson, M. (2002) "Meet the Metrosexual." *Salon*, 2 July. www.salon.com/2002/07/22/metrosexual/ (accessed 14 September 2004).

Slater, D. (1997) *Consumer Culture and Modernity*. Cambridge: Polity Press.

Stevens, L. and Maclaran, P. (2007) "The Carnal Feminine: Womanhood, Advertising and Consumption." In S. Borghini, M.A. McGrath and C. Otnes (eds), *European Advances in Consumer Research*. Duluth, MN: Association for Consumer Research, pp. 169–74.

Stevens, L. and Ostberg, J. (2012) "Gendered Bodies: Representations of Femininity and Masculinity in Advertising Practices." In L. Penaloza, N. Toulouse and L. Visconti (eds), *Marketing Management: A Cultural Approach*. New York: Routledge, pp. 392–407.

Tuncay, Linda (2005) *How Male Consumers Construct and Negotiate their Identities in the Marketplace: Three Essays*. University of Illinois dissertation.

West, C. and Zimmerman, D.H. (1987) "Doing Gender." *Gender & Society* 1(2): 125–51.

II

The dynamic self: Transformation, change, support and control

II.I

Self-transformation

14

CONFLICTING SELVES AND THE ROLE OF POSSESSIONS

A process view of transgenders' self-identity conflict

Ayalla A. Ruvio and Russell W. Belk

The meaning of possessions as part of the extended self has long been established in the consumer behavior literature (e.g. Belk 1988, 1992, 2010; Hirschman and Labarbera 1990; Kleine and Baker 2004; Richins 1994). The underlying assumption of the concept of the extended self is that the individual has an atomized self that radiates out into the world by means of tangible objects and consumption rituals (Belk 2010). Studies from this perspective have generally focused on the meaning of possessions as reflecting a holistic self or specific aspects of the self. However, as Erikson (1968) notes, all individuals experience conflicts between different aspects of their self-identity throughout their lifetime. Though some argue that possessions play an important role in cases of self-conflict (Csikszentmihalyi and Rochberg-Halton 1981; Kates 2004; Tian and Belk 2005), there has been very little research on this subject. This ethnographic study explores the role possessions play in the formation and development of, coping with, and resolution of conflict between different selves using an extreme instance of self-conflict – gender identity.

Gender is one of the most defining characteristics of the self (Gagné *et al.* 1997). When the individual's gender identity is not congruent with his or her genital configuration, he or she will experience a gender identity conflict. Since gender identity is established early in life, it is an internalized aspect of the self and is thought to be virtually immutable, but those who experience a gender identity conflict must develop an alternative gender identity and enact a gender presentation that does not coincide with their sex. They are identified as transgenders (Gagné *et al.* 1997). Our study is built on in-depth, unstructured interviews with seven male-to-female transgenders, using a grounded theory approach (Corbin and Strauss 1990). We assert that insights gathered from this extreme example of self-conflict can educate us about more common or usual behaviors (O'Guinn and Faber 1989; Kates 1998).

The formation of an alternative gender identity is similar to the "coming-out" process of gay individuals (Kates 1998). However, transgenders need not just come out, but must also cross over either temporarily or permanently from one sex/gender category to another (Gagné *et al.* 1997; Lev 2004). In Western society, dominated by the binary perception of gender, the act of crossing over challenges the cultural and structural social order, exposing the individual to social sanctions. Building on Erikson's (1968) social development theory, several multiple-stage models have been used to describe the act of crossing over. Although these models vary in the number of stages they envision, they all reflect the influence of social surroundings on the development of the new gender identity (Erikson 1968). They discuss the conflict that accompanies the process of emergence from a clinical, therapeutic and medical perspective. Together they still provide us with a useful theoretical framework for understanding the conflict. Integrating these models, we propose a five-stage model that includes: 1 conflict emergence; 2 negotiating identities – exploration of one's self; 3 acceptance – coming out to one's self; 4 sharing one's new identity – coming out to others; and 5 identity resolution. We will discuss the role possessions play in each of these stages.

Method

Data generation and sample

A total of seven transgender males-to-females (MtoF) interviews were conducted over the course of a year. Some of the interviews were conducted in public places (e.g. restaurants), while others were conducted in the privacy of the participants' homes. The interviews ranged in length from one hour to three and a half hours. The interviews focused on the meaning of possessions and other consumption rituals as part of their conflict development and resolution.

Data interpretation

The interviews were transcribed and were read by both authors several times, identifying narrative themes from the collective text (Hirschman 1992) that illustrate the role of possessions and consumption rituals in the gender conflict experienced by our informants. The themes that emerged were organized and presented within the context of the crossing-over process of transgender participant.

Results

While presenting the conflict development in stages might suggest that it is a linear process, it should be noted that our informants moved back and forth between stages, skipped stages, or failed to complete the process and reach a resolution (Ettner *et al.* 2007; Lev 2004).

Stage 1: conflict emergence

Conflict emergence refers to the period when the transgendered person first experiences an awareness of his or her identity incongruence, but has not yet labeled these feelings. In the case of transgenderism, there is a discrepancy between the physical configuration of the body and the psychological structuring of gender identity. At this stage, this discrepancy causes profound discomfort and confusion about the person's birth sex and what it means. Nancy told us, "It's a very clear understanding that you are not in the right place." For transgenders, the failure to conform to societal values and norms associated with their biological sex leads to feelings of being inherently defective and different (Bockting and Coleman 2007; Gagné and Tewksbury 1999). Most of our informants reported that they felt as if something was wrong with them and that they did not "fit in" (Bockting and Coleman 2007; Kates 1998). They felt shame, fear, confusion and alienation as a result of living in a world that ignored or refused to acknowledge their "authentic" identity.

Gender-identity conflict often emerges during childhood, when children incorporate the social norms and perceptions about gender into their self-identity (Gagné *et al.* 1997; Lev 2004). "It was clear to me that … a boy couldn't be a girl and a girl couldn't be a boy," said Maria, remembering her childhood perceptions. Society expects children to conform to their assigned gender roles. Appropriately gendered possessions and consumption behavior define the boundaries of socially accepted behaviors. Children learn that using possessions the "wrong way" will result in an act of correction or even punishment from others. Those who refuse to conform and choose to act out their "true selves" run the risk of outright rejection and contempt from others (Bockting and Coleman 2007).

In order to minimize their conflict, our informants sometimes proved to be resourceful con artists during their childhood. Lying, stealing, and deceptive behaviors were reported as a means to ease the conflict between their public and private selves, their personal desires and societal norms, their current identity and their desired identity. For example, Maria remembered how she satisfied her desire for dolls as a boy: "Sometimes I stole them from other girls who were playing outside, but then I had to hide them so my parents wouldn't find them. That was basically when I was little." Mary used to "memorize where everything was in the [her sister's] closet so I could put it back exactly where it belonged and no one would know that anything had been moved."

Finally, using gendered possessions allows children to engage in initial cross-gender exploration. Using possessions such as clothing and make-up helped them achieve what in their eyes was a desirable appearance, at least temporarily. These experimental rituals provided them with the initial visualization of crossing over to the other sex. Like Erica, who was socialized into the secret side of female performance by classmates: "These were girls who were teaching me how to dress and look … [and] all the little secrets that girls do in order to look their best but don't tell anyone else."

Stage 2: negotiating identities - exploration of one's self

This phase is characterized by the transsexual's quest for self-meaning and self-labeling. Positioned between conflict awareness and acceptance, the person strives to answer questions such as: "Who am I?" "Who do I want to be?" The identity negotiation process, when the individual explores different identities, has been posited as driven by a search for the "true self" and "authenticity." The emergence of a new identity occurs within the constraints of the current perceptions of social norms. Thus, while these questions typify identity conflict in general, the social stigma associated with gender conflict makes these questions harder to answer. Identity incongruity normally motivates informants to search for information that will help them understand their inner self-conflict.

Some of our older informants felt that today's young transgenders are much more knowledgeable than ever before. They have access to resources, such as the Internet, that did not exist in the past, which makes it easier for them to cope with their identity conflict. Online communication also enables them to contact their peers, as well as to experiment with alternative identities and post informational inquiries without posing a threat to their existing identity and relationships (Gagné *et al.* 1997). They can build a "virtual identity" in an effortless and relatively safe manner: " … virtual reality allowed me to say that I was a transgender without revealing my personal details … I had my own online nickname that I used" (Mary).

All of our informants reported that information seeking led them to the discovery that "there are others in the world like me." This was a liberating feeling for them which helped to alleviate their sense of alienation and being a deviant. It also helped our informants experience a sense of self-recognition and identity reinforcement needed for their next step of acceptance. These "similar others" became a symbol of possible identities (Bockting and Coleman 2007; Henry and Caldwell 2006), and contributed to identity clarification by providing them with alternatives. Mary remembered the first time she went to a transgender gathering in a public coffee shop: "All of them looked like women, talked like women, and behaved like women, and I didn't. It wasn't until the end of the evening that I decided that apparently this is what I wanted for myself."

Revelation is a double-edged sword. While the person feels a sense of relief at solving the puzzle of his/her identity crisis, she or he "suddenly discovers or finally admits belonging to this stigmatized group" (Hanley-Hackenbruck 1988: 22). This duality often results in the creation of a parallel, secret world where the person practices the desired cross-gender identity. Ruth, who did mandatory military service as a man, recalled: "I ... kept my little perversion for the evening ... in the morning I was the best damn fighting man in the world ... but at night I would dress up like a woman. Put on make-up. Even the perfume I used at night was different from the aftershave I used in the morning." Possessions played a crucial part in this masquerade as they created an invisible border between identity worlds. Some objects were used only in one world while others symbolized the parallel one. Possessions were used in the "public" world used to create a socially acceptable identity, but at the same time were perceived as costumes. Cross-dressing is a common practice during this stage (Bockting and Coleman 2007). However, unlike in the awareness phase, where cross-dressing is performed unintentionally just because it "feels right," in this stage cross-dressing becomes a purposeful act of passing into the other sex in order to "essentially express my true me" (Erica).

Stage 3: acceptance – coming out to one's self

In this stage the long journey of acknowledging and accepting one's new identity begins. Nancy noted that "this process of self-acceptance, the improvement of one's femininity [or masculinity], is a long process that takes time ... I was exploring my boundaries." Acceptance is the last in a series of coping strategies aimed at internalizing the new insight generated in the previous stage and its meaning. According to Bockting and Coleman (2007), the developmental task in this stage is to overcome and resolve the confusion associated with identity crises and achieve self-acceptance. Here possessions can help the person engage in a variety of coping strategies as a response to their stressful self-revelation (Carver *et al.* 1989; Henry and Caldwell 2006; Lazarus and Folkman 1984).

The literature on coping emphasizes two general types of strategies for coping with stressful situations. The first is problem-focused coping, which involves taking action to solve the problem or alter the source of the stress. The second type is emotion-focused coping, which seeks to reduce or manage the emotional distress that is associated with the problem (Carver *et al.* 1989; Folkman and Lazarus 1985). Our informants reported utilizing both types of coping strategies.

Acknowledging the transgendered identity is emotionally demanding. As Donna wondered, "Why the hell did this happen to me? Why me? There is a lot of anger in this process. Relief, but also a lot of anger." The enormity of the revelation often drove our informants to find ways of actively coping with this discovery. Some continued to perfect their secret world. Others ran away to remote places (such as foreign countries and cities) to seek temporary relief from their stressful existence and to practice their alternate identity under the protective wings of anonymity.

Denial was another common strategy experienced by all of our informants at this stage or another. For our informants denial meant completely ignoring their conflict. Most of them tried to live the "normal" lives socially expected of them. They created a performance that would seem aligned with their physical configuration, so no questions regarding their true identity would be asked. Possessions played a key role in the design of this performance.

Coping with the new insight usually involves moving back and forth from periods of experimenting to periods of suppression, in attempts to limit the conflict and control it. However, "sooner or later everything collapses and you come to understanding that you can't run away anymore" (Nancy). Acceptance usually involves a beginning of developing and managing the public presentation of their new gender identity, with the final goal of being able "to pass" as the other sex in public. In its broader sense, "passing" is a concept that reflects a set of activities employed by the person with a stigmatic identity in order to manipulate social meaning and the impression others have of their self-identity as "normal" or non-deviant. For that reason, "passing" for our informants was the ultimate test of their new gendered identity and they regarded achieving it as a victory (Bockting and Coleman 2007; Lev 2004). The act of stepping out into the street as the other sex seemed to many of them to be an unreachable goal. Indeed, their greatest fear was to be "read" or recognized as someone who was a cross-dresser (Lev 2004).

A convincing "passing" image required buying items to support the new gender identity, including clothes, make-up, shoes, accessories, and sometimes the beginning of bodily alterations (Kates 1998). Buying these items was often a ritual in itself, as our informants felt uncomfortable and even horrified buying cross-gender goods in public. These feelings affected their buying behaviors such as their choice of shopping places and the way they interacted with the sales person in the store: "I didn't say it was for me … I said it was for my sister" (Erica), or "for my girlfriend" (Ruth). Using these items was, in many cases, even harder than buying them. Although some of our informants had previous experience in using female-oriented items in their early childhood and adolescence, for most of them creating an entirely new look, one that bridged their identity incongruence in a convincing way, was an extremely excruciating process.

Stage 4: sharing one's new identity – coming out to others

For our informants, reaching full self-acceptance of their new identity led to sharing it with significant others (e.g. spouses, children, family, friends and colleagues). All of them reported this stage to be an emotionally demanding one, which often led to rejection (Lev 2004). They were aware of the possible negative consequences of their choice, which sometimes held them back from revealing their true identity, as Ruth expressed it: "From my point of view, it meant I had to give up a lot, a lot … Family, a very good position that I had worked hard to get … " Sometimes they reached out for help from professionals, who were not always very supportive. Others, like Erica, received support from friends but not from family: "My whole life I was with people who knew about me, who helped me … The biggest problem was with my parents, not with the environment."

The moment and the place of revelation were carefully chosen and planned. Our informants truly felt the burden of years of "proper" gender performance, as well as the knowledge of what happens when someone does not conform to gender normality. However, at this point they felt that they could no longer hide their "true" selves. The cost of living a lie was much greater for them than the cost of revealing their true identity. In sharing their new identity with others, our informants felt the need to present a convincing public image of their cross-gender identity, which was more than just "passing." While in the previous stage their public appearance was mainly to legitimize their identity, at this stage they did not want to be perceived as a transgender person. They wanted to be perceived and accepted as a person of the other sex (Gagné *et al.* 1997). As Ruth noted, "I saw myself as a woman. I presented myself to the world as a woman and people accepted me as a woman." In this stage, possessions must be presented as a coherent ensemble embedded in the new gender identity. In addition, the individual needs to demonstrate the proper use of these items.

Once the secret was out, our informants did not feel the need to manage parallel lives and parallel presentations of the self. Most of them reported getting rid of possessions that were not congruent with their new identity. "I took a bag of clothes and shoes and burned them … Watching my clothes burn was like a kind of cleansing for me" (Ruth). In addition to the disposal of possessions, other signals of the old identity were replaced with new ones. For example, six out of our seven informants reported changing their names.

Other alterations included the modification of physical appearance. At this point alterations would be much more profound and permanent. Some of our informants underwent a full transformation to the other sex, including a sex-change operation as well as taking hormones. Others just took hormones with no genital reconstruction. Some felt more comfortable using possessions to construct their cross-gender performance without doing any bodily alterations. Fully crossing over to the other sex requires structuring a new daily routine that reflects their new identity (Bockting and Coleman 2007; Gagné *et al.* 1997). Unremarkable things that would never have been considered before become problematic. How you sit, how you walk, how you carry yourself, how you talk – all of these mannerisms become issues to deal with on a daily basis and for a long period of time. It is a day-after-day, hour-after-hour form of learning how to present a coherent image of the new identity.

> It sounded funny that you could hear me coming because the shoes made noise on the floor when I walked. That kind of thing doesn't generally happen with men's shoes. It made me very self-conscious because all of a sudden everyone could hear me.
>
> *(Mary)*

Stage 5: identity resolution

This stage revolves around identity emergence and consolidation. The goal is to come to terms with one's "true" identity. Public and private identities must reach congruence and present a positive self-image. Labeling also becomes less important and is governed by the person's overall identity. The transgender reaches a deeper level of self-acceptance and – confidence: "Today I don't say to myself that I'm a woman. I say that I'm Erica" (Erica). Shameful feelings turn into pride and self-esteem. Identity authentication and self-legitimization lose their grip on the person's everyday behaviors. They are no longer driven by the need to prove their gendered identity. Their daily performance becomes automatic at different levels. For transgenders, that means that they have a holistic new identity, of which transgenderism is one part.

At this stage, possessions are no longer perceived as a means to project gender identity but as a means to project a new self-identity. When the transgender at this stage gets up in the morning, and he or she picks out his or her clothes based on personal preferences and not based on their "passing" qualities, this is an indication of identity consolidation and integration. The person is less sensitive to the gendered subtexts of possessions and he or she is less conscious of the gendered meaning of possessions. At this point they engage in consumption rituals that are rooted in the new "true" self. Style and mannerisms come to reflect the person's preferences. "I have my own style … someone once told me that when I get up from a table, I instinctively fix my blouse. That comes out of my socialization as a woman" (Nancy).

Another important task the transgender faces at this stage is to come to terms with the past and integrate it into the new identity. Some of them closed the door behind them on their painful past, never incorporating it into their new identity. Others made their past a major focal point of their new self by becoming activists for the transgender community. The informants' relationships with their memories of their previous selves were reflected in their behavior with their possessions. While some of them chose to dispose of anything associated with their previous identity, others kept certain items that helped them cope in hard times with their conflict. For most of our informants, however, a successful transformation process implied that some or all of their material objects simply became irrelevant to their new identity and were replaced by others. Not all of our informants managed to solve their identity conflict and several are still struggling with the basic questions of who they are and who they want to become. As Ed conveyed, "I'm not really sure about my final identity. I'm still learning who I am and who I am not as a person."

Discussion

This ethnographic research contributes to the theory of the extended self, the literature on identity conflict, and the knowledge about transgenderism. Our findings enrich understanding of the important role that possessions play in our lives. They demonstrate that possessions are not just an extension of one's self-identity, but are also a reflection of the conflict between different identities. The symbolic power of possessions causes such identity conflict to surface to the level of consciousness. Possessions also help people to cope with their conflict in different ways, and reflect the conflict's resolution in the formation of a new self-identity.

We argue that the role possessions play in gender-identity conflict can be generalized to other self-conflicts. Therefore, the relevance of our findings may be applied to other identity conflict research. The transgenders literature, like other identity-conflict research, acknowledges the fact that possessions and consumer rituals are an inherent part of the conflict's development (Gagné *et al.* 1997). However, these studies have failed to build a comprehensive picture of the dynamic role possessions play in activating the conflict, helping suppress or disguise it, managing it, and helping to resolve it. We believe that our findings can shed new light on the identity-conflict research and ultimately promote a more clinical understanding of this phenomenon.

In sum, according to our findings, possessions play an important role in a transgender's self-conflict process. The symbolic power of possessions causes the conflict to surface to the level of consciousness. Possessions help individuals cope with the conflict in different ways, and reflect the conflict's resolution and the formation of a new self-identity. The role possessions play in the gender-identity conflict can be generalized to other self-conflicts. Thus, the present work contributes to the literatures on the extended self, identity conflict and transgender identity.

References

Belk, Russell W. (1988) "Possessions and the Extended Self." *Journal of Consumer Research* 14 (September): 139–68.

——(1992) "Attachment to Possessions." In Irwin Altman and Setha Low (eds), *Human Behavior and Environment: Advances in Theory and Research, Vol. 12, Place Attachment*. New York: Plenum Press, pp. 37–62.

——(2010) "Sharing." *Journal of Consumer Research* 37 (February): 1–20.

——(forthcoming) "Possessions and the Self." In Richard Bagozzi and Ayalla Ruvio (eds), *Consumer Behavior, Wiley International Encyclopedia of Marketing*. New York: Wiley.

Benjamin, Harry (1966) *The Transsexual Phenomenon*. New York: Ace Books.

Bockting, Walter O. and Coleman, Eli (2007) "Developmental Stages of the Transgender Coming-out Process: Toward an Integrated Identity." In Randi Ettner, Stan Monstrey and Evan Eyler (eds), *Principles of Transgender Medicine and Surgery*. New York: The Haworth Press.

Carver, Charles S., Scheier, Michael F., and Weintraub, Jagdish K. (1989) "Assessing Coping Strategies: A Theoretically Based Approach." *Journal of Personality and Social Psychology* 56(2): 267–83.

Corbin, Juliet M. and Strauss, Anselm (1990) "Grounded Theory Research: Procedures, Canons, and Evaluative Criteria." *Qualitative Sociology* 13: 3–21.

Csikszentmihalyi, Mihaly and Rochberg-Halton, Eugene (1981) *The Meaning of Things: Domestic Symbols and the Self*. Cambridge: Cambridge University Press.

Erikson, Erik H. (1968) *Identity: Youth and Crisis*. New York: Norton.

Ettner, Randi, Monstrey, Stan, Eyler, Evan (2007) *Principles of Transgender Medicine and Surgery*. New York: Haworth Press.

Folkman, Susan and Lazarus, Richard S. (1985) "If it Changes it Must be a Process: A Study of Emotion and Coping During Three Stages of a College Examination." *Journal of Personality and Social Psychology* 48: 150–70.

Freud, Sigmund (1900) *The Interpretation of Dreams*. Translated by A.A. Brill (1911).

Gagné, Patricia and Tewksbury, Richard (1999) "Knowledge and Power, Body and Self: An Analysis of Knowledge Systems and the Transgendered Self." *Sociological Quarterly* 40: 59–83.

Gagné, Patricia, Tewksbury, Richard, and McGaughey, Deanna (1997) "Coming Out and Crossing Over: Identity Formation of Proclamation in the Transgender Community." *Gender and Society* 11(4): 478–508.

Hanley-Hackenbruck, Peggy (1988) "Psychotherapy and the 'Coming Out' Process." *Journal of Gay and Lesbian Psychotherapy* 1(1): 21–40.

Henry, Paul C., Caldwell, Marylouise (2006) "Self-empowerment and Consumption: Consumer Remedies for Prolonged Stigmatization." *European Journal of Marketing* 40(9/10): 1031–48.

Hirschman, Elizabeth (1992) "The Consciousness of Addiction: Toward a General Theory of Compulsive Consumption." *Journal of Consumer Research* 19: 155–79.

Hirschman, Elizabeth C. and Labarbera, Priscilla A. (1990) "Dimensions of Possession Importance." *Psychology and Marketing* 7(3): 215–33.

Kates, Steven M. (1998) *Twenty Million New Customers: Understanding Gay Men's Consumer Behavior*. New York: The Haworth Press.

——(2004) "The Dynamics of Brand Legitimacy: An Interpretive Study in the Gay Men's Community." *Journal of Consumer Research* 31 (September): 455–64.

Kleine, Susan Schultz and Baker, Stacey Menzel (2004) "An Integrative Review of Material Possession Attachment." *Academy of Marketing Science Review* 1: 1–39.

Lazarus, Richard S. and Folkman, Susan (1984) *Stress, Appraisal, and Coping*. New York: Springer.

Lev, Arlene (2004) *Transgender Emergence: Therapeutic Guidelines for Working with Gender-Variant People and Their Families*. New York: The Haworth Clinical Practice Press.

Markus, Hazel and Nurius, Paula (1986) "Possible Selves." *American Psychologist* 41: 954–69.

O'Guinn, Thomas C. and Faber, Ronald J. (1989) "Compulsive Buying: A Phenomenological Exploration." *Journal of Consumer Research* 16:2 (September): 147–57.

Richins, Marsha L. (1994) "Valuing Things: The Public and Private Meaning of Possessions." *Journal of Consumer Research* 21: 504–21.

Tian, Kelly and Belk, Russell (2005) "Extended Self and Possessions in the Workplace." *Journal of Consumer Research* 32 (September): 297–310.

15

SELF-TRANSFORMATION AND AIDS POSTER CHILDREN

Ingeborg Astrid Kleppe and Marylouise Caldwell

Not everyone can become an AIDS poster child. Very few people possess the courage, determination and self-control needed to evolve into such a publicly accountable role. AIDS poster children are HIV+ consumers who spearhead HIV/AIDS health campaigns by acting as highly visible role models for disease prevention and/or treatment. Their effectiveness lies in their capacity to provide ongoing proof that the strenuous lifestyle changes needed to combat the disease are possible (Corby *et al.* 1996). Magic Johnson is the epitome of an AIDS poster child. Johnson was a huge basketball star in 1991 when he publicly declared his HIV+ status. Thereafter he used his celebrity, good health, and successful business and family life to disprove many of the preconceptions about living with HIV/AIDS (Casey *et al.* 2003)

In Botswana, the site of our study, very few consumers ever go public with their HIV/AIDS status. Although the Botswana government has vigorously fought HIV/AIDS over the past quarter century, including openly acknowledging the disease and making HIV testing and counseling widely available, socio-cultural factors have historically limited openly living with the disease. Such factors include elevated denial and stigma, a preference for traditional rather than Western biomedicine and a bias towards tribal rather than democratically elected government rule. However overwhelming evidence that the anti-retroviral drugs distributed via the public health system save lives has led to a decline in stigma and more people living publicly with the disease (Physicians for Human Rights 2007).

Our study is of relevance to consumer research for two reasons. First, we study enforced identity change prompted by a life-threatening illness. Second, we study consumers who become public endorsers for a stigmatized health issue in a socio-political context offering them limited support. Our research departs from previous consumer research which tends to focus on identity work that is voluntary, pleasurable, driven by feelings of fantasy, fun and/or self-fulfillment, and has the capacity to signal affluence and social prestige (Arnould and Thompson 2005). In contrast, consumer identities that emanate from illness experiences are typically stigmatizing, involving life-long, anxiety-ridden efforts to manage physical and/or mental pain so that patients can cope with everyday living. In this chapter we shed light on the identities and related activities that AIDS poster children manifest in a context where such consumer behavior is rare.

AIDS poster child pageants

In exploring these issues we conducted an extended ethnographic study of the 2005 Miss HIV/ Stigma Free and 2006 and 2008 Mister Positive Living beauty pageants in Botswana. Since 2003, local nongovernmental organizations (NGOs) wanting to promote the well-being of HIV+ consumers have hosted such pageants regularly, with the aim of facilitating the emergence of individuals who could serve as AIDS poster children for government health programs, especially Positive Living. Positive Living is a constellation of consumption practices, including testing to know one's HIV status, always engaging in safe sex and, if one is HIV+, adhering to prescribed medication, monitoring disease progression, following a well-balanced diet and limiting excessive drinking and smoking. Positive Living also involves addressing stigma and discrimination and remaining a productive member of society (n.a. 2011).

We collected data from multiple sources. In November 2005 we interviewed participants and made field notes at the Global Health Conference and Women's Affairs Gender Office in Gaborone, Botswana. In March–April 2006 we video-taped interviews in Botswana with two participants from the 2005 Miss HIV Stigma Free Beauty Contest, six participants in the 2006 Mr Positive Living Contest, five HIV/AIDS experts working in the public health sector, a national leader of an HIV+ persons' support group, a Pentecostal pastor and a volunteer youth leader. In 2009 and 2010 we re-interviewed some of our original participants as well as Mr Positive Living 2008. Two Botswana experts with substantial experience working in the HIV/ AIDS sector in Botswana checked our findings for face validity and reliability.

Becoming an AIDS poster child

The identity work of AIDS poster children starts with an HIV+ diagnosis. Subsequently they experience a serious biographical disruption; they no longer know who they are or what their future will be (Bury 1982). They ask themselves fundamental questions such as: "Who am I? Why am I here on Earth? What is my role now? (Courtney *et al.* 1998). This stage is followed by a long period of self-reconstruction. Many years are typically required to come to terms with their diagnosis, educate themselves about the disease, normalize treatment and achieve self- and social acceptance (Royer 1998). Eventually AIDS poster children move beyond their individual concerns, to become public figures who strive to help and educate others and larger society about HIV (Zoller 2005). A major part of this activity is to provide living proof that the radical, often undesirable behavioral changes required to cope with HIV/AIDS are worth it (Berger and Rand 2008). The overall process is one of increasing self-transcendence (Coward 1995) in which consumers garner the skills, experience, social support and courage to act as health advocates within regional, national and international domains.

"I must accept"

> I found out 28th December 2004. I could not believe that I was HIV+. I thought they were lying to me, to frighten me.
>
> *(Andrew)*

Acceptance of an HIV+ diagnosis is essential in becoming an AIDS poster child, being linked to the many changes necessary to survive and prosper with the disease, especially adherence to drug regimes that limit disease progression (Nam *et al.* 2008). Acceptance is not easy because an HIV+ diagnosis means one's life has irrevocably changed. Acceptance is expedited when AIDS poster children acknowledge prior to testing the existence of the disease and their past risky behavior. Yet acceptance is not always immediate, with some AIDS poster children, like Andrew, initially denying their HIV+ status. Such reactions are not surprising. By excluding highly threatening aspects of reality from consciousness, denial facilitates the maintenance of self-esteem and the misconception that one can continue life as before. For men particularly in Botswana acceptance of HIV+ status may be especially difficult; a widespread belief exists that women, not men, are susceptible to the disease. Itumeleng, a consultant to the Ministry of Health in Botswana explains: "The man is in control … He is so macho, he cannot actually get HIV and AIDS."

However, AIDS poster children eventually overcome denial, most notably after their adherence to biomedical treatment coincides with the Lazarus Effect, or near-miraculous recovery, from a prolonged period of pernicious infections.

> In the beginning of 1993 I got very sick. I had boils which were coming on and off and terrible headaches … On the 17th of April, 1993 I took the test and the results were released on the 28th of April, 1993. That is when I learned about my sero-positive status. I was put on medication and began to get better … [Thirteen years later] I am still kicking, fit and strong like anybody else!
>
> *(Donald)*

Acceptance of status is accelerated if one responds proactively and rejects victim status: "Yeah it shocked me you know, mildly. To say, am I one of these victims, now? Why? And I quickly said: 'No. Let me not ask myself where this thing is from.' You know when you find a snake in your room? You don't ask yourself where it is from! You start doing something with it" (Paul). A different but nevertheless productive response is when AIDS poster children abdicate personal responsibility, attributing their infection to the rich tapestry of life: "I must accept. As much as many other illnesses are being handled that are brought by nature … This is just a condition I acquired. I couldn't do anything because I never made an application to it. But then as fate would have it I got struck down the line" (Paul).

Research suggests that other responses made by AIDS poster children are likely to lead to acceptance of their status. Disclosure of their HIV+ status to significant others is such an activity; hearing themselves say the diagnosis out loud adds credibility to the diagnosis and can lead to acceptance by others and hence self-acceptance (Reeves *et al.* 1999). "I never had to go through the experience of … discrimination. [After receiving my diagnosis] I immediately told the people that I was with; the same girl friend of mine that I went on that particular trip with. We were with her sister too, so I told both of them … They're my friends; this is how my status came out … " (Amogalang).

Altruism can lead to acceptance of one's status, with AIDS children regarding such behavior as a means of salvaging a spoiled identity. "When I was first informed of the status, three things came to mind. One was to commit suicide. The second, I thought, was that life was a gift from God and that I should not take it out by myself. The third was, I thought, let me go back to Botswana and educate them" (Donald). When HIV+ people help others with the disease, they develop feelings of self-validation and greater life satisfaction (Reeves *et al.* 1999).

Accepting an HIV+ diagnosis does not always associate with AIDS poster children addressing their disease in a timely manner. Sometimes they appear to oscillate between acceptance and denial of their status, failing to treat their disease in a consistent fashion. Precious's story is a case in point. After accepting her status, Precious becomes more and more terrified, unable to develop the mental equanimity required to take her anti-retroviral drugs as prescribed. Consequently she develops resistance her to anti-retrovirals and is struck down by serious opportunistic infections. Her physical condition deteriorates to such a point, that she is derided by others for having full-blown AIDS. She is driven to attempt suicide. Fortunately she recovers, but reports that the experience has made her truly afraid of death. She vows from then on to follow her doctors' orders. Precious goes on to win the Miss HIV Stigma Beauty contest, becoming Botswana's most successful AIDS poster child, a living embodiment of Positive Living.

Not surprisingly AIDS poster children's acceptance of their status can be complicated by elevated fear and uncertainty about how others will react to their HIV+ status. "I was thinking what people are going to say when they hear that I have HIV … I knew that telling one individual would automatically lead to a chain reaction … Because of that worry, it's a huge burden for an individual" (Otsile). AIDS poster children are sometimes subject to horrific mockery and denigration by their peers. "How is it living with HIV? We know you are going to die!" (Precious). Such negative treatment likely originates in the intense fear surrounding the disease. Up until recently HIV/AIDS was considered a death sentence in Botswana, with most of the population having direct experience of others succumbing to the disease (Heald 2006). The denial surrounding the disease also means that some people still believe that HIV/AIDS belongs to a highly stigmatized other – the poor, the uneducated, the promiscuous – never one's immediate social circle.

"I am a human being"

> I am not a victim, because a victim is powerless. I am not a sufferer because suffering is nothing but a helpless prayer. I am not a statistic because statistics are nothing but numbers. I am a human being with flesh and breath.
>
> *(Precious (pseudonym), in* Colors Magazine *2005/6)*

In this stage AIDS poster children engage in a process of de-stigmatizing themselves and establishing themselves on an equal footing to others. They strive to rid themselves of the AIDS victim label, instead casting themselves as people living with HIV/AIDS who have the right, like other human beings, to fully participate in society, free from stigma and discrimination (Robins 2009). A first step involves disclosing one's status to the people one believes are most likely to be accepting: friends and family. For most AIDS poster children this event goes smoothly, especially if other family members are infected or have died from the disease. In other cases family members become worried about the negative impact of an HIV diagnosis on a family's reputation, especially loss of employment. With sexual partners it's quite different; AIDS poster children universally experience immediate rejection, which is not unexpected since HIV is primarily transmitted via sexual contact.

When AIDS poster children inform significant others, they typically receive strong encouragement from members of their support groups. "After meeting with the leader of the support group, she told me she herself is HIV+. That she is public and open about her positive living with HIV for many years. That encouraged me to be open and tell my friends about my HIV+ status" (Otsile). AIDS poster children rationalize that such disclosures assist them in normalizing their condition, reducing any stress likely to negatively impact their health. "It's really going to relieve the burden on us. People will know that we have HIV. We don't need to hide anymore. We are still living like others" (Bontle, wife of an AIDS poster child).

Denial can be so strong that people do not always believe AIDS poster children are HIV+. Donald, Botswana's first AIDS poster child and director of a nationwide support network, reports that people could not believe it when they saw him walking in the streets. Instead of someone looking frail and weak, they saw a healthy person. He was even accused of lying about his status. Up until this point, HIV/AIDS in Botswana was associated with full-blown

AIDS, with an asymptomatic person being a contradiction in terms. Other AIDS poster children report similar incidences. They are accused of working for the government by pretending they are HIV+. To prove their status, they must frequently resort to showing hospital records.

AIDS poster children encounter stigma in their communities. "I was at a club, a girl, she was pointing at me and said: 'Look she's the one; she's the one. She's HIV+.' I think they were thinking I was not supposed to be at the club" (Amogalang). One way AIDS poster children cope with stigma is by asserting that they are superior to others because at least they know their status. "If they are pointing their fingers at me, they don't know their status" (Andrew). AIDS poster children then propose that as a consequence such people don't access treatment early enough and end up seriously ill. "Many people who have been stigmatizing to other people, I saw them to the hospital, critical sick" (Joseph). When condemning stigma, AIDS poster children can appeal to notions of Christian sisterly/brotherly love. "It's very bad because Jesus loves us. God loves us. He loves everyone, whoever you are. You must accept that any human being is your brother, is your sister, is your mama, is your child" (Joseph).

To maintain community respect, AIDS poster children need to present convincing evidence of always engaging in safe sex. If they do not, AIDS poster children may be accused of spreading the virus. They also know that unprotected sex with infected others, including marital partners, can increase their viral loads and lead to re-infection with new viral strains. As a result their medication may become less effective, because HIV drugs are customized to different viral strains and viral loads. AIDS poster children and their spouses report using condoms although they admit difficulty at first. Joseph initially rationalizes that being asked to wear a condom by his wife implies that she is straying. "In the beginning I was worried she is falling in love with someone but in the end I heard what the counselors said ... Then I started to talk to my wife. It's better to put ourselves in a good mood. Use condoms instead of using flesh to flesh, because flesh to flesh is no good" (Joseph). Other AIDS poster children express a preference for mutual masturbation, because they do not like condoms. They clarify their view using a well-known Botswana saying: "A sweet is never eaten with the wrapper – you have to uncover the sweet and then it becomes – sweet" (Paul). Finally, AIDS poster children sometimes indicate they have decided to totally refrain from sex. They explain they do not trust condoms and are far too frightened of re-infection.

AIDS poster children link excessive drinking to sexually irresponsible behavior, explaining that drunkenness leads to a lack of inhibition, unsafe sex and spreading the virus. To overcome this problem, AIDS poster children deliberately create substitutes for hanging out in bars. Otsile forms a football team in his local village, which holds practice sessions twice a week and participates in a regional competition. Together with his friends he also constructs a home-made gym from abandoned car parts in which he regularly works out. Other AIDS poster children make conscious decisions to drink moderately at home with family and friends, or become teetotalers.

"I belong to the world outside"

> Since I was crowned Miss HIV Stigma Free my life has changed in a way ... you are a celebrity in a way, because most of the people they know me. And I don't belong to my family, now I belong to the world outside.
>
> *(Precious)*

When AIDS poster children decide to act more publicly in their fight against the disease, they manifest at least three distinct identities: 1 caring buddy; 2 publicly accountable role model; and 3 political advocate for people living with HIV/AIDS. Acting as a caring buddy involves helping, on a voluntary one-to-one basis, persons newly diagnosed with HIV/AIDS (clients), to adapt to living with the disease, especially disease treatment. Buddies are necessary in countries such as Botswana, where although antiretroviral drugs are free, stigma, fear and poverty keep many from taking advantage of government-sponsored help. A buddy is there "to give a sick person love, care, and support. You make time to remind and to visit your client, to check how well he or she is keeping up" (Paul). As they share a common plight, buddies and clients identify with each other. However, as buddies have more, they can anticipate problems and help in a more proactive and effective way. Paul explains that the buddy-client relationship works both ways. Buddies get positive self-confirmation while clients access compassionate advice from someone they can identify and trust.

Buddies are "the foot soldiers of global health" as they vernacularize biomedical ideas and practices into cultural contexts that otherwise may not be able to absorb them (Robins 2009). Such behavior is a form of active citizenship where individuals fill in the gaps created by inadequate government services, especially outside the main urban hubs. "Even when I did find a doctor willing to come to the country, [he or she] wasn't willing to live in remote rural areas ... So the answer must be that we use already existing people ... living in these communities in new and creative ways" (Dr Ernest Darkoh, Former Operations Manager, Botswana's Treatment Program for HIV/AIDS). Community care-givers of this caliber have proven crucial in Botswana because global health interventions typically fail to provide localized interpretations of prevention and treatment that facilitate conversion to the biomedical principles of Positive Living.

Acting as a publicly accountable public role model comes with many challenges and obligations. AIDS poster children have to be able to identify with their subjects and inspire them, through positive example, to believe in their lifestyle. Precious instructs contestants in the Mr Positive Living Contest: "Positive living means that, as a person living with HIV, you should actively be involved in social activities, but in a positive way. Have a positive impact, attend funeral services, community services, be involved general to the level of your capacity ... be an inspiration, you know, you guys are going to be role models." Donald underscores this point by offering the following warning: "Those young men [Mr Positive Living contestants], who are in the pageant, if they don't change their behavior, people won't believe them. If they go back and become drunk, people won't believe them ... [They] have to be an example to people of what is supposed to be happening!" Of course, becoming a public person is completely new to most AIDS poster children. Not only are they going public with their HIV status, which is rare in itself, but they are committing themselves to be role models of Positive Living. AIDS poster children indicate that such a change is not "an overnight thing." Some of them find comfort in believing that they are among the few who had been chosen for this task by God. Acting as an exemplary HIV role model is their purpose in life.

Becoming a political advocate for people living with HIV/AIDS adds to the mission of AIDS poster children, with political health advocacy being necessary to change social and political power structures and improve government services for the afflicted (Zoller 2005). The opening statement of the 2006 Mr HIV/AIDS Positive Living pageant acknowledges that HIV is a political matter. "You don't have AIDS. I don't have AIDS. We have AIDS. Botswana has AIDS." Precious takes up this mantle when she seeks to raise awareness among the village chiefs, important gatekeepers in disseminating information and changing attitudes about HIV/AIDS. In a village meeting she challenges the chiefs to go and get tested and in doing so become role models for their villagers. An AIDS glass ceiling exists in Botswana, with no public person, politician or wealthy person ever admitting that they have tested positive. Hence HIV/AIDS is regarded as a disease of the poor, which is a paradox for Precious, since she knows that "AIDS does not discriminate." Anyone could get the disease and politicians and the chiefs must join the collective fight against the disease. Changing power relations requires concerted efforts, with AIDS poster children helping to pave the way for greater understanding of the socio-political ramifications of HIV/AIDS.

AIDS poster children understand that they must collaborate with the authorities rather than come into undue conflict with them. They must act as tempered radicals, refraining from "biting the hand that feeds them." For example, they should put to good use the free medication supplied by the government and remain in the workforce. "It is sad that all the time when the national budget is announced … [a]ll our revenue goes to AIDS [and] we refuse to adhere to medication, also refusing to work for ourselves, pretending to be sick. My friends we are not sick, we live with the virus. As HIV+ persons we have a dependency syndrome tendency" (Precious, HIV+ spokesperson). Activists are therefore different to radical anti-consumption activists who think that they must always aggressively confront their adversaries otherwise they cannot convince non-activist consumers and the corporate elite. AIDS poster children have much more demanding advocacy roles as they need to be knowledgeable about, understand, and effectively interact with multiple players, including politicians, scientists, healthcare providers and voting constituents, on most of whom they heavily depend for life-giving resources.

Discussion

How can some individuals – themselves very ill – become effective AIDS poster children for radical behavioral change? Magic Johnson is a success story, but we know little about what it took him to transform from a basketball megastar into a longstanding, highly respected HIV/AIDS spokesperson. Our study suggests that AIDS poster children engage in substantial identity work before taking up such a public role. They embark on a long journey of renaissance, in which they rediscover self-worth and purpose in life. During this process they benefit hugely from free, highly effective biomedical treatment that allows them to lead healthy, productive lives. They also derive much advantage from government-subsidized support groups and buddy networks, where they learn from others by sharing common experiences. Over time they achieve the insights and knowledge that form the basis of their collective and political health identities. Upon entering AIDS poster children pageants, they are often more than ready to become AIDS poster children.

Significantly, some AIDS poster children in Botswana extended their influence into the international arena. Their buddy program became a regional success, with Amogalang, Precious, pageant contestants and national HIV/AIDS sector leaders acting as pioneers in exporting the buddy concept to Swaziland, Lesotho and Namibia. Some of these same AIDS poster children also recounted their stories in television documentaries distributed internationally and represented HIV+ persons in Botswana at global HIV/AIDS conferences held in the USA, Canada and Thailand.

Further reading

Brown, P., Zavestoski, S., McCormick, S., Mayer, B., Frosca, R.M. and Altman, R.G. (2004) "Embodied Health Movements: New Approaches to Social Movements in Health." *Sociology of Health and Illness* 26 (1): 50–80.

Caldwell, M., Kleppe, I., Watson, S., with Matlho, K. (n.d.) *Walk the Talk.* 35-minute documentary, vimeo.com/15311998.

Nolan, S. (2007) *28 Stories of AIDS in Africa.* New York: Walker Publishing Company.

Pisani, E. (2008) *The Wisdom of Whores: Bureaucrats, Brothels and the Business of AIDS.* New York: W.W. Norton and Company.

References

Arnould, E.J. and Thompson, C.J. (2005) "Consumer Culture Theory (CCT): Twenty Years of Research." *Journal of Consumer Research.* 31 March: 868–82.

Berger, J. and Rand, L. (2008) "Shifting Signals to Help Health: Using Identity Signaling to Reduce Risky Health Behaviors." *Journal of Consumer Research* 35 (October): 509–18.

Bury, M. (1982) "Chronic Illness as Biographical Disruption." *Sociology of Health and Illness* 4: 167–82.

Casey, M.K., Allen, M., Emmers-Sommer, T., Sahstein, E., DeGooyer, D., Winters, A.M., Wagner, A.E., and Dun, T. (2003) "When a Celebrity Contracts a Disease: The Example of Earvin 'Magic' Johnson's Announcement that he was HIV positive." *Journal of Health Communication* 8: 249–65.

Colors Magazine (2005/06) "Botswana HIV." Issue 67. sites.colorsmagazine.com/67/index.php?page=3.

Corby, N.H., Enguidanos, S.M. and Kay, L.S. (1996) "Development and Use of Role Model Stories in a Community Level HIV Risk Reduction Intervention." *Public Health Reports* 111(1): 54–58.

Courtney, B.C., Merriam, S.B., and Reeves, P.M. (1998) "The Centrality of Meaning-making in Transformational Learning: How HIV-positive Adults Make Sense of their Lives." *Adult Education Quarterly* 48: 65–84.

Coward, D.D. (1995) "The Lived Experience of Self-Transcendence in Women with AIDS." *Journal of Obstetric, Gynecologic, and Neonatal Nursing* (0884–2175), 24(4): 314.

Heald, S. (2006) "Abstain or Die: The Development of HIV/AIDS Policy in Botswana." *Journal of Biological Science* 38: 29–41.

n.a. (2011) *A Positive Life: Living with HIV.* www.apositivelife.com/livingwithhiv/living-with-hiv.html (accessed 7 June 2011).

NACA (2009) *October to December 2008 Quarterly Report.* Botswana.

Nam, S., Fielding, K., Avalos, A., Dickinson, D., Galothe, T., and Geissler, P.W. (2008) "The Relationship of Acceptance or Denial of HIV-status to Antiretroviral Adherence Among HIV Patients in Urban Botswana." *Social Science & Medicine* 67: 301–10.

Physicians for Human Rights (2007) *Epidemic of Inequality Women's Rights and HIV/AIDS in Botswana & Swaziland* (data collected 2004). Cambridge, MA. hrbaportal.org/?p=403 (accessed 3 January 2010).

Reeves, P.M., Merriam, S.B., and Courtenay, B.C. (1999) "Adaptation to HIV Infection: The Development of Coping Strategies Over Time." *Qualitative Health Research* 9: 344–61.

Robins, S. (2009) "Foot Soldiers of Global Health: Teaching and Preaching Science and Modern Medicine on the Frontline." *Medical Anthropology* 28(1): 81–107.

Royer, A. (1998) "Living with Chronic Illness: Social and Psychological Dimensions." *Research in Sociology of Health Care* 12: 25–48.

Zoller, H.M. (2005) "Health Activism: Communication Theory and Action for Social Change." *Communication Theory* 15(4): 341–64.

16

COSMETIC SURGERY AND SELF-TRANSFORMATION

Shay Sayre

For most women of the world, there is nothing more integral to identity than physical appearance. Although global cultures dictate their own desirable facial and body preferences, Western mass media and celebrity worship have influenced the creation of beauty standards that are emulated by audiences worldwide. Many of these standards are acquired through cosmetic surgery.

Statistics verify that cosmetic surgery in the USA generates around $20 billion each year (Elliott 2009). Even in a downturn economy, women have opted for cosmetic surgery to enhance both their public and private images, and to increase their competitiveness in an ever-shrinking job market. Elliott (2009) attributes surgery's growing popularity to a celebrity culture and advanced surgical technology, while others (Tait 2007; Heyes 2007) suggest that television has contributed too and reflect the processes through which such surgery has become normalized across cultural and global contexts.

Most researchers agree that body image is a social construction that dictates acceptability based upon how a person looks. Much of what has transpired over several decades of study on altering body image through cosmetic surgery has been derived from second-hand narratives and/or statistical reports of post-surgical degrees of satisfaction. This study, however, builds upon a previous self-narrative to develop a longitudinal reflection of plastic surgery as it applies to personal transformation.

First person perfect

Fifteen years ago, when I had plastic surgery, basic surgical procedures produced rudimentary and painful facial reconstruction. In 2011 laparoscopic techniques have all but eliminated the pain and recovery time previously needed to accomplish physical makeovers. What has remained consistent over time, however, is the desire for enhancing one's physical identity through surgical procedures.

By revisiting my self-narrative surrounding the decision to undergo cosmetic surgery (Sayre 2000), this article begins with a synopsis of the introspective chronicle of a first-hand consumption experience that resulted in a personal construction of self. Self, expressed through that self-narrative, represented the sum total of temporal phases (early childhood, adolescence, adulthood) and influencers (media, family, friends, geography, economy) of the author, then in her fifties. Based on Schouten's (1991) notion that plastic surgery is a form of symbolic consumption, that narrative used introspection (Gould 1993) to investigate the surgical consumption experience.

Personal experience as the object of research is an extension of autobiographical consumer research (Hirschman 1990) and literature (Levy 1994; Stern 1989) where researcher-as-subject allows a much richer description of the consumption experience than other types of investigation. Using photographs, objects and text to elicit memories tucked away in the subconscious, I employed a dataset of documents including tape recordings, diaries, photographs and eyewear to serve as tangible and systematic forms of analysis and interpretation. That consumption experience was corroborated by mediated data that occurred concurrently with the author's narration.

Rather than invoking secondary observations or covert research (Langer and Beckman 2005) to detail identity reconstruction, my narrative used author as informant to remove the aberrant signification typical of symbolic communication between researcher and respondent. Researcher as subject allowed a rich description of the consumption experience (cf. Brown 1998). My narrative differed from past auto-ethnographic experiences (Holbrook 1995; Rose 1990; Reid and Brown 1996) in that it drew extensively from Gould's (1993) process of combining introspection with retrospection while simultaneously engaging in analysis of the phenomenon itself.

For authentication, I relied on detailed recordings of the experience as it occurred, using photographs, objects and text to elicit memories that resided in my subconscious. The narrative suggested that past experiences and daily transformations such as social interaction play equal roles in a person's sense of self (Kleine and Kernan 1991). Each individual person negotiates with plastic surgery differently, as each body is different and contains its own unique characteristics. I purport that personal motivations and the meanings associated with cosmetic surgery can only be understood by studying the context in which it was consumed. This chapter reviews those contextual milestones that motivated me to undergo plastic surgery and presents the longitudinal impact it had on my personal identity over time.

What motivated my need for cosmetic surgery? What sort of transformation resulted? How did physical alteration affect my life after 15 years? These questions are approached here by incorporating a review of past narratives with a self-assessment of transformative outcomes.

Previous studies

The literature on cosmetic surgery is voluminous. Recent studies relevant to patients' motivations and self-image are summarized here by motivations, media culture and celebrity, identity, and outcomes.

Motivations for surgery

Although motivations for self-transformation are varied, studies of surgery patients reveal several common themes. A retrospective study of motivations for surgery by Thorpe *et al.* (2004), found that "age appropriateness," "body integrity," and "wanting to look normal" were the prevalent themes.

Slevec and Tiggemann (2010) investigated factors that influence attitudes toward cosmetic surgery in middle-aged women. A sample of 108 women, aged 35 to 55 years, revealed that appearance investment, aging anxiety, and television exposure were unique predictors of endorsement of social motivations for cosmetic surgery. Body dissatisfaction, appearance investment, and television exposure were found to be unique predictors of actual consideration of cosmetic surgery.

Previously, most feminist scholars have railed out against plastic surgery; recently, that view has changed. Negrin (2002: 435), for instance, argues that cosmetic surgery is a "strategy that enables women to exercise a degree of control over their lives in circumstances where there are very few other opportunities for self-realization."

Media culture and celebrity

Media are often cited as motivational factors for considering cosmetic surgery. Goodman's (1996: 67) study of 24 women who underwent cosmetic surgery concluded that the "steady growth of cosmetic surgery as a recourse to bodily discontent or visible signs of aging stems from the media-idealization of women in our culture." Two later studies indicated that television reality shows have stimulated desire for cosmetic alterations in young women (Nabi 2008). Using a detailed analysis of "Extreme Makeover," Heyes (2007: 24) argued that the show "created homogeneous bodies by representing cosmetic surgery as enabling personal transformation through its narratives of intrinsic motivation and authentic becoming, and its deployment of fairy tale tropes."

After analyzing "Nip-Tuck" and "Extreme Makeover," Tait (2007) found that such programs contributed to the process of domesticating cosmetic surgery in a globalized context. By publicizing its benefits, "Makeover" promotes the ability to erase undesirable body and facial features. Both shows, she suggests, contribute to a post-feminist mediascape that renders an inevitability of our culture's surgical turn. Franco's (2008) cross-national analysis of the Dutch, Flemish, and British versions of "Makeover" alerts us to cultural differences in terms of aesthetic allegiances but suggests that the formulaic narrative structure of the reality television format transcends local culture and perpetuates normative gender and class regimes, particularly in combination with other popular reality shows aimed at female spectators.

Elliott (2009) suggested the rise of cosmetic surgical culture results from a celebrity culture and the consumer industries, contending that surgical culture has become increasingly interwoven with major institutional changes of the global electronic economy. People worldwide seeking to reinvent themselves in the image of celebrities and improve their lives are doing so through cosmetic surgery.

Even the popular press offers consumer-oriented approaches to the phenomenon of cosmetic surgery. Surgeon Norman Leaf (2010) presents a history of his experiences over 30 years of doing cosmetic surgery in *Are Those Real?: True Tales of Plastic Surgery from Beverly Hills*, while *The New York Times* reporter Kuczynski's (2006) documentary-like narrative *Beauty Junkies: Inside Our $15 Billion Obsession with Cosmetic Surgery* portrays the quest for self-transformation using plastic surgery.

Surgery and identity

Researchers Askegaard *et al.* (2002) used interviews with 15 women who had cosmetic surgery to examine what motivated their decision to have surgery and ways in which the operation subsequently influenced their lives and self-identity. They found that cosmetic surgery was understood to be part of the individual's reflexive construction of self-identity that led to a focus on issues such as self-determination, self-esteem, and the relationship between body and identity.

Physicians with psychiatric and psychological specialties have also studied the relationship between cosmetic surgery and identity. One study used interview data of 20 female clients of a New York plastic surgeon. Results suggest that cosmetic surgery allows women who undergo these procedures to successfully reposition their bodies as normal bodies. At the same time, it also requires them to "create accounts that reattach the self to the surgically-corrected – but potentially inauthentic – body by invoking both essentialist notions of the self and corresponding notions of the body as accidental, inessential, or degenerated from a younger body that better represented who they truly are" (Gimlin 2000: 62).

Surgical outcomes

Some 37 relevant studies of cosmetic surgery that utilized disparate methodologies suggest that patients overall appeared generally satisfied with the outcome of their procedures (Honigman *et al.* 2010). Physicians' assumptions that a positive change in a patient's physical appearance leads to an improvement in both their self-confidence and self-esteem are not always the case. Two issues of satisfaction emerged from previous studies: patient satisfaction with procedures, and changes in psychosocial status (parameters pertaining to functioning in social and work/study domains). In other words, patients can be satisfied with their appearance change following surgery but may experience no change in psychological characteristics.

A psychological study of 50 female facelift patients (Goin *et al.* 1980) with an average age of 56 years found a 54% rate of psychological disturbance post-operatively with transient depression in a third of patients. Factors that appeared to be associated with poor outcomes included demographic factors, psychological factors such as depression, relationship issues, unrealistic expectations regarding the outcome of the procedure, and previous surgical procedure with which the patient was dissatisfied; this study, however, did not follow patients beyond six months after the operation, with longer-term outcomes remaining unknown.

Whether successful cosmetic intervention actually results in measurable and meaningful improvement in psychosocial satisfaction over time is still unclear. Scant literature on the long-term outcomes of cosmetic intervention as it relates to identity enhancement suggests that this issue deserves further investigation. In an effort to add to the literature of post-surgical impact in personal identity, this section takes a longitudinal perspective to analyze the issue.

Surgery in context

Like the 1960s show "This is Your Life," my narrative of the self incorporated visual devices to re-create life experiences and evoke emotional responses. Introspective self-narration helped me to understand my motivations for electing to undergo cosmetic surgery. I used photo-elicitation (Heisley and Levy 1991; Rook 1991) and object elicitation as stimuli for recollection and understanding. Invoking visual empiricism in a narrative mode to structure my data into accounts, I used photos from friends and family, a high school yearbook, an eyewear archive of my previously worn glasses, and media images from the 1950s and 1960s to act as elicitation devices in a technique discussed by van der Does *et al.* (1992). A collection of spectacles revealed my "extended self" (Belk 1988). These tools were used to evoke recollections of events where meanings lay, recalled for what they revealed about the contextual and motivational reasons for seeking physical change.

Contextual aspects of cosmetic surgery

A few significant events that led to my decision to consider cosmetic surgery are recalled here to characterize the decades of my life (1960s through 1990s) and their impact on my personal evolution.

A photo of myself at age four triggered my earliest clear memory of neighbor children making fun of my spectacles. Elementary school snapshots revealed a transformation from a boyish figure to boys themselves. Junior high was characterized by DA haircuts and hockey skates. In high school I was photographed in cashmere sweaters and pearls for my yearbook.

Those yearbook pages are evidence that body cathexis was an identity factor for my age cohorts. Large breasts were in and fashionable, dictating the use of augmentation devices for those of us who were not naturally endowed. Wearing falsies – a requirement for a flat-chested girl's socially acceptable sexuality – resulted in countless moments of photographic humiliation. Guys always knew who wore falsies and who didn't. My set looked like the fins of a '57 Chevy.

Even during my formative years, fitting into the prevailing trends was a requirement of survival. The type of glasses frames, garment fabric and physical attributes were factors of blending into society as perceived by suburban Clevelandites in the 1950s. So the transition from fads to fantasy was not difficult – we were primed to accept prevailing changes, including those involving physical surgery.

After 20 years of marriages, children and state-hopping, I moved to southern California to teach and nestled into a less cerebral single existence near the beach, which brought me to the point of considering personal indulgence in the form of facial reconstruction. Not that I wanted to be somebody different – just somebody younger. At fifty-something, age was beginning to rear its ugly head and I got caught up in the competitiveness of being a single woman in a sunshine state.

Motivational aspects of cosmetic surgery

Confounded by oppositional pulling typical of cognitive dissonance, I identified six circumstantial factors that contributed to my decision to consider plastic surgery. First and foremost was *where I lived.* According to Wells (1997), we are seriously influenced by where we live and whom we live near. My cosmetic purchase is best understood in the context of southern California, where appearance was (and still is) the established medium of exchange. Living near the beach necessitated constant exposure to youth, physical prowess, and beauty. Weather encouraged abbreviated dress, demanded fitness, and required youthfulness. Who could be oblivious to appearance in the capital of "hedonic consumption" (Hirschman and Holbrook 1982)?

Certainly not me. Every glance in the mirror, every visit to the cosmetic counter screamed the gruesome three-letter word, O-L-D. Simultaneously I felt challenged, threatened and pressured. Visiting my 100-year-old grandmother gave me a slap from the time glove – the inevitable forecast of family genes. At a class reunion in Cleveland, pudgy, pasty people who used to be my peers bulged out of their clothes, exposing tiny blue and red veins. Unlike the residents of Ohio, Orange County folks focused on looking good.

Today, I look around at other aging baby boomers and don't feel so out of place. Only Jane Fonda and Diane Keaton remind us how beauty can be retained simply by undergoing yet another surgical procedure to remove wrinkles, fat and age spots.

The second motivation for considering cosmetic surgery were the *people I knew.* Social influences began with friends who dropped names of plastic surgeons, suggested anti-aging treatments, and recalled their own transformative experiences. A visual census of group norms revealed implant acquisitions, dating much younger men, hair transplants, liposuctioned thighs, and Grecian Formula-improved men who dated women younger than their children.

Today, group norms consist of discussing ailments, wearing sweats and – with the help of blurring vision – seeing others as fait accompli. On the downward slope of 60, priorities change and we become more content with our status quo.

A third influential motivation were the *media*, both past and present. A quick review of media cohorts of the 1950s suggests that females were preoccupied with snagging men (Rosen 1979), and that television's Jeannie ("I Dream of … ") and Samantha ("Bewitched") dedicated their lives to looking good for the men they loved. During what might be called this age of "commercialized feminism" (Ewen 1988), women were encouraged to emulate the fabricated perfection depicted by advertising's ivory complexions, Breck-girl hair and Coke-bottle figures. Culturally conditioned by advertising and the media in the 1950s and 1960s, this pre-baby boomer was socialized to be overly conscious of appearance.

Current mass media provide visual justifications to reinforce perfection norms. Magazine advertisements show men conquering baldness with hair transplants and women enjoying new popularity with saline or silicone implants. Video and film personalities are ageless reminders of the power of surgical restoration. Media images literally scream synchronized endorsements of physical enhancements. According to Slevec and Tiggemann (2010), television exposure is a unique predictor of actual consideration of cosmetic surgery. Baudrillard (1994) may have been on to something: after all is said and done, simulacra is becoming reality for us all – not a copy of the real, but a truth in its own right. One's originality (pre-surgery face) becomes a totally meaningless concept.

A fourth motivation for considering surgery was my *family*. My sister was a devout advocate of surgical solutions to nature's mistakes. She believed the myth of eternal youth and had no intention of abandoning it for reality. She had subjected many parts of her body to the knife: breast implants, facelift and browlift, liposuction. She acted as head cheerleader for me going under a knife.

Today, that sister battles cancer that lurks within her surgically enhanced body. Health and homeopathy are priorities. As hair turns gray and breasts sag, we tend to use our recollection of what we were rather than what we can become.

Finally, the fifth motivation for considering cosmetic surgery was *timing*. Two circumstances existing concurrently with the decision process were tenure review with its economic uncertainty and the departure of a significant other. In the seasons of my life, this was the dead of winter. I recall thinking that if only I were more attractive, more youthful, I could find companionship in a younger person. After all, the men my age were either having their third set of children with "boys with breasts" (Wolf 1998) or fighting off an addiction in group therapy. It was then or never for the business of male-snaring. Most important, I had the money, which is the ultimate enabler of "self-gifting" (Mick and DeMoss 1990).

Today, self-gifting may include eliminating a drooping eyelid or age spot, but our bouts with beauty have subsided. Because being retired takes one out of the public eye, seclusion from all but the media allows us to get comfortable with our aging selves.

Concurrently, the youth culture of California, a physically enhanced peer group, years of media images, an urging sibling, and access to sufficient funds figured prominently in my decision to undergo a facelift. Personal retrospection suggests that external influences had as much to do with surgical consumption as did my self-image. The ideology of youth and narcissism was the engine that drove my decision to consume, and I was caught in the riptide of trends and self-imposed pressure existing within the prevailing social culture.

Outcomes of cosmetic surgery

Immediately following surgery and healing, my self-confidence increased and I felt truly transformed. To my surprise, no one seemed to notice the improvement. No increased flirting from men and no envy from other women. Results of my self-gifting were appreciated internally but were almost devoid of external validation.

Struck by the consumption imagery that filled my diaries, memorabilia and photographs, I now understand why I and my cohorts resorted to cosmetic surgery in hopes of a personal transformation. Aging is not cool, and "senior citizens" were supposed to be parents, not contemporaries. However, as the population ages, beauty is being redefined. Sally Fields, formerly the Flying Nun, appears in pharmaceutical ads and on the cover of *AARP Magazine*. Rock stars of the 1950s continue to attract thousands of young fans, and 60 has become the new 50. As stars from my era re-emerge as youthful examples of the cosmetic age, boomers use their Visa cards to charge mini-facelifts and youth-enhancing procedures like dermabrasion. What was once a secret drastic measure is today an open, normal procedure.

As presented by Askegaard *et al.* (2002), my reflexive identity is deeply inscribed in a social logic. Consumers of cosmetic surgery maintain that "they do it for themselves," yet social pressures – as experienced in my personal narrative – and the accessibility and normalization of a remedy against what was formerly considered to be fate, is strongly constraining the experienced freedom to change one's own looks. In other words, if one *can* do something about one's looks, one *probably* should.

For critics of cosmetic surgery, a manufactured identity is proof that women are victims of a male-dominated society where physical beauty is preeminent. For me, this facelift was just another acquisition, another factor of my personal expression, helping to solidify an unstable and changing self-concept. Rather than a transformation, surgery became a necessary rite of passage that allowed me to blend into the beautiful people of Orange County. It enabled me to snare a younger man for my sixth husband.

Perhaps my positive attitude towards the surgical experience is due to the fact that I did not suffer any factors previously associated with poor outcomes of cosmetic surgery (Honigman *et al.* 2004): no history of anxiety or personality disorder; no need to save a dying relationship; no unrealistic expectations; and no unsuccessful previous surgical procedures.

Typical of previous study results, I was satisfied with my appearance change following surgery but experienced no change in psychological characteristics. The post-surgical impact on my personal identity after 15 years is negligible. Surgery served as a confidence-booster, delivered a feeling of "fitting in" with my friends who were likewise having surgery, and gave me time to focus on inward rather than outward personal attributes.

I'd like to believe that time has revealed the insignificance of cosmetic surgery in transforming my self-image. Sure, I like my mirror reflection more than before surgery, but time has all but erased the improvement. Even thoughts of a "touch up" have surfaced; a recent visit to the same physician determined that, for a mere $17,000, he could inject fat from my stomach into my face to replace dwindling collagen, and suggested some laser resurfacing to remove the prevalent crevices in my cheeks.

At this writing, I view my own surgical transformation as a *rite of passage*, successfully and necessarily completed; a momentary interruption of the aging process. However, most importantly, the experience provided me the opportunity to come to terms with the psychology of acquisition and consumption that ground self-transformation through the alteration of one's physical appearance.

Further reading

Elliott, A. (2008) *Making the Cut: How Cosmetic Surgery is Transforming our Lives*. London: Reaktion Books. (Impact of global body enhancement.)

Featherstone, M. (2010) "Body, Image and Affect in Consumer Culture." *Body & Society* 16(1): 193–221. (Discusses the affective body image and its potential greater visibility through new media technologies with examples taken from digital video art.)

Haiken, E. (1999) *Venus Envy: A History of Cosmetic Surgery*. Baltimore, MD: Johns Hopkins University Press. (An historical perspective of the topic.)

Heyes, C.J. and Jones, M. (2009) *Cosmetic Surgery: A Feminist Primer*. Burlington, VT: Ashgate. (Feminist-based arguments surrounding the topic of cosmetic surgery.)

References

Askegaard, S., Gertsen, M.C., and Langer, R. (2002) "The Body Consumed: Reflexivity and Cosmetic Surgery." *Psychology & Marketing* 19(10): 793–812.

Baudrillard, J. (1994) *Simulation and Simulacra*. Ann Arbor, MI: University of Michigan Press.

Belk, Russell W. (1988) "Possessions and the Extended Self." *Journal of Consumer Research* 14 (September): 139–68.

Brown, S. (1998) "The Wind in the Willows: Literary Theory, Autobiographical Criticism and Subjective Personal Introspection." In J.W. Alba and W. Hutchinson (eds), *Advances in Consumer Research* XXV. Provo, UT: Association of Consumer Research, pp. 25–30.

Elliott, A. (2009) "Drastic Plastic and the Global Electronic Economy." *Humanities, Social Science and Society* 46(4): 357–62.

Ewen, S. (1988) *All Consuming Images*. New York: Basic Books.

Franco, J. (2008) "Extreme Makeover: The Politics of Gender, Class and Cultural Identification." *Television and News Media* 24: 21–34.

Gimlin, D. (2000) "Cosmetic Surgery: Beauty as Commodity." *Qualitative Sociology* 23(1): 77–89.

——(2010) "Imagining the Other in Cosmetic Surgery." *Body & Society* 16(4): 57–76.

Goin, M.K., Burgoyne, R.W., and Goin, J.M. (1980) "A Prospective Psychological Study of 50 Female Facelift Patients." *Plastic Reconstructive Surgery* 65: 436.

Goodman, M. (1996) "Culture, Cohort and Cosmetic Surgery." *Journal of Women and Aging* 8(2): 55–73.

Gould, S. (1993) "The Circle of Projection and Introjection: An Introspective Investigation of Introspection as a Method in Consumer Research: Applications, Issues and Implications." *Journal of Consumer Research* 21 (March): 719–22.

Grosz, E. (1994) Volatile Bodies: Toward a Corporeal Feminism. Bloomington, IN: Indiana University Press.

Heyes, C.J. (2007) "Cosmetic Surgery and the Television Makeover: A Foucauldian Feminist Reading." *Feminist Media Studies* 7(1): 17–32.

Heisley, D. and Levy, S. (1991) "Autodriving: A Photoelicitation Technique." *Journal of Consumer Research* 18 (December): 257–72.

Hirschman, E. (1990) "Consumption Styles of the Rich & Famous." *Association of Consumer Research* 17: 85–155.

Hirschman, E. and Holbrook, M. (1982) "Hedonic Consumption: Emerging Concepts, Methods and Propositions." *Journal of Marketing* 46: 92–101.

Hogue, T. (2009) "Body Modification and Popular Culture." In V. Pitts-Taylor (ed.), *Becoming/Being a Cosmetic Surgery Patient: Semantic Instability and the Intersubjective Self.* Inquiry@Queen's: An Undergraduate Journal 2.

Holbrook, M. (1995) *Consumer Research: Introspective Essays on the Study of Consumption*. Thousand Oaks, CA: Sage.

Honigman, R.J., Phillips, K.A. and Castle, D.J. (2004) "A Review of Psychosocial Outcomes for Patients Seeking Cosmetic Surgery." *PubMed Central*, ncbi.nlm.nih.gov/pmc/articles/PMC1762095/.

——(2010) "A Review of Psychological Outcomes for Patients Seeking Cosmetic Surgery." *Plastic Reconstructve Surgery* 113(4) (April): 1229–37.

Kleine, R. and Kernan, J. (1991) "Contextual Influences on the Meanings Ascribed to Ordinary Consumption Objects." *Journal of Consumer Research* 18 (December): 311–24.

Kuczynski, Alex (2006) *Beauty Junkies: Inside Our $15 Billion Obsession with Cosmetic Surgery*. New York: Doubleday.

Langer, R. and Beckman, S. (2005) "Sensitive Research Topics: Netnography Revisited." *Qualitative Market Research: An International Journal* 8(2): 189–203.

Leaf, Norman (2010) *Are Those Real?: True Tales of Plastic Surgery from Beverly Hills*. Bloomington, IN: iUniverse.

Levy, S.J. (1994) "Interpreting Consumer Mythology: Structural Approach to Consumer Behavior Focuses on Story Telling." *Marketing Management* 2(4): 4–9.

Mick, D.G. and DeMoss, M. (1990) "Self Gifts: Phenomenogical Insights from Four Contexts." *Journal of Consumer Research* 17 (December): 322–32.

Nabi, R.L. (2008) "Cosmetic Surgery Makeover Programs and Intentions to Undergo Cosmetic Enhancement: A Consideration of Three Models of Media Effects." *Human Communication Research* 35 (1): 1–27.

Negrin, L. (2002) "Cosmetic Surgery and the Eclipse of Identity." *Body and Society* 8(4): 21–42.

Reid, R. and Brown, S. (1996) "I Hate Shopping! An Introspective Perspective." *International Journal of Retail and Distribution Management* 24, 4: 4–16.
Rook, D. (1991) "I Was Observed (in Absentia) and Autodriven by the Consumer Behavior Odyssey." In Russ Belk (ed.), *Highways and Buyways*. Provo.
Rose, D. (1990) *Living the Ethnographic Life*. Newbury Park, CA: Sage.
Rosen, M. (1979) "Popcorn Venus or How the Movies Have Made Women Smaller Than Life." In P. Erens (ed.), *Sexual Stratagems: The World of Women in Film*. New York: Horizon Press.
Sayre, S. (2000) "Using Self-narrative to Analyze Consumption: A Case of Plastic Surgery." *Consumption, Markets and Culture* 3(2): 99–127.
Schouten, J. (1991) "Selves in Transition: Symbolic Consumption in Personal Rites of Passage and Identity Reconstruction." *Journal of Consumer Research* 17: 412–25.
Slevec, J. and Tiggemann, M. (2010) "Attitudes Toward Cosmetic Surgery in Middle-Aged Women: Body Image, Aging Anxiety and the Media." *Psychology of Women Quarterly* 34(1): 65–74.
Stern, B. (1989) "Literary Criticism and Consumer Research: Overview and Illustrative Analysis." *Journal of Consumer Research* 16 (December): 322–34.
Tait, S. (2007) "Television and the Domestication of Cosmetic Surgery." *Feminist Media Studies* 7(2): 119–35.
Thorpe, S.J., Ahmed, B., and Steer, K. (2004) "Reasons for Undergoing Cosmetic Surgery: A Retrospective Study." *Sexualities, Evolution and Gender* 6 (2&3): 75–96.
van der Does, P., Edelaar, S., Gooskens, I., Liefting, M., and van Mierlo, M. (1992) "Reading Images: A Study of a Dutch Neighborhood." *Visual Sociology* 7(1): 4–60.
Wells, J. (1997) quoted in "Inside Out." J. Kaplan. *Coast Magazine* (July), 50.
Wolf, Tom (1998) *Bonfire of the Vanities*. New York: McMillan.

II.II

Life cycle and self-change

17

ADOLESCENT CONSUMPTION AND THE PURSUIT OF "COOL"

David B. Wooten and James A. Mourey

In a scene from the 1995 movie *Billy Madison*, Adam Sandler plays the main character, an irresponsible slacker who must go back to school and pass grades 1–12 on his own over a 24-week period to earn the right to run the family business. Along the way he discovers that a classmate had an embarrassing "accident" during a school field trip. An empathetic Billy comes to the rescue by splashing water on the front of his own pants, thereby attracting the children's attention, who begin teasing him about wetting his pants. Without hesitation, Billy exclaims, "Of course I peed my pants! Everybody my age pees their pants; it's the coolest! You ain't cool unless you pee your pants!" Instantly, a behavior that people normally shun becomes the popular thing to do, as every child proceeds to have "accidents." Upon witnessing these bizarre events, the elderly woman conducting the field trip responds, "If peeing your pants is cool, consider me Miles Davis."

This humorous scene illustrates two challenges associated with efforts to understand and reproduce the impression of being "cool." First, not everyone can influence coolness perceptions (Belk *et al.* 2010). Second, even after objects are designated as cool, market responses to them can be unpredictable (Gladwell 1997). To address these challenges, savvy marketers have tried to identify arbiters of cool (Nancarrow *et al.* 2002) and have them endorse their products (Lacayo and Bellafante 1994). Unfortunately, many have found that coolness is a moving target that is reinforced by imitation (Belk *et al.* 2010), but threatened by duplication (Lacayo and Bellafante 1994). In this chapter, we discuss the characteristics of coolness as it has been defined in the literature and performed by adolescents.

Adolescence is typically marked by confusion, ambivalence, emotional instability, and low self-esteem (Majors and Billson 1992). Adolescents are often obsessed with independence, uniqueness, and identity (O'Donnell and Wardlow 2000). For this group, being cool often is a pivotal criterion for acceptance by their peers (Majors and Billson 1992). We begin this chapter by highlighting relevant findings from previous efforts to illuminate the nature of coolness, along with its characteristics and contradictions, such as how too much duplication of cool can result in uncool. We offer insights from primary data focusing on the characteristics of cool and uncool products, sources of information about cool brands, and interpersonal feedback about uncool possessions. We conclude by synthesizing previous research with our original data to shed light on two distinct, but interdependent types of coolness: "standing-out cool" and "fitting-in cool."

What is cool?

Belk *et al.* (2010) describe cool as a particular impression-related verbalized and embodied performance that requires validation by an audience and represents an important source of status in consumer culture, especially among adolescents. Majors and Billson (1992: 3–4) cite the *Dictionary of American Slang*'s definition of cool as being "in complete control of one's emotions; hip but having a quiet, objective, aloof attitude; indifferent to those things considered non-essential to one's individual beliefs, likes, and desires." In addition, their concept of "cool pose" recognizes the performance-oriented nature of coolness. According to Danesi (1994: 38), "Coolness entails a set of specific behavioural characteristics that vary in detail from generation to generation, from clique to clique, but which retain a common essence." Nonchalance, composure, indifference, detachment, confidence, and control are important parts of this essence, as is the ability to disguise awkward or embarrassing behaviors (Danesi 1994). These definitions, combined with associations of coolness with marginalized groups and adolescent subcultures, highlight some interesting and contradictory characteristics of coolness, especially as enacted by adolescents through their consumption practices.

Coolness requires an appearance of indifference toward others. This appearance is exemplified by the efforts of black jazz musicians like Miles Davis and Charlie "Yardbird" Parker to distance themselves from their white audiences (Ellison 1964). Interestingly, acting cool involves an effortless display of indifference toward others' reactions, but being cool requires validation by an audience (Belk *et al.* 2010), often consisting of those toward whom one supposedly is indifferent. Of course, coolness among adolescents often involves indifference, if not defiance, toward adult audiences, but validation by audiences consisting of peers.

Coolness also has been defined as composure (Smitherman 1994), the outward appearance of an inner quality. Interestingly, adolescents appear to be more concerned about outward appearances than inner qualities, as they look for cool in the marketplace more than within themselves (Belk *et al.* 2010). Examples include the increased importance of branded clothing during adolescence (Piacentini and Mailer 2004) and other wearable markers of cool like Livestrong wristbands and Silly Bandz. Moreover, emotional expression undermines coolness perceptions (Majors and Billson 1992), but artistic or stylistic expression enhances it. For example, the signature moves and celebratory behaviors of African-American athletes (Majors and Billson 1992), the "bling" associated with hip hop artists (Smith and Beal 2007), and the creative movements of African-American dancers during the break-dancing era (Majors and Billson 1992), are all cases in point. Contemporary examples include the elaborately staged performances by musicians like Kanye West, Lady Gaga, and Nikki Minaj, in which the artists push creative boundaries yet appear outwardly indifferent to their extreme spectacles.

Coolness also has been characterized as an enviable quality that few people possess, but many pursue (Belk *et al.* 2010). Because marketers have attempted to commoditize coolness, the envy associated with it tends to be actionable, emulative, and, therefore, benign (Belk 2011). Imitation is part of the validation process required for something or someone to be recognized as being cool. However, duplication can threaten perceptions of coolness (Lacayo and Bellafante 1994). As a result, manifestations of coolness tend to vary over time and across groups (Danesi 1994). For example, the roles of opinion leadership and emulation, the trickle-down effect, and the pressures on the elite to innovate are consistent with the process theorized in the sociology of fashion (Simmel 1904). Because imitation appears to have both facilitative and inhibitory effects on coolness, the relationship between the number of imitators and coolness perceptions may resemble an inverted U-shaped curve. A good example is the rise and fall of Livestrong wristbands. Although they originally sold for $1, their popularity led to online auction sites selling them for $10 each. However, once too many people had access to the wristbands, their popularity faded and they were no longer cool (Berger 2008).

Coolness has been associated with blacks (Hebdige 1979) and adolescents (Danesi 1994), and viewed as a coping mechanism or form of rebellion, respectively. Associations of coolness with groups that have had limited access to traditional status hierarchies and limited rule-making authority has led some scholars to theorize style as an example of the status float phenomenon (e.g. Field 1970) and others to view it as an alternative status hierarchy (e.g. Heath and Potter 2004). Interestingly, efforts to commoditize coolness (Gladwell 1997) and the tendency of high-profile celebrities to tout luxury brands in their displays of coolness (Smith and Beal 2007) has resulted in income playing a greater role in the performance of coolness (Belk *et al.* 2010).

In sum, coolness involves indifference toward others (Danesi 1994) and validation by others (Belk *et al.* 2010), sometimes the same others toward whom one supposedly is indifferent. It has been characterized as an outward display of an inner quality, but mainstream consumers tend to pursue the outward symbols more actively than the inner quality they supposedly convey (Belk *et al.* 2010). Coolness should be devoid of emotional expression (Danesi 1994), but often is infused with stylistic expression (Majors and Billson 1992). It provokes imitation, but resists duplication (Lacayo and Bellafante 1994). It is rooted in marginalized groups and youth countercultures, but has been diluted by mainstream values. Because this chapter addresses the interplay between coolness and consumption, we focus our exploration of coolness on its material symbols, the role of imitation, and the threat imposed by duplication.

Brand coolness perceptions

We surveyed 180 college students to explore their perceptions of cool and uncool brands and to identify factors that shape their perceptions. Social factors, which play an important role in identity construction, are among the dominant themes that emerged from our data analyses.

Themes of popularity, prestige, and uniqueness emerge from respondent comments about cool brands, whereas themes of popularity and inferiority surface from comments about their uncool counterparts. The notion that the coolness of brands is affected by associations with certain types of people and that coolness coincides with status emerge from comments about brands at both ends of the coolness continuum. The nexus between brand coolness perceptions and the status of brand users is evident in assertions that brands like Ferrari are cool because they are expensive, endorsed by celebrities, or associated with wealthy people. Alternatively, brands like Payless and Wizards of the Coast were characterized as uncool because of their associations with people with limited wealth or social skills. That is, brands were identified as cool or uncool when they were viewed as part of the consumption constellations of aspirational or dissociative groups, respectively.

Consumption constellations are clusters of products, brands, or consumption activities associated with a social role (Solomon and Assael 1987). Our data suggest that the status of the social role affects the perceived coolness of the brand with which the role is associated. Endorsement or possession by high-status consumers enhances perceived coolness, whereas associations with or accessibility to low-status consumers threatens it. The notion that limited accessibility to low-income consumers enhances a brand's coolness perceptions supports Belk *et al.*'s (2010) contention that economic capital is increasingly needed for consumers to acquire coolness as a form of cultural capital. Associations with age cohorts that are viewed as immature (e.g. tweens) or unfashionable (e.g. senior citizens) also threatened coolness perceptions.

We observed two notable inconsistencies in respondents' perceptions of cool and uncool brands. First, conflicting themes of uniqueness and popularity surfaced in their comments about cool brands. Second, popularity shaped perceptions of brands at both ends of the coolness continuum. On one hand, popularity is a sign of acceptance that enhances a brand's coolness perceptions. On the other hand, popularity diminishes uniqueness, thereby threatening some notions of coolness. To adolescents, certain brands lose their cool when *everyone* uses them, especially parents and younger siblings. Adolescents care about the identities of brand users. They favor brands that are embraced by their peers, but reject those that are adopted by the wrong people (Berger and Heath 2007). Before we address the roles of uniqueness and popularity in shaping brand coolness perceptions, we consider how adolescents learn and apply behavioral guidelines in their efforts to determine who is cool enough to emulate or accept.

Determining the coolness of others

Interviews of 43 young adults (aged 18–23) and critical incident reports from 79 adolescents (aged 15–17) are the primary sources of insights for this section. The interviews address how informants develop an interest in certain brands, how peer influences shape these interests, and how negative feedback from peers shapes brand meanings and acceptance. These data shed light on informants' efforts to find and follow those who are cool and detect and avoid those who are not. The critical incident reports focus on specific interactions in which respondents are targets, observers, or perpetrators of ridicule about consumption choices. These data, which include descriptions of the parties involved in the focal interaction, help illuminate the qualities of uncool possessions, as well as the tensions between cool and uncool consumers.

Looking up to cool others

Given the tendency of adolescents to infer the coolness of brands from the attributes of users, it is not surprising that they look to others to find cool brands. Informants report engaging in such surveillance efforts as watching celebrities, observing popular peers, and emulating or consulting older siblings or close friends. Some describe iterative processes involving observations of socially distant others and conversations with more accessible others in order to identify cool products and have peers validate their judgments.

The notion that peer validation is essential to being perceived as cool is evident in the feedback informants reportedly receive about their consumption choices. For instance, one informant was applauded by his "Jordan-crazy" peers for buying the latest Air Jordan sneakers whereas another was ridiculed for buying a pair that was endorsed by Hakeem Olajuwon and sold at Payless. The different responses to the two products could not be justified by differences in the talent of their respective endorsers alone. At the time, both were premier athletes, but only Jordan was a trendsetter. Olajuwon was not even cool enough for his signature shoe to overcome the stigma associated with the store in which it was sold. The perception of Payless as uncool is consistent with the notions that coolness is an inaccessible quality (Belk *et al.* 2010).

Observing cool others is to adolescents as cool hunting is to marketers. Cool hunting involves observing trendsetters in order to find the next cool thing quickly enough for marketers to introduce their own version and capitalize on its coolness by taking it to a larger mass market (Belk *et al.* 2010). Similarly, adolescents attempt to learn from role models in order to reduce the risk of making uncool choices. Emulating role models also serves as a means by which members of the early and late majority validate the coolness of innovators and early adopters.

Looking down on uncool others

Informants' efforts to acquire behavioral guidelines are accompanied by attempts to apply these lessons to self and others. Some allude to unwritten rules specifying the proper way to display desired brands. For example, informants from Metropolitan Detroit describe the concept of "perping" as a specific type of rule violation that enables insiders to detect imposters (Wooten 2006). Those who are "in the know" do not mix or match brands that have clashing logos or brand images. Violating this rule is seen as "trying too hard" to impress others or "perpetrating a fraud." Violators unwittingly reveal their lack of coolness through their failed attempts to pass themselves off as cool. Insider knowledge aids recognition of cool ideas (Gladwell 1997), enhances the credibility of cool performances (Belk *et al.* 2010), and enables those who belong to distinguish themselves from those who do not (Wooten 2006).

The discussion of perping is consistent with the notion that effortlessness (Nancarrow *et al.* 2002) and authenticity (Southgate 2003) are indicators of coolness. Effortlessness, like nonchalance and indifference, aids in the performance of coolness (Danesi 1994). It also enhances perceptions of authenticity, another quality associated with coolness (Southgate 2003). Inauthentic behavior in the presence of others is antithetical to the notion that coolness reflects indifference toward others. Why should people modify their behaviors in response to others toward whom they are indifferent?

Efforts to detect and avoid uncool others follow from the associative nature of coolness perceptions, especially among adolescents who appear to apply a "cool by association" heuristic. Consumers abandon options that become too popular (Berger and Heath 2007), especially with the wrong crowd (Escalas and Bettman 2005). Thus, cool is a complex and dynamic construct. Adolescents pursue it by monitoring the behaviors of cool and uncool others, emulating the former and avoiding the latter.

Two types of cool

In this section, we synthesize insights from previous studies with findings from our own research to examine the distinction between "standing-out cool" and "fitting-in cool," two types of coolness identified by Belk *et al.* (2010). This distinction may help explain our findings of contradictory themes associated with cool brands, and the same theme associated with brands at different ends of the coolness continuum. The distinction also may help explain why some adolescents pronounce and use the label "cool" differently at different times. The difference between "cooool" and "cool" is like the difference between awesome and acceptable. Below we discuss the distinction and relationship between standing-out cool and fitting-in cool.

Standing-out cool

Standing-out cool is a form of positive deviance that reflects a seemingly effortless display of style and composure. It is consistent with characterizations of coolness as showing detachment from or indifference toward others (e.g. Danesi 1994) and is associated with efforts to distinguish oneself through innovative consumption behaviors (Tian *et al.* 2001). Those who exemplify this type of coolness are likely to be innovators or early adopters of products or styles. Their nose for cool products is sought by cool hunters (Gladwell 1997) and their sense of style is envied by others (Belk 2011). As arbiters of cool, their product endorsements and brand choices provide stamps of approval. Objects are perceived as cool through their associations with these consumers.

Efforts by these consumers to display their individuality and uniqueness lead them to try new things and abandon old ones that become too popular (Berger and Heath 2007). This type of coolness is the focus of discussions about the elusiveness of cool (Lacayo and Bellafante 1994). Marketers try to understand it (Gladwell 1997) and consumers try to emulate it (Belk *et al.* 2010), but their efforts are complicated by the fact that standing-out cool is a moving target.

The resources needed to achieve this type of coolness include creativity, confidence, and charisma in order to identify and adopt new styles that will be validated and copied by others. Anyone can adopt styles that are new and different, but few can do so in a way that provokes the envy of their peers. Those who display uniqueness, but lack charisma, are likely to be dismissed as weirdoes or free spirits.

Fitting-in cool

In contrast to standing-out cool, which involves effortlessness and deviance, fitting-in cool is more effortful and compliant. It is characterized by efforts to gain acceptance through emulative consumption behaviors. In comparison to their standing-out cool counterparts, those who pursue this type of coolness are likely to be more socially anxious (Fenigstein *et al.* 1975), susceptible to interpersonal influence (Bearden *et al.* 1989), and attentive to social comparison information (Lennox and Wolfe 1984). Concerns about fitting in are likely to surface during the early and late majority phases of the new product adoption process, as new styles gain popularity (Rogers 1962). For those who pursue this type of coolness, there are social risks involved with adopting new styles too early or too late. Because these consumers lack the ability to predict the next cool thing and the charisma to influence it, early adoption may lead to fewer hits than misses. However, because being "behind the times" is associated with being uncool, laggards risk being characterized as economically disadvantaged or ostracized as social misfits (Wooten 2006).

Desires to gain approval or avoid disapproval from peers prompt these impressionable consumers to seek safety in numbers when making consumption choices. That is, adolescents attempt to purchase popular brands, if their parents can afford them and are willing to indulge their children. In contrast to their standing-out cool counterparts, who play a role in making brands cool, these consumers attempt to use popular brands to make themselves appear cool. However, as with standing-out cool, economic resources can facilitate efforts to fit in. It may not be necessary for them to be at the top of the economic ladder to achieve this type of coolness, but it may be difficult for those at the bottom of the ladder to do so, especially if it requires spending money to "keep up with the Joneses."

The relationship between types of coolness

The relationship between standing-out and fitting-in cool is like the symbiotic relationship between leaders and followers: each depends on the other for validation of their respective statuses. Standing-out cool is validated by acclamation by a group of adherents, often in the form of emulative behaviors by those who aspire to fit in. Fitting-in cool, on the other hand, is validated by social acceptance by influential others, which often includes those who stand out. Imitation is not only a form of flattery and validation, but also a threat to uniqueness. Consequently, standing-out cool is, by necessity, a moving target as efforts to achieve distinction motivate consumers to abandon old styles in search of new ones. Fitting-in cool also is a moving target, but a more slowly moving one. For this type of coolness, movement is driven by efforts to adopt styles that catch on in the marketplace and distinguish oneself from laggards who eventually adopt and contaminate popular styles. Thus, it is important to consider how the two types of coolness co-exist.

Discussion

In this chapter, we identified the major characteristics associated with coolness, explored the tension between differentiation and conformity evident in various articulations or performances of coolness, and found evidence to support Belk *et al.*'s (2010) distinction between "standing-out" and "fitting-in" cool. We argue that there is a symbiotic relationship between the two types of coolness such that each plays a role in validating the other. However, aspirants of the two types differ markedly in their social motivations and the timing of their product adoptions.

Other tensions also surface in definitions or enactments of coolness. For example, with the commodification of cool, economic capital plays a greater role in acquiring a form of social capital that is most closely associated with groups that historically have had limited access to economic capital (Belk *et al.* 2010). The potential for economic capital to facilitate acquisition of coolness as social capital may depend on local social structures and the type of coolness that one pursues. The relationship between coolness and expressivity also warrants greater attention, especially with the visibility of products as identity signals (Berger and Heath 2007). On one hand, perceptions of coolness coincide with shows of aloofness or detachment (Danesi 1994) – that is, little outward display of emotion. On the other hand, Majors and Billson's (1992) discussion of the roles of stylistic expression and artistic flare in demonstrations of coolness suggests a complex relationship between coolness and expressivity that varies across domains.

Future research also is needed to identify and explore other tensions that are reflected in conflicting definitions of coolness. The forces that give rise to these tensions also warrant further exploration. For example, mass mediated images contribute to the globalization of youth culture, but styles are translated, appropriated, and creolized to fit into local social structures and issues (Kjeldgaard and Askegaard 2006). Coolness, like youth culture in general, also may reflect a balance of global and local influence. Moreover, ascribed characteristics like race or ethnicity have the potential to shape perceptions and constrain performances of coolness (Wooten 2006).

Conclusion

Marketers and adolescents look to each other to find the coolness that often eludes them. Marketers consult "cool hunters" to find opinion leaders to certify the coolness of their offerings (Gladwell 1997). For them, the path to coolness runs through brand associations with consumers on the cutting-edge of cool. If successful, these products "trickle down" to imitators (Simmel 1904). Adolescents monitor trends and consult others to find cool brands to use as props in their social performances. For them, the path to coolness runs through the market to brands that are associated with cool people. That is, they emulate those who are cooool in order to be recognized as cool. Thus, just as coolness inherently involves interactions among the standing-out and fitting-in cool, creating cool seems equally reliant on a symbiotic relationship between marketers and consumers such that understanding the interactions of these two groups is critical to understanding the construct of cool, itself.

Further reading

Danesi, M. (1994) *Cool: The Signs and Meanings of Adolescence.* Toronto: University of Toronto Press. (A thoughtful examination of the behaviors associated with coolness among teenagers.)

Hebdige, D. (1979) *Subculture: The Meaning of Style.* London: Methuen. (A classic treatment of the meanings behind the styles of youth sub-cultures in the UK.)

Majors, R. and Billson, J.M. (1992) *Cool Pose: The Dilemmas of Black Manhood in America.* New York: Lexington. (A comprehensive examination of characteristics and consequences of coolness among inner-city youths.)

References

Bearden, W.O., Netemeyer, R.G., and Teel, J.E. (1989) "Measurement of Consumer Susceptibility to Interpersonal Influence." *Journal of Consumer Research* 15: 473–81.

Belk, R.W. (2011) "Benign Envy." *AMS Review* 1: 117–34.

Belk, W., Tian, K., and Paavola, H. (2010) "Consuming Cool: Behind the Unemotional Mask." In R.W. Belk (ed.), *Research in Consumer Behavior*. Bingley: Emerald Group Publishing Ltd, vol. 12, pp. 183–208.

Berger, J. (2008) "Identity Signaling, Social Influence, and Social Contagion." In M.J. Prinstein and K.A. Dodge (eds), *Understanding Peer Influence in Children and Adolescents*. New York: Guilford Press, pp.181–99.

Berger, J. and Heath, C. (2007) "Where Consumers Diverge from Others: Identity-Signaling and Product Domains." *Journal of Consumer Research* 34: 121–34.

Danesi, M. (1994) *Cool: The Signs and Meanings of Adolescence*. Toronto: University of Toronto Press Incorporated.

Ellison, R. (1964) *Shadow and Act*. New York: Random House.

Escalas, J.E. and Bettman, J.R. (2005) "Self-Construal, Reference Groups, and Brand Meaning." *Journal of Consumer Research* 32: 378–89.

Fenigstein, A., Scheier, M.F., and Buss, A.H. (1975) "Public and Private Self-Consciousness: Assessment and Theory." *Journal of Consulting and Clinical Psychology* 43: 522–27.

Field, G.A. (1970) "The Status Float Phenomenon: The Upward Diffusion of Innovation." *Business Horizons* 13: 45–52.

Gladwell, M. (1997) "The Coolhunt." *The New Yorker* 73: 78–88.

Heath, J. and Potter, A. (2004) *Nation of Rebels: Why Counterculture Became Consumer Culture*. New York: Harper Business.

Hebdige, D. (1979) *Subculture: The Meaning of Style*. London: Methuen.

Kjeldgaard, D. and Askegaard, S. (2006) "The Glocalization of Youth Culture: The Global Youth Segment as Structures of Common Difference." *Journal of Consumer Research* 33: 231–47.

Lacayo, R. and Bellafante, G. (1994) "If Everyone is Hip … is Anyone Hip?" *Time* 144: 48–55.

Lennox, R.D. and Wolfe, R.N. (1984) "Revision of the Self-Monitoring Scale." *Journal of Personality and Social Psychology* 46: 1349–64.

Majors, R. and Billson, J.M. (1992) *Cool Pose: The Dilemmas of Black Manhood in America*. New York: Lexington.

Nancarrow, C., Nancarrow, P., and Page, J. (2002) "An Analysis of the Concept of *Cool* and its Marketing Implications." *Journal of Consumer Behaviour* 1: 311–22.

O'Donnell, K.A. and Wardlow, D.L. (2000) "A Theory on the Origins of Coolness." In S.J. Hoch and R. J. Meyer (eds), *Advances in Consumer Research*. Duluth, MN: Association for Consumer Research, vol. 27, pp. 13–18.

Piacentini, M. and Mailer, G. (2004) "Symbolic Consumption in Teenagers' Clothing Choices." *Journal of Consumer Behavior* 3: 251–62.

Rogers, E. (1962) *Diffusion of Innovations*. New York: Free Press.

Simmel, G. (1904) "Fashion." *International Quarterly* 10: 130–55.

Smith, M.M. and Beal, B. (2007) "'So You Can See How the Other Half Lives': MTV 'Cribs' Use of 'the Other' in Framing Successful Athletic Masculinities." *Journal of Sport and Social Issues* 31: 103–27.

Smitherman, G. (1994) *Black Talk: Words and Phrases from the Hood to the Amen Corner*. New York: Houghton Mifflin Company.

Solomon, M.R. and Assael, H. (1987) "The Forest or the Trees?: A Gestalt Approach to Symbolic Consumption." In J. Umiker-Sebeok (ed.), *Marketing and Semiotics: New Directions in the Study of Signs for Sale*. Berlin: Mouton de Gruyter, pp. 189–217.

Southgate, N. (2003) "Coolhunting with Aristotle." *International Journal of Market Research* 45: 167–89.

Tian, K.T., Bearden, W.O., and Hunter, G.L. (2001) "Consumers' Need for Uniqueness: Scale Development and Validation." *Journal of Consumer Research* 28: 50–66.

Wooten, D.B. (2006) "From Labeling Possessions to Possessing Labels: Ridicule and Socialization Among Adolescents." *Journal of Consumer Research* 33: 188–98.

18

SELF-BRAND CONNECTIONS IN CHILDREN

Development from childhood to adolescence

Deborah Roedder John and Lan Nguyen Chaplin

Individuals use consumer goods to define and communicate their self-concepts to others (Belk 1988; Kleine *et al.* 1995; Sirgy 1982; Solomon 1983; Wallendorf and Arnould 1988). Brands, in particular, are well suited for this purpose given the large number of available brands and the distinctive brand images they reflect (Fournier 1998; Gardner and Levy 1955; Muñiz and O'Guinn 2001; Schouten and McAlexander 1995). For example, some brands of watches are associated with a sophisticated personality (Cartier), while others are thought of as fun (Swatch) or adventurous (Rolex Mariner). By owning and using these brands, consumers can appropriate the associations of sophistication, fun, or adventure into their self-concepts. In this way, consumers form connections between brands and their self-concepts, referred to as self-brand connections (Escalas and Bettman 2003).

Although this line of research has advanced our understanding of adult consumers, we know relatively little about how children use brands to define, express, and communicate their self-concepts. When do children start to make self-brand connections? Are there differences in the type of self-brand connections made by younger versus older children? Prior research has provided important insights into children's knowledge of brands, social meanings they attach to brands, and use of brands to develop perceptions of other people (John 1999). Studies in the area of consumer symbolism, for example, have revealed that children increasingly understand the symbolic meanings attached to owning certain possessions (e.g. fancy house), combinations of possessions, or certain brands (e.g. Nike) – and use this knowledge to judge others by the possessions and brands they own (Achenreiner and John 2003; Belk *et al.* 1984; Chaplin and Lowrey 2010). However, research focusing on the incorporation of possessions and brands into children's self-concepts has been extremely limited.

In this chapter, we examine the development of self-brand connections from childhood to adolescence. Our interest lies in understanding at what age children begin to incorporate brands into their self-concepts and how these self-brand connections change in qualitative ways as children move from middle childhood into adolescence. We present our view of how self-brand connections develop during this important developmental window, and summarize the available evidence from our research regarding changes in self-brand connections from middle childhood to early adolescence.[1] We conclude with discussion of a future research agenda for studying self-brand connections in children and adolescents, identifying research issues that are important in furthering our understanding in the area.

Development of self-brand connections

How are self-brand connections formed? The prevailing view is that consumers engage in a matching process to identify products or brands that are congruent with their self-image (e.g. Birdwell 1968; Dolich 1969; Gardner and Levy 1955). Sirgy (1982) offers self-image/product-image congruity theory as a process explanation. Product cues that evoke certain images (e.g. prestige) are viewed as activating similar beliefs about the self (e.g. high status), which prompts a comparison process to determine whether the product and self-image are congruent. Escalas and Bettman (2003) adopt a prototype matching view, where individuals imagine prototypical users of alternative brands and select ones that maximize similarity to their actual or desired self-concept, thereby forging a self-brand connection.

Underlying these processes are three prerequisites that set the stage for making self-brand connections. First, consumers must have representations of brands that include brand associations – such as personality traits, user characteristics, and reference groups – that can be related to the self. Second, consumers must have a representation of their self-concept that includes characteristics and traits that can be aligned with those possessed by brands. Third, consumers must be able to engage in a comparison process to match brand associations to aspects of their self-concept.

Although we can safely assume that these prerequisites are met by most adult consumers, the same cannot be said for youngsters. In fact, research in psychology and consumer behavior shows that these elements are characterized by age differences, emerging as children move through early and middle childhood. Because these elements are necessary for the formation of self-brand connections, we propose that self-brand connections are also characterized by age differences. Specifically, we propose that self-brand connections develop in nature and scope throughout childhood and only become fully formed by adolescence. Below, we review research relevant to each of these prerequisites and then present our view of how self-brand connections develop in children.

Self-concepts, brand representations, and comparison processes

Major changes occur in the *representation of self-concepts* between early childhood and adolescence (Rosenberg 1986). First, as children grow older, they conceptualize the self in less concrete and more abstract terms. Toddlers and preschoolers construct concrete representations of observable features of the self ("I am a girl"), referred to as "single representations" (Fischer 1980; Griffin 1992). As children approach middle childhood, they are able to see connections between single representations ("I like to laugh" – "I like to joke"), although they typically do not integrate them into a higher-order construct ("I am a jovial person"). This capability emerges during middle-to-late childhood.

Second, self-concepts become more complex as children mature, with a greater variety of self constructs used to describe themselves (Montemayor and Eisen 1977). Research in this area has also found that the content of self-concepts varies with age. Studies analyzing children's descriptions of their self-concepts have found that possessions become a more salient part of the self-concept between early childhood and adolescence, while mentions of other descriptors such as personal characteristics and activities remain constant (Dixon and Street 1975; Snyder 1972). For example, in the Dixon and Street (1975) study, possessions were not part of self-concept descriptions for six-to-eight year olds but surfaced and increased in importance from eight to 16 years of age.

Similar age differences characterize *representations of brands*. Children recognize brands at an early age, as young as three or four years of age. By the time they reach middle childhood (seven-to-eight years of age), children can name multiple brands in many product categories, mention brand names as an important type of product information, and often request products by brand name (John 1999). More changes lie ahead from middle childhood into adolescence. Instead of thinking about brands on a perceptual level – focusing on readily observable concrete features of a product – children begin to understand brands on a conceptual level – composed of more abstract brand associations such as personality traits, user stereotypes, and reference group usage (Achenreiner and John 2003). Developments in cognitive abilities underlie this shift, as children become more analytical in nature and more able to think abstractly about objects in their environment (Ginsburg and Opper 1988).

Social skills in areas such as impression formation and perspective taking are also implicated. Many brand images relate to social status, prestige, and group affiliation, but these brand meanings are understood only when children gain a better understanding of impression formation (Barenboim 1981) and are able to see how these brand cues might be used to form impressions of other people (Selman 1980). The evidence to date suggests that these changes are in place by late childhood, between 10 and 12 years of age (Achenreiner and John 2003; Belk *et al.* 1984; Chaplin and Lowrey 2010).

Finally, age differences also characterize children's *comparison abilities*. Of particular interest to our discussion are findings about the types of dimensions and attributes children use to compare and classify objects. Researchers find that children younger than seven-to-eight years of age focus on perceptual dimensions, whereas older children also consider more abstract unobservable attributes (Denney 1974; Markman 1980; Whitney and Kunen 1983). For example, in a study examining product categorization in children, John and Sujan (1990) found that children four-to-seven years old used perceptual cues (shape, package color), whereas older children (eight-to-ten year olds) used non-observable conceptual cues (taste) as a basis for classifying products.

Self-brand connections from middle childhood to early adolescence

Based on our discussion of developmental changes in three elements – representations of self-concepts, representations of brands, and comparison processes – we propose that self-brand connections develop in the following way. By middle childhood, around seven-to-eight years of age, children define themselves primarily in terms of concrete associations (e.g. physical attributes). However, they are beginning to think more abstractly, which opens up the possibility of defining themselves in more complex and psychological terms (e.g. happy, nerdy). Self-concepts also begin to include possessions, although the abstract and symbolic meanings of possessions (especially brands) are not well understood. Comparisons of the self-concept with brands take place on a concrete level, without consideration of unobservable qualities such as brand personalities and user stereotypes. As a result, self-brand connections are modest in number and are relatively straightforward in nature. For example, self-brand connections might be made on the basis of simply being familiar with or owning a brand.

By the time children approach adolescence, starting around 11–12 years of age, developments in the representation of their self-concepts and brands facilitate the formation of self-brand connections. A heightened appreciation for subtle meanings imbedded in brand images converges with a trend toward defining the self in more abstract and complex terms. The end result is a meeting of self-concepts and brands, where brands gain recognition as useful devices for characterizing the self in terms of personality traits, user characteristics, and reference groups. A greater understanding of the self, combined with social pressures to "fit in" and signal group membership, leads adolescents to be more vigilant about the social implications of owning certain brands. As a result, self-brand connections are more numerous and more abstract, reflecting personal traits and characteristics shared with brand images.

To summarize, our view is that self-brand connections develop from early childhood to adolescence. Specifically, the number of self-brand connections increases from middle childhood through early adolescence. Also, the type of self-brand connections varies by age. In middle childhood, self-brand connections are characterized by concrete and surface-level associations, such as being familiar with or owning a brand. By early adolescence, self-brand connections are characterized by abstract and symbolic associations, such as personality traits, user stereotypes, and reference group membership.

Research on age differences in self-brand connections

Research focusing on self-brand connections in children is quite sparse. Below, we summarize findings from several studies we have conducted with 8–13 year olds to better understand the development of self-brand connections.

In one of our first studies, we examined changes in self-brand connections in children aged eight-to-nine years versus 12–13 years using a standard methodology for eliciting self-concepts from children, called the "who am I?" test (Kuhn and McPartland 1954; Stipek and MacIver 1989; Wang *et al.* 1998). Typically, participants are asked to construct 20 statements to describe themselves ("I am ... ").We modified the test to make it less demanding for younger children by allowing participants to answer the "who am I?" question in any format they wished. Children's responses were content analyzed into five major categories: traits, favorite television/movie characters, hobbies, sports, and clothing brands. Of interest was the fact that clothing brands were the only brands mentioned. Also of interest was the finding that the number of self-brand connections varied by age group, with eight-to-nine year olds mentioning fewer brands than did 12–13 year olds.

In a follow-up study, we examined changes in self-brand connections with the same age groups using measurement methods designed to make the task easier for younger children. First, we asked children the "who am I?" question, but prompted responses with five categories (traits, television/movie characters, hobbies, sports, and clothing brands) that were mentioned by children in the first study. Category prompts were added to reduce the difficulty of retrieving self-descriptive elements for young children. Respondents were allowed to describe themselves in any way they wished – using some, all, or none of the categories provided. The number of brands mentioned by each respondent served as the measure of self-brand connections. The results showed age differences in the number of self-brand connections, similar to those found in the first study, with eight-to-nine year olds mentioning fewer brands than did 12–13 year olds.

Second, we designed a totally new approach for measuring self-brand connections to provide more structure and rely less on verbalization skills, making the task less difficult for younger participants. We asked children to answer the "who am I?" question by making a collage using words and pictures from the five categories identified earlier. Participants were shown five Post-it boards, each one representing a different theme: hobbies, television/movie characters, brand names, sports, and personality traits (see Figure 18.1). Placed on each board were 20 laminated labels and pictures that represented the theme. For example, musical instruments and ballet were included on the "hobbies" board, Gap and Nike were listed on the "brand names" board, and "happy" and "athletic" were placed on the "personality traits" board. Items on the boards were selected on the basis of pilot tests to be familiar to most children in each age group and to

Figure 18.1 Brand name board

resonate with children across ages and genders. For example, most of the brands chosen were popular across age and gender (e.g. Gap, Nike), a few more popular with younger girls (e.g. Limited Too), a few more popular with older girls (e.g. Express), a few more popular with younger boys (e.g. Starter), and a few more popular with older boys (e.g. Fubu).

Participants were asked to look at the labels and pictures on each board and pull off ones unfamiliar to them, providing a measure of how familiar each age group was with the various stimuli, especially brand names. Respondents were then asked to construct their collage by choosing among the familiar pictures and labels and placing them on their collage board, which was a blank Post-it board with adhesive allowing children to easily move pictures and labels from board to board as well as to arrange the elements on their "who am I?" collage as they wished (see Figure 18.2 for an example collage). To ensure that participants were not limited by the choices on the theme boards, blank cards and markers were made available for making up new entries for the self-brand collages.

When completed, photographs of the collages were taken and two measures of self-brand connections were computed: 1 total number of brands placed on a collage; and 2 total number of brands placed on a collage divided by the number of items placed on the collage. Both measures revealed age differences in the number of self-brand connections. More brands appeared on the collages of 12–13 year olds versus eight–nine year olds, even after controlling for any differences in brand familiarity. Analyses of the number of brands as a percentage of total number of collage items revealed the same pattern.

We also examined age differences in the types of self-brand connections using children's explanations for why certain brands were placed on their collages. As expected, explanations from eight–nine year olds suggested concrete types of self-brand connections, usually referring

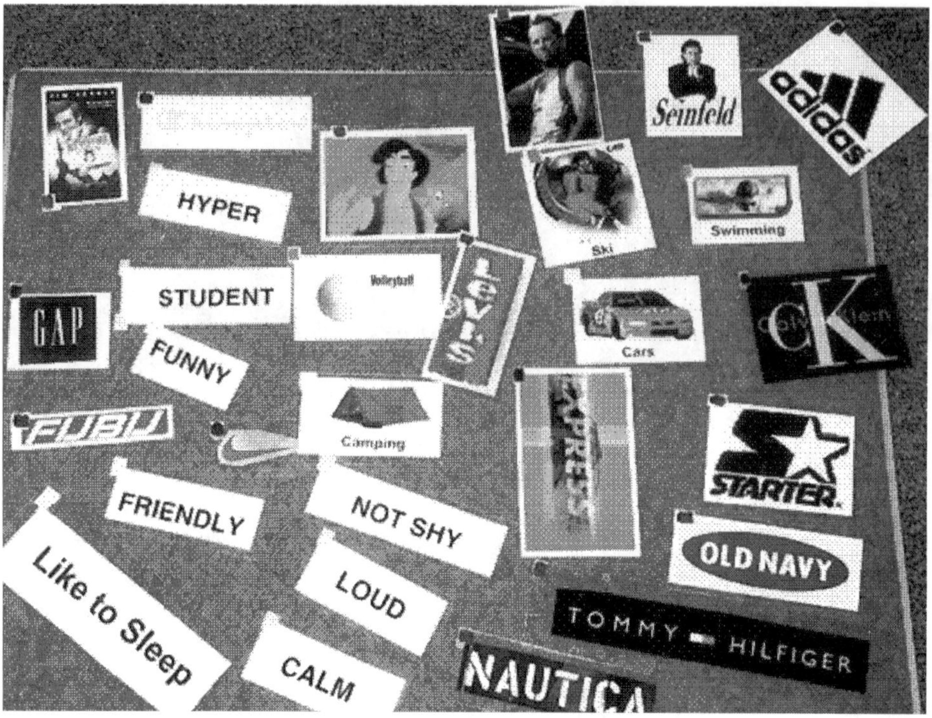

Figure 18.2 Example "who am I" collage

to having or wearing clothes with the brand name. For example, when asked why she put Gap on her collage, a third-grade girl responded, "My mom buys me things from there." In contrast, older respondents provided explanations that were more sophisticated, demonstrating knowledge of the brand's personality or user stereotypes and how that image fit with their self-concept. For example, when asked why Gap was on her collage, a 12-year-old girl responded by saying, "Gap has really clean, preppie clothes. I like to dress preppie so I like the clothes they make." Similar trends were evident when participants were asked to explain why certain brands were not placed on their collages. Explanations from eight-to-nine year olds noted concrete reasons why certain brands were not seen as good descriptors of themselves, often referring to not having or wearing clothes with the brand name ("Because I don't have any clothes from there"). In contrast, 12–13 year olds provided explanations that demonstrated a deeper appreciation for brands and how they compared to their self-image ("It's [Fubu] really for urban boys – you know, the type that wear real baggy pants and talk slang. I'm more of a prep so I go for stuff from places like Gap").

In sum, across studies, our findings show the number and type of self-brand connections change between middle childhood and early adolescence. With increasing age, self-brand connections become more numerous and exhibit a more sophisticated sense of brands and self.

A future research agenda

Our findings provide insight into the development of self-brand connections in children, yet many questions remain unanswered. Here, we focus on two critical questions that warrant attention in future research: What social factors influence the development of self-brand connections? How do self-brand connections change from early to late adolescence?

Social factors influencing self-brand connections

Our research to date has been focused on age (as a proxy for cognitive development) as a factor influencing the development of self-brand connections. It is quite likely, however, that a number of social factors will also shape the development of these connections. Evidence for factors other than age is apparent in our data. For example, we noticed variation among third graders with regard to brand familiarity, number and type of self-brand connections, and sophistication of brand collages. There were a few children in this age group that responded in ways more similar to older children. Why are these children different? Perhaps they are simply ahead of their peers in conceptual abilities or social development. Or, it may be that their social environment provides more experience with brands or more exposure to brands through older siblings or parents. By examining the sources of within-age group differences, we might be able to untangle factors related to cognitive development versus experience versus environment.

In doing so, there are several candidates for immediate examination. First on the list is family environment, which includes factors such as socioeconomic class and presence of older siblings. Our research was conducted with children and adolescents from middle-class homes, and it is possible that lower-income children might develop self-brand connections at a later age due to a relative inability to obtain brands they could connect to their self-concept. Also, the presence of older siblings, who serve as models for the consumption of brands as a way to develop and communicate their self-images, might facilitate the development of self-brand connections at a much earlier age.

A second category worthy of investigation is the media environment. Exposure to traditional forms of advertising and newer forms of social media increases children's awareness of brands, which could spur the development of self-brand connections. Media images of celebrities wearing certain brands elevates the connections of brands with celebrity personalities, which could further the development of self-brand connections. Finally, brand placements in movies, television, online entertainment, and video games is another method of making children and teens more brand aware, and perhaps more likely to embrace brands as ways to develop and express their own self-concepts.

Self-brand connections from early to late adolescence

In our research, we have focused on the development of self-brand connections from middle childhood to early adolescence. Changes in self-brand connections emerging during adolescence promise to be just as interesting. Exploratory findings from our research suggest that the difference between younger and older adolescents is likely to be found in the qualitative nature of their self-brand connections.

We asked a sample of 12–13 and 16–18 year olds to complete the same "who am I?" tasks described earlier. Responses to the open-ended "who am I?" question indicated a similar number of mentions of brands they used to describe *who they are*. However, the 16–18 year olds also mentioned brands in describing *who they are not*. These trends were corroborated by results from the "who am I?" collage task, where the number of brands placed on the collages to reflect *who they are* was similar across age groups. However, age differences surfaced when participants were asked to describe why they had placed brands on their collage. Early adolescents develop connections with brands that help them fit it. For example, a 12-year-old boy says, "My soccer team wears Adidas jerseys so it looks odd if I'm the only one who doesn't … no, it [Adidas] doesn't really mean anything except that you play soccer." Similarly, a 12-year-old girl explains why she chose the brand Abercrombie and Fitch: "All the kids at school have it and so it just feels good to have it." By late adolescence, self-brand connections are made to stand out more so as to blend in. Older teenagers are more confident in who they are (and who they are not), note that having brands to "fit in" is a phase that younger teens go through, and voice the opinion that it is more important to be you and be distinctive. For example, talking about brands, a 17-year-old boy says, "It's like you get noticed more when you are different. It's more important being who you are … Don't bug your parents for things just because you want to be like other people when you don't even feel like it's you." Taking the same tone, a 17-year-old girl says, "I have a *Coach* bag that no one has. I just can't stand it when a group of friends wears the same shoes, same jeans, same everything … I have to be myself."

These initial results reveal that there are qualitative age differences in self-brand connections throughout adolescence that deserve more attention. Further research on adolescent populations would not only help clarify the qualitative differences in self-brand connections, but also would add to a very small but growing literature on adolescent consumer behavior (Ritson and Elliott 1999; Solomon 2003).

Concluding comments

The area of self-brand connections in children rests on less than a handful of studies, but promises an exciting research agenda. We have presented our view of how children forge self-brand connections from middle childhood through adolescence, but have underscored the need for more research. We hope our research agenda is met with enthusiasm, as the proposed studies should help clarify how self-brand connections develop across a wider age range of young consumers as well as how they are influenced by family and media environments.

Note

1 Portions of this chapter were reprinted from Lan Nguyen Chaplin and Deborah Roedder John (2005) "The Development of Self-brand Connections in Children and Adolescents." *Journal of Consumer Research* 32 (June): 119–25.

Further reading

Achenreiner, G.B. and John, D.R. (2003) "The Meaning of Brand Names to Children: A Developmental Investigation." *Journal of Consumer Psychology* 13(3): 205–19. (A key article examining age differences in children's understanding of the perceptual versus symbolic meanings of brands.)

Belk, R.W., Mayer, R.N., and Driscoll, A. (1984) "Children's Recognition of Consumption Symbolism in Children's Products." *Journal of Consumer Research* 10(3): 386–97. (An early influential article examining children's understanding of the symbolic meaning of products.)

Chaplin, L.N. and John, D.R. (2005) "The Development of Self-brand Connections in Children and Adolescents." *Journal of Consumer Research* 32(6): 119–28. (The key article examining self-brand connections in children.)

Chaplin, L.N. and Lowrey, T.M. (2010) "The Development of Consumer-based Consumption Constellations in Children." *Journal of Consumer Research* 36(2): 757–77. (Article examining children's understanding of consumption symbolism and consumer identity.)

John, D.R. (1999) "Consumer Socialization of Children: A Retrospective Look at Twenty-five Years of Research." *Journal of Consumer Research* 26(11): 183–213. (A comprehensive review of how children's knowledge and understanding in consumer matters develops throughout childhood and adolescence.)

References

Achenreiner, G.B. and John, D.R. (2003) "The Meaning of Brand Names to Children: A Developmental Investigation." *Journal of Consumer Psychology* 13(3): 205–19.

Barenboim, C. (1981) "The Development of Person Perception in Childhood and Adolescence: From Behavioral Comparisons to Psychological Constructs to Psychological Comparisons." *Child Development* 52(3): 129–44.

Belk, R.W. (1988) "Possessions and the Extended Self." *Journal of Consumer Research* 15(9): 139–68.

Belk, R.W., Mayer, R.N., and Driscoll, A. (1984) "Children's Recognition of Consumption Symbolism in Children's Products." *Journal of Consumer Research* 10(3): 386–97.

Birdwell, A. (1968) "A Study of the Influence of Image Congruence on Consumer Choices." *Journal of Business* 41(1): 76–88.

Chaplin, L.N. and John, D.R. (2005) "The Development of Self-brand Connections in Children and Adolescents." *Journal of Consumer Research* 32(6): 119–28.

Chaplin, L.N. and Lowrey, T.M. (2010) "The Development of Consumer-based Consumption Constellations in Children." *Journal of Consumer Research* 36(2): 757–77.

Denney, N.W. (1974) "Evidence for Developmental Changes in Categorization Criteria for Children and Adults." *Human Development* 17(1): 41–53.

Dixon, J. and Street, J. (1975) "The Distinction Between Self and Not-self in Children and Adolescents." *Journal of Genetic Psychology* 127(12): 157–62.

Dolich, I. (1969) "Congruence Relationships Between Self Images and Product Brands." *Journal of Marketing Research* 6(2): 80–4.

Escalas, J.E. and Bettman, J.R. (2003) "You Are What They Eat: The Influence of Reference Groups on Consumers' Connections to Brands." *Journal of Consumer Psychology* 13(3): 339–48.

Fischer, K. (1980) "A Theory of Cognitive Development: The Control and Construction of Hierarchies of Skills." *Psychological Review* 87(11): 477–531.

Fournier, S. (1998) "Consumers and Their Brands: Developing Relationship Theory in Consumer Research." *Journal of Consumer Research* 24(3): 343–73.

Gardner, B.B. and Levy, S.J. (1955) "The Product and the Brand." *Harvard Business Review* 33(4): 33–9.

Ginsburg, H.P. and Opper, S. (1988) *Piaget's Theory of Intellectual Development.* Englewood Cliffs, NJ: Prentice-Hall.

Griffin, S. (1992) "Structural Analysis of the Development of their Inner World: A Neo-structural Analysis of the Development of Intrapersonal Intelligence." In R. Case (ed.), *The Mind's Staircase.* Hillsdale, NJ: Erlbaum, pp. 123–46.

John, D.R. (1999) "Consumer Socialization of Children: A Retrospective Look at Twenty-five Years of Research." *Journal of Consumer Research* 26(12): 183–213.

John, D.R. and Sujan, M. (1990) "Age Differences in Product Categorization." *Journal of Consumer Research* 16(3): 452–60.

Kleine, S.S., Kleine, R.E., III, and Allen, C.T. (1995) "How is a Possession 'Me' or 'Not Me?' Characterizing Types and an Antecedent of Material Possession Attachment." *Journal of Consumer Research* 22(12): 327–43.

Kuhn, M.H. and McPartland, T. (1954) "An Empirical Investigation of Self-attitudes." *American Sociological Review* 19(2): 68–76.

Markman, E.M. (1980) "The Acquisition and Hierarchical Organization of Categories by Children." In R.J. Spiro, B.C. Bruce and W.F. Brewer (eds), *Theoretical Issues in Reading Comprehension.* Hillsdale, NJ: Erlbaum, pp. 371–406.

Montemayor, R. and Eisen, M. (1977) "The Development of Self-conceptions from Childhood to Adolescence." *Developmental Psychology* 13(4): 314–19.

Muñiz, A.M., Jr and O'Guinn, T. (2001) "Brand Community." *Journal of Consumer Research* 27(3): 412–32.

Ritson, M. and Elliott, R. (1999) "The Social Uses of Advertising: An Ethnographic Study of Adolescent Advertising Audiences." *Journal of Consumer Research* 26(3): 260–77.

Rosenberg, M. (1986) "Self-concept from Middle Childhood Through Adolescence." In J. Suls and A. Greenwald (eds), *Psychological Perspectives on the Self.* Hillsdale, NJ: Erlbaum, pp. 107–36.

Schouten, J.W. and McAlexander, J.H. (1995) "Subcultures of Consumption: An Ethnography of the New Bikers." *Journal of Consumer Research* 22(6): 43–61.

Selman, R.L. (1980) *The Growth of Interpersonal Understanding.* New York: Academic Press.

Sirgy, M.J. (1982) "Self-concept in Consumer Behavior: A Critical Review." *Journal of Consumer Research* 9(3): 287–300.

Snyder, E.E. (1972) "High School Student Perceptions of Prestige Criteria." *Adolescence* (Spring Issue): 129–36.

Solomon, M. (1983) "The Role of Products as Social Stimuli: A Symbolic Interactionism Perspective." *Journal of Consumer Research* 10(12): 319–29.

——(2003) *Conquering Consumerspace: Marketing Strategies for a Branded World.* New York: Amacom.
Stipek, D. and MacIver, D. (1989) "Developmental Change in Children's Assessment of Intellectual Competence." *Child Development* 60(6): 521–38.
Wallendorf, M. and Arnould, E. (1988) "My Favorite Things: A Cross-cultural Inquiry into Object Attachment, Possessiveness, and Social Linkage." *Journal of Consumer Research* 14(3): 531–47.
Wang, Q., Leichtman, M., and White, S. (1998) "Childhood Memory and Self-description in Young Chinese Adults: The Impact of Growing Up an Only Child." *Cognition* 69(11): 73–103.
Whitney, P. and Kunen, S. (1983) "Development of Hierarchical Conceptual Relationships in Children's Semantic Memories." *Journal of Experimental Child Psychology* 35(4): 278–93.

19
AGING AND CONSUMPTION

Carolyn Yoon, Ian Skurnik and Stephanie M. Carpenter

Introduction

Older consumers do not comprise a monolithic, undifferentiated group. They are heterogeneous with respect to socioeconomic status, health, and cognitive abilities, and come from diverse racial, ethnic and cultural backgrounds. One way of distinguishing among older adults is by age cohort. Members within each age cohort group share a significant number of experiences, goals and values, insofar as they have lived through the same distinctive sequence of societal events. Cohort effects are acknowledged by researchers as being potentially useful for studying aging consumers (Moschis 2009); however, they are infrequently studied because of stringent data and methods requirements needed to disentangle the effects of the cohort from age and life events. Other more common approaches to studying older consumers have characterized aging in terms of changes in biological (e.g. chronological age, physical status), psychological (e.g. self-concept, cognitive age) and social (e.g. social roles, social relationships) states. In the present chapter, we adopt a mix of these perspectives on aging to consider how identity affects consumption in later life.

We provide a review of the extant literature related to age identity. Specifically, we begin by presenting what is known about self-concepts and self-stereotypes among older adults. We then discuss findings that speak to the effects of age and identity on consumption. We focus primarily on three broad areas relevant to consumption: memory and decision-making processes, communication, and consumer expenditures and satisfaction. In so doing, we identify gaps in knowledge and suggest directions for future research.

Age and identity

At the core of identity is the notion of self-concept. We define self-concept broadly as a person's knowledge and beliefs about her- or himself, along with how the person evaluates the knowledge and beliefs. Self-concept can thus refer to an overall, summary evaluation of the self, or to thoughts and evaluations of certain self-attributes. The self-concept in older adulthood embraces not only the actual current self concept, but also remembered past and projected future self-concepts, as well as imagined "ideal" or "ought" selves (Ryff 1991).

Knowledge and evaluations of the self can arise from many sources. A person's own experience is an obvious source of the self-concept: people learn something about their own abilities and preferences by interacting with the world around them. An individual's self-concept is therefore formed in part with reference to other people. Cooley, in one of the earliest psychological investigations into the self-concept, christened the term "looking-glass self" (Cooley 1902) to refer to the process of defining ourselves through others' reactions to us. More recently, social identification theories propose that people's self-concepts are bound up with group membership, and that what a person thinks of her- or himself as an individual depends on the groups to which the person belongs (and on the groups to which the person does not belong; e.g. Tajfel and Turner 1986). As a result, some aspects of a person's self-concept vary or change as interaction partners change, and can change over time as other people react differently to the person. For older adults, the impact of a comparison group on self-concept may increase if the size of the group shrinks, or if contact is lost with other comparison groups from earlier social life.

The extent to which other people determine an individual's self-concept seems driven in part by cultural norms, such as the difference between individualism and collectivism. In more individualistic cultures, people tend to define the self in contrast to others, by selecting and emphasizing distinctive features of the self. In contrast, in more collectivist cultures, people tend to define the self with reference to shared group memberships, deemphasizing differences with close others (e.g. Nisbett 2003). These differences in self-concept have implications for product preferences and marketing promotion: more collectivist consumers, for example, favor advertising messages showing a product's benefit to members of the consumer's close groups, rather than focusing on the benefits to the consumer in isolation (Markus and Kitayama 1991).

It may make more sense to craft marketing appeals to older consumers' self-concepts even when those self-concepts deviate from the perceptions of outsiders. For instance, Barak and Schiffman (1981) report that consumers' own perceived age, rather than chronological age, drives many behaviors and attitudes. Older adults tend to think of themselves as younger than their actual chronological age. According to a survey conducted by the National Council on Aging (2002), 42% of people aged 65 and older considered themselves to be middle-aged or younger.

Possessions and other external objects can also play a role in defining an individual's self-concept (Belk 1988). Consumers may include personal possessions in their self-concept, echoing aphorisms such as "you are what you wear." External possessions that consumers might include in their self-concepts range from individually owned possessions, like clothing and automobiles, to group-dependent experience goods, such as sports team performances.

Stereotypes often distort the self-concepts of individuals of all ages. Because many (not all) stereotypes of old age are negative, the impact of such stereotypes on the self-concepts of older adults can be detrimental. In an influential study that suggests the pervasiveness of such aging stereotypes in society, Bargh *et al.* (1996) demonstrated that younger participants primed with concepts related to elderly stereotypes (e.g. lonely, Florida) walked more slowly down a hallway compared to those primed with control words (e.g. thirsty, private). To the extent that other people view an older adult negatively, or expect negative performance (e.g. declining memory), older adults may integrate these views into their own self-concepts, differentially notice their own behaviors that may seem consistent with a stereotype, and eventually behave in a way consistent with the stereotype. We discuss the effects of stereotypes further in the section on communication.

Hence even the mere mention of a negative stereotype, without applying the stereotype to any particular individual, can affect behavior through the threat created by the stereotype (Steele 1997). Knowledge of the stereotype may create anxiety in a member of a stereotyped group about performance on a stereotype-relevant task. This anxiety can lead to reduced performance on the task, and may eventually lead to self-blame for poor performance, self-handicapping, or withdrawal of effort. As a hypothetical example, consider the role that memory stereotypes of older adults might play in consumer contexts. In purchase decisions that rely heavily on recall of product attributes (e.g. where there is a long delay between learning the attributes and making a purchase, or a product comparison with many complex attributes such as among smartphones), any subtle reminder of a negative stereotype about age can reduce memory performance and may result in a suboptimal decision. Stereotypes about aging also affect older adults externally, as discussed in the later section on communication.

Effects of age

Memory and decision making

Cognitive declines due to normal aging are pervasive and have real consequences for both memory processes and decision-making abilities. Different types of memory processes are differentially influenced by cognitive declines associated with normal aging. Working (short-term) memory tends to be more sensitive to such declines than long-term memory, and explicit memory processes (i.e. conscious and purposeful memory) are more influenced than implicit (i.e. non-conscious) memory processes (see Yoon *et al.* 2009, for a review).

Because working memory is especially sensitive to aging, performance on tasks that rely heavily on working memory ability decline to the greatest extent. Cognitive declines associated with working memory processing can hinder task performance when older adults are instructed to compare several alternatives within a decision context (Cole and Houston 1987). All adults perform better on decision-making tasks when presented with fewer options, but this effect is greatest among older populations (Tanius *et al.* 2009). Older adults also tend to focus more specifically on a narrow range of option dimensions (Abaluck and Gruber 2009), and construct smaller consideration sets while making consumption decisions (Lambert-Pandraud *et al.* 2005). Such findings highlight how memory and information search can influence the choice process, and suggest that older consumers may have better decision performance when presented with fewer choice options.

Explicit memory is also likely to decline across the lifespan, with older adults having worse source memory (e.g. for specific context, speaker) and greater difficulty inhibiting task-irrelevant information, as well as locating relevant information within complex environments. Semantic memory, on the other hand, is often associated with long-term memory processes and general knowledge and is relatively preserved across the lifespan (see Yoon *et al.* 2009, for a review).

Older adults also tend to spontaneously rely on schema-based or heuristic processing more than younger adults (Kim *et al.* 2005). However, the way in which the message is framed can greatly influence the manner of information processing, such that older adults will use a systematic approach to decision making when specifically instructed to consider the reasons for their decisions.

Certain conditions, such as time of day, also lead older adults to process information more systematically (Yoon 1997). Individual differences in patterns of circadian arousal have an influence on memory and decision-making performance (May *et al.* 1993; Yoon 1997). Specifically, peak circadian arousal is associated with peak decision performance, and tends to occur for older and younger adults at different times of day. Older adults typically reach this peak level of circadian arousal in the morning, whereas younger adults peak in the afternoon or evening. These findings suggest that older adults may perform better on complex tasks that require more detailed or elaborate information processing in the morning, while younger adults may benefit from engaging in similarly complex tasks in the afternoon or evening.

Memory for information may also reflect changes in emotion goals that occur across the lifespan. The socio-emotional selectivity theory of aging (Carstensen 1992) proposes that older adults focus on strategies that enhance positive emotion goals by directing their attention away from negative stimuli (e.g. an image of a snake), and toward positive stimuli (e.g. an image of a butterfly). Due to this selective attention for positive information, older adults' memory tends to skew more positive (i.e. the "positivity effect" or "bias") than that of younger adults who typically skew toward a negativity bias (Mather and Carstensen 2005). One proposed driver of this positivity bias in memory among older adults is emotion regulation processing that occurs during the encoding of information (Mather and Knight 2005), which lends support to the notion that the positivity bias is associated with greater cognitive control and preserved cognitive functioning.

Although most forms of memory decline to some extent across the lifespan, familiarity facilitates the ease with which older adults process information involving highly familiar tasks (e.g. shopping at a preferred store). In general, information that has become familiar through repeated exposure is easier to perceive, recognize, learn, and remember than unfamiliar information. The relationship between ease of processing and perceived familiarity has important consequences when designing ways to convey information to older adults; information should be framed in familiar or easy-to-process formats, for example. This relationship also has a number of potentially negative consequences. One of these is the "illusion of truth" effect whereby repeating a statement increases its perceived truth, and familiar information is more likely to be misremembered as true (Begg *et al.* 1992; Hasher *et al.* 1977). This effect is particularly pronounced among older adults (Law *et al.* 1998), and relying on familiarity to infer truth can lead to the negative consequence of misremembering false information as true. Research has suggested, for instance, that being repeatedly exposed to a false health-related claim can lead to misremembering that false claim as true at a later time (Skurnik *et al.* 2005). Such effects have implications for the importance of framing information in a manner that reduces the occurrence of memory distortion.

Judging the truth of information based on its familiarity is a strategy that people use to compensate for less-than-perfect memory retrieval. When detailed records of the past are not available in memory, people often turn to naïve theories about whether the past matches the present, without realizing that they are doing so. For example, McFarland and Ross (1987) had people rate their current dating partner on dimensions such as honesty and intelligence. Two months later, the people rated their partners again, and tried to recall their initial ratings. In many cases people changed their ratings over the two-month period. However, they didn't recall their previous ratings well, and tended to report that the initial ratings – whether more positive or more negative than the later ratings – were consistent with the later ones. Not realizing how their assessments had changed over time, people assumed that their past assessments matched their present feelings.

Naïve theories about consistency of the self across time can exaggerate inconsistency as well. Conway and Ross (1984) found that in response to an ineffective study skills workshop, people (mis)recalled their initial assessments, taken before the study skills program, to be much worse than they actually were. In other words, there was no difference in their before- and after-program performance, but people assumed that the program was effective, which biased their memory reports. For older adults, as memory functions such as recall decline, the influence of theories, such as a belief that the past was consistent with the present, may increase. Because people seem unaware that their memories are inaccurate in such cases, the influence of naïve theories may pass completely unnoticed. In a consumer context, this makes reports of past purchase behavior more difficult to interpret, and may lead to over- or underestimations of brand loyalty in purchase behavior.

Communication

When people communicate with one another, they tend to change their speech patterns to match the perceived needs of their audience in relation to themselves. For instance, sometimes people try to accommodate interaction partners by changing their speech to match the tone, speed, etc., that they expect will be appreciated by the person with whom they are speaking. At other times, people change their speech to enhance their distinctiveness from an interaction partner (Giles *et al.* 1990). When younger adults communicate with older adults, they tend to over-accommodate their speech (Ryan and Cole 1990). That is, younger adults tend to slow their speech rate, raise the pitch of their voices, exaggerate intonations, use tag question formations, and simplify their vocabulary when talking to noticeably older adults – in general, to engage in a variety of "baby talk."

This change in speech patterns is not driven by an actual need or preference for these accommodations by older adults. As with certain effects on self-concept and performance discussed earlier, the change in speech patterns is driven mostly by stereotypes about age, in this case the stereotypes of older adults held by younger adults rather than those held by the older adults themselves. Apart from some hearing loss, the conversational skills of older adults tend not to decline, making many of these conversational over-accommodations unnecessary and potentially patronizing to older adults. In a consumer context, the risk of over-accommodation when communicating with older adults could play a role throughout the purchase decision process, especially where extended interaction is involved. For instance, personal selling is likely to be ineffective with older adults if a salesperson unintentionally engages in "baby talk" with a prospective client. Similarly, follow-up service on a purchase may leave older consumers unsatisfied if the person providing the service over-accommodates their speech based on a poorly calibrated stereotype.

Consumer expenditures and satisfaction

It has traditionally been assumed that older adults are concerned primarily with simple and necessary consumption (e.g. clothing, food, housing, fuel, energy) (Goldstein 1968). More recent accounts, however, indicate increased consumer spending by older adults being directed toward nonessential goods such as leisure, entertainment, personal care, luxury goods, and holiday travel (Ransome 2005). According to survey data of US households collected from 1984 to 2010, expenditure on simple consumption by people aged 65–74 years remained relatively constant (compared to the national household average), while the proportion spent on nonessential goods increased from 66% to nearly 90% of the national household average (US Bureau of Labor Statistics 2010).

A small number of studies suggest that older adults actively engage in consumption patterns that create, change, or expand their identities. For example, older people purchase goods and services that promote lifestyles to ignore or deny the identification of self with what it means to be old chronologically (Gilleard 1996; Szmigin and Carrigan 2000). Consistent with this finding, Schau *et al.* (2009) describe a "consumer identity renaissance," via consumption of leisure goods and services (e.g. travel, entertainment) by older adults (aged 61–83 years). In the financial domain, the wide availability and marketing of services such as long-term care insurance, investment portfolios, and reverse mortgages, speaks to the importance of financial security in later life (Brennan and Ritch 2010).

A better understanding of consumer satisfaction across the lifespan is becoming increasingly important as the number of older adult consumers continues to grow. This includes heightening awareness of products and services in which older consumers may be interested, as well as facilitating older adult satisfaction with the choices that they make. A recent examination by Yoon *et al.* (2010) of cross-sectional data from the American Consumer Satisfaction Index (ACSI) (Fornell *et al.* 1996) reported a phenomenon referred to as the "older and more satisfied" effect. The ACSI is a database containing information on consumer satisfaction with products and services representing more than 200 companies in 45 industries, as well as government agencies (see Yoon *et al.* 2010, for a review). In this report, older adults (aged 65 and above) self-reported higher satisfaction across all product and service categories, with the exception of "media" categories such as television programming, movies, and radio.

The observed increase in self-reported consumer satisfaction across domains is still not well understood, and is likely caused by several factors. Proposed explanations include older adults having extensive experience with products and services and a better sense of their own preferences, as well as the fact that current technologies are more advanced now than ever before. Older adults may also be more likely to satisfice than younger adults if the product or service meets their minimum requirements (Yoon *et al.* 2010).

This higher self-reported satisfaction observed across the lifespan, while certainly providing benefits for consumer well-being, may also lead to detriments in decision quality. This is particularly true if older adult decisions result from memory distortions or challenges experienced due to processing new, unfamiliar information. Areas of the prefrontal cortex associated with deliberative and executive functioning, including working memory, speed of processing, and decision making, have all been shown to follow predictable declines in older adult populations (Mather and Knight 2005). Such declines in cognitive functioning may increase the difficulty that older adults experience when processing and remembering complicated product and purchase information, which could hinder decision quality, increase older adult susceptibility to marketing deception and scams, and decrease post-choice satisfaction.

Conclusions and directions for future research

We have summarized the current state of knowledge from recent research on aging as it relates to identity and consumption. Cognitive deficits caused by aging include physical processes as well as mechanisms involving the effects of negative age stereotypes on older adults and their communications. Even the mention of a negative stereotype can adversely impact the physical and cognitive performance of older people. Older adults are able to compensate for cognitive deficits caused by normal aging through a variety of strategies, including deliberate use of their optimal time of day (usually morning) for cognitively taxing tasks like complex decisions, examination of their reasons for a decision to prime their deliberative thought processes, and consideration of a smaller set of options at a time. Not surprisingly, there are substantial changes in consumption patterns across the life span. Finally, we report that older adults experience greater consumer satisfaction and are more likely to satisfice once their minimum requirements are met.

In general, there is still a dearth of empirical research on consumption in later life. More work is needed to understand consumption motivation and consumption patterns in consumer domains. Much research on age differences focuses on performance that declines with age. It is important to note that for some consumer decisions, older adults may be better off than their younger counterparts. For example, if older adults are more likely than younger adults to satisfice when making a complex purchase decision, it may be that older adults are also less susceptible to certain decision-related problems. Specifically, perhaps older adults' choices do not suffer from having "too many" decision options (Iyengar 2000). If older adults perceive an advantage over younger adults in decision making (i.e. that younger consumers sometimes have trouble focusing on "what's important"), then older adults may adopt this difference as a positive part of their age-related self-concepts.

Another area that deserves further exploration is the role of consumption in shaping and sustaining social identities and relationships. As the consumption rate for consumer goods falls with increasing age, the role that possessions play in defining the self-concept may change as well. Fewer possessions could lead to diminished opportunities to tie the possessions to the self-concept, or it could heighten the importance of the possessions that remain part of an older adult's life. So far, research into issues such as these has just begun to describe the lives of older adults as consumers, and how consumption affects the identities of older adults.

References

Abaluck, J.T. and Gruber, J. (2009) "Choice Inconsistencies Among the Elderly: Evidence from Plan Choice in the Medicare Part D Program." The National Bureau of Economic Research Working Paper No. 14759.

Barak, B. and Schiffman, L.G. (1981) "Cognitive Age: A Nonchronological Age Variable." In K. B. Monroe (ed.), *Advances in Consumer Research* (Vol. 8). Provo, UT: Association for Consumer Research.

Bargh, J.A., Chen, M. and Burrows, L. (1996) "Automaticity of Social Behavior: Direct Effects of Trait Construct and Stereotype Activation on Action." *Journal of Personality and Social Psychology* 71: 230–44.

Begg, I.M., Anas, A. and Farinacci, S. (1992) "Dissociation of Processes in Belief: Source Recollection, Statement Familiarity, and the Illusion of Truth." *Journal of Experimental Psychology: General* 12: 446–58.

Belk, R.W. (1988) "Possessions and the Extended Self." *Journal of Consumer Research* 15(2): 139–68.

Brennan, C. and Ritch, E. (2010) "Capturing the Voice of Older Consumers in Relation to Financial Products and Services." *International Journal of Consumer Studies* 34: 212–18.

Carstensen, L.L. (1992) "Social and Emotional Patterns in Adulthood: Support for Socioemotional Selectivity Theory." *Psychology and Aging* 7: 331–8.

Cole, C.A. and Houston, M.J. (1987) "Encoding and Media Effects on Consumer Learning Deficiencies in the Elderly." *Journal of Marketing Research* 11: 551–63.

Conway, M. and Ross, M. (1984) "Getting What You Want by Revising What You Had." *Journal of Personality and Social Psychology* 47: 738–48.

Cooley, C.H. (1902) *Human Nature and the Social Order*. New York: Scribner's.

Fornell, C., Johnson, M.D., Anderson, E.W., Cha, J. and Bryant, B.E. (1996) "The American Consumer Satisfaction Index: Nature, Purpose, and Findings." *Journal of Marketing* 60: 7–18.

Giles, H., Coupland, N. and Coupland, J. (1990) "Evaluative Perceptions of Interpersonal Communication with Elders." In H. Gile, N. Coupland, and J. M. Wiemann (eds), *Communication, Health, and the Elderly*. Manchester: Manchester University Press.

Gilleard, C. (1996) "Consumption and Identity in Later Life: Toward a Cultural Gerontology." *Ageing & Society* 16: 489–98.

Goldstein, S. (1968) "The Aged Segment of the Market, 1950 and 1960." *Journal of Marketing* 32: 62–68.

Hasher, L., Goldstein, D. and Toppino, T. (1977) "Frequency and the Conference of Referential Validity." *Journal of Verbal Learning and Verbal Behavior* 16: 107–12.

Iyengar, S.S. (2000) "When Choice is Demotivating: Can One Desire Too Much of a Good Thing?" *Journal of Personality and Social Psychology* 79(6): 995–1006.

Kim, S., Goldstein, D., Hasher, L. and Zacks, R.T. (2005) "Framing Effects in Younger and Older Adults." *The Journal of Gerontology: Series B: Psychological Science and Social Sciences* 60B: 215–18.

Lambert-Pandraud, R., Laurent, G. and Lapersonne, E. (2005) "Repeat Purchasing of New Automobiles by Older Consumers: Empirical Evidence and Interpretations." *Journal of Marketing* 69: 97–103.

Law, Sharmistha, Hawkins, Scott A. and Craik, Fergus I.M. (1998) "Repetition-Induced Belief in the Elderly: Rehabilitating Age-Related Memory Deficits." *Journal of Consumer Research* 24 (September): 91–107.

McFarland, C. and Ross, M. (1987) "The Relation Between Current Impressions and Memories of Self and Dating Partners." *Personality and Social Psychology Bulletin* 13: 228–38.

Markus, H. and Kitayama, S. (1991) "Culture and the Self: Implications for Cognition, Emotion, and Motivation." *Psychological Review* 98: 224–53.

Mather, M. and Carstensen, L.L. (2005) "Aging and Motivated Cognition: The Positivity Effect in Attention and Memory." *Trends in Cognitive Sciences* 9: 496–502.

Mather, M. and Knight, M.R. (2005) "Goal-directed Memory: The Role of Cognitive Control in Older Adults' Emotional Memory." *Psychology and Aging* 20: 554–70.

May, C.P., Hasher, L. and Stoltzfus, E.R. (1993) "Optimal Time of Day and the Magnitude of Age Differences in Memory." *Psychological Science* 4: 326–30.

Moschis, G.P. (2009) "Generational Marketing." In I.R. Jones, P. Higgs, and D.J. Ekerdt (eds), *Consumption and Generational Change*. London: Transaction Press.

National Council on Aging (2002) *Survey*. www.ncoa.org (accessed 1 November 2011).

Nisbett, R.E. (2003) *The Geography of Thought: How Asians and Westerners Think Differently … and Why*. New York: The Free Press.

Ransome, P. (2005) *Work, Consumption, and Culture: Affluence and Social Change in the Twenty-First Century*. London: Sage.

Ryan, E.B. and Cole, R.L. (1990) "Evaluative Perceptions of Interpersonal Communication with Elders." In H. Giles, N. Coupland, and J.M. Wiemann (eds), *Communication, Health, and the Elderly*. Manchester: Manchester University Press.

Ryff, Carol D. (1991) "Possible Selves in Adulthood and Old Age: A Tale of Shifting Horizons." *Psychology and Aging* 6(2): 286–95.

Schau, H.J., Gilly, M., and Wolfinbarger, M. (2009) "Consumer Identity Renaissance: The Resurgence of Identity-inspired Consumption in Retirement." *Journal of Consumer Research* 36: 255–76.

Skurnik, I., Yoon, C., Park, D.C., and Schwarz, N. (2005) "How Warnings About False Claims Become Recommendations." *Journal of Consumer Research* 31: 713–24.

Steele, C.M. (1997) "A Threat in the Air: How Stereotypes Shape Intellectual Identity and Performance." *American Psychologist* 52(6): 613–29.

Szmigin, I. and Carrigan, M. (2000) "The Older Consumer as Innovator: Does Cognitive Age Hold the Key?" *Journal of Marketing Management* 16: 505–27.

Tajfel, H. and Turner, J. (1986) "The Social Identity Theory of Inter-group Behavior." In S. Worchel and L.W. Austin (eds), *Psychology of Intergroup Relations*. Chicago, IL: Nelson-Hall.

Tanius, B.W., Wood, S., Hanoch, Y., and Rice, T. (2009) "Aging and Choice: Applications to Medicare Part D." *Judgment and Decision Making* 4: 92–101.

US Bureau of Labor Statistics (2010) Current Expenditure Table (1984 through 2010). www.bls.gov/cex/2010/Standard/age.pdf (accessed 1 December 2011).

Yoon, C. (1997) "Age Differences in Consumers' Processing Strategies: An Investigation of Moderating Influences." *Journal of Consumer Research* 24: 329–42.

Yoon, C., Cole, C.A., and Lee, M.P. (2009) "Consumer Decision Making and Aging: Current Knowledge and Future Directions." *Journal of Consumer Psychology* 19: 2–16.

Yoon, C., Feinberg, F., and Schwarz, N. (2010) "Older Consumers and Satisfaction." In A. Drolet, N. Schwarz, and C. Yoon (eds), *The Aging Consumer: Perspectives from Psychology and Economics*. London: Taylor and Francis.

II.III

Self-esteem and self-support

20

EXISTENTIAL INSECURITY AND THE SELF

Aric Rindfleisch and James E. Burroughs

> No one wants to die. Even people who want to go to heaven don't want to die to get there. And yet death is the destination we all share.
>
> (Steve Jobs 2005)

The self is a fragile thing. Our being is fraught with constant challenges, not the least of which is our need to deny our own death (Becker 1973). The threat of existential insecurity is a fundamental human condition and a frequent theme across art, literature, religion, and science (Kubler-Ross 1969). For example, nearly all of the major players in the Christian *Bible*, ranging from Adam to Jesus, are encased within a narrative of existential angst, the cause and resolution of which provides the meta-narrative for Christianity itself.

Within the realm of social science, this threat has been most systematically explored within the domain of terror management theory (TMT). In brief, TMT posits that, as humans, we are uniquely aware of our impending mortality and that this is a terrifying thought. Thus, in order to function effectively in daily life, we need some means of keeping this terror at bay. According to TMT, protection from existential insecurity is mainly provided by our sense of self in general and the concept of self-esteem in particular. Indeed, as noted by Pyszczynski *et al.* (2004: 436), "the initial impetus for the development of TMT was to address the question of why people need self-esteem." TMT's answer to this question is that self-esteem "provides a buffer against the omnipresent potential for anxiety engendered by the uniquely human awareness of mortality" (ibid.: 435).

Thus, in essence TMT is a theory about the self and how our notion of self is not only threatened by the specter of death, but also provides protection from this terror. In fact, one of TMT's main postulates is the "anxiety-buffer hypothesis," which asserts that strong self-esteem and a positive self-image are important tools for assuaging the fear of death (Greenberg *et al.* 1992). Over the past two decades this hypothesis has received considerable empirical support, as a large and diverse body of research has found that high levels of self-esteem reduce death anxiety across a wide variety of contexts (Pyszczynski *et al.* 2004; Solomon *et al.* 2004).

In sum, prior TMT research has provided a clear conceptual and empirical linkage between existential insecurity and the self. Collectively, TMT's theory and findings suggest that existential insecurity is terrifying because it threatens our sense of self and that this threat can be reduced by bolstering our sense of self-esteem. Our chapter begins by outlining this thesis in more detail and reviewing some of the major findings in this body of research. Despite its conceptual elegance and strong empirical support, TMT has also been the subject of several critiques. In order to provide a balanced perspective, we briefly examine these critiques and discuss their implications for research about the self. We conclude with an attempt to enrich the scope of inquiry between existential insecurity and the self by offering an expanded version of the self. This expanded view is motivated by the premise that TMT's view of the self (i.e. self-esteem) is overly circumscribed and would benefit from a broadened perspective. We present such a perspective and use this expanded view to offer a research agenda for future inquiry into the relationship between existential insecurity and the self.

The terror of existential insecurity and the buffering role of self-esteem

The concept

The concept of self-esteem has played a central role in modern psychology, and has been used to explain a wide range of phenomena from altruism to aggression, individualism to collectivism, and adaptation to learned helplessness (Branden 2001). Although the explanatory role of self-esteem is well established, little is known about self-esteem's ontology. In other words, why is self-esteem necessary? Most (if not all) animals lack a self-concept, yet manage to function quite well. As noted by Pyszczynski *et al.* (2004), it is rather ironic that psychologists have employed self-esteem to explain many *other* things, without extensively considering the explanation of self-esteem's existence.

Terror management theory is one of a handful of psychological theories that examines the "why" of self-esteem, and in so doing, provides a grand narrative of human behavior (Kirkpatrick and Navarrete 2006). The essential premise of TMT is remarkably simple, but profound in its implications: humans are uniquely aware of their mortality, this awareness is terrifying, and this terror drives all thought and activity, including the construction of the self (Greenberg *et al.* 2008; Solomon *et al.* 2004).

According to TMT, over the course of human evolution, as our cognitive capacities developed, we gained the unique ability to contemplate the meaning and finality of our existence. From such contemplations sprang the horrifying possibility that "humans are merely transient animals groping to survive in a meaningless universe, destined only to die and decay" (Pyszczynski *et al.* 2004: 436). If this unsettling premise is true, our lives are no more than a cosmic series of unfolding chemical reactions and all of our thoughts and actions are, in the end, meaningless. Hence, TMT posits that in order to achieve a sense of meaning, we construct a wide variety of "cultural worldviews" (e.g. art, science, religion), which, if ascribed closely, enhance our sense of self-esteem. In short, these worldviews impose order on the universe and signify our position within it. "Thus, for TMT, self-esteem is ultimately a culturally based construction that consists of viewing oneself as living up to specific contingencies of value" (Pyszczynski *et al.* 2004: 437). This striving for cultural validation, in turn, reduces existential insecurity by providing the self with a sense of either literal or symbolic immortality by, "carving out a place in nature, by building an edifice that reflects human value, a temple, a cathedral, a totem pole, a sky scraper, a family that spreads over three generations" (Becker 1973: 5).

The evidence

Over the past two decades, the existential premise of TMT has been empirically tested among hundreds of published studies across more than a dozen cultures (see Burke *et al.* 2010, for a recent review). The majority of these studies employ a simple, yet elegant manipulation which asks participants to answer the question: "What do you think will happen to you after you die?" This condition is typically contrasted with an unpleasant, but not life-threatening, control condition such as experiencing dental pain. The mere act of writing out an answer to the question of one's death typically evokes a powerful response among most participants and primes self-esteem striving and defense of cultural worldviews (Solomon *et al.* 2004). Manifestations of cultural worldview defense encompass a broad array of effects, ranging from increased prejudice to higher levels of prosocial behavior (Mikulincer *et al.* 2003).

A substantial number of TMT experiments have found that high levels of self-esteem (either measured or manipulated) reduce the accessibility of death-related thoughts, attenuate worldview defense, and lessen existential insecurity (Pyszczynski *et al.* 2004). For example, in one of the earliest studies in this domain, Greenberg *et al.* (1992) found that the degree of anxiety induced by viewing graphic videos of death was lower among participants who had their self-esteem boosted via positive affirmation vs. participants in a control condition. Likewise, Harmon-Jones *et al.* (1997) showed that TMT's standard mortality awareness manipulation had a strong effect upon death thought accessibility among participants in a control condition but little effect among those who had their self-esteem stroked by positive feedback. In aggregate, a substantial amount of empirical evidence suggests that self-esteem serves as a strong buffer against existential threats.

In addition to these direct effects, a growing body of research (some of which has been conducted by consumer researchers) indicates that self-esteem also plays an important role as a moderator of the impact of mortality awareness upon worldview defense mechanisms, particularly as they relate to consumer behavior and the concept of the self. For example, Ferraro *et al.* (2005) found that the standard TMT manipulation led participants to make more indulgent and less socially conscious consumption choices, but only when the consumption domain was not an important source of self-esteem. Similarly, Mandel and Smeesters (2008) found that inducing mortality salience prompted participants to purchase (and consume) greater amounts of food. However, this effect primarily occurred among low self-esteem individuals. In interpreting their findings, Mandel and Smeesters suggested that this overconsumption among low self-esteem participants represents an attempt to escape death awareness. Most recently, Rindfleisch *et al.* (2009), found that existential insecurity was related to the degree of self-brand connections among individuals high in materialism but not among those low in materialism. Although materialism is distinct from self-esteem, prior research has shown a clear connection between these constructs (see Burroughs *et al.* 2012 for a review). In sum, the extant TMT literature provides strong evidence that self-esteem serves as both an effective buffer to existential insecurity as well as a moderator of the impact of this insecurity upon a variety of consumption-related outcomes.

Critiques of terror management theory

Despite its conceptual elegance and strong empirical support, TMT has been the subject of numerous critiques (Bonsu and Belk 2003; Cozzolino 2006; Kirkpatrick and Navarrete 2006; Leary and Scherindorfer 1997; Muraven and Baumeister 1997; Proulx and Heine 2006; Rindfleisch and Burroughs 2004). Given TMT's conceptual ambition as a theory that purports to explain nearly the entirety of human motivation and behavior (Becker 1973), this criticism is perhaps not unexpected. In aggregate, these critiques tend to fall into one of three categories: 1 TMT fails to adequately rule out or subsume other theories of human motivation; 2 TMT's assumptions run counter to evolutionary theory; and 3 TMT's traditional means of manipulating mortality salience presents an abstract, and incomplete, view of the death experience. We briefly review each of these critiques in turn.

Alternative explanations critique

A common critique of TMT is that it is just one of many explanations of human motivation and behavior such as self-efficacy theory, sociometer theory, and the meaning maintenance model (Leary and Scherindorfer 1997; Proulx and Heine 2006). According to this critique, humans are confronted by an uncertain and complex world which they must try and make sense of and successfully navigate. This sense making task requires ordering the world into categories, causal effects, and expectancies. When this order is violated, humans experience considerable distress, which forces us to either reinterpret the situation or revise our beliefs (Proulx and Heine 2006). Thus, the fear of death is but one of many potential sources of distress, and hence, TMT may over-emphasize the impact of existential insecurity as a motivating influence. For example, Bonsu and Belk (2003) find that West African communal death rituals help transcend the fear of death by providing a powerful cultural narrative that places death "as part of a broader process of social recognition and identity negotiation" (ibid.: 52). As a corollary, this critique also implies that self-esteem is but one path by which humans can achieve a sense of order and meaning in life.

Evolutionary theory critique

Another critique has been raised by evolutionary psychologists (Kirkpatrick and Navarrete 2006; Navarrete and Fessler 2005). These scholars have expressed two key concerns about TMT. According to TMT, our elaborate coping mechanism (i.e. crafting cultural worldviews), is necessary because without it, the fear of death would become overwhelming and incapacitating. Thus, death anxiety can be viewed as an evolutionary adaptation for survival and self-preservation (Solomon *et al.* 2004). This assumption has been called into question by recent evolutionary research (Navarrete and Fessler 2005). Why would we evolve an adaptation (mortality awareness) that subsequently requires the evolution of another mechanism to counter it? Moreover, humans often sacrifice their life for others (e.g. a mother who runs into a burning building to save her children, a soldier who jumps on a hand grenade to save his comrades). These instances of extreme altruism are not unique to humans; bees will readily sacrifice their lives in defense of the colony. Thus, some evolutionary theorists suggest that we have evolved to preserve our species, but not necessarily ourselves (Kirkpatrick and Navarrete 2006).

This broadened view of the self-preservation instinct presents a potential challenge to TMT's core premise that existential insecurity is hardwired in human evolution. Even if a self-preservation instinct does exist, some evolutionary psychologists question the reason why humans would evolve a response (i.e. death awareness) that is maladaptive. Indeed, from an evolutionary perspective, it seems odd that awareness of death would motivate self-preservation, yet result in existential terror (Kirkpatrick and Navarrete 2006). In terms of the self, this critique directly questions the degree to which self-esteem, in the form of an instinct for self-preservation, is a key component of existential insecurity.

Mortality manipulation critique

As noted earlier, much of the extant TMT research has employed a common manipulation, which asks participants to answer the question: "What do you think will happen to you after you die." This manipulation is designed to induce mortality salience and has successfully produced a wide array of interesting outcomes (Solomon *et al.* 2004). In aggregate, most prior studies have focused on defensive (and self-centered) outcomes such as anger, prejudice, and greed, as participants seek to protect their worldview and maintain their sense of self-esteem (Burke *et al.* 2010). Over the past decade, a growing number of TMT scholars have sought a more expansive array of outcomes, and have found that depending on one's value system, existential anxiety can also lead to positive (and other-centered) outcomes, such as prosocial attitudes and charitable donations (Jonas *et al.* 2002; Joireman and Duell 2005). In aggregate, these findings suggest that both selfish and selfless worldviews can bolster self-esteem when our sense of self is challenged by mortality salience.

In an effort to understand this duality, Cozzolino (2006) has proposed the notion of "dual-existential systems." In essence, he suggests that "individuals process their existence either via a specific and personal existential system, or via an abstract and categorical existential system" (Cozzolino 2006: 278). More specifically, he views TMT's standard mortality salience manipulation as operating via an abstract system and argues that simply asking participants to contemplate their death is likely to lead to a fairly shallow level of cognitive processing that is prevention-focused in nature. To counteract this tendency, Cozzolino and his colleagues (Cozzolino *et al.* 2004) developed a new "death reflection" manipulation designed to operate via a concrete system, leading to deeper levels of cognitive processing and a promotion-focused orientation. This new manipulation was inspired by the phenomenology of individuals who have experienced near-death experiences, which in contrast to the typical TMT experiment, usually exhibits low levels of existential insecurity and high levels of self-esteem. Specifically, this new manipulation is considerably longer than the standard TMT manipulation and seeks to transport participants into a graphic scenario of dying in a high-rise apartment fire. This depiction is replete with graphic details such as "the choking smell of smoke," eyes "filled with tears from the smoke," and a room that is "nearly entirely in flames" (Cozzolino *et al.* 2004: 290). In Cozzolino's scenario escape is not possible and is designed to focus thoughts on the moment of death, as opposed to standard TMT manipulation in which partecipants often focus on what happens after they die. As susch it is designed to be more self-reflective than forward oriented.

To reiterate, Cozzolino and colleagues (Cozzolino *et al.* 2004) argue that their more detailed manipulation operates via a concrete system and leads to a deep level of cognitive processing that is promotion-focused in nature. Their empirical results appear to support this claim; participants treated with their death reflection manipulation exhibit higher levels of prosocial behavior compared to participants treated with TMT's standard mortality salience manipulation. Based on these results, they suggest that "whereas mortality salience leads to worldview defense, death reflection leads to worldview capitulation" (Cozzolino *et al.* 2004: 288). Thus, their theory and results suggest that TMT's emphasis on the role of self-esteem may be overstated, as individuals who deeply reflect upon their death appear to achieve a transcendent state in which selfish strivings give way to selfless acts.

An expanded view of the self

To recap, TMT places considerable emphasis on the role of self-esteem as a means by which humans seek protection from existential insecurity. This foundational premise has received considerable empirical support across a wide range of studies in which mortality is made salient via a brief and abstract manipulation. On the other hand, this premise has received a healthy degree of (both conceptual and empirical) criticism, which suggests that TMT's emphasis on self-esteem may be overstated and/or misplaced. Thus, in the remainder of this chapter we seek to enrich TMT in specific and the concept of existential insecurity in general by offering an expanded view of the self.

Although terror management theory devotes substantial attention to the role and importance of self-esteem, it is largely silent about the broader notion of the self. Indeed, it appears that for TMT scholars, the self is little more than an agent of self-esteem. According to Pyszczynski *et al.* (2004: 435), self-esteem is defined as "a person's evaluation of, or attitude toward, him- or herself." This evaluation is largely determined by the degree to which an individual adheres to culturally approved worldviews, which helps keep the thought of death at bay. Thus, in the realm of TMT, the self is essentially a cognitive entity. Indeed, outside of the use of the term "physically die" in its standard mortality salience manipulation, the bodily aspect of the self is largely absent from the TMT literature. This neglect of the bodily aspect of the self is congruent with TMT's dictum that our minds provide the most effective means of coping with the reality of our physical death.

Hence, TMT can be thought of as a grand narrative of the mind versus the body. In essence, our mortal body is a terrifying entity and this terror can only be abated via a mind fed by a continual stream of self-esteem. Hence, TMT largely views the self as an adaptive cognitive entity that rules our physical body. This dichotomy between the mind and body is illustrated by Pyszczynski *et al.* (2004: 435), who suggest that human culture "is fabricated and given meaning by the mind, a meaning that was not given by physical nature."

The relationship between mind and body is a vexing issue that predates and transcends TMT. Indeed, this deeply ontological issue has engaged many of history's greatest philosophers, including Descartes, James, Kant, and Plato, and is currently being debated across a wide array of scholarly domains, ranging from artificial intelligence to neuropsychology. Although there are many flavors to this debate, mind-body discourse is anchored by two opposing perspectives: one side views the mind as separate from the body (disembodiment) while the other side views mind and body as a broader integrated system (embodiment). Interestingly, neither perspective has received much attention in the extant TMT literature. Thus, in the remainder of this section, we briefly review each perspective and offer some thoughts about its implications for TMT, existential anxiety, and the self.

The disembodied self

As noted earlier, TMT implies that the mind is the (temporary) cure to the problem of the (mortal) body. Thus, TMT scholars appear to view the mind and body as two distinct entities. However, it is largely silent regarding the issue of where the mind resides in relation to the body. This issue is the central focus of scholars who advance the notion of the disembodied self, as they view mind and body as distinct not only in function but also in terms of location (Irwin 2000; Morse and Mitcham 1998; Lenggenhager *et al.* 2007). Specifically, proponents of the disembodied self argue that our notion of self in specific and our mind in general, may reside outside of our physical bodies.

The notion of the disembodied self has been most fervently advanced by scholars (across both psychology and medicine) who have examined near-death experiences (Parnia 2006; Ring 1982). These researchers have found that a substantial number of individuals who have survived medical death experience an awareness of their self as being remote from their (dead) body. This type of out-of-body experience (OBE) goes beyond those who have survived near death, as similar effects have been attained via lucid dreaming, meditation, and hallucinatory drugs (Twemlow *et al.* 1982). According to Irwin (2000), approximately one-third of adults will have an OBE during their lifetime.

Due to its heavy reliance on case studies and self-reports, research on the disembodied self has had difficulty obtaining scientific legitimacy. However, recent advances in technology have now made it possible to create OBE in the laboratory. In one of the first such studies Lenggenhager *et al.* (2007) used virtual reality technology to induce OBE by presenting participants with conflicting visual and somatic stimuli. Their results indicate that "humans systematically experience a virtual body as if it were their own," and thus, "selfhood can be dissociated from one's physical body position" (ibid.: 1098).

The concept of a disembodied self raises a number of interesting questions regarding how the self is affected by existential insecurity. Most importantly, if the self is located outside the body, then it seems possible that it may "survive" physical death. The idea of life after death is found across most cultures, and, even today, is a widely held belief (Bering 2006). In the parlance of TMT, this belief is termed "literal immortality" and is typically regarded as a cultural worldview (Solomon *et al.* 2004). However, this perspective is challenged by Dechesne *et al.* (2003), who find that belief in an afterlife significantly attenuates the impact of mortality salience on worldview defense.

Thus, it appears that how individuals view the location of their self (i.e. within or outside of their body) is an important, but largely untapped, topic in TMT scholarship. Hence, future research on the impact of existential insecurity on the self should reach beyond self-esteem and examine the extent to which the fear of death motivates worldview defense when the self is viewed as a disembodied entity. It would also be intriguing to assess the degree to which self-esteem serves as a buffer against existential insecurity among individuals who experienced an OBE or have strong afterlife beliefs. Another interesting direction for future research is the development of alternative mortality salience manipulations that vary the degree to which they focus on the death of the physical body vs. the death of the self.

The embodied self

In essence, the embodied self is the antithesis of the disembodied self. Although this thesis has been most strongly advanced by cognitive psychologists (Glenberg and Robertson 2000; Wilson 2002), it has also been endorsed by scholars from a diverse set of domains, ranging from philosophy to artificial intelligence (Brooks 1999; Merleau-Ponty 1962). The notion of the embodied self was first formalized by James (1890), who suggested that the self encompasses two distinct but interrelated concepts: me and mine. This interrelationship between these two concepts provides the theoretical foundation for Belk's (1988) seminal treatise on the extended self. Although Belk's essay focuses on the role of possessions as an extension of the self, he notes that our body parts are the elements of "mine" that are most closely related to "me." This observation is closely aligned with Merleau-Ponty's (1962) concept of embodiment as the "bodily aspects of human subjectivity."

According to proponents of the embodied self perspective, all aspects of our cognition (including our sense of self) are strongly influenced by the nature of our bodies (Lakoff and Johnson 1999). As noted by Wilson (2002: 625), "[t]here is a growing commitment to the idea that the mind must be understood in the context of its relationship to a physical body that interacts with the world." One of the most interesting applications of this idea comes from the field of artificial intelligence (AI), which after reaching the limits of disembodied AI, is now rallying around the belief that true AI can best be attained via robots that embody sensory and motor skills in addition to cognitive ones (Brooks 1999). In recent years, the notion of the embodied self has received empirical verification from a series of experiments in which various sensory-motor manipulations have been shown to impact cognitive processes (Schubert and Koole 2009; Stel *et al.* 2012). For example, Schubert and Koole (2009) find that males (but not females) who briefly make a fist exhibit higher perceptions of power, assertiveness and self-esteem. Interpreting these results, they conclude that "cognitive representations and operations are fundamentally grounded in their physical context" (ibid.: 828).

The concept of an embodied self raises intriguing questions regarding how the self is affected by existential insecurity. As noted earlier, traditional TMT theory views self-esteem as essentially a cognitive process (Pyszczynski *et al.* 2004). However, if the self is truly embodied, self-esteem may also have a bodily component. Thus, by utilizing cognitive-based measures (or manipulations) of self-esteem, extant TMT theory may mis-estimate the degree to which self-esteem protects against existential insecurity. To address this concern, future research should consider employing more organic assessments of self-esteem such as physical observation or asking participants to look at a mirror. Likewise, TMT's standard mortality salience manipulation is largely cognitive in orientation ("what do you think will happen to you after you die?"). Thus, it would be interesting to assess the degree to which the results of this manipulation are influenced by various sensory-motor manipulations such as laying still or engaging in physical exercise.

Concluding thoughts

As detailed through the many chapters in this book, the self is a multi-faceted entity shaped by a broad array of influences. According to TMT, the most basic and primitive of these influences is the self's awareness of its impending mortality. For most, this awareness is frightening. Thus, to manage this terror, the self engages in a quest to bolster esteem by seeking a sense of meaning through a set of cultural beliefs. This simple yet profound theory has attracted a considerable degree of both support and criticism. Our own stance lies somewhere in between, as we acknowledge TMT's impressive amount of empirical support, yet caution against its reductionary view of the self. As a means of enriching TMT in specific and our understanding of the influence of existential insecurity in general, we propose that greater attention should be paid to the concept of embodiment, and the role of both the mind and the body as components of self and hazards of existential insecurity. Although we illustrate the role of embodiment by contrasting two opposing perspectives (i.e. the disembodied self and the embodied self), there are clearly various shades in between (Morse and Mitcham 1998). Each self is unique and some may be more or less embodied than others. Locating where we fall along this continuum should enhance both our personal and collective ability to manage the terror of existential insecurity. Indeed, as noted by Illich (1995: 1653), "The ability to die one's death depends on the depth of one's embodiment."

References

Becker, E. (1973) *The Denial of Death*. New York: Free Press.

Belk, R.W. (1988) "Possessions and the Extended Self." *Journal of Consumer Research* 15 (June): 139–68.

Bering, J.M. (2006) "The Folk Psychology of Souls." *Behavioral and Brain Sciences* 29: 453–98.

Bonsu, S.K. and Belk, R.W. (2003) "Do Not Go Cheaply into That Good Night: Death-Ritual Consumption in Asante, Ghana." *Journal of Consumer Research* 30 (June): 41–55.

Branden, N. (2001) *The Psychology of Self-Esteem: A Revolutionary Approach to Self-Understanding that Launched a New Era in Modern Psychology*. San Francisco: Jossey-Bass.

Brooks, R.A. (1999) *Cambrian Intelligence: The Early History of the New AI*. Cambridge, MA: MIT Press.

Burke, B.L., Martens, A., and Faucher, E.H. (2010) "Two Decades of Terror Management Theory: A Meta Analysis of Mortality Salience Research." *Personality and Social Psychology Review* 14 (May): 155–95.

Burroughs, J.E., Chaplin, L.N., Pandelaere, M., Norton, M., Ordabayeva, N., Gunz, A., and Dinauer, L. (forthcoming 2012) "Using Motivation Theory to Develop a Transformative Consumer Research Agenda for Reducing Materialism in Society." *Journal of Public Policy and Marketing*.

Cozzolino, P.J. (2006) "Death Contemplation, Growth, and Defense: Converging Evidence of Dual-Existential Systems?" *Psychological Inquiry* 17(4): 278–87.

Cozzolino, P.J., Staples, A.D., Meyers, L.S., and Samboceti, J. (2004) "Greed, Death, and Values: From Terror Management to Transcendence Management Theory." *Personality and Social Psychology Bulletin* 30 (March): 278–92.

Dechesne, M., Pyszczynski, T., Arndt, J., Ransom, S., Sheldon, K.M., van Knippenberg, A., and Jannsen, J. (2003) "Literal and Symbolic Immortality: The Effect of Evidence of Literal Immortality on Self-Esteem Striving in Response to Mortality Salience." *Journal of Personality and Social Psychology* 84(4): 722–37.

Ferraro, R., Shiv, B. and Bettman, J.R. (2005) "Let Us Eat and Drink, for Tomorrow We Shall Die: Effects of Mortality Salience and Self-Esteem on Self-Regulation in Consumer Choice." *Journal of Consumer Research* 32 (June): 65–75.

Glenberg, A.M. and Robertson, D.A. (2000) "Symbol Grounding and Meaning: A Comparison of High-Dimensional and Embodied Theories of Meaning." *Journal of Memory & Language* 43: 379–401.

Greenberg, J., Pyszczynski, T., Burling, J., Simon, L., Solomon, S., Rosenblatt, A., Lyon, D., and Pinel, E. (1992) "Why Do People Need Self-Esteem? Converging Evidence that Self-Esteem Serves an Anxiety-Buffering Function." *Journal of Personality and Social Psychology* 63(6): 913–22.

Greenberg, J., Solomon, S., and Arndt, J. (2008) "A Basic but Uniquely Human Motivation: Terror Management." In J.Y. Shah and W.L. Gardner (eds), *Handbook of Motivation Science*. New York: Guilford, pp.114–34.

Harmon-Jones, E., Simon, L., Greenberg, J., Solomon, S., Pyszczynski, T. and McGregor, H. (1997) "Terror Management Theory and Self-Esteem: Evidence that Increased Self-Esteem Reduces Mortality Salience Effects." *Journal of Personality and Social Psychology* 72(1): 24–36.

Illich, I. (1995) "Death Undefeated." *British Medical Journal* 311 (23–30 December): 1652–3.

Irwin, H.J. (2000) "The Disembodied Self: An Empirical Study of Dissociation and the Out-of-Body Experience." *Journal of Parapsychology* 64(3): 261–77.

James, W. (1890) *The Principles of Psychology*. London: Macmillan.

Jobs, Steve (2005) *Commencement speech to Stanford University*. news.stanford.edu/news/2005/june15/jobs-061505.html, or watch it at www.youtube.com/watch?v=D1R-jKKp3NA.

Joireman, J. and Duell, B. (2005) "Mother Teresa Versus Ebenezer Scrooge: Mortality Salience Leads Proselfs to Endorse Self-Transcendent Values (Unless Proselfs are Reassured)." *Personality and Social Psychology Bulletin* 31 (March): 307–20.

Jonas, E., Schimel, J., Greenberg, J. and Pyszczynski, T. (2002) "The Scrooge Effect: Evidence that Mortality Salience Increases Prosocial Attitudes and Behaviors." *Personality and Social Psychology Bulletin* 28 (October): 1342–53.

Kirkpatrick, L.A. and Navarrete, C.D. (2006) "Reports of My Death Have Been Greatly Exaggerated: A Critique of Terror Management Theory from an Evolutionary Perspective." *Psychological Inquiry* 17(4): 288–98.

Kubler-Ross, E. (1969) *On Death and Dying*. New York: Simon and Schuster.

Lakoff, G. and Johnson, M. (1999) *Philosophy in the Flesh: The Embodied Mind and Its Challenge to Western Thought*. New York: Basic Books.

Leary, M.R. and Scherindorfer, L.S. (1997) "Unresolved Issues with Terror Management Theory." *Psychological Inquiry* 8(1): 26–9.

Lenggenhager, B., Tadi, T., Metzinger, T. and Blanke, O. (2007) "Video Ergo Sum: Manipulating Body Self-Consciousness." *Science* 317 (24 August): 1096–9.

Mandel, N. and Smeesters, D. (2008) "The Sweet Escape: Effects of Mortality Salience on Consumption Quantities for High- and Low-Self-Esteem Consumers." *Journal of Consumer Research* 35 (August): 309–23.

Merleau-Ponty, M. (1962) *Phenomenology of Perception*. London: Routledge.

Mikulincer, M., Florian, V., and Hirschberger, G. (2003) "The Existential Function of Close Relationships: Introducing Death into the Science of Love." *Personality and Social Psychology Review* 7(1): 20–40.

Morse, J.M. and Mitcham, C. (1998) "The Experience of Agonizing Pain and Signals of Disembodiment." *Journal of Psychosomatic Research* 44(6): 667–80.

Muraven, M. and Baumeister, R.F. (1997) "Suicide, Sex, Terror, Paralysis, and Other Pitfalls of Reductionist Self-Preservation Theory." *Psychological Inquiry* 8(1): 36–40.

Navarrete, C.D. and Fessler, D.M. (2005) "Normative Bias and Adaptive Challenges: A Relational Approach to Coalitional Psychology and a Critique of Terror Management Theory." *Evolutionary Psychology* 3: 297–325.

Parnia, S. (2006) *What Happens When We Die*. Carlsbad, CA: Hay House.

Proulx, T. and Heine, S.J. (2006) "Death and Black Diamonds: Meaning, Mortality, and the Meaning Maintenance Model." *Psychological Inquiry* 17(4): 309–18.

Pyszczynski, T., Solomon, S., Greenberg, J., Arndt, J., and Schimel, J. (2004) "Why Do People Need Self-Esteem? A Theoretical and Empirical Review." *Psychological Review* 130(3): 435–68.

Rindfleisch, A. and Burroughs, J.E. (2004) "Terrifying Thoughts, Terrible Materialism? Contemplations on a Terror Management Account of Materialism and Consumer Behavior." *Journal of Consumer Psychology* 14(3): 219–24.

Rindfleisch, A., Burroughs, J.E., and Wong, N. (2009) "The Safety of Objects: Materialism, Existential Insecurity, and Brand Connection." *Journal of Consumer Research* 35 (June): 1–16.
Ring, K. (1982) *Life After Death: A Scientific Investigation of the Near-Death Experience.* New York: Quill.
Schubert, T.W. and Koole, S.L. (2009) "The Embodied Self: Making a Fist Enhances Men's Power-Related Self-Conceptions." *Journal of Experimental Social Psychology* 45: 828–34.
Solomon, S., Greenberg, J., and Pyszczynski, T. (2004) "The Cultural Animal: Twenty Years of Terror Management Theory and Research." In J. Greenberg, S.L. Koole, and T.A. Pyszczynski (eds), *Handbook of Experimental Existential Psychology.* New York: Guilford, pp. 13–34.
Stel, M., van Dijk, E., Smith, P.K., van Dijk, W.W., and Djalal, F.M. (2012) "Lowering the Pitch of Your Voice Makes You Feel More Powerful and Think More Abstractly." *Social Psychological and Personality Science* 3: forthcoming.
Twemlow, S.W., Gabbard, G.O., and Jones, F.C. (1982) "The Out-of-Body Experience: A Phenomenological Typology Based on Questionnaire Responses." *American Journal of Psychiatry* 139 (April): 450–5.
Wilson, M. (2002) "Six Views of Embodied Cognition." *Psychonomic Bulletin & Review* 9(4): 625–36.

21
COMPENSATORY CONSUMPTION

Derek D. Rucker and Adam D. Galinsky

A core theme surrounding consumption is that people do not consume products and services based solely on their functionality and for utilitarian purposes (Belk *et al.* 1982). One's home, car, clothes, and music often hold additional psychological value to the consumer. As elegantly detailed throughout this book, such consumption opportunities serve as a reflecting pool for the self and one's identity (Chapter 8 and Chapter 9, this volume). In addition, consumption is also a stage on which individuals signal their identity to others as well as indicate their connections to groups and other individuals in society (Chapter 27, this volume).

In the present chapter we focus on a particular use of consumption: the reliance on consumption as a tool to ward off psychological threats. Specifically, we discuss the idea that consumption can be motivated in an effort to assuage a broad range of psychological threats from one's intellectual ability to a sense of mastery over one's environment. The aim of the chapter is to familiarize the reader with the concept of compensatory consumption, provide a sample of the type of threats that are compensated, discuss representative moderators of consumers' engagement in compensatory consumption, and speak to the psychological value of consumption in response to threats.

Compensatory consumption

We use the term *compensatory consumption* to define the desire for, acquisition, or use of products to respond to a psychological need or deficit. By compensatory, we mean that consumption is undertaken, implicitly or explicitly, to offset a threat to one's identity or preferred psychological state. By consumption, we refer to both the physical consumption of goods (e.g. wearing clothing, eating a meal) as well as consumers' product preferences (e.g. wanting a particular brand, preferring one snack to another).

The theoretical roots of compensatory consumption are partially based in the work of Wicklund and Gollwitzer (1981, 1982) on symbolic self-completion. In their writings, Wicklund and Gollwitzer suggest that at times individuals' identities come under fire. For instance, when academics have a paper rejected, it can lead them to question their intellectual scholarship, or athletes who finish last in a race may question their own athleticism. One response to such a threat would be to address or cope with the threat in a direct fashion. For example, the academic might rewrite the paper for another journal, or the athlete might train harder for the next race.

However, according to Wicklund and Gollwitzer (1981), people can engage in behaviors that allow them to symbolically signal mastery, competence, or completeness of the threatened dimension. That is, individuals can seek out what they termed, "symbols of completeness." Indeed, Harmon-Jones *et al.* (2009) found that professors who were not ranked highly in research – assessed via publications, citations, and their department ranking – were more likely to refer to professional titles such as professor or PhD in their email signatures.

Consumption of products and services provides one venue by which individuals can symbolically demonstrate mastery of a threatened dimension – that is, the acquisition or display of certain consumer products can serve as symbols of completeness. For example, the rejected scholar might buy a frame to publicly display his PhD even though this does not address his rejected paper. Similarly, the athlete might overhaul her athletic wardrobe even though this does little to affect her loss on the field. Indeed, in an early demonstration of consumption as a compensatory tool, Wicklund and Gollwitzer (1982) found that MBA students who lacked certain indicators of business success (e.g. a high GPA, multiple job offers), were more inclined to display other indicators of business success (e.g. expensive suits and watches). In such circumstances, although consumption did not change the reality of the MBA's performance, it may mitigate or eliminate the threatened aspect of the self.

Evidence for compensatory consumption

In this section we review evidence for compensatory consumption. Importantly, we provide evidence across a broad array of threat as a testimony to the broad and flexible use of consumption as a compensatory device (see also Chapter 22, this volume, for a more detailed identity perspective). Specifically, we review work that suggests consumption can be used as a means to respond to threats to one's masculinity, intelligence, power, personal freedom, and system beliefs. It is also worth noting that this set of findings is not meant to be an exhaustive list, but to offer an ample foundation for the claim that consumers use consumption in a compensatory manner.

Threats to one's masculinity

Willer *et al.* (2010) examined men's preference for masculine products when their identity as a man was threatened. Male and female participants were given feedback that they had masculine or feminine identities. Subsequently, participants were asked to choose their favorite vehicle from a selection of four cars, one with a strong association with masculinity (i.e. an SUV) and three that did not have a strong association (i.e. minivan, coupe, and sedan). When asked to choose their favorite vehicle, Willer *et al.* (2010) found that males who had been told they had a feminine identity were much more inclined to choose the SUV. For such males, only the SUV had the ability to restore their shaken sense of masculinity. No differences were found among females whose femininity was threatened, presumably because none of the vehicles were associated with femininity and thus the choice did not serve as an opportunity to compensate through consumption.

Threats to one's intelligence

Threats need not be trigged by blatant shortcomings in performance or clear feedback, as in the case of Willer and colleagues (2011). For example, Gao *et al.* (2009) have shown it is possible to threaten college students' intelligence in an incidental fashion to produce compensatory consumption. In their work, participants wrote about their intelligence using their dominant or non-dominant hand. The logic was that using one's non-dominant hand would lead to doubt about whatever was written about (see Briñol and Petty 2003), in this case one's intelligence. Subsequently, participants were given a choice to select a product associated with intelligence (i.e. a fountain pen) or a product with no association with intelligence (i.e. a pack of candy). Participants who had written about their intelligence with their non-dominant hand, and thus had doubt associated with their intelligence, were more likely to choose the product associated with intelligence.

Threats to one's power

Having control and mastery over one's environment has been posited to be a basic human need (Rotter 1966). Building on this insight, Rucker and Galinsky (2008) proposed that when people's sense of control is undermined with respect to power – their relative control over others or valued resources (Magee and Galinsky 2008) – they seek to restore their sense of power. In particular, given that one input into power is the status and esteem one has in the eyes of others (French and Raven 1959), Rucker and Galinsky proposed that one means for individuals to restore their lost sense of power would be to acquire status objects. Consistent with this hypothesis, when individuals were placed into a state of low power they reported a greater willingness to pay for products that were associated with status (e.g. a silk tie, a rare portrait). Importantly, however, these individuals were not willing to pay more for more mundane objects (e.g. a microwave, a common portrait). This latter finding supports the notion that consumers guided their consumption habits specifically toward products that could compensate for the threatened dimension.

Threats to personal freedom

Recent work by Levav and Zhu (2009) has suggested that being placed in confining spaces can produce a threat to individuals' personal freedom. Furthermore, Levav and Zhu posit that, in an effort to restore their personal freedom, people can use choice as a means for doing so (see Kim and Drolet 2003). Specifically, Levav and Zhu suggested that threatened individuals could re-establish their freedom by making more varied and unique consumption decisions. To test this hypothesis, in one experiment participants were given the opportunity to choose three candy bars from a set of six different options. Importantly, the room was constructed such that the candy bars were featured at the end of an aisle. In the low threat to personal freedom condition participants walked down an aisle that was 7 feet wide. In the high threat to personal freedom condition participants walked down an aisle that was only 3.5 feet wide, and thus impinged upon participants' personal space. Levav and Zhu found that participants selected a greater variety of candy bars when their physical space was threatened (i.e. the narrow aisle) compared to when it was not (i.e. the wide aisle). They suggested that this occurred because variety seeking in consumption was one means by which individuals could psychologically restore their sense of freedom that had been threatened.

System threats

In addition to a psychological need for control, people also seek to bolster and defend the social systems to which they belong in an effort to see the world as good, legitimate, and desirable (Kay and Jost 2003). Building off of this idea and tying it to the consumption literature, Cutright *et al.* (2011) examined how people use consumption to deal with threats to the social system of the USA. They found that when consumers heard negative comments about the USA, they consumed in a manner that would support the country. For example, threatened consumers were more likely to favor US brands (e.g. Nike, Chevy) over foreign brands (e.g. Adidas, Toyota).

When does compensatory consumption occur

Although there is considerable evidence for the argument that compensatory consumption is a real response to threat, this does not mean all threats affect consumption. Here we discuss initial work that suggests when consumption is more or less likely to be used as a compensatory device.

Importance of the threatened domain

Perhaps the most logical observation is that compensatory consumption is more prone to occur when the dimension under threat is important versus unimportant to the individual (see Wicklund and Gollwitzer 1982). For example, although there is a basic need for governance over one's environment (Rotter 1966), this need may be stronger in some individuals than others. Consistent with this proposition, Rucker *et al.* (2011) found that individuals threatened with a loss of power were willing to pay a greater amount for status-signaling objects, particularly when they were accustomed to having power.

Similarly, Braun and Wicklund (1989) presented evidence for this proposition with respect to tennis players. Braun and Wicklund reasoned that novice tennis players with a strong commitment to tennis should be more prone to experience threat when they made mistakes during games. Consistent with the authors' hypothesis, participants who were both novices in tennis *and* reported that playing tennis was important to them were most inclined to exhibit a strong preference for a specific brand of apparel.

Ability and motivation to rebuke the threat directly

Compensatory consumption is a surrogate means of addressing threats. In some cases individuals could address a threat directly and completely resolve it. However, whether consumers address a threat head on or indirectly through consumption may hinge on their perceived ability and motivation to effectively dispel a threat. For example, if an MBA's business success is threatened by a poor grade on a finance exam they could choose to either study harder for the next exam or to adorn themselves with finely crafted suits and ties to signal their success. However, the route people choose may depend strongly on their perception that studying harder would actually produce a desired outcome on the exam.

Cutright *et al.* (2011; experiment 4) provide a recent illustration of the role of ability in how people respond to threat. In this experiment the authors first measured individuals' confidence in the USA as a system. Subsequently, participants were exposed to an article purportedly written by a British journalist that threatened their beliefs about the USA. Participants were then given the opportunity to evaluate both the writer and to make a choice between national and international brands. Two interesting results emerged. Among participants who had low, as opposed to high, confidence in the system there was a stronger preference for national over international brands, consistent with the idea that they used consumption as a means to compensate for the threat. In contrast, among participants who had high, as opposed to low, confidence in the system, there was a stronger derogation of the British journalist. Thus, having confidence in the system appeared to give participants the psychological gusto to address the threat in a more direct manner, whereas those with low confidence relied on the more indirect and less confrontational method of consuming products made in the USA.

The conspicuous nature of compensatory consumption

In writing on symbolic self-completion, Wicklund and Gollwitzer (1982) put forth the idea that others govern symbolic completion of the self. Specifically, they use the term "social reality" to relate the point that defining aspects of the self are only given meaning when they are accepted and acknowledged by others. As a consequence, one can infer that compensatory consumption might be more likely to occur when that consumption can be observed and witnessed by others in one's social environment. Indeed, work suggests, at least for some types of threats (see Lee and Shrum 2012) the conspicuousness of consumption is important.

For example, work examining the influence of a low-power state on status speaking also offers evidence favoring conspicuous consumption in response to threat. Specifically, research has found that individuals in a low state of power not only desire status-related objects, but they desire objects that are more likely to be seen and recognized by others as such (i.e. objects with physically larger brand logos) (Rucker and Galinsky 2009). Furthermore, Charles *et al.* (2009) find that minority groups spend a disproportionate amount of their income on conspicuously displayed goods (e.g. cars, jewelry) as a means to elevate their own status within society. Similarly, Dubois *et al.* (in press) manipulated how visible consumption was and found that loss of power led participants to consume more only when the consumption was visible to others.

The restorative power of consumption

Why do consumers engage in consumption in response to threats? Perhaps the simplest answer to this question is that compensatory consumption can alleviate the threat experienced by consumers. Indeed, several independent findings suggest that compensatory consumption assuages the threatened aspect of the self.

For example, in one experiment by Gao and colleagues (Gao *et al.* 2009), participants' intelligence was threatened. Subsequently, participants engaged in a sequential choice task. In the first choice task half of the participants first chose from a set of objects associated with intelligence (e.g. bookstore gift certificates) or a set of objects unrelated to intelligence. In the second choice task, all participants chose between a product either related to intelligence (i.e. a fountain pen) or unrelated to intelligence (i.e. candy). When threatened participants had first chosen from a set of objects associated with intelligence they did not differ in their second choice between the fountain pen and candy. However, if they had selected an object from a set of objects unrelated to intelligence objects, then threatened participants displayed a preference for the pen in the subsequent choice task. The authors suggest that in the former case the choice of a product symbolizing intelligence alleviated the threat and eliminated the need to compensate.

Elsewhere, Rucker and colleagues (Rucker *et al.* 2011) report an experiment where the acquisition of a status object restored participants' self-reported feelings of power. Participants were induced into a low- or high-power state and then given a pen that had been advertised in terms of either status or performance. Before receiving the pen individuals in the low-power condition reported feeling less powerful than high-power participants. However, after the pen had been physically received, low-power participants felt more powerful, but only when given the pen associated with status and not when the pen was associated with performance. Thus, physically acquiring an object was enough to eliminate the experienced threat.

Finally, although much of the research to date has examined compensatory consumption in the threatened domain, it should be noted that this is not the only means by which consumption can ward off threat. Mandel and Smeesters (2008) found that consumption can also distract individuals from threat by serving as an escape from self-awareness. In their study, when individuals' mortality was threatened (i.e. they were reminded that they would someday die) they ate more cookies. The eating of more cookies does not serve to eliminate concerns with death; rather, the action provides a means to escape thinking about the loss of the self. This finding, of course, raises an important direction for future research with respect to when consumers seek out products that specifically address the threat at hand and when they engage in greater consumption to distract oneself from the threat.

Future directions

Our final section proposes several promising questions to be tackled by future research efforts in understanding the nature of compensatory consumption.

Mapping compensatory efforts

One important goal for research in the domain of compensatory consumption is to map out the various psychological needs consumers have and the type of products and attributes that are sought in response to these needs. At first blush this might seem like a relatively easy task if one assumes that consumers seek out products that are clear manifestations of the dimension under threat. For example, if one assumes that when athletic ability is threatened people seek to demonstrate their athleticism the implications are straightforward. However, recent work reveals that constructs that do not have such immediate explicit connections can share a more common motive.

Consider the following two examples. First, work has found that a basic human motive for control underlies threats related to both lacking choice and lacking power (see Inesi *et al.* 2011). As a consequence, what initially appeared to be two separate and distinct literatures, one on the intrapersonal domain of choice and the other on the interpersonal domain of power, were found to share a common thread that allows substitution between them: a lack of choice can increase the desire for products that offer power, whereas a lack of power can lead to a preference for greater choice in selecting one's products. Second, research by Levav and Zhu (2009), noted earlier, has shown that when consumers feel physically confined (e.g. when surrounded by narrow aisles in a grocery store) they are more likely to seek variety in their purchases because variety provides a sense of freedom. However, prior to that work, a clear and direct link between threats to personal freedom and variety seeking was not apparent.

Clearly, understanding the dynamic interplay between various threats and the type of consumption that alleviates those threats warrants further consideration.

Threat-specific versus general consumption

As reviewed here, the bulk of the work in the literature suggests that consumption tends to increase in a threat-specific fashion. That is, whatever the specific nature of the threat (e.g. intelligence, power), people consume in a manner that signals one standing of that dimension. However, the work reported by Mandel and Smeesters (2008) suggests that consumption can sometimes increase regardless of whether it specifically relates to the threatened dimension or not by serving as a means of distraction.

An important challenge for the literature on compensatory consumption is to understand when people consume in a threat-specific fashion as opposed to increasing their consumption more generally. In response to this issue, Kim and Rucker (2011) proposed that general versus threat-specific consumption might sometimes be observed as a function of whether consumers state preferences or engage in actual behavior. Specifically, they proposed that when asked for their preferences consumers would tend to prefer products that specifically resolved the threatened aspect of their identity. However, when given the opportunity to engage in actual consumption of products, they hypothesized consumers might spend more time consuming to allow them to distract themselves from the threat.

To test this idea, participants were first given feedback that they had performed poorly on a task related to intelligence. Subsequently, participants took part in an evaluation task related to music. Half the participants were told the music was associated with increasing intelligence (threat-related), whereas the other half were told the music was associated with calmness (threat-unrelated). Participants were either: 1 asked to state how long they would prefer to listen to music; or 2 given the opportunity to actually listen to music. Relative to a no-threat condition, when simply asked for their preferences, threatened participants wanted to listen to the music longer only when it was framed in terms of intelligence. However, when given the opportunity to actually listen to the music, threatened participants listened to the music longer than unthreatened participants, regardless of its association to the threat.

This finding represents one initial moderator of threat-specific versus general consumption, and future research should be guided to examining other potential moderators.

Successfulness of threat reduction

Although research has suggested that consumption can attenuate needs induced via states of threats (see Gao *et al.* 2009; Rucker *et al.* 2011), less work has examined the various boundary conditions that affect the degree or duration of threat reduction. For example, although a single occasion of consumption might be effective in alleviating a temporary induced effect, in the presence of recurring threats (e.g. bullying at school, social rejection) it may require continual consumption. As a consequence, what may initially begin as efforts to alleviate threats through consumption may give way to habitual overspending and overconsumption that can produce crippling credit card debt or obesity.

In addition, even when consumption appears to remedy threat, it may only lead to a temporary alleviation of the threat rather than a complete resolution. If consumption merely alleviates the symptoms of the threats, this could have unintended consequences of allowing the threat to come back more strongly. The plausibility of such an occurrence has roots in research in the area of stereotype suppression that has found that individuals who successfully suppress stereotypes during one task demonstrate enhanced accessibility of those stereotypes in a subsequent task (Galinsky and Moskowitz 2000; Macrae *et al.* 1995). These remain important questions to explore to more fully understand the efficacy of compensatory consumption.

Conclusion

The work reviewed in the present chapter is a testament to the powerful role consumption can play in responding to psychological threats. Central to the theme of this book, consumption offers a means to respond to threats that attempt to carve away important components of one's identity. We also reviewed boundary conditions for when compensatory consumption does and does not occur, with the importance of the domain under threat, people's ability to address the threat, and the conspicuousness of the consumption serving as important moderators. When compensatory consumption does transpire, it can indeed serve to reduce the experience of threat. The present chapter hopefully serves as both a primer on the topic of compensatory consumption and a cradle for new ideas and directions in this burgeoning area of research.

References

Belk, R.W., Bahn, K.D., and Mayer, R.N. (1982) "Developmental Recognition of Consumption Symbolism." *Journal of Consumer Research* 9: 4–17.

Braun, O.L. and Wicklund, R.A. (1989) "Psychological Antecedents of Conspicuous Consumption." *Journal of Economic Psychology* 10: 161–87.

Briñol, P. and Petty, R.E. (2003) "Overt Head Movements and Persuasion: A Self-validation Analysis." *Journal of Personality and Social Psychology* 84: 1123–39.

Charles, K.K., Hurst, E., and Roussanov, N. (2009) "Conspicuous Consumption and Race." *Quarterly Journal of Economics* 510: 425–67.

Cutright, K.M., Wu, E.C., Banfield, J.C., Kay, A.C., and Fitzsimons, G.J. (2011) "When Your World Must Be Defended: Consuming to Justify the System." *Journal of Consumer Research* 38: 62–77.

Dubois, D., Rucker, D.D., and Galinsky, A.D. (in press) "Super Size Me: Product Size as a Signal of Status." *Journal of Consumer Research.*

French, J.R.P., Jr, and Bertram, R. (1959) "The Bases of Social Power." In Dorwin Cartwright (ed.), *Studies in Social Power.* Ann Arbor, MI: Institute for Social Research, pp. 150–67.

French, J. and Raven, B. (1959) "In the Bases of Social Power." In Dorwin Cartwright (ed.), *Studies in Social Power.* Ann Arbor, MI: Institute for Social Research, pp. 150–67.

Galinsky, A.D. and Moskowitz, G.B. (2000) "Perspective Taking: Decreasing Stereotype Expression, Stereotype Accessibility and In-group Favoritism." *Journal of Personality and Social Psychology* 78: 708–24.

Gao, L, Wheeler, S.C., and Shiv, B. (2009) "The 'Shaken Self': Product Choices as a Means of Restoring Self-view Confidence." *Journal of Consumer Research* 36: 29–38.

Gordijn, E.H., Hindriks, I., Koomen, W., Dijksterhuis, A., and Knippenberg, A.V. (2004) "Consequences of Stereotype Suppression and Internal Suppression Motivation: A Self-regulation Approach." *Personality and Social Psychology Bulletin* 30: 212–24.

Harmon-Jones, C., Schmeichel, B.J., and Harmon-Jones, E. (2009) "Symbolic Self-completion in Academia: Evidence from Department Web Pages and Email Signature Files." *European Journal of Social Psychology* 39: 311–16.

Inesi, E., Botti, S., Dubois, D., Rucker, D.D., and Galinsky, A.D. (2011) "Power and Choice: Their Dynamic Interplay in Quenching the Thirst for Personal Control." *Psychological Science* 22: 1042–8.

Kay, A.C. and Jost, J.T. (2003) "Complementary Justice: Effects of 'Poor but Happy' and 'Poor but Honest' Stereotype Exemplars on System Justification and Implicit Activation of the Justice Motive." *Journal of Personality and Social Psychology* 85: 823–37.

Kim, H.S. and Drolet, A. (2003) "Choice and Self-expression: A Cultural Analysis of Variety Seeking." *Journal of Personality and Social Psychology* 85: 373–82.

Kim, S. and Rucker, D.D. (2011) "Salting the Sidewalk Just in Case the Snowstorm Hits: Effects of Potential Versus Experienced Threat on Consumption." Unpublished manuscript, Northwestern University.

Lee, Jaehoon and Shrum, L.J. (2012) "Conspicuous Consumption versus Charitable Behavior in Response to Social Exclusion: A Differential Needs Explanation." *Journal of Consumer Research* 30: 530–44.

Levav, J. and Zhu, R. (2009) "Seeking Freedom Through Variety." *Journal of Consumer Research* 36: 600–10.

Macrae, C.N., Bodenhausen, Galen V., and Milne, A.B. (1995) "The Dissection of Selection in Person Perception: Inhibitory Processes in Social Stereotyping." *Journal of Personality and Social Psychology* 69: 397–407.

Magee, J.C. and Galinsky, A.D. (2008) "Social Hierarchy: The Self-reinforcing Nature of Power and Status." *Academy of Management Annals* 2: 351–98.

Mandel, N. and Smeesters, D. (2008) "The Sweet Escape: Effects of Mortality Salience on Consumption Quantities for High- and Low-self-esteem Consumers." *Journal of Consumer Research* 35: 309–23.

Rotter, J.B. (1966) "Generalized Expectancies for Internal Versus External Control of Reinforcement." *Psychological Monographs* 80: 1–28.

Rucker, D.D. and Galinsky, A.D. (2008) "Desire to Acquire: Powerlessness and Compensatory Consumption." *Journal of Consumer Research* 35: 257–67.

——(2009) "Conspicuous Consumption versus Utilitarian Ideals: How Different Levels of Power Shape Consumption." *Journal of Experimental Social Psychology* 45: 549–55.

Rucker, D.D., Galinsky, A.D., and Dubois, D. (2011) "Power and Consumer Behavior: How Power Shapes Who and What Consumers Value." *Journal of Consumer Psychology*. doi:10.1016/j.jcps.2011.06.001.

Wicklund, R.A. and Gollwitzer, P.M. (1981) "Symbolic Self-completion, Attempted Influence, and Self-deprecation." *Basic and Applied Social Psychology* 2: 89–114.
——(1982) *Symbolic Self-completion*. Hillsdale, NJ: Erlbaum.
Willer, R., Rogalin, C.L., Conlon, B., and Wojnowicz, M.T. (2010) "Overdoing Gender: A Test of the Masculine Overcompensation Thesis." Unpublished manuscript. University of California Berkeley.

22
SELF-THREATS AND CONSUMPTION

Jaehoon Lee and L.J. Shrum

The self-concept – how we view ourselves – is multifaceted and complex. We view ourselves the way we think others view us, what Cooley termed the looking-glass self (Cooley 1902). We have multiple selves (e.g. parent, scientist, woman) that may be activated by situational cues or social roles (Mead 1934; Tajfel and Turner 1986). Moreover, each of these selves may consist of actual ones and ideal ones, and discrepancies between the two can lead to significant discomfort (Higgins 1987). It is thus unsurprising that we spend a significant amount of time and energy constructing and maintaining our sense of self.

One way in which we manage our self-concept is through self-presentation. Because our self-concept is a function of how we think other people see us, good construction and maintenance of the self requires constant attention to managing our appearance to others. We do this by managing the myriad signals that indicate who we are: how we look, where we eat, who we hang out with, what groups we belong to, and what we own – what Belk (1988) refers to as the extended self (see Chapter 8 and Chapter 9, this volume). People are attracted to products and brands that are consistent with their identity, form impressions of those who use those products and services (Kleine *et al.* 1993; Shavitt and Nelson 1999), construct their identity by associating themselves with signs, symbols, material objects, and places (Schau and Gilly 2003), and seek identity-relevant possessions to signal their identity to others (Schouten 1991; Wicklund and Gollwitzer 1981). Thus, in a consumer context, people strive to achieve or maintain their identity through symbolic products and brands. Put simply, a significant portion of self-concept management occurs through the consumption of goods and services (Shrum *et al.* 2012).

A considerable literature thus exists documenting how people use possessions and other related concepts to manage their self-concepts. In this chapter we explore a particular aspect of self-concept maintenance: self-concept repair. We investigate what happens when our self-concepts are threatened, what aspects of the self are threatened under particular situations, and how consumption is used to compensate for these threats and repair the self-concept (compensatory consumption) (for a detailed discussion, see Chapter 21, this volume).

Sources of self-threats and responses to self-threats

Identity threat

In forming identity, there are two central dimensions: social and personal (Harré 1983). The social dimension is based on the groups to which people belong. People generally have several social identities that are a function of the groups to which they belong, and any of these identities can be activated by situational cues (Deaux 1991). In contrast, personal identity refers to intra-personal traits, characteristics, and goals that the person finds self-descriptive (Deaux 1993) and which are not formulated as connected to membership in a social group or relationship (Oyserman 2009).

However, what happens when social or personal identities are threatened? In such instances, people will attempt to bolster their self-concepts by thinking and acting in identity-consistent ways and defend important group or personal core values in response to the identity threats. In the following sections we review research on social and personal identity threats and their consequences in a consumer context.

Social identity threat

People tend to classify themselves and others into various social categories such as organizational membership, religious affiliation, gender, and age cohort (Tajfel and Turner 1986). Social identities are depersonalized representations of the self and are derived primarily from group membership (Brown 2000). People achieve a positive social identity by making favorable distinctions between their own group and some other group (Deaux 1993).

However, social identity can be threatened when people are aware that they have the potential to be stereotyped negatively or devalued because of their membership in a particular social group, a phenomenon termed stereotype threat (Steele *et al.* 2002; see Chapter 11, this volume). It is important to note that the same group membership may be seen either as identity-enhancing or identity-jeopardizing, depending on whether it compares favorably or unfavorably to other groups. Thus, it is the social context, rather than specific group features, that determines the evaluative flavor of any given group membership (Ellemers *et al.* 2002). For example, women, relative to men, are often judged as less competent in quantitative domains, leading them to feel identity-threatened, whereas they are often judged as more competent in qualitative domains, leading them to feel identity-safe. Social identity threat generates various psychological and behavioral consequences such as powerlessness and inhibition (Cook *et al.* 2011), cognitive vigilance (Pinel 1999), depleted working memory (Schmader and Johns 2003), and poor task performance (Spencer *et al.* 1999).

In a consumer context, social identity threat can occur in diverse marketplace settings. For example, Baker *et al.* (2008) investigated the effects of race on perceptions of a service failure (e.g. slow service). They asked both Black and White participants to read a scenario of a service failure, and manipulated social cues (e.g. race of service provider, race of other customers) that might be expected to activate stereotype threat, and then asked the participants to indicate what they would expect in terms of service recovery (e.g. apology, refund). The researchers found that Black participants perceived more discrimination and required more in service recovery than White participants when the service provider and all the other customers were White. However, when the racial composition of the other customers was mixed, Black and White participants showed no differences in perceptions or expectations. Presumably, the all-White composition condition primed stereotype threat and led to greater perceptions that race was a factor in the service failure and greater requirements for service recovery.

Recent research has also demonstrated negative effects of gender stereotype threat. Lee *et al.* (2011) primed male and female participants with subtle cues expected to activate the stereotype that women are bad at math or know nothing about cars. They then asked participants to view an advertisement for a service provider (e.g. financial advisor, car salesperson), but manipulated the gender of the service provider. As they expected, under stereotype-threat conditions, women (but not men) showed lower purchase intentions when the service providers were male than when they were female. However, when no stereotype cues were present, women showed no preference between the male and female service providers.

The previous two examples of social identity threat were externally induced. That is, the threats to self came from situational cues in the environment. However, ironically, people can in fact threaten themselves! Research has shown that people purchase products that are consistent with their own identity (Reed 2004). However, imagine a situation in which you must purchase a gift for a close friend who has quite a different social identity? Do you purchase a product consistent with the friend's identity, or consistent with your own, and does the choice have implications for self-concept (identity) repair? Ward and Broniarczyk (2011) examined this question. They asked participants to consider a situation in which they were buying a gift for either a close or distant friend, and they manipulated whether the friend was part of the participants' in-group (attends the same university) or out-group (attends a rival university). They then gave participants a choice of choosing either an identity-verifying or identity-contrary product. When participants chose an identity-contrary gift for a close (but not distant) friend, they were more likely to subsequently engage in identity-verifying behaviors than when they chose an identity-verifying gift.

Personal identity threat

Personal identity is characterized as inner identity or the inside self, and is often described in terms such as intelligent, kind, compassionate, and independent (Jones and McEwen 2000). Although conceptually distinct from social identity, personal and social identities are interrelated in that personal identity can derive from group memberships, and social categories can be infused with personal meaning (Deaux 1993).

Recent research indicates that when certain aspects of personal self-identity are threatened, people attempt to repair the threatened identity through various means. For example, Tetlock and colleagues (Tetlock *et al.* 2000) showed that when people's moral values are threatened, they quite understandably express moral indignation, but they also respond in ways that bolster those moral values. When participants read a scenario in which they were confronted with a tradeoff of advocating that a hospital save a life through an expensive organ transplant versus save the money for other purposes, participants were more likely to volunteer their time to campaign for organ donation, compared to participants who did not have their moral values threatened.

In a study that explored product purchase effects resulting from threatened self-views, Gao *et al.* (2009) temporarily "shook" self-views and observed how participants behaved. In one experiment they asked participants to write down examples of three personal characteristics that indicate they are intelligent individuals. They manipulated participants' confidence in their intelligence by having some participants write with their dominant hand, but others with their nondominant hand (Briñol and Petty 2003). They found that people who had their confidence in their intelligence shaken (writing with their nondominant hand) were more likely to choose a pen (intelligence-affirming) over candy, whereas there was no difference in preference for pen or candy when their self-confidence was not shaken. Thus, when identities are threatened, people will seek out products that reaffirm their self-image. However, some research suggests that these effects may be confined to people who consider personal (as opposed to social) characteristics as self-defining. For example, when induced to feel uncertain about themselves, individualists (but not collectivists) rated their favorite possessions (e.g. jeans, cars) as more self-expressive than when self-uncertainty was not induced (Morrison and Johnson 2011).

Threats to fundamental identity needs

Although there are numerous perspectives on fundamental human needs (Maslow 1954; Max-Neef *et al.* 1991), we focus on four needs in particular that are identity-related: the need to belong; to have power and control over one's environment; to maintain high self-esteem; and to feel one's existence is meaningful (see Williams 2009, for a review). As with identity in general, when these specific identity-related needs are threatened, people will attempt to bolster those need (e.g. enhance feelings of power, self-esteem, belonging, and meaningfulness), and this often occurs through consumption-related activities. In the following sections, we discuss needs threat in the context of situations that may threaten particular needs. These include threats that are activated indirectly through particular fears (physical death, social death), and threats that are activated directly by situations.

Fear of physical death: mortality salience

People are often confronted with reminders of their own mortality. One need look no further than the news, which seems to be dominated by tragic reports of terror, wars, natural disasters, car accidents, and terminal illnesses. As a result, the salience of the inevitability of death may often be high. Terror management theory (Greenberg *et al.* 1997) suggests that when people are reminded of their own inevitable death, they are motivated to maintain self-esteem and faith in their cultural worldviews, and to defend both of these mechanisms against threats.

The theory thus posits that self-esteem and cultural worldviews function to protect an individual from the potential for existential anxiety that is engendered by awareness of the inevitability of death (see Chapter 20, this volume). Consequently, when mortality salience is increased, people express stronger beliefs in their cultural worldviews and increase the desire for self-esteem. In support of these propositions, making mortality salient led participants to bolster their cultural worldview and produce more aggressive responses to those who had different political beliefs by allocating more hot sauce for a person whom they thought did not like spicy foods (McGregor *et al.* 1998), to give more negative evaluations to those who criticized their country and more positive evaluations to those who praised it (Greenberg *et al.* 1990), and to place more blame on a car manufacturer for an accident when it was a foreign manufacturer than when it was a domestic one (Nelson *et al.* 1997). Mortality salience also caused participants to bolster self-esteem by increasing activities central to their self-concept. For example, it increased intention to work out by those who valued fitness (Arndt *et al.* 2003) and increased performance on a handgrip exercise for those who valued strength (Peters *et al.* 2005).

Responses to mortality salience and existential threat also play out in the consumer domain. For example, when mortality was made salient, consumers who valued their body or their virtue as a source of self-esteem chose a less indulgent food (e.g. fruit salad) and increased donations and other charitable behavior compared to when mortality was not made salient (Ferraro *et al.* 2005). In contrast, consumers with low self-esteem increased the quantity of food they ate in response to mortality salience, but those with high self-esteem were little affected (Mandel and Smeesters 2008). Mortality salience has also been shown to increase the desire to acquire wealth and possessions (Kasser and Sheldon 2000; see Arndt *et al.* 2004 for a review), purchase luxury items (Mandel and Heine 1999), and form strong brand connections (Rindfleisch *et al.* 2009) as means of bolstering self-esteem. In addition, death-related media contexts led consumers to become more patriotic, focus on the brands' country of origin, increase their preference for domestic brands, and decrease their preference for foreign brands to defend their cultural worldviews (Liu and Smeesters 2010).

Fear of social death: social exclusion

In addition to fears of physical death, fears of social death can be a source of threat. An example of social death is social exclusion (Williams 2009). Social exclusion occurs when people are excluded from a group. This may occur through explicit rejection, implicit ignoring, or extreme ignoring through ostracism. On the most general level, social exclusion threatens the fundamental need to belong (Baumeister and Leary 1995). On a more specific level, it threatens four needs noted earlier in this section: self-esteem, power and control, belongingness, and meaningful existence (Williams 2009).

Social exclusion has been shown to produce a variety of effects. For example, it has been shown to increase aggressive, antisocial behavior. Compared to non-excluded people, socially excluded people allocated more hot sauce to others whom they thought disliked spicy foods (Ayduk *et al.* 2008), gave unappealing snacks to interaction partners (Chow *et al.* 2008), and provided more negative job evaluations to someone who insulted them (Twenge *et al.* 2001). However, in other cases, social exclusion produced more prosocial, affiliative responses. Compared to non-excluded people, excluded people were more interested in working with others (Maner *et al.* 2007), engaged in more behavioral mimicry (Lakin *et al.* 2008), showed more conformity to group perceptions (Williams *et al.* 2000), and were more socially attentive (Gardner *et al.* 2000).

Like the other self-threats we have reviewed, consumer researchers have also documented social exclusion effects. For example, when participants were excluded (ostracized) in a computer-generated three-way ball toss, they showed increased preferences for nostalgic products (Loveland *et al.* 2010). The consumption of nostalgic products repaired threats to belongingness by providing a reconnection with the past and shared consumption experiences. Other research has documented similar consumption behaviors intended to bolster one's feeling of belongingness. Across a series of experiments, Mead *et al.* (2011) demonstrated that being socially excluded increased spending that facilitated affiliation with others. Excluded participants, compared to non-excluded ones, were more likely to buy products that signified group membership, adjusted their spending to conform to preferences of their interaction partner, and were even willing to consume illegal narcotics if it increased their chances of social inclusion.

However, reactions to social exclusion do not always promote prosocial, affiliative consumer responses. In a series of recent experiments, Lee and Shrum (2012) demonstrated that social exclusion can produce both prosocial responses and self-focused responses. Which outcome is produced depends on which needs are threatened. When relational needs (e.g. self-esteem, belonging) are most threatened, prosocial responses result, consistent with Mead *et al.* (2011) and Loveland *et al.* (2010). However, when efficacy needs (e.g. power and control, meaningful existence) are most threatened, more self-focused, antisocial responses result. To demonstrate this, Lee and Shrum manipulated whether exclusion was explicit (rejected) or implicit (ignored). Being rejected has been shown to threaten relational needs, whereas being ignored threatens efficacy needs (Molden *et al.* 2009). Their results showed that being ignored increased conspicuous consumption (self-focused), but being rejected did not. In contrast, being rejected increased charitable donations and intentions to help others (prosocial), but being ignored did not. They also provided explicit links to the repair of threatened needs. In a test of what they term the differential needs hypothesis, they demonstrated that when relational needs such as self-esteem were bolstered, the effects of being rejected on helping behavior were eliminated, but the effects of being ignored on conspicuous consumption were unaffected. In contrast, when efficacy needs such as power and meaningful existence were bolstered, the effects of being ignored on conspicuous consumption were eliminated, but the effects of being rejected on helping behavior were unaffected. Thus, the specific consumer behaviors were clearly intended to repair the particular needs that were threatened.

Direct threats to needs

People may also experience direct threats to particular needs. One example is direct threats to feelings of power. Feelings of low power can induce uncertainty (Anderson and Galinsky 2006) and learned helplessness (Seligman 1975). When people experience such threats to power, they will attempt to repair their threatened needs, and one way of doing so is through consumption. For example, when participants were induced to have feelings of low power, they increased their willingness to pay for high-status but not low-status products (Rucker and Galinsky 2008), and conversely, acquiring a status object increased feelings of power (Rucker *et al.* 2011). Similarly, feelings of low power caused people to choose larger products (e.g. portion sizes), which were associated with higher status (Dubois *et al.* 2012).

Future directions

It is well established in consumer research that people use products and services to develop and maintain their identities. It is also well established in psychological research that when people's identities are threatened, they go to great lengths to shore up their identities. However, it is only recently that researchers have begun to put these two well-known facts together to investigate how consumers react to identity threats through their consumption behavior. As the research we have reviewed attests, consumer reactions to self-threats can explain diverse types of consumer behavior, including conspicuous consumption, luxury product purchase, nostalgic product demand, materialism, spending on products that indicate affiliation, and charitable donations.

However, despite the accumulation of research to date, relatively little is known about the underlying processes and reasons for specific reactions in particular situations. We expect that the future research will focus on understanding the particular conditions that contribute to identity threat. For example, when fundamental identity needs are threatened, what is the range of consumption activities that serve to repair the threatened needs? Answering this question requires a deeper understanding of what products mean to people. Moreover, the question is complicated because people often are not consciously aware of the meaning certain products have for their identity.

Another useful direction for future research is understanding precisely what aspects of identity are threatened by particular situations. For example, social exclusion has been shown to produce a number of different responses, many of which appear to be contradictory (e.g. prosocial and antisocial). It may be that particular types of social exclusion threaten multiple needs, and which is most salient to an individual may be a function of both personal and situational characteristics. More research is needed to understand both the main effects and the interaction of personal and situational factors. A better understanding of why consumers are motivated to purchase as a function of identity threat may help them make better purchase decisions.

References

Anderson, C. and Galinsky, A.D. (2006) "Power, Optimism, and Risk-Taking." *European Journal of Social Psychology* 36: 511–36.

Arndt, J., Schimel, J., and Goldenberg, J.L. (2003) "Death Can Be Good for Your Health: Fitness Intentions as a Proximal and Distal Defense Against Mortality Salience." *Journal of Applied Social Psychology* 33: 1726–46.

Arndt, J., Solomon, S., Kasser, T., and Sheldon, K.M. (2004) "The Urge to Splurge: A Terror Management Account of Materialism and Consumer Behavior." *Journal of Consumer Psychology* 14: 198–212.

Ayduk, Ö., Gyurak, A., and Luerssen, A. (2008) "Individual Differences in the Rejection-Aggression Link in the Hot Sauce Paradigm: The Case of Rejection Sensitivity." *Journal of Experimental Social Psychology* 44: 775–82.

Baker, T.L., Meyer, T., and Johnson, J.D. (2008) "Individual Differences in Perceptions of Service Failure and Recovery: The Role of Race and Discriminatory Bias." *Journal of the Academy of Marketing Science* 36: 552–64.

Baumeister, R.F. and Leary, M.R. (1995) "The Need to Belong: Desire for Interpersonal Attachments as a Fundamental Human Motivation." *Psychological Bulletin* 117: 497–529.

Belk, R.W. (1988) "Possessions and the Extended Self." *Journal of Consumer Research* 15: 139–68.

Briñol, P. and Petty, R.E. (2003) "Overt Head Movements and Persuasion: A Self-Validation Analysis." *Journal of Personality and Social Psychology* 84: 1123–39.

Brown, R. (2000) "Social Identity Theory: Past Achievements, Current Problems and Future Challenges." *European Journal of Social Psychology* 30: 745–78.

Chow, R.M., Tiedens, L.Z., and Govan, C.L. (2008) "Excluded Emotions: The Role of Anger in Antisocial Responses to Ostracism." *Journal of Experimental Social Psychology* 44: 896–903.

Cook, J.E., Arrow, H., and Malle, B.F. (2011) "The Effect of Feeling Stereotyped on Social Power and Inhibition." *Personality and Social Psychology Bulletin* 37: 165–80.

Cooley, C.H. (1902) *Human Nature and the Social Order*. New York: Scribner.

Deaux, K. (1991) "Social Identities: Thoughts on Structure and Change." In R.C. Curtis (ed.), *The Relational Self: Theoretical Convergences in Psychoanalysis and Social Psychology*. New York: Guilford Press.

——(1993) "Reconstructing Social Identity." *Personality and Social Psychology Bulletin* 19: 4–12.

Dubois, D., Rucker, D.D., and Galinsky, A.D. (2012) "Super Size Me: Product Size as a Signal of Status." *Journal of Consumer Research* 38: 1047–62.

Ellemers, N., Spears, R., and Doosje, B. (2002) "Self and Social Identity." *Annual Review of Psychology* 53: 161–86.

Ferraro, R., Shiv, B., and Bettman, J.R. (2005) "Let Us Eat and Drink, for Tomorrow We Shall Die: Effects of Mortality Salience and Self-Esteem on Self-Regulation in Consumer Choice." *Journal of Consumer Research* 32: 65–75.

Gao, L., Wheeler, S.C., and Shiv, B. (2009) "The 'Shaken Self': Product Choices as a Means of Restoring Self-View Confidence." *Journal of Consumer Research* 36: 29–38.

Gardner, W.L., Pickett, C.L., and Brewer, M.B. (2000) "Social Exclusion and Selective Memory: How the Need to Belong Influences Memory for Social Events." *Personality and Social Psychology Bulletin* 26: 486–96.

Greenberg, J., Pyszczynski, T., Solomon, S., Rosenblatt, A., Veeder, M., Kirkland, S., and Lyon, D. (1990) "Evidence for Terror Management II: The Effects of Mortality Salience on Reactions to Those Who Threaten or Bolster the Cultural Worldview." *Journal of Personality and Social Psychology* 58: 308–18.

Greenberg, J., Solomon, S., and Pyszczynski, T. (1997) "Terror Management Theory of Self-Esteem and Social Behavior: Empirical Assessments and Conceptual Refinements." In M.P. Zanna (ed.), *Advances in Experimental Social Psychology*. New York: Academic Press, 29: 61–139.

Harré, H.R. (1983) *Personal Being*. Oxford: Basil Blackwell.

Higgins, E.T. (1987) "Self-Discrepancy: A Theory Relating Self and Affect." *Psychological Review* 94: 319–40.

Jones, S.R. and McEwen, M.K. (2000) "A Conceptual Model of Multiple Dimensions of Identity." *Journal of College Student Development* 41: 405–14.

Kasser, T. and Sheldon, K.M. (2000) "Of Wealth and Death: Materialism, Mortality Salience, and Consumption Behavior." *Psychological Science* 11: 348–51.

Kleine, R.E., Kleine, S.S., and Kernan, J.B. (1993) "Mundane Consumption and the Self: A Social-Identity Perspective." *Journal of Consumer Psychology* 2: 209–35.

Lakin, J.L., Chartrand, T.L., and Arkin, R.M. (2008) "I Am Too Just Like You." *Psychological Science* 19: 816–22.

Lee, J. and Shrum, L.J. (2012) "Conspicuous Consumption versus Charitable Behavior in Response to Social Exclusion: A Differential Needs Explanation." *Journal of Consumer Research* 39: 530–44.

Lee, K., Kim, H., and Vohs, K.D. (2011) "Stereotype Threat in the Marketplace: Consumer Anxiety and Purchase Intentions." *Journal of Consumer Research* 38: 343–57.

Liu, J. and Smeesters, D. (2010) "Have You Seen the News Today? The Effect of Death-Related Media Contexts on Brand Preferences." *Journal of Marketing Research* 47: 251–62.

Loveland, K.E., Smeesters, D., and Mandel, N. (2010) "Still Preoccupied with 1995: The Need to Belong and Preference for Nostalgic Products." *Journal of Consumer Research* 37: 393–408.

McGregor, H.A., Lieberman, J.D., Greenberg, J., Solomon, S., Arndt, J., Simon, L., and Pyszczynski, T. (1998) "Terror Management and Aggression: Evidence That Mortality Salience Motivates Aggression against Worldview-Threatening Others." *Journal of Personality and Social Psychology* 74: 590–605.

Mandel, N. and Heine, S.J. (1999) "Terror Management and Marketing: He Who Dies with the Most Toys Wins." In E.J. Arnould and L.M. Scott (eds), *Advances in Consumer Research*. Provo, UT: Association for Consumer Research.

Mandel, N. and Smeesters, D. (2008) "The Sweet Escape: Effects of Mortality Salience on Consumption Quantities for High- and Low-Self-Esteem Consumers." *Journal of Consumer Research* 35: 309–23.

Maner, J.K., DeWall, C.N., Baumeister, R.F., and Schaller, M. (2007) "Does Social Exclusion Motivate Interpersonal Reconnection? Resolving the 'Porcupine Problem'." *Journal of Personality and Social Psychology* 92: 42–55.

Maslow, A.H. (1954) *Motivation and Personality*. New York: Harper and Row.

Max-Neef, M.A., Hopenhayn, M., and Elizalde, A. (1991) *Human Scale Development: Conception, Application and Further Reflections*. New York: Apex Press.

Mead, G.H. (1934) *Mind, Self, and Society*. Chicago, IL: University of Chicago Press.

Mead, N.L., Baumeister, R.F., Stillman, T.F., Rawn, C.D., and Vohs, K.D. (2011) "Social Exclusion Causes People to Spend and Consume Strategically in the Service of Affiliation." *Journal of Consumer Research* 37: 902–19.

Molden, D.C., Lucas, G.M., Gardner, W.L., Dean, K., and Knowles, M.L. (2009) "Motivations for Prevention or Promotion Following Social Exclusion: Being Rejected Versus Being Ignored." *Journal of Personality and Social Psychology* 96: 415–31.

Morrison, K.R. and Johnson, C.S. (2011) "When What You Have Is Who You Are: Self-Uncertainty Leads Individualists to See Themselves in Their Possessions." *Personality and Social Psychology Bulletin* 37: 639–51.

Nelson, L.J., Moore, D.L., Olivetti, J., and Scott, T. (1997) "General and Personal Mortality Salience and Nationalistic Bias." *Journal of Personality and Social Psychology* 23: 884–92.

Oyserman, D. (2009) "Identity-Based Motivation and Consumer Behavior." *Journal of Consumer Psychology* 19: 250–60.

Peters, H.J., Greenberg, J., Williams, J.M., and Schneider, N.R. (2005) "Applying Terror Management Theory to Performance: Can Reminding Individuals of Their Mortality Increase Strength Output?" *Journal of Sport & Exercise Psychology* 27: 111–16.

Pinel, E.C. (1999) "Stigma Consciousness: The Psychological Legacy of Social Stereotypes." *Journal of Personality and Social Psychology* 76: 114–28.

Reed, A. (2004) "Activating the Self-Importance of Consumer Selves: Exploring Identity Salience Effects on Judgments." *Journal of Consumer Research* 31: 286–95.

Rindfleisch, A., Burroughs, J.E., and Wong, N. (2009) "The Safety of Objects: Materialism, Existential Insecurity, and Brand Connection." *Journal of Consumer Research* 36: 1–16.

Rucker, D.D. and Galinsky, A.D. (2008) "Desire to Acquire: Powerlessness and Compensatory Consumption." *Journal of Consumer Research* 35: 257–67.

Rucker, D.D., and Galinsky, A.D., Dubois, D. (2012) "Power and Consumer Behavior: How Power Shapes Who and What Consumers Value." *Journal of Consumer Psychology* 22: 352–68.

Schau, H.J. and Gilly, M.C. (2003) "We Are What We Post? Self-Presentation in Personal Web Space." *Journal of Consumer Research* 30: 385–404.

Schmader, T. and Johns, M. (2003) "Converging Evidence That Stereotype Threat Reduces Working Memory Capacity." *Journal of Personality and Social Psychology* 85: 440–52.

Schouten, J.W. (1991) "Selves in Transition: Symbolic Consumption in Personal Rites of Passage and Identity Reconstruction." *Journal of Consumer Research* 17: 412–25.

Seligman, M.E. (1975) *Helplessness: On Depression, Development, and Death*. New York: W.H. Freeman/ Times Books/Henry Holt & Co.

Shavitt, S.E. and Nelson, M.R. (1999) "The Social Identity Function in Person Perception: Communicated Meanings of Product Preferences." In G.R. Maio and J.M. Olson (eds), *Why We Evaluate: Functions of Attitudes*. Mahwah, NJ: Erlbaum, pp. 37–57.

Shrum, L.J. *et al.* (2012) "Reconceptualizing Materialism as Identity Goal Pursuits: Functions, Processes, and Consequences." *Journal of Business Research*. http://dx.doi.org/10.1016/j.jbusres.2012.08-010.

Spencer, S.J., Steele, C.M., and Quinn, D.M. (1999) "Stereotype Threat and Women's Math Performance." *Journal of Experimental Social Psychology* 35: 4–28.

Steele, C.M., Spencer, S.J., and Aronson, J. (2002) "Contending with Group Image: The Psychology of Stereotype and Social Identity Threat." In M.P. Zanna (ed.), *Advances in Experimental Social Psychology*. San Diego, CA: Academic Press, 34: 379–440.

Tajfel, H. and Turner, J.C. (1986) "The Social Identity Theory of Intergroup Behavior." In S. Worchel and W.G. Austin (eds), *The Psychology of Intergroup Relations*. Chicago, IL: Nelson-Hall.

Tetlock, P.E., Kristel, O.V., Elson, S.B., Green, M.C., and Lerner, J.S. (2000) "The Psychology of the Unthinkable: Taboo Trade-Offs, Forbidden Base Rates, and Heretical Counterfactuals." *Journal of Personality and Social Psychology* 78: 853–70.

Twenge, J.M., Baumeister, R.F., Tice, D.M., and Stucke, T.S. (2001) "If You Can't Join Them, Beat Them: Effects of Social Exclusion on Aggressive Behavior." *Journal of Personality and Social Psychology* 81: 1058–69.

Ward, M.K. and Broniarczyk, S.M. (2011) "It's Not Me, It's You: How Gift Giving Creates Giver Identity Threat as a Function of Social Closeness." *Journal of Consumer Research* 38: 164–81.

Wicklund, R.A. and Gollwitzer, P.M. (1981) "Symbolic Self-Completion, Attempted Influence, and Self-Deprecation." *Basic and Applied Social Psychology* 2: 89–114.

Williams, K.D. (2009) "Ostracism: A Temporal Need-Threat Model." In M.P. Zanna (ed.), *Advances in Experimental Social Psychology*. New York: Academic Press, pp. 275–314.

Williams, K.D., Cheung, C.K.T., and Choi, W. (2000) "Cyberostracism: Effects of Being Ignored over the Internet." *Journal of Personality and Social Psychology* 79: 748–62.

II.IV

Controlling the self

23

SELF-CONTROL AND SPENDING

Lauren G. Block and Keith Wilcox

Introduction

One of the most fundamental tradeoffs consumers face is how to spend their money and on what to spend it. With a limited supply of funds, but an unlimited supply of spending opportunities and desires, we must continually negotiate with ourselves regarding expenditures. Should we purchase a new high-definition television or put the money instead into a college savings account? Even the most ordinary decisions, like whether to lunch at a restaurant or pick up a cheaper deli sandwich often reflect a conscious tradeoff between spending vs. saving money. Such decisions often require us to subdue our hedonic or short-term desires in favor of more utilitarian or longer-term options. In other words, such desires require our conscious use of self-control. Our capacity to exert self-control is one of the foundations of the human self (Muraven *et al.* 1998) and drives our behavior across almost all domains of human life.

In this chapter, we examine the relationship between self-control and consumer spending. We highlight both the similarities and differences between general self-control and self-control over spending. Additionally, we examine the factors that enhance and reduce consumers' ability to regulate their spending. The chapter begins with a discussion of self-control, its relationship to spending control and the consequences of failing to control spending. We then discuss how consumers control their spending and the factors that lead to spending control failures. Finally, we conclude with ways to bolster consumers' ability to regulate their spending.

What is self-control?

The ability to control one's behavior – in other words to resist temptation, break habits, and maintain discipline – enables people to live healthful, happy and successful lives. One of the best definitions of self-control by scholars studying this construct is "the overriding or inhibiting of automatic, habitual, or innate behaviors, urges, emotions, or desires that would otherwise interfere with goal directed behavior" (Muraven *et al.* 2006). Our capacity to exert self-control is perhaps the most powerful adaptive mechanism in maintaining social order (Tangney *et al.* 2004).

Over a decade of research on self-control has ruled out varying accounts of how self-control works, including self-control as a knowledge structure similar to a master schema and self-control as a learned skill, in favor of a strength model. This model posits that effective self-control depends on three-components: standards, monitoring and the capacity to regulate one's behavior (Baumeister 2002). Standards refer to goals and other guidelines that a person hopes to achieve. Without clear and appropriate goals, self-control can be undermined, as is often the case when consumers have conflicting goals (e.g. the desire to save versus the desire to purchase). Monitoring refers to the process through which consumers track their behavior to ensure that it remains consistent with their standards. Finally, effective self-control requires the strength or willpower to resist temptation and prevent immediate gratification.

Consistent with this strength model, studies have shown that utilizing self-control actually results in physiological arousal, which implies effortful exertion (Wegner *et al.* 1990). A strength model also implies that one's capacity for self-regulation is a limited resource. At any point in time, there is a fixed amount of capacity, so that each act of self-regulation depletes from a fixed amount, resulting in poorer self-regulatory performance and ability with each successive act of self-control. Unlike other limited capacity models, like attention, the strength model suggests that exertion leads to fatigue. With attention, once the immediate demands of the task are eliminated, one's attention returns to full capacity. However, the depletion of regulatory capacity lasts for a period of time until it can be built up again. Imagine a consumer exerting self-control in deciding to forgo an unnecessary purchase, say a new iPad. Even once this decision has been made and the consumer continues on her way through the electronics store, her regulatory resources are depleted such that she has less self-control or willpower to draw on for the next spending decision. Ironically enough, this same consumer who just demonstrated self-control in avoiding an unnecessary purchase (i.e. the iPad) is now at greater risk of succumbing to the next test of willpower, say an impulse purchase near the store exit.

Importantly, an additional assumption of the self-control model is that all self-regulation tasks draw from the same fixed pool of regulatory resources. This has important implications for consumers, since it suggests that exerting self-control in one domain may reduce the ability to self-regulate in another. Think of the repercussions of this reality for consumer spending decisions. If the electronics store shopper had exerted self-control by not ordering lunchtime dessert prior to the shopping trip, this shopper is now less able to exert spending control in the store and might just have ended up with the iPad. With each repeated act of self-control, regardless of context or domain – not ordering dessert, not engaging in conflict with rude people – unnecessary purchases are more likely.

Self-control and spending control

The relationship between self-control and spending has recently received attention in the consumer behavior literature (Haws *et al.* 2011; Vohs and Faber 2007; Wilcox *et al.* 2011a). Vohs and Faber (2007) explore how resource availability affects impulsive buying. Related to our discussion above, when participants' general self-regulatory resources were depleted by simply having them control their thoughts during a shopping task, they felt stronger urges to buy, were willing to spend more and actually did spend more on impulse purchases.

It is important to note that research studies have identified trait differences in self-control, such that some people are better able to maintain control than others, and that this generalized trait level of control crosses domains. For example, some people are better than others at saving money, concentrating at work and maintaining a regular exercise routine (Baumeister and Heatherton 1996; Rick *et al.* 2008; Tangney *et al.* 2004). Indeed, inherent individual differences in self-control represent a stable personality characteristic, so much so that "conscientiousness, control or constraint" is conceptualized as one of the five personality traits in the five-factor taxonomy (Goldberg 1990). Tangney and colleagues' scale to measure general self-control

(Tangney *et al.* 2004) captures this general personality trait by focusing on general temptation resistance and self-discipline, and has been reliably used across a variety of domains including spending behavior. Wilcox *et al.* (2011a) used this scale to demonstrate that lower levels of general self-control are associated with greater credit card debt and lower credit scores.

Haws *et al.* (2011) recently developed a more specific conceptualization and measure of self-control within the spending domain. They define consumer spending self-control (CSSC) as "the ability to monitor and regulate one's spending-related thoughts and decisions in accordance with self-imposed standards." Their 10-item, one-factor model of CSSC provides an additional and more parsimonious tool for researchers interested in studying self-control specifically in the spending domain.

Consequences of failing to control spending

Failures of spending self-control have large and varied individual and societal ramifications. Breakdowns in spending self-control naturally affect personal savings, bankruptcy rates and other financial consequences like less access to credit and funding (Bearden and Haws 2011). At the societal level, the consequences can be dire. The recent mortgage crisis, for instance, has been attributed to a lack of self-control (Thaler and Sunstein 2008). The crisis was so widespread that a significant portion of the defaults that occurred were attributed to those who previously had relatively solid credit histories (Goodman and Healey 2009).

Beyond the obvious financial consequences, failures in spending self-control can have downstream influence on people's social, physical and psychological well-being. Failures in spending control can result in strained relationships with friends and family (Bearden and Haws 2011). Psychological consequences like stress, shame and guilt all manifest as direct results of spending self-control failures (Bearden and Haws 2011). Financial stress due to credit card debt is associated with greater physical impairment (Drentea and Lavrakas 2000). Consumers who are able to improve their financial control through credit counseling display less stress and improved overall health (O'Neil *et al.* 2005).

How consumers exert spending control

Mental budgeting

Consumers' ability to control their spending often is based on their ability to set and stay within a budget. According to Heath and Soll's (1996) model of mental budgeting, consumers create mental budgets for various categories of expenses (e.g. clothing, entertainment and food). Once their budget within a category is reached, consumers resist spending on products related to the category. Thus, mental budgeting serves as a self-control mechanism (Thaler and Shefrin 1981) and it shares many of the same characteristics as general self-control. Consumers control their spending by setting a budget (i.e. a standard), tracking their expenses (i.e. monitoring their behavior) and controlling future spending to remain consistent with their budget (i.e. regulating their behavior).

When consumers create mental budgets they earmark money for categories of expenses in advance of actual consumption. However, this psychological earmarking can sometimes lead to overconsumption. For instance, O'Curry (1996) finds that when people receive an unexpected discount on beer, they are more likely to use the discount to buy a more expensive brand of beer, thus negating the price reduction and spending their "beer budget" anyway; note that they would not buy the more expensive brand if the same amount of money were received as a gift (see also Heilman *et al.* 2002). More recently, Stilley *et al.* (2010) found that when consumers set mental budgets for specific shopping trips they often budget more than their planned purchases because they have learned from past shopping behavior to leave some "slack" for unplanned purchases.

The expense tracking process is efficient when expenses are highly typical of specific categories, making it easier for consumers to regulate their spending. For instance, consumers are less likely to purchase sports tickets, which are clearly for entertainment, when their budget for entertainment has been reached (Heath and Soll 1996). However, Cheema and Soman (2008) find that when a purchasing opportunity arises that is ambiguous in terms of its category, consumers' mental accounting process becomes malleable. Consumers use this flexibility in assigning the expenses to justify the purchase, which can lead them to display less spending control compared to when the expense is unambiguous.

Pain of payment

The pain of paying refers to the psychological impact associated with making a purchase. It plays a central role in consumers' ability to exercise spending control (Rick *et al.* 2008). While consumers may experience pain for a variety of purchases, certain expenses are more painful than others. For example, the purchase of hedonic luxuries is associated with frivolous consumption, which often leads consumers to restrict their spending on hedonic luxuries in favor of utilitarian necessities. Okada (2005) finds that the purchase of hedonic products is associated with guilt so the purchase of indulgences often needs to be justified to overcome the pain associated with their purchase. Kivetz and Simonson (2002) argue that many consumers suffer from over-control or "hyperopia" when it comes to spending on indulgences. Often hyperopia can lead to regret over time because consumers begin to feel that they have missed out on life's pleasures (Kivetz and Keinan 2006). Consequently, anticipating regret can lower self-control and increase consumer spending on indulgences (Keinan and Kivetz 2008).

Payment mode can also have an effect on the pain of paying and consumers' ability to regulate their spending. Research on the credit card effect demonstrates that the use of a credit card can lead to greater spending and more unnecessary purchases compared to other payment options like cash or a personal check (Feinberg 1986; Hirschman 1979; Inman *et al.* 2009; Prelec and Loewenstein 1998; Prelec and Simester 2001; Raghubir and Srivastava 2008; Soman 2001). For example, Hirschman (1979) demonstrates that consumers spend more on the same item when it is paid for by credit card. Inman and colleagues find that credit cards increase the likelihood of making an unnecessary purchase (Inman *et al.* 2009). The credit card effect is attributed to the temporal separation of the purchase from payment (Prelec and Loewenstein 1998). With cash, payment occurs during the purchase, which accentuates the pain of paying. Credit cards, however, are paid at the end of the month, which decouples the payments from the purchase. Consequently, purchases made using a credit card are less painful than cash, which leads to greater spending.

Bagchi and Block (2011) demonstrate that pain of payment affects *what* is purchased and not just overall dollars spent. Over a series of studies, they demonstrate that when consumers purchase food items for immediate consumption, the greater the pain of payment (i.e. higher imputed cost), the more indulgent the foods chosen (higher in calories, fat, and sugars). Since cash is more painful than credit, consumers purchase higher-calorie, less-healthy food when paying with cash vs. credit. Importantly, these researchers demonstrate that it is the imputed cost, not the mode of payment (cash vs. credit) that drives differences in purchase. They include studies that vary only imputed cost, but keep method of payment the same, by comparing cash conditions that manipulate imputed costs to be high or low by varying how difficult or easy it was to earn this money. Findings support the theorizing that consumers indulge more when imputed costs are higher, regardless of whether that is derived from cash (vs. credit) or difficult-to-earn cash (vs. easy-to-earn cash). Their findings also show that consuming indulgent foods actually alleviates the pain of payment and leads to greater positive affect.

Failures in spending control

Many of the same mechanisms that influence self-control in other domains also influence consumers' ability to regulate their spending. For instance, research on self-control demonstrates that consumers are more likely to indulge after a mentally taxing task. Thus, when consumers are cognitively depleted they feel stronger urges to buy and are willing to spend more on products (Vohs and Faber 2007). Additionally, focusing on past accomplishments or virtuous behavior can lead to more indulgent spending decisions (Wilcox *et al.* 2011b). Finally, consumers' goals can play a strong role in their ability to exercise spending restraint. Laran and Wilcox (2011) demonstrate that priming an indulgence goal increases consumers' preference for frivolous luxuries. However, priming a regulation goal leads them to prefer necessities. Similarly, Soman and Cheema (2011) find that focusing consumers on their saving goal can increase the amount that they save for retirement.

Although budgets and goals play a vital role in regulating spending, they may also undermine consumers' spending control when they are violated. Soman and Cheema (2004) find that when consumers exceed a set monthly budget, they display less spending control by being more likely to make an unnecessary purchase compared to if they had stayed within their budget. That is, even though they may spend more initially, those who violate their budget abandon their spending restraint. This occurs because failing to achieve a behavioral goal (e.g. staying within a budget) has a psychological cost, which leads consumers to abandon their goal in an effort to overcome the pain of failure (Soman and Cheema 2004). Often failure leads to a complete loss of restraint and a pattern of overindulgence in the opposite direction that is often referred to as the "what the hell" effect (Cochran and Tesser 1996).

Although the "what the hell" effect has been primarily shown in the eating domain, there is increasing evidence that the same effect emerges in consumer spending decisions when a mental barrier has been violated. Dhar *et al.* (2007) demonstrate that making an initial purchase can relax spending control and increase the likelihood of making an unplanned purchase. Research on the denomination effect finds that even though consumers are less likely to make a purchase when given money in large denominations, if they decide to "break" the larger bill they will spend more on the purchase compared to if they had used a bill with a smaller denomination (Raghubir and Srivastava 2009).

The different spending pattern from larger, compared to smaller, denominations is consistent with the literature on the salience of available resources, which suggests that making more consumption resources salient can undermine spending control. This occurs because the more resources individuals actually have available for consumption, the lower the psychological impact of the consumption (Ando and Modigliani 1963). Consequently, simply focusing people on greater available resources can increase spending. For example, Morewedge *et al.* (2007) found that people spend more when they focus on how much money they have in their retirement account compared to how much money they have in their wallet.

Interestingly, differences in consumption resources can also increase spending control, particularly once a goal has been violated. Wilcox *et al.* (2011a) demonstrate consumers will display the "what the hell" effect and spend more on their credit card when they have an outstanding balance on the card compared to not having an outstanding balance on the credit card.

However, they find that spending control can be restored by increasing consumers' resources for consumption through their available credit. Specifically, they find that at low levels of available credit consumers with outstanding balances on their credit card spend more in actual auctions, are more likely to purchase higher-priced products and spend more on their credit card per month compared to those who do not have an outstanding balance on their credit card. This effect is mitigated when consumers have high levels of available credit because the greater resources reduce the psychological impact of incurring an outstanding balance on their credit card.

How to improve spending control

One way to control spending is by controlling consumers' access to consumption. Cheema and Soman (2008) argue that partitioning a resource into smaller units introduces a small transaction cost to consumption, which allows consumers to better control spending. For example, placing money into four envelopes versus one large envelope reduces the amount people spend on risky gambles. More recently, Soman and Cheema (2011) found that low-income consumers are more effective at saving money when it is partitioned into two accounts compared to being pooled into one account.

Finally, since elaboration often has a positive effect on self regulation (Nenkov *et al.* 2009), spending control can improve by focusing on future consequences. Haws *et al.* (2011) find that prompting people to think about potential outcomes of spending behavior improves spending control. Importantly, this effect primarily emerges in those who are relatively low in spending control. Similarly, Spiller (2011) finds that when consumers consider how purchasing something now will affect what they can purchase in the future, it reduces consumption by leading them to consider the opportunity cost of consumption.

Conclusion

Self-control is one of the most powerful mechanisms for maintaining social order and well-being (Tangney *et al.* 2004). Recently, the relationship between self-control and spending has received considerable attention because failing to control spending can have dire consequences. Although it is clear that people differ in their ability to regulate their spending, the ability to control spending begins with setting a budget and spending within the budget. However, budgets may have a counterproductive effect on spending when consumers violate them since people often spend more when they exceed their budget compared to when they remain within their budget. Thus, some of the same mechanisms consumers use to regulate their spending can also undermine their spending control.

Thus, while we have come a long way in understanding spending control in the last few years, as the credit crisis of 2008–9 illustrates, we have a long way to go to help consumers effectively control their spending. Much of the research to date is focused on a single purchase opportunity or a static moment in time. We feel that the next step is to identify ways to improve consumers' spending control over the long term. Additionally, future research should continue to explore the relationship between consumer spending control and self-control in other domains. Doing so will not only make consumers more financially responsible, but will also contribute to their overall well-being.

References

Ando, Albert and Modigliani, Franco (1963) "The 'Life Cycle' Hypothesis of Saving: Aggregate Implications and Tests." *American Economic Review* 53 (March): 55–84.

Bagchi, Rajesh and Block, Lauren G. (2011) "Chocolate Cake Please! Why Do We Indulge More When it Feels More Expensive?" *Journal of Public Policy & Marketing* 30(2): 294–306.

Baumeister, Roy F. (2002) "Yielding to Temptation: Self-control Failure, Impulsive Purchasing, and Consumer Behavior." *Journal of Consumer Research* 28(4): 670–76.

Baumeister, Roy F. and Heatherton, Todd F. (1996) "Self-Regulation Failure: An Overview." *Psychological Inquiry* 7(1): 1–15.

Bearden, William O. and Haws, Kelly (2012) "How Low Spending Control Harms Consumers." *Journal of the Academy of Marketing Science* 40(1): 181–93.

Cheema, Amar and Soman, Dilip (2008) "The Effect of Partitions on Controlling Consumption." *Journal of Marketing Research* 45(6): 665–75.

Cochran, Winona and Tesser, Abraham (1996) "The 'What the Hell Effect': Some Effects of Goal Proximity and Goal Framing on Performance." In Leonard L. Martin and Abraham Tesser (eds), *Striving and Feeling: Interactions Among Goals. Affect, and Self-Regulation.* Mahwah, NJ: Erlbaum, pp. 99–120.

Dhar, Ravi, Huber, Joel, and Khan, Uzma (2007) "The Shopping Momentum Effect." *Journal of Marketing Research* 44(3): 370–78.

Drentea, Patricia and Lavrakas, Paul J. (2000) "Over the Limit: The Association Among Health, Race and Debt." *Social Science and Medicine* 50: 517–29.

Feinberg, Richard A. (1986) "Credit Cards as Spending Facilitating Stimuli: A Conditioning Interpretation." *Journal of Consumer Research* 13 (December): 348–56.

Ferber, Robert (1962) "Research on Household Behavior." *American Economic Review* 52 (March): 19–63.

Fishbach, Ayelet and Dhar, Ravi (2005) "Goals as Excuses or Guides: The Liberating Effect of Perceived Goal Progress on Choice." *Journal of Consumer Research* 32(3): 370–7.

Goldberg, Lewis R. (1990) "An Alternative 'Description of Personality': The Big-Five Factor Structure." *Journal of Personality and Social Psychology* 59(6): 1216–29.

Goodman, P.S. and Healy, J. (2009) "Job Losses Push Safer Mortgages to Foreclosure." *The New York Times*, 25 May: A1.

Haws, Kelly, Bearden, William O., and Nenkov, Gergana Y. (2012) "Consumer Spending Self-Control Effectiveness and Outcome Elaboration Prompts." *Journal of the Academy of Marketing Science* 40(1): 695–70.

Heath, Chip and Soll, Jack B. (1996) "Mental Budgeting and Consumer Decisions." *Journal of Consumer Research* 23(1): 40–52.

Heilman, Carrie M., Nakamoto, Kent, and Rao, Ambar (2002) "Pleasant Surprises: Consumer Response to Unexpected In-store Promotions." *Journal of Marketing Research* 39 (May): 242–51.

Hirschman, Elizabeth (1979) "Differences in Consumer Purchase Behavior by Credit Card Payment System." *Journal of Consumer Research* 6 (June): 58–66.

Inman, Jeffrey J., Winer, Russell S. and Ferraro, Rosellina (2009) "The Interplay Among Category Characteristics, Customer Characteristics, and Customer Activities on In-Store Decision Making." *Journal of Marketing* 73(5): 19–29.

Keinan, Anat and Kivetz, Ran (2008) "Remedying Hyperopia: The Effects of Self-Control Regret on Consumer Behavior." *Journal of Marketing Research* 45(6): 676–89.

Khan, Uzma and Dhar, Ravi (2006) "Licensing Effect in Consumer Choice." *Journal of Marketing Research* 43(2): 259–66.

Kivetz, Ran and Keinan, Anat (2006) "Repenting Hyperopia: An Analysis of Self-control Regrets." *Journal of Consumer Research* 33(2): 273–82.

Kivetz, Ran and Simonson, Itamar (2002) "Self-control for the Righteous: Toward a Theory of Precommitment to Indulgence." *Journal of Consumer Research* 29(2): 199–217.

Laran, Juliano and Wilcox, Keith (2011) "Choice, Rejection, and Elaboration on Preference-Inconsistent Alternatives." *Journal of Consumer Research* 38(2): 229–41.

Morewedge, Carey K., Holtzman, Leif, and Epley, Nicholas (2007) "Unfixed Resources: Perceived Costs, Consumption, and the Accessible Account Effect." *Journal of Consumer Research* 34(4): 459–67.

Muraven, Mark, Shmueli, Dikla, and Burkley, Edward (2006) "Conserving Self-control Strength." *Journal of Personality and Social Psychology* 91(3): 524–37.

Muraven, Mark, Tice, Diane M., and Baumeister, Roy F. (1998) "Self-Control as Limited Resource: Regulatory Depletion Patterns." *Journal of Personality and Social Psychology* 74(3): 774–89.

Nenkov, Gergana Y., Inman, Jeffrey J., Hulland, John S., and Morrin, Maureen (2009) "The Impact of Outcome Elaboration on Susceptibility to Contextual and Presentation Biases." *Journal of Marketing Research* 46 (December): 764–76.

O'Curry, Sue (1996) *Income Source Effects.* Working paper. Chicago, IL: DePaul University.

Okada, Erica Mina (2005) "Justification Effects on Consumer Choice of Hedonic and Utilitarian Goods." *Journal of Marketing Research* 42(1): 43–53.

O'Neil, Barbara, Sorhaindo, Benoit, Xiao, Jing J., and Garman, E. Thomas (2005) "Health, Financial Well-being, and Financial Practices of Financially Distressed Consumers." *Consumer Interests Annual* 51: 80–82.

Prelec, Drazen and Loewenstein, George (1998) "The Red and the Black: Mental Accounting of Savings and Debt." *Marketing Science* 17(1): 4–28.

Prelec, Drazen and Simester, Duncan (2001) "Always Leave Home Without It: A Further Investigation of the Credit-Card Effect on Willingness to Pay." *Marketing Letters* 12(1): 5–12.

Raghubir, Priya and Srivastava, Joydeep (2008) "Monopoly Money: The Effect of Payment Coupling and Form on Spending Behavior." *Journal of Experimental Psychology: Applied* 14(3): 213–25.

——(2009) "The Denomination Effect." *Journal of Consumer Research* 36 (December): 701–13.

Rick, Scott I., Cryder, Cynthia E., and Loewenstein, George (2008) "Tightwads and Spendthrifts." *Journal of Consumer Research* 34(6): 767–82.

Schelling, Thomas C. (1992) "Self-Command: A New Discipline." In George Loewenstein and Jon Elster (eds), *Choice over Time*. New York: Sage, pp. 167–76.

Shefrin, Hersh M. and Thaler, Richard H. (1988) "The Behavioral Life-Cycle Hypothesis." *Economic Inquiry* 26(4): 609–43.

Soman, Dilip (2001) "Effects of Payment Mechanism on Spending Effects: The Role of Rehearsal and Immediacy of Payments." *Journal of Consumer Research* 27 (March): 460–74.

Soman, Dilip and Cheema, Amar (2002) "The Effect of Credit on Spending Decisions: The Role of the Credit Limit and Credibility." *Marketing Science* 21(1): 32–53.

——(2004) "When Goals are Counterproductive: The Effects of Violation of a Behavioral Goal on Subsequent Performance." *Journal of Consumer Research* 31(1): 52–62.

——(2011) "Earmarking and Partitioning: Increasing Saving by Low-income Households." *Journal of Marketing Research.*

Spiller, Stephen A. (2011) "Opportunity Cost Consideration." *Journal of Consumer Research* 38(4): 595–610.

Stilley, Karen M., Inman, Jeffrey J., and Wakefield, Kirk L. (2010) "Planning to Make Unplanned Purchases? The Role of In-Store Slack in Budget Deviation." *Journal of Consumer Research* 37(2): 264–78.

Tangney, June P., Baumeister, Roy F., and Boone, Angie Luzio (2004) "High Self-control Predicts Good Adjustment, Less Pathology, Better Grades, and Interpersonal Success." *Journal of Personality* 72(2): 271–324.

Thaler, Richard and Sunstein, Cass (2008) "Human Frailty Caused This Crisis." *The Financial Times.*

Thaler, Richard H. and Shefrin, Hersh M. (1981) "An Economic Theory of Self-Control." *Journal of Political Economy* 89(2): 392–406.

Vohs, Kathleen D. and Faber, Ronald (2007) "Spent Resources: Self-regulatory Resource Availability Affects Impulse Buying." *Journal of Consumer Research* 33(4): 537–47.

Wegner, Daniel M., Shortt, Joann W., Blake, Anne W., and Page, Michelle S. (1990) "The Suppression of Exciting Thoughts." *Journal of Personality and Social Psychology* 58(3): 409–18.

Wertenbroch, Klaus (2001) *Self-Rationing: Self-Control in Consumer Choice.* Working paper.

Wilcox, Keith, Block, Lauren, and Eisenstein, Eric (2011a) "Leave Home Without It? The Effects of Credit Card Debt and Available Credit on Spending." *Journal of Marketing Research* 48 (November).

Wilcox, Keith, Kramer, Thomas, and Sen, Sankar (2011b) "Indulgence or Self-Control: A Dual Process Model of the Effect of Incidental Pride on Indulgent Choice." *Journal of Consumer Research* 38 (June): 157–63.

24

CULTURE AND SELF-REGULATION

The influence of self-construal on impulsive consumption

L.J. Shrum and Yinlong Zhang

Culture and identity are fundamentally intertwined. Shared cultural values – those integrated systems of attitudes, beliefs, perceptions, and behaviors – dictate the norms for interactions among group members. They also provide a blueprint for acceptable means of expressing identity.

The expression of cultural values and cultural identity takes many forms. One of those forms, which is the focus of this volume, is consumption. As several other chapters in this volume suggest, cultural differences in self and identity can be seen across a large spectrum of consumer behaviors. In this chapter, we focus on the relation between cultural orientation and impulsive consumption, and the underlying processes of self-regulation. More specifically, we discuss the cultural identity of self-construal – how members of a culture view themselves in relation to other members – and how it influences self-expression and self-regulation, and the corresponding effects these constructs have on impulsive consumption.

Cultural orientation and self-construal

Culture is a complex construct that represents ways of engaging with the world. Although often thought of in terms of people and their values and traditions, it also comprises those things that people of a culture make, such as structures and institutions (Oyserman and Lee 2007). Cross-cultural researchers have noted the systematic ways in which cultures differ on how their people interact with each other and the environment. Numerous dichotomies have been noted that capture some of these differences, such as masculine/feminine (Hofstede 1980), loose/tight (Triandis 1995), and short/long-term orientations (Chinese Culture Connection 1987). The most prominent distinction, and the one on which we focus in this chapter, is individualism/collectivism (Hofstede 2005; Oyserman and Lee 2007). Individualistic cultures view the individual as independent and autonomous, put emphasis on individual initiative, value emotional independence, self-reliance, and freedom of choice, and stress rights over duties. In contrast, collectivistic cultures give priority to group goals over personal goals, define the self in relation to the group, value conformity and in-group harmony, and stress sharing, duties, and obligations over personal rights (Hofstede 1980; Triandis 1995; see also McCarty and Shrum 2001).

Although individualism and collectivism are viewed as cultural level constructs that represent opposite ends of a continuum, more contemporary models suggest that the concepts can be both operationalized and measured at the individual level (Singelis 1994; Triandis 2009; Triandis *et al.* 1988; Zhang 2004; Zhang *et al.* 2006; Zhang and Mittal 2007). Moreover, the constructs can be viewed as orthogonal ones that coexist within the same culture and within each person. The internalization of these cultural values influences how the self is viewed. In their seminal paper on self-construal, Markus and Kitayama (1991) distinguished between independent and interdependent self-construals (for a more in-depth discussion, see Chapter 1, this volume). People with an independent self-construal (independents) view themselves as autonomous, self-contained, and distinct from the group, and tend to place high value on uniqueness, achievement, and individual accomplishments. In contrast, people with an interdependent self-construal (interdependents) see themselves in terms of their connectedness to the larger group, stress conformity and group harmony, and place high value on safety and security. These differences in self-construal in turn manifest themselves in attitudes and behaviors. The behavior of independents tends to be guided more by attitudes and internal dispositions, whereas the behavior of interdependents is guided more by subjective norms (Abrams *et al.* 1998; Ybarra and Trafimow 1998). Independents take more social risks but interdependents take more financial risks (Mandel 2003; Hsee and Weber 1999), and independents tend to be more promotion-focused and seek to maximize gains, whereas interdependents tend to be more prevention-focused and seek to minimize losses (Aaker and Lee 2011).

Markus and Kitayama (1991) note the link between the cultural level constructs of individualism and collectivism, and self-construal. It is well established that individuals have multiple selves (Kihlstrom and Cantor 1984), and this is true of self-construals. Individuals typically hold both self-construals simultaneously, and cultures differ in the extent to which their members have a particular self-construal that is chronically accessible, activated most often, and the predominant guide to behavior. People in individualistic cultures (e.g. Western cultures such as American and European) tend to hold predominantly independent self-construals, whereas people in collectivistic cultures (e.g. Eastern cultures such as Asian) tend to hold predominantly interdependent self-construals. However, contextual cues can also make a particular self-construal temporarily accessible (Oyserman and Lee 2007). Thus, self-construals can be manipulated so that even those with chronically independent or interdependent selves can be situationally primed to take the opposite perspective (Trafimow *et al.* 1991; for a review, see Oyserman and Lee 2008).

Self-construal and self-regulation

The attributes associated with independent and interdependent self-construals have clear implications for self-regulation. For independents, one of their primary motivations is self-expression. Independents strive to be unique and stand out from others. They give priority to personal goal pursuit, tend to "do what is fun" (Triandis 2009: 190), and are relatively unconcerned about how such behaviors affect others, compared to interdependents. The case for interdependents is quite different. Interdependents strive for group cohesion and harmony, and work to fit in with (rather than stand out from) the group. They are particularly vigilant about how their actions and expressions affect others, and less concerned about pursuing personal goals that are distinct from group goals.

It is the differences between interdependents and independents in vigilance, monitoring, and concern about the impact of one's actions on others that translate into differences in self-regulation. Because independents are more concerned about self-fulfillment and acting on their own thoughts and feelings, their behavior tends to follow the pleasure principle, they choose actions based on benefits versus costs, and they are less concerned about the impact of their actions on others (Triandis 1995). Consequently, they are less likely to regulate their thoughts, feelings, or behaviors. In contrast, because interdependents are concerned about how their actions affect others, they are more likely to suppress expressions and behaviors that would be considered disruptive. This act of suppression suggests a high level of self-regulation. In fact, self-regulation and impulse control are fundamental to Confucian philosophy. When asked how to live a good life, Confucius replied that it is important to subdue one's impulses and desires, then return to ritual, and all will ascribe the goodness to a man who can control himself (Tu 1978).

Research in a number of domains supports this cultural difference in self-regulation. For example, interdependent cultures tend to regulate emotions more so than do independent cultures (Eisenberg and Zhou 2000; Morelli and Rothbaum 2007). Emotions that may be disruptive, such as pride, anger, or frustration, are viewed more negatively in Eastern than Western cultures (Kitayama *et al.* 2004). Based on scores on the Minnesota Multiphasic Personality Inventory, Chinese people are more emotionally reserved and practice more self-restraint than do people from a Western culture (Song 1985). These differences have also been documented in the workplace, with Chinese managers endorsing the concept of emotional moderation and conflict avoidance more so than British managers (Westwood *et al.* 1992). In a study that examined cultural differences in emotional regulation in the context of interpersonal conflict, Tsai and Levenson (1997) measured physiological response and self-reported affect of European-American and Chinese-American dating couples while the couples discussed the main source of conflict in their relationships. Their results showed that the European-American couples exhibited greater variability and positivity in reported affect and more variable cardiac interbeat intervals than the Chinese-American couples, suggesting less self-regulation for those with more independent self-construals.

Other research on self-regulation, particularly with children, has shown similar cultural differences. For example, in a study of preschoolers, North American children responded to hypotheticals of interpersonal conflict with more indicators of anger and aggression than did Japanese children (Zahn-Waxler *et al.* 1996). In another study of adolescents, Western children showed more aggression and less guilt and shame than did Japanese children (Kornadt *et al.* 1992).

Philosophical writings, ethnographic studies, and experimental research have all produced consistent evidence for cultural differences in self-regulation across a variety of situations. In the next section, we discuss the implications of this research for impulsive consumption, and discuss several studies, including work in progress, that have directly assessed the relation between cultural orientation (self-construal) and impulsive consumption.

Self-construal and impulsive consumption

Thus far we have presented evidence of cultural differences in self-regulation. In particular, we have discussed research indicating that individuals with a predominantly interdependent self-construal tend to self-regulate to a greater degree than do individuals with a predominantly independent self-construal. We now consider the proposition in the context of what is generally considered to be a self-regulatory failure: impulsive consumption. Impulsive consumption (or time-inconsistent preferences) can be thought of as a self-control problem that results from a conflict between desires to consume (e.g. a product or an experience) and the willpower to resist (Hoch and Loewenstein 1991). Willpower is the strength of will or self-control to resist an impulse, and is a function of both the ability and motivation to exert this willpower (Zhang and Shrum 2009).

Impulsive consumption often poses serious problems for both individuals and societies. Some have estimated that about 62% of supermarket sales and 80% of luxury-goods sales in the US are attributed to impulsive buying and consumption (Agins 2004). New technologies that promote instant gratification through immediate access to goods and services (e.g. ATM machines, online and home television shopping, etc.) are thought to be one source of the problem (Hoch and Loewenstein 1991; Rook 1987; Vohs and Faber 2007). Impulsive behavior is often associated with negative traits such as lower intelligence, immaturity, and poor value systems, and can lead to problematic outcomes (e.g. financial problems, lower self-esteem, post-purchase dissatisfaction) (Rook 1987; Rook and Fisher 1995). It has also been linked to high debt-to-income ratios in the US (Vohs and Faber 2007).

Underlying mechanisms

When given the choice of consuming a hedonic product or experience, consumers often experience a conflict between two competing goals: pleasure seeking and self-regulation (Zhang and Shrum 2009). Individuals may differ on the relative accessibility of those goals in memory (Ramanathan and Menon 2006), such that those who are considered chronically high in impulsivity are ones whose pleasure-seeking goals tend to be more accessible than self-regulation goals. Situational factors can also impact the activation of these goals. For example, when self-regulatory resources are in ample supply, both high and low impulsives may be able successfully to resist a strong impulse to consume. However, if those self-regulatory resources become depleted, high impulsives are more likely to succumb to the impulse than low impulsives (Shiv and Fedorikhin 1999).

The notion of individual differences in goal activation (pleasure seeking vs. self-regulation) has implications for the possible relation between self-construal and impulsive consumption. We have reviewed research showing that independents and interdependents differ on which goals are chronically accessible. Independents are oriented toward goals of expressing individuality and acting on their attitudes and emotions (Trafimow *et al.* 1991), whereas interdependents are oriented toward goals of conformity to social norms and group cohesion. Given that impulsive consumption is generally considered a vice that reflects immaturity, then individuals who have more accessible interdependent self-construals should be inclined to activate the goal of suppressing behaviors that are considered normatively inappropriate and may disrupt social cohesion, which should reduce impulsive consumption. In contrast, those with independent self-construals should be inclined to act on their attitudes and emotions and worry less about the normative inappropriateness of the behavior, and thus should be more likely than interdependents to give into the impulse.

In the next section, we review both survey and experimental research that has addressed this proposition. We also discuss research in progress that is aimed at better understanding some of these processes.

Kacen and Lee (2002): culture and impulsive buying

In one of the first studies to investigate the relation between culture and impulsive consumption, Kacen and Lee tested the hypothesis that collectivists would be more successful than individualists at resisting impulsive consumption tendencies. They reasoned that humans are for the most part similar in their preferences for pleasure over pain. When they see something that gives them pleasure, they will likely want it. Thus, Kacen and Lee surmised that there would be few cultural differences in trait impulsiveness; those feelings are more innate and uncontrollable. They also expected that trait impulsiveness would be predictive of impulsive buying. However, where they did expect to see cultural differences was in suppressing those impulsive urges. That is, they expected that collectivists would be less likely than individualists to act on their impulses.

To test this proposition, they conducted surveys in five different countries that differed on whether they scored high on Hofstede's (2005) ranking of individualism (Australia, US) or collectivism (Singapore, Malaysia, Hong Kong). The surveys asked respondents to complete measures of buying impulsiveness tendencies (trait measure) and indicate how often they actually did end up buying things on impulse (behavioral measure). The surveys also measured respondents' level of self-construal (independent and interdependent). As expected, they found virtually no differences between the individualistic and collectivistic countries on their scores on the trait buying impulsiveness. They also found that although trait buying impulsiveness was indeed predictive of impulsive buying behavior for both cultures, individualists showed a significantly stronger correlation than collectivists between the trait measure of buying impulsiveness and their actual impulsive buying. The same was true when measured levels of self-construal were considered. This pattern of results suggests that independents and interdependents have similar levels of impulsive tendencies, but interdependents are less likely to act on those impulses, and thus suppress their impulsive urge to buy.

These results support the hypothesis of cultural differences in impulsive consumption. However, there are two important questions left unanswered. The first pertains to causality. It may be that other variables that are correlated with both the cultural orientations and the impulsive measures are driving the results (e.g. other cultural values, such as power distance or horizontality–verticality; Oyserman and Lee 2008; or impression management and socially desirable responding; Lalwani *et al.* 2009). The second question pertains to the underlying processes. Why are interdependents more successful than independents at resisting their impulsive tendencies? Are they more motivated to do so, simply better at it, or both? These possibilities were addressed by Zhang and Shrum (2009).

Zhang and Shrum (2009): self-construal and impulsive alcohol consumption

Alcohol use and abuse has been consistently linked to impulsivity. Impulsivity has been found to be positively correlated with drinking behavior (Acton 2003) and negatively correlated with serotonin levels in people with alcohol disorders (Soloff *et al.* 2000). Other traits related to impulsivity, such as lack of willpower (Hoch and Loewenstein 1991), sensation-seeking (Grau and Ortet 1999), and need for stimulation (Gerbing *et al.* 1987), have also been linked to alcohol consumption.

Based on these findings, Zhang and Shrum (2009) conducted a series of studies to test the hypothesis that self-construal is related to impulsive consumption. In the first two studies they used secondary data to examine the relation between individualism and alcohol consumption. In the first study, they obtained data indicating the per capita beer consumption of 42 countries, and then correlated these data with each country's individualism scores (Hofstede 2005). In the second study they obtained data pertaining to problem alcohol consumption, published by the Center for Disease Control and Prevention (CDC 2004), which provides the data broken out by US states. They then correlated each state's measured level of individualism (Vandello and Cohen 1999) with three separate problem alcohol consumption measures: percentage of teens reporting drinking alcohol in the last month; percentage of teens reporting heavy drinking in the last month; and percentage of adults reporting binge drinking (five or more drinks) in the last month.

As expected, individualism was positively correlated with per capita beer consumption in the first study ($\beta = 0.38$), and this relation was significant even when other potential confounding variables were controlled (e.g. masculinity, power distance, uncertain avoidance, income, climate, religiosity). The results for the second study were even more dramatic. Individualism was positively correlated with teen drinking ($\beta = 0.83$), teen heavy drinking ($\beta = 0.44$), and adult binge drinking ($\beta = 0.42$), and the results again held when control variables (income, temperature) were included in the analysis.

Although consistent with hypotheses, these studies were also correlational and cannot speak confidently to the issue of causality, and also say nothing about the underlying processes.

To address these issues, Zhang and Shrum conducted two experiments that manipulated participants' self-construal. To accomplish this, in one of the experiments Zhang and Shrum had participants write about either enjoying themselves (independent self-construal) or enjoying relationships (interdependent self-construal). This procedure has been shown to prime the respective concepts (Hamilton and Biehal 2005). Following that, participants were asked to provide their attitudes toward drinking beer at that moment. In addition, to address the question of why the effect occurred, the researchers also manipulated the context of the drinking, either with peers (friends) present or not. Having peers present was expected to increase motivations for beer consumption among independents, but decrease the motivations for interdependents.

The results were as predicted, and suggest that greater motivation to suppress impulsive consumption tendencies on the part of interdependents can explain the previous findings. These findings were further confirmed in a second experiment. The design of this experiment was identical to the previous one except for one change: some of the participants were given a task that reduced their self-regulatory resources (and hence their ability to resist tempting impulses). Thus, under these circumstances, even those who were motivated to resist impulsive feelings (interdependent) would be unable to do so. As expected, this manipulation eliminated the effect of peer presence on alcohol consumption preferences.

The findings of Zhang and Shrum (2009) indicate that interdependents do in fact exert more self-control, and resist impulsive tendencies more than independents. In addition, consistent with Kacen and Lee (2002), these differences can be traced to a greater motivation to suppress impulsive tendencies on the part of interdependents. Combined, the two sets of studies provide consistent results using multiple research methods across different impulsive consumption domains. Moreover, not only do both laboratory experiments and field surveys provide convergent findings, but similar relations can be noted in aggregate consumption data.

Future research

Although the research just reviewed provides compelling evidence of cultural differences in impulsive consumption, there are still some additional unanswered questions. One that we are in the process of investigating is the extent to which these cultural differences can be attributed to motivation versus ability. The studies by Zhang and Shrum provide clear evidence that motivation is at least one component. However, it may be that ability to resist temptation also plays a role. Some models of self-regulation consider it analogous to a muscle (Muraven and Baumeister 2000). Self-regulatory resources are limited, and thus self-regulatory strength can be depleted when self-regulation is engaged (exercised). When self-regulatory strength is depleted, the ability to self-regulate is decreased. This explains why in Zhang and Shrum (2009: study 3), independents and interdependents behaved similarly after a self-regulatory resource-depletion manipulation, even though interdependents were more motivated to self-regulate when peers were present.

However, there is also some evidence that, like human muscles, the self-regulatory muscle can be strengthened through exercise (Muraven *et al.* 1999). That is, practice at self-regulation can increase the ability to self-regulate. If so, then people who regularly engage in self-regulation and impulse control (e.g. people who are chronically interdependent) should show a greater ability to resist temptation than those who would habitually self-regulate relatively less. There is some evidence to support this proposition. In an experiment that manipulated self-regulatory resources, chronic interdependents exhibited more self-control (took fewer chocolates) than independents, even after their self-regulatory resources were depleted (Arsena *et al.* 2010). Seeley and Gardner (2003) also found that chronic interdependents do not get as depleted as independents following a self-regulation task (see also Seeley and Gardner 2006). Zhang *et al.* (2010) reported similar self-regulation effects as a function of power distance. We are currently conducting experiments in the US and China to further untangle the effects of motivation and ability to self-regulate and resist impulsive consumption tendencies.

In sum, although research on cultural differences in impulsive consumption is in its infancy, the results to date compellingly argue for these differences, at least in terms of Eastern versus Western cultures. However, there are many cultures, and many cultural variables, other than the ones that have been a focus of research thus far. Future research would benefit from an exploration of these other types of cultural differences, particularly ones that take a more nuanced view of cultural differences. For example, most research on cultural values looks at the effects of one or more cultural value, either in isolation or simultaneously. However, relatively little research investigates how cultural values interact and places these effects within a theoretical framework (for an exception, see Triandis and colleagues' research on vertical and horizontal dimensions of individualism and collectivism; Triandis 1995; Triandis and Gelfand 1998; for a review, see Shavitt *et al.* 2006). Understanding cultural differences beyond the main effects of cultural values should contribute to a deeper understanding of the effects of culture and identity on consumer behavior.

Acknowledgement

The authors thank Kathleen Vohs for excellent comments on an earlier version of this chapter.

References

Aaker, J.L. and Lee, A.Y. (2011) "'I' Seek Pleasures and 'We' Avoid Pains: The Role of Self-regulatory Goals in Information Processing and Persuasion." *Journal of Consumer Research* 28(6): 33–49.

Abrams, D., Ando, K., and Hinkle, S. (1998) "Psychological Attachment to the Group: Cross-cultural Differences in Organizational Identification and Subjective Norms as Predictors of Workers' Turnover Intentions." *Personality and Social Psychology Bulletin* 24(10): 1027–39.

Acton, G.S. (2003) "Measurement of Impulsivity in a Hierarchical Model of Personality Traits: Implications for Substance Use." *Substance Use and Misuse* 38(1): 67–83.

Agins, T. (2004) "For Men, Fancier Pants – and Pricier Boxers." *Wall Street Journal*, 3 September: W.12.

Arsena, A.R., Lee, J., Shrum, L.J., Zhang, Y., and Row, J.L. (2010) "Differences in Self-regulatory Strength as a Function of Self-construal." In M.C. Campbell, J. Inman and R. Pieters (eds), *Advances in Consumer Research*. Duluth, MN: Associate for Consumer Research, pp. 750–1.

CDC (2004) *Behavioral Risk Factor Surveillance System: Prevalence Data*. Atlanta, GA: Centers for Disease Control and Prevention. apps.nccd.cdc.gov/brfss/.

Chinese Culture Connection (1987) "Chinese Values and the Search for Culture-free Dimensions of Culture." *Journal of Cross-Cultural Psychology* 18: 143–64.

Eisenberg, N. and Zhou, Q. (2000) "Regulation from Developmental Perspective." *Psychological Inquiry* 11(3): 166–71.

Gerbing, D.W., Ahadi, S.A., and Patton, J.H. (1987) "Toward a Conceptualization of Impulsivity: Components Across the Behavioral and Self-report Domains." *Multivariate Behavioral Research* 22(7): 357–79.

Grau, E. and Ortet, G. (1999) "Personality Traits and Alcohol Consumption in a Sample of Non-alcoholic Women." *Personality and Individual Differences* 27(12): 1057–66.

Hamilton, R.W. and Biehal, G.J. (2005) "Achieving Your Goals or Protecting Their Future? The Effects of Self-view on Goals and Choices." *Journal of Consumer Research* 32(9): 277–83.

Hoch, S.J. and Loewenstein, G.F. (1991) "Time-inconsistent Preferences and Consumer Self-control." *Journal of Consumer Research* 17(3): 492–507.

Hofstede, G. (1980) *Culture's Consequences: International Differences in Work-Related Values*. Beverly Hills, CA: Sage.

——(2005) *Cultural Dimensions*. www.geert-hofstede.com/hofstede_dimensions.php.

Hsee, C.K. and Weber, E.U. (1999) "Cross-national Differences in Risk Preference and Lay Predictions." *Journal of Behavioral Decision Making* 12(2): 165–79.

Kacen, J.J. and Lee, J.A. (2002) "The Influence of Culture on Consumer Impulsive Buying Behavior." *Journal of Consumer Psychology* 12(2): 163–76.

Kihlstrom, J.F. and Cantor, N. (1984) "Mental Representations of the Self." *Advances in Experimental Social Psychology* 17: 1–47.

Kitayama, S., Karasawa, M., and Mesquita, B. (2004) "Collective and Personal Processes in Regulating Emotions: Emotion and Self in Japan and the United States." In P. Philippot and R.S. Feldman (eds), *The Regulation of Emotion*. Mahwah, NJ: Erlbaum, pp. 251–73.

Kornadt, H.J., Hayashi, T., Tachibana, Y., Trommsdorff, G., and Yamauchi, H. (1992) "Aggressiveness and its Developmental Conditions in Five Cultures." In S. Iwawaki, Y. Kashima, and K. Leung (eds), *Innovations in Cross-cultural Psychology*. Amsterdam: Swets & Zeitlinger, pp. 250–68.

Lalwani, A.K., Shrum, L.J., and Chiu, C.Y. (2009) "Motivated Response Styles: The Role of Cultural Values, Regulatory Focus, and Self-consciousness in Socially Desirable Responding." *Journal of Personality and Social Psychology* 96(4): 870–82.

McCarty, J.A. and Shrum, L.J. (2001) "The Influence of Individualism, Collectivism, and Locus of Control on Environmental Beliefs and Behavior." *Journal of Public Policy & Marketing* 20(1): 93–104.

Mandel, N. (2003) "Shifting Selves and Decision Making: The Effects of Self-construal Priming on Consumer Risk-taking." *Journal of Consumer Research* 30(6): 30–40.

Markus, H.R. and Kitayama, S. (1991) "Culture and the Self: Implications for Cognition, Emotion and Motivation." *Psychological Review* 98(4): 224–53.

Morelli, G.A. and Rothbaum, F. (2007) "Situating the Child in Context: Attachment Relationships and Self-regulation in Different Cultures." In S. Kitayama and D. Cohen (eds), *Handbook of Cultural Psychology*. New York, NY: Guilford Press, pp. 500–27.

Muraven, M. and Baumeister, R.F. (2000) "Self-regulation and Depletion of Limited Resources: Does Self-control Resemble a Muscle." *Psychological Bulletin* 126(2): 247–59.

Muraven, M., Baumeister, R.F., and Tice, D. (1999) "Longitudinal Improvement in Self-regulation Through Practice: Building Self-control Strength Through Repeated Exercise." *Journal of Social Psychology* 139(4): 580–91.

Oyserman, D. and Lee, S.W. (2007) "Priming 'Culture': Culture as Situated Cognition." In S. Kitayama and D. Cohen (eds), *Handbook of Cultural Psychology*. New York: Guilford Press, pp. 255–79.

——(2008) "Does Culture Influence What and How We Think? Effects of Priming Individualism and Collectivism." *Psychological Bulletin* 134(3): 311–42.

Ramanathan, S. and Menon, G. (2006) "Time-varying Effects of Chronic Hedonic Goals on Impulsive Behavior." *Journal of Marketing Research* 43(11): 628–41.

Rook, D.W. (1987) "The Buying Impulse." *Journal of Consumer Research* 14(9): 189–99.

Rook, D.W. and Fisher, R.J. (1995) "Normative Influences on Impulsive Buying Behavior." *Journal of Consumer Research* 22(12): 305–13.

Seeley, E.A. and Gardner, W.L. (2003) "The 'Selfless' and Self-regulation: The Role of Chronic Other-orientation in Averting Self-regulatory Depletion." *Self & Identity* 2: 103–17.

——(2006) "Succeeding at Self-control Through a Focus on Others: The Roles of Social Practice and Accountability in Self-regulation." In Kathleen D. Vohs and E.J. Finkel (eds), *Self and Relationships: Connecting Intrapersonal and Interpersonal Processes*. New York: Guilford.

Shavitt, S., Lalwani, A.L., Zhang, J., and Torelli, C.J. (2006) "The Horizontal/Vertical Distinction in Cross-cultural Consumer Research." *Journal of Consumer Psychology* 16(4): 325–56.

Shiv, B. and Fedorikhin, A. (1999) "Heart and Mind in Conflict: The Interplay of Affect and Cognition in Consumer Decision Making." *Journal of Consumer Research* 26(12): 278–92.

Singelis, T. (1994) "The Measurement of Independent and Interdependent Self-construals." *Personality and Social Psychology Bulletin* 20(10): 580–91.

Soloff, P.H., Lynch, K.G., and Moss, H.B. (2000) "Serotonin, Impulsivity, and Alcohol Use Disorders in the Older Adolescent: A Psychobiological Study." *Alcoholism: Clinical and Experimental Research* 24(11): 1609–19.

Song, W. (1985) "A Preliminary Study of the Character Traits of the Chinese." In W.S. Teng and D. Wu (eds), *Chinese Culture and Mental Health*. Orlando, FL: Academic Press.

Trafimow, D., Triandis, H., and Goto, S.G. (1991) "Some Tests of the Distinction Between the Private Self and the Collective Self." *Journal of Personality and Social Psychology* 60(5): 649–55.

Triandis, H. (1995) *Individualism and Collectivism*. Boulder, CO: Westview Press.

——(2009) *Fooling Ourselves: Self-deception in Politics, Religion, and Terrorism*. Westport, CT: Praeger.

Triandis, H., Bontempo, R., Villareal, M., Asai, M., and Lucca, N. (1988) "Individualism and Collectivism: Cross-cultural Perspectives on Self-in Group Relationships." *Journal of Personality and Social Psychology* 54(2): 323–38.

Triandis, H. and Gelfand, M.J. (1998) "Converging Measurement of Horizontal and Vertical Individualism and Collectivism." *Journal of Personality and Social Psychology* 74: 118–28.

Tsai, J. and Levenson, R.W. (1997) "Cultural Influences on Emotional Responding Chinese American and European American Dating Couples During Interpersonal Conflict." *Journal of Cross-Cultural Psychology* 28(5): 600–25.

Tu, W. (1978) *Humanity and Self-Cultivation: Essays in Confucian Thought*. Boston, MA: Asian Humanities Press.

Vandello, J.A. and Cohen, D. (1999) "Patterns of Individualism and Collectivism Across the United States." *Journal of Personality and Social Psychology* 77(8): 279–92.

Vohs, K.D. and Faber, R.J. (2007) "Spent Resources: Self-regulatory Resource Availability Affects Impulse Buying." *Journal of Consumer Research* 33(3): 537–47.

Westwood, R.I., Tang, S., and Kirkbride, P.S. (1992) "Chinese Conflict Behavior: Cultural Antecedents and Behavioral Consequences." *Organization Development Journal* 10(2): 13–19.

Ybarra, O. and Trafimow, D. (1998) "How Priming the Private Self or Collective Self Affects the Relative Weights of Attitudes and Subjective Norms." *Personality and Social Psychology Bulletin* 24(4): 362–70.

Zahn-Waxler, C., Friedman, R.J., Cole, P.M., Mizuta, C., and Hiruma, N. (1996) "Japanese and United States Preschool Children's Responses to Conflict and Distress." *Child Development* 67(5): 2462–77.

Zhang, Y. (2004) *The Impact of Self-construal on Consumer Decision-making*. Thesis (PhD). University of Pittsburgh.

Zhang, Y., Feick, L., and Price, L.J. (2006) "The Impact of Self-construal on Aesthetic Preference for Angular Versus Rounded Shapes." *Personality and Social Psychology Bulletin* 32(6): 794–805.

Zhang, Y. and Mittal, V. (2007) "The Attractiveness of Enriched and Impoverished Options: Culture, Self-construal, and Regulatory Focus." *Personality and Social Psychology Bulletin* 15(8): 588–98.

Zhang, Y. and Shrum, L.J. (2009) "The Influence of Self-construal on Impulsive Consumption." *Journal of Consumer Research* 35(5): 838–50.

Zhang, Y., Winterich, K., and Mittal, V. (2010) "Power-distance Belief and Impulsive Buying." *Journal of Marketing Research* (10): 945–54.

25

REMINDERS OF MONEY CHANGE THE SELF-CONCEPT

Kathleen D. Vohs

State of knowledge

The love of money seems to bring psychological illness, whereas having money seems to be a benefit to psychological health. It is a rare concept that has such disparate twinning effects.

When I started thinking about the psychology of money, I did as good scholars do and I read the literature. Money had been studied in economics, health, sociology, and anthropology rather extensively and somewhat so in consumer behavior and psychology; however, this did not speak to the question that I had about money. I was searching for evidence related to the hypothesis that when people were around money they acted in a more self-oriented fashion than when they were not around money. I found no empirical evidence that even came close to addressing that question, so I wrote a grant application on the idea and with the help of a young, promising student (Nicole Mead), I started conducting experiments.

In the 10 years since, my colleagues and I have conducted close to 60 experiments on the psychology of money. Yet, even with all these data, we lack evidence on key issues and have more questions now than ever before. We have, however, come to some conclusions about how the concept of money affects people's behavior.

Behavioral correlates of money

The small but important literature that has investigated money and psychological states has almost exclusively examined the relation between money and well-being. Research on money and well-being has primarily construed money in terms of financial strain, personal income, materialism, or importance.

A review of the literature suggested that wanting money exerted negative effects on the self, whereas having money largely aided the self (Vohs *et al.* 2008). Research on money attitudes consistently has shown that money importance is negatively related to well-being (e.g. Srivastava *et al.* 2001). Materialism, a personality dimension that describes the importance of obtaining material objects relative to the importance of other life domains, is also associated with lower well-being (e.g. Kasser and Ryan 1993). Burroughs and Rindfleisch (2002; also Chapter 20, this volume) demonstrated that materialism relates to lower well-being in part because placing a great deal of importance on material objects conflicts with placing importance on communal values (e.g. family, religion). In short, feeling a strong desire for money or what money can buy portends problems for happiness and life satisfaction.

In contrast, having money seems to make life better (up to a point) relative to not having money. People who have money report feeling positive emotions more and negative emotions less than others who do not have money (Diener and Seligman 2004). Research on financial strain shows that a lack of money is associated with detrimental mental and physical outcomes. Research on unemployment found that financial strain was tied to heightened depression, poor health, and a sense of losing control (Price *et al.* 2002). Price *et al.* further revealed that financial strain and personal control decrements were responsible for the rise in depression after job loss.

The effects of money (as income) can also be seen in research on physical health outcomes. One review noted that income exerts a clearly positive effect on overall health and mortality (Adler and Snibbe 2003). This effect has been explained by invoking lower perceived personal control among people with low income or low socioeconomic status (SES), of which income is a major determinant. Research indicates that people who are low in SES but who feel that they possess high personal control have mental and physical health outcomes similar to people who are high in SES, suggesting that a lack of money can elicit feelings of powerlessness and helplessness, which bring about problematic mental and physical costs. A large-scale twins study suggests that money protects people from the unfortunate and unforeseen events that occur in life, mainly through control over the outcomes (Johnson and Krueger 2006).

The concept of money

My work uses an experimental approach to study the effects of money across a spectrum of emotions, thoughts, and behavior. My colleagues and I systematically expose some people to the idea of money while others are not exposed to the idea of money. Then we test people's behaviors and see how they differ as a function of earlier exposure to the idea of money. This method allows for an examination of the effects of money without implying income, love of money, or material goods, and therefore offers a more precise understanding of its psychological effects than conjecturing about money's effects on the self while studying concepts only somewhat related to money.

It is useful to describe how we activate the idea of money in participants' minds. We have used four basic types of procedures. In one, participants' rooms contain the board game Monopoly™. Sometimes participants play the game, whereas in other experiments they do not. In all experiments participants who have been randomly assigned to the money condition sit in a room where the board game has only been cleaned up partway, leaving a large amount ($4,000) of play money left behind, in plain view of participants. In the non-money condition, no play money is left behind. Another type of experiment exposes participants to the idea of money through a finger dexterity task. Participants who had been randomly assigned to the money condition count 80 pieces of hard currency, whereas those in the non-money condition count 80 pieces of paper. A third manipulation builds on Srull and Wyer's (1979) classic supraliminal priming technique of having participants put together meaningful phrases. In our experiments, money condition participants solve phrases that pertain to money ("one hundred-dollar bill") whereas non-money participants solve phrases that are unrelated to money ("I wrote the letter"). In a fourth procedure, participants sit in front of a computer monitor or at a desk where images of money or non-money concepts (e.g. fish, flowers) are present, typically in participants' visual periphery.

All four procedures are quite different on the surface, and yet they accomplish one goal very well: they remind participants of the concept of money. They do so without endowing the participants with money or tying it to their behavior or performance. That these dissimilar procedures all yield similar patterns of behavior implies that a great number of cues can activate the idea of money.

What is the purpose of money?

To understand what psychological processes follow from activating the concept of money, it is instructive to consider the function of money; that is, how people use money in their daily lives. People use money to obtain objects or experiences that they want but do not have. Framing the purpose of money in this manner suggests that the idea of money is linked to the psychological concepts of goal achievement and control over one's outcomes. Control over outcomes was apparent in the extant literature on money-related topics, such as income and socioeconomic status. When people lacked money, they felt that they had less control over what was happening in their lives, and when they had money a feeling of control was bolstered.

Our data also support the idea of money being linked to a need for control and goal striving. In the first set of studies that my colleagues and I performed (Vohs *et al.* 2006), we found clear and strong evidence that people reminded of money worked longer and harder than others on personal goals.

Reminders of money enhance pursuit of personal goals

One of the first hypotheses we set out to test was that reminders of money motivate people to pursue their goals. That money is exceptional in its ability to motivate people has been recognized many times. One recent analysis is by Stephen Lea and Paul Webley (Lea and Webley 2006), who wrote that money is motivating because it activates the desire for trade. With the globalization of money came attendant openings for trade (Lea and Webley 2006). Trade exists to help people satisfy their basic needs (be that for the self or others), and therefore if money is strongly linked to trade, it can be understood as representing satisfaction of a personal goal (to obtain the desired good).

My colleagues and I made use of these ideas in forming the hypothesis that even small reminders of money would inspire people to work hard to achieve their goals. In several experiments in the laboratory, we saw precisely that.

In one study, participants were given a reminder of money in the form of a word puzzle that contained phrases that pertained to money, whereas other participants completed a neutral version of the task. Then participants were given a challenging but solvable task that comes from cognitive science's work on insight effects. A quality of insight problems is that working on them does not yield a feeling of making progress; typically the answer comes after some time in a flash of insight (hence the name). We used this task to see how long participants would work at a challenge, and in doing so we gave them the instructions to work on it until they solved it or gave up trying. The experimenter then offered to provide tips or hints if participants wanted them. This procedure was in place so that we could test how quickly participants gave up on solving the tasks themselves and turned to the experimenter to get help. The results showed that people reminded of money worked longer and harder on the difficult task relative to their peers who were not reminded of money, suggesting that they were reticent to ask for help.

A similar experiment was conducted with an unsolvable task, with the additional change that in the experiment participants were given the opportunity to ask a peer for help. The results were parallel to the prior study's results, in that participants reminded of money worked longer on an unsolvable task relative to participants in the neutral condition. Statistically, participants reminded of money worked almost 150% as long as participants in the non-money condition (averaged across both experiments). We concluded from these and several other experiments that when people are reminded of money, they seek to achieve personal goals.

The concept of money is seen as a means of control

Recent work has tested the idea that people sometimes view money as a means to have control. Such a view makes sense because money can veridically help people control their outcomes. Consider a hungry person. In order to obtain the desired outcome of being sated, money can be used to buy food. We hypothesized in these experiments that when people felt a loss of control, they would view money as a way to have control more than would others whose sense of control had not been perturbed.

Half of the participants were given a task, such as writing about an event from one's life or playing a game with others, that made them feel socially ostracized. Other participants were given a task that did not make them feel ostracized. We chose social isolation as a way to temporarily reduce feelings of control based on much prior research that feelings of ostracism (being shunned or ignored by others) upset people's sense of control (Williams 2007), which our experiments also supported.

After exclusion or inclusion, participants rated their agreement with statements about whether money could offer control in life (Wen Wan *et al.* under review). As predicted, participants who felt socially isolated agreed more strongly than other participants with the idea that money can offer control. More tellingly, though, was the finding that the more people thought of money as a way to have control, the less they wanted to spend it.

Perhaps the more interesting findings were those pertaining to the opportunity to spend money on an experience of control. Recall that the general effect was that people who felt socially excluded wanted to hold on to their money to increase their sense of control. Notably, these effects were obtained when nothing else was available to give participants real control. When we gave participants options that offered the experience of control, we found that socially ostracized people were willing to let go of their money in order to obtain those experiences. To favor the experience of control over the possibility of control that money offers is intriguing because it suggests that ostracized people are responding to the experience of losing control in a fairly rational manner. These studies also highlight money's ability to be a coping mechanism for people seeking control.

Interpersonal ramifications of money

There are many studies that link money to interpersonal disharmony, especially in terms of correlational data. Our experiments tested the idea of interpersonal consequences after reminders of money by measuring helpfulness toward others. Helpfulness was measured in some cases in terms of giving time, such as when the experimenter asked participants if they could help her as a research assistant or when a confused peer (a confederate working for the lab, in reality) asked for help on a puzzle task she was given (Vohs *et al.* 2006). Participants who had not been reminded of money said that they would help the experimenter for almost twice as long as participants reminded of money. When it came to helping a confused peer, non-money participants were helpful (behaviorally) more than twice as long as participants reminded of money.

To further test whether money reminders reduced people's helpfulness, we asked whether money-reminded participants would be willing to help others if helpfulness involved donating money. It could be that activating the idea of money made it appealing to use money to solve problems, such as helping others. Participants in this study were unconsciously reminded of money or neutral constructs. Then they were given a private opportunity to donate to the University Student Fund. However, it was not the case that being reminded of money made helpfulness in the form of donating money appealing. Participants who had been reminded of money donated less than others – by a lot. Money-conditioned participants donated on average 57% of what others did.

The data in our laboratories point to the harm to social inclusion that reminders of money can produce. We found tantalizing evidence that money may psychologically substitute for social acceptance. In one study, we found that when people have been socially rejected, their desire for money goes up (Zhou *et al.* 2009). We also found evidence of the reverse – that reminders of money lessen the pain of social rejection (Zhou *et al.* 2009). In that experiment, participants performed a finger dexterity task in which they either handled hard currency or pieces of paper. They then played an online game with players whose behavior was controlled by the computer. In some cases, participants were left out of much of the game and therefore were socially ostracized. Later we asked participants how the game made them feel and found that participants who had handled money reported less distress about the ostracism relative to participants who had handled paper. This work suggests that people treat money and social acceptance as substitutes, an idea that continues to stimulate research in our laboratories.

Outstanding questions and calls for research

The work that I have described has focused exclusively on motivation and cognition. What about the role of emotion when people are reminded of money? The experiments thus far have measured emotion in terms of self-reported feelings on standardized scales, which by and large have yielded no statistically significant effects. One notable exception involves feelings of inner strength. Current (Akpinar and Vohs in progress) and past work (Zhou *et al.* 2009) repeatedly found that reminders of money elicit a sense of inner confidence, strength, and efficacy. Although this effect has not been thoroughly integrated into our working theories of the psychology of money, my sense is that it derives from money's ability to get people what they want and need (i.e. achieve their goals and exert control).

A proper test of how emotions affect behavior when people are reminded of money would include subtle forms of emotion measurement. One such method that my colleagues and I have started to use instructs participants to sit at a computer and look at a flash of light that they are told is a word that their subconscious can "read." A short list of words appears next and participants are told to trust their gut feelings in order to guess which word it was that appeared as the flash of light (Liu *et al.* 2011; comes from DeMarree *et al.* 2005). We used the method for a slightly different purpose, but nonetheless found that when participants reminded of money suspected that someone was trying to influence them, they chose more threat-related words than did others. While this finding does not (and cannot) answer the question of whether reminders of money elicit global, but subtle, shifts in mood, the method is promising. The broader point is that reminders of money may alter people's feelings in small ways, which might offer insights into the structure of the concept of money in people's minds.

Our studies have produced a mass of null results when we test for the effects of moderating variables, such as culture, age, income, expected income, family of origin income, and SES (Vohs *et al.* 2008). At this point, we might want to conclude that such global factors might not be where individual differences lie, and more nuanced dimensions could be assessed (e.g. childhood background, experiences with money).

A nagging question for me has been why there are negative interpersonal consequences when the idea of money is activated. The data that we have gathered clearly suggest that interpersonal relationships can be harmed by the indifference that money-reminded people show to others. However, why money might get in the way of interpersonal harmony is not immediately apparent.

If the purpose of money is to provide a route for people efficiently to get what they want, then this description seems orthogonal as to whether people who use money will have happy, successful, stable relationships. This question is worth pursuing, and here are a few theories.

Is it because the personal self gets activated in the pursuit of personal goals and in doing so, shuts out the influence of others? While this is what often occurs when people are reminded of money, it is not a theory about why that happens so much as a re-description of what happens.

My favorite theory has to do with money's ability to act as a source of control and an aid to goal completion. Because money is linked so strongly with goal completion, the strong ties between money and control might bear on the social relationship. Yet interpersonal outcomes are not well achieved by overt control and indeed often backfire (Overall *et al.* 2006). Hence, if money promotes a desire to control outcomes, interpersonal problems could arise because people use money to reach goals that would be better reached by other means, such as with affection, attention, time, respect, or loyalty.

Concluding notes

To manipulate experimentally the activation of the concept of money is a promising and nascent route to studying money. My colleagues and I have found that when people are reminded of money, they seem to be reminded of lots of money. The concept propels people toward their personal goals and away from being sensitive to others. One explanation for these patterns is that money fundamentally is used for control over outcomes and goal attainment, which suit the motives of the personal self very well – but are incongruent with those of the social self.

Our work shows that there are changes in the behavior of individuals reminded of money, and some concordant changes in their self-concept. On the one hand, people reminded of money feel strong and efficacious – and reminders of money that one no longer possesses (because it has been spent) leave people feeling weak (Zhou *et al.* 2009). People work longer and harder toward their own goals and are willing to take on more work than is necessary (Vohs *et al.* 2006). They do not mind physical or social pain. These findings suggest that the self that is activated when people are reminded of money is tough, competent, and motivated. On the other hand, when people are reminded of money, their preferences and behavior seem to disregard others' wants and needs. They prefer to work alone, do not help very much when it is called for, and view others' attempts at affiliation to be a threat (Liu *et al.* 2011; Vohs *et al.* 2006). In summary, the picture that these findings paint is of a self-sufficient person who can live without help and operates as if others should do the same.

There is much more work to be done to understand how the concept of money has these effects, including whether there are ways to bridge the personal and interpersonal divide and possible emotion consequences. There is much more to know about money and the human psyche, and I encourage readers to join me in studying it. Money continues to shape modern society and will for the foreseeable future.

Further reading

Johnson, W. and Krueger, R.F. (2006) "How Money Buys Happiness: Genetic and Environmental Processes Linking Finances and Life Satisfaction." *Journal of Personality and Social Psychology* 90: 680–91. (A twin study that details the role of monetary resources in gene expression.)

Lea, S.E.G. and Webley, P. (2006) "Money as Tool, Money as Drug: The Biological Psychology of a Strong Incentive." *Behavioral and Brain Sciences* 29: 161–209. (A comprehensive theory of money as a powerful incentive.)

Liu, J.E., Smeesters, D., and Vohs, K.D. (in press) "Reminders of Money Elicit Feelings of Threat and Reactance in Response to Social Influence." *Journal of Consumer Research.* (Experiments showing that people reminded of money mostly seem immune to others but react oppositionally if there is a hint of others attempting social influence.)

Vohs, K.D., Mead, N.L., and Goode, M.R. (2006) "The Psychological Consequences of Money." *Science* 314: 1154–56. (The first experiments to systematically remind people of the concept of money and test their subsequent behaviors.)

Zhou, X., Vohs, K.D., and Baumeister, R.F. (2009) "The Symbolic Power of Money: Reminders of Money Alter Social Distress and Physical Pain." *Psychological Science* 20: 700–6. (These experiments show that money and social acceptance seem to work as substitutes, such that lacking one prompts a need to obtain the other.)

References

Adler, N.E. and Snibbe, A.C. (2003) "The Role of Psychosocial Processes in Explaining the Gradient Between Socioeconomic Status and Health." *Current Directions in Psychological Science* 12: 119–23.

Akpinar, E. and Vohs, K.D. (in progress) "Can Religion and Money Substitute for Each Other." Rotterdam, Netherlands: Erasmus University.

Burroughs, J.E. and Rindfleisch, A. (2002) "Materialism and Well-Being: A Conflicting Values Perspective." *Journal of Consumer Research* 29: 348–70.

DeMarree, K.G., Wheeler, S.C., and Petty, R.E. (2005) "Priming a New Identity: Self-Monitoring Moderates the Effects of Nonself Primes on Self-Judgments and Behavior." *Journal of Personality and Social Psychology* 89: 657–71.

Diener, E. and Seligman, M.E.P. (2004) "Beyond Money: Toward an Economy of Well-Being." *Psychological Science in the Public Interest* 5: 1–31.

Horan, R.D., Bulté, E., and Shogren, J.F. (2005) "How Trade Saved Humanity From Biological Exclusion: An Economic Theory of Neanderthal Extinction." *Journal of Economic Behavior & Organization* 58: 68–76.

Johnson, W. and Krueger, R.F. (2006) "How Money Buys Happiness: Genetic and Environmental Processes Linking Finances and Life Satisfaction." *Journal of Personality and Social Psychology* 90: 680–91.

Kasser, T. and Ryan, R.M. (1993) "A Dark Side of the American Dream: Correlates of Financial Success as a Central Life Aspiration." *Journal of Personality and Social Psychology* 65: 410–22.

Lea, S.E.G. and Webley, P. (2006) "Money as Tool, Money as Drug: The Biological Psychology of a Strong Incentive." *Behavioral and Brain Sciences* 29: 161–209.

Liu, J.E., Smeesters, D., and Vohs, K.D. (2011) "Reminders of Money Elicit Feelings of Threat and Reactance in Response to Social Influence." *Journal of Consumer Research* (forthcoming).

Overall, N.C., Fletcher, G.J.O., and Simpson, J.A. (2006) "Regulation Processes in Intimate Relationships: The Role of Ideal Standards." *Journal of Personality and Social Psychology* 91(4): 662–85.

Pareto, V. (1972) *Manual of Political Economy*. Trans. A.S. Schwier. London: Macmillan.

Price, R.H., Choi, J.N., and Vinokur, A.D. (2002) "Links in the Chain of Diversity Following Job Loss: How Financial Strain and Loss of Personal Control Lead to Depression, Impaired Functioning, and Poor Health." *Journal of Occupational Health Psychology* 7: 302–12.

Srivastava, A., Locke, E.A., and Bartol, K.M. (2001) "Money and Subjective Well-Being: It's Not the Money, It's the Motives." *Journal of Personality and Social Psychology* 80: 959–71.

Srull, T.K. and Wyer, R.S. (1979) "Role of Category Accessibility in the Interpretation of Information About Persons – Some Determinants and Implications." *Journal of Personality and Social Psychology* 37: 1660–72.

Vohs, K.D., Mead, N.L., and Goode, M.R. (2006) "The Psychological Consequences of Money." *Science* 314: 1154–56.

——(2008) "Merely Activating the Concept of Money Changes Personal and Interpersonal Behavior." *Current Directions in Psychological Science* 17: 208–12.

Weatherford, J.M. (1998) *The History of Money*. New York: Three Rivers Press.

Wen Wan, E., Zhansheng, C., and Vohs, K.D. (under review) "Money is Viewed as a Source of Control After Social Exclusion." *Journal of Personality and Social Psychology*.

Williams, K.D. (2007) "Ostracism." *Annual Review of Psychology* 58: 425–52.

Zhou, X., Vohs, K.D., and Baumeister, R.F. (2009) "The Symbolic Power of Money: Reminders of Money Alter Social Distress and Physical Pain." *Psychological Science* 20: 700–6.

III

Social and cultural aspects of self and consumption

III.I

Other vs. self in consumers' behavior

26
SOCIAL INFLUENCE AND THE SELF

Richard P. Bagozzi

> To know who I am is a species of knowing where I stand. My identity is defined by the commitments and identifications … with which I can try to determine … what is good, or valuable, or what ought to be done, or what I endorse or oppose.
>
> (Taylor 1989: 27)

It might be said that consumption begins and ends with the self. We are interested in social influence primarily because of its ability to move the self to action (i.e. in buying and consuming products and services) and its use or exemplification by the self in moving others to so act. However, what the self is and its relation to social influence are both complex and ambiguous issues and will require some unpacking and repacking.

The chapter begins with an analysis of the self and its relation to consumption. Next we consider social influence and its manifestation in marketing. It will become evident that the self is both constituted by, and reciprocally and reflexively connected to, cognitive processes and emotions. Moreover, social influence both shapes and is shaped by the self. The chapter closes with directions for future research.

The self

Marketing and the social sciences are filled with a plethora of self references: self-esteem, self-concept, self-knowledge, self-confidence, self-efficacy, self-deception, self-respect, and many more. The impression is that the self is subdivided into a seemingly unlimited number of self-aspects or even that there are multiple selves. So it is useful to address the conceptual confusion that permeates scientific and everyday usage.

I consider the self to be a real entity, although I allow for some meaning to accrue from interpretive perspectives based on narrative and self- or social constructions (e.g. Dennett 1991; Hermans and Kempen 1993; McAdams 1997). To give a working definition, I consider the self to be the set of central values, goals, and commitments a person has (e.g. Taylor 1989), which are reflected in one's beliefs, dispositions, emotions, choices, and personal and group relationships with others.

By real, I mean that the self is not a fiction or illusion but rather actually exists and can be (imperfectly) measured so as to enter into scientific hypotheses of what it is, what determines or influences it, and what implications it has. From my perspective, there is only one real self, although it sometimes appears that multiple selves exist (cf. James 1890; Neisser 1988). The apparent existence of multiple selves arises, I maintain, because first, any person can intentionally or unintentionally convey multiple selves, or second, observers of others attribute multiple selves to others because of the information others convey. In a sense, self and others engage in the art of simulation and dissimulation. Thus, I make a distinction between the real self and the presented self (or selves). Such a distinction allows us to speak meaningfully about discrepancies between the real and an ideal self, between the real and presented self/selves, and between an ideal self and presented self/selves. Such discrepancies undergird social comparison processes and social identity processes, and provide motivation for personal and social agency and for succumbing to or resisting social influence.

Two important aspects of any self are the independent-based and interdependent-based self (e.g. Markus and Kitayama 1991). Some researchers tend to see these as being mutually exclusive and suggest, or at least imply, that people are largely characterized by one or the other in relatively fixed senses. For example, it has been claimed that people indigenous to most Western societies follow an independent-based self construal, whereas those indigenous to many Eastern or group-based societies exhibit an interdependent-based self. While this point of view sometimes captures the preponderant mode of behavior for many people in each society, I believe that such a characterization is at best a static picture and at the same time obscures a dynamic aspect of the self that occurs universally. That is, I claim that it is valid to conceive of any self as comprising a tension between the independent-based and interdependent-based self.

By tension, I mean that at any point in time a person is confronted with internal and external pressures to see oneself as, or to choose to act from, independent or interdependent exigencies or requisites. A person in effect reconciles the tension by choosing one extreme or another, or else, perhaps less frequently, blends together a persona with multiple attributes chosen from each extreme. At different points in time, the same person might exemplify an independent-based or an interdependent-based self as a matter of degree, or exhibit a self with characteristics from both independent-based and interdependent-based selves. Thus the degree of independence or interdependence can change for an individual in any society over time, and indeed some persons in so-called independent-based societies might display characteristics indicative of so-called interdependent-based societies, and vice versa. The aforementioned tension can have profound effects for susceptibility to social influence and for self-generated action, in consumption contexts.

The independent-based self is an individualistic perspective where one tends to see oneself as separate from others and self-reliant; self-focus is upon one's unique traits or attributes, personal goals, and individual achievements. The orientation of such a style is on one's personal identity, and the predominant motivation is self-interest (Brickson 2000). Thus consumers with a strong independent-based self see possessions as extensions of the individual self (Belk 1988), and social relations with others are largely used as a means to stand out from others (Markus and Kitayama 1991) or function to restore threatened power or status by motivating people to spend more on goods or to purchase luxury goods for themselves (Rucker and Galinsky 2008). Materialistic urges and self-indulgence tend to be more characteristic of the independent- as opposed to interdependent-based self.

The interdependent-based self is a social orientation marked by more mutuality than are social relations under an independent-based self-construal. Here a person sees oneself as linked inseparably to others and jointly dependent on these others in some fashion; self-focus is upon one's shared traits or attributes, common goals, and group achievements. The orientation of such a style is on one's social identity, and the predominant motivation is one of shared interests (Brickson 2000). This is manifest in one of two ways, depending on the nature of social relations. For interpersonal or dyadic relations, the social motivation is to enhance the benefits of the partner. For relationships with a group and members of the group to which one belongs, the social motivation is collective welfare. Thus consumers with a strong interdependent-based self see possessions as ways to build or maintain ties under a social self-construal, and social relations with others in the group focus on fitting in and reducing power or status disparities. Purchases are often made with group harmony in mind, yet one's group may also strive to outpace a rival group through the goods it consumes. We will have more to say below about the role of the independent-based and interdependent-based self when we consider social influence.

A little-recognized aspect of the self is the role of emotions. Indeed, I propose that emotions infuse the very meaning of the self and function to link the self to products and brands, individuals and groups, and social influence. In so doing, they serve to regulate how one thinks about the self, how one relates to other people and groups, and what one decides or chooses to do, or not do, in relation to products, services, and brands.

First, of course, are the so-called basic emotions (e.g. joy, anger, sadness, and fear) (see Lazarus 1991). The basic emotions are hard-wired, so to speak, in our brains and have genetic as well as learned properties. Much of our automatic response to advertising and product/service attributes arises in response to the pain or pleasure, or conditioning, that these stimuli or cues produce in our brains, which are linked to various regions in the brain associated with the basic emotions (e.g. fear responses especially occur in the amygdala and hippocampus). At the same time, the basic emotions enter decision making when we deliberate about product/service and brand choices, and lend affective/evaluative weight to so-called reasoned processes (e.g. Damasio's (1994) somatic marker hypothesis seems to be operative in such cases).

The basic emotions or their effects can be regulated to a certain extent (e.g. sometimes as consumers we experience weakness of will, resist temptation, delay gratification, or in some other way counteract desires with "second order desires") (see Bagozzi 2006a, 2006b), but for the most part they seem to be relatively immutable aspects of the self and operate automatically. More pertinent to the self as I conceive it herein are, first, the self-conscious emotions, and second, the moral emotions. Let me briefly consider these and their relation to the self.

The self-conscious emotions include pride, shame, guilt, embarrassment, envy, and jealousy (e.g. Tangney and Fischer 1995). They develop later in early life than the basic emotions and involve more learning, requiring a lot of socialization and well-defined developmental processes. Very early physiological developmental processes also appear to play a role, for people with autism or Asperger's syndrome exhibit lack of development in such regions of the brain as the medial prefrontal cortex, temporo parietal junction, and temporal poles. That is, the self-conscious emotions entail theory of mind capabilities where a person infers the thoughts, feelings, or intentions of people with whom they interact. People differ in these capabilities and can be placed perhaps on a continuum going from low capabilities (e.g. autism) to "normal" capabilities, to high capabilities (e.g. "super-normal" skills, say).

More than the basic emotions, the self-conscious emotions require evaluations of the self (and others) and the ability for self-representation in order to experience and cope with these emotions. It is beyond the scope of this chapter to discuss all the self-conscious emotions, but some comments on (self-)pride convey the unique functioning of these emotions. Tracy and Robins (2007) suggest that pride has a number of adaptive functions. Pride reinforces behaviors that give proud feelings and increase self-esteem. Pride serves also to communicate one's successes, thus boosting one's social status for an individual-based self or group acceptance for an interdependent-based self. Advertisers might explicitly prime pride or remind purchasers of the pride they felt on a previous purchase occasion, for example, so as to increase positive word-of-mouth communication or stimulate sales. A recent study even showed that viewing pride in others increases product evaluations and the willingness to buy, for people who value possessions as extensions of the self, envy the observed proud person, or desire power or status (Ruvio and Bagozzi 2012). Tracy *et al.* (2010) explore two senses of pride (i.e. authentic pride, based on one's focus on his/her achievements, and hubristic pride, based on egocentric beliefs that one is superior to others), and propose that authentic pride evolved to motivate one to achieve prestige, whereas hubristic pride arose to motivate one to attain dominance. Thus depending on whether one exhibits either form of pride as a trait, or one can prime one or the other as a manipulation, different products or brands might have distinct appeals when they fit one emotional aspect of the self or the other. The study by Ruvio and Bagozzi (2012) showed that audiences viewing pride or hubris in a spokesperson actually demonstrated stronger effects for hubris than pride, which might be counterintuitive since the former is generally seen to be a negative trait, whereas the latter is seen to be positive. Group pride can be a motivating force for consumption, too, such as when group members purchase products or brands to express group identity, or members use purchases to create group solidarity, compete with other groups or in some other way benefit the group.

The moral emotions include contempt, anger, disgust, gratitude, awe, and elevation (e.g. Tangney *et al.* 2007). They occur either when moral values or virtues are violated or confirmed due to actions committed by others as perceived by a person. In other words, moral emotions are aspects of the self and when activated can motivate consumers to act in ways punishing or rewarding bad or good behavior of others. For example, Romani *et al.* (2012) showed that positive practices by corporations in terms of maintaining the dignity of workers, protecting the environment, and respecting community values in cities where the companies operate, influence positive actions by consumers toward the companies (e.g. positive word of mouth, intentions to buy), as mediated by feelings of gratitude. On the other hand, violations of worker dignity, the environment, and community led to negative actions toward companies (e.g. negative word of mouth), as mediated by felt contempt, anger, and disgust by consumers, to the extent that consumers exhibited altruistic values (Grappi *et al.* 2012).

There is another sense that emotions function morally even for the so-called self-conscious emotions. Pride, shame, and envy are cases in point. An essential part of human agency is to make practical choices. Such choices are made in response to social influence through deliberative processes, yet can be mediated or moderated by moral considerations. This occurs both prescriptively and evaluatively as kinds of normative behavior. For example, dispositional pride (pridefulness) might dispose a consumer to be positively affected by an advertisement extolling how proud one might feel purchasing the advertised brand (because my purchase benefits the poor, say). Anticipated shame, on the other hand, might function to prevent me from making a risky purchase because of an expected threat to my core self, if I were to appear foolish or a spendthrift. Envy, by contrast, might motivate me as a customer to demand a refund from a seller that I observed another customer get, and might even reflect jealousy to the extent that I felt the seller favored the other customer, whom I perceived to be less worthy than I of the refund. All this is to say that pride, shame, and envy (or jealousy) can reinforce or counteract normal reasoning processes. Indeed, I speculate that these emotions, in morally tinged contexts, serve to bolster or sustain the self. The social and moral emotions function dynamically in human agency to regulate behavior in order to promote or protect a particular self-construal.

The moral and self-conscious emotions are important for the self in two senses. First, they govern a kind of moral ownership, and accountability for one's own actions. This is an aspect of one's self-reflective self that becomes a part of one's self-consciousness and part of one's dispositions to act properly in the right circumstances. Second, they contribute to the interdependent self through their promotion of obligations and responsibilities towards others. Both mechanisms will be seen below to function in brand community behavior in relation to both fellow community members and the companies to which the members and brands are connected. It might be argued that the value and validity of the concept of self inheres in moral and self-conscious emotions and their role in everyday practical choices.

Empathy is yet another mental condition defining the nature of the self and bridging the relationship of people to social influence. Empathy consists of a triad of mental reactions: the ability to take the perspective of others, to feel compassion for others, and to maintain the self-other distinction in proper balance so as not to experience dysfunctional distress. Various regions of the brain are implicated in empathetic processes, including the mirror neuron system, precuneus, insula, and amygdala. Empathy is a prime aspect of caring for others and functions to build rapport between interaction partners. Through empathy, one is shaped by, and shapes, social influence, where it functions not only as a tool of influence but its object as well.

In sum, the self is the nucleus of consumption decisions. It is the raison d'être for consumption in that basic emotions function to initiate and evaluate consumption alternatives; self-conscious and moral emotions regulate transactions with sellers so as to protect, maintain, or strengthen the self; human empathy facilitates communication and fosters social exchanges; and all this happens in social situations where individual, relational, and collective orientations facilitate or constrain the expression of the self. We turn now to how the self links to social influence.

Social influence

Conceptualization

Kelman (1958, 1974) distinguished between three modes of social influence: compliance, internalization, and identification. In each case, reflecting the individualistic and interpersonal perspectives of the time, the modes of influence were conceived as ways in which attitudes of individual persons change under persuasive communication. Thus compliance entails interpersonal or mass market influence (e.g. peer pressure, subjective normative effects) where the response of a target is based on the need for approval or the desire to gain particular rewards or avoid punishment from someone whose opinion one values; internalization reflects responses of individuals based on felt common values or goals (i.e. intrinsic rewards) with the source of persuasive communication; and identification consists of acting so as to establish or maintain a satisfying, self-defining relationship with a source of persuasive communication.

Bagozzi and Lee (2002; see also Bagozzi 2005) reconceived social influence mechanisms as group processes. That is, the aim of social influence was specified to affect shared decisions, which were depicted as we-intentions (i.e. shared decisions of group members to act together to achieve a group goal), or group-based I-intentions (i.e. a member's intention to act as an agent or in a role so as to contribute to group ends). We-intentions and group-based I-intentions mediate between the effects of mutual desires for a group goal and joint actions to achieve that goal. Mutual desires, in turn, are functions of first, social influence reconceptualized as group-based forms of compliance, internalization, and identification, and second, attitudinal and anticipated and anticipatory emotions, framed as shared psychological reactions and expressed in a group-based model of goal-directed action.

Marketing theory and practice have had limited enquiry of social influence, until quite recently, to interpersonal or one-way (i.e. mass media to target person) instances of social influence. Although such approaches to social influence are obviously important and have generated a large body of findings over a long period of time under the rubrics of persuasive communication and audience effects in the advertising literature, they fail to address a type of social influence that occurs frequently in the marketplace and which I characterized above as group-based social influence. The need for a shift to a complementary form of social influence parallels the rationale behind social identity theory. Tajfel (1978; see also Hogg and Abrams 1988) introduced social identity theory as a new paradigm for study because he felt that the dominant paradigms of the day (i.e. individual psychology and interpersonal psychology) did not account for forms of social behavior occurring in groups, organizations, and certain collectivities. Indeed, he claimed that much of group behavior cannot be reduced to properties or states of individuals, or even to what transpires between individuals, but rather exists in social categorization and social identity processes by members within a group and in cross-group processes, where such processes are at a fundamentally different level of analysis. My colleagues and I have taken this a step further by integrating social identity theory with the notion of intentional social action borrowed from philosophy (e.g. Gilbert 1989; Tuomela 1995), wherein people within groups or social relations jointly pursue mutual ends (e.g. Bagozzi 2000, 2005). Not only does group-based social influence entail different levels of conceptualization, but new methods of analysis are required as well (e.g. Algesheimer, Bagozzi, and Dholakia, 2012), though most empirical studies to date have not fully used the new methods of analysis.

Contexts of social influence

A number of researchers have identified a small number of venues where social influence occurs in consumption and where the self plays a central role. One of these is termed a *subculture of consumption*, which Schouten and McAlexander (1995: 43) define as "a distinctive subgroup of society that self-selects on the basis of a shared commitment to a particular product class, brand, or consumption activity." Schouten and McAlexander (1995) conducted an ethnography of Harley-Davidson motorcycle owners and found that the subculture therein had: 1 a well-defined social structure comprising an informal hierarchy of officers and based on both within-group status (which in turn is a function of members' commitment to the group's ideology of consumption) and across-group status (which is a function of the group's appraisal of other groups' authenticity in the sense of representativeness of the overall subculture); 2 dominant values (e.g. personal freedom, patriotism and American heritage, and machismo); and 3 transformation of self into a biker, where motives for involvement and commitment to the subculture deepen. Explicit social influence processes found in subcultures of consumption have been tested by Bagozzi and Dholakia (2002, 2006a, 2006b). In a field study of Camp Jeep participants, Schouten *et al.* (2007: 357) identified transcendent customer experiences where "aspects of flow and/or peak experiences ... generate lasting shifts in beliefs and attitudes, including subjective *self-transformation*" (emphasis added).

Another context where social influence happens is a *brand fest*. Brand fests are "corporate-sponsored events provided primarily for the benefit of current customers" (McAlexander and Schouten 1998: 379). Consisting of large collectivities, where participants come together in one location for a few days once a year, such gatherings typically include entertainment, food and drink, product demonstrations, contests, competitive activities, and opportunities to purchase products or brand-related paraphernalia, all in a holiday-like atmosphere. Such venues can be huge: witness Ducati week where upwards of 60,000 enthusiasts gather. Other brand fests are much smaller and even occur frequently in a year and at different locations, such as Jeep Jamborees, where 30-odd off-road weekend adventures happen in a typical year for upwards of as many as 600 people in attendance at a time. McAlexander and Schouten's (1998) ethnography of brand fests revealed that "participation in such brand-intensive galas often leads consumers to extraordinary and memorable experiences with the brand – experiences that become virtual watersheds of attitude change and purchase intention" (ibid.: 378), and "grant marketers incredible access to consumer consciousness ... in contexts that are relevant ... to key aspects of the consumer's identity" (ibid.: 380). By definition, social influence in brand fests is geographically bounded and mediated face to face.

By contrast, a *brand community* has come to be construed as "a specialized, nongeographically-bound community, based on a structured set of relationships among admirers of a brand" (Muñiz and O'Guinn 2001: 412). According to Muñiz and O'Guinn (2001: 415), such communities are large, geographically dispersed, mass mediated, and commercial in nature. Moreover, such communities exhibit three key personal and social characteristics: shared consciousness, rituals and traditions, and a sense of moral responsibility to each other. Often such communities form and express themselves in virtual communities through online venues (e.g. e-mail lists, bulletin boards, Usenet newsgroups, online chat groups, and web-based chat rooms).

McAlexander *et al.* (2002: 39) provide a different perspective on brand communities and propose a *customer-centric model*, stressing that the "existence and meaningfulness of community inhere in customer experience." This experience plays out in the relationship a customer has with a brand, product, marketer, and other customers, and can be described in four dimensions: geography (concentrated, scattered, or virtual), social context (face-to-face, electronically mediated, mass media-based), temporality (stable, temporary, periodic), and basis of identification (e.g. leisure pursuits, occupational connections, religious beliefs). This is a broad conception of brand communities that encompasses a range of different forms of consumption.

Schau *et al.* (2009) identified 52 articles investigating brand communities and discovered 12 common practices committed in value creation by community members, which are organized into four interlocking categories: impression management (evangelizing, justifying), social networking (welcoming, empathizing, governing), community engagement (documenting, badging, mile-stoning, staking), and brand use (customizing, grooming, commoditizing). As Schau *et al.* (2009: 35) note, "an emergent sense of membership and identity arises from the trajectory, or the development of practices that foster the exchange of collectively defined and valorized resources." The common practices obviously involve formation and expression of the self and serve as routes to social influence.

An important special case of brand communities is the *small-group brand community*. These typically have a handful or two of members, involve face-to-face interactions among friends who are aficionados of a brand, and often include web-based interactions as well. In contrast to most studies of subcultures of consumption, brand fests, and brand communities to date, which have had different purposes and have used qualitative methods primarily, the small-group brand community studies done so far have tested specific hypotheses and have done so generally in survey contexts according to a comprehensive model of intentional social action and group behavior.

Ten studies have been done to date examining small-group brand communities. These studies have tested portions of the comprehensive model described in Bagozzi (2006a, 2006b), and some have also incorporated additional variables as well. It is beyond the scope of this chapter to describe the studies, but the reader is referred to Algesheimer *et al.* (2005), Bagozzi and Dholakia (2002), Dholakia *et al.* (2004), Bagozzi and Dholakia (2006a, 2006b), Bagozzi *et al.* (2006), Bagozzi *et al.* (2007), Zaglia and Bagozzi (2012), Zaglia *et al.* (2012), and Tsai and Bagozzi (2012).

Conclusion

Social influence and the self constitute much of the content of everyday consumption. The self is both reflective and reflexive, entails a tension between independent-based and interdependent-based self-construals, is intimately related to basic, self-conscious, and moral emotions, and is driven by, and linked through, empathy, caring, and love to social influence. Social influence, in turn, is itself a group-based process. The venues we considered were subcultures of consumption, brand fests, virtual brand communities, and small-group brand communities. These complement traditional conceptions of social influence, which are more mass media-based (e.g. advertiser to audience).

Directions for future research

One area for future research is consideration of how consumers acquire a self and self-concepts and the implications of such development for consumption. Press and Arnould (2011) study one aspect of the formation of consumer identification with, and its consequences for, firms. More work is needed in terms of the formation of emotions and how these, along with moral considerations, help regulate consumer behavior.

Second, inquiry is needed into contexts for social or group behavior and how they function to constrain and facilitate consumption. To the venues we considered above might be added dyadic relations, pressure or protest groups, and informal organizations or associations where social influence occurs and where the self is implicated in novel ways.

A third opportunity for research resides in the phenomena of chains or networks of identity. Consumers express the self through webs of interconnections and identifications, but we know little about their implications for consumption.

Fourth, the role of brain processes in the formation and regulation of the self and social influence are promising avenues for research. Here neuroscience, genetic, and hormonal processes are at work.

Finally, James's (1890) enduring notions of "me and mine" deserve consideration by consumer researchers. Among other areas, these seem to have relevance for the study of consumer materialism and spiritual aspects of consumption, as well as self and identity more generally.

Further reading

Seigel, J. (2005) *The Idea of the Self.* Cambridge: Cambridge University Press. (A fine and comprehensive historical and philosophical coverage of the self since the 17th century that is at the same time sensitive to modern psychological perspectives.)

Sorabji, R. (2006) *Self: Ancient and Modern Insights About Individuality, Life, and Death.* Chicago, IL: University of Chicago Press. (Nice introduction to classical and modern philosophical points of view of the self.)

References

Abrams, D. and Hogg, M.A. (1990) "An Introduction to the Social Identity Approach." In D. Abrams and M.A. Hogg (eds), *Social Identity Theory: Constructive and Critical Advances.* New York: Harvester Wheatsheaf, pp. 1–9.

Algesheimer, R., Dholakia, U.M. and Hermann, A. (2005) "The Social Influence of Brand Community: Evidence from European Car Clubs." *Journal of Marketing* 69: 19–34.

Bagozzi, R.P. (2000) "On the Concept of Intentional Social Action in Consumer Behavior." *Journal of Consumer Research* 27: 388–96.

——(2005) "Socializing Marketing." *Marketing – Journal of Research and Management* 1: 101–11.

——(2006a) "The Role of Social and Self-Conscious Emotions in the Regulation of Business-to-Business Relationships in Salesperson-Customer Interactions." *Journal of Business and Industrial Marketing* 21: 453–57.

——(2006b) "Explaining Consumer Behavior and Consumer Action: From Fragmentation to Unity." *Seoul Journal of Business* 12, 2: 111–43.

Bagozzi, R.P. and Dholakia, U.M. (2002) "Intentional Social Action in Virtual Communities." *Journal of Interactive Marketing* 16: 2–21.

——(2006a) "Antecedents and Purchase Consequences of Customer Participation in Small Group Brand Communities." *International Journal of Research in Marketing* 23: 45–61.

——(2006b) "Open Source Software User Communities: A Study of Participation in Linux User Groups." *Management Science* 52: 1099–115.

Bagozzi, R.P., Baumgartner, H., and Pieters, R. (1998) "Goal-Directed Emotions." *Cognition and Emotion* 12: 1–26.

Bagozzi, R.P., Dholakia, U.M., and Mookerjee, A. (2006) "Individual and Group Bases of Social Influence in Online Environments." *Media Psychology* 8: 95–126.

Bagozzi, R.P., Dholakia, U.M., and Klein Pearo, L.R. (2007) "Antecedents and Consequences of Online Social Interactions." *Media Psychology* 9: 77–114.

Bagozzi, R.P. and Lee, Kyu-Hyun (2002) "Multiple Routes for Social Influence: The Role of Compliance, Internalization, and Social Identity." *Social Psychology Quarterly* 65: 226–47.

Bagozzi, R.P. and Warshaw, P.R. (1990) "Trying to Consume." *Journal of Consumer Research* 17: 127–40.

Baumgartner, H., Pieters, R., and Bagozzi, R.P. (2008) "Future-Oriented Emotions: Conceptualization and Behavioral Effects." *European Journal of Social Psychology* 38: 685–96.

Belk, R.W. (1988) "Possessions and the Extended Self." *Journal of Consumer Research* 15: 139–68.

Brickson, S.L. (2000) "The Impact of Identity Orientation on Individual and Organizational Outcomes in Demographically Diverse Settings." *Academy of Management Review* 25: 82–101.

Damasio, A. (1994) *Descartes' Error: Emotion, Reason, and Human Brain.* New York: Putnam.

Dennett, D. (1991) *Consciousness Explained.* Boston, MA: Little, Brown, & Co.

Dholakia, U.M., Bagozzi, R.P., and Klein Pearo, L.R. (2004) "A Social Influence Model of Consumer Participation in Network- and Small-Group-Based Virtual Communities." *International Journal of Research in Marketing* 21: 241–63.

Gilbert, M. (1989) *On Social Facts.* London: Routledge.

Grappi, S., Romani, S., Bagozzi, R.P. (forthcoming 2012) "Consumer Responses to Corporate Irresponsible Behavior: The role of Moral Emotions and Virtues." *Journal of Business Research.*

Hermans, H. and Kempen, H. (1993) *The Dialogical Self: Meaning as Movement.* New York: Academic Press.

Hogg, M.A. and Abrams, D. (1988) *Social Identification: A Social Psychology of Intergroup Relations and Group Processes.* London: Routledge.

James, W. (1890) *Principles of Psychology.* Vols 1 and 2. New York: Henry Holt.

Kelman, H.C. (1958) "Compliance, Identification, and Internalization: Three Processes of Attitude Change." *Journal of Conflict Resolution* 2: 51–60.

——(1974) "Social Influence and Linkages Between the Individual and the Social System: Further Thoughts on the Processes of Compliance, Identification, and Internalization." In J. Tedeschi (ed.), *Perspectives on Social Power.* Chicago, IL: Aldine, pp. 125–71.

Lazarus, R.S. (1991) *Emotion and Adaptation.* New York: Oxford University Press.

McAdams, D. (1997) "The Case for the Unity in the (Post)modern Self: A Modest Proposal." In R. Ashmore and L. Jussim (eds), *Self and Identity: Fundamental Issues.* Oxford: Oxford University Press, pp. 46–78

McAlexander, J.H. and Schouten, J.W. (1988) "Brandfests: Servicescapes for the Cultivation of Brand Equity." In J.F. Sherry, Jr (ed.), *Servicescapes: The Concept of Place in Contemporary Markets.* Chicago: American Marketing Association, pp. 377–402.

McAlexander, J.H., Schouten, J.W., and Koenig, H. (2002) "Alumni and Their Alma Mater: A Partial Test of the Reformulated Model of Organizational Identification." *Journal of Organizational Behavior* 13: 38–54.

Markus, H.R. and Kitayama, S. (1991) "Culture and the Self: Implications for Cognition, Emotion, and Motivation." *Psychological Review* 98: 224–53.

Muñiz, A. and O'Guinn, T. (2001) "Brand Community." *Journal of Consumer Research* 27: 412–32.

Neisser, U. (1988) "Five Kinds of Self-knowledge." *Philosophical Psychology* 1: 37–59.

Romani, S., Grappi, S., and Bagozzi, R.P. (forthcoming 2012) "Explaining Consumer Reactions to Corporate Social Responsibility: The Role of Gratitude and Altruistic Values." *Journal of Business Ethics.*

Rucker, D.D. and Galinsky, A.D. (2008) "Desire to Acquire: Powerlessness and Compensatory Consumption." *Journal of Consumer Research* 35: 257–67.

Ruvio, A. and Bagozzi, R.P. (2012) "The Influence of Communicator Pride and Hubris on Product Evaluations and Purchase Likelihood." Unpublished working paper. University of Michigan.

Schau, H.J., Muñiz, A., Jr, and Arnould, E.J. (2009) "How Brand Communities Create Value." *Journal of Marketing* 73: 30–51.

Schouten, J.W. and McAlexander, J.H. (1995) "Subcultures of Consumption: An Ethnography of the New Bikers." *Journal of Consumer Research* 22: 43–61.

Schouten, J.W., McAlexander, J.H., and Koenig, H.F. (2007) "Transcendent Customer Experience and Brand Community." *Journal of the Academy of Marketing Science* 35: 357–68.

Tajfel, H. (1978) *Differentiation Between Social Groups: Studies in the Social Psychology of Intergroup Relations.* New York: Academic Press.

Tangney, J.P. and Fischer, K.W. (eds) (1995) *The Self-Conscious Emotions: Shame, Guilt, Embarrassment, and Pride.* New York: Guilford.

Tangney, J.P., Stuewig, J. and Mashek, D.J. (2007) "Moral Emotions and Moral Behavior." *The Annual Review of Psychology* 58: 345–72.

Taylor, C. (1989) *Sources of the Self: The Making of the Modern Identity.* Cambridge, MA: Harvard University Press.

Tracy, J.L. and Robins, R.W. (2007) "The Nature of Pride." In J.L. Tracy, R.W. Robins, and J.P. Tangney (eds), *The Self-Conscious Emotions: Theory and Research.* New York: Guilford, pp. 263–82.

Tracy, J.L, Shariff, A. and Cheng, J.T. (2010) "A Naturalist's View of Pride." *Emotion Review* 2: 163–77.

Tsai, H.-T. and Bagozzi, R.P. (2012) "Contribution Behavior in Virtual Communities: Cognitive Emotional, and Social Influences." Unpublished working paper. University of Michigan.

Tuomela, R. (1995) *The Importance of Us: A Philosophical Study of Basic Social Notions.* Stanford, CA: Stanford University Press.

Zaglia, M. and Bagozzi, R.P. (2012) "Building Brand Equity Through Small-group Brand Communities." Unpublished working paper. University of Michigan.

Zaglia, M., Bagozzi, R.P. and Matzler, K. (2012) "Cognitive and Emotional Processes Within Brand Support and Loyalty." Unpublished working paper. University of Michigan.

27

SHARED POSSESSIONS/ SHARED SELF

Russell W. Belk and Rosa Llamas

Sharing is a process of communion. What is mine becomes ours. It can be thought of as cooperative consumption (Widlok 2005), or collaborative consumption (Botsman and Rogers 2010). Drawing on Ingold (1986) and Widlok (2004), Belk (2010) distinguishes between two types of sharing: sharing in and sharing out. In sharing in, we make those with whom we share a part of our extended self (Belk 1988). When we regard someone as a part of our aggregate extended self we experience something of their pleasures and pains as our own. We take pride in their successes and suffer shame in their failures. Those who harm them harm us, while those who help them help us. We most commonly think of sharing in with family, relatives, and close friends. However, we also practice this type of sharing with the companion animals with which we may share our home, food, and other resources. Like others who are included within our aggregate sense of self, we also feel pride and shame at their accomplishments and faux pas (Sanders 1990).

Sharing out may sometimes be an equally sincere effort to help others, but it is done at arm's length and we don't regard these others as part of our extended self. Natural and humanitarian disasters like the earthquake, tsunami, and Fukushima nuclear leaks in Japan in March of 2011 triggered a wave of sharing. Citizens of the world went online to contribute money and other forms of aid. At the other extreme from this major emotional outpouring of help in times of disaster are many minor forms of sharing out that we take for granted on a daily basis. We are usually willing to share directions with someone who is lost, to give the time of day to someone who requests it, to share information in an online forum in which we participate, and to share public resources like sidewalks, roads, parks, and libraries, even if we begrudge paying taxes to support them. Even though we don't make those with whom we share such resources a part of our most immediate extended self, we may still feel a vague sense of imagined community with them (Anderson 1983). Community and even national identity may be enhanced by these and other public goods such as monuments, airports, and stadia.

Because sharing in seems natural and automatic, we often don't even regard it as a choice. Of course our children can sit on the sofa, of course they can take food from the refrigerator, and of course they can turn on the lights so they can read. We may give more thought to a friend's request to make a call on our mobile phone or borrow our umbrella, but these, too, are fairly automatic and unquestioned acts. Because we take such sharing in as natural, we are unlikely to feel particularly virtuous as a result. Our sharing out on the other hand may be more likely to shape our self-identity as being helpful, generous, kind, and thoughtful. However, some of these behaviors where we have no choice or where they are quite minor, like sharing parks and public roads or sharing directions and the time of day, also come to be thought of as natural and unworthy of reflection. Giving a few coins to a beggar or a busker is likely to fall somewhere between these natural acts and more major acts of sharing out that would be labeled philanthropy.

What we begin to see in thinking about what we share and with whom is that not only is self-identity and the extended self an impetus for sharing, but our self-perceptions are also affected by our observations of our own sharing out behavior. This can even be true with mandated sharing out, depending on the attitude with which we share. Do we pay our taxes willingly or grudgingly? Do we serve our turn on work committees happily or with bitterness? Do we graciously share the road with bicycles and pedestrians or fume as they cause us to swerve or brake our car? Such reactions also reflect on our identity.

In the discussion that follows we take up some more aggregate effects of sharing. Moving beyond the effects of sharing on personal identity, we ask how sharing may affect our sense of community identity and how this sense of community identity may affect our sharing within the community. In doing so we consider various types of communities, including virtual communities. We also consider different types of sharing, and especially non-profit versus for-profit sharing. We begin with a delineation of the different types and forms of things that may be shared. We consider the role of technologies like the Internet and mobile phones in facilitating sharing, and the role of structural variables like economic conditions as they relate to our sharing tendencies. We conclude with an appraisal of the prospects for greater sharing and its bearing on our individual and aggregate sense of self.

What may be shared?

Broadly speaking, we may share resources that we possess collectively or individually. Possession need not involve ownership. We may possess knowledge of directions or a seat at a bus stop or the ability to translate from one language to another. Even though we do not own these things we can still share them with others. There is also often a considerable difference between owning things collectively or "in common" and owning them individually (Hyde 2010), and this differs over times and cultures. Mander (1992: 215) observes that contemporary indigenous people share possessions and, to the extent they have not been overwhelmed by non-indigenous people, "[t]hey still engage in collective production, share commodities, and live in extended families… Traditionally they had no private ownership of land, water, minerals, or plant life. No concept of selling land. No inheritance."

Without notions of private property, joint possession by indigenous people previously involved sharing in and might or might not abide de facto sharing out to other groups, including colonialists (Murray 2000). In the latter case differing property systems inevitably led to conflicts between notions of private property and perceptions of gift giving versus common ownership and sharing (Murray 2000; Parry 1986).

Individual resources that we might share include our time, money, labor, ideas, companionship, knowledge, possessions, and social capital or links to other people. Some of these are tangible things while others are intangible. Some are more central to our sense of self (e.g. blood, bone marrow, bodily organs) and others less so. Some are fungible commodities (e.g. money), while others are more unique and singular (Kopytoff 1986). When objects are singular, to think about them as a resource, much less as a commodity, seems inappropriate. For most people a wedding ring or an urn with our dead parent's ashes is regarded as a sacred, inalienable possession rather than a resource. It is reasonable to assume that possessions that are more central to our sense of self and more singular are seen as more precious by the person potentially sharing them and most likely by the persons with whom they may be shared. Even a seemingly fungible commodity like money can be singular when it has special meanings like an inheritance (Zelizer 1994). When objects are sufficiently central and singular to us, they are unlikely to be shared at all. Scarcity should be another factor affecting the degree to which we regard a possession as sharable. It is easier to share an apple when we own an orchard full of apple trees than when it is our last scrap of food in the house.

There are some objects that are sufficiently abundant and inexhaustible that economists call them non-rivalrous goods (Benkler 2006). Use of these goods by one person does not diminish their availability for others. Examples are news, information, music, and films. If I listen to a broadcast by the BBC, CBC, or NPR, it does not need to be produced again for others. Nevertheless the music and film industries as well as many others have been insistent on intellectual property rights and a market-based system for accessing these goods rather than an intellectual commons where these goods are freely available to all. They call the free sharing of such goods piracy. Intellectual property wars are as old as the first printed books (Johns 2009), but they have accelerated considerably with the file-sharing capabilities enabled by the Internet. Benkler (2004) suggests two characteristics for goods to be potentially shareable: lumpiness and granularity (see also Rose and Poynor 2007). A lumpy good can only be had in certain amounts or capacities, such as a computer available only with a certain range of speeds and storage capacities as opposed to just the amount we need. Granularity refers to the cost and affordability of a good. Large-grained goods like power-generating turbines are so massive and expensive that very few individuals could afford to own one, while finer-grained goods like a donut or a cup of coffee are small and inexpensive enough that most of us can afford to buy them for individual use.

According to Benkler (2004, 2006), the ideal goods for sharing are lumpy and mid-grained. This would include both automobiles and personal computers, for example. Both have excess capacity beyond what we can use. Although there are examples of both of these consumer goods being shared, through car-sharing organizations like Zipcar and distributed computing projects like SETI@Home (Search for Extraterrestrial Intelligence), most of us seem unwilling to share either our automobiles or our computers. A key reason seems to be that even though our cars and computers are eminently shareable and it makes excellent environmental sense that we do so, we regard both as quite central to our sense of self. As noted in Chapter 8 in this volume, if you don't regard your computer as central to your identity, envision how uncomfortable you might be turning over all your computer files, social media passwords, e-mails, contacts, music, bookmarked Internet links, and other information on your computer to someone else. Goods that are more central to our extended sense of self are less likely to be shared, even though it might be quite beneficial to the community if we did share them.

So there are a variety of tangible and intangible goods and services that might be shared. It appears that our willingness to do so depends not only on the type of good or service, but how scarce it is and how central to our sense of self is the object. Lumpiness and granularity help understand what types of goods make sense to share, but if the good is highly singular or a key part of our self-definition, we are unlikely to do so.

How do we share things? Alternative models

Gansky (2010) suggests that high-cost, infrequently used objects should be shareable. She uncovered more than 1,500 cooperatives, non-profit organizations, and for-profit corporations that facilitate such sharing. Product and service categories that these sharing organizations help distribute to those who need them include clothing, homes, toys, travel, transportation, food, and finance. There is a flurry of sharing activity at the moment, much of which has been made possible or much easier thanks to the Internet (Botsman and Rogers 2010). The first to discover the sharing possibilities of the Internet were those who shared digital music via Napster and other file-sharing systems (Giesler 2006). While intellectual property rights (IPR) battles have shut down many of these sites, such file sharing continues to thrive. Many people today would not think of buying music or films that they can download for free with relatively little effort. In other cases sites like YouTube, Flickr, and Vimeo have sprung up and allow consumers to freely upload and share their own content. In the first five years after its 2005 founding, YouTube made more than 150 million videos available, making it the largest film archive in the world (Kessler and Schäfer 2010; Prelinger 2010). Such sharing is rarely compensated, except by whatever fleeting fame it might bring those who post their productions.

At the same time, we no longer just use the Internet to share digital goods that can be transferred online (like music, films, documents, photos, and videos). Sharing sites like Freecycle, Craigslist, Kijiji, and eBay act like giant swap meets that allow users to sell, give away, loan, or trade resources with each other. They are so successful that they have largely put newspaper classified sections out of business. The major revenue stream for these sites is from banner advertising or AdWords, so that those who use them pay no fees. Other sites like Bag, Borrow, or Steal, and Netflix operate with a business model in which users pay a subscription fee that allows them to sequentially access a variety of purses or movies, respectively. Still others like Couchsurfing.org (free housing for travelers) and various community-supported agriculture sites like Local Harvest, operate as non-profit cooperatives. As we will see, for-profit sharing versus sharing through cooperatives may have a differential impact on sense of extended self and community.

Most of these sites and sharing organizations facilitate sharing at arm's length between largely anonymous or distant people. In that sense they are examples of sharing out rather than sharing in. There are, however, several other ways to share things and several other types of sharing that are inherently closer to sharing in. One type of organization is a neighborhood sharing organization like thesharehood.org or sharability.org. These groups, at a surface level, help neighbors share things that they only occasionally need like paint shakers, garden tillers, repair tools, and ladders. Beneath the surface, though, a broader purpose of these organizations is to help recreate a sense of community. In an era when next-door neighbors don't even know one another's names (Putnam 2000), this is not only a way to create the trust needed to share resources, but also to create the neighborhood sense of extended self that we now see as largely a thing of the past.

Another type of sharing organization that can build a different type of community is that of Wikipedia and open-source software movements like Linux. In both cases people contribute their labor with no immediate personal benefit. The collective results in these examples are an encyclopedia and computer software that would have been impossible for any of the individuals to create on their own (Kelty 2008; Lévy 1997; Sunstein 2006). Moreover, there is a broader sense of unity and trust that results from such joint volunteerism (Bergquist 2003; Ghosh 2005). In these cases the lack of a profit orientation provides an added sense of working for a noble cause. It could also be the case, however, that enthusiasts rallying together to form an online brand community or fan community feel a similar sense of oneness and virtual community (e.g. Cova *et al.* 2007; Jenkins 2006; Muñiz and O'Guinn 2001). In this case, extended self is enhanced by the understanding that these are people "just like me." Regardless of their age, race, class, or religion, "we all believe in the same thing" in this domain.

A comparison can be made in some cases between the effects of for-profit versus non-profit sharing organizations and their apparent effects on extended sense of self and feelings of community. One case where this is possible, is between the cooperative car-sharing organization of

Majorna in Sweden (now renamed Göteborgs Bilkoop) and the for-profit Zipcar car-sharing corporation in North America and some European cities. Majorna is a voluntary organization with 340 members and 29 cars (Jonsson 2007). The members share the tasks of maintaining the cars and pay an initial fee, a yearly fee, and bills corresponding to their actual use of the cars. Zipcar has a similar fee structure, but is a much larger organization with 275,000 members, $130 million in revenues, and 5,500 cars in 2009 (Botsman and Rogers 2010). Zipcar members are not required to help maintain the car they use other than filling the gas tank with a credit card that is included in the cars. With more locations in a wider array of major metropolitan locations, Zipcar is more convenient and has a wider range of "hipper" cars than the more utilitarian cars of Majorna. In terms of actual operations, both organizations are similar from the user's perspective; they reserve cars online, pick them up and drop them off at designated locations, and use a smartcard or smartphone to unlock the vehicles. Furthermore, members of both organizations claim to have been motivated to join for similar reasons of saving money by having the convenience of a car when they need one without the burdens of ownership. Both groups are happy with their experience in their respective car-sharing groups, but beyond these similarities there are fundamental differences.

Members of the Swedish group mostly know one another and get to know others better as they work together on the various maintenance committees. Some members have begun to worry that with 340 members the group has gotten too big and it is more difficult to know all the other members. They lament this because they enjoy the sense of community they experience with the group (Jonsson 2007). Zipcar has tried to instill a sense of community in its members as well. They name the cars and give them personalities, engage in camaraderie-building ads, sponsor get-togethers, and seek feedback from members for improvements. However, the members want nothing to do with the other members of Zipcar (Bardhi and Eckhardt 2010). When they pick up or drop off a car, they do not want to see other members and do not want to see signs of former drivers left in the car. They have functional suggestions for improving the service but generally have no desire to form a brand community around Zipcar. There are multiple possible explanations for this sharp difference, including different cultures and different size organizations, but perhaps a key reason is that Majorna's is a non-profit cooperative while Zipcar is a for-profit corporation. It is too early to say whether this difference in feeling a sense of community and extended self will generalize to other sharing organizations with similar organizational structures, but it suggests that sharing based on sharing out (e.g. Zipcar) is less likely to enfold members in a sense of community than is sharing based on sharing in (e.g. Göteborgs Bilkoop). However, since there are strong virtual brand communities where members only "know" one another online, more work is needed to untangle these differences.

In a different context the so-called Arab Spring revolutions in Tunisia, Egypt, and elsewhere during 2011 were hailed by many as having been brought about by social media like Facebook and Twitter. Governments in the Middle East temporarily shut down access to these sites and China blocks them entirely. In October 2010, reflecting on uprisings in Iran and Moldova, Malcolm Gladwell (2010) wrote a *New Yorker* article arguing that social media are not sufficiently high in involvement to foment a revolution. His argument is that social media are great at spreading news and rallying people to engage in low-risk behaviors, but not in precipitating the high-risk behavior of actual revolution. He draws on Granovetter's (1973) work on social networks to argue that social media activate many people with only weak ties to one another. Using the US civil rights movement as an example, Gladwell (2010) emphasizes that the strong ties of real face-to-face relationships are needed in order to generate the high-risk activism required for political revolution. Or, stated in terms of sharing, risk is something that can be shared out when it is small, but when the risk is large it requires sharing in. Gladwell's argument has generated counterarguments and the power of social media is likely more complex than acting simply for or against democracy (Cottle 2011; Pollock 2011; Rosen 2011). However, the question of just what sort of sense of community social media create is a valid one. While our hundreds or thousands of Facebook "friends" may contribute to, validate, and help shape our identity, this does not mean that we would be willing to share our home, car, or clothes with all of them.

There is also an apparent impact of new media on sharing and identity that differs between close sharing in groups and distant sharing out groups. Consider photographs, for example. Whereas analog print photos are easy to share within the home and difficult to share outside of it, the opposite is true of digital photos. Digital photos typically either reside on a computer in a home office, in an online "cloud," or on the small screen of a mobile device (Nunes *et al.* 2009). None of these facilitates face-to-face sharing. Furthermore, there may be a generation gap between the "Kodak generation" and the "Flickr generation" (Kray *et al.* 2009). As a result, the change to digital photography is seen to result in less photo sharing within the immediate family. On the other hand, the ease of sharing digital photos among distant people may facilitate making these people more a part of our aggregate extended self (Schwartz 2010). That is, through the self-disclosure of posting our own photos on social media or photo sharing sites as well as being "tagged" by those who recognize us in the photos that others have posted, we may begin to make strangers into friends and distant others into a part of our extended self.

Conclusion

As this brief look at sharing and identity suggests, the closeness of someone within our extended sense of self affects not only our willingness to share with them but also the type of things we are willing to share. At the same time, as with sharing Internet photos or tools within our neighborhood, this sharing also brings others closer to our aggregate sense of self and generates stronger ties and feelings of community. Thus, the Internet, sharing, and identity are intimately linked. As natural disasters, economic recessions, and wars or hostilities draw us closer together, they also create conditions in which we may be more willing to share. However, more work is needed to better understand the types of sharing that such conditions facilitate. It seems reasonable that natural disasters create more permeable self-boundaries and greater sharing out, while wars create less permeable self-boundaries and more sharing in. We have also seen that there may be differences according to the particular model of sharing that is involved. Although commercially facilitated sharing with distant others may be an efficient model of sharing, it may do little to foster an aggregate sense of self or build a sense of community around the group or brand. There are likely many cultural differences that affect both the preponderance of individual versus group self-definitions, but also related sharing tendencies, group boundaries, and feelings of ethnocentrism. Under the right circumstances, "you are what you own" might just become "you are what you share."

Acknowledgment

We thank Yun Mi Antorini and Albert Muñiz for their very helpful comments on this chapter.

References

Anderson, Benedict (1983) *Imagined Communities*. London: Verso.

Bardhi, Fleura and Eckhardt, Giana (2010) "Market-Mediated Collaborative Consumption in the Context of Car Sharing." *Advances in Consumer Research* 37, online edition.

Belk, Russell W. (1988) "Possessions and the Extended Self." *Journal of Consumer Research* 15 (September): 139–68.

——(2010) "Sharing." *Journal of Consumer Research* 37 (February): 715–34.

Benkler, Yochai (2004) "Sharing Nicely: On Shareable Goods and the Emergence of Sharing as a Modality of Economic Production." *Yale Law Journal* 114 (November): 273–358.

——(2006) *The Wealth of Networks: How Social Production Transforms Markets and Freedom*. New Haven, CT: Yale University Press.

Bergquist, Magnus (2003) "Open Source Software Development as Gift Culture: Work and Identity Formation in an Internet Community." In Christina Garsten and Helena Wulff (eds), *New Technologies at Work: People, Screens and Social Virtuality*. Oxford: Berg, pp. 223–41.

Botsman, Rachel and Rogers, Roo (2010) *What's Mine is Yours: The Rise of Collaborative Consumption*. New York: HarperCollins.

Cottle, Simon (2011) "Media and the Arab Uprisings of 2011: Research Notes." *Journalism* 12(15): 647–59.

Cova, Bernard, Kozinets, Robert, and Shankar, Avi (2007) *Consumer Tribes*. Oxford: Butterworth-Heinemann.

Gansky, Lisa (2010) *The Mesh: Why the Future of Business is Sharing*. New York: Portfolio Books.

Ghosh, Rishab Aiyer (ed.) (2005) *CODE: Collaborative Ownership and the Digital Economy*. Cambridge, MA: MIT Press.

Giesler, Markus (2006) "Consumer Gift System: Netnographic Insights from Napster." *Journal of Consumer Research* 33 (September): 283–90.

Gladwell, Malcolm (2010) "Small Change: Why the Revolution will not be Tweeted." *The New Yorker*, 4 October, online edition.

Granovetter, Mark (1973) "The Strength of Weak Ties." *American Journal of Sociology* 78(6): 1360–80.

Hyde, Lewis (2010) *Common as Air*. New York: Farrar, Straus and Giroux.

Ingold, Tim (1986) *The Appropriation of Nature: Essays on Human Ecology and Social Relations*. Manchester: Manchester University Press.

Jenkins, Henry (2006) *Fans, Bloggers, and Gamers: Exploring Participatory Culture*. New York: NYU Press.

Johns, Adrian (2009) *Piracy: The Intellectual Property Wars from Gutenberg to Gates*. Chicago, IL: University of Chicago Press.

Jonsson, Pernilla (2007) "A Tale of a Car Sharing Organization." In Helene Brembeck, Karin M. Ekströ, and Magnus Mörck (eds), *Little Monsters: (De)coupling Assemblages of Consumption*. Berlin: Lit Verlag, pp. 149–63.

Kelty, Christopher (2008) *Two Bits: The Cultural Significance of Free Software*. Durham, NC: Duke University Press.

Kessler, Frank and Schäfer, Mirko Tobias (2010) "Navigating YouTube: Constituting a Hybrid Information Management System." In Pelle Snickars and Patrick Vonderau (eds), *The YouTube Reader*. Stockholm: National Library of Sweden, pp. 275–91.

Kopytoff, Igor (1986) "The Cultural Biography of Things: Commitization as Process." In Arjun Appadurai (ed.), *The Social Life of Things: Commodities in Cultural Perspective*. Cambridge: Cambridge University Press, pp. 64–93.

Kray, Christian, Rohs, Michael, Hook, Jonathan, and Kratz, Sven (2009) "Bridging the Gap Between the Kodak and Flickr Generations: A Novel Interaction Technique for Collocated Photo Sharing." *International Journal of Human-Computer Studies* 67: 1060–72.

Lévy, Pierre (1997) *Collective Intelligence: Mankind's Emerging World in Cyberspace*. Trans. Robert Bonono. Cambridge, MA: Perseus Books.

Mander, Jerry (1992) *In the Absence of the Sacred: The Failure of Technology and the Survival of the Indian Nations*. San Francisco, CA: Sierra Club Books.

Muñiz, Albert M., Jr and O'Guinn, Thomas C. (2001) "Brand Community." *Journal of Consumer Research* 27 (March): 412–32.

Murray, David (2000) *Indian Giving: Economies of Power in Indian-White Exchanges*. Amherst, MA: University of Massachusetts Press.

Nunes, Michael, Greenberg, Saul, and Neustaedter, Carmen (2009) "Using Physical Memorabilia as Opportunities to Move into Collocated Digital Photo Sharing." *International Journal of Human-Computer Studies* 67: 1087–111.

Parry, Jonathan (1986) "*The Gift*, the Indian Gift and the 'Indian Gift'." *Man* 21: 466–71.

Pollock, John (2011) "Streetbook: How Egyptian and Tunisian Youth Hacked the Arab Spring." *Technology Review* (September/October). www.technologyreview.com/web/38379/.

Prelinger, Rick (2010) "The Appearance of Archives." In Pelle Snickars and Patrick Vonderau (eds), *The YouTube Reader*. Stockholm: National Library of Sweden, pp. 268–74.

Putnam, Robert D. (2000) *Bowling Alone: The Collapse and Revival of American Community*. New York: Simon and Schuster.

Rose, Randall and Poynor, Catherine (2007) "Mi Casa es Whose Casa? An Experimental Investigation of Consumers' Propensity to Participate in a Multilateral Sharing System." *Advances in Consumer Research* 34: 342–44.

Rosen, Rebecca J. (2011) "So, Was Facebook Responsible for the Arab Spring After All?" *The Atlantic* (3 September). Online edition.

Sanders, Clinton (1990) "Excusing Tactics: Social Responses to the Public Misbehavior of Companion Animals." *Anthrozoös* 4(2): 82–90.

Schwartz, Ori (2010) "On Friendship, Boobs, and the Logic of the Catalogue: Online Self-Portraits as a Means of Exchange of Capital." *Convergence: The International Journal of Research into New Media Technologies* 16(2): 163–83.

Sunstein, Cass R. (2006) *Infotopia: How Many Minds Produce Knowledge*. Oxford: Oxford University Press.

Widlok, Thomas (2004) "Sharing by Default: Outline of an Anthropology of Virtue." *Anthropological Theory* 4(1): 53–70.

——(2005) "Introduction." In Thomas Widlock and Wolde Gossa Tadesse (eds), *Property and Equality, Volume 1: Ritualisation, Sharing, Egalitarianism*. New York: Berghahn Books, pp. 1–17.

Zelizer, Viviana (1994) *The Social Meaning of Money*. New York: Basic Books.

28

THAT IS SO NOT ME

Dissociating from undesired consumer identities

Lea Dunn, Katherine White and Darren W. Dahl

Nicole "Snookie" Polizzi from MTV's *Jersey Shore* was well known for always being photographed with her Coach purse. In August 2010 she received media attention for shunning her trademark Coach for a Gucci bag instead. The interesting part of the story, however, was not that she had a sudden change in brand preference, but that Coach had carefully orchestrated the switch: by sending her their competition's products Coach hoped to decrease the undesirable associations of having Snookie seen using their brand! Similarly, in August 2011 clothing brand Abercrombie & Fitch paid Mike "The Situation" Sorrentino (another *Jersey Shore* celebrity) to stop wearing their clothes because they were " ... deeply concerned that Mr. Sorrentino's association with [their] brand could cause significant damage to [their] image" (Heller 2011); that is, they were worried that other consumers might avoid the Abercrombie brand because of these undesirable identity associations. These two incidents demonstrate preemptive marketing strategies to mitigate customer dissociation tendencies (i.e. the avoidance of products and/or brands that are associated with undesired social identities).

Marketers often position brands in order to highlight positive brand aspects, while simultaneously differentiating themselves from the competition. One way to accomplish this is by linking the brand identity with a group that has positive associations for the consumers, such as a positive reference group. The majority of past research on reference groups has examined the influence of positive reference groups on consumer decisions (Bearden and Etzel 1982; Childers and Rao 1992; Escalas and Bettman 2003). This work finds that consumers generally prefer products associated with positive reference groups such as their own membership group or an aspirational group. However, how do consumers respond to products associated with negative reference groups such as out-groups or dissociative groups (e.g. reference groups with which an individual wishes to avoid being associated)? Escalas and Bettman (2005) examined the differences between in-groups and out-groups as they relate to self-brand connections and found that consumers form stronger self-brand connections with symbolic brands associated with the in-group and weaker self-brand connections with brands associated with the out-group. This research shows that even groups to which people do not belong have significant impact on their feelings of connection with the brand. This chapter will explore the nature of dissociation, circumstances that can produce dissociation, the boundary conditions to dissociation, and applications of this research.

Dissociation: what is it?

Dissociation is the act of avoiding or disparaging products and brands that represent undesired groups or identities. Consumers purchase and use products as a means of constructing and presenting their self-concept to others (Belk 1988; Kleine *et al.* 1993). Thus, consumers choose to associate with groups and purchase products that allow them to be seen in a positive light (Escalas and Bettman 2003) and avoid or disparage those that are seen negatively (White and Dahl 2006, 2007; Berger and Heath 2007). Research in this area has been approached from two different viewpoints: one using social identity theory (Tajfel and Turner 1979) and one using optimal distinctiveness theory (Brewer 1991).

White and Dahl (2006, 2007) focus on dissociation using social identity theory as a starting point (Tajfel and Turner 1979) and see identity as comprising both personal identity (i.e. individual sense of self) and social identity (i.e. related to the groups to which one belongs or is affiliated). Shifts in situational factors cause certain social identities to become active and thus an individual may see themselves in terms of their group memberships. These group memberships become a crucial part of one's self-concept; therefore, consumers desire to see not just the self positively, but also their groups positively. To maintain this positive view, consumers rely on different strategies such as decreasing affiliations with groups that do not confer positive associations and differentiating between in-groups and out-groups (Marques *et al.* 1998).

White and Dahl (2006, 2007) demonstrate that dissociation occurs not just with out-groups (e.g. a reference group to which one does not belong), but with a specific type of reference group: a dissociative group. A dissociative (or negative) group is one with which an individual wishes to avoid being associated and "disidentifies" (Englis and Solomon 1995; Turner 1991). In essence, a dissociative group is a group of which the consumer does not want to be a member. For White and Dahl (2006, 2007), consumers are more likely to differentiate from a dissociative identity group than from an out-group more generally. For example, men are more likely to avoid and negatively evaluate a steak portion when it is associated with a dissociative group (i.e. women via "ladies' cut steak") than when associated with a neutral group (i.e. "chef's cut steak") (White and Dahl 2006). To further demonstrate that consumers avoid dissociative groups, White and Dahl (2007) found that Canadians only form weak self-brand connections to and negatively evaluate products that symbolically represent a dissociative group (e.g. Americans), but not an out-group (e.g. Belgians) or a neutral brand. Together, these articles show that consumers do avoid products associated with undesirable groups, but dissociative groups are more likely to result in dissociation than out-groups more generally. Dissociation, therefore, does not simply differentiate in- from out-groups, but is an attempt to actively avoid associations with undesired consumer identities.

Berger and Heath (2007, 2008), on the other hand, view dissociation from a convergence and divergence perspective centered in optimal distinctiveness theory (Brewer 1991). Optimal distinctiveness theory proposes that consumers desire to be a member of, but also differentiate from, a group (Brewer 1991). This is especially demonstrated when people have a higher need for uniqueness (Snyder and Fromkin 1980; Tian *et al.* 2001), or when situational cues threaten differentiation (Byrne and Griffith 1969). Berger and Heath theorized that consumers show more taste abandonment in certain domains than in others, and hypothesized that consumers diverge not just to seem unique, but also to signal specific identities to others. Their identity signaling approach explains why consumers abandon product preferences when the product in question is adopted by an out-group. Abandonment occurs not because the consumers no longer feel unique, but because they want to avoid the social cost of being misidentified as a member of a group to which they do not belong. Both perspectives lead to the conclusion that consumers are driven to avoid undesired affiliations and that this desire motivates consumers to dissociate from products that symbolically represent these groups.

Factors that lead to dissociation

Dissociation is a social process in that it is driven by a desire to avoid association with particular social group identities. Due to the social nature of dissociation, there are several factors that lead consumers toward diverging consumption practices.

Symbolic brands/products

Certain product domains are more capable of communicating user traits than others. Compared to utilitarian products, identity-relevant or symbolic products are more likely to elicit dispositional information about another person or group (Shavitt and Nelson 1999). As groups converge use on a single brand or product, the brand becomes a representation of the group and the traits the group possesses (McCracken 1989). When considering product consumption, consumers think about what their purchase communicates to others. Dissociation research has found that products that are more symbolic in nature (e.g. clothing, music, etc.) result in greater divergence than non-symbolic products (e.g. utilitarian products) (White and Argo 2011; Berger and Heath 2007, 2008; White and Dahl 2007).

Private vs. public consumption

Both Berger and Heath (2007) and White and Dahl (2006) agree that dissociation can be a self-presentational process (e.g. selectively choosing products to ensure that the consumer is seen by others in a positive light). Due to this social component, divergence is more likely to occur in public than in private consumption decision contexts. For example, White and Dahl (2006) found that while male consumers were more likely to rate the "ladies' cut" steak more negatively in public, there was no difference in preference or evaluation between steak cuts when the decision context was private. Berger and Heath (2007) similarly showed that when consumers anticipated having to defend their product preference in public, they were more likely to abandon their initial product choice if this choice was preferred by the majority. In addition, individual differences in self-presentation tendencies such as public self-consciousness have been shown to moderate the strength of dissociation (White and Dahl 2006, 2007). It appears that consumers with a heightened desire to present a positive self-image to others, either through situational cues or individual differences, are more likely to demonstrate product or brand dissociation.

Identity activation and importance

One component of social identity theory is that, when activated, one's social identity becomes a salient, important component of the self (Tajfel and Turner 1979). One result of this is that when one's own identity is made salient or is chronically important to the self, consumers are more likely to avoid products linked to dissociative groups (White and Dahl 2007). For example, when national identity was primed, Canadians were more likely to negatively evaluate the "American" (dissociative) branded pen than a "Belgian" (out-group) pen. White and Argo (2009), however, found that when it is one's own social identity that is viewed negatively, those consumers who strongly value and identify with the in-group (high collective self-esteem individuals) are less likely to distance themselves from the threatened identity. Instead, these consumers are more likely to reaffirm ties to the threatened group identity. Therefore, the salience and importance of the identity influences whether or not consumers engage in dissociation behavior.

Social or self-identity threat

Dissociation responses have also been shown to occur in ways that allow for the avoidance of an aspect of one's own social identity when it is viewed negatively or threatened in some way. In cases such as this, dissociation appears to reaffirm self-worth. For example, White and Argo (2009) examined how identity threat impacts consumer preferences. They found that participants whose own gender identity was threatened were subsequently more likely to avoid purchasing products associated with the female identity. In addition, collective self-esteem (e.g. the degree to which the individual sees the self as a worthy member of the social group, values social identity, and sees the social identity as important to the self-concept) (Luhtanen and Crocker 1992) moderated dissociation outcomes. Consumers with low collective self-esteem (CSE) are more focused on the individual self and, thus, more likely to seek ways to protect self-worth when an identity is threatened. In the case of a threatened social identity, those low in CSE may distance themselves from products affiliated with the threatened trait in order to protect self-worth. Those with high CSE, conversely, did not display these dissociation effects under threat.

Other work provides evidence that social identity threat activates the desire for dissociation. For example, White *et al.* (2012) find that self-construal influences consumer response to social identity threat. Self-construal refers to the extent to which the self is viewed as being separate and distinct from, or interconnected with, others (Singelis 1994). Consumers with an independent self-construal focus on individual-level goals, while consumers with an interdependent self-construal value social identities and exhibit strong bonds to their social groups (Trafimow *et al.* 1991). In particular, the authors find that consumers with independent self-construals are likely to respond to social identity threat in a manner consistent with self-enhancement motives (e.g. the desire to enhance positive self-concept and to protect the self from negative information) (Sedikides 1993). Independent self-construals respond to identity threat by avoiding products that symbolize the threatened dimension while interdependent self-construals respond to identity threat by evaluating associated products positively. The authors argue that the mechanisms behind these different responses vary depending on the activated self-construal. Independent self-construals see social identity threat as a threat to individual self-worth and restore this self-worth by avoiding the threatened identity. Interdependent self-construals, however, see social identity threat as a threat to their sense of belonging and satisfy their need to belong by activating multiple memberships.

Importantly, the aforementioned research demonstrates that not only do consumers dissociate to avoid signaling undesirable affiliations, but they also dissociate to maintain positive self-worth by avoiding threatened identities. Dissociation serves several different purposes including maintaining a positive image in the eyes of others (White and Dahl 2006, 2007), ensuring that there is no misidentification from others (Berger and Heath 2007, 2008), and maintaining positive self-worth by creating distance from a threatened aspect of one's own social identity (White and Argo 2009; White *et al.* 2011).

There are several promising areas for future research. For example, when considering social threat, are there more permanent outcomes of dissociation? If an identity is persistently under threat, will consumers consistently avoid these products? In addition, previous research suggests that dissociation effects are stronger in public than in private. However, how does the social audience impact dissociation? Will dissociation occur if the audience is an out-group or one with ambiguous group affiliation? For example, preliminary work suggests that consumers might strengthen their preferences for identity-linked products when an aspect of their own social identity is threatened by a dissociative out-group (as opposed to an in-group or a neutral group) (Mathews 2010). However, if the situation is such that no threat is involved and the consumer has the option to use/choose a product with dissociative associations in front of different audiences, consumers' self-presentation tendencies might shift as well. Consumers may become neutral toward the dissociative product or even accepting of it if the choice is made in front of members of a dissociative group.

When dissociation differs

The previous sections discussed common occurrences of consumer dissociation as well as factors that motivate consumers to dissociate. This section will discuss both circumstances that motivate consumers to dissociate, not from an out-group but from an in-group, and situations in which consumers are motivated to approach out-group products.

When consumers dissociate from the in-group

Optimal distinctiveness theory (Brewer 1991) states that people have two opposing needs – assimilation with others (i.e. a need to belong) and a need for differentiation from others (i.e. a need for uniqueness). Commonly, people maintain an optimal balance of these needs through their social group memberships. Assimilation is achieved by conforming to the tastes and behaviors of in-group members while uniqueness is achieved by differentiating from the out-group (Brewer 1991, 2003). One way to achieve differentiation, therefore, would be to avoid communicating undesired out-group identities as facilitated through symbolic consumption (Berger and Heath 2007, 2008; White and Dahl 2006, 2007).

Recently, researchers have examined circumstances in which threatened distinctiveness does not lead to dissociation from out-groups but dissociation at an in-group level. Chan *et al.* (2011) explore how consumers simultaneously satisfy both their need to belong and their need for uniqueness at an in-group level. The authors find that consumers are likely to purchase a brand that is associated with the in-group as a way to communicate assimilation, while simultaneously differentiating themselves from the in-group along the product dimension (e.g. choosing the least favorable color option). Chan and colleagues demonstrate that the goal of dissociation is not necessarily to avoid undesirable identities but could also be to maintain a sense of distinctiveness (Chan *et al.* 2011).

Similarly, White and Argo (2011) examine circumstances in which consumers engage in dissociation responses with a similar, not a dissimilar, other. As stated above, people desire to maintain a balance between assimilation and differentiation. Often consumers pursue products that are affiliated with similar others, while avoiding those associated with dissimilar others. However, when distinctiveness is threatened at an individual level, consumers are motivated to reassert their uniqueness. White and Argo (2011) assert that possession mimicry (e.g. having a product choice copied) by a similar other motivates consumers to dissociate from that product to reaffirm uniqueness. In particular, consumers for whom distinctiveness concerns are paramount (i.e. who have an independent self-construal primed or who are high in need for uniqueness) and who are mimicked by a similar other tend to abandon, re-customize, or exchange the mimicked product. For White and Argo (2011) dissociation is not driven by negative associations towards the other person, but by a desire to enhance a sense of distinctiveness from similar others.

Future research directions could examine other circumstances that lead to dissociation from in-group products. Perhaps there are circumstances in which actions by an in-group member might lead to dissociation. For example, if a female consumer strongly identifies with her gender identity, would seeing another female acting inappropriately lead her to dissociate from in-group products? Would the dissociation consist of products used by this one exemplar or spread to the group? Would the strength of the act change consumption behavior? For example, would the consumer dissociate from all products or simply think of the act as a one-time occurrence and not change her consumption behaviors?

When consumers approach the dissociative group

While dissociation appears to be driven by a desire for distinction from an out-group, there are circumstances in which consumers will actively seek out products used by out-groups. Focusing on within-group differentiation, Dommer *et al.* (2011) suggest that consumers can distinguish themselves through horizontal and vertical differentiation. Horizontal differentiation occurs when consumers go against reference group norms and seek out products that distance them from the in-group. Vertical differentiation implies seeking out ways to be superior to the reference group. The authors examine how social exclusion and inclusion interact with self-esteem to create a preference for out-group brands and products. For example, socially excluded, low self-esteem individuals will seek out alternative social relationships to fulfill their need to belong (Maner *et al.* 2007). Specifically, low self-esteem individuals dissociate from in-group products and approach out-group products as a means of asserting acceptance from another social group. High self-esteem individuals, on the other hand, will reassert their social connection from the in-group by avoiding out-group products and choosing in-group-affiliated products. Under situations of social inclusion, low self-esteem individuals continue to attempt to affirm their self-worth by choosing products associated with desirable traits like high-status products. By making themselves seem more desirable, low self-esteem individuals are able to elicit greater approval and acceptance from the reference group.

Another line of research further explored consumer motivations to pursue products used by undesirable groups. Looking at dissociation from a social comparison perspective, Shalev and Morwitz (2011) identify a form of social influence called the comparison-driven self-evaluation and restoration (CDSER). CDSER involves consumers evaluating their standing on specific traits by observing the possessions of others. For example, when a consumer notices an undesirable individual (i.e. a low socioeconomic-status consumer) using a high-status product, instead of avoiding that product, the consumer may conclude that his or her relative standing on that high-status trait is lower than he or she originally thought. This change in self-evaluation motivates the consumer to restore his or her relative standing on the trait by purchasing the same product. Counter to previous dissociation research which shows avoidance of the undesirable other, this study illuminates circumstances in which an undesirable other can positively affect an observer's intentions to purchase a target product. In addition, other work shows that while consumers learn that an out-group (vs. an in-group) is performing well on a prosocial dimension (e.g. composting), they will be more inclined to engage in that activity when their behaviors are public as opposed to private in nature (White *et al.* 2012). These lines of work reveal that out-groups do not always lead to dissociation, but can lead to associative effects too.

Future research in this area could examine other circumstances that lead consumers to approach products used by dissociative groups. One area could look at how publicized preemptive action on the part of the brand to prevent undesirable consumers from using their products impact consumer reactions and purchase intentions. For example, does Abercrombie publically offering

"The Situation" money to stop wearing their clothes motivate consumers to avoid or purchase Abercrombie? Does the status of the dissociative group change opinions about products? Would a celebrity member of an undesirable group have the same impact on dissociation? Celebrities have the potential to either magnify dissociation due to their public persona or they could mitigate the effects due to the status of being a celebrity.

Applications of dissociation research

In this section, we will discuss practical applications of dissociation research. Research has begun to examine the public policy implications of dissociative influence. Research shows that marketers can improve the behavioral outcomes of health advertising by using dissociative others as a reference point. For example, to convince consumers to avoid risky behaviors like smoking or excessive drinking (Berger and Rand 2008; White *et al.* 2006), simply aligning these behaviors with a dissociative other can reduce both risky behavioral intentions and actual behavior, a finding that is heightened among those who are prevention-focused (White *et al.* 2006). Further, highlighting the positive performance of dissociative others on a prosocial dimension (e.g. composting) ironically might increase inclinations to engage in that behavior (White *et al.* 2011). Future research might profitably explore other ways in which dissociative influence might be harnessed to encourage positive behaviors.

In summary, dissociation is the act of avoiding or disparaging products that are associated with undesired social identities. Dissociation can arise from a number of factors including the desire to avoid undesirable associations with symbolic products in public consumption settings, when an aspect of the consumer's identity is important and salient, and in circumstances of identity threat where dissociation is a means of protecting self-worth. There are also circumstances in which consumers do not show traditional forms of dissociation, but instead actively dissociate from their own membership groups or alternately approach dissociative group products. All in all, whether as a means of avoiding an undesirable identity, reaffirming self-worth or reasserting uniqueness, researchers and companies alike need to be aware that dissociation can be an important motivator for consumers in the marketplace.

References

Bearden, W.O. and Etzel, M.J. (1982) "Reference Group Influence on Product and Brand Purchase Decisions." *Journal of Consumer Research* 9(2): 183–94.

Belk, R.W. (1988) "Possessions and the Extended Self." *Journal of Consumer Research* 15: 139–67.

Berger, J. and Heath, C. (2007) "Where Consumers Diverge from Others: Identity Signaling and Product Domains." *Journal of Consumer Research* 34: 121–34.

——(2008) "Who Drives Divergence? Identity Signaling, Outgroup Dissimilarity, and the Abandonment of Cultural Tastes." *Journal of Personality and Social Psychology* 95(3): 593–607.

Berger, J. and Rand, L. (2008) "Shifting Signals to Help Health: Using Identity Signaling to Reduce Risky Health Behaviors." *Journal of Consumer Research* 35: 509–18.

Brewer, M.B. (1991) "The Social Self: On Being the Same and Different at the Same Time." *Personality and Social Psychology Bulletin* 17(5): 475–82.

——(2003) "Optimal Distinctiveness, Social Identity, and the Self." In M. Leary and J. Tangney (eds), *Handbook of Self and Identity*. New York: Guilford Press, pp. 480–91.

Byrne, D. and Griffith, W. (1969) "Similarity and Awareness of Similarity of Personality Characteristic Determinants of Attraction." *Journal of Experimental Research in Personality* 3(3): 179–86.

Chan, C., Berger, J. and van Boven, L. (2011) "Differentiating the 'I' in 'In-Group': How Identity-Signaling and Uniqueness Motives Combine to Drive Consumer Choice." *Journal of Consumer Research.*

Childers, T.L. and Rao, A. (1992) "The Influence of Familial and Peer-Based Reference Groups on Consumer Decisions." *Journal of Consumer Research* 19(2): 198–211.

Dommer, S.L., Swaminathan, V., and Ahluwalia, R. (2011) "Blending in by Standing Out? The Paradox of Self-Differentiating with Brands to Signal a Desire to Belong." Unpublished manuscript.

Englis, B.G. and Solomon, M.R. (1995) "To Be or Not to Be? Lifestyle Imagery, Reference Groups, and the Clustering of America." *Journal of Advertising* 24: 13–28.

Escalas, J.E. and Bettman, J.R. (2003) "You Are What You Eat: The Influence of Reference Groups on Consumers' Connections to Brands." *Journal of Consumer Psychology* 13(3): 339–48.

——(2005) "Self-Construal, Reference Groups, and Brand Meaning." *Journal of Consumer Research* 32(3): 378–89.

Heller, L. (2011) "Abercrombie to The Situation: Stop Wearing Out Clothes!" *Forbes*. www.forbes.com/sites/lauraheller/2011/08/17/abercrombie-to-the-situation-stop-wearing-our-clothes/.

Kleine, R.E., Kleine, S.S., and Kernan, J.B. (1993) "Mundane Consumption and the Self: A Social-Identity Perspective." *Journal of Consumer Psychology* 2(3): 209–35.

Luhtanen, R. and Crocker, J. (1992) "A Collective Self-Esteem Scale: Self-Evaluation of One's Social Identity." *Personality and Social Psychology Bulletin* 18(3): 302–18.

McCracken, G. (1989) "Who is the Celebrity Endorser? Cultural Foundations of the Endorsement Process." *Journal of Consumer Research* 16(12): 310–21.

Maner, J.K., DeWall, C.N., Baumeister, R.F., and Schaller, M. (2007) "Does Social Exclusion Motivate Interpersonal Reconnection? Resolving the 'Porcupine Problem'." *Journal of Personality and Social Psychology* 92(1): 42–55.

Marques, J., Abrams, D., and Paez, D. (1998) "The Role of Categorization and In-Group Norms in Judgments of Groups and Their Members." *Journal of Personality and Social Psychology* 75(4): 976–88.

Mathews, M. (2010) "Choosing Identity: Situational influences of Social Identity Threat on Product Choice." Unpublished honors thesis. University of Calgary.

Sedikides, C. (1993) "Assessment, Enhancement, and Verification Determinants on the Self-Evaluation Process." *Journal of Personality and Social Psychology* 65: 317–38.

Shalev, E. and Morwitz, V.G. (2011) "Influence via Comparison-Driven Self Evaluation and Restoration: The Case of the Low-Status Influencer." *Journal of Consumer Research.*

Shavitt, S. and Nelson, M.R. (1999) "The Social Identity Function in Person Perception: Communicated Meanings of Product Preferences." In G.R. Maio and J.M. Olson (eds), *Why We Evaluate: Function of Attitudes*. Mahwah, NJ: Erlbaum, pp. 37–57.

Singelis, T.M. (1994) "The Measurement of Independent and Interdependent Self-Construals." *Personality and Social Psychology Bulletin* 20(5): 580–91.

Snyder, C.R. and Fromkin, H.L. (1980) *Uniqueness*. New York: Plenum.

Tajfel, H. and Turner, J.C. (1979) *An Integrative Theory of Intergroup Conflict*. Monterey, CA: Brooks/Bole.

Tian, K.T., Bearden, W.O., and Hunter, G.L. (2001) "Consumers' Need for Uniqueness: Scale Development and Validation." *Journal of Consumer Research* 28: 50–66.

Trafimow, D., Triandis, H.C., and Goto, S.G. (1991) "Some Tests of the Distinction Between the Private Self and the Collective Self." *Journal of Personality and Social Psychology* 60(5): 649–55.

Turner, J.C. (1991) *Social Influence*. Buckingham: Open University Press.

White, K. and Argo, J.J. (2009) "Social Identity Threat and Consumer Preferences." *Journal of Consumer Psychology* 19: 313–25.

——(2011) "When Imitation Doesn't Flatter: The Role of Consumer Distinctiveness in Responses to Mimicry." *Journal of Consumer Research* 38(4): 677–80.

White, K., Argo, J.J., and Sengupta, J. (2012) "Dissociative Versus Associative Responses to Social Identity Threat: The Role of Consumer Self-Construal." *Journal of Consumer Research* (December), forthcoming.

White, K., Cunningham, K., and Dahl, D.W. (2006) "The Effect of Dissociative Reference Groups on Evaluations of a Health-Marketing Campaign." Society for Personality and Social Psychology conference, Palm Springs, CA.

White, K. and Dahl, D.W. (2006) "To Be or Not Be? The Influencer of Dissociative Reference Groups on Consumer Preferences." *Journal of Consumer Psychology* 16(4): 404–14.

——(2007) "Are All Out-Groups Created Equal? Consumer Identity and Dissociative Influence." *Journal of Consumer Research* 34: 525–36.

White, K., Simpson, B., and Argo, J. (2011) "I Can Do Anything Better than You: Ironic Effects of Dissociative Influence." Manuscript in preparation. University of British Columbia.

III.II

Family, community, and self

29

SELF-EXTENSION, BRAND COMMUNITY, AND USER INNOVATION

Yun Mi Antorini and Albert M. Muñiz, Jr

For thousands of years, people have pondered the quintessential questions "who are we?" and "what can we be?" Lately, with the rise of the consumer society, another question has risen in prominence, one which concerns how people's lives are shaped and socially connected through the things they consume and possess. To illuminate this complex relationship between self and mass goods, consumer behavior researchers have developed a stream of literature that focuses on how people extend individual and group self through the use of specific products and brands.

Belk (1987, 1988, 1989) summarizes that self-extension takes place in three primary ways: via controlling and mastering the object, via knowing the object, and by creating the object. While the first two ways of self-extension are quite well documented (Belk 1990; Hill *et al.* 2008; Epp and Price 2008; Hirschman 1994; Kleine *et al.* 1995; Sivadas and Venkatesh 1995; Tian and Belk 2005), surprisingly few studies have looked into how people extend self via the things they themselves create (Claiborne and Ozanne's (1990) study of custom-made homeowners, and Belk's (1988) references to craftspeople and artists being notable exceptions). This particular omission is all the more noteworthy given the phenomenal rise of and scholarly interest in consumer co-creation (Prahalad and Ramaswamy 2004; von Hippel 2005). Consumer behavior researchers suggest that the participatory actions by consumers, such as the customizations and improvements they make, create much value for other consumers (Schau *et al.* 2009). However, in the extended-self literature we find little to illuminate the question of how social contexts influence creative and self-definitive processes.

To address these gaps, in this chapter we explore how members of the organic Adult Fans of LEGO (AFOL) community extend self through user innovation and community membership. In addition to making contributions to the consumer behavior literature we add new perspectives to the user innovation literature, which has been concerned with how user innovation happens and what motivates it, but which has so far not dealt with the relationship between identity negotiation and consumers' creations.

Self-extension and ways of self-extension

Central to the extended-self construct is the notion of a reciprocal relationship between consumers' view of self and their possessions. Consumers are construed as possessing a proximal or core self that is extended into possessions while those possessions, in turn, infuse consumers' identities (Belk 1987, 1988, 1989). Through extending self into products that are consumed, possessions come to act as symbols (Belk 1988: 144) or artifacts of the self (Kleine *et al.* 1995: 341). These symbols give the individual the possibility to gain feedback from others who may otherwise be reluctant to respond to the unextended self (Belk 1988). As we will show, the solicitation and provision of feedback are processes that play out quite powerfully in the AFOL community.

Not all possessions are candidates for being perceived as part of self nor do all possessions reflect the same kind of potential "me-ness." Generally, the possessions people consider "me" and "mine," feel emotionally attached to and are satisfied with are more likely to become part of self (Sivadas and Venkatesh 1995). This is because such possessions are invested with psychic energy that links the owner with important feelings, experiences and life projects (Belk 1988, 1990; Epp and Price 2008; Hill *et al.* 2008; Hirschman 1994; Tian and Belk 2005). As such, possessions have the capability of integrating experiences and relationships from the past into the present life story (Epp and Price 2008; Kleine *et al.* 1995). As we will demonstrate, user innovations, too, can facilitate these processes.

Kleine *et al.*'s (1995) findings further suggest that possession attachments are usually past or present oriented. That is, people rarely become attached to products that represent emerging aspects of themselves. Similarly, consumers feel less of an attachment with possessions that mark what the consumer wishes to avoid becoming (Morgan 1993). Despite having lost their ability to mark current self, such possessions still signify identity (Kleine *et al.* 1995). These processes, too, are evident in the user-innovation activities of AFOL.

Belk (1988) suggested that one of the ways people appropriate objects is by overcoming, controlling, and mastering them. For example, as we learn to ride a bike, climb a mountain, manipulate a new computer system, or find our way in an unfamiliar subway system, we gain control and mastery over (and by) the thing. In these processes, our self figuratively extends to include these things (Belk 1988: 150). As we will show, consumer innovation represents a potent form of control and mastery.

Another way of incorporating objects into self is via the accumulation of deep knowledge of a thing, such as the consumer who has a profound and passionate knowledge of his collection of products, the way these products function, their history, and new offerings on the marketplace of relevance to his or her collection (Belk 1988). Such knowledge, in most cases, would precede efforts at innovation. Hill *et al.*'s (2008) study vividly illustrates how passionately knowing a thing can be tied up with both very positive but also very difficult and sad emotions, like for example when one is being forced to end the relationship. In addition, their findings suggest that knowing is typically associated with attachment and satisfaction with the thing. However, as our findings show, the sense of closeness may also result in the opposite – i.e. feelings of devaluation in cases where other members of the community criticize the creation.

Finally, people may incorporate objects into self via creation. Belk (1988: 151) suggests that "handcrafted pieces to the craftsperson, and artworks to the artist, may become part of extended self, because we have intentionally worked upon or created these things, investing both energy and self in them." Belk (1988: 149) discusses the possibility that handcrafted items come to possess more of the creator's self compared to mass-produced items. Similarly, people are known to retain identity in the creation via marking the object (if the object is physical) or by codifying it though patent (if the thing represents a mental creation such as an idea for a product). None of the few studies available have studied the processes through which integration via creation happens and how consumers subscribe meaning to these processes. Neither have they been centered on mundane and mass-produced consumption objects of the kind that are consumed most frequently. Our study addresses these gaps.

Research site and method

In 1998 the children's toy firm LEGO launched the product line, LEGO Mindstorms Robotic Invention System. Sales data for this system revealed quite a surprise: it was mainly adult males who bought and used the product. Also surprising was the extent to which these adult consumers, without any encouragement from the firm, re-engineered and wrote new code for the programmable control unit that came with the set. These consumers thought of themselves as belonging to the self-organized global AFOL community exhibiting the cultural and social hallmarks of brand community (Muñiz and O'Guinn 2001). Today, this community comprises over 70,000 members (LEGO Group, interview, April 2011).

User creativity and product innovation have always been central activities of the AFOL community. AFOLs innovate all aspects of the LEGO consumption activity (Antorini 2007; Bender 2010; Baichtal and Meno 2011). For example, they innovate new LEGO models, new play concepts, and technologically based products, all with the purpose of going "beyond what comes in the box." They also innovate social spaces and means of communication that allow for online as well as offline interaction. Between 2003 and 2010 we engaged in a multi-site, multi-method research program to examine community development and user-innovation in the AFOL community. The multi-site, multi-method program allowed us to study self-identity in different contexts and situations.

We observed AFOL in two contexts: 1 at conventions and locally arranged events; and 2 on community forums and sites. We participated in seven conventions in North America, Denmark and Germany, which amounted to 82 hours of observation. The conventions had between 50 and 400 AFOL. At these events, AFOL displayed their most impressive user innovations and participated in presentations, workshops, competitions, auctions, and roundtable discussions. We also observed AFOL at smaller and locally arranged events such as visits to the LEGO factory and the LEGOLAND park in Billund, Denmark, monthly LEGO user group meetings and locally arranged LEGO shopping trips. At the end of each observation, impressions were consolidated into field notes that included descriptions of the physical frames of the event venue, the kinds of innovations and creations that were on display, the nature of the social interactions, and the language and jargon we observed. Becoming increasingly aware of the relationship between user innovation and self-extension, we followed several LEGO online forums and we collected member profiles uploaded by members of the LEGO User Group Network (Lugnet.com). In total, we collected 1,016 pages of double-spaced text.

To further elaborate the ideas that were associated with AFOL group self and to study the "me" and the "mine" that was associated with the things AFOL created, we conducted 25 depth interviews with members of the community that we met at conventions and events. The interviews typically lasted between one and two hours. In total, interview transcripts yielded 672 pages of double-spaced text. The interviews offered an opportunity to further elaborate the findings that had emerged through the observations and to expand the opinions and experiences that AFOL had previously brought up in the message board threads.

Data were analyzed using the constant comparative method (Miles and Huberman 1984; Strauss and Corbin 1998), where we engaged in an iterative procedure of transcribing, interpreting, pursuing new questions and paths, collecting additional data, and challenging, affirming, and refining emerging themes until we achieved sufficient interpretive convergence.

Findings

AFOL self-extension through creation

Being creative is for AFOL an important component of self. Consider the following comments:

> Creativity is what I, and I suspect others [AFOL], value. It does not matter how much [LEGO] you have but what you do with what you have.
>
> *(Christina, f, interview)*

> I think of LEGO as a creative outlet. I tell people I am creative but I am not artistic. I cannot draw, paint or sculpt or play music. But LEGO gives me a real creative outlet because I can look at something and start thinking about how I would build it. If it does not turn out the best part is that you take it apart and try again. That to me is the essence of LEGO. Being able to express something that I see in my head so that other people can see it.
>
> *(John, m, interview)*

As the above comments illustrate, creating new things, seeing other AFOL's self-designed work, and discussing innovative ways of using LEGO elements represent the things most appreciated about being AFOL.

AFOL generally think of creativity along two interdependent dimensions: creativity as related to mental and inner cognitive processes ("something I see in my head," "your uniqueness," as AFOL mentioned in interviews), and creativity as a collectively negotiated process in which social interaction and exchange of viewpoints in the form of feedback appear to be an important source of attraction. Consider these narratives:

> I find that there's a sort of a cycle where I build, share it, hear what people say about it, see what other people are building, talk about it, then go back and build again. Ideas tend to get passed around that way, and different people will use the idea in different ways and generate new ideas. It becomes a highly creative experience for me.
>
> *(AFOL posting from Lugnet.com)*

> The audience I build for is Builder's Lounge [a members-only forum for a group of very experienced and proficient AFOL] and a few other non-members I highly respect too. Sure, I build primarily for fun, but if I can get those select people to comment on something I did, I know I have achieved something great.
>
> *(AFOL posting from The Brothers Brick)*

As the above narratives illustrate, everything that makes AFOL uniquely them are incorporated into their creation, but in such a way that it is attuned with the taste of other community members. Feedback, in this respect, plays a key role in the reciprocal relationship between the AFOL creation and sense of self.

Through these iterative processes, an otherwise anonymous pile of LEGO elements transform into a symbol and artifact of the creator's self but also, because of the integration of other members' ideas and tastes, the group self. For example, we observed that AFOL would oftentimes show other AFOL's work to non-LEGO people as a way of testifying what AFOL as a group are capable of creating. In other words, we saw a strong sense of ownership and identification with other AFOL's work. Consequently, creation among AFOL is very much a social process made possible through the many community meeting spots (online and offline). The social aspect is also reflected in the way AFOL talk about their work, which they commonly refer to as MOC, an abbreviation for "my own creation."

Self-extension and the role of the MOC

With the emphasis on *my own*, AFOL want to clearly distinguish their creative work from LEGO models produced by the LEGO Group. To qualify as a good MOC it needs to be perceived as novel and not just a variation of the known, or worse, a copy of someone else's work. As John (m, interview) mentions, and which represents a typical viewpoint among AFOL:

> You know, there are so many ways to put the bricks together that somebody is always coming up with something new. And for a lot of people that's a really cool thing. Finding a new way to do something.
>
> *(John, m, interview)*

This desire for novelty is closely linked with AFOL's collective quest to move the hobby "beyond what comes in the box," as it said on the cover of an AFOL-produced book about AFOL LEGO creations. Also, though, by praising the novel MOC as "a really cool thing" and by motivating one another to create new work, with each new MOC, AFOL are able to experience new sides of the self. As postmodernists have noted, the ability to experience new sides of the self through acquisition of new products is perhaps the most powerful driver of consumption in our times (Lipovetsky 2006). For AFOL specifically, it explains their high level of engagement in the MOC specifically and in innovation more generally.

While AFOL are generally happy to see others incorporate their work as symbols of the shared AFOL self, they also want to maintain a sense of self in the creation. Thus, similar to when people mark and patent their work, AFOL signal individual ownership over MOCs by writing elaborate descriptions of the model(s) they display and show others, by giving particular (brand) names to their work, and by using particular building styles that identify them as the creator. We observed several examples of AFOL who openly frowned and discredited those who, for whatever reason, had incorporated part of an MOC in their creation and displayed it as his or hers but without crediting the original creator. We see this as a self-defensive act that strives to protect the "me" that has been invested in the MOC. To AFOL, these self-defensive acts are anything but trivial and mundane. By posing as the inventor, the copyist threatens to "wash away" (Belk 1988: 159) the identity of the original creator.

Being no longer capable of claiming self through the MOC, the true creator can no longer gain feedback from others who may otherwise be reluctant to respond to the unextended self (Belk 1988). He or she becomes a "have-not" (Sayre and Horne 1996: 323). Clearly, there is much at stake when a copyist tries to claim work he or she did not do. It's not just that people can't respond to the creators' self if the MOC no longer is associated with him or her. Other deeper parts of the creator's identity risks being "washed away" too. Thus, we found that the MOC links AFOL with important self-defining experiences that concern first, AFOL's past, and second, the sense of engaging in constant self-improvement.

User creations as links to AFOL's past and self-improvement

MOCs connect AFOL with the past that is for many associated with a strong sense of creative freedom. Freedom to lose oneself entirely in the joy-filled act of expressing whatever idea came to mind, where one did not have to deal with, as many AFOL pointed out to us, current "stresses of life," "deadlines," and "grown-up life of working, having a mortgage, etc." The past is clearly the time when AFOL were their "ideal self" (Belk 1990: 670). So strong is this need to create distance from the anti-self (associated with "grown-up life of work, having a mortgage, etc.") and to be connected with the ideal self that AFOL have created – a sacred myth that is centered on the idea that being innovative with LEGO elements represents, in the words of AFOL, a "fountain of youth" that offers the "chance to never stop being a kid." The myth is not about achieving immortality or staying the same forever. Rather, it is about connecting the current self with freely chosen, creative practices of the past.

By creating and sharing their MOCs with others, AFOL transfer and situate their ideal self in the present. Self-extension via the MOC, consequently, allows AFOL to express themselves and it helps them resolve current life theme-related tensions and emotional inconsistencies that exist between AFOL's desire for unrestricted creative self-expression and the limitations and constraints that are associated with grown-up life. Innovation and MOC creation thus help affirm the harmony and integrity of the self (McAdams 1993: 112).

Our findings support Belk's (1990) observation that people are especially concerned with the past when current identities are challenged and that possessions can act as security objects that help overcome life theme-related tensions. We build on Belk's (1990) findings by accentuating the role of creation in coupling past self with current self, and how the physical and mental involvement in a creation process enable people to actually act on the gaps that may exist between the two. Thus, our findings suggest a more agentic and dynamic view of the relationship between past, possessions, and the self.

Our findings also suggest, as the following will further illustrate, that social contexts play a key role in coupling these dimensions and giving them a future-oriented direction. Consider Stefan's (m, interview) comments:

STEFAN: The feedback I get most excited about is the one that takes time to dissect and analyze and deconstruct my model … That gives me something to think about, something to, you know, that makes me excited, starts getting the mental resources pumping and makes me think about, you know, how to improve it. It makes me very energetic, very, "OK, all right, I know I can do this, and this, and this, and this," 'cause then I have a laundry list to go back to look through the monolog.

R: What does it tell about you as a person that you have this kind of, you know, or you have this wish to … ?

STEFAN: Hopefully, that I like improving myself, that I like improving my creations, that I hold myself to a high standard … If it's [the feedback] something that just says, oh this sucks, but it doesn't tell me why, then it will either make me very … it'll make me feel bad, obviously, but it will make me feel discouraged and disheartened. But the lack of feedback will also do the same because I go: "OK, well, this isn't impressive enough to make anybody care to post. So I have to go back and make it more impressive. I have to find a way to make it more attention-grabbing." So there can be discouragement and depression when you don't get any response to your model, be it good or bad.

Feedback allows Stefan to think about how his work can be improved and how, as a result, he as a person can change and evolve. Creativity becomes part of an ongoing narrative of personal development and future visions of the self (Morgan 1993). The MOC couples past self with current self-identities but it is also instrumental to the development of the self, what the individual member and AFOL as a collective are hoping they will be in the eyes of others. As one

AFOL explained to us in an interview: people not in the LEGO hobby generally "have fond memories [of LEGO play] and that is all," but they "do not understand that this is a very complex and deep hobby and the possible creations you can make out of LEGO parts are endless." MOCs are perceived as instrumental to the path toward legitimizing the hobby as they demonstrate the complex nature of the hobby.

These findings contrast previous findings (Klein *et al.* 1995) which suggested that people rarely become attached to objects that represent emerging aspects of self. We find that people do become attached to such objects. We also find that the meanings inherent in these objects – i.e. their capacity to help people couple the past, the current, and future vision of self – represent a powerful motivation to innovate. By creating new MOCs, AFOL show to the world that they are evolving, consistently holding themselves, as Stefan emphasized, to a higher standard. The attitude: "I have to go back and make it more impressive," resonates with the self-view-bolstering dynamics described by Gao *et al.* (2009) and Belk (1988), where demand for new products and/or periods of creativity may follow loss of one's possessions. In the case of AFOL whose MOCs are being criticized or are simply ignored, the loss is not a tangible one but a symbolic loss related to the MOC's incapability to reflect how the creator has improved. We can see why Stefan and other AFOL are willing to work so hard to improve their work, and we can see why self-extension via creation can be a risky and time-consuming task that requires cognitive competencies and skills, but also attention to the social contexts of which the creator is a part.

Clearly, physically building with LEGO elements represents the most obvious way in which AFOL actively and intentionally incorporate LEGO products into self. However, incorporation also happens via control and mastering, and through knowing the brand. For example, AFOL's wide use of consumer-developed building techniques, various 3D-modeling software and parts library systems enable them to gain a high degree of control and mastery over the LEGO System. Through years of collecting and building with the LEGO System, AFOL have come to know the LEGO brand passionately. In some cases, AFOL know the brand better than employees of the LEGO Group itself, a fact noted by LEGO managers (Koerner 2006). Yet it is in the physical interaction and manipulation with LEGO elements that the subject arises and that the MOC can truly act as a symbol of self which other people can relate to, comment on, and acknowledge.

Discussion: self-extension, brand community, and user innovation

One of our main contributions to the extended-self theory is that self-extension projects sometimes fail (marking the creator as a "have-not") and that successful self-extension through creation depends on the individual's ability to incorporate the collectively negotiated taste that is shared by community members (and which in our case involves a taste for the novel creation). Compared to the unchanging objects that are typically examined in the extended-self literature (like furniture, houses and clothing), which are integrated into self through knowing, controlling, and/or mastery, self-extension via creation is a tricky and quite complicated task.

In the context of brand community, successful self-extension through creation happens not simply because the creator has intentionally worked upon or created a thing (Belk 1988). It happens because the creator is also able to reflect and incorporate the collectively negotiated taste in his or her creation. This is because, as we show, creation is very much a social process which involves a great deal of interaction and negotiation among members. In addition, we found that other members readily incorporate a creation as theirs when the creation testifies to what members appreciate and value as a community. These findings represent significant extensions of current literature which focuses mainly on the person-thing-person relationship and which depicts self-extension processes as largely under the control of the individual. We find that others exert considerable influence on individual members' self-extension projects. We also find that through these processes the community creates a communal sense of self: what it means to belong to the AFOL community.

Another main finding concerns the role of innovations as narratives of self. It contributes to extant user innovation literature by illuminating the overlooked aspect of how identity relates to the innovations users conceive. Overall, user innovation scholars identify the following motives for why users innovate: a strong need for the thing which is not on the market (von Hippel 2001; Lüthje 2004; Hienerth 2006), peer recognition (Jeppesen and Molin 2003; Jeppesen and Frederiksen 2006), and intrinsic motives like it is fun to innovate (Franke and Shah 2003; Füller 2006; Füller *et al.* 2006; Shah 2006). We propose that something deeper is at stake. Operating in the intersection between the "inside" and the real world, consumer innovations are at one and the same time "creative work of the imagination" and "grounded in the real world" (McAdams 1993: 112). We assert that these characteristics make consumer innovations especially good for telling stories of self. In fact, we find that the creation of identity through the expression of "inner" and unique ideas represents the ultimate in self-definition. Regarding the question of what inspires consumer innovation, we assert that the realness and authenticity of consumer innovations, that they are objects that can be touched, looked upon, and discussed, help stabilize and confirm the existence of self. Innovations literally and symbolically provide answers. They offer new perspectives on things, new ideas to believe in, and new solutions to be enthusiastic about and share. As such, one implication of this study for user innovation and consumer research is to acknowledge the creative and productive sides of consumption and of identity construction that go on "far removed from the corporation" (Holt 2002: 86), where companies no longer act as cultural authorities but are instead used as "original cultural material" (ibid.: 88) by the "unruly bricoleurs who," like AFOL, "engage in nonconformist producerly consumption practices" (ibid.: 88). In sum, we believe that the reason consumers find the innovation process to be fun, engaging, and exciting (Franke and Shah 2003; Füller 2006; Füller *et al.* 2006; Jeppesen and Frederiksen 2006) is because consumers are creating solutions to real-life problems that help them execute their consumption activity more effectively (Lüthje 2004; von Hippel 2001). However, viewing consumer innovations from an identity perspective, we assert that what makes the innovation process profoundly meaningful, and what makes consumers innovate not once but several times and over a long period, is the fact that in the process, individual and communal self is created and experienced anew.

References

Antorini, Yun Mi (2007) *Brand Community Innovation. An Intrinsic Case Study of the Adult Fans of LEGO Community*. PhD Series 35.2007.

Baichtal, John and Meno, Joe (2011) *The Cult of LEGO*. San Francisco, CA: No Starch Press.

Belk, Russell W. (1987) "Presidential Address: Happy Thought." In Melanie Wallendorf and Paul Anderson (eds), *Advances in Consumer Research*, Vol. 14. Provo, UT: Association for Consumer Research, pp. 1–4.

——(1988) "Possessions and the Extended Self." *Journal of Consumer Research* 15 (September): 139–68.

——(1989) "Extended Self and Extending Paradigmatic Perspective." *Journal of Consumer Research* 16(1): 129–32.

——(1990) "The Role of Possessions in Constructing and Maintaining a Sense of Past." In Marvin E. Goldberg *et al.* (eds), *Advances in Consumer Research*, Vol. 17. Provo, UT: Association for Consumer Research, pp. 669–76.

Bender, Jonathan (2010) *LEGO – A Love Story*. Hoboken, NJ: John Wiley & Sons.

Claiborne, C.B. and Ozanne, Julie L. (1990) "The Meaning of Custom-Made Homes: Home As a Metaphor for Living." *Advances in Consumer Research* 17(19): 367–74.

Epp, Amber M. and Price, Linda L. (2008) "Family Identity: A Framework of Identity Interplay in Consumption Practices." *Journal of Consumer Research* 35(1): 50–70.

Franke, Nikolaus and Shah, Sonali (2003) "How Communities Support Innovative Activities: An Exploration of Assistance and Sharing Among End-users." *Research Policy* 32: 157–78.

Füller, Johann (2006) "Why Consumers Engage in Virtual New Product Developments Initiated by Producers." *Advances in Consumer Research* 33: 639–46.

Füller, Johann, Jawecki, Gregor, and Mühlbacher, Hans (2006) "Innovation Creation by Online Basketball Communities." *Journal of Business Research* 60(1): 60–71.

Füller, Johann, Matzler, Kurt, and Hoppe, Melanie (2008) "Brand Community Members as a Source of Innovation." *Journal of Product Innovation Management* 25(6): 608–19.

Gao, Leilei, Wheeler, S. Christian, and Shiv, Baba (2009) "'The Shaken Self': Product Choices as a Means of Restoring Self-View Confidence." *Journal of Consumer Research* 36 (June): 29–38.

Hienerth, Christoph (2006) "The Commercialization of User Innovations: The Development of the Rodeo Kayak Industry." *R& d Management* 36(3): 273–95.

Hill, Ronald Paul, Gaines, Jeannie, and Wilson, Mark R. (2008) "Consumer Behavior, Extended-self, and Sacred Consumption: An Alternative Perspective from our Animal Companions." *Journal of Business Research* 61(5): 553–62.

Hirschman, Elizabeth C. (1994) "Consumers and Their Animal Companions." *Journal of Consumer Research* 20(4): 616–32.

Holt, Douglas B. (2002) "Why Do Brands Cause Trouble? A Dialectical Theory of Consumer Culture and Branding." *Journal of Consumer Research* 29 (June): 70–90.

Jeppesen, Lars Bo and Frederiksen, Lars (2006) "Why do Users Contribute to Firm-Hosted User Communities? The Case of Computer Controlled Music Instruments." *Organization Science* 17: 45–63.

Jeppesen, Lars Bo and Molin, Mans J. (2003) "Consumers as Co-developers: Learning and Innovation Outside the Firm." *Technology Analysis & Strategic Management* 15(3): 363–83.

Kleine, Susan Schultz, Kleine, Robert E., and Allen, Chris T. (1995) "How is a Possession 'Me' or 'Not Me'? Characterizing Types and an Antecedent of Material Possession Attachment." *Journal of Consumer Research* 22(3): 327–43.

Koerner, Brendan I. (2006) "Geeks in Toyland." *Wired* Issue 14.02, February.

Lipovetsky, Gilles (2006) *The Time of the Hyper-consumer.* Essay presented at the ESOMAR Congress, London, 17–20 September.

Lüthje, Christian (2004) "Characteristics of Innovating Users in a Consumer Goods Field. An Empirical Study of Sports-Related Product Consumers." *Technovation* 24: 683–95.

McAdams, Dan P. (1993) The Stories We Live By: Personal Myths and the Making of the Self. New York: The Guilford Press.

Miles, Matthew B. and Huberman, A. Michael (1984) *Qualitative Data Analysis: A Sourcebook of New Methods.* Beverly Hills, CA: Sage.

Morgan, Amy J. (1993) "The Evolving Self in Consumer Behavior: Exploring Possible Selves." *Advances in Consumer Research* 20(1): 429–33.

Muñiz, Albert M., Jr, and O'Guinn, Thomas C. (2001) "Brand Community." *Journal of Consumer Research* 27 (March): 412–32.

Prahalad, C.K. and Ramaswamy, V. (2004) *The Future of Competition. Co-creating Unique Value with Customers.* Boston, MA: Harvard Business School Press.

Sayre, Shay and Horne, David (1996) "I Shop, Therefore I Am: The Role of Possessions for Self Definition." *Advances in Consumer Research* 23: 323–28.

Schau, Hope Jensen, Muñiz, Albert M., Jr, and Arnould, Eric J. (2009) "How Brand Community Practices Create Value." *Journal of Marketing* 73 (September): 30–51.

Shah, Sonali (2006) "Motivation, Governance, and the Viability of Hybrid Forms in Open Source Software Development." *Management Science* 52(7): 1000–14.

Sivadas, Eugene and Venkatesh, Ravi (1995) "An Examination of Individual and Object-specific Influences on the Extended Self and its Relation to Attachment and Satisfaction." *Advances in Consumer Research* 22(1): 406–12.

Strauss, Anselm and Corbin, Juliet (1998) *Basics of Qualitative Research: Techniques and Procedures for Developing Grounded Theory.* Thousand Oaks, CA, and London: Sage.

Tian, Kelly and Belk, Russell W. (2005) "Extended Self and Possessions in the Workplace." *The Journal of Consumer Research* 32(2): 297–310.

von Hippel, Eric (2001) "Innovation by User Communities: Learning from Open-Source Software." *MIT Sloan Management Review* (Summer): 82–86.

——(2005) *Democratizing Innovation.* Cambridge, MA: MIT Press.

30

MOTHER POSSESSING DAUGHTER

Dual roles of extended self

Junko Kimura and Mototaka Sakashita

Various forms of consumption help consumers to create their own self-image (McCracken 1986; Saren 2007). The conceptualization of extended self by Belk (1988) has introduced the idea that consumers own their core self and often try to extend it through possessions, and in such cases certain types of objects become a part of the extended self (Belk 1988; Mittal 2006). There has been a wide variety of distinctive objects identified as extended selves by numerous scholars. Examples of such objects are body parts in plastic surgery (Schouten 1991), personal websites (Schau and Gilly 2003), things in the workplace (Tian and Belk 2005), loved objects (Ahuvia 2005), and pets (Kravets and Tari 2008; Hill *et al.* 2008). There are also the special cases of extended selves introduced by Belk (1988): collections, money, pets, other people, and body parts.

The focus of this chapter is on other people as extended selves, and it tries to understand the unique relationship between Japanese mothers and their own daughters from their standpoint. In doing so, it identifies two seemingly different roles played by Japanese daughters as being part of their own mothers' extended selves. First, mothers treat daughters as mere objects of possession, especially when mothers are simply enjoying shopping with them. On some occasions, daughters are regarded as mothers' "Barbie dolls," and mothers try to choose their own preferred outfits for their daughters. Second, mothers treat their daughters' existence as highly important, trying to turn their daughters into their extended selves, and accomplish the mothers' unachieved desires.

Theoretical background

Viewing people as extended selves

Two viewpoints are crucial when looking at the case of other people as extended selves. First, other people are often seen as non-human objects without any free will. To illustrate, some people try to create their own ideal self-images by "wearing" their own friends or lovers as if they were beautiful clothing. Also, typically seen in divorce cases, children are often treated as possessions (Derdeyn 1979; Hobart 1975). In an effort to understand the distinctive nature of relationships with other people, this notion of treating others as mere objects without consideration is very important.

Second, especially when part of oneself, other people can be extremely important. For example, children or grandchildren can deliver a sense of immortality (Lifton 1973). Moreover, it is said that people tend to be more willing to share with others when they have made them a part of their extended selves (Belk 2010). Also, any negative events, such as the injury or loss of close friends or spouses, are known to hurt the original self-concept. For example, sexual infidelity of spouses or lovers delivers a severe wound to the ego, resulting in a feeling of self-loss (Clanton and Smith 1977). Death of family members usually creates loss of self (Doka 1986).

Mother-daughter relationships in Japan

Based on the self-in-relations model by Surry (1985), the self is developed and maintained in the context of significant relationships. In women's case, this significant relationship often involves their mothers (Surry 1985), and daughters' attitudes are formed by mothers as primary socializing agents (Bohannon and Blanton 1999). Findings from intergenerational transmission of attitudes reveal that generally parents' attitudes, especially mothers' attitudes, predict those of their daughters (Acock and Bengston 1978; Bohannon and Blanton 1999).

According to symbolic interaction theorists, people are born asocial into a world of meanings that are translated to each child by interacting with significant and generalized others who are the primary socializing agents for each new generation (Mead 1934). Parents are identified as one of the most influential socializing agents for their children (Cooley 1902; Sullivan 1947; Turner 1962). Similarly, mothers are significant socializers to their daughters, and try to control them with social power; in many cases, parents force their children to identify with them (McDonald 1977, 1980).

As a concept, identification of a mother and a daughter has drawn academic interest (Chodorow 1978; Boyd 1985). Chodorow (1978) discussed that mothers' behaviors, values, thoughts, and meanings are internalized by their daughters. Mothers reinforce daughters to become like themselves (Weitzman 1984). Even after growing up, daughters still identify themselves with their care-giving mothers, in which mother-daughter relationships are maintained. Since daughters identify themselves with their mothers for longer periods, they perceive themselves as similar to their mothers more often than sons perceive themselves as similar to their fathers (Chodorow 1978).

In contemporary Japan, as Nobuta and Ueno (2008) argued, identification with mothers does not necessarily mean daughters identifying with their actual mothers. Rather, mothers try to control their daughters to identify with their ideal selves. Mothers are said to have several unachieved goals in their lives. In Nobuta and Ueno's study, mothers were in their late forties or early fifties. They had received higher education under the post-war liberalism school system in Japan. Different from their own mothers in the so-called pre-war generation, they were allowed their own free will even after getting married and having children. Unfortunately for them, however, in their actual lives, just as for their mothers, they are persuaded to suppress their will and live for their husbands and children. There are things they could not achieve; more precisely, they were forced to give up their dreams (Nobuta and Ueno 2008).

This is one of the reasons why Japanese mothers hold enormous expectations for their daughters. Daughters, who have higher education and usually do not get married until their middle thirties, are expected to achieve their mothers' ideals (Nobuta and Ueno 2008). Sometimes mothers even use social power in order to control their daughters to identify with the mothers' ideal selves.

Research proposition

As argued in the previous literature, daughters serve as their mothers' extended selves. Two different ideas emerge when understanding another person as an extended self (see Figure 30.1).

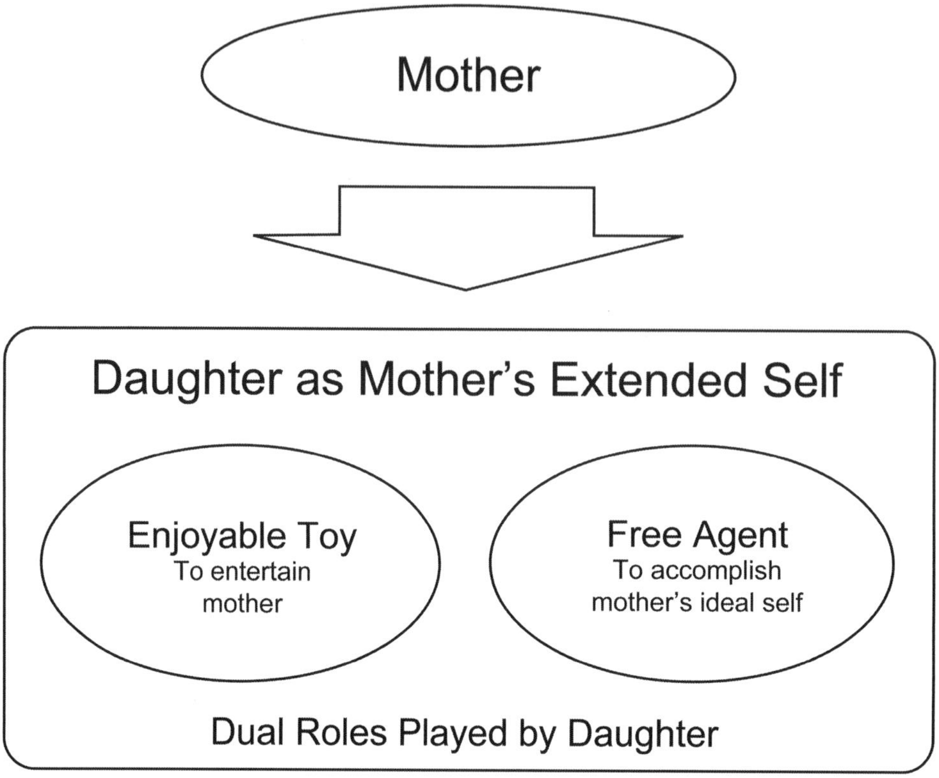

Figure 30.1 Daughter as mother's extended self

First, mothers in contemporary Japan treat their own daughters as possessions. Second, mothers anticipate that their own daughters will become the mothers' ideal selves. There seem to exist these two contradictory roles that daughters will play as mothers' extended selves. However, there are various kinds of mother-daughter relationships in Japan, the phenomena and practices of which are expected to show a heterogeneous nature.

Methodology

This study used two interpretive approaches: 1 direct observation using camcorders to gather data of actual shopping processes; and 2 semi-structured interviews after the observation. Direct observation can provide more accurate assessment of varying modes of interaction than direct measurement such as self-reports in controlled laboratory conditions (Atkin 1978).

Six mother-daughter pairs performed catalog shopping, where they could freely look for and talk about outfits in a real fashion magazine. They were to choose one ideal outfit for the daughter, in an attempt to improve her present image. The context of catalog shopping was a relatively natural setting, where we could expect to gather richer data of interactions between mothers and daughters.

The six daughters were either 22 or 23 years old, in the junior or senior year in college, and starting to prepare for their approaching new careers after graduation. Therefore, both mothers and daughters tended to choose outfits that were more or less related to the daughters' new careers. Table 30.1 describes general information about the six daughters (Hina, Yuna, Erika,

Table 30.1 Informant descriptions

Mother-daughter pair		*Age*		*Daughter's year*	*Daughter's siblings*	*Date of study*
Pair 1	Hina	Daughter	early 20s	university senior	oldest of the three (one brother and one sister)	6 December 2007
	U	Mother	early 50s			
Pair 2	Yuna	Daughter	early 20s	university senior	younger of the two (one sister)	6 December 2007
	V	Mother	early 50s			
Pair 3	Erika	Daughter	early 20s	university junior	younger of the two (one brother)	6 December 2008
	W	Mother	early 50s			
Pair 4	Mayu	Daughter	early 20s	university junior	younger of the two (one brother)	15 December 2008
	X	Mother	early 50s			
Pair 5	Yu	Daughter	early 20s	university junior	younger of the two (one sister)	24 November 2008
	Y	Mother	late 40s			
Pair 6	Airi	Daughter	early 20s	university junior	no siblings	16 December 2008
	Z	Mother	early 50s			

Mayu, Yu, and Airi) and their mothers. Before starting this study, we conducted two pre-tests in order to decide first, the catalog shopping purpose, and second, catalog shopping material, using different female students. We found that the shopping purpose of "choosing a more sophisticated outfit for the daughters, which would create a different image of her as a professional working woman" could promote more active communication between the informants. The mail order shopping magazine *VOI*, issued by one of the largest fashion retailing stores, Marui, was selected because the store was very popular among female college students in Japan.

All of the catalog shopping processes and interviews after they came to a decision were recorded by camcorder. Each catalog shopping event took around 30–40 minutes and one interview took about one hour. Each mother-daughter pair was given 10,000 JPY (about $125) for their cooperation. They were told to spend the money for actual purchase of the ideal outfit they had chosen in the magazine. Four coders documented all verbal data from shopping observations and interviews. For reliability of documented data, two different researchers checked the documents several times.

Description

The interpretation is described below, organized by the role the daughter plays in the mother's extended self: 1 mothers possessing daughters as objects; and 2 mothers treating daughters as agents of their own desires.

Mothers possessing daughters as objects

When their daughters were little, the mothers enjoyed dressing them. During the interaction with their daughters in catalog shopping, the mothers were reminded of the days when they were able to choose their daughters' clothes according to their own preferences.

One item of clothing in the magazine reminds Mother U of several items of clothing in which she used to dress her daughter Hina in her childhood.

DAUGHTER HINA: This is pretty. You don't like it so much, do you?
MOTHER U: Well, it is just like the one you wore when you were little.

Mothers like to play dress-up dolls using their daughters in their twenties. Daughters are just like Barbie dolls for their mothers. For Mother Y, it is more enjoyable to go out shopping for her daughter's clothes, than for her own clothes. Choosing and putting clothes on her daughter is just like dress-up doll play.

INTERVIEWER: Why is shopping with your daughter fun?
MOTHER Y: It is like a dress-up doll play. Ha-ha.
DAUGHTER YU: I didn't know that.
MOTHER Y: It is always more fun to see products for my daughter.
INTERVIEWER: Then was today also a dress-up doll play?
DAUGHTER YU: You put this on me, and that on me,
MOTHER Y: Yes. [Puts clothes on her daughter in gesture.] Umm … How are these clothes on her?

Daughter Mayu believes that the color pink is not for her and does not wear it. Mother X says that she used to make Mayu wear pink-colored clothing when she was a child. She seems to have fun dressing Mayu in pink during the process.

DAUGHTER MAYU: Among these, this pink one is the best. I don't wear pink. Pink is cute but I don't suit the color.
MOTHER X: I used to make you wear pink when you were a child.

Mothers treating daughters as agents of their own desires

Mothers find their past selves in their daughters

Mother Z wants her daughter to wear check-patterned clothes because she liked and used to wear check-patterned clothes when she was young and dating; therefore, she wants her daughter to feel the same way.

MOTHER Z: When I was young, I always wore check-patterned clothes. Lately, check has become a trend. It reminds me of those days and …
DAUGHTER AIRI: You wanted to make me look like you?
MOTHER Z: Right.
INTERVIEWER: Why do you want to make your daughter wear check-patterned clothes?
MOTHER Z: Because I like check. I have an image of youth in check. Though I like check, I cannot possibly wear it at my age any longer.
DAUGHTER AIRI: You don't have the guts to wear it?
MOTHER Z: No, I don't. Thus I want my daughter to wear it instead.
INTERVIEWER: Ha-ha.
DAUGHTER AIRI: Pushing, pushing me [smiling].
MOTHER Z: Since I myself wore it, I want my daughter to have the same feeling.

Mother Z mentions a bow-tie blouse in the interview. It came into fashion when she was young. Though it was a long time ago, she still remembers the actual price of it, which was about 4,000 Yen. Recently the same style has come back into fashion. Airi does not know what a bow-tie is, so Mother Z explains it to her. Mother Z says that she saw it in the magazine while they were doing the catalog shopping.

She also says that she wants her daughter to choose it because she used to wear the same style in her twenties. Airi understands her mother's expectations and likes to listen to her mother's old memories. In her eyes, her mother is not her mother but a sentimental girl just like her. During the observation, Airi tries to identify with her mother's previous self.

Mothers' own ideal selves dominate those of their daughters

Though it is the choosing process for her daughter, Mother Y is unconsciously choosing clothes that she likes to wear herself.

MOTHER Y: I was almost choosing the one for myself.
DAUGHTER YU: I see you choosing what you like to wear.

Then Daughter Yu sees her mother checking several types of outfits, but she knows that her mother is still looking for something for herself.

DAUGHTER YU: These clothing here are to your taste, aren't they?
MOTHER Y: [nods]

Later, when Daughter Yu and her mother are browsing other clothing, Daughter Yu points out that her mother is trying to prevent her from choosing the items her mother dislikes. Mother Y laughs and admits it. During the interview, Mother Y recognizes that she was pushing her preferences on her daughter.

For her daughter, Mother W tries to choose clothes she would like to wear if she were younger. Mother W describes the choosing process as "pseudo experience."

MOTHER W: Because now that I am too big to wear what I like to wear, I always try to make my daughter wear what I like to wear, imagining I would be wearing it if I were younger.
INTERVIEWER: Why do you want to make your daughter wear what you like to wear?
MOTHER W: I don't know. Maybe it is a pseudo experience. I naturally think she should wear it.
INTERVIEWER: Can you explain what you mean by pseudo experience?
MOTHER W: I would be like this [pointing at her daughter], seeing my daughter wear it.
DAUGHTER AIRI: Ha-ha.
MOTHER W: I would be like this if I were younger.
INTERVIEWER: I see.
MOTHER W: When I go out shopping with my daughter, I say, "You look good in this."
DAUGHTER AIRI: You are forcing me against my will. Ha-ha.

Mother W says that she cannot wear what she likes, because she is not young and slim enough. By making her daughter wear her favorite clothing, Mother W is able to see herself in her daughter, just as if she were looking at herself in the mirror.

Mothers fulfill their own ideal selves through their daughters

During the observation process, the mothers remember not only the time when their daughters were little but also the time when they themselves were young and unmarried. The catalog shopping reminds the mothers of the actual past, as well as their own unaccomplished ideal lives. The mothers wonder, "what if I had continued working? What would be happening in my life?"

Mother W dreams of an imaginary life as a working woman. In the interview, she explains that she recently met a former colleague who was still working. When she met her, she imagined what her life would be like if she also had kept working. She is confident that she would be in a superior status than her former colleague in the office, which makes her regret this because she cannot have her wish granted. Therefore, this unachieved dream should be fulfilled by her daughter. For Mother W, the shopping process in the study is quite enjoyable because she keeps imagining herself working in an office and becoming a successful businesswoman.

INTERVIEWER: What kind of woman would you like your daughter to become in her future?

MOTHER W: A career woman.

DAUGHTER ERIKA: Ha-ha.

MOTHER W: I want her to keep her job and I will take care of her children. I want her to keep her job even after her marriage. Since the economic crisis, getting a job is even tougher, though. I want her to work very hard.

INTERVIEWER: Did you have a similar career? After your marriage?

MOTHER W: No. I was such a hard worker, but stopped working after my marriage. I always wonder what it would be like if I hadn't stopped working then. It might be wrong to reflect my dream onto my daughter, but I always wanted her to continue working whatever happened, such as marriage or anything.

INTERVIEWER: What kind of job did you have?

MOTHER W: I used to work in human resources at one of the department stores. I hired employees and part-time workers there. It was such a challenging and meaningful job. I quitted the job when I got married. Maybe I had a dream to become a full-time housewife. I sometimes have a chance to meet my former colleague and hear about her job, wondering if I were still working there if I would be her supervisor. Thus, I want my daughter to keep working.

Mother Z says that she is "given to wild fancies" during the study. She is imagining her daughter achieving her ideal-self image. She herself was working in Otemachi, the financial district in Tokyo, and wants her daughter to become a smart, professional office worker as well.

MOTHER Z: It may be a fantasy but I want my daughter to go to the office after she loses her weight and becomes smart and brisk.

DAUGHTER AIRI: Ha-ha.

MOTHER Z: I wonder why I chose these clothes today. I think it seems like typical "OL" [office lady], Marunouchi [the biggest and most popular office district in Tokyo] OL [giggling].

...

INTERVIEWER: Is the desire your daughter's? Or is it your will?

MOTHER Z: I used to work in the Otemachi area. Those areas around Tokyo station, such as Ginza and Yurakucho, are ... Is it my will?

DAUGHTER AIRI: [giggling].

INTERVIEWER: Is it the mother's will?

MOTHER Z: [nodding] It may be my will.

DAUGHTER AIRI: Is it? Ha-ha.

MOTHER Z: [nodding] Yes, it is my will.

DAUGHTER AIRI: [giggling].

MOTHER Z: I noticed it while I was talking right now.

INTERVIEWER: I see. It is the mother's will.
MOTHER Z: You are right. You are right. I understood it while I was talking.

Discussion

Summary of findings

Two interesting findings emerge from the interpretation. The most important finding is that daughters play dual roles for their own mothers, as being a part of the mothers' extended selves. First, mothers treat their own daughters as possessions, as if they were the mothers' enjoyable toys. Second, mothers see their own daughters' existence as highly important, as they make their daughters part of their own extended selves. Here, daughters are expected to vicariously accomplish mothers' unfulfilled ideal selves. The profound and complex nature of mother-daughter relationships in Japan is best described by these two seemingly contradictory ideas about daughters: that is, daughters as objects of possession, and daughters as agents for mothers' unaccomplished ideal selves. This finding helps further to understand the distinctive nature of other people's roles in the extended-self literature.

Also, the unique methodology used in this study – the in-pairs catalogue shopping observation and the in-depth interview – allowed us to capture the actual interaction process between mothers and daughters at the stage of a real purchasing conversation, in a relatively natural setting. Through the careful interpretation of the verbal data gathered from the direct observation of their communication process, the puzzling relationships between Japanese mothers and daughters were better understood. In other words, the complexity of mother-daughter relationships is best described as a dynamic interaction. In essence, the relationship between consumers and their extended selves becomes highly interactive, especially when another person with her own free will becomes part of the extended self. A unique methodology was necessary to gain some insight into the dynamic nature of this distinctive relationship.

Limitations and future research directions

This study faces three limitations. First, although we recorded both audio and visual data in observations and interviews, we only used verbal accounts for interpretation. We should have included the non-verbal data interpretation, such as nodding or laughing. This would make it possible for us to generate richer interpretation.

Second, this study only describes the mothers' points of view. We should interpret daughters' points of view in order to enrich deep understanding of mother-daughter relationships. We noticed that several daughters were feeling emotional pressure from their mothers when they were expected to fulfill their mothers' unaccomplished ideal selves. If we focus on the daughters' struggle, we can further understand the complex and profound nature of mother-daughter relationships.

Third, as self-concept changes depending on person and time period (Schenk and Holman 1980; Belk 1989), we should focus on different natures of the relationships in different settings in future studies. Though thoroughly interpreting the data, we could only deal with six mother-daughter pairs; however, even this small number of informants showed heterogeneity. In fact, the relationship of Pair Six was very different from that of Pair Three. Further investigation needs to be done using informants in different cultural settings or at different life stages. As shown in this chapter, a mother-daughter relationship is a puzzling, yet interesting phenomenon. Research focusing on this special relationship should be continued in future studies.

Further reading

Belk, Russell W. (1988) "Possessions and the Extended Self." *Journal of Consumer Research* 15: 139–68.

Doi, Tateo (2001 [1971]) *The Anatomy of Dependence*. Tokyo: Kodansha International.

Sirgy, Joseph M. (1982) "Self-Concept in Consumer Behavior: A Critical Review." *Journal of Consumer Research* 9 (December): 287–300.

References

Acock, Alan C. and Bengston, V.L. (1978) "On the Relative Influence of Mothers and Fathers: A Covariance Analysis of Political and Religious Socialization." *Journal of Marriage and the Family* 40: 519–30.

Ahuvia, C. Aaron (2005) "Beyond the Extended Self: Loved Objects and Consumers' Identity Narratives." *Journal of Consumer Research* 32 (June): 171–84

Arnould, Eric J. and Thompson, Craig J. (2005) "Consumer Culture Theory (CCT): Twenty Years of Research." *Journal of Consumer Research* 31 (March): 868–82.

Atkin, Charles K. (1978) "Observation of Parent-Child Interaction in Supermarket Decision-Making." *Journal of Marketing* 42 (October): 41–5.

Belk, Russell W. (1988) "Possessions and the Extended Self." *Journal of Consumer Research* 15: 139–68.

——(1989) "Extended Self and Extending Paradigmatic Perspective." *Journal of Consumer Research* 16 (June): 129–32.

——(2010) "Sharing." *Journal of Consumer Research* 37 (February): 715–34.

Bohannon, Judy Rollins and Blanton, Priscilla White (1999) "Gender Role Attitudes of American Mothers and Daughters Over Time." *Journal of Social Psychology* 139(2): 173–9.

Boyd, Carol (1985) "Toward an Understanding of Mother-Daughter Identification Using Concept Analysis." *Advances in Nursing Science* 7(3): 78–86.

Chodorow, Nancy (1978) *The Reproduction of Mothering*. Berkeley, CA: University of California Press.

Clanton, Gordon and Smith, Lynn G. (1977) "The Self-Inflicted Pain of Jealousy." *Psychology Today* 3 (March): 45–7.

Cohen, Joel B. (1989) "An Over-Extended Self?" *Journal of Consumer Research* 16 (June): 125–8.

Cooley, C.H. (1902) *Human Nature and the Social Order*. New York: Scribner.

Derdeyn, Andre P. (1979) "Adoption and Ownership of Children." *Child Psychiatry and Human Development* 9 (Summer): 215–26.

Doka, Kenneth J. (1986) "Loss upon Loss: The Impact of Death After Divorce." *Death Studies* 10(5): 441–9.

Hill, Ronald Paul, Gaines, Jeannie, and Wilson, Mark R. (2008) "Consumer Behavior, Extended-self, and Sacred Consumption: An Alternative Perspective from Our Animal Companions." *Journal of Business Research* 61: 553–62.

Hobart, Charles W. (1975) "Ownership of Matrimonial Property: A Study of Practices and Attitudes." *Review and Analysis of Sociology and Anthropology* 12(4), Part I: 440–52.

Kravets, Olga and Tari, Berna (2008) "A Friend and/or A Foe?: Exploring Activeness of Objects in Consumption." *Advances in Consumer Research* 35: 771–2.

Lifton, Robert J. (1973) "The Sense of Immortality: On Death and the Continuity of Life." *American Journal of Psychoanalysis* 33(1): 3–15.

McCracken, Grant (1986) "Culture and Consumption: A Theoretical Account of the Structure and Movement of the Cultural Meaning of Consumer Goods." *Journal of Consumer Research* 13 (June): 71–84.

McDonald, G.W. (1977) "Parental Identification by the Adolescent: A Social Power Approach." *Journal of Marriage and the Family* 39 (November): 289–96.

——(1980) "Parental Power and Adolescents' Parental Identification: A Reexamination." *Journal of Marriage and the Family* 42 (May): 705–19.

Mead, George Herbert (1934) *Mind, Self, and Society*. C.W. Morris (ed.). Chicago, IL: University of Chicago.

Mittal, Banwari (2006) "I, Me, and Mine: How Products Become Consumers' Extended Selves." *Journal of Consumer Behavior* 5: 550–62.

Nobuta, Sayoko (1997) *Ichiransei Oyako na Kankei* [Relationships of Mother and Daughter as Identical Twins]. Tokyo: Shufunotomosha.

Nobuta, Sayoko and Ueno, Chizuko (2008) "Suraimu Haha to Hakamori Musume" [Slime Mother and Graveyard Watcher Daughter]. *Eureka* (December), Tokyo: Seidosha:73–88.

Saren, Michael (2007) "To Have is To Be? A Critique of Self-Creation Through Consumption." *The Marketing Review* 7(4): 343–54.

Schau, Hope Jensen and Gilly, Mary C. (2003) "We Are What We Post? Self-Presentation in Personal Web Space." *Journal of Consumer Research* 30 (December): 385–404.

Schenk, Carolyn Turner and Holman, Rebecca H. (1980) "A Sociological Approach to Brand Choice: The Concept of Situational Self Image." *Advances in Consumer Research* 7: 610–14.

Schouten, John W. (1991) "Selves in Transition: Symbolic Consumption in Personal Rites of Passage and Identity Reconstruction." *Journal of Consumer Research* 17 (March): 412–25.

Sirgy, Joseph M. (1982) "Self-Concept in Consumer Behavior: A Critical Review." *Journal of Consumer Research* 9 (December): 287–300.

Smith, T.E. (1970) "Foundation of Parental Influences upon Adolescents: An Application of Social Power Theory." *American Sociological Review* 36 (October): 860–72.

Sullivan, H.S. (1947) *Conceptions of Modern Psychology*. Washington, DC: William A. White Psychiatric Foundation.

Surry, J.L. (1985) "Self-in-Relation: A Theory of Women's Development." Work in progress. Stone Center for Development Services and Studies, Wellesley College.

Tian, Kelly and Belk, Russel W. (2005) "Extended Self and Possessions in the Workplace." *Journal of Consumer Research* 32 (September): 297–310.

Turner, R.H. (1962) "Role-Taking Process versus Conformity." In Arnold Rose (ed.), *Human Behavior and Social Processes: An Interactionist Approach*. Boston, MA: Houghton Mifflin.

Weitzman, Lenore (1984) "Sex-Role Socialization: A Focus on Women." In Jo Freeman (ed.), *Women: A Feminist Perspective*. Third edition. Palo Alto, CA: Mayfield Publishing.

31
FAMILY STUFF
Materiality and identity

Linda L. Price

The purpose of this chapter is to uncover the nuanced interplay of individual, relational and collective identities in the practices and meanings surrounding "family stuff." My journey to understand family stuff has been fraught with mystery played out against the materiality, meanings and practices of my own striving to be a family and myself. Are we the kind of family who covers our refrigerator with family pictures or not? Am I the kind of person who, for the sake of family, might do this? Would we be a better or a different family if we did?

My journey is also played out against sweeping changes in how we think about and immerse ourselves in the material world – a complex system shaped by a breakdown between the animate and inanimate, material and immaterial, organic and inorganic, matter and energy (Coole and Frost 2010; Urry 2005). This is a world in which information and symbols circulate in a state of relative or total independence from the corporeal and material world (Bendle 2002; Hayles 1999), fundamentally changing myriad constructs such as ownership, intellectual property, identity, and indexicality. Processes of dematerialization now characterize many of our most important socio-material practices – from music, photo and book collections to numerous leisure and life-pursuits. How will these shifts shape future relationships between materiality, family and identity?

I begin with an introduction to individual, relational and collective identities in the context of family life and my use of the term "family stuff." "Family stuff" foreshadows what I see as a significant reprisal of materialism such that "materiality is always something more than 'mere' matter: an excess, force, vitality, relationality, or difference that renders matter active, self-creative, productive, unpredictable" (Coole and Frost 2010: 9; Miller 2010). This view forces a reconsideration of a popular constructivist stance that "matter is inert stuff awaiting cultural imprint" (Coole and Frost 2010: 25). While our material lives are always culturally mediated, material forces also exert agentic capacities within complex interactive systems, and stuff is continually redefined and reassembled in new and unexpected forms (Epp and Price 2010; Miller 2010). Next, I draw on a personal vignette to highlight the individual experience of family stuff – the complex way that stuff gets layered on from one generation to the next as well as displaced and transformed. I conclude with challenges for future research surrounding the complex interplay of materiality with individual and collective identity, and uncover implications of our new socio-material practices for consumer theory.

Being we, being me

Although a large body of research focuses on collective and individual identity, how these terms are understood is quite different depending on disciplinary roots. In this chapter, I underscore the tensions, paradoxes and fluidity associated with collective and individual identity. In this view, collective identity is shared as meaningful, but is discursively produced and reproduced through individual and collective practices and in concert with the material world (Hardy *et al.* 2005; Thomas *et al.* 2012). Hence, consistent with a broader reframing of "the social," collective identity does not designate a thing but a type of connection and trail of associations between heterogeneous elements that "might be assembled anew in some given state of affairs" (Latour 2005: 5). Similarly, my view of individual identity highlights consumers trying (or sometimes not) to construct coherent narratives across the tensions, paradoxes and fluidity that comprise their lives and in interaction with their varied and changing life worlds (Ahuvia 2005; Arnould and Price 2000; Firat and Venkatesh 1995; Schau *et al.* 2009; Schouten 1991). My focus is primarily on the "we" that is family, and the many individual and coalitional identities that comprise and interplay with that collective, which are described next.

Only a limited amount of recent consumer theory and research highlights family identity as a distinct "we" made up of motives, discourses, practices and temporal interplays that are collectively shaped and enacted (Epp and Price 2008, 2010, 2011a, 2011b). This is a significant departure from prior consumer research focused on how individuals negotiate outcomes within a family, influence other family members or represent family as aspects of their extended selves (Commuri and Gentry 2005; Cotte and Wood 2004; Epp and Price 2008: 51; Moore *et al.* 2002; Tian and Belk 2005). This view of family recognizes that while the "we" is distinct and meaningful to members, like other identities it is negotiated, revised and transformed and members may have distinct and differing experiences in relationship to this collective. As compared with prior generations, this "we" is also far more elective with individuals or coalitions opting in or out of their family of origin and blending families in unique and fluid ways (Giddens 1992). As compared with past generations, this "we" is often mediated through technologies and practiced across temporal and geographic divides (Epp *et al.* 2011; Urry 2007). Moreover, in many consumer societies, this "we" is carved out against a market landscape that prizes individual pursuits and happiness over collective goals and customizes offerings to optimize individual rather than collective well-being (Epp and Price 2011a; Gergen 1994). The "we" that constitutes family identity is further complicated by the amalgam of individual and coalitional identities within the collective, each with distinct identity projects that may compete with family practices and goals (Connell and Schau 2011; Epp and Price 2011a, 2011b).

Individual identities interplay with collective identity and are also complex (Reed and Bolton 2005). Theory and research questions modernist notions of a unified self, highlighting the complexity of individual identity projects circumscribed by particular historical and social processes and internally negotiated, managed and transformed in part through consumption, and narratives and dreams of consumption (Ahuvia 2005; Arnould and Price 2000; Markus and Nurius 1986; Shankar *et al.* 2009; Belk *et al.* 2003). While much prior research has emphasized consumers' active construction and communication of identity partly through the symbolic resources of consumer culture (Belk 1988), in this chapter I foreground consumers as embedded within socio-material contexts, especially families, with identities that develop and unfold across time (Heisley and Cours 2007; Shankar *et al.* 2009). Consumers' identities are not just couched within systems of cultural, social and economic capital that are more or less fungible (Bourdieu 1984), but rather they are tightly threaded with and uniquely shaped by interactions with material objects, ideas, and others (Brothers 1997). As an idealized and realized cultural form, families (whether embraced, denied or viewed with ambivalence) consequentially shape us and we shape them (Epp and Price 2008, 2011b).

Hence as we look at family, we see a collective identity that is meaningful to its members, but in intricate interplay with individual and coalitional identities among, between and beyond the family, that are also complex, navigated, negotiated and fluid. For example, being a family is challenged by other individual and collective identity enactments that interrupt family dinner, family vacation and family spaces (Epp and Price 2010, 2011a, 2011b). Being a family is important, but so are soccer practice, earning a black belt, and playing World of Warcraft (WOW) with my guild. Not surprisingly, most consumer research has highlighted how a single collective identity (rarely the family) is meaningful in the mind of an individual, rather than tackling this complex array of "we" and "me" enactments. The interlocking practices of "being we" and "being me" offer a rich theoretical landscape for consumer researchers to explore, and have to date received little focal attention. In this chapter, I'm particularly interested in how materiality interfaces with family and individual identity, and again, the answer is complicated.

"Family stuff"

I use the term "family stuff" to capture the fluid materiality of daily family life that includes transient, non-durable, de-materialized, iconic, indexical and inalienable objects intricately interwoven with each other and with the people, relationships and practices that give them weight.[1] Family stuff is "not simply the hapless bearers of symbolic projection," but actors in relational networks of associations (DeLanda 2006; Latour 2005). We mature in "the light of things that come down to us from the previous generations," these direct us and "are the landscapes of our imagination" (Miller 2010: 53). The term is ambiguous to connote how our objects, practices and minds get stuffed with family, and how materiality bleeds across material and non-material domains, across temporal anchors of past, present and future, residing as much in our imaginations as in our dining rooms. It gives a nod to common usage where when asked what we're thinking, we reply, "Oh, just family stuff," implying both weight and privacy fences. The stuff of family occupies ground from the ordinary to the sacred and inalienable; from stuff that creates and means family to stuff that disrupts and fragments them; and from stuff that constitutes "we" to stuff that becomes and is "me."

Theory and research recognize that materiality and human relationships are inextricably intertwined, sometimes foregrounding one, sometimes the other (Miller 2010). Moreover, research implicitly recognizes that goods are sought and valued because of the way they support human relatedness. However, our focus on possessions and consumption sometimes leads us to attribute greater importance to materiality than to the social relations they function to facilitate (Miller 2010; Jenkins *et al.* 2011; Shankar *et al.* 2009). For example, research on possessions has most often focused on what's special, what's important, what's irreplaceable, what's collected, what's saved, what's put on the mantelpiece, what's authentic, what's really me (Belk 1988, 1991, 1992, 1995; Belk *et al.* 1988; Beverland and Farrelly 2010; Curasi *et al.* 2004; Csikszentmihalyi and Rochberg-Halton 1981; Grayson and Shulman 2000; Kleine *et al.* 1995; Hurdley 2006; Price *et al.* 2000). This has uncovered much about person-object relationships and the significant and nuanced relationships between possessions, well-being and identity (Kleine and Baker 2004; Miller 1987, 2001, 2005, 2008). However, various other questions remain unanswered. In particular, despite a recent surge in research employing consumer practice theory (cf. Halkier *et al.* 2011; Money 2007; Warde 2005), the way in which objects are inserted and insert themselves in the practices of individual and collective identity interplays is still underexplored.

Asking object questions foregrounds objects over identity, and person-object relationships over person-person relationships. Emergent from prior research is a view that privileges durable, indexical, sacred, and even inalienable objects, suggesting that such stuff is truly the important stuff in our lives. It answers questions of how stuff uses relationships to gain importance, become irreplaceable, the symbolic material of self and family (Curasi *et al.* 2004). Not surprisingly, relationships are often *why* objects are treasured, saved and passed forward, but the lens is typically on how relationships figure in what makes objects important rather than how objects figure in relationships. Similarly, consumers desire goods as a means to create, sustain and enhance relationships (Belk *et al.* 2003); however, when we focus on consumer desire, we may foreground material longings over longings in which materiality is absent or in the background (Jenkins *et al.* 2011). That is, we learn how relationships inform desired consumption rather than whether and how consumption figures in desired relationships. When we reframe the question to ask about positive imagined futures the picture changes, and we see "the primacy of relationships and the implied emotional experience of a practice or event," as the focus of individuals' desires and imaginings (Jenkins *et al.* 2011: 270).

Moreover, empirical focus on objects renders a demarcation between stuff and identity, material and de-material, ownership and use that may be overstated, misleading and changing (Belk 2010; Hayles 1999; Warde 2005). For example, the socio-material practices of everyday life are dramatically different than even 10 years ago, with profound implications for how and what stuff is animated by and animates family identity. As we re-examine past assumptions about materiality we also uncover how these assumptions potentially constrained theorizing about mundane socio-material processes in much prior consumer research. The ability to create vivid and efficacious selves in virtual spaces (freed of gender, race, species, family and much of how we think about material), and to use virtual spaces (in interaction with human and non-human others) to create and resolve world problems changes how we think about the powers and constraints exerted by the corporeal, material world (re-enlivening de Beauvoir, Sartre and Marx critiques) (Bendle 2002; Kruks 2010). For example, Sartre describes a house as a "vampire object" that constantly absorbs human action, lives on the blood taken from him and finally lives in symbiosis with him (Sartre 1976). This experience of the vampire object can be extended to the collective assemblage that inhabits the home. Hence, while we have perhaps sometimes accorded singularized objects too much importance within the family, celebrating them as indexical carriers of individual and collective identities, we have also not fully examined objects' agentic capabilities in interaction with other material and relational systems (DeLanda 2006; Epp and Price 2010; Miller 2010). These agentic capabilities are not new but re-imagined as technologies transgress "fixed boundaries" previously "regarded as vital to civilization," making clear the complex symbiotic relationship of humans and matter in which neither has mastery (Bendle 2002: 58). Moreover, as we encroach on the limits of our material world we are forced to reconsider this complex symbiotic network of evolving and unpredictable power relations (Coole and Frost 2010).

Emerging views of materiality challenge us with new vocabularies and causalities with which I am just beginning to grapple and about which there is considerable debate. By looking at the practices of everyday life elaborated by both meanings and networks of actors we may begin to engage with mundane materiality in different ways (Epp and Price 2010; Warde 2005). Only recently has consumer research begun in earnest to investigate the everyday practices of networks of actors in complex, dynamic assemblages, and such research continues to offer fertile theoretical and empirical ground. In the next section I use a personal vignette to elaborate on the individual phenomenological experience of family stuff.

The individual experience of family stuff

Box 31.1 describes a personal practice saturated with individual and collective identity and intertwined with materiality. It is a phenomenological narrative of material meanings and only hints at the vast actor networks in which my personal experience is located. Nonetheless, referencing it I hope to highlight porous boundaries and underexplored flows between alienable and sacred; objects and practices; material, de-material and imagined worlds; and self and collective identities.

Box 31.1 Personal vignette: playing the piano

Playing the piano is a small thing and monumental: aspirational and nostalgic; family and me; possible and unrealized worlds. With notes of ecstasy and tears, in a flow of a two bar reach and resolution my piano seeks me out – an amazing chord, a surprise that delights again and again. Brahms is my mother's goodnight kiss and the way her hope lingers on the chords that tumble beyond my hand's reach, the same way the lessons she scrambled tumbled across the reach of our family income. Bach is my father's call to logic, the power of repetition and resolve – a melody playing against itself in a fugue of purpose – a purpose to envision something different, better, beyond. Mozart is the playful, frenetic engagement with possibility; Chopin the gurgling Wyoming brook of my youth that plays a watery trill against a stone – a rhythm, first complicated, next simple. My brothers tumble with me in an intricate play of water, rocks, imagination and beaver-like energy. Our sandy improvised dams can't stop the water's music.

This, my piano, is the stuff of my life. It is the stuff of my family. It is a history of what was, is and might have been. It is sadness and promise, the hope and lost hope of family. It is "we," it is me; it is what I distill from the growing up that left me as I am. It is possession and practice. I stroke it, polish it, and tune it (well I don't but I see to it as I would my child's dental appointment). You might imagine that I play it well, but I don't. You might imagine that I play it often, but I don't. You might imagine that it is expensive and irreplaceable, but it's not. You might imagine my children embrace it as sacred, but they won't. Yet it occupies my life and traces across its keys the life of my family. My piano is sacred, but not as an object. It is sacred as a thread of consciousness that takes me to a privileged place of beauty, discipline, and elevation. I hope my children chart a course there. I do not think it will be on the piano. Their fingers across digital paper seek those heights of ecstasy through other objects and practices.

My piano stands in for things it's not: it is nicer than the one I had growing up, and yet it cost me much less than my childhood piano cost my parents who made monthly payments to put this dream inside our reach. It reigns over my living room and conquers the majestic mountain horizon outside my windows with its black enamel splendor. Yet it is still the ironic hovering remnants of my parents' dreams. My mother imagined I would be a preacher's wife and play hymns in a church. She was impatient with how slowly I learned God's voice in four flats. My father sometimes envisioned an uncompromising future for me, in his life filled with compromises. In truth, he bet on me like the hopeless buy lottery tickets – I was ticket number three of four children, and a girl.

In general, consumer research surrounding possessions has stressed consequential differences between alienable and cherished or special objects (Belk *et al.* 1989; Belk *et al.* 1988; Grayson and

Shulman 2000; Grayson and Martinec 2004; Curasi *et al.* 2004). Cherished possessions may be further distinguished as sacred or inalienable either to an individual and/or a kin group. Sacred, inalienable objects hold imaginary power over the individual or group such that they are withheld from exchange often from generation to generation and imbued with identity, authority and mythology. As consumers cultivate and invest attention and layer meanings on select possessions they become distinct from other objects and may give them a kind of agency such that they are difficult to divest (Epp and Price 2010; Lastovicka and Fernandez 2005; Price *et al.* 2000). Longitudinally objects move from alienable to sacred and vice versa based on changing social functions, uses and meanings, but the boundary is sticky – typically a significant crossing in both directions (Belk 1992; Godelier 1999; Kopytoff 1986).

Sacred and inalienable objects are typically also viewed as indexical and irreplaceable, marked by a factual and spatio-temporal link with something else that is valued or important (Grayson and Martinec 2004; Grayson and Shulman 2000), and which distinguishes them from copies (Benjamin 1969). For example, my childhood piano (which maybe still sits in my childhood home) is indexical, with a strong evidentiary link to collective practices that imbued playing the piano with identity, authority and mythology. Yet, in this case, it is the *practice* not the indexical object that holds sway, and the rich layered meanings of care and use of the object have not made the object sacred or inalienable. It is interesting to contemplate why not. We know from prior work that sometimes when an indexical object is displaced practices get displaced as well (Epp and Price 2010), but here the practices are more sacred and inalienable than the object. Through the practices the iconic piano (not the original) is capable of carrying the weight of my family legacy in its notes. In this case, as in contemporary virtual worlds, it is possible to separate the meanings and practices from the indexical object.

In summary, three threads of meaning can be garnered from this personal vignette. First is the way temporality is stretched across the integrated practice and object such that it includes a past, a present and a future (Curasi *et al.* 2004a). There is nothing surprising about this since it inhabits our everyday life experiences. Yet the imagined future potentialities that are poured into the present experience of objects and practices remain understudied in consumer research. Especially significant, in this vignette, a collective identity is implicated that is not constituted in a practice or object but a shared modality of being, or ephemeral consciousness negotiated across patterns of people, objects, ideologies and practices. Perhaps there is value in examining not how objects *or* practices are passed from generation to generation, but how the pattern of relationships between objects and practices are assembled and reassembled within and over time to enact the contingent co-evolution of collective identities (DeLanda 2006; Goode 2007).

A second related thread is the interplay of the material and immaterial that characterizes the object-practice-identity web. As Coole and Frost (2010: 1) observe, "there is an apparent paradox in thinking about matter: as soon as we do so, we seem to distance ourselves from it, and within the space that opens up, a host of immaterial things seems to emerge." Sometimes the imaginative capacity of practices and people create relative independence from the material object. For example, Hélène Grimau prior to a concert will sometimes mentally practice all of her pieces without touching the piano (*New Yorker* 2011). Again, this is consistent with our everyday experience, but has received relatively little attention in consumer research (MacInnis and Price 1987). Hence, we might examine not just the material and expressive capacities of actors within the object-practice-identity web (DeLanda 2006), but also their imaginative capacities. Imaginative capacity describes an actor's power to interact with social entities in a way that transcends corporeal presence. Because playing the piano involves the repetitive interaction of a sound, touch, visual image of keyboard and music, as a practice it may interactively acquire substantial imaginative capacity – the power to be reassembled without a corporeal presence. Thinking of objects, people, practices and identity performances in terms of their imaginative capacities could enliven our understanding of how family identity is assembled and reassembled across material absences, virtual spaces and time (Epp *et al.* 2011; Urry 2007). For example, indexical objects may have more imaginative capacity than iconic or alienable objects because they facilitate the reliving of experiences, and some people may be thought to have more imaginative capacity than others (MacInnis and Price 1987). At the same time, compared to indexical objects or complex rituals, simple, iconic objects or practices may be more transportable into virtual spaces because their meanings don't require rich tapestries of sensory information (Epp *et al.* 2011).

Third, we observe the power of a practice over a durable object (often considered inalienable as represented in the film *The Red Violin*). In this case, the practice is more sacred and enduring for the individual and within the collective than an object. Many mundane examples support the value of examining the give and take of practices and objects in identity enactments. For example, reading children's books at bedtime on a parent's iPad or Kindle Fire may enliven the experience in myriad ways, but the practice shifts many other material experiences – the experience of ownership, sharing, collection, and agency to name a few. At the same time the practice itself evolves and shifts as well, pushing further changes in the material experience. How will this change the future meanings of materiality? The co-evolution of practices and objects in the context of identity enactments is worthy of more research attention. In particular, the implications of these shifts for the role and meaning of indexical objects is ripe for renewed inquiry. Despite his brilliant analysis, Walter Benjamin (1969) could not have anticipated the shifting power of the indexical object that we have experienced in the past decade.

My journey to understand family identity and materiality began when my daughter's grandfather gave and read to her a tattered *Peter Rabbit* book from his childhood, and I wondered, "What is this about?" It's entirely appropriate that as I read my favorite childhood stories to my grandnephews on my iPad, I'm still bewildered and enchanted with how materiality interplays with individual and collective identity – how the intricate filigrees of objects, practices and identities are assembled and reassembled from generation to generation.

Family stuff: challenges for future research

In this chapter I outlined a personal perspective on objects, practices and individual and collective identities that embraces rather than diminishes their complexity, heterogeneity and co-evolution. The focus of my story is on family stuff, which includes the object-practice-identity networks of associations that make up a "we" and its shifting, contingent, component parts.

I argued that our theories and experience of materiality and identity have changed in dramatic ways with myriad consequences that represent opportunities for future investigation and research. Prior research evokes a rich narrative of how identity and possessions are linked, but this narrative is incomplete. In particular, we need to know more about the interlocking practices of being "me" and being "we" as they are navigated across persons, objects, places, temporalities, and our individual and social imaginings. While I have focused predominantly on the fluid and negotiated "we" that is family and its component parts, a more significant hurdle is to envision how a variety of "me" and "we" enactments interplay within and beyond family.

Similarly, I focused on some of the easier ways that we might re-envision object-practice-identity relationships, but the real challenge is to examine how their agentic capabilities (material, expressive and/or imaginatively imbued) and their patterns of associations affect whether and how they assemble and reassemble over time and space. Critically, an actor (human or non-human) never acts alone. "Its efficacy or agency always depends on the collaboration, cooperation, or interactive interference of many bodies and forces" (Bennett 2010: location 431).

In pragmatic terms, I proposed some immediate avenues for research. I argued there is much to be learned by shifting our focus from what makes possessions special to how possessions are special in our lives. The way in which objects are inserted and insert themselves in the practices of individual and collective identity is underexplored. We have not fully examined objects' agentic capabilities in interaction with other material and relational systems. Such investigations would likely uncover the agentic capabilities of mundane, non-indexical objects as well as highlighting how various assemblages of objects and practices transform identity. Such research would help us uncover how objects and practices inform and transform each other within the context of family life.

I also suggested more investigation of the porous boundaries between stuff and identity, material and de-material, ownership and use that may be overstated, misleading and changing. These porous boundaries are made salient by new research and theory around matter, but are also relevant in our own individual and collective life experiences. For example, the imaginative capacities within object-practice-identity webs could be fruitfully investigated as a different lens for understanding than, for example, indexicality or attachment.

Importantly, we could explore how socio-material practices of dematerialization and the increasing independence of information and symbols from the corporeal and material world alter our understandings of family identity. For example, how do these socio-material processes affect the pattern of relationships between objects and practices that are passed from generation to generation, or the practices of families who are geographically and temporally dispersed? Miller observes that the media are most certainly stuff and there is a dialectical relationship in which "people are simultaneously creating a relationship with each other and with the media" (Miller 2010: 121). While he charts some changing patterns of kinship enactment with the spread of the Internet in Trinidad and the mobile phone in Jamaica, he has just begun to scratch the surface. We need further exploration of whether and how family consumption practices and identity are created, lost and transformed in these technologically mediated spaces (Epp *et al.* 2011; Urry 2007).

Acknowledgments

The author would like to thank Austen Arnould for many late-night discussions related to this chapter and Amber Epp for comments on a previous version.

Note

1 After I decided on the term "family stuff" I read Daniel Miller's provocative book *Stuff* in which he resolutely refuses to define the term, but consistent with my approach in this chapter challenges our oppositions between "the person and the thing, the animate and inanimate" (Miller 2010: 5).

Further reading

Belk, R.W. (1988) "Possessions and the Extended Self." *Journal of Consumer Research* 15 (September): 139–68. (This is the essential first piece to read!)

Coole, D. and Frost, S. (eds) (2010) *New Materialisms: Ontology, Agency and Politics*. Durham, NC: Duke University Press. (This book brings together a variety of important new perspectives on materiality.)

DeLanda, M. (2006) *A New Philosophy of Society: Assemblage Theory and Social Complexity*. New York: Continuum Books. (This is an accessible version of the theory and an important rethinking of collectives and materiality.)

Miller, D. (2010) *Stuff.* Cornwall: Polity Press. (This is a charming read that also encapsulates much of Miller's writing on this topic.)

Warde, Alan (2005) "Consumption and Theories of Practice." *Journal of Consumer Culture* 5(2): 131–53. (This paper provides a good introduction to practice theory in consumer research.)

References

Ahuvia, A.C. (2005) "Beyond the Extended Self: Loved Objects and Consumers' Identity Narratives." *Journal of Consumer Research* 32 (June): 171–85.

Arnould, E.J. and Price, L.L. (2000) "Authenticating Acts and Authoritative Performances: Questing for Self and Community." In S. Ratneshwar, David Glen Mick and Cynthia Huffman (eds), *Postmodernity, Dimensions of Consumers Motives, Goals, and Desires: Emerging Perspectives and Applications for a New Century.* New York and London: Routledge.

Belk, R.W. (1988) "Possessions and the Extended Self." *Journal of Consumer Research* 15 (September): 139–68.

——(1991) "Possessions and the Sense of Past." In Russell W. Belk (ed.), *Highways and Buyways: Naturalistic Research from the Consumer Behavior Odyssey.* Provo, UT: Association for Consumer Research, pp. 114–30.

——(1992) "Moving Possessions: An Analysis Based on Personal Documents from the 1847–69 Mormon Migration." *Journal of Consumer Research* 19 (December): 339–61.

——(1995) *Collecting in a Consumer Society.* New York: Routledge.

——(2010) "Sharing." *Journal of Consumer Research* 36 (February): 715–34.

Belk, R.W., Ger, G., and Askergaard, S. (2003) "The Fire of Desire: A Multisited Inquiry into Consumer Passion." *Journal of Consumer Research* 30(3): 326–51.

Belk, R.W., Sherry, J.F., Jr, and Wallendorf, M. (1988) "A Naturalistic Inquiry into Buyer and Seller Behavior at a Swap Meet." *Journal of Consumer Research* 14(4): 449–70.

Belk, R.W., Wallendorf, M., and Sherry, J.F., Jr (1989) "The Sacred and Profane in Consumer Behavior: Theodicy on the Odyssey." *Journal of Consumer Research* 16 (June): 1–38.

Bendle, M.F. (2002) "Teleportation, Cyborgs and the Posthuman Ideology." *Social Semiotics* 12:1: 45–62.

Benjamin, W. (1969) *Illuminations.* New York: Harcourt, Brace & World.

Beverland, M.B. and Farrelly, F.J. (2010) "The Quest for Authenticity in Consumption: Consumers' Purposive Choice of Authentic Cues to Shape Experienced Outcomes." *Journal of Consumer Research* 36 (5): 838–56.

Bourdieu, P. (1984) *Distinction: A Social Critique of the Judgment of Taste.* London: Routledge.

Brothers, L. (1997) *Friday's Footprint: How Society Shapes the Human Mind.* New York: Oxford University Press.

Commuri, S. and Gentry, J.W. (2005) "Resource Allocation in Households with Women as Chief Wage Earners." *Journal of Consumer Research* 32 (September): 185–95.

Connell, P.M. and Schau, H.J. (2011) "Synergy and Discord in the Intergenerational Transfer of Consumption Practices (ITCP): The Role of Individuals and Coalitions within Families." Working paper, Stony Brook University.

Coole, D. and Frost, S. (eds) (2010) *New Materialisms: Ontology, Agency and Politics.* Durham, NC: Duke University Press.

Cotte, J. and Wood, S.L. (2004) "Families and Innovative Consumer Behavior: A Triadic Analysis of Sibling and Parental Influence." *Journal of Consumer Research* 31(1): 78–86.

Csikszentmihalyi, M. and Rochberg-Halton, E. (1981) *The Meaning of Things: Domestic Symbols and the Self.* New York: Cambridge University Press.

Curasi, C.F., Arnould, E.J., and Price, L.L. (2004) "Ritual Desire and Ritual Development: An Examination of Family Heirlooms in Contemporary North American Households." In C. Otnes and T. Lowrey (eds), *Contemporary Consumption Rituals: A Research Anthology.* Matwah, NJ: Lawrence Erlbaum Press.

Curasi, C.F., Price, L.L., and Arnould, E.J. (2004) "How Individuals' Cherished Possessions Become Families' Inalienable Wealth." *Journal of Consumer Research* 31 (December): 609–22.

DeLanda, M. (2006) *A New Philosophy of Society: Assemblage Theory and Social Complexity.* New York: Continuum Books.

Epp, A.M. and Price, L.L. (2008) "Family Identity: A Framework of Identity Interplay in Consumption Practices." *Journal of Consumer Research* 35 (June): 50–70.

——(2010) "The Storied Life of Singularized Objects: Forces of Agency and Transformation." *Journal of Consumer Research* 36(5): 820–37.

——(2011a) "Designing Solutions Around Customer Network Identity Goals." *Journal of Marketing* 75 (March): 36–54.

——(2011b) "Family Time in Consumer Culture: Implications for Transformative Public Policy." In David Mick, Simone Pettigrew, C.P., and J. Ozanne (eds), *Transformative Consumer Research Handbook*. New York: Routledge.

Epp, A.M., Schau, H.J., and Price, Linda L. (2011) "Connected Families: How Consumption Practices Survive Distance." *Marketing Science Institute Working Paper* (4–1618), November.

Firat, A.F. and Venkatesh, A. (1995) "Liberatory Postmodernism and the Reenchantment of Consumption." *Journal of Consumer Research* 22 (December): 230–67.

Gergen, K.J. (1994) *Realities and Relationships*. Cambridge, MA: Harvard University Press.

Giddens, A. (1992) *The Transformation of Intimacy: Sexuality, Love, and Eroticism in Modern Societies*. Stanford, CA: Stanford University Press.

Godelier, M. (1999) *The Enigma of the Gift*. Chicago, IL: University of Chicago Press.

Goode, J. (2007) "Whose Collection is it anyway? An Autoethnographic Account of 'Dividing the Spoils' Upon Divorce." *Cultural Sociology* 1(3): 365–82.

Gram-Hanssen, K. (2009) "Standby Consumption in Households Analyzed with a Practice Theory Approach." *Journal of Industrial Ecology* 14(1): 150–65.

Grayson, K. and Martinec, R. (2004) "Consumer Perceptions of Iconicity and Indexicality and Their Influence on Assessments of Authentic Market Offerings." *Journal of Consumer Research* 31 (September): 296–312.

Grayson, K. and Shulman, D. (2000) "Indexicality and the Verification Function of Irreplaceable Possessions: A Semiotic Analysis." *Journal of Consumer Research* 27(1): 17–30.

Halkier, B., Katz-Gerro, T., and Martens, L. (2011) "Applying Practice Theory to the Study of Consumption: Theoretical and Methodological Considerations." *Journal of Consumer Culture* 11(1): 3–13.

Hardy, C., Lawrence, T.B. and Grant, D. (2005) "Discourse and Collaboration: The Role of Conversations and Collective Identity." *Academy of Management Review* 30(1): 58–77.

Hayles, N.K. (1999) *How We Became Posthuman: Virtual Bodies in Cybernetics, Literature, and Informatics*. Chicago, IL: University of Chicago Press.

Heisley, D.D. and Cours, D. (2007) "Connectedness and Worthiness for the Embedded Self: A Material Culture Perspective." *Consumption, Markets and Culture* 10(4): 425–250.

Hurdley, R. (2006) "Dismantling Mantelpieces: Narrating Identities and Materializing Culture in the Home." *Sociology* 40(4): 717–33.

Jenkins, R., Nixon, E., and Molesworth, M. (2011) "'Just Normal and Homely': The Presence, Absence and Othering of Consumer Culture in Everyday Imagining." *Journal of Consumer Culture* 11(2): 261–81.

Kleine, S.S. and Baker, S.M. (2004) "An Integrative Review of Material Possession Attachment." *Academy of Marketing Science Review* 8(4): 1–35.

Kleine, S.S., Kleine, R.E., III, and Allen, C.T. (1995) "How is a Possession 'Me' or 'Not Me'? Characterizing Types and an Antecedent of Material Possession Attachment." *Journal of Consumer Research* 22 (December): 327–43.

Kopytoff, I. (1986) "The Cultural Biography of Things: Commoditization as Process." In Arjun Appadurai (ed.), *The Social Life of Things*. Cambridge: Cambridge University Press, pp. 64–94.

Kruks, S. (2010) "Simone de Beauvoir: Engaging Discrepant Materialisms." In Diana Coole and Samantha Frost (eds), *New Materialisms: Ontology, Agency and Politics*. Durham, NC: Duke University Press, pp. 258–80.

Lastovicka, J.L. and Fernandez, K. (2005) "Three Paths to Disposition: The Movement of Meaningful Possessions to Strangers." *Journal of Consumer Research* 31(4): 813–23.

Latour, B. (2005) *Reassembling the Social: An Introduction to Actor-Network-Theory*. New York: Oxford University Press.

MacInnis, Deborah J. and Price, Linda L. (1987) "The Role of Imagery in Information Processing: Review and Extensions." *Journal of Consumer Research* 13 (March): 473–91.

Markus, Hazel and Nurius, Paula (1986) "Possible Selves." *American Psychologist* 41: 954–69.

Max, T.D. (2011) "Her Way: A Pianist of Strong Opinions." *The New Yorker*, Nov. 7th.

Miller, D. (1987) *Material Culture and Mass Consumption*. Oxford and New York: Basil Blackwell.

——(2001) "Possessions." In Daniel Miller (ed.), *Home Possessions*. Oxford: Berg Press, pp. 107–21.

——(2005) *Materiality*. Durham, NC: Duke University Press.

——(2008) *The Comfort of Things*. Cambridge: Polity Press.

——(2010) *Stuff*. Cambridge: Polity Press.

Money, A. (2007) "Material Culture and the Living Room: The Appropriation and Use of Goods in Everyday Life." *Journal of Consumer Culture* 7(3): 355–77.

Moore, E.S., Wilkie, W.L., and Lutz, R.J. (2002) "Passing the Torch: Intergenerational Influences as a Source of Brand Equity." *Journal of Marketing* 66 (April): 17–37.

Price, L.L., Arnould, E.J., and Curasi, C.F. (2000) "Older Consumers' Disposition of Special Possessions." *Journal of Consumer Research* 27 (September): 179–201.

Reed, A., II and Bolton, L.E. (2005) "The Complexity of Identity." *MIT Sloan Management Review* (Spring): 18–22.

Sartre, J. (1976) *Critique of Dialectical Reason*. Vol. 1. Translated by Alan Sheridan-Smith. London: New Left Books.

Schau, H.J., Gilly, M.C., and Wolfinbarger, M.F. (2009) "Consumer Identity Renaissance: The Resurgence of Identity-inspired Consumption in Retirement." *Journal of Consumer Research* 36 (August): 255–76.

Schouten, J.W. (1991) "Selves in Transition: Symbolic Consumption in Personal Rites of Passage and Identity Reconstruction." *Journal of Consumer Research* 17 (March): 412–25.

Shankar, A., Elliott, R., and Fitchett, J.A. (2009) "Identity, Consumption and Narratives of Socialization." *Marketing Theory* 9(1): 75–94.

Thomas, T.C., Price, L.L., and Schau, H.J. (2012) "When Differences Unite: Resource Interdependence in Heterogeneous Consumption Communities." *Journal of Consumer Research* (forthcoming).

Tian, K. and Belk, R.W. (2005) "Extended Self and Possessions in the Workplace." *Journal of Consumer Research* 32 (September): 297–310.

Urry, J. (2005) "The Complexity Turn." *Theory, Culture and Society* 22(5): 10–14.

——(2007) *Mobilities*. Cambridge: Polity Press.

Warde, Alan (2005) "Consumption and Theories of Practice." *Journal of Consumer Culture* 5(2): 131–53.

III.III

Culture and self

32

DEATH STYLES AND THE IDEAL SELF

Elizabeth C. Hirschman, Ayalla A. Ruvio and Russell W. Belk

Introduction

> With Socrates and Plato, the human being discovered … a mystery that clears a path to the Ultimate Goodness … From the viewpoint of the evolution of consciousness, this conceptual development signals … the discovery of the ideal self … The ideal self is not a given. It is what the human being seeks and aspires to attain.
>
> *(Obayashi 1992: xiii)*

The human tendency to focus on mortal aspects of life is well reflected in the consumer behavior literature. With rare exceptions (e.g. Bonsu and Belk 2003; Brown, Bell, and Carson 1996; La Barbara 1987; Turley 1998), studies have been grounded in earthly concerns, whether mundane or exalted, celebratory or routine. The few studies that do involve the end of life focus on the sacred, but stop well short of envisioning life after death. Although consumer research has delved into a multitude of earthly consumption locales, in all of these the pull of cultural realities and responsibilities exerts its force upon both the consumer and the inquirer.

As a result, both consumers and theorists are confined to the present, hemmed in by resource and opportunity limitations, and bounded by mortality. This has narrowed our theoretical vision to the reasonable, the prudent, and the possible. What if this limitation were removed from the horizon of both the observed and the observer? What if the realm of personal ideals were limitless; what if we could fulfill our fondest desires without constraints or worries; what then might be observed?

For many people there is a genuine sense that one's ideals and desires will be made real after death. Our aim here is to venture into the land of the dead with the hope of discovering the *ideal self*. We believed that gaining deeper knowledge of consumers' images of the material and non-material aspects of the afterlife could provide new insights into what consumers believe to be the perfect or ideal lifestyle, absent earthly constraints. What we learned is that heaven, for many, is a place where their loved ones consume much as they did in life, but in happier, more ideal circumstances. For others it is a place where personal deficiencies, material absences and missed opportunities are "made whole" and made perfect. For yet others it is a place where the forbidden, the desired, and the quested for can finally be possessed without guilt, shame or penalty. We tentatively account for these visions using a rewards-based model of consumption joined with the Platonic Ideal. However, our study primarily is intended to open doors to different ways of thinking – and our hope is that many other researchers will choose to go through them.

Consumption: beyond the here and now to the hereafter

Attitudes toward death have changed over the centuries (Ariès 1974; Elias 1982; Moller 1996). Because humans fear death, one reaction is to become more materialistic when thinking of mortality in an effort to defy death (e.g. Rindfleisch *et al.* 2009; Solomon *et al.* 2004). Another tactic, suggested by Ernest Becker (1973), is to initiate an "immortality project" that denies the fact of death. One common type of immortality project is to sustain a belief that after death, life will go on as we have known it on earth, but in another realm known as heaven.

Since humans first gained consciousness of their own mortality approximately 60,000 years ago, we have developed expectations of life after death (Mithen 1996). Evidence of these beliefs is based upon the internment of several types of grave goods with the deceased (ibid.). Among these are weapons, jewelry, apparel, eating utensils, decorative objects, and tools that apparently were deemed to have value to the decedent in the life to come. More contemporary post-mortem consumer goods for the deceased to use in the afterlife are found in the paper replicas of branded luxury goods, travel documents, foods, and drinks burned for the dead in Chinese cultures (Zhao and Belk 2008).

As human societies evolved in complexity, correspondingly complex beliefs about a life after death developed. For example, in the *Mesopotamian* afterlife, the role of the deceased human is to serve the needs and desires of the gods. However, there are status differentials among the deceased, with those who had more children (especially sons) becoming "companions to the gods" and experiencing pleasure and leisure. As Cooper (1992: 26) comments, a deceased individual's "worth" in Mesopotamian religious beliefs seems to be based upon his/her fecundity in life. Evidently in ancient Mesopotamia, the ability to produce healthy children was seen as morally and socially desirable. In this calculus we see one version of a justice system in which rewards and punishments in an afterlife are computed based on a reckoning of "deservingness" during life – the beginnings of envisioning a correspondence between "the good life" and "the good afterlife."

Ancient *Egyptian* culture was the first known to develop the concept of a universal moral order (*Ma'at*, also meaning "justice") and established a mortuary cult ideology which guided the inhabitants' views about and preparations for the afterlife (Murnane 1992). For their own burials, the Egyptian elite prepared elaborate tombs containing both artifacts believed necessary for functioning in the afterlife (e.g. food, tools, weapons, apparel), and murals depicting the social structure in which the decedents had been, and expected to be, embedded – that is, servants, slaves, children, animals, soldiers, and so forth (Murnane 1992).

Hindu religious beliefs evolved over millennia into intricate patterns that defy simple schemata or categorization (Pearson 1998). Among the conceptual oppositions embraced are dualism between god (Brahma) and the material world (Ma'sumian 1995). Although it is unlikely than any present-day Hindu is conversant across the entire body of philosophy, two concepts, *karma* (the principle of reciprocal justice) and *samsara* (the transmigration of the human spirit into different human and animal forms), are accepted by most adherents (Pearson 1998). Within the *Rig-Veda*, heaven is reserved for those who have practiced asceticism, made offerings to the priests, followed the holy law, or died in battle (Pearson 1998).

As with Hindu adherents, *Buddhists* represent a wide range of religious thought. Most Buddhist precepts originated in the teachings of the historical Buddha, known as *Gautama*, *Sidhartha*, or *Shakyamuni* (Klein 1998: 47). In a spiritual epiphany, Gautama saw all living entities cycling through a series of births, deaths and re-births based upon the moral quality of their life during each cycle. Within Buddhist thought, individuals also cycle repeatedly through heaven(s) and hell(s), just as they do through earthly, mortal existences. Once again we can discern notions of various afterlives contingent on the merit earned during life on earth.

The prophet Zarathustra developed a novel religious philosophy, *Zoroastrianism*, between the 17th and 15th centuries BCE (Cooper 1989), which formed the intellectual substrata for Judaism, Christianity, and Islam (see e.g. Choksy 1998). One central tenet is an ethical and moral dualism between *asha* (righteousness) and *druj* (falseness) (ibid.).

Zoroastrian philosophy proposes that upon death, the soul separates from the physical body and must pass through a critical judgment. If the soul is found to be virtuous and good, it passes to heaven, where it sojourns for eternity. Souls of persons who have led evil, sinful lives are sent to *drujo-denamo*, a dark, fiery place where they are tormented eternally (Choksy 1998; Ma'sumian 1995).

Judaism evolved over a 5,000-year history, absorbing elements of the Mesopotamian religions, and later Zoroastrian and Greek beliefs as it transitioned from a polytheistic fertility tradition to abstract monotheism. The Hebrew *Torah* does not propose the existence of a paradise or heaven that mortals enter after death. Instead heaven is described as the "dwelling place of God" (Isaiah 66:1), while a place called *Sheol* (Job 17:16) is described as the "resting place of the dead." However, by the first century, Judaic teachings had developed to include the idea that those found worthy would go to dwell in a beautiful Garden (*Gan*) with God for eternity.

Entry to the *Christian* heaven is contingent upon belief in the divinity of Jesus as Christ/the Messiah. Following a Day of Judgment, the Christian faith proposes that the souls of all humans will be sent either to heaven to dwell with God, or to Hell to suffer for eternity. Contemporary fundamentalist Christian writers provide vividly detailed descriptions of heaven: "A place of unlimited pleasure, unlimited happiness and unlimited joy" (DeStefano 2003: 1). Alcorn (1999: 12) describes the Christian heaven as "home-like" and "a place of marvellous smells and tastes, fine food and great conversation … a place of unprecedented freedom and adventures."

As Ashton and Whyte (2001), Casey (2009), and Gardiner (1989) have observed, the concept of heaven is both elaborately described and deeply inscribed in *Islam*. The term *alakhira* ("here-after") occurs 113 times in the *Qur'an* and is believed to be entered immediately after one's death. The righteous decedent arrives in an eternal world of gardens and pleasures (Blair and Bloom 1991) and is greeted by radiant angels, while the unfaithful are dragged to the Underworld by repulsive and ugly creatures.

These religious concepts are summarized in Table 32.1.

Table 32.1 Summary of the religious concepts of the afterlife

	Afterlife perceptions	*Consumption-related practices*
The Egyptian view	Developed a universal mortal order that regards death as a continuum of life.	There is no difference in the way of living before or after death. Therefore, the deceased needs the exact same possessions for a successful functioning in the afterlife.
Hindu and Buddhist view	Heaven is a temporary residence for the soul in the journey from one material body to another.	Heaven is a magical place full of light, music and delicious food. The soul can enjoy times without any sorrow and misery.
Zoroastrianism	Development of dualism perspective of good and bad. The soul is judged and sent to heaven/hell accordingly.	Heaven is a light, joyful place full of virtuous pleasures. Hell is a dark place, where the soul is tormented forever.

Table 32.1 (continued)

	Afterlife perceptions	*Consumption-related practices*
Judaism	Death is a temporary state until the soul and the body resurrect, when the Messiah arrives.	Unmaterialistic perception of all that is divine and holy. All men are buried equal in plain, white wraps.
Christianity	Materialist view of heaven.	The ultimate luxurious place, which poses no boundaries or constraints to pleasurable experiences and living.
Islam	A dual perspective of good/evil that corresponds to heaven/hell. A manly perception of heaven.	A lavish place that offers pure enjoyment of all five senses and no suffering of any kind.

Method

Sample and procedure

In-depth interviews were conducted with 60 adults ranging in age from 22 to 81 in three eastern American states. The interviewees represented a wide range of economic, social, ethnic and religious backgrounds. The people conducting the interviews were graduate students trained in interpretive research techniques. Those whom they interviewed were friends or relatives who had lost a loved one recently. In each case the interview was conducted in the participant's home and recorded either on audiotape or in field notes. Each interviewer constructed an interpretation of the data s/he had collected; usually these were informed by personal knowledge of the individuals being interviewed. These analyses, together with the original transcriptions and field notes, were used as source material to construct the present analysis.

Analysis

Analysis was conducted by a bi-gender, bi-cultural research team of three. We individually read and coded material and discussed differences. The analysis was hermeneutic and ongoing, being informed by iterations of the analysis as well as interrogations of relevant literature. Of the 60 interviews conducted, only three respondents reported that their deceased loved one was not residing in heaven in bodily form. One Jewish woman believed her relative was "decomposing in the ground," because "there is no Jewish heaven." Two others reported their deceased loved ones were in the form of an "energy field" capable of observing behavior on earth. In one of these cases, a man reported his great-grandfather was "an orb of energy" floating near his great-grandmother's orb and looking down on their family.

The other 57 interviewees reported that their deceased loved ones were in an afterlife and engaging in various activities using specific abilities, services and products. In other words, they were *continuing to be consumers* even in the afterlife. Our analysis focused upon understanding how and what informants believed was being consumed by these decedents with the intention of gaining greater understanding of the ideal self.

Findings

Although not all descriptions of what loved ones were doing in heaven involved material consumption, the majority did. We concentrate on the consumption-related scenarios here.

Across the set of interviews, there were two major styles of afterlife consumer behavior reported. These we have labeled the "enhanced" and the "limitless." Both were viewed by the informants as ideal self-outcomes for their loved one in heaven.

The enhanced death style

Just like life on earth, only better

A common view among the informants is that their deceased relative is leading an enhanced consumer lifestyle, which is more properly now termed a "death style." Among those believing in such an enhanced death style, the deceased loved one is described as now living under much the same conditions in heaven as s/he did on earth. The alterations are, first, that the individual is younger and in a more physically and emotionally perfect form. Any deterioration in health, happiness or appearance suffered during the individual's years on earth, e.g. from Alzheimer's, cancer, diabetes, accidents, has been remedied, and s/he is joyous, alert, attractive and mobile. This is believed to be the condition in which they will exist through eternity. Thus, in keeping with theological teachings common to Zoroastrianism, Christianity and Islam, the afterlife provides the opportunity for one to become his/her ideal self, at least in emotional and physical terms, and remain that way forever.

The loved one is further envisioned as having access to his/her favorite possessions, dwellings, friends (deceased), and activities, while no negative events, accidents or unhappiness can occur – forever. One young woman, whose father had passed away after an extensive struggle with cancer, now sees him in heaven dressed in his favorite button-down plaid shirt, smiling, and wearing his Transition® eyeglasses. She pictures him "doing all the things he loved doing in life: floating in the middle of the pool, talking on his cell phone, … sitting in his favorite chair watching the news, … eating his favorite foods." His dwelling place in heaven is a replica of his former house on earth, because "he would stay in the house he loved so much."

Another respondent believes that her recently deceased Grandma Clare, an excellent cook on earth, is "without a doubt still cooking away today; perhaps she even has her own bakery up in heaven" (Anne-Marie). Notably, in both these cases the loved one is also believed to be "looking down" and "guiding" or "protecting" loved ones still on earth. Here we see that for many consumers, the positive aspects of their loved one's earthly lives are seen as perfect or ideal. There is no need or desire to greatly improve upon them in eternity.

No consumption problems

A second aspect of this theme provides insight into consumers' beliefs about consumption problems commonly experienced in mortal life. One middle-aged woman reported that her deceased parents do not feel pain, hunger, thirst, or anxiety about employment or bills, and do not experience time pressure. These appear to be what are viewed as the primary deterrents to happiness on earth.

Helping others

A third novel insight is provided by a respondent whose mother "lived hand-to-mouth in Kartarpur [India]." Her son, who immigrated to the USA, believes that his deceased mother is making clothing, specifically Indian *saris*, "which she gives to her children, close friends and the poor." The mother got great joy during her lifetime from creating the *saris*, designing each one to suit the unique taste of the individual for whom she was making it. He believes she also celebrates all the traditional Hindu festivals and maintains her strict vegetarianism in the afterlife (Bhalla).

From considering the enhanced death style, we learn that favorite earthly possessions and dwelling places are deemed to be central to the ideal self. These consumers' sense of their loved ones' perfect, immortal selves is bound-up in – and bounded by – the consumption activities undertaken during life. We also learn that anxieties about meeting basic human needs for food and shelter, financial obligations, maintaining their residence and jobs "haunt" consumers here on earth, but are removed in the afterlife. Mortal life is but a degraded version of that envisioned for the informant's ideal self.

The limitless death style

The concept of a limitless consumption style after mortal death represents the extreme end of the continuum of possibilities our participants reported. In these scenarios, the ideal self differs dramatically from what had been experienced on earth. A materially grandiose view of the afterlife is reported by a young woman whose deceased single mother raised her amidst impoverished conditions. The daughter reported that in the afterlife she has "a beautiful new home with granite countertops, marble floors, and modern decor; her new kitchen includes a stovetop island and extensive wine bar; a chef and housekeeper are available fulltime." In her mother's "walk-in closet is overhead lighting which illuminates racks of designer dresses, purses and other apparel. She is driven about by her chauffer and flies in private jets" (Andrea, Filipino).

Such projective images may be compensatory for the deceased's prior life (e.g. Bonsu and Belk 2003) or expressive of the fanciful and materialistic personal ideals detected by Fournier and Guiry (1993). They also resonate with depictions of the "good life" portrayed in the media (e.g. Shrum *et al.* 2005). Providing a philosophical rationale for the emphasis on obtaining material luxuries in the afterlife, a young man who had grown up in an impoverished area of Appalachia with drug-addicted parents proposed that, "Everyone gets what they desire in heaven. There are wide-open spaces; everyone lives in mansions, … has nice cars, a PlayStation 3, a big-screen TV, and anything else they want … In heaven, your work is done. You just get to relax and chill" (Jayson).

Rewarding prior austerity

While the previous three informants were Christians, the same sentiment was found among those from other religious traditions. One young woman, discussing the afterlife her recently deceased father was now enjoying, commented:

> Our faith is Islam and our background is Egyptian, which has a huge influence on our view of the afterlife … [My] father is in heaven due to all the great deeds he has done for society and the dedication he had towards his faith, family, and work … [In heaven] Father would have good health, youth, and would never sense pain …
>
> Material things that were unattainable to my father in life would be at his hands in the blink of an eye … Alcohol would be allowed … Trees will be growing around my father's mansion, and as soon as his appetite causes him to crave a specific food, it will grow on the trees. Food will fulfill cravings and not cause my father to feel too full or sick.
>
> *(Sheren)*

Here we see the post-mortem availability of consumption behaviors that were impermissible or unattainable during life, such as drinking alcohol. It becomes impossible to over-consume and experience negative consequences, such as obesity or satiation. Activities that once were forbidden as sinful now become rewards for prior moral behavior.

A final set of examples extends the notion of the unlimited ideal self into more experiential and self-developmental aspects of consumption. One informant reported that her friend, who died in middle age, was now:

> seeing new places, meeting new people and learning about different cultures, [because she] was a very open-minded and friendly person, loved exploring exotic countries … [She] owns a huge collection of paintings by some of the world's most famous artists.

A 40-year old deceased man is reported to have:

> loved music to the day he passed away … [He] is in the afterlife playing with famous musicians and surrounded by people who share his passion for music. He is now riding through the universe on his new motorcycle.
>
> *(Greg)*

In these passages we glimpse the hoped-for ideal self of lives that ended "too soon." To die in middle age is not only tragic, but viewed as unjust: the person did not receive his/her full due of mortal happiness. Perhaps to assuage this sense of injustice, these deceased friends and relatives are envisioned as living out the rest of their lives in idealized fulfillment of their earthly dreams.

The death of Calvinism, the triumph of the Id

One of the most emotionally and intellectually challenging aspects of many religious teachings – and current consumer behavior theorization (Lehrer 2009) – is that postponing gratification will result in a heightened sense of gratification. Asceticism and self-constraint are lauded as virtues, while receiving things without "earning" them, instant gratification, impulsivity, unchecked hedonism and over-indulgence are cast as the "dark side" of consumer behavior and human existence (e.g. Benson 2000; Hirschman 1992). Indeed, Western Christian culture is largely centered around the Calvinist ethic of industriousness on earth equating with salvation in heaven. However, as the following section suggests, some consumers may now go even further in rejecting piety on earth and see the ideal parts of life as the activities that often are condemned as socially inappropriate and damaging.

To sin is human; to sin forever is divine!

A subset of our interviews provide a remarkable view of the ideal self. This type of content was hinted at earlier in excerpts suggesting heaven may be a place where the forbidden or sinful becomes acceptable and enjoyed. However, the accounts that follow are more explicit and detailed. One informant described his deceased uncle as follows:

> [He was] bright, outgoing, and always willing to "stir the pot" … [In heaven], he's probably gambling, drinking and spending time with hookers … I bet [he] would fly his private jet to Vegas every day and start out by getting a couple of "girlfriends" to take with him to the casino … Next to him would be a bottomless glass of straight vodka with a lime that never lost its flavor. One of the girlfriends would be standing at the table giving him a neck massage and the other one would be under [the table] …

The wife of a recently deceased man who died of smoking-induced emphysema reported she is certain that in heaven her late husband "is having a party. I'm sure he's gambling, smoking and drinking ... He's probably with all his old friends ... " The activities that led to his death now are viewed as constructing his ideal self in heaven.

If self- or socially destructive activities are viewed as sinful, wrong, harmful, and bad on earth, by what process do they become the ideal self for some in the afterlife? There are two, possibly three, eschatological foundations for these beliefs.

One position is that the afterlife provides an *eternal reward* for self-control during mortal life. We can sense this philosophical underpinning across Christianity, Islam, Hinduism and Zoroastrianism (see Table 32.1). The person who denies him/herself material and sensual pleasures during life in order to demonstrate his/her virtue will be permitted to indulge in an unbounded manner during the afterlife.

The second position, intertwined in some religious philosophies with the first, is that *sensuality and materialism* are part and parcel of a fully lived mortal life and to not partake of them within certain boundaries is not fulfilling God's purpose for the individual on earth. Judaism and Islam encourage sensuality and material abundance during life, whereas the Calvinist Protestant tradition eschews sensuality, but celebrates material acquisition during one's lifetime as evidence of divine blessing (Weber 1958).

A third position is that consumption activities during life are continued intact into the next world. All the pleasures, foods, statuses, and companions enjoyed as a mortal are available when one gains immortality. Thus, if the logic of Egyptian eschatology is followed, individuals would find in the afterlife a direct continuation of their former life. Viewed in this way, the logic of a drinking, gambling, and Harley-riding eternity is supportable.

Discussion

In today's consumer culture, the ideal self seems to be a physically perfect and emotionally content existence enjoying leisure time and material goods with no fear of the consequences.

One's pursuits in heaven can be custom-tailored to recreate – or even enhance – one's most desired activities in life. We are free to become our ideal selves – although that ideal self may be construed as sinful by earthly standards (Sandage 2005). It is no longer necessary, in the terms of Mischel's "marshmallow" studies, to forgo the pleasures of one marshmallow now in order to be rewarded with two later (Shoda *et al.* 1990). Heaven is the time and place to eat all the marshmallows we want, now and forever. This may be one of the reasons consumption seems to beckon to many in the afterlife. Possessions, consumer activities, leisure pursuits, having fun, experiencing adventures are what we see as the best part of ourselves.

References

Alcorn, Randy (1999) *In Light of Eternity: Perspectives on Heaven*. Colorado Springs, CO: Waterbrook Press.

Ariès, Philippe (1974) *Western Attitudes Towards Death: From the Middle Ages to the Present*. Baltimore, MD: Johns Hopkins University Press.

Ashton, John and Whyte, Tom (2001) *The Quest for Paradise: Visions of Heaven and Eternity in the World's Myths and Religions*. New York: Harper Collins.

Becker, Ernest (1973) *The Denial of Death*. New York: Simon and Schuster.

Belk, Russell (1988) "Possessions and the Extended Self." *Journal of Consumer Research* 5(2) (September): 139–68.

Benson, April Lane (ed.) (2000) *I Shop, Therefore I Am: Compulsive Buying and the Search for Self*. Northvale, NJ: Jason Aronson.

Blair, Sheila S. and Bloom, Jonathan M. (1991) *Images of Paradise in Islamic Art*. Hanover, NH: Hood Museum, Dartmouth University.

Bonsu, Samuel and Belk, Russell (2003) "Do Not Go Cheaply into That Good Night: Death Ritual Consumption in Asante Ghana." *Journal of Consumer Research* 30 (June): 41–55.

Botsman, Rachel and Rogers, Roo (2010) *What's Mine is Yours: The Rise of Collaborative Consumption*. New York: HarperCollins.

Brown, Stephen, Bell, Jim, and Carson, David (eds) (1996) *Proceedings of the Marketing Eschatology Retreat*. Belfast: University of Ulster.

DeStefano, Anthony (2003) *A Travel Guide to Heaven*. New York: Doubleday.

Elias, Norbert (1982) *The Loneliness of the Dying*. Trans. Edmund Jephcott. London: Blackwell.

Foucault, Michel (1977 [1995]) *Discipline and Punish: The Birth of the Prison*. New York: Vintage Books.

——(1978 [1991]) "Governmentality." In Graham Burchell, Colin Gordon, and Peter Miller (eds), *The Foucault Effect: Studies in Governmentality*. Hemel Hempstead: Harvester Wheatsheaf, pp. 87–104.

Fournier, Susan and Guiry, Michael (1993) "'An Emerald Green Jaguar, a House on Nantucket, and an African Safari': Wish Lists and Consumption Dreams in Materialist Society." In Leigh McAlister and Michael L. Rothschild (eds), *Advances in Consumer Research*. Vol.20. Provo, UT: Association for Consumer Research, pp. 352–58.

Freke, Timothy (1996) *Heaven: An Illustrated History of the Higher Realms*. Hants: Godsfield Press.

Gardiner, Eileen (ed.) (1989) *Visions of Heaven and Hell Before Dante*. Ithaca, NY: Ithica Press.

Ger, Güliz and Belk, Russell (1999) "Accounting for Materialism in Four Cultures." *Journal of Material Culture* 4 (July): 183–204. University of Kansas Press.

Hirschman, Elizabeth (1992) "The Consciousness of Addiction: Toward a General Theory of Compulsive Consumption." *Journal of Consumer Research* 19 (September): 155–79.

Johnson, Christopher Jay and McGee, Marsha G. (1998) *How Different Religions View Death and the Afterlife*. Second edition. Philadelphia, PA: Charles Press.

Kozinets, Robert V. (2001) *Utopian Enterprise: Articulating the Meanings of Star Trek's Critical Essays in American History, 1880–1980*. New York: Pantheon, pp. 1–38.

La Barbara, Priscilla (1987) "Consumer Behavior and Born Again Christianity." In Jagdish Sheth and Elizabeth Hirschman (eds), *Research in Consumer Behavior*, Vol. 2. Greenwich, CT: JAI Press, pp. 193–222.

Ma'sumian, Farnaz (1995) *Life After Death: A Study of the Afterlife in World Religions*. Los Angeles, CA: Kalimat Press.

Miller, Lisa (2010) *Heaven: Our Enduring Fascination with the Afterlife*. New York: HarperCollins.

Miller, Vincent (2004) *Consuming Religion: Christian Faith and Practice in a Consumer Culture*. New York: Continuum.

Noble, David F. (1999) *The Religion of Technology: The Divinity of Man and the Spirit of Invention*. New York: Penguin.

Obayashi, Hiroshi (1992) *Death and Afterlife: Perspectives of World Religions*. Westport, CT: Praeger.

Pfeiffer, John E. (1985) *The Emergence of Humankind*. New York: HarperCollins.

Rindfleisch, Aric, Burroughs, James E., and Wong, Nancy (2009) "The Safety of Objects: Materialism, Existential Insecurity, and Brand Connection." *Journal of Consumer Research* 36 (June): 1–16.

Sandage, Scott A. (2005) *Born Losers: A History of Failure in America*. Cambridge, MA: Harvard University Press.

Segal, Alan F. (1989) *Life After Death: A History of the Afterlife in the Religions of the West*. New York: Doubleday.

Shrum, L.J., Burroughs, James E., and Rindfleisch, Aric (2005) "Television's Cultivation of Material Values." *Journal of Consumer Research* 32 (December): 473–79.

Solomon, Sheldon, Greenberg, Jeffrey L., and Pyszczynski, Thomas A. (2004) "Lethal Consumption: Death-Denying Materialism." In Tim Kasser and Allen D. Kanner (eds), *Psychology and Consumer Culture: The Struggle for a Good Life in a Materialistic World*. Washington, DC: American Psychological Association, pp. 127–46.

Turley, Darach (1998) "A Postcard from the Very Edge: Mortality and Marketing." In Stephen Brown and Darach Turley (eds), *Consumer Research: Postcards from the Edge*. London: Routledge, pp. 350–77.

Twitchell, James B. (1999) *Lead Us Into Temptation: The Triumph of American Materialism*. New York: Columbia University Press.

——(2007) *Shopping for God: How Christianity Went from in Your Heart to in Your Face*. New York: Simon and Schuster.

Weber, Max (1958) *The Protestant Ethic and the Spirit of Capitalism*. Trans. Talcott Parsons. New York: Charles Scribner's Sons.

Zelinsky, Wilbur (1976) "Unearthly Delights: Cemetery Names and the Map of the Changing American Afterworld." In David Lowenthal and Martyn J. Bowden (eds), *Geographies of the Mind: Essays in Historical Geography*. New York: Oxford University Press, pp. 171–95.

Zhao, Xin and Belk, Russell (2008) "Desire on Fire: A Naturalistic Inquiry of Chinese Death Ritual Consumption." *European Advances in Consumer Research* 45.

33

SOCIAL BRANDING AND THE MYTHIC REINVENTION OF ETHNIC IDENTITY

Siok Kuan Tambyah and Craig J. Thompson

In this chapter we analyze consumers' ethnic identifications as a social brand that is constructed and promoted through a network of family myths. Our participants' mythic reinvention of ethnic identity manifests a subtle reaction against the democratizing tendencies of the consumer culture's identity market. Through these myths, our participants construct their ethnic identity as a deeply rooted, familial connection to their immigrant history. However, consumers' relationships to this social brand vary across generations, sometimes contentiously so, owing to different viewpoints on how best to maintain the authenticity of this social brand.

Studies of consumer ethnicity have highlighted several key postmodern motifs, such as hybridization, code switching, and the continual reinvention of (simulated) traditions that suggest consequential changes in the way in which ethnic identifications are represented and enacted (e.g. Askegaard *et al.* 2004; Bouchet 1995; Mehta and Belk 1991; Oswald 1999; Peñaloza 1994; Peñaloza and Gilly 1999). We suggest that these postmodern shifts have created important continuities between forms of ethnic identification that are largely symbolic in nature (Gans 1979, 1994) and consumption-centered, elective forms of community (Celsi *et al.* 1993; Kozinets 2001; McAlexander *et al.* 2002; Muñiz and O'Guinn 2001).

Historically, ethnic identifications have been regarded as a major pillar of traditional communities (Thompson 1989). By traditional community structure, we mean situations where the experiential characteristics of community – consciousness of kind, moral responsibility to members, shared rituals and traditions – are directly reflected in the social space of a neighborhood. For example, geographic propinquity and concentration among ethnics (as in the classic ethnic enclave) is conducive to making ethnic traditions, values, and norms an omnipresent feature of everyday life (Peñaloza 1994). This everyday socio-cultural immersion greatly increases the likelihood that an ethnic tradition will become a habituated and fully embodied aspect of personal identity (see Hall 1992), and that it will be a pervasive and naturalized feature of individuals' social networks.

In the USA, traditional ethnic neighborhoods historically also have been communities of necessity, owing to the dual factors of economic hardship and socially enforced segregation (Model 1990; Peñaloza 1994; Portes and Manning 1986). However, as immigrant groups' economic and social options become less limited by social stigmas, cultural barriers, and forms of institutionalized prejudice, their members become less dependent upon the contextualized social, economic, and cultural capital offered by an immigrant enclave, and they also gain greater latitude in how they construct their identities and the relative centrality their ethnic heritage plays in their identity projects.

Under these conditions, ethnicity can easily become a situational aspect of personal identity (Stayman and Deshpande 1989), or as Bouchet (1995) argues, a highly personalized bricolage construction that individuals cull together from a kaleidoscope of ethnic images offered up by the postmodern marketplace. Bakalian (1993) characterizes this difference as one between being ethnic and feeling ethnic. In this latter case, individuals experience their ethnic heritage as less binding on their life choices (including marriage partners) and personal outlooks, less central to their self-conceptions, and something recalled and enacted primarily through consumption symbolism (see Gans 1979; Mehta and Belk 1991; Oswald 1999).

This cross-generational process of socioeconomic assimilation had long been assumed to precipitate an attenuation of ethnic traditions (the so-called melting-pot effect). In recent years, however, post-assimilation theorists have shown that ethnicity is a protean cultural resource, rather than a timeless set of characteristics, which is continuously reinvented in relation to changing social circumstances (Askegaard *et al.* 2004; Guss 2000; Peñaloza 1994; Peñaloza and Gilly 1999). From this post-assimilationist perspective, the collective memories and traditional practices that constitute an ethnic heritage increasingly become nostalgic markers, abstracted from their historical mooring, which are volitionally used to symbolize an affiliation with a particular immigrant legacy (Gans 1979; Ger and Østergaard 1998; Mehta and Belk 1991).

The symbiosis between symbolic ethnicity and postmodern consumer culture is more intensive and extensive than suggested by the now familiar idea that individuals represent their ethnicity through consumption symbols and ethnic brands (i.e. Progresso means Italian, Goya means Mexican). Ethnic traditions are now increasingly dependent upon commercial representation, touristic performances, and continual practices of cultural reinvention and re-telling to maintain their cultural vibrancy and relevance (Wood 2008). For example, consider the legions of Americans who travel to Ireland or visit Irish heritage museums in hopes of reconnecting with their often quite distant Hibernian heritage (Brown *et al.* 2000).

In this chapter we argue that symbolic ethnicity organized around self-chosen consumption activities, social events, and material symbols more closely resemble brand communities than more traditional, geographically segregated and economically circumscribed ethnic communities. Practices of social branding have become necessary to maintain and to revitalize ethnicity in the postmodern marketplace where ethnic heritage is one of many cultural possibilities through which consumers can construct their personal and communal identities. In other words, the much-discussed process of ethnic reinvention does not just happen as a matter of course. Rather, it is embedded in active processes of social branding that are geared toward recruiting younger members back into the ethnic fold and finding a viable niche for ethnic identifications in a postmodern marketplace replete with identity brands (e.g. Holt 2002).

Conceptualizing ethnic identity as a social brand is not meant to trivialize this complex socio-cultural phenomenon. On the contrary, our research aligns with a growing body of studies suggesting that brands (and their associated meanings) are very significant aspects of personal identity that help individuals cope with many of the ambiguities and dilemmas posed by the complexities of postmodern life (Fournier 1998; O'Guinn and Muñiz 2005; Luedicke *et al.* 2010; Muñiz and Schau 2005). We contend that the idea of a social brand is better able to account for the experiential significance, narrative complexity, and generational differences that characterize our participants' relationships to their ethnic heritage than other formulations, such as situational ethnicity (Stayman and Deshpande 1989) or code switching (Oswald 1999), which also theorize the complexities of ethnic identification that are no longer anchored in the proximities of place and the impetus for collective solidarity provided by socioeconomic limitations.

Social branding also brings to the analytic foreground the identity projects that consumers are pursuing by embracing an ethnic heritage and the kinds of experiential benefits (and travails) that they receive through this expansive form of brand relationship (e.g. Fournier 1998). A postmodern paradox that runs throughout our analysis is that the cultural conditions which enable individuals to feel ethnic, rather than being bound and constrained by a stigmatized ethnic identity, give rise to many activities that seek to reinforce and habituate these ethnic identifications so that they are not merely situational. Conversely, our participants, particularly those who have become self-appointed caretakers of the heritage, are also attempting to recruit younger generations into a more dutiful commitment to these traditions. In this latter case, the goals are not only to perpetuate these ethnic traditions but also to promote an ethnic-centered conceptualization of identity rather than the multi-faceted, bricolage identities that have become emblematic of global youth culture (Kjeldgaard and Askegaard 2006).

Context and method

The context for this study is an age- and class-stratified community of Italian-Americans in a mid-western city in the USA. Italian-Americans, as one of the most culturally and structurally assimilated ethnic groups in America, may be in the "twilight phase" of their ethnicity because they have lost many of the distinctive cultural traits that were once attributed to Italian immigrants (Alba 1988). Although there are some general characteristics for different generations of Italian-Americans, several scholars have highlighted the need to recognize the diversity of the Italian-American population in terms of their range of socioeconomic positions, lifestyles, personal values and adjustments to life in American society (e.g. Bellioti 1995; Juliani 1994). Other scholars have also drawn attention to how a multiplicity of Italian-American identities can exist, instead of one Italian-American identity (Vecoli 1985).

We use the general term "Italian-American" somewhat reluctantly as a convenient label. Some of our participants would more readily identify themselves as Sicilians or Albanians. Others would simply use the term "Italian" or "American." These preferences and sensitivities highlight that ethnic identifications are less organized by nation-state identifications than a diverse array of intersecting heritages, grounded in regional traditions and even guild-organized clans. However, the Italian-American classification reflects the historic position of this community as a minority group and it also serves distinctive politics of identity functions, enabling this community to marshal its collective capital (i.e. social, cultural, and economic) toward common goals, such as sustaining a cultural heritage threatened by the gradual demise of its core second-generation members, geographic mobility among its younger members, and dilution via inter-ethnic marriage.

Methodological approach

In-depth interviews focusing on how the participants understood and experienced their ethnic heritage formed the backbone of the data-collection process. Some 32 participants from 13 families were recruited after six months of rapport-building within the Italian-American community. Every effort was made to interview at least two generations within the families so as to explore the inter-generational processes related to the maintenance and reinvention of ethnic traditions. The interviews, ranging from 45 minutes to two and a half hours, were audiotaped and transcribed. All participants received a copy of the transcripts for verification and feedback. The transcripts were analyzed and interpreted using a hermeneutic process (Thompson 1997).

We sought a holistic understanding of individual transcripts while noting similarities or differences across transcripts. Individual transcripts were closely read several times, and a summary profile of salient themes expressed was developed for each participant. Next, the transcripts were grouped according to families and subjected to further close readings, with a particular focus on the inter-generational dynamics within these ethnic identification and consumption processes.

Findings

While many themes have emerged from this research, in this chapter we focus on how our participants use family myths to construct a sense of their ethnic heritage. Myths are culturally salient stories that convey valued meanings, ideals, and moral values in a compelling and resonant way (Stern 1995). Myths pervade popular culture and are particularly important to the process of branding and brand building (Holt 2004). By mythologizing their ethnic heritage, our participants create a hybrid identity that melds a more general notion of Italianness, and which is steeped in a nostalgic view of old world values.

We argue that this mythic re-telling and reinvention of their heritage is also a reaction against the unconstrained identity experimentation and spirit of consumer sovereignty promoted by postmodern consumer culture (Holt 2002). Whereas these postmodern cultural tendencies tend to militate against invariant commitments to binding cultural traditions (Bauman 2007), our participants turn to their ethnic heritage to generate feelings of rootedness, stability, and immutability that are anchored in a distinctive genealogical legacy.

Family myths

Being "family-oriented" has often been described as a distinguishing cultural trait of Italians (Johnson 1985; di Leonardo 1984). For Italian-Americans in present times, the family has been mythologized as the means through which they can protect their ethnic identity from being subsumed by the larger American society (Gallo 1981). This veneration of the family also usually involved ideals of family loyalty, respect for and care of the elderly, and most of all, nostalgic reflections on the close-knit extended Italian family which bonded the generations together and provided unfailing support to all its members.

This mythic construction aligns Italianness with meanings of intimacy, stability, and immutability that are highly coveted in a postmodern world characterized by endless contingencies, impermanence, and feelings of uprootedness (Bauman 2007). For Katerina, the family bonds she attributes to her Italian heritage provide an important symbolic (and identity-affirming) distinction to her "more Americanized" husband:

> Family is very important. My husband, he is also from an ethnic background but very Americanized. It's hard for him to understand sometimes what is this family? And it's not my parents, it's the extended family, everyone. [I want] to be closer to the family and to be involved in, to have the choice to be part of all the events that go on, and just to be here. I grew up with my cousins right in the neighborhood, so they were my friends and I'd like to reconnect with them.
>
> *(Katerina Simeti-Ewers, third generation, working mother)*

The Italian family is further mythologized as a repository of sacrosanct values that must be passed on to the next generation. Through stories about their family heritage, our older participants hope to instill in their grandchildren a sense of respect and admiration for the perseverance and strength of character displayed by their immigrant forebears that will translate into a deep pride in their ethnic heritage:

> I want them to be proud of it [i.e. their Italian heritage], I like them to know what my mother and father went through to get us where we are, that includes me and them. Because without my mother and my father, none of this would have happened ... Every parent sacrifices, everyone does.
>
> *(Mario Ross, second generation, retired)*

These family myths also express a claim to *indexical authenticity* (Grayson and Martinec 2004: 298) that suggests a factual and spatio-temporal link between contemporary symbols and re-enactments of Italianness and the ways of life of their first- and second-generation immigrant forebears. Through this linkage, our participants insinuate themselves into an historical legacy that seems neither arbitrary nor available to anyone. This lineage is represented and passed on through family heirlooms but perhaps even more significantly through the stories related by older family members about life in Italy and the noble character of their immigrant ancestors who settled in America.

Many of our participants are also actively seeking connections to their roots through family trees, family history projects, and pilgrimages to their ancestral towns and villages in Italy. These authenticating acts (Arnould and Price 2000) were particularly important to our participants whose grandparents and other older members of their family had already passed away. Members of older generations provide living links between abstract ethnic traditions and richly storied family histories. In lieu of this authenticating presence, several participants like Helen Raimond took it upon themselves to pass this legacy on to future generations.

> I had this interest [in my husband's family history] and one day I thought if I don't sit down and do this, someday we'll be gone. Their grandparents are already gone, and great grandparents. And these generations coming up are going to know nothing about the past, nothing about the Raimonds that came to America. I gave them copies of the original information that I did, the packet that I did. It's called "We Remember." It tells them the family tree and gives them some family recipes. I had some of the family members talk about other family members who have passed away so that they would know. I'll like to pass on the interest of their ethnic background ... And I have things put away that I'm hoping some day, somebody in the family will be interested enough to keep and pass on.
>
> *(Helen Raimond, second generation, semi-retired)*

Interestingly, while we might expect younger ethnics to have more latitude of freedom to enact bricolage ethnicities (Bouchet 1995), some participants rejected this kind of unencumbered identity play and gravitated toward more fixed notions of identity and pride in a singular ethnic heritage:

> I just think that it is sad that people are not more proud of where they come from. They say America is a melting pot because there are so many cultures here. There are but people all want to be American, they want to blend in, they don't want to be special anymore. They all want to be the same, they want to be mainstream, they want to fit in. And they don't think it's not OK to not fit in anymore. So I don't necessarily want to fit in. I need to be a little bit unique. And so I think being Italian is part of that.
>
> *(Jamie Capadona, third generation, young working adult)*

> I'm so glad that I'm not a complete mish-mash of cultures. A lot of my friends are. You know when people say "oh, I'm a mutt," they have this and this and whatever in them. I'm so glad for that one solid, pure-bred half of me that is Italian. Because that's actually like some roots, something definite that I can just delve into. I always like that part of me that is actually rooted to a specific country, instead of four or five. Their ways of life make so much more sense to me than some of the things we do.
>
> *(Isabella Johnson, second generation, but closer in age to third-generation participants, student)*

This rejection of "mish mash" and "blended" cultures serves an identity project of enhancing personal distinctiveness and creating a symbolic distinction to the mainstream, which is construed as being an indiscriminate mix of heritages. However, this symbolic distinction necessitates considerable interpretive work to sustain, such as Isabella focusing on her one-half pure-bred side. In these narratives, the ideal of ethnic purity is not utilized in a racist manner, but rather becomes a metaphor for authenticity and an identity anchored in a timeless heritage. Our younger informants are at the stage of life where identity issues tend to become tantamount and their identification with Italianness helps to allay anxieties over who they are and should be. Beyond this generational effect, this embrace of heritage and flight from identity play also assuage existential anxieties that can ensue from the reflexive awareness about the malleability of personal identity (cf. Giddens 1991) and the vast range of identity choices that confront individuals in a postmodern consumer society.

Food is family

Stories about the preparation of food and family meals are a recurrent motif in our participants' family myths. Immigrant groups have long used culinary traditions to sustain and reinforce collective identifications (e.g. Barthes 1975; Douglas 1971; Powdermaker 1932) and to negotiate their symbolic boundaries to a host culture (Oswald 1999; Peñaloza 1994; Wallendorf and Reilly 1983). Among southern Italian immigrants, the preparation and sharing of food has been one of the most central family rituals (Levenstein 1988). As Rachel puts it, Italian food has a deeper meaning because of its symbolic connections with family myths:

> When I think of my Italian traditions, I think of food, I think of plenty of food, I think of wonderful food. And I think of all of those family gatherings and the fact that most of it was centered around food and maybe it wasn't the consumption of food, but it was the fact that everybody was there. And the family is not only your family, it was extended family because everybody was also welcome to be there. It didn't make any difference. If you were there, you were part of the family.
>
> *(Rachel Bremer, third generation, working mother)*

Despite the significance attributed to the large family meal replete with traditional Italian fare, our participants' ritual enactment of their ethnic heritage through food is largely confined to Christmas holidays and special occasions. By being separated from the quotidian routine of cooking, the traditional foods served during Christmas (especially Italian cookies, rice balls and cannolis) take on an even greater symbolic significance. These dishes materially represent memories of their family's immigrant past, and perhaps most importantly, are viewed as a form of cross-generational transfer (Price *et al.* 2000) that will enrich future generations and keep their ethnic heritage alive:

> The Italian foods, we have to have those. Otherwise it's not Christmas. Like if I don't make cookies, what? You'll think he [my husband] was a little kid, what, no cookies? We still have Christmas, 28 of us. And that's just my family. And if we don't get together, if something would happen and someone's sick, they would say "it's not like Christmas, we are not all together." We are to the point now where my husband and I, we are the older members of the family. And while we still can, we want to keep these things. So my grandchildren and then some day, their children will know this is what we did, this is how we did it.
>
> *(Marge Parisi, second generation, retired)*

On a culturally significant holiday such as Christmas, some families make the extra effort to prepare Italian meals or to incorporate ethnic traditions and symbols. The consumption of their ethnic foods sets them apart from other American families who celebrate Christmas the conventional way. For our participants, the symbolic meanings embodied in these quintessential Italian dishes are pride in being Italian, a desire to honor the heritage of their immigrant forebears, and an appreciation of their own family's ethnic traditions. In their narratives, the term "Americanized" is used to indicate a contamination of tradition or a loss of authenticity that needs to be overcome by incorporating more ethnic elements into their holiday celebrations. Italian culinary traditions thus encompass more than just learning recipes for everyday and holiday meals – they embody family values, ethnic group and family history, and other symbolic meanings that need to be passed on as well.

Discussion

This analysis addresses postmodern transformations in the nature of ethnic identification. We argue that ethnicity functions as a social brand that fosters feelings of communal solidarity and that provides a form of existential grounding consumers often find lacking in the flux of postmodern life. This social brand is also used by self-appointed caretakers and promulgators of the ethnic heritage to heighten interest in its constituent traditions and to enhance their own status within the community.

Prior studies on consumers' brand relationships (Fournier 1998; Holt 2002) and brand communities (O'Guinn and Muñiz 2005; Muñiz and O'Guinn 2001) converge on the finding that perceptions of authenticity are fundamental to the power of brands to serve as anchors for identity and community. Similarly, the perceived authenticity of ethnicity as a social brand is based on antiquarian notions of blood, kinship, and deeply rooted connections to immigrant history. Through this mythic construction of authenticity (and the legitimating imprimatur of family elders and familial artifacts), our participants feel that they have a privileged access to a rich cultural heritage that is not generally available in the identity marketplace. Once freed from the imperatives of political and socioeconomic limitations and geographic segregation (and the corresponding necessity to collectively pool the available social and economic capital), however, ethnicity becomes something akin to a lineage brand (Olsen 1993), which is passed down from one generation to the next and the continued (identity) equity of which is dependent upon practices of intergenerational transfer (Moore *et al.* 2002).

We suggest that our participants are seeking to realize an authentic form of identity that is not contingent, malleable, or merchandisable. In our participants' narratives, their ethnic heritage is consistently portrayed in sanctified terms that stand apart from the mainstream of American culture. This mythic rendering of symbolic ethnicity is expressive of a broader and much-documented consumer project to experience forms of authenticity that seem lacking in most quarters of the commercial marketplace (Arnould and Price 2000; Brown *et al.* 2000; Grayson and Martinec 2004; Kozinets 2002; Peñaloza 2001; Thompson and Tambyah 1999). For our participants, the historical authenticity attributed to their ethnic heritage is a resource for the authentication of selfhood. That is, it provides an immanent identity pillar that seems impervious to the shifting tides of fashion, status consciousness, and the fickle whims of consumer preferences.

Throughout the course of 20th-century American popular culture, the ideal of authenticity has been aligned with morally redemptive meanings of revitalizing emotional immediacy (echoing the strains of ecstatic spirituality), genuineness of actions, and virtuous necessity. These venerated meanings stand in diametric opposition to the improbities of artifice, conspicuous consumption, calculated acts of impression management, and avaricious wants (Lears 1994). This cultural formulation emanates from a fairly pervasive sense of disenchantment that arose in the modern era of industrialization, standardization, mass advertising, and the depersonalization of the marketplace, and that continues into the present day through a variety of anti-marketing, anti-corporate sentiments (Holt 2002; Kozinets 2002).

A much less discussed cultural dimension of this quest for authenticity is that it also represents a dialectical pushback against the so-called democracy of goods offered by the contemporary marketplace (see Marchand 1985) and its myriad opportunities for identity experimentation and reconstruction. In other words, democratized identities and the brands through which they are symbolized can readily acquire an aura of commercialized inauthenticity (Holt 2002). This dilemma is quite apparent in the case of successful prestige brands, the cultural cachet of which makes them increasingly popular until they are pushed into the sullied sphere of *populuxe* (see Twitchell 2002). More generally, consumers have become increasingly critical toward the ubiquitous advertising claim that specific products and brands can function as modern-day talismans for conjuring personal distinctiveness (see Holt 2002).

The assimilation of the Italian community, the privatized nature of suburban lifestyles, and the multiplicity of identity options available to contemporary consumers have all worked to divorce ethnicity from the socioeconomic conditions that once necessitated its social reproduction. In so doing, ethnic traditions also become less and less vital to the practices of everyday life and instead emerge periodically as symbolic gestures that are volitionally undertaken at special times and places. As our study shows, a considerable degree of interpretive work is needed to buttress these tenuous and malleable connections to an ethnic past and to mythically reconstruct practices of symbolic ethnicity as expressions of an authentic and timeless core identity.

Acknowledgment

This research benefited from financial support provided by the National University of Singapore and the Sheth Foundation.

References

Alba, Richard (1988) "The Twilight of Ethnicity Among Americans of European Ancestry: The Case of Italians." In Richard D. Alba (ed.), *Ethnicity and Race in the USA: Toward the Twenty-first Century*. New York: Routledge, pp. 134–58.

Arnould, Eric J. and Price, Linda (2000) "Authenticating Acts and Authoritative Performances: Questing for Self and Community." In S. Ratneshwar, David Glen Mick, and Cynthia Huffman (eds), *The Why of Consumption*. New York: Routledge, pp. 140–63.

Askegaard, Søren, Arnould, Eric J., and Kjeldgaard, Dannie (2004) "Post-Assimilationist Ethnic Consumer Research: Qualifications and Extensions." *Journal of Consumer Research* 31 (December): 160–70.

Bakalian, Anny (1993) *Armenian-Americans: From Being to Feeling Armenian*. New Brunswick, NJ: Transaction Publishers.

Barth, Fredrik (1969) "Introduction." In Fredrik Barth (ed.), *Ethnic Groups and Group Boundaries*. Boston, MA: Little & Brown.

Barthes, Roland (1975) "Towards a Psychosociology of Contemporary Food Consumption." In Elborg Forster and Robert Forster (eds), *European Diet from Pre-Industrial to Modern Times*. New York: Harper and Row, pp. 47–59.

Bauman, Zygmunt (2007) *Consuming Life*. Malden, MA: Polity.

Bellioti, Raymond A. (1995) *Seeking Identity: Individualism versus Community in an Ethnic Context*. Lawrence, KS: University of Kansas Press.

Bouchet, Dominique (1995) "Marketing and the Redefinition of Ethnicity." In Janeen Costa and Gary Bamossy (eds), *Marketing in a Multicultural World*. Thousand Oaks, CA: Sage, pp. 68–104.

Brown, Stephen, Hirschman, Elizabeth C., and MacClaren, Pauline (2000) "Presenting the Past: On Marketing's Reproduction Orientation." In Stephen Brown and Anthony Patterson (eds), *Imagining Marketing*. New York: Routledge, pp. 145–91.

Celsi, Richard, Rose, Randall, and Leigh, Thomas (1993) "An Exploration of High-Risk Leisure Consumption through Skydiving." *Journal of Consumer Research* 20 (June): 1–21.

di Leonardo, Micaela (1984) *The Varieties of Ethnic Experience: Kinship, Class and Gender Among California Italian-Americans*. Ithaca, NY: Cornell University Press.

Douglas, Mary (1971) "Deciphering a Meal." In Clifford Geertz (ed.), *Myth, Symbol and Culture*. New York: Norton, pp. 61–81.

Fournier, Susan (1998) "Consumers and Their Brands: Developing Relationship Theory in Consumer Research." *Journal of Consumer Research* 24 (March): 343–73.

Gallo, Patrick J. (1981) *Old Bread New Wine*. Chicago, IL: Nelson-Hall.

Gans, Herbert (1979) "Symbolic Ethnicity: The Future of Ethnic Groups and Cultures in America." In Herbert Gans, N. Glazer, J.R. Gusford and Christopher Jencks (eds), *On the Making of Americans: Essays in Honor of David Riesman*. Philadelphia, PA: University of Pennsylvania Press, pp. 193–220.

——(1994) "Symbolic Ethnicity and Symbolic Religiosity: Towards a Comparison of Ethnic and Religious Acculturation." *Ethnic and Racial Studies* 17 (October): 577–92.

Ger, Güliz and Østergaard, Per (1998) "Constructing Immigrant Identities in Consumption: Appearance among Turko-Danes." In Joseph W. Alba and J. Wesley Hutchinson (eds), *Advances in Consumer Research*. Vol. 25. Provo, UT: Association for Consumer Research, pp. 48–52.

Giddens, Anthony (1991) *Modernity and Self-Identity: Self and Society in the Late Modern Age*. Stanford, CA: Stanford University Press.

Grayson, Kent and Martinec, Radan (2004) "Consumer Perceptions of Iconicity and Indexicality and Their Influence on Assessments of Authentic Market Offerings." *Journal of Consumer Research* 31 (September): 296–313.

Guss, David M. (2000) *The Festive State: Race, Ethnicity, and Nationalism as Cultural Performance*. Berkeley, CA: University of California Press.

Hall, John (1992) "The Capital(s) of Cultures: A Nonholistic Approach to Status Situations, Class, Gender, and Ethnicity." In Michele Lamont and Marcel Fournier (eds), *Cultivating Differences*. Chicago, IL: University of Chicago Press, pp. 257–88.

Holt, Douglas B. (1998) "Does Cultural Capital Structure American Consumption?" *Journal of Consumer Research* 25 (June): 1–26.

——(2002) "Why Do Brands Cause Trouble? A Dialectical Theory of Consumer Culture and Branding." *Journal of Consumer Research* 29 (June): 70–90.

——(2004) *How Brands Become Icons: The Principles of Cultural Branding*. Cambridge, MA: Harvard Business School Press.

Johnson, Colleen Leahy (1985) *Growing Up and Growing Old in Italian-American Families*. New Brunswick, NJ: Rutgers University Press.

Joy, Annamma, Hui, Michael, Kim, Chankon, and Laroche, Michel (1995) "The Cultural Past in the Present: The Meaning of Home and Objects in the Homes of Working-Class Italian Immigrants in Montreal." In Janeen Costa and Gary Bamossy (eds), *Marketing in a Multicultural World*. Thousand Oaks, CA: Sage, pp. 145–79.

Juliani, Richard N. (1994) "*Al Ricupero di una Tradizione Perduta*: Toward the Recovery of a Lost Tradition." In Harral E. Landry (ed.), *To See the Past More Clearly: The Enrichment of the Italian Heritage 1890–1990*. Austin, TX: Nortex Press, pp. 33–50.

Kjeldgaard, Dannie and Askegaard, Søren (2006) "The Glocalization of Youth Culture: The Global, Youth Segment as Structures of Common Difference." *Journal of Consumer Research* 33 (September): 231–47.

Kozinets, Robert V. (2001) "Utopian Enterprise: Articulating the Meaning of Star Trek's Culture of Consumption." *Journal of Consumer Research* 28 (June): 67–89.

——(2002) "Can Consumers Escape the Market? Emancipatory Illuminations from Burning Man." *Journal of Consumer Research* 29 (June): 20–38.

Lears, Jackson (1994) *Fables of Abundance: A Cultural History of Advertising in America.* New York: Basic Books.

Levenstein, Harvey (1988) "New Reformers and New Immigrants." In *Revolution at the Table: The Transformation of the American Diet.* New York: Oxford University Press, pp. 98–108.

Luedicke, Marius, Thompson, Craig J., and Giesler, Markus (2010) "Consumer Identity Work as Moral Protagonism: How Myth and Ideology Animate a Brand-Mediated Moral Conflict." *Journal of Consumer Research* 36 (April): 1016–32.

McAlexander, James H., Schouten, John W., and Koenig, Harold (2002) "Building Brand Community." *Journal of Marketing* 66 (January): 38–54.

Marchand, Roland (1985) *Advertising the American Dream: Making Way for Modernity, 1920–1940.* Berkeley, CA: University of California Press.

Mehta, Raj and Belk, Russell W. (1991) "Artifacts, Identity, and Transition: Favorite Possessions of Indians and Indian Immigrants to the United States." *Journal of Consumer Research* 17 (March): 398–411.

Model, Susan W. (1990) "Work and Family: Blacks and Immigrants from South and East Europe." In Virginia Yans-McLaughlin (ed.), *Immigration Reconsidered.* New York: Oxford University Press, pp. 130–59.

Moore, Elizabeth S., Wilkie, William L., and Lutz, Richard J. (2002) "Passing the Torch: Intergenerational Influences as a Source of Brand Equity." *Journal of Marketing* 66 (April): 17–37.

Muñiz, Albert and O'Guinn, Thomas C. (2001) "Brand Communities." *Journal of Consumer Research* 27 (March): 412–32.

Muñiz, Albert M., Jr and Schau, Hope Jensen (2005) "Religiosity in the Abandoned Apple Newton Brand Community." *Journal of Consumer Research* 31(4): 737–47.

O'Guinn, Thomas C. and Muñiz, Albert M. (2005) "Communal Consumption and the Brand." In David Glen Mick and S. Ratneshwar (eds), *Inside Consumption: Frontiers of Research on Consumer Motives, Goals, and Desires.* New York: Routledge, pp. 252–72.

Olsen, Barbara (1993) "Brand Loyalty and Lineage: Exploring New Dimensions for Research." In Leigh McAlister and Michael L. Rothschild (eds), *Advances in Consumer Research.* Vol. 20. Provo, UT: Association for Consumer Research, pp. 276–84.

Oswald, Laura R. (1999) "Culture Swapping: Consumption and the Ethnogenesis of Middle-Class Haitian Immigrants." *Journal of Consumer Research* 25 (March): 303–18.

Peñaloza, Lisa (1994) "Atravesando Fronteras/Border Crossings: A Critical Ethnographic Study of the Consumer Acculturation of Mexican Immigrants." *Journal of Consumer Research* 21 (June): 32–53.

——(2001) "Consuming the American West: Animating Cultural Meaning at a Stock Show and Rodeo." *Journal of Consumer Research* 28 (December): 369–98.

Peñaloza, Lisa and Gilly, Mary (1999) "Marketer Acculturation: The Changer and the Changed." *Journal of Marketing* 63 (July): 84–104.

Portes, Alejandro and Manning, Robert D. (1986) "The Immigrant Enclave: Theory and Empirical Examples." In Susan Olzak and Joanne Nagel (eds), *Competitive Ethnic Relations.* Orlando, FL: Academic Press, pp. 47–68.

Powdermaker, Hortense (1932) "Feasts in New Ireland: The Social Functions of Eating." *American Anthropologist* 34: 236–47.

Price, Linda L., Arnould, Eric J., and Curasi, Carolyn Folkman (2000) "Older Consumers' Disposition of Special Possessions." *Journal of Consumer Research* 27 (September): 179–201.

Schau, Hope Jensen, Muñiz, Albert M., Jr, and Arnould, Eric J. (2009) "How Brand Community Practices Create Value." *Journal of Marketing* 73 (September): 30–51.

Stayman, Douglas M. and Deshpande, Rohit (1989) "Situation Ethnicity and Consumer Behavior." *Journal of Consumer Research* 16 (December): 361–71.

Stern, Barbara B. (1995) "Consumer Myths: Frye's Taxonomy and the Structural Analysis of Consumption Text." *Journal of Consumer Research* 22 (September): 165–85.

Thompson, Craig J. (1997) "Interpreting Consumers: A Hermeneutical Framework for Deriving Marketing Insights from the Texts of Consumers' Consumption Stories." *Journal of Marketing Research* 34 (November): 438–55.

Thompson, Craig J. and Tambyah, Siok Kuan (1999) "Trying to Be Cosmopolitan." *Journal of Consumer Research* 26 (December): 214–41.

Thompson, Richard H. (1989) *Theories of Ethnicity: A Critical Appraisal.* Westport, CT: Greenwood Press.

Twitchell, James B. (2002) *Living it Up: Our Love Affair with Luxury.* New York: Columbia University Press.

Vecoli, Rudolph J. (1985) "The Search for an Italian American Identity: Continuity and Change." In Lydio Tomasi (ed.), *Italian Americans: New Perspectives in Italian Immigration and Ethnicity.* Staten Island, New York: Center for Migration Studies, pp. 88–112.

Wallendorf, Melanie and Reilly, Michael D. (1983) "Ethnic Migration, Assimilation, and Consumption." *Journal of Consumer Research* 10 (December): 292–302.

Wood, W. Warner (2008) *Made in Mexico: Zapotec and the Global Ethnic Art Market.* Bloomington, IN: Indiana University Press.

34
THE GLOBAL SELF

Søren Askegaard and Dannie Kjeldgaard

Introduction

What is the global self? The sheer formulation – a global self – seems to carry with it an inherent contradiction, since self refers to a profound existential individuality which hardly lends itself easily to a global scope and character. One possible interpretation could be based on Lovelock's (1979) "Gaia hypothesis," presenting the world's biosphere as one interconnected cybernetic system that works like a single organism forming (if unharmed) a global equilibrium. With a point of departure in the Gaia hypothesis, the global self seen in connection with issues concerning identity and consumption would presumably be a consuming self in respectful harmony with this delicate global equilibrium. While such a sustainable global consuming self may be one of the most important political and economic goals for humankind in these years, it is not the focus of this chapter.

A second understanding of the global self is the self that is global not so much in a biological and ecological perspective, but in a cultural perspective. This self, often called a cosmopolitan self (cf. Thompson and Tambyah 1999), is global in the sense that its cultural orientation is not confined to a particular socio-historical, national and/or ethnic context, but consciously searching an openness toward the multiculturalism of the contemporary global society.

In the two already mentioned types of global selves, it has been the global that was in focus and the self more of a consequence or a qualifier of the global character of phenomena. The global self addressed in this chapter focuses more on the self and uses the global as a qualifier that describes a process: the globalization of the self as idea and project. In other words, what we are going to discuss is the self as a global ideoscape (Appadurai 1990). Needless to say, it is beyond the scope of this single chapter to address this idea at its fullest. This volume addresses relationships between identity and consumption. One of the most obvious and proliferating fields in which this connection appears in the marketplace is in the consumption of self-actualization techniques. We will therefore focus on the global idea of self as it unfolds in terms of consumption of technologies of self (Foucault 1990).

Not only is the figure of the self-actualizing subject global to the extent that it diffuses globally as part of global consumer culture, but it is global in the sense that it diffuses to more and more aspects of social life. Subjects are increasingly cast as choosing individual consumer-citizens in different institutional settings – in the roles as workers, voters, users of the welfare state, etc.

Moreover, the figure of self-actualization permeates socialization in institutional settings, for example in pre-school individual "learning plans." The consequence is that the self-actualizing self is global both "extensionally" (geographically) and "existentially" (that is, as a fundamental existential condition in contemporary modern life). Modernity leads to a life politics in which searching for answers to the question "Who am I?" becomes central to our approaches to how we organize our lives (Lury 2011). This chapter is about the global presence of the self-project as a consumption motivator.

We therefore take our point of departure in possibly one of the most fundamental characters of contemporary consumer culture: the character of the self-actualizing consumer. As we will argue, this character has a mythological aspect to it. The central narrative of this mythology is that the goal of human existence is, to borrow a formulation from Nietzsche (2005), "to become what one is" through the unfolding of the true and natural self via a number of self-actualizing activities and therapies. In this way, the myth of self-actualization unites Thompson's (2004) core marketplace mythologies of nature and technology, the Romantic and the Gnostic *mythos*.

The myth of self-actualization intensified and diffused on an increasingly global scale through the combination of the popularity of humanistic psychology and new-age orientation toward Eastern philosophical and religious practices among Western cultural movements of the 1960s and 1970s. Far from being a globalization of a Western conception of "self," the global self in focus here is simultaneously a consequence of the easternization of the West (Campbell 2007) and what Campbell calls the human potential movement and the casting of such Eastern holistic approaches to the realization of natural human potential in a mold of Western, humanistic (self-help) psychology. Paradoxically the focus on individual emancipation and self-realization of this largely anti-capitalist movement fits the core ideology of consumer culture.

The commercialization of the myth of self-actualization takes two forms: one general and one specific. The general form is the way in which all kinds of references to the role of products, brands and consumption in consumers' self-enhancement and self-actualization are prevalent in modern commercial vernacular. In its most specific form, this concerns the huge and growing industry of self-actualization through self-help books, courses, coaching, etc., and increasingly, through lifestyle programming on TV. The discourse of the self-actualizing industries more often than not evokes the idea of a monadic self, whose goal is to try to liberate itself from social norms and expectations (Brinkmann 2005). It is thus linked to a Rousseau-inspired anthropocentrism of an unspoiled, immediate natural state of being. However, the modern idea of the individual is not an ahistorical concept, as Dumont (1980) reminds us. The basic function of the myth in society is exactly to naturalize that which is culturally instituted, thereby legitimizing it and providing it with a status of profound truth.

The myth of consumer self-actualization is also part of modern management paradigms and the request of corporate capitalism for a flexible workforce and the constant self-development of the individual as an attractive employee in a post-industrial economy. The generalized myth of self-actualization is thus found in the sphere of consumption as well as in the sphere of production. The consequence of this is a myth and identity script that promotes the idea of an unfinished self (Bauman 2004). In the myth of self-actualization the subject stands in an instrumental relation to the self-identity both in the role of employee and consumer.

One might hypothesize that even the intimate sphere of family-making and procreation is subject to the myth of self-actualization. An indication of its prevalence in contemporary society might be found in the growing importance of single households in North America as well as Europe and the increasing focus on children as pre-planned vehicles for self- (and family) actualization.

In the following we explore the roots of the myth of the global self in terms of the development of the idea of individualization as an outcome of Western modernity and in the Western appropriation of Eastern thought systems into humanistic psychology and therapeutic culture. Following that we discuss the diffusion of the figure of the self-realizing self in diverse market settings globally.

Individualization and reflexivity

Concepts such as identity, lifestyle, health, body and youthfulness are central to contemporary global ideoscapes (Appadurai 1990) of middle-class consumer society patterns, and they are central in the forming of consumer practices, especially in the Western world of Europe and North America, but increasingly also outside these core consumer cultures. These constructs are all based on a high degree of individualism, and they are born from and in turn nurture the reflexive identity projects of modern consumer culture selves (Giddens 1991). As argued by Rindfleish (2005), there is an almost perfect fit between the modern consumer subject and the various forms of commodified productions of self-actualization.

Giddens's starting point is the disembedding mechanisms characteristic of living in late modernity and the consequences this has for the management of individual lives. Giddens's claim is that the frameworks for meaning creation are upheaved from the local and are re-embedded in new institutions that are becoming increasingly global in nature. This can be said to have two overall consequences for individual life handling: 1 the certainty of identity which characterized both traditional and early modern (industrial) society is eroded; and 2 this emancipates the individual from given identities to which he/she has access. The consequence is that in late modernity identity is left to the choices of the individual which at the same time gains access to a much greater variety of lifestyle options. So, first of all the individual is left with seemingly free choice of identity construction, and second, it is facing a pluralization of options made available by increasingly global markets. The local frameworks are disembedded from their locality and new forms are re-embedded in the locality. Giddens's (1991) analysis focuses on the existential challenges this development poses for individuals and does not so much analyze the nature and extent of diffusion of symbols and lifestyle options that become available. The paradoxes inherent in the individualization strategy of identity point to the notable reflexivity that must be part of the individual's life projects in late modernity.

The therapeutic ethic and the spirit of modern consumerism

The accelerating process of individualization as rigid social structures disappear as frames for identity are taken up by Furedi (2004), in his discussion of therapy culture. Therapeutic culture is not just reflective of the individualization process, says Furedi, but is recasting the individual "true" self in an emotional form. Contemporary emotionalism, he argues, is prevalent in a variety of strategies for generating emotional authenticity and/or to successfully manage one's emotions for personal optimization. Consequently, from this perspective self-actualization becomes translated into furthering positive and exorcizing negative emotions. This emotionalism is thus deeply linked to an idealized self-determining self as proposed by humanistic psychology. Therapeutic (consumer) culture, paradoxically, provides all sorts of market-based means in order to cultivate and optimize this autonomous and authenticating self in the form of social technologies of self offered to the individual in a process, which Furedi calls a professionalization of everyday life. Again, we see the mythological blend of romantic naturalness and optimizing technologies that constitute a cornerstone in contemporary (alternative) belief systems (Thompson 2004).

The roots of the contemporary marketplace mythology of self-actualization lie in the humanistic psychology of the 20th century, and even if psychology has evolved as a science, one may argue that the humanistic psychology with its focus on self-actualization in the tradition of notably Maslow (1954) and Rogers (1961), has developed into the most prevalent popular psychology and, thus, to a cornerstone of a modern lifestyle (Smith 1997). According to Brinkmann (2005), there are three major consequences of this humanistic ethos: hypostasis, therapeutization, and subjectivization. Hypostasis indicates that the self becomes conceived in material terms as a resource or a commodity. Therapeutization refers to the degree to which life becomes a therapeutic project and subjectivization is indicative of a tendency to consider moral values as inner and private rather than externally given.

All of these are profoundly linked to consumer culture. Hypostasis to the extent that self is seen as an object for consumption as in "working with one's self" through a number of mind and body regimes: controlling one's caloric intake and one's exercise level and managing one's fashionability in terms of clothes, shoes, hair and make-up. Therapeutization is linked to consumer culture in the general idea that products and brands are there to help the consumer cope, to solve problems occurring in daily social life. Finally, subjectivization is reflected in the philosophy that "the customer is always right," that the ultimate judgment of the appropriate character of some kind of solution rests on the acceptance of the user/customer/client.

Furthermore, the therapeutic culture (here understood in a more narrow sense of psychological forms of therapy) cast subjects as both patients and consumers (Illouz 2008). Therapeutic industry has a performative dimension in that its core ideology of an eternally incomplete self and an insistence on a universal right for individuals to become "whole persons" are fuelling the market for therapy and the therapeutic logic. Illouz exemplifies this with, for example, an industry for third-generation trauma self-help groups. Illouz furthermore points out that this market for therapy increasingly constitutes a new system for social stratification in terms of a Bordieuan power game – that is, in contemporary consumer culture it marks "emotional health [as] a new commodity produced, circulated, and recycled in social and economic sites that takes the form of a field" (Illouz 2008: 171), constituting in turn new forms of capital and habitus.

However, one might argue that the therapeutic narrative stretches way beyond the psychologically based forms of therapy. Turning to the contemporary marketplace, the therapeutic narrative is found in industries that help consumers become "better" consumers, whether morally (e.g. voluntary simplicity consultants), or in terms of competencies (e.g. HOG groups (Harley owners group), DIY courses, wine-tasting courses). Such phenomena point to an autotelic and reflexive relation toward the self. Consumption in a self-actualizing perspective must be seen both as authenticating acts – consuming techniques for actualizing the "true" self – and authoritative performances – sustaining practices of the collective identity (Arnould and Price 2000). There is, we should add, the significant difference that whereas Arnould and Price situate the authoritative performances on the collective level, our self-actualizing consumer often overlooks the significance of the Other as mirror for as much authoritative performances as well as for authenticating acts. The project of the consuming self is the self itself and the self comes from within! Consumption and consumption objects (whether physical goods or therapeutic services in one form or another) thus get a different kind of instrumentality than in the ideas of possessions as extensions of selves. Consumption as extensions of selves assume a stable self-identity. However, the dominant logic of individualization in contemporary consumer culture is that the self is constantly in need of revision and articulation (Beck and Beck-Gernsheim 2002). Actualizing the "true self" thus becomes a never-completed process engendering existential frustration and a constant problematization of the self-esteem (Furedi 2004), an aspect which has also given rise to the qualification of the predominant therapeutic personality as a narcissist (Lasch 1979).

A global myth of me?

As the values and ideals of Western modernity diffuse though the global ideoscape (Appadurai 1990), so does the ensuing cultural transformation towards a reflexive self-realizing consumer subject in a range of "modernizing" and marketizing cultural contexts. We would like, though, to caution that, as with other elements of global consumer culture, this is not a homogenization writ large. The appropriation of the global ideoscape is always both semantic as well as pragmatic (Appadurai 1990) – that is, these appropriations always occur in a dialectic with local cultural contexts. As we have demonstrated elsewhere, the appropriation of the individualized identity among Greenlandic youth occurs in a dialectic with post-colonial and traditional Inuit cultural models of the self (Kjeldgaard and Askegaard 2006). We will illustrate this local as well as global character of the myth of self-actualization with a range of examples in diverse cultural settings. We are aware that such snapshots do not provide any firm ground on which to conclude on the globality of the global self discussed here; however, to the best of our understanding, they do witness the global impact of contemporary ideas of the self-as-project and self-actualization and their global instantiations.

In a recent study also addressing the interplay between easternization and westernization, Askegaard and Eckhardt (2012) analyze the re-appropriation of yoga as a consumer practice in contemporary India. They demonstrate how the renewed popularity of yoga in India is linked both to the fact that it symbolizes local cultural heritage but also because it ties into modern self-management techniques. Yoga is thus considered by some as a stress-relieving technique necessitated by the chores and demands of modern work life under conditions of global competition. By others it is characterized as a health and fitness technique, which is instrumental in altering old normative schemes for what constitutes the attractive body and also helping promote a new normativity of "lean and fit." The practice of yoga is thus gaining renewed popularity in the Indian middle classes as a modern self-help technique, endorsed by Western celebrity yoga practitioners such as Sting and Madonna as well as by Western yoga teachers in India who at times demonstrate more yoga cultural capital than locals. Yoga classes are found in the urban health and fitness centers, where they are positioned and marketed as yet another way of the self-actualizing consumer to live a life of physical and mental health and balance. Varman and Belk (2008), in their study of subaltern consumers in India, find a weakening of traditional bonds and a rise in anomie, a fascination with and aspiration for a modern consumer lifestyle, as well as a longing for rural village lifestyles as a more pure and authentic way of living. This contradiction is interpreted in terms of balancing out the challenges of modernity, and it might very well be, but it is also and simultaneously a greenhouse of factors for promoting ideals of self-actualization, admittedly still a luxury for these consumers. We are here talking about the global creation of the right ideoscape for cultivation of the self rather than an already ongoing process.

China, the other booming Asian mega-economy, may seem less prone to such modernist conceptions of self with its ancient collectively focused Confucian and Taoist philosophy. Nevis (1983) concluded in a study of Maslow's hierarchy of needs in the People's Republic of China that he found little evidence for the importance of the upper, self-actualizing layers of the hierarchy in the Chinese context. However, China has been changing rapidly and already in 1989, Tse, Belk and Zhou found evidence of a growing importance of hedonistic values in advertising also in the back-then only recently marketizing China (Tse *et al.* 1989). This finding, while not directly pointing toward the significance of self-actualization, illustrates the growing importance of a modern consumer subject. In another study of media impact in China, Wei and Pan (1999) isolated three value factors – conspicuous consumption, *aspirations for self-fulfillment and self indulgence*, and worship of Western lifestyles – to be strongly represented at least among the people in Shanghai, and in the better-educated, upper-middle classes. Finally, and possibly most significantly, there is the upsurge of new self-actualization movements. While the political and historical context of the rise and crackdown of the Falun Gong movement is too complex to be reduced to just a matter of self-actualization, its holistic anti-scientist but also anti-traditionalist character, its skilful use of Internet recruitment and communication and not least its aspiration to provide a meaning of life in what is experienced as an ideological vacuum makes it a valid global representative of contemporary self-actualization movements (Chan 2004).

Jafari and Goulding's (2012) recent study of Iranian consumers underlines the decisive role of the project of the self in contemporary Iranian consumption patterns. There is arguably a big distance between Iranians' attempts at consumer resistance to the anti-Western policy of the Iranian government to a post-materialist, wellness-oriented, self-actualizing Western consumer. However, we see the underlying logics of the global self-project as similar in the primacy of the self-project as a basic motivating factor for consumption practices.

Wattanasuwan and Elliott (1999) studied the identity discourses among teenage Buddhists in Thailand. Their findings indicate that despite a Buddhist conception of self that seeks to avoid an understanding of the self as intrinsic, fixed or transcendental, their informants nevertheless articulate such an understanding of the self in relation to consumption practices (although within the narrow confines of a Buddhist sect). Their study indicates the presence of a Western conception of the self, despite the fact that it is being practiced within a local religious structure.

However, new trends toward a global myth of "me" is not just an Asian phenomenon. One of the predominant areas in which we see the global diffusion of the self-realizing consumer is in the area of gender. Kjeldgaard and Nielsen (2010), for example, demonstrate how the traditionally dominant ideology of *marianismo* in a Mexican context is challenged in young women's consumption of popular culture to break with traditional family-oriented notions of femininity. Femininity in this context is cast in a virgin-whore dualism which constitutes the basic discursive space of the local gender culture interacting with modern ideals and discourses of identity. In psychotherapy the *marianismo* ideology has been identified as a significant source of trauma and personal inner conflict among therapeutic clients in Mexico and to some extent among migrant Hispanic women in the USA, to the extent that self-help books are marketed on how to deal with *marianismo* in a modern society (e.g. Gil and Vazquez 1996).

In an African context, the logic behind the (un)holy marriage between the Pentecostal mission in Ghana and liberalist consumer culture and its focus on personal wealth and material reward for faith, as analyzed by Bonsu and Belk (2010), is hardly distinguishable from the logic applied by self-actualization guru Rhonda Byrnes in her bestseller *The Secret*, where positive thinking is presented as the direct road to promotions, better salaries, increasing wealth and "the good life" in general. The wrapping of the individual self-actualizing consumer logic in Pentecostalism may be ascribed to the "incurably religious African" thesis, but its religious wrapping does not alter the fact that Pentecostalism represents a particular kind of economic imperialism and proposes a "significant interaction between religion and consumption" (Bonsu and Belk 2010: 321). An ideology of personal happiness and accomplishment, we might add.

Conclusion

The present chapter has argued for a global diffusion of a particular socio-cultural figure of the self originating in Western modernity and its therapeutic ethos, but in itself formed by processes of global exchanges between East and West (Campbell 2007). As underlined initially, it is not the only possible perspective on the global(izing) self. However, given that the premises for the chapter are given by the title of the volume – identity and consumption – we consider it one of the most obvious and proliferating. To paraphrase Fuat Firat, a consumer identity is identity consumed, and this is nowhere more obvious globally than in the explosion of consumption of various self-actualizing or self-help technologies. The reinforcement of consumption of and as self-actualization seems to follow wherever consumer culture is on the rise, albeit with differences in its local political, social, and spiritual instantiations.

The rise of the self-actualizing consumer and the industries catering to him/her carries with it its own particular models of governance and is fundamentally inscribed in an individualistic and emancipative ideology of the primacy of the personal self as the ultimate authority on his/her own life. The lure of the movement is its great promise of (consumer) empowerment and its logical consequence a promotion of a hyper-responsible self in a fundamentally neoliberal societal mode (Rimke 2000). The downside to this, however, is the relative negation of the influence of social structures of repression and inequality, oftentimes resulting in the continued deprivation of poor and subaltern consumers and in generating increasing existential anxieties based on the ephemeral formulation of the end goal (when can I be sure that my self is actually actualized?) (Brinkmann 2005), and so the promise of individual autonomy through self-actualization is highly dubious (Rimke 2000). Consequently, we find this discussion to be crucial in a context of elaborating the relationship between identity and consumption.

Further reading

Bauman, Z. (2004) *Identity*. Cambridge: Polity Press. (Postmodern conditions for identity under scrutiny.)

Dumont, L. (1991) *Essays on Individualism*. Chicago, IL: University of Chicago Press. (A set of anthropological demonstrations that the "individual" is not a natural category.)

Furedi, Frank (2004) *Therapy Culture*. London: Routledge. (A sociological discussion of the contemporary therapeutic ethos.)

Illouz, E. (2008) *Saving the Modern Soul. Therapy, Emotions, and the Culture of Self Help*. Berkeley, CA: University of California Press. (Sociological discussion of the self-help culture and industry.)

Lasch, C. (1979) *The Culture of Narcissism*. New York: Warner. (A now classical discussion of the narcissistic personality and its shallowness.)

References

Appadurai, A. (1990) "Disjuncture and Difference in the Global Cultural Economy." In M. Featherstone (ed.), *Global Culture: Nationalism, Globalization and Modernity*. London: Sage, pp. 295–310.

Arnould, E.J. and Price, L. (2000) "Authenticating Acts and Authoritative Performances." In S. Ratneshwar, D.G. Mick, and C. Huffman (eds), *The Why of Consumption*. London: Routledge, pp. 140–63.

Askegaard, S. and Eckhardt, G.M. (2012) "Glocal Yoga: Re-Appropriation in the Indian Consumptionscape." *Marketing Theory* 12: 45–60.

Bauman, Z. (2004) *Identity*. Cambridge: Polity Press.

Beck, U. and Beck-Gernsheim, E. (2002) *Individualization*. London: Sage.

Bonsu, S.K. and Belk, R.W. (2010) "Marketing a New African God: Pentecostalism and Material Salvation in Ghana." *International Journal of Nonprofit and Voluntary Sector Marketing* 15: 305–23.

Brinkmann, S. (2005) "Selvrealiseringens etik." In S. Brinkmann and C. Eriksen (eds), *Selvrealisering – kritiske diskussioner af en grænseløs udviklingskultur*. Århus: Klim, pp. 41–64.

Campbell, C. (2007) *The Easternization of the West*. Boulder, CO: Paradigm Publishers.

Chan, C.S.(2004) "The Falun Gong in China: A Sociological Perspective." *The China Quarterly* 179: 665–83.

Dumont, L. (1980) *Homo Hierarchicus*. Chicago, IL: University of Chicago Press.

Foucault, Michel (1990 [1976]) *The History of Sexuality. An Introduction, Volume 1*. New York: Vintage Books.

Furedi, F. (2004) *Therapy Culture*. London: Routledge.

Giddens, A. (1991) *Modernity and Self-Identity*. Stanford, CA: Stanford University Press.

Gil, R.M. and Vazquez, C.I. (1996) *The Maria Paradox: How Latinas Can Merge Old World Traditions With New World Self-Esteem*. East Rutherford, NJ: Putnam.

Illouz, E. (2008) *Saving the Modern Soul. Therapy, Emotions, and the Culture of Self Help*. Berkeley, CA: University of California Press.

Jafari, A. and Goulding, C. (2012) "Globalization, Reflexivity and the Project of the Self: A Virtual Intercultural Learning Process." *Consumption, Markets & Culture.*

Kjeldgaard, D. and Askegaard, S. (2006) "The Globalization of Youth Culture: The Global Youth Segment as Structures of Common Difference." *Journal of Consumer Research* 22: 231–47.

Kjeldgaard, D. and Nielsen, K. (2010) "Global Gender Identities in Market Places of Transition. Marianismo and the Consumption of the Telenovela Rebelde." *Marketing Theory* 10: 29–44.

Lasch, C. (1979) *The Culture of Narcissism*. New York: Warner.

Lovelock, J.E. (1979) *Gaia*. Oxford: Oxford University Press.

Lury, C. (2011) *Consumer Culture*. Second edition. Cambridge: Polity Press.

Maslow, A. (1954) *Motivation and Personality*. New York: Harper & Row.

Nevis, E.C. (1983) "Using an American Perspective in Understanding Another Culture: Toward a Hierarchy of Needs for the People's Republic of China." *Journal of Applied Behavioral Science* 19: 249–64.

Nietzsche, F. (2005 [1888]) *Ecce Homo. How One becomes What One Is*. London: Penguin.

Rimke, H.M. (2000) "Governing Citizens Through Self-Help Literature." *Cultural Studies* 14: 61–78.

Rindfleish, J. (2005) "Consuming the Self: New Age Spirituality as 'Social Product' in Consumer Society." *Consumption, Markets and Culture* 8: 343–60.

Rogers, C. (1961) *On Becoming a Person*. Boston, MA: Houghton Mifflin.

Smith, R. (1997) *The Norton History of Human Sciences*. New York: W.W. Norton.

Thompson, C.J. (2004) "Marketplace Mythology and the Discourse of Power." *Journal of Consumer Research* 31: 162–80.

Thompson, C.J. and Tambyah, S.K. (1999) "Trying to Be Cosmopolitan." *Journal of Consumer Research* 26: 214–41.

Tse, D.K., Belk, R.W., and Zhou, N. (1989) "Becoming a Consumer Society: A Longitudinal and Cross-Cultural Content Analysis of Print Ads from Hong Kong, the People's Republic of China and Taiwan." *Journal of Consumer Research* 15: 457–72.

Varman, R. and Belk, R.W. (2008) "Weaving a Web: Subaltern Consumers, Rising Consumer Culture, and Television." *Marketing Theory* 8: 227–52.

Wattanasuwan, K. and Elliott, R. (1999) "The Buddhist Self and Symbolic Consumption: The Consumption Experience of the Teenage Dhammakaya Buddhists in Thailand." In *Advances in Consumer Research* 26. Provo, UT: Association of Consumer Research, pp. 150–5.

Wei, R. and Pan, Z. (1999) "Mass Media and Consumerist Values in the People's Republic of China." *International Journal of Public Opinion Research* 11: 75–96.

35
CONSTRUCTING "MASCULINE" IDENTITIES
Consuming "feminine" practices

Deirdre Duffy

This chapter explores how young men negotiate the matriarchal domain of fashion consumption and self-presentation, observing techniques adopted to navigate this "feminine" world and construct their own masculine identities.

The research adopts poststructuralist, postmodern thought to consider the sociology of men, placing emphasis on how men's sense of identity is "validated through dominant discursive practices of self, and how this identity work connects with (gender) power and resistance" (Whitehead and Barrett 2001: 15). In particular, the works of social theorist Michel Foucault are drawn upon to consider the discursive subject of masculinity and self-identity.

Consumption, gender and identity

The act of consumption as a social activity, and particularly the consumption of fashion in Western culture has long been associated with women and femininity (Delhaye 2006). This longstanding dominance of women in self-styling has rendered men's interest in fashion and appearance "suspect of effeminacy or, even worse, of homosexuality" (Rinallo 2007).

Reported shifts in stringently prescribed gender roles and culturally defined behavioral norms (An and Kim 2007), suggests the opening up of the fashion sphere to the participation of mankind is imaginably a pre-conclusion. Nonetheless such shifts, if inevitable, are gradual and complex.

Regarding fashion consumption, one's mode of dress forms an integral link between individual identity and the body, facilitating one's performance of identity (Entwistle 2000). Thus dress can be considered a "visual metaphor for identity" (Davis 1992: 25). However the presentation of self is subject to social pressure, with individuals managing their dress in rather more mundane and routine ways (Entwistle 2001), making dress choices within the confines of specific social contexts (Tseëlon 1997) rather than in the sole interest of self-expression.

More specifically, fashion has been charged as playing a crucial role in policing the boundaries of sexual difference (Entwistle 2001: 39). Gender roles are prescribed by Connell as a set of culturally defined behavioral norms associated with males and females respectively, in a given social group (Connell 1987: 165). Understood as such, a role is essentially performative whereby one learns how to play a masculine or feminine role, one learns what is acceptable and what is not, and one learns how one should think, behave and evaluate oneself and others in a gendered manner. Butler (1990) proposes that it is the repetitive act of the performance that produces gender and gives the impression of it being something constant, something that individuals possess. Wilson targets the fashion magazine in particular as being "obsessed with gender," whereby styles of dress are so clearly gendered thus facilitating this repetitious production of gender (Wilson 1985: 117).

In a similar vein, Whitehead (2002: 33) criticizes the way the sociology of masculinity has represented masculinity and femininity as universal truths – what Connell terms "gender order." Gender ordering has been labeled "patriarchy" by Women's Liberation whereby woman is subordinate to the dominant man (Connell 2005: 74). This positioning of men versus women places them within a political arena. Men as a gender class within the patriarchal system are privileged with power and prestige over their subordinate female counterpart.

Traditionally, in order to understand masculinity it was located in the wider field of gender relations, or rather in relation to femininity. However, contemporary thought seeks a more plural model of power relations. Nixon contends it is more useful to shift away from the opposing male dominant/female subordinate dichotomy toward a model that allows for multiple lines of power, positioning varying masculinities and femininities in relation to each other at different times. He maintains that patriarchal hierarchy is lacking when it comes to considering power relations between different masculinities, and so his key thinking behind this re-conceptualization is that it "allows us to consider dominant, subordinate and oppositional forms of masculinity" (Nixon 1997: 300).

In relation to fashion, while Entwistle identifies challenges to the status quo, to include cross-dressing and "gender-bending," she concludes that although the regime of representations of masculinity and femininity are certainly broadening, they are "nonetheless resolutely gendered and fashion continues to play on gender, even while it periodically deconstructs it" (Entwistle 2000: 180).

Introducing "the consumptionisto"

Five young Irish men between 22 and 27 years of age were selected for this research and interviewed based on their active interest in the discursive regime of self-presentation. This includes practices of "dress code, language, phraseology, physique, body posture, hair-style [and] general grooming" (Whitehead 2008: 236). Following consideration of the "maleness" of the group, and the predominance of the act of consumption in the formulation and performance of self-identity (Slater 1997), I coin the phrase "consumptionisto" to describe these young men.

Taking a constructionist approach, each interview text is read with the awareness that the interview is operating within a certain discourse or "a certain network of practices of power and constraining institutions" (Foucault 1988: 17). Consequently, rather than seeking to uncover an informant's "essential self," instead a narrative analysis approach is interested in how the speaker selects, organizes, connects and evaluates events they deem meaningful for the social interaction of an interview (Riessman 2008: 3). The respondent is constructing their identities through storytelling: "Identities are narratives, stories people tell themselves and others about who they are (and who they are not)" (Yuval-Davis 2006: 202). These narratives, when taken as social artifact, can reveal much about the society and culture within which young men exist.

Furthermore, Foucault was concerned with how power produces discourses of "truth," often as a consequence of multiple forms of constraint policing "what may and may not be uttered" (DeAngelis 2008: 121). The following research considers Foucault's assertion to explore how young men negotiate constructing their identity through discursive practices of fashion consumption and self-presentation.

The matriarch's domain

As discussed, within traditional, patriarchal society, the binary of "masculine" and "feminine" is omnipresent, whereby men are repeatedly given privilege in various cultural settings over subordinated women (Connell 2005). However, while much literature on power documents the patriarchal male as the dominant discourse, and the feminine matriarch as the counter discourse, one exception to this "rule" has been alluded to: consumption culture and fashion, which have for some time reigned as "feminine domains *par excellence*" (Delhaye 2006: 88, original emphasis). So in discussing the performances and practices of the consumptionistos, I take as a starting point an inverted perspective of the commonplace binary logic – that men's existence within the field of consumption is as subordinate to the privileged female in this particular cultural setting. This position is explored, extended and challenged later. Contesting feminist Simone de Beauvoir's (1974) positioning of women as the unnatural pole that requires an explanation because it departs from the "norm," this research takes into account the site of exploration, i.e. consumption and self-presentation, and thus allows for the positioning of men (and not uniformly women) as the less-privileged "other" in this particular domain.

To take a positive rather than oppressive stance on workings of power, let us consider what Foucault terms "reverse" discourse. That is, by fact of a dominant discourse existing, it allows for a counter-discourse to come about – the dominant discourse in time (unwittingly) reproduces rather than eradicates the subordinate (Foucault 1978: 101–2). Applied to the context of the traditionally feminine field of consumption/fashion, and considering the productive workings of power relations, this logic infers the male, rather than being annihilated in this domain, can actually be rejuvenated by the dominant feminine. The fashionable male consumer can come into existence by virtue of the fashionable female existing. The subordinate takes the language of the dominant and comes to legitimate or "naturalize" themselves through using their categories of existence (Foucault 1984: 101).

In terms of men appropriating once feminine grooming practices, consumptionisto Sean wonderfully captures this gradual "trickling-down" process in a story recollected from high school days. He remembers buying GHD hair straighteners when they were primarily marketed to women. He transformed his trademark curly hair to a sleek, straight style. At school he got stick from the lads; however, he believes his pioneering endeavor eventually led to other guys following suit:

SEAN: … it sounds kind of big-headed but I really think I was the first one in my school, absolutely for definite, because no one did it before that and then, as you can see now, like rugby players, guys, they do it all the time, and then I saw it trickling down in school, guys were coming and they had straight hair and they were like, "Oh yeah, I got that straightener" and I was like, "Oh really, did you?" And these were the same guys that were giving me stick, you know, a year ago … so it was kind of the starting of metrosexual kind of beginnings I suppose.

Just as Brickell argued for emerging fashion trends as opening up spaces and providing "linguistic resources" for women through which "new understandings of themselves and their lives" could come about (Brickell 2002: 264), in a similar vein, men can negotiate the available resources in consumption culture, blending them with their own living experiences, to create new understandings of themselves.

This concept of men borrowing from the dominant discursive practices of women in order to consider new fashionable possibilities for themselves can be evidenced in conversations with the consumptionisto group. They consult various "female" domains to source fashion advice. Sean and Patrick follow women's fashion blogs and magazines as they find them more "fashion-forward," stating these trends only "drip-feed" into men's fashion eventually in a diluted manner. Meanwhile Joe prefers purchasing ladies' apparel, as he favors "tight clothing."

While the emergence of the "new man" in the consumption field is well documented (see Edwards 2006; Mort 1996; Nixon 1996), it is the merging of these male and female spheres (Boni 2002), or "blurring of the traditional gender dichotomy" (Whitehead 2008: 236), and indeed men's negotiation of this traditionally matriarchal arena in contemporary society, that is of interest here.

So from here on in, a Foucauldian perspective of power relations is adopted. This alternative viewpoint allows one to consider power as circulating the social web with both positive and negative forces, the process of which produces privileged and subordinated discourses and knowledge (Whitehead and Barrett 2001: 17), allowing a shift away from the gender dichotomy and opening up for consideration the multiple possibilities of masculinity (Nixon 1997: 300).

Techniques in negotiating the matriarch's domain: the arts

Foucault ascribes "technologies of the self" as techniques "which permit individuals to effect by their own means or with the help of others a certain number of operations on their own bodies … to transform themselves … " (Foucault 1988: 18). This mode of thought acknowledges the individual as a work in progress, so to speak. It accepts the individual considers themselves "flawed, inadequate or at least incomplete"; however, there are "appropriate tools, practices and experts" available to solve the "problem of self-production" (Smith Maguire and Stanway 2008: 65). Not least, the act of consumption is one such technique the individual can avail of in their self-project, enabling "the construction and expression of identity" (ibid.: 66). Certainly the consumptionistos referred to multiple self-enhancement techniques consumed, to include hair straightening, eyebrow plucking, chest waxing, manicures and fake tanning, to name but a few.

While some consider identity and self-production as individual endeavors and responsibilities, a by-product of this individualistic era of reflexive modernity (Giddens 1991; Shilling 1993), it is inconceivable that the individual can detach themselves from their lived existence in society, and make "pure" individual decisions. So it is the individual male-as-consumer, existent within his own social surroundings, or interpretive community, which is of salience to this theme. Certainly Thompson and Haytko would propose, rather than the individual operating within a social vacuum, consumers do "appropriate (i.e. adapt, combine and transform) culturally shared fashion discourses to fit the circumstances of their immediate social settings and their sense of personal history, interests, and life goals" (Thompson and Haytko 1997: 18). However, individuals do this in an active manner, "negotiating, reformulating and rejecting prescribed meanings and uses [of commodities] through, for example, tactics, bricolage and symbolic creativity" (Smith Maguire and Stanway 2008: 67).

The following extract exemplifies how Joe negotiates his social surroundings and takes "cues" from external influences:

JOE: … I used to wear a V-neck T-shirt but had like, quite a generously hairy chest and I really felt self-conscious about it, but I never had the, I suppose, I just didn't think it was socially acceptable to get rid of my chest hair … My brother last year moved from Holland and he, like, he goes to the gym every day ... and he started shaving his chest because everybody did it over in Holland and once he did it, I felt like I could do it. He is my younger brother, he is like five years younger than me, and I was taking cues on it from my brother. But anyway, so I did that, and I was delighted.

So while the discursive practice of consumption provides a means through which individuals can come to create their selves, just as with any discourse, it also suggests very strongly "what can and cannot be spoken at a given time or in a given cultural setting" (Whitehead and Barrett 2001: 21). In particular, one's gender mediates ways in which consumption is accessed and practiced (Scanlon 2000). This highlights how gendered norms circulating society can restrain participants by regulating "the appropriateness and exchange value of self-attention and self-presentation" (Smith Maguire and Stanway 2008: 68). It is this insidious policing of gender performance which the consumptionistos must negotiate when accessing the feminine realms of self-presentation.

Coincidentally, one technique, unanimously adopted by all respondents, was the use of music and the arts to act as a gateway into the creative fashion arena. This linkage has historic founding in popular culture, with Delhaye recording analogies between fashion and the arts in women's fashion magazines in the late 19th century (Delhaye 2006). The quest for "the authentic and expressive individual" (Delhaye 2006: 108), proposed to stem from Romantic idealism, continues to percolate consumer society, with consumer goods the "tools in self-authentication" (Smith Maguire and Stanway 2008: 73).

While the consumptionistos were sourced solely based on self-presentation practices, it emerged four of these men are highly involved in various music scenes. Within the first minutes of each interview respondents had aligned their interest in fashion and own "individual" style, with their musical tastes, proffering various musicians as sources of fashion inspiration. This immediate alignment of themselves, and their interest in fashion, through the appropriation of music can be seen as techniques adapted to recontextualize their appreciation of fashion away from any feminine domain and into a context wherein it is more socially acceptable for men to engage in self-expressive practices – music. Through this medium, they more confidently express their own style, acting as a bricoleur, borrowing from their musical role models, in describing their fashion. In particular, Joe's "self-style" clearly borrows from musical genres, but also exemplifies the exhaustive minefield negotiated to arrive at the correct version of "individual" style.

JOE: I guess it's like indie-rock band kind of style ... it would be an aspect of like, hipster, the sort of much frowned-upon hipster in London, singing with the loafers with no socks and like, sort of rolled-up jeans, just very tight-fitting and like, elements of vintage ... you have to find a middle ground between looking like you're trying to be too cool and then not caring at all.

So these men can access the traditionally feminine domain of fashion through appropriating cultural resources more familiar to them, such as music, and by so doing, involve themselves more comfortably in the discursive practice of fashion and self-presentation.

However, men can also adapt "self-construction" strategies, as we shall see, which can be construed as resistance to the feminine.

Techniques in negotiating the matriarch's domain: the art of irony

The proliferation of new lad magazines in the 1990s have been identified as promulgating "new" forms of masculinity through the adoption of what is termed "new sexism" discourses (Benwell

2007). The emergence of the "sexist and regressive new lad" evidenced in lad magazine literature is proposed by some as a backlash to the "politically sensitive and feminist new man" of the preceding decade, instigating a return to a more "natural" gender order emphasizing "biological essentialism and polarized difference" (Benwell 2004: 6). Feminist critique argues that such media constructions of masculinity are a cynical recycling of patriarchy (Chapman 1988).

Benwell identifies one particular "new sexism" device – the use of irony, as strategically adapted in men's publications to legitimize their participation in the "feminized" realm of consumption (Benwell 2007: 540). Viewed from this arguably pessimistic stance, the use of ironic discourse can be considered a technique in the field of consumption wherein males can reconfigure meanings of hegemonic masculinity so as to engage in "feminine" practices, all the while facilitating their dominant patriarchal position.

Meanwhile a less cynical view of irony in men's magazines considers the ambiguous space it opens up, enabling readers "to explore mediated forms of masculinity in a period of social change" (Jackson *et al.* 2001: 104). Taking the latter approach, the use of irony as a discursive resource could be seen as constructive, enabling men to consider themselves in multiple new and creative ways.

Let us consider tactical techniques of irony adapted by the consumptionistos, and explore the possibilities and restrictions facilitated by such linguistic resources.

Consumptionistos Brian and Patrick are public figures in Irish media. They have forged successful careers, Brian both in national sport and a music career, and Patrick in national sport. While both men have excelled in the stereotypically masculine realm of male team sports, rugby and football, they do not express stereotypical habits such as hypermasculinity often associated with such team sports (Messner 1990). Instead they challenge the status quo by embracing "feminine" practices of fashion and grooming. Their contradiction to the norm presents an opportunity to open up the realms of possibilities for the male stereotype and potentially dissolve gendered codes of practice. These young men can be seen as innovators in Irish grooming and dress practices through their "unique" self-presentations circulating the Irish media. However, beyond self-presentation, what is more particular to this theme is the mode of narrative these men adapt to communicate with other men. That is, through the linguistic art of irony.

As discussed, discourses can subtly suggest what may or may not be uttered in certain social settings. The adaptation of irony by these young spokespersons in their discussions of fashion is explored to understand this satirical strategy and whether it serves to facilitate new modes of being for young men, or whether it merely keeps them locked, perhaps unwittingly, into the "lad's mag" trope accused of sustaining the gender binary logic.

In particular, Brian is vocal in holding the national TV broadcaster, RTÉ, culpable in maintaining fashion in the feminine realm, and as such, sustaining the gender binary logic:

BRIAN: 'cos the media don't get behind it [men's fashion] … I mean RTÉ, like Off The Rails … That is so women-orientated … There's nothing about men any time …

Brian's frustration at the lack of media is palpable, whereby the potential male fashion consumer is subjugated in this female-dominant sphere. He articulates anxieties men experience negotiating feminine spaces, including the risk of emasculation or being accused of homosexuality. After criticizing the gendered norms upheld by RTÉ programming, Brian proceeds to use the same binary logic to hypothesize a "liberating" new fashion program for men, incorporating "sexist" strategies toward women, in opposition to the current RTÉ fashion program:

BRIAN: To do a fashion program about men, you've got to be careful. You don't want men to think anyone that sees them watching it think they're fucking woofters, you've got to make it masculine ... Look at GQ magazine. I have no problem reading that. That's purely at men, fashion for men, and ... 'cos it's funny and it's a little bit, it pulls the piss out of women a little bit in it in terms of, which is fine because women fucking absolutely eat us alive too, like, I mean, don't, Jesus Christ, every man who has seen Loose Women, like, if that was the other way around and there was four men on the panel, we'd be ... but I mean, GQ is, we'll say sexist, it kind of pulls the piss a little. You need something like that ...

Brian's proposal is reminiscent of Whitehead's (2002) discussion of gender, whereby futile issues of power struggles recur between the sexes in the pretext of a search for equality. In particular, his justification of sexism, by retorting that ITV broadcast *Loose Women* [a UK show hosted by women for a female audience, which can be derogatory of men], wonderfully captures exactly the "type" of liberation against which Foucault warns – a reversal of power positions. Rather, Foucault encourages "practices of freedom" – that is, practices that will in turn shape new attitudes and new behaviors, creating new spaces for individuals.

As long as Brian's proposal for a new program is considered in opposition to female programming, it can be considered redundant in opening up new modes of being. However, when Brian then describes his proposed fashion program for an Irish male audience, his narrative may be considered from a less sinister position. In this instance he contemplates a solely male domain, describing how a male voice could reach a male audience, to discuss men's fashion. To achieve this, he proposes techniques of ironic discourse:

BRIAN: You need someone like ... a lad, someone like Baz [Irish TV personality] who has no clue about fashion, bring him in, coax him and like actually pull the piss out of how little about fashion he [knows], but bring in experts and make it, like, almost like he's being lectured in every series ... pull the piss out of yourself a little, rather than make it really obvious. That's what men do ... It's, 'cos like, men need to feel masculine, and to watch Off The Rails is not a masculine thing to do, whatever way you look at it.

The omnipresent power of discourse, in this case gendered discourse, becomes clear once again as we see how even a fashion-forward consumptionisto still has a consciousness of what is and is not acceptable in Irish social settings.

Of note, Irish society, culture and identity in a holistic and historical sense, was reproached by the consumptionistos as being ultimately responsible for Irish men's lack of fashion and style. They feel Irish men are culturally "afraid to look good" and so their style is "very stunted." In considering such suppressive social surroundings that limit possibilities of self-expression, the acquisition of satire to attempt to challenge these boundaries seems less threatening, and perhaps a necessary tool, if it succeeds in opening up the creative realm of fashion and grooming to the male domain.

Bridging the arch between matri and patri

The traditional gender dichotomy was adapted as a starting point to consider discourse; however, its reducing properties became evident when considering gender power relations. Moving away from the binary logic instead allows for multiple possibilities to emerge, challenging the gendered norms circulating and sometimes restricting society. Whilst shifts in the representations of gendered male bodies circulate the mass media, such shifts are not a foregone conclusion, but are gradual and complex – as consumptionisto Sean suggests, it is a "trickling-down" process.

Within this process, subordinates can take the language of the dominant to legitimate their self. However, this is negotiated in conjunction with their own living experiences and their adaptation of techniques through which they can come to know and create their self-identity. In this case, the young men adapted strategic techniques from the arts, and the art of irony to renegotiate social relationships and consider new meanings and behaviors for themselves in the traditionally feminized sphere of consumption and self-presentation.

References

An, D. and Kim, S. (2007) "Relating Hofstede's Masculinity Dimension to Gender Role Portrayals in Advertising: A Cross-cultural Comparison of Web Advertisements." *International Marketing Review* 24(2): 181–207.

Benwell, B. (2004) "Ironic Discourse: Evasive Masculinity in Men's Lifestyle Magazines." *Men and Masculinities* 7(1): 3–21.

——(2007) "Reader's Responses to the Use of Irony in Men's Magazines." *Journalism Studies* 8(4): 539–49.

Boni, F. (2002) "Framing Media Masculinities: Men's Lifestyle Magazines and the Biopolitics of the Male Body." *European Journal of Communication* 17(4): 465–78.

Brickell, C. (2002) "Through the (New) Looking Glass: Gendered Bodies, Fashion and Resistance in Postwar." *Journal of Consumer Culture* 2(2): 241–69.

Butler, J. (1990) *Gender Trouble: Feminism and the Subversion of Identity*. New York: Routledge.

Chapman, R. (1988) "The Great Pretender: Variations on the New Man Theme." In R. Chapman and J. Rutherford (eds), *Male Order: Unwrapping Masculinity*. London: Lawrence and Wishart.

Connell, R.W. (1987) *Gender and Power: Society, the Person and Sexual Politics*. Palo Alto, CA: Stanford University Press.

——(2005) *Masculinities*. Cambridge: Polity Press.

Davis, F. (1992) *Fashion, Culture, and Identity*. Chicago, IL: The University of Chicago Press.

DeAngelis, P. (2008) "C.G. Prado, Searle and Foucault on Truth (Cambridge: Cambridge University Press, 2006)." *Foucault Studies* (5): 118–22.

de Beauvoir, S. (1974) *The Second Sex*. New York: Vintage.

Delhaye, C. (2006) "The Development of Consumption Culture and the Individualization of Female Identity." *Journal of Consumer Culture* 6(1): 87–115.

Edwards, T. (2006) *Cultures of Masculinity*. London: Routledge.

Entwistle, J. (2000) *The Fashioned Body*. Cambridge: Polity Press.

——(2001) "The Dressed Body." In J. Entwistle and E. Wilson (eds), *Body Dressing*. Oxford: Berg, pp. 33–58.

Foucault, M. (1978) *The History of Sexuality, Volume 1: An Introduction*. London: Penguin Books Ltd.

——(1988) "Technologies of the Self." In L.H. Martin, H. Gutman, and P.H. Hutton (eds), *Technologies of the Self: A Seminar with Michel Foucault*. Amherst, MA: The University of Massachusetts Press, pp. 16–49.

Giddens, A. (1991) *Modernity and Self-Identity: Self and Society in the Late Modern Age*. Cambridge: Polity Press.

Jackson, P., Stevenson, N., *et al.* (2001) *Making Sense of Men's Magazines*. Cambridge: Polity Press.

Messner, M. (1990) "When Bodies are Weapons: Masculinity and Violence in Sport." *International Review for the Sociology of Sport* 25(3): 203–18.

Mort, F. (1996) *Cultures of Consumption: Masculinities and Social Space in Late Twentieth-Century Britain*. London: Routledge.

Nixon, S. (1996) *Hard Looks; Masculinities, Spectatorship & Contemporary Consumption*. London: Routledge.

——(1997) "Exhibiting Masculinity." In S. Hall (ed.), *Representation: Cultural Representations and Signifying Practices*. London: Sage Publications, pp. 291–336.

Riessman, C. Kohler (2008) *Narrative Methods for the Human Sciences*. Los Angeles, CA: Sage Publications.

Rinallo, D. (2007) "Metro/Fashion/Tribes of Men: Negotiating the Boundaries of Men's Legitimate Consumption." In B. Cova, R. Kozinets and A. Shankar (eds), *Consumer Tribes: Theory, Practice, and Prospects*. Oxford: Elsevier/Butterworth-Heinemann, pp. 76–92.

Scanlon, J. (ed.) (2000) *The Gender and Consumer Culture Reader*. New York: New York University Press.

Shilling, C. (1993) *The Body and Social Theory*. London: Sage.

Slater, D. (1997) *Consumer Culture & Modernity*. Cambridge: Polity Press.

Smith Maguire, J. and Stanway, K. (2008) "Looking Good: Consumption and the Problems of Self-production." *European Journal of Cultural Studies* 11(1): 63–81.

Thompson, C.J. and Haytko, D.L. (1997) "Speaking of Fashion: Consumers' Uses of Fashion Discourses and the Appropriation of Countervailing Cultural Meanings." *Journal of Consumer Research* 24: 15–42.

Tseëlon, E. (1997) *The Masque of Femininity*. Cambridge: Polity Press.

Whitehead, S.M. (2002) *Men and Masculinities*. Cambridge: Polity Press.
——(2008) "Metrosexuality! Cameron, Brown and the Politics of 'New Masculinity'." *Public Policy Research* 14(4): 234–39.
Whitehead, S.M. and Barrett, F.J. (2001) *The Masculinities Reader*. Cambridge: Polity Press.
Wilson, E. (1985) *Adorned in Dreams: Fashion and Modernity*. London: Virago.
Yuval-Davis, N. (2006) "Belonging and the Politics of Belonging." *Patterns of Prejudice* 40(3): 197–214.

IV

Marketing and the self

IV.I

Brands and self-identity

36

BRAND RELATIONSHIPS AND SELF

Vanitha Swaminathan and Alokparna (Sonia) Basu Monga

Consumers often purchase products and brands in symbolic ways in order to express their identities. The idea that possessions often constitute the "extended self" has been described extensively in the literature (e.g. Belk 1988; Kleine *et al.* 1995; Reed 2004). Marketers often link aspects of brands with a target consumer's identity to increase consumers' favorable perceptions of a brand and to strengthen consumers' loyalties toward a brand. Brands can both reflect the consumers' identities and help shape these identities.

The symbolic use of brands by consumers has been an important theme in the literature. Researchers have characterized the interactions between brands and consumers using an interpersonal relationship metaphor (e.g. Fournier 1998; Aggarwal and Law 2005). Further, research has also suggested that relationships with brands (i.e. self-concept connection) can vary based on consumers' identity goals, for example a desire for self-differentiation versus belongingness. For instance, Escalas and Bettman (2005) suggest that brands consistent with one's in-group enhance self-brand connections for consumers; further, Escalas and Bettman (2005) argue that brands that are consistent with an out-group have a greater negative impact on independent (versus interdependent) consumers.

Although identity theory within consumer behavior has tended to view identity as a unidimensional construct or has tended to focus on one or two levels (e.g. the individual or collective identity), the social psychology literature has recently demonstrated that identity comprises at least three levels: individual, relational and collective. How do brands help reflect consumers' identities at these three levels? In turn, how do consumers' own individual, relational and collective identities influence their choice of brand names? What are the moderators of brand preferences at these varying levels? Building on this three-part conceptualization of an individual's identity, we examine how brand names can affirm individual, relational and collective identities. We also synthesize the literature to examine the role of various moderators (e.g. culture, type of brand) in the use of brands by consumers for identity self-expression. We conclude by highlighting areas for future research.

Levels of self-representation and consumer-brand relationships

Building on cross-cultural perspectives (Markus and Kitayama 1991), as well as recent research on social identities which argue that belongingness to social groups is a fundamental human motivation (Baumeister and Leary 1995). Brewer and Gardner (1996) describe the extent to which individuals define themselves in terms of their unique self (i.e. individual self) or in terms of their relationships to close others (i.e. interpersonal or relational self) as well as larger social groups (i.e. collective self). The *unique or individual self* is composed of those aspects of an individual's identity that pertain to the self as distinct from others. The *relational self* is made up of intimate dyadic relationships with family members and close friends. Finally, the *collective self* is determined by assimilation to the in-groups. Both interpersonal and collective social identities are based on the perception of self as a part of a social category, the interpersonal self presupposes personal connections with close others whereas collective social identities do not presuppose personal relationships among group members. The next section reviews the literature on brand relationships and the individual self.

Brand relationships and the individual self

The development of self-brand connections

In order for self-brand connections to form, consumers must be aware of appropriate brand information (e.g. user imagery), they must have a self-concept (e.g. actual self), and they must engage in a comparison process to identify congruent brands (Chaplin and John 2005). Typically, among children, brand relationships tend to emerge in middle childhood and adolescence. Older children think about the brand in a way (e.g. in terms of group membership, or personalities) that allows them to form linkages between the brand and the self concept (Chaplin and John 2005). Interestingly, not all consumers are interested in incorporating brands into the self-concept and differences in propensity to do so are also known as brand engagement in the self-concept (BESC) (Sprott *et al.* 2009). Some consumers with strong brand relationships tightly couple the brand's performance to their own performance – also known as the "brand as self" conceptualization (Cheng *et al.* 2011). Because of this, consumers with strong brand relationships respond to brand failures as they do to personal failure – they experience a threat to the self-concept.

Brand personality and the consumer's personality

Brand personality and the consumer's personality strongly influence how brands are used for self-expression. Brand personality refers to the "set of human characteristics associated with a brand" (Aaker 1997: 347). For example, Hallmark and Coke are sincere brands, whereas Yahoo, Virgin, MTV are examples of exciting brands (Aaker *et al.* 2004). Aaker (1999) found that attitudes toward brands highly descriptive on a particular personality dimension (e.g. excitement – Benetton, CKOne) are more favorable for individuals who consider excitement to be central to their self-definition than those who do not. Further, attitude toward brands highly descriptive on a particular personality dimension (e.g. excitement – Benetton, CKOne) are more favorable when situational cues that promote that personality are salient (e.g. going to a hip club on a date). This research reveals that consumers' self-concepts are highly malleable and consumers appear to be self-expressing with different kinds of brands depending on what the situation demands of them.

More recently, Malär *et al.* (2011) examined whether brand personalities targeted at the actual self, versus the ideal self, would elicit stronger brand relationships. For example, most cosmetics companies try to target the consumers' ideal self-concept ("become more beautiful"), whereas the Unilever's Dove campaign has targeted the actual self-concept (by using models who are more average in appearance). Interestingly, Malär *et al.* (2011) found that brands that targeted the actual self, generated stronger brand relationships, an effect which was magnified when consumers were heavily involved with the product or when they were high in self-esteem. Presumably, this occurred because brands that targeted the actual self were perceived to be psychologically closer than brands that targeted the ideal self

More recently, researchers have investigated whether brand personalities actually change a consumer's self-perception in line with the brand's personality (Park and John 2010). They distinguish between entity theorists who believe that personal qualities of an individual are fixed and incremental theorists who believe that personal qualities are malleable. They find that entity theorists perceive themselves to be more good-looking, feminine and glamorous after using a Victoria's Secret shopping bag. In contrast, incremental theorists' self-perceptions did not change after using the bag. Apparently, entity theorists use brand experiences (e.g. Victoria's Secret shopping bag) as a signaling mechanism which leads to more positive self-perceptions (i.e. more feminine and glamorous).

Summary

According to Brewer and Gardner (1996), the personal self is the differentiated, individuated self-concept. It appears that consumers integrate brands into the individual self-concept (Sirgy 1982; Escalas and Bettman 2000), even at a very early age (Chaplin and John 2005). Doing so allows consumers to express themselves as unique individuals. Several factors can affect the formation of self-brand connections. First, the nature of the brand matters: brands that are congruent with the consumer are more likely to be integrated into the self-concept (Chaplin and John 2005). Second, the nature of the consumer matters: consumers who are high (vs. low) in BESC tend to have more (vs. few) brands connected to the self-concept. Consumers with high self-brand connections tightly couple the brand to the self-concept, such that they respond to brand failures as they would to personal failures (Cheng *et al.* 2011).

Brands allow consumers to be consistent across situations (Aaker 1999). Since personality traits are generally positive, expressing the self-concept through brands can make consumers feel more positive about themselves (Aaker 1999). Both of these needs increase self-esteem and help in self-presentation (Aaker 1999). Malär *et al.* (2011) showed that brands targeted at the actual self (rather than the aspiration self) elicited stronger brand relationships. Importantly, the findings also suggest that the notion of authenticity and "my true self" is particularly important to consumers in their brand relationships, and brands that allow consumers to express their true self are likely to be rewarded with strong attachments. Finally, Park and John (2010) showed that certain consumers use brands as a signaling mechanism and are more likely to change their own self-perceptions after using a brand. This provides direct evidence of how the individual self is shaped by brand usage.

Brand relationships and the relational self

The previous section highlights the role of brand relationships in influencing the individual self. We now shift our focus to the role of relational self in shaping brand relationships. There is considerable research in consumer behavior on how interpersonal relational selves impact the number and strength of brand relationships. An important theoretical perspective from inter-personal relationship theory that has been applied to a brand context is attachment theory. Attachment theory has its roots in the work of Bowlby (1969), who suggested that interactions with caregivers in early childhood form the foundation for systematic differences in relationships formed in later life. Attachment theory has identified two dimensions of attachment style based on the individuals' view of self and view of others, which are expected to influence the type of relationships in which they engage (Bartholomew and Horowitz 1991).

Following Bartholomew and Horowitz (1991), attachment theory focuses on classifying individuals based on two dimensions: anxiety and avoidance. The anxiety dimension refers to the extent a person's view of self is positive or negative, whereas the avoidance dimension is based on the extent to which one's view of others is positive or negative. These two dimensions of attachment theory have been shown to impact consumer-brand relationships as well. Thomson and Johnson (2006) investigated the role of attachment dimensions on relationships with brands. They find that because anxious people perceive their relationships as bad, they also view their relationships as inconsistent. People who registered high levels of avoidance reported a diminished experience of reciprocity as well as lower levels of satisfaction, commitment and involvement. Paulssen and Fournier (2007) have also looked at attachment in consumer-brand relationships. Specifically, they use attachment theory and longitudinal data regarding brand relationships with automotive service dealers to empirically derive *consumer* attachment. Their results regarding consumer attachment parallel those found in interpersonal relationship settings. In this way, the research by Paulssen and Fournier (2007), and Thomson and Johnson (2006) provide initial evidence that attachment theory can be applicable to a consumer-brand relationship context.

Attachment styles have also been shown to influence how consumers choose brands and how they react to transgressions involving brands (Swaminathan *et al.* 2009; Dommer *et al.* 2011). Swaminathan and colleagues examine the manner in which brand personality and attachment style differences systematically influence brand outcomes including brand attachment, purchase likelihood and brand choice (Swaminathan *et al.* 2009). Results show that anxiously attached individuals are more likely to be differentially influenced by brand personalities. Across a series of studies, they show that the level of avoidance predicts the types of brand personality that are most relevant to anxious individuals. Specifically, under conditions of high avoidance and high anxiety, individuals exhibit a preference for exciting brands; however, under conditions of low avoidance and high anxiety, individuals tend to prefer sincere brands. The differential preference for sincere (versus exciting) brand personality emerged in public consumption settings, when interpersonal relationship expectations were high, suggesting that brand personality was being used by anxious individuals as a signaling mechanism, to signal to potential relationship partners. Dommer *et al.* (2011) linked consumers' interpersonal attachment styles to their propensities to forgive a company following a product recall, as well as to their responses to recovery efforts. Their results demonstrated that avoidant users of a brand were more likely to have lower brand evaluations following a transgression incident, and forgiveness appeared to mediate these results. Park and colleagues (2010) extended our understanding of brand attachment further by describing differences between brand attachment and brand attitude, and focusing on separation distress, a key construct in the interpersonal relationships literature. Thus, it appears that various constructs such as attachment to brands and separation distress involving brands have many of the same properties as those described in the relationship context.

Brand relationships also share many of the same antecedents as those that have been shown to be important in the interpersonal relationships context. For example, personality traits such as self-monitoring have been shown to moderate individuals' propensities to engage in conspicuous consumption (Ratner and Kahn 2002). Self-construal has also been shown to moderate the extent to which consumers form relationships with brands that strengthen either unique self or collective self (Escalas and Bettman 2005; Swaminathan *et al.* 2007). Finally, as described previously, attachment style has also been shown to predict consumer-brand relationships (Swaminathan *et al.* 2009). We turn next to the collective self and the role it plays in shaping brand relationships.

Summary

Taken together, the findings regarding relational self appears to suggest that relational selves have an important impact as an antecedent to brand relationship formation. Additionally, relational selves moderate the types of brand relationships that consumers form. Individuals who are avoidant in their personal relationships appear to avoid brand relationships as well. In addition, those who are highly anxious in their interpersonal relationships appear to rely more on brand personality to convey a desired image to others. Priming interpersonal relationship constructs (e.g. communal or exchange) has an impact on subsequent choices made by consumers (Aggarwal and Law 2005; Aggarwal and Zhang 2006). Future research should examine other facets of interpersonal relationships and how they impact brand preferences.

Brand relationships and the collective self

Reference groups

A significant body of research shows the important role played by reference groups in shaping brand relationships and building consumers' identity (Escalas and Bettman 2005; White and Dahl 2007). Reference groups are defined as social groups that are important to the consumer and against which s/he compares himself or herself. For example, if a consumer considers herself to be rugged and adventurous and she is a member of a reference group that tends to use brands like Jeep and Patagonia, she may choose to drive Jeep or wear Patagonia clothing as a reflection of how rugged she is and thus form a strong brand relationship with Jeep and Patagonia. In fact, Escalas and Bettman (2005) find that students are more likely to form relationships when there is a strong usage association between the member reference group (e.g. athletes) and the brand (e.g. Nike), and consumers perceive a strong similarity between the membership group and their own self. Further, Escalas and Bettman (2005) find that brands that are consistent with an out-group are less likely to form self-brand connections than brands inconsistent with an out-group.

More recently, White and Dahl (2007) showed that products associated with a dissociative reference group tend to have a more negative effect on brand relationships than out-groups in general. For example, Canadians evaluated a pen more negatively when it was associated with a dissociative reference group (American pen) than when it was neutral (vintage pen) or associated with an out-group (Belgian pen) when their own identity was salient. Such dissociative influences stem from public self-image concerns (White and Dahl 2006) as well as private self-image concerns (White and Dahl 2007). Relatedly, Berger and Heath (2008) showed that consumers often diverge from others in order to avoid sending undesired identity signals to others. They found that undergraduates stopped wearing a particular wristband when members of the "geeky," academically focused dorm next door started wearing them. Thus, by selectively associating or dissociating with appropriate kinds of brand relationships, consumers appear to be building, enhancing and signaling their collective self-concept.

Self-construal and culture

Much research in social cognition shows that individuals in different cultures tend to vary in terms of their self-concepts (Markus and Kitayama 1991). Westerners tend to focus on the personal self and focus on unique personal traits and attributes (independent self-construal), whereas Easterners tend to focus on how the self is related to other people (interdependent self-construal).

When faced with negative information about a brand, self-construal determines the degree to which consumers rely on self-concept connection (the brand's contribution to one's identity and values) (Fournier 1998) versus country-of-origin connection (how the brand contributed to social identity) in making judgments about the brand (Swaminathan *et al.* 2007). When self-concept connection is high, consumers tend to undervalue the negative information, but this occurs more for independent self-construal. Apparently, an independent self-construal increases the impact of self-concept connection, since both are focused on the brand's contribution to building personal identity. Further, a brand country-of-origin connection also allows consumers to tolerate the negative information, but this tends to be stronger for an interdependent self-construal. An interdependent self-construal increases the salience of country-of-origin connection, since both are focused on using brands differentiating between in-group and out-group members. Thus, consumers with different kinds of self-construal appear to be focusing on different brand relationship dimensions (self-concept connection vs. country-of-origin) to bolster their thoughts about the brand in the face of negative publicity.

Relatedly, Monga and Lau-Gesk (2007) examine how self-complexity affects responses to co-brands that are composed of two parent brands with different personality dimensions (sophistication and excitement), versus those that are composed of parent brands with the same personality dimension (sophistication only or excitement only). When a more complex aspect of the self is activated (independent self for Caucasians; interdependent self for Hispanics), consumers prefer a co-brand exuding both sophistication and excitement. Presumably, activation of self-complexity leads consumers to perceive themselves as more complex and therefore they prefer the complex, dual personality co-brand over the single personality co-brand.

Summary

As suggested earlier, brand relationships can serve a social function by reflecting social connections to one's family, community or culture (Wallendorf and Arnould 1988; Kleine *et al.* 1995). For example, brands associated with an in-group are more likely to be incorporated into the self-concept (Escalas and Bettman 2005), whereas brands associated with a dissociative reference group are less likely to be incorporated into the self-concept (White and Dahl 2007; Berger and Heath 2008). Presumably consumers are signaling their association or dissociation with different social groups using their brand relationships. Further, consumers with different kinds of self-construal focus on different aspects of brand relationships in the face of negative information. Those with an interdependent self-construal focus on brand country-of-origin information whereas those with an independent self-construal focus on self-concept connection to bolster their thoughts about the brand. Monga and Lau-Gesk (2007) reveal that activating a more complex aspect of the self leads to self-expression with a more dual personality co-brand (exuding both sophistication and excitement). Thus, brand relationships can be used to project a certain image about the self to others.

Future research

There are a wide variety of research questions that could advance our understanding of self in brand relationships. Research in the area of culture suggests that consumers in Asian cultures tend to incorporate more inconsistency in their self-concepts than consumers in Western cultures (Spencer-Rodgers *et al.* 2010). This suggests the interesting possibility that the range of brand personalities used by Asian consumers to express themselves may indeed be far broader and include conflicting brand personalities than those used by Western consumers. Examining these effects would advance our understanding of self-expression in different cultures.

There is reason to believe that self-construals may affect how consumers respond to a transgression in a brand relationship. One of the important distinctions between the independent and interdependent self-construals is the desire for harmony in relationships (Markus and Kitayama 1991). This suggests the interesting possibility that in the face of a transgression (e.g. your brand accidentally deletes all of your personal pictures) (Aaker *et al.* 2004), those with an interdependent (vs. interdependent) self-construal may be more willing to engage in actions that promote harmony in the relationship, which may include forgiving the brand.

Although much research has examined how the content of the self-concept affects brand relationships, very little research addresses other structural properties of the self-concept. Self-concept clarity (SCC) is defined as the extent to which the contents of an individual's self-concept (e.g. perceived personality attributes) are clearly and confidently defined, internally consistent and temporally stable (Campbell *et al.* 1996). Following a self-threat (e.g. failure), hostility is particularly strong among those with low rather than high SCC (Stucke and Spore 2002). We know that consumers with high self-brand connection respond to negative brand information as they do to personal failure – they experience a self-threat and lower their self-esteem (Cheng *et al.* 2011). This raises the possibility that these effects are likely to be even stronger among consumers with low SCC. Such consumers are likely to be even more hostile when their favorite brands face negative publicity.

Although self-construal has received much attention within the realm of brand relationships, most studies have been focused on monocultural consumers. However, research shows that bicultural consumers are not only increasing across the globe, but that they tend to be different from monocultural consumers (Lau-Gesk 2003). Bicultural consumers have an equally developed independent and interdependent self and can access either independence or interdependence depending on cues embedded in the environment (Lau-Gesk 2003). Within biculturals, researchers have distinguished between alternators and integrators. Alternators temporally access only one cultural disposition as a way to cope with the contradiction that exists with being affiliated with two cultures. In contrast, integrators share and balance both cultural meaning systems within the same context (Lau-Gesk 2003). This suggests the interesting possibility that biculturals in general may have a greater variety of brands incorporated into the self-concept in order to relate to two different cultural selves (independence and interdependence). Importantly, integrators may use a similar set of brand relationships for self-expression regardless of context, whereas alternators may have different sets of brand relationships for self-expression depending on the context. Researching these ideas would give us a fuller understanding of the many ways in which brand relationships affect consumer behavior.

Further reading

Aaker, J.L. (1999) "The Malleable Self: The Role of Self-expression in Persuasion." *Journal of Marketing Research* 36: 45–57. (This paper provides the basis for understanding how individual attributes interact with personality of the brand to influence brand attitude favorability, and the moderating role of self-monitoring.)

Escalas, J.E. and Bettman, J.R. (2005) "Self-Construal, Reference Groups, and Brand Meaning." *Journal of Consumer Research* 32: 378–89. (An important paper that sets the stage for how self-construal interacts with reference groups in influencing brand meaning.)

Fournier, S. (1998) "Consumers and Their Brands: Developing Relationship Theory in Consumer Research." *Journal of Consumer Research* 24: 343–73. (This paper provides important theoretical arguments for consumer-brand relationships.)

Swaminathan, V., Page, K.L. and Gürhan-Canli, Z. (2007) "'My' Brand or 'Our' Brand: The Effects of Brand Relationship Dimensions and Self-construal on Brand Evaluations." *Journal of Consumer Research* 34: 248–59. (This research examines how self-construal and brand dimensions interact to influence consumer-brand relationships.)

Swaminathan, V., Stilley, K. and Ahluwalia, R. (2009) "When Brand Personality Matters: The Moderating Role of Attachment Styles." *Journal of Consumer Research* 35: 985–1002. (This research shows that individuals' attachment styles influence their propensity to choose different brand personalities.)

References

Aaker, J.L. (1997) "Dimensions of Brand Personality." *Journal of Marketing Research* 34: 347–56.

——(1999) "The Malleable Self: The Role of Self-expression in Persuasion." *Journal of Marketing Research* 36: 45–57.

Aaker, J.L., Fournier, S. and Brasel, S. (2004) "When Good Brands Do Bad." *Journal of Consumer Research* 31: 1–16.

Aggarwal, P. and Law, S. (2005) "Role of Relationship Norms in Processing Brand Information." *Journal of Consumer Research* 32: 453–64.

Aggarwal, P. and Zhang, Meng (2006) "The Moderating Effect of Relationship Norm Salience on Consumers' Loss Aversion." *Journal of Consumer Research* 33: 413–19.

Bartholomew, K. and Horowitz, L.M. (1991) "Attachment Styles Among Young Adults: A Test of a Four-category Model." *Journal of Personality and Social Psychology* 61: 226–44.

Baumeister, R.F. and Leary, M.R. (1995) "The Need to Belong: Desire for Interpersonal Attachments as a Fundamental Human Motivation." *Psychological Bulletin* 117: 497–529.

Belk, R.W. (1988) "Possessions and the Extended Self." *Journal of Consumer Research* 15: 139–68.

Berger, J. and Heath, C. (2008) "Who Drives Divergence? Identity Signaling, Out-group Similarity, and the Abandonment of Cultural Tastes." *Journal of Personality and Social Psychology* 95: 593–607.

Bowlby, J. (1969) *Attachment and Loss: Vol. 1. Attachment.* New York: Basic Books.

Brewer, M.B. and Gardner, W.L. (1996) "Who is This "We"? Levels of Collective Identity and Self Representations." *Journal of Personality and Social Psychology* 71: 83–93.

Campbell, J.D., Trapnell, P.D., Heine, S.J., Katz, I.M., Lavallee, L.F., and Lehman, D.R. (1996) "Self-concept Clarity: Measurement, Personality Correlates, and Cultural Boundaries." *Journal of Personality and Social Psychology* 70: 141–56.

Chaplin, L.N. and John, D.R. (2005) "The Development of Self-brand Connections in Children and Adolescents." *Journal of Consumer Research* 32: 119–29.

Cheng, S.Y.Y., White, T.B. and Chaplin, L.N. (2011) "The Effects of Self-brand Connections on Responses to Brand Failure: A New Look at the Consumer-brand Relationship." *Journal of Consumer Psychology*. doi:10.1016/j.jcps.2011.05.00.

Dommer, S.L., Swaminathan, V., and Gürhan-Canli, Z. (2011) "Who Forgives When Companies Err? Applying Attachment Theory to Explain Consumer Responses to Company Transgressions." Working paper. The Joseph M. Katz Graduate School of Business, University of Pittsburgh.

Escalas, J.E. and Bettman, J.R. (2000) "Using Narratives to Discern Self Identity Related Consumer Goals and Motivations." In R. Ratneshwar, D. Mick, and C. Huffman (eds), *The Why of Consumption: Perspective on Consumer Motives, Goals, and Desires.* New York: Routledge Press.

Escalas, J.E. and Bettman, J.R. (2005) "Self-Construal, Reference Groups, and Brand Meaning." *Journal of Consumer Research* 32: 378–89.

Fournier, S. (1998) "Consumers and Their Brands: Developing Relationship Theory in Consumer Research." *Journal of Consumer Research* 24: 343–73.

Hazan, C. and Shaver, P.R. (1987) "Romantic Love Conceptualized as an Attachment Process." *Journal of Personality and Social Psychology* 52: 511–24.

Kleine, S.S., Kleine, R.E., and Allen, C.T. (1995) "How is a Possession "Me" or "Not Me"? Characterizing Types and an Antecedent of Material Possession Attachment." *Journal of Consumer Research* 22: 327–43.

Lau-Gesk, L. (2003) "Activating Culture Through Persuasion Appeals: An Examination of the Bicultural Consumer." *Journal of Consumer Psychology* 13: 301–15.

Malär, L., Krohmer, H., Hoyer, W.D. and Nyffenegger, B. (2011) "Emotional Brand Attachment and Brand Personality: The Relative Importance of the Actual and the Ideal Self." *Journal of Marketing* 75: 35–52.

Markus, H.R. and Kitayama, S. (1991) "Culture and the Self: Implications for Cognition, Emotion and Motivation." *Psychological Review* 98: 224–53.

Monga, A.B. and Lau-Gesk, L. (2007) "Blending Co-brand Personalities: An Examination of the Complex Self." *Journal of Marketing Research* 44: 389–400.

Park, J.K. and John, D.R. (2010) "Got to Get You into My Life: Do Brand Personalities Rub Off on Consumers?" *Journal of Consumer Research* 37: 655–69.

Park, C.W., MacInnis, D.J., Priester, J., Eisingerich, A., and Iacobucci, D. (2010) "Brand Attachment and Strong Positive Brand Attitudes: Conceptual and Empirical Differentiation of Two Critical Brand Equity Drivers." *Journal of Marketing* 74: 1–17.

Paulssen, M. and Fournier, S. (2007) "Attachment Security and the Strength of Commercial Relationships: A Longitudinal Study." Manuscript in preparation. Boston University School of Management.

Pierce, T. and Lydon, J. (1998) "Priming Relational Schemas: Effects of Contextually Activated and Chronically Accessible Interpersonal Expectations on Responses to a Stressful Event." *Journal of Personality & Social Psychology* 75: 1441–48.

Ratner, R.K. and Kahn, B.E. (2002) "The Impact of Private Versus Public Consumption on Variety-seeking Behavior." *Journal of Consumer Research* 29: 246–57.

Reed, A., II (2004) "Activating the Self-importance of Consumer Selves: Exploring Identity Salience Effects on Judgments." *Journal of Consumer Research* 31: 286–95.

Sirgy, J. (1982) "Self-concept in Consumer Behavior: A Critical Review." *Journal of Consumer Research* 9: 287–300.

Spencer-Rodgers, J., Boucher, H.C., Mori, S., Peng, K., and Wang, L. (2009) "The Dialectical Self-concept: Contradiction, Change, and Holism in East Asian Cultures." *Personality and Social Psychology Bulletin* 35: 29–44.

Spencer-Rodgers, J., Williams, M.J., and Peng, K. (2010) "Cultural Differences in Expectations of Change and Tolerance for Contradiction: A Decade of Empirical Research." *Personality and Social Psychology Review* 14: 296–312.

Sprott, D., Czellar, S., and Spangenberg, E. (2009) "The Importance of a General Measure of Brand Engagement on Market Behavior: Development and Validation of a Scale." *Journal of Marketing Research* 46: 92–104.

Stucke, T.S. and Spore, S.L. (2002) "When a Grandiose Self-image is Threatened: Narcissism and Self-concept Clarity as Predictors of Negative Emotions and Aggression Following Ego-threat." *Journal of Personality* 70: 509–32.

Swaminathan, V., Page, K.L., and Gürhan-Canli, Z. (2007) "'My' Brand or 'Our' Brand: The Effects of Brand Relationship Dimensions and Self-construal on Brand Evaluations." *Journal of Consumer Research* 34: 248–59.

Swaminathan, V., Stilley, K., and Ahluwalia, R. (2009) "When Brand Personality Matters: The Moderating Role of Attachment Styles." *Journal of Consumer Research* 35: 985–1002.

Thomson, M. and Johnson, A.R. (2006) "Marketplace and Personal Space: Investigating the Differential Effects of Attachment Style Across Relationship Contexts." *Psychology & Marketing* 23: 711–26.

Thomson, M., MacInnis, D.J. and Park, C.W. (2005) "The Ties That Bind: Measuring the Strength of Consumers' Emotional Attachments to Brands." *Journal of Consumer Psychology* 15: 77–91.

Wallendorf, M. and Arnould, E.J. (1988) "My Favorite Things: A Cross-cultural Inquiry into Object Attachment, Possessiveness, and Social Linkage." *Journal of Consumer Research* 14: 531–47.

White, K. and Dahl, D. (2006) "To Be or Not To Be? The Influence of Dissociative Reference Groups on Consumer Preferences." *Journal of Consumer Psychology* 16: 404–14.

——(2007) "Are All Outgroups Created Equal? Consumer Identity and Dissociative Influence." *Journal of Consumer Research* 34: 525–36.

37

THE BRAND IS "ME"

Exploring the effect of self-brand connections on processing brand information as self-information

Jennifer Edson Escalas and James R. Bettman

Introduction

People use products and brands in part to create and represent desired self-images and to present these images to others or to themselves. That is, consumers value psychological and symbolic brand benefits because these benefits can help them construct their self-identity and/or present themselves to others. Brands can act as symbols of personal accomplishment, provide self-esteem, allow one to differentiate oneself and express individuality, and help people through life transitions. Brands can also be used as tools for social integration or to connect us to the past. In the process of using brands to construct self-identities, the set of brand associations may become linked to the consumer's mental representation of self. We conceptualize and operationalize this linkage at the aggregate level as self-brand connections, the extent to which individuals have incorporated specific brands into their self-concepts.

Our framework is based on the idea that people engage in consumption behavior in part to construct their self-concepts and to create their personal identities (Richins 1994; McCracken 1989; Belk 1988). As a result of this process, the brand and its associations become linked with the consumer's mental representation of the self. For especially close connections, one can assert that the brand becomes part of the self-concept. Below, we report on a series of studies that explore how the incorporation of brands into the self-concept influences how information about those brands is processed, replicating well-established effects for how information about the self is processed, to provide empirical evidence of our assertion that the brand is indeed thought of as part of the self-concept. In our study, we find that consumers blame the situation, rather than the brand, in the face of brand failure, replicating self-serving biases (Miller and Ross 1975). Additionally, we find that failure of the brand to achieve ought expectations results in agitation-related emotions, while ideal brand discrepancies result in dejection-related emotions, consistent with self-discrepancy theory (Higgins *et al.* 1986).

Self-brand connections

For a particular individual, there are at least two aspects of what a brand means. First, there is the brand's image, which is primarily a function of marketers' actions and other external influences, such as culture. McCracken's (1986) model of meaning transfer asserts that meanings "get into" a brand through advertising, the fashion system, and other cultural influences. Second, what a brand means to a particular consumer is influenced by his or her personal experiences with the brand. Consumers bring their own life experiences with them to every encounter with a brand or communication about a brand. While theoretically difficult to capture, idiosyncratic aspects of brand meaning are important. Hirschman (1980) found that roughly one-fourth of meaning was idiosyncratic (see also Richins 1994). Rather than approaching "meaning" as a set of specific associations with a brand, the self-brand connection concept allows consumers to ascribe their own meanings to brands and examines the intensity of the relationship between the brand and the consumer's self-concept.

Consumers value products and brands for different reasons. One reason is for a product's instrumental features or attributes, which provide tangible benefits. For example, cars provide transportation, and salt adds flavor to food. On the other hand, sometimes consumers form a special, self-brand connection with products or brands. Consumers ascribe these brands with an intrinsic meaning that makes them worth more than the value of their features or instrumental benefits. As an example of special meaning, many people have become particularly attached to their iPhone. The phone's features allow them to connect to others via calling, texting, and applications such as Facebook. Important memories become associated with the phone, in part because the phone takes and stores photos and videos, but also because the phone becomes part of personal experiences of the consumer. Based on more than just functional features, the phone gives its owners a community with other owners with which they can bond, by sharing phone experiences, pictures, and apps. Beyond the iPhone, phone owners may also feel part of the more general Apple community. The phone also has an innovative, trendy, stylish image that consumers can appropriate for themselves: the phone reflects that they too are "cool." As an expensive device, the phone may also symbolize status and/or accomplishment. Given the many apps available on the phone, it also can facilitate social interactions and help meet needs for affiliation. Based on any or all of these factors, the consumer may come to associate positive feelings and memories with the iPhone. Obviously, the phone's functional performance needs to be strong as well, but while many other brands of phone may perform equally well and offer the same features, for this consumer the iPhone may become incorporated into the consumer's sense of self. It represents a part of who that consumer is and can be used to communicate this identity to others.

How does this meaning become associated with the brand? In order to understand this process, we must recognize that brands have symbolic properties that extend beyond their functional benefits (Levy 1959). As such, brands can be used to meet higher order, psychological needs, such as self-construction, social integration, self-differentiation, and self-presentation (e.g. Kleine *et al.* 1995; Richins 1994; Ball and Tasaki 1992; Shultz *et al.* 1989; McCracken 1989; Belk 1988). Levy (1959) claims that brands, as symbols, take on meaning when they join with, add to, and reinforce the way consumers think about themselves.

McCracken's (1986) model of meaning transfer asserts that meaning originates in the culturally constituted world, moving into goods via the fashion system, word of mouth, reference groups, subcultural groups, celebrities, and the media. Next, meaning moves from goods to consumers, as consumers construct themselves through their brand choices based on congruency between brand image and self-image. Thus, the meaning and value of a brand is not just its ability to express the self, but also its role in helping consumers create and build their self-identities (McCracken 1989).

In order to study these meanings of brands, we must be able to measure the relationship between the brand and the consumer's sense of self. This relationship between consumers' self-concepts and brands is referred to as self-brand connections because these brands become associated with, or connected to, consumers' mental representations of self. We focus on self-brand connections, rather than specific brand associations, because we believe that brand meaning is most often dependent upon the entire constellation, or gestalt, or the set of brand associations. In sum, the self-brand connection scale comprehensively examines the link between brands and consumers' self-concepts, treating consumers' interactions with brands as a constructive, active process.

Our research has provided a series of empirical demonstrations of McCracken's (1989) ideas by demonstrating that reference group brand usage and celebrity endorsement are sources of symbolic brand meaning (e.g. Escalas and Bettman 2009). Consumers connect with the symbolism associated with the reference group or celebrity and the brands they use or endorse, transferring these meanings from the brand to themselves as they actively construct themselves by selecting brands with meanings relevant to an aspect of their self-concept.

In our reference group research, we find that consumers are more likely to develop a self-brand connection when there is a strong usage association between a reference group and the brand *and* there is a strong connection between the reference group and the consumer's self-concept (Escalas and Bettman 2003). When this scenario exists, the consumer may appropriate user imagery and psychological benefit associations of the brand to meet a self-need, such as self-enhancement or self-verification. In the case of self-verifiers, member groups have a larger effect on self-brand connections, while for self-enhancers, the effect of aspiration groups on self-brand connections is greater. Thus, consumers are motivated by their self-needs to utilize brand associations derived from different types of groups to construct their self-concepts, behaving consistently with their predominant self-motivations.

Our studies also show that consumers report higher self-brand connections for brands with images that are consistent with (versus inconsistent with) the image of an in-group (Escalas and Bettman 2005). Further, we find that self-brand connections are lower for brands with images that are consistent with (versus inconsistent with) the image of an out-group. In these studies we also find that independent versus interdependent self-construals interact with group congruency to determine the level of self-brand connections: the negative effect of out-group brand associations on self-brand connections is stronger for independent consumers than for interdependent consumers, due to the stronger needs of more independent consumers to differentiate themselves from out-groups (Kampmeier and Simon 2001). We also find that our effects are moderated by degree of brand symbolism, such that brands that communicate something about the user yield stronger effects than brands that do not.

Finally, in our research on celebrity endorsement, we argue that consumers appropriate brand meanings from celebrity endorsement to construct their self-concepts (Escalas and Bettman 2009). Our studies show that consumers report higher self-brand connections for brands with images that are consistent with the image of a celebrity whom they aspire to be like, particularly in the case when the image of the celebrity and the brand match. We also find that celebrity endorsement effects are moderated by brand symbolism, such that brands that communicate something about the user yield stronger effects than brands that do not. Finally, we find that for consumers with active self-enhancement goals, the effect of celebrity endorsement on self-brand connections is stronger, both more positive in the aspirational celebrity condition and more negative in the non-aspirational celebrity condition, compared to consumers who do not have active self-enhancement goals. Thus, our research empirically demonstrates McCracken's (1986) theory of meaning movement, revealing two cultural sources of brand meaning – reference group usage and celebrity endorsement – that consumers appropriate to meet self-needs.

Processing brand information as self-information

While our research to date has focused on the antecedents of self-brand connections (SBC), we feel it is important to support empirically the conceptualization of the SBC construct. One of the key tenets of the notion of self-brand connections is that this linkage represents the incorporation of the brand into one's mental representation of self. Similar to Belk's (1988) research on special possessions, we assert that brands with high SBC become part of one's extended self. While some research has begun to look at how this incorporation of a brand into the self influences how brand information is processed (Ahluwalia *et al.* 2000; Cheng *et al.* in press), we felt it was important to provide empirical evidence that brands indeed become part of the extended self. To do this, we build on some well-established psychological theories about how attributions about performance and the self are biased and how certain types of self-discrepancies evoke particular emotions to demonstrate that information about brands with high self-brand connections is processed in the same manner as information about the self.

Self-serving biases in attributions

The self-serving bias is reflected in attribution of successes to the self and failures to external causes (Miller and Ross 1975). In addition, people see their successes as due to stable factors and their failures as due to unstable factors. In this research, we explore whether brands with high self-brand connections will lead to attributions consistent with the self-serving bias.

Study methodology

To test whether the precepts of self-serving biases extend to brands considered to be part of the self, we conducted a web-based study with 344 participants. First, we asked participants to list four brands: one high and one low self-brand connection car brand and clothing brand, described as "representing who you are as a person" or "NOT representing who you are as person." Next, SBCs were assessed using the seven-item Escalas (2004) scale ($\alpha = 0.98$) (see Table 37.1). Brands listed as being highly representative of the self have significantly higher SBC scores than those listed as not being representative of the self (high = 72.08, low = 7.32, $F(1, 340) = 15.50$, $p < 0.001$, with product category not having a significant or interactive effect on SBC levels).

Participants were then presented with either a success or failure scenario (see Box 37.1), which incorporated one of the four brands (randomly assigned across high/low SBC and car/

Table 37.1 Self-brand connection scale items

Scale items	
This brand reflects who I am	0 (strongly disagree)–100 (strongly agree)
I can identify with this brand	
I feel a personal connection to this brand	
I use this brand to communicate who I am to other people	
I think this brand helps me become the type of person I want to be	
I consider this brand to be "me" (it reflects who I consider myself to be or the way that I want to present myself to others)	
This brand suits me well	

clothing products) into the scenario. Next, participants indicated their attributions for the success or failure on two dimensions: locus of causality (internal vs. external) and stability (stable vs. unstable) (SDSII scale, three items per dimension, $0.63 < \alpha < 0.79$) (McAuley *et al.* 1992). High values for locus of causality correspond to attributions to more internal causes, and high values for stability correspond to attributions to more stable causes.

Box 37.1 Stimulus materials: self-serving biases

Success condition

You are reading your local newspaper and in the business section you see the following article:

> Over the last year, *Brand* has launched a number of new products onto the marketplace that have received a large number of very favorable reviews from critics and customers alike.

The article goes on to discuss the details of the favorably reviewed new products.

Failure condition

You are reading your local newspaper and in the business section you see the following headline:

> Over the last year, *Brand* has launched a number of new products onto the marketplace that have received a large number of very unfavorable reviews from critics and customers alike.

The article goes on to discuss the details of the unfavorably reviewed new products.

Results

Our results confirm the proposition that brands with high SBC are considered to be part of the self. Our model crosses scenario (success vs. failure) by SBC (high vs. low), using product category as a covariate. We find a significant scenario by SBC interaction for locus of causality and attributions of stability ($F(1, 343) > 15.30$, $p < 0.001$). Participants make higher internal attributions of causality for high SBC brand success versus failure ($F(1, 343) = 15.50$, $p < 0.001$), and this relationship does not exist for low SBC brands ($F(1, 343) < 1.0$, *NS*) (see Figure 37.1). Similarly, participants feel that high SBC brand success is stable, but failure is not ($F(1, 343) = 5.78$, $p < 0.05$). The situation is reversed for low SBC brands (see Figure 37.2); failure is stable, but success is not ($F(1, 343) = 5.62$, $p < 0.05$). Thus, individuals make attributions for success and failure consistent with the idea that brands that are high in SBCs are considered to be part of the self. High SBC brand success is considered to be caused by the brand and to be stable, while failure is not considered to be caused by the brand and is less stable. These results parallel years of similar findings in psychology for self-serving attributions regarding one's own success and failure.

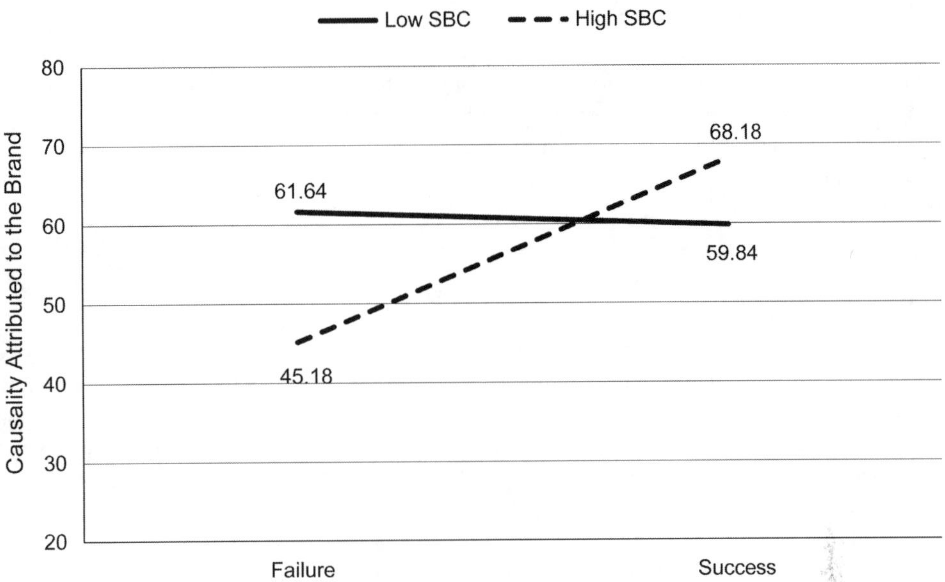

Figure 37.1 Brand locus of causality attributions replicate the self-serving bias for brands high in SBC

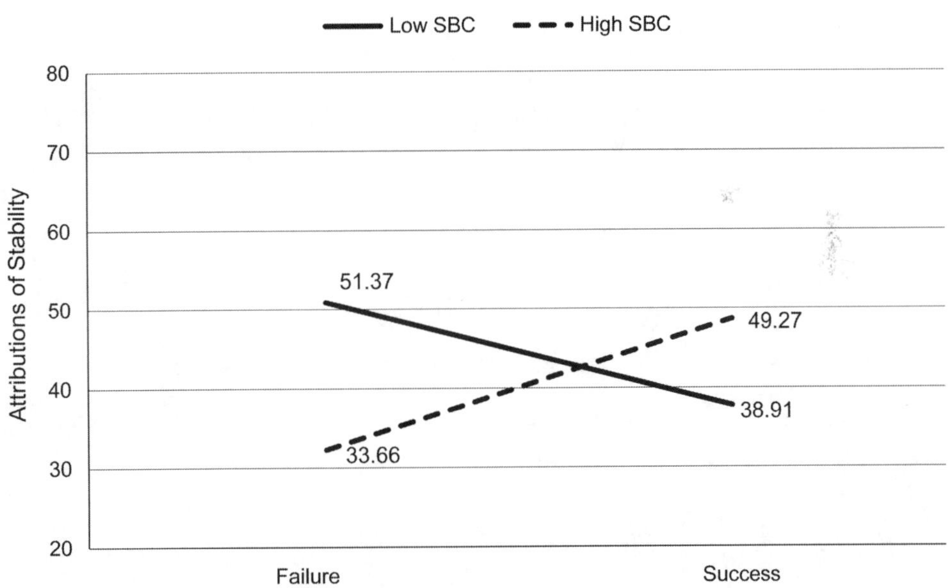

Figure 37.2 Brand stability attributions replicate the self-serving bias for brands high in SBC

Self-discrepancy theory

Higgins's self discrepancy theory predicts what type of emotion is experienced based on how well our actual selves measure up to our ideal selves (who we desire to be) or our ought selves (who we should be or believe others want us to be) (Higgins 1987). When discrepancies exist between who we actually are and who we believe we ought to be or ideally would like to be, negative affect arises. Specifically, differences between the actual self and the ought self lead to agitation-related emotions, such as fear, restlessness, or anxiety. Differences between the actual self and the ideal self lead to dejection-related emotions, such as disappointment, dissatisfaction, or sadness (Higgins *et al.* 1986). In this chapter, we explore whether brands with high self-brand connections will lead to the same type of negative emotion when actual brand behavior does not live up to either ideal or ought brand behavior, which would indicate that brands with high SBCs are considered to be part of the self.

Study methodology

To test whether the self-discrepancy theory extends to brands considered to be part of the self, we included additional conditions in the same web-based study with 344 participants described above. After the success vs. failure scenario used in the analysis above, we presented participants with a second scenario, randomly assigning a second brand from the high/low SBC, car/clothing categories elicited at the beginning of the study. This second scenario manipulated discrepancies between actual brand behavior and either ideal brand behavior or ought brand behavior (see Box 37.2). Afterwards, we asked participants to rate the extent to which they experienced agitated (anxious, guilty, relaxed [reversed], Replacement = 0.69) and dejected (disappointed, ashamed, unworthy, $\alpha = 0.73$) feelings while reading the scenario.

Box 37.2 Stimulus materials: self-serving biases

Please imagine that you read or hear the following story about *Brand* in a respected magazine or from a friend. Assume for the sake of this study that the scenario you are reading is true (when, in fact, it is fictional).

Ideal condition

Brand has let down many of its customers. BLA surveyed its customers and found that their customers felt that a company would ideally support a social cause, such as cancer research. As a result, BLA created a special program where 1% of all sales would be donated to the American Cancer Foundation. However, it has since been discovered that BLA only donated half of 1% to the American Cancer Foundation. Customers are reeling from the fact that BLA did not live up to their ideals.

Ought condition

Brand has let down many of its customers. BLA surveyed its customers and found that customers felt that a company ought to support a social cause, such as cancer research. As a result, BLA created a special program where 1% of all sales would be donated to the American Cancer Foundation. However, it has since been discovered that BLA only donated half of 1% to the American Cancer Foundation. Customers are reeling from the fact that BLA did not behave as it ought to have.

Results

Our results confirm the proposition that brands with high SBC lead to emotional reactions consistent with those displayed for the self. In the actual-ideal brand discrepancy condition, participants in the high SBC condition experienced more dejection than those in the low SBC condition (high = 49.88, low = 42.96, $F(1, 170) = 3.42$, $p < 0.05$, one-tailed). In the actual-ought brand discrepancy condition, participants in the high SBC condition experienced marginally more agitation than those in the low SBC condition (high = 27.60, low = 23.30, $F(1, 173) = 2.28$, $p = 0.066$, one-tailed). Thus, the more closely the brand is linked to the self-concept, the greater the experience of the negative emotions predicted by Higgins's self-discrepancy theory. Individuals feel dejected when a brand that is considered to be part of the self does not live up to its ideals and they feel agitated when a brand included in the self-concept does not behave as it ought, paralleling the findings for self-discrepancy in psychology.

Conclusion

In this chapter we explore self-brand connections as a linkage between brands and consumers' self-concepts. We propose that consumers form self-brand connections, which represent the extent to which consumers have incorporated the brand into their mental representation of self, when they use brands to create their self-identity and communicate it to others. We have reviewed our previous research on reference groups and celebrities as providers of cultural meaning for brands, meaning which consumers then appropriate for themselves by adopting, and ultimately forming connections to, these brands. We have also reported on a new study that explores how the incorporation of brands into the self-concept influences how information about those brands is processed, replicating well-established effects for how information about the self is processed. In our study, the more closely a brand is linked to the self, the more we find that consumers attribute brand success to factors internal to the brand and blame the situation, rather than the brand, in the face of brand failure, replicating the self-serving bias (Miller and Ross 1975). Additionally, we find that the more the brand is linked to the self, the more the failure of the brand to achieve ought expectations results in agitation-related emotions, while ideal brand discrepancies result in dejection-related emotions, consistent with Higgins's (1987) self-discrepancy theory. These results empirically support our conceptualization of self-brand connections as the incorporation of a brand into one's self-concept, becoming part of one's extended self (Belk 1988).

We close by encouraging future research on self-brand connections. In particular, how self-brand connections arise is an important topic that has seen too little work to date. For example, there may be differences in self-brand connections that develop due to personal experiences with the brand as opposed to connections formed based on the symbolic meaning of the brand. These different sources of connection then may play different roles in identity construction and/or maintenance. For instance, connections formed based on shared symbolic meanings (McCracken 1986) may more readily communicate that meaning to others, whereas connections based on personal experiences may initially be more effective in developing one's own private sense of identity. After this development has taken place, the individual can then attempt to communicate the meaning of such experiences to others. In addition to work on the antecedents of self-brand connections, important issues remain regarding consequences for identity. For example, consumers with a strong tendency to form self-brand connections (BESC) (Sprott *et al.* 2009) may use relationships with brands to compensate for either chronic or acute identity threats. Finally, there may be important cross-cultural differences in the formation and outcomes of self-brand connections, with independent versus interdependent individuals favoring different types of connections or using them to meet differing identity needs.

References

Ahluwalia, R., Burnkrant, R.E., and Unnava, H.R. (2000) "An Integrative Model of Market-Related Negative Information Processing: The Context of Negative Publicity." *Journal of Marketing Research* 37 (May): 203–14.

Ball, A.D. and Tasaki, L.H. (1992) "The Role and Measurement of Attachment in Consumer Behavior." *Journal of Consumer Psychology* 1(2): 155–72.

Belk, R.W. (1988) "Possessions and the Extended Self." *Journal of Consumer Research* 15 (September): 139–68.

Cheng, Y., White, T., and Chaplin, L. (in press) "The Effects of Self-Brand Connections on Responses to Brand Failure: A New Look at the Consumer-Brand Relationship." *Journal of Consumer Psychology*.

Escalas, J.E. (2004) "Narrative Processing: Building Consumer Connections to Brands." *Journal of Consumer Psychology* 14(1 and 2): 168–79.

Escalas, J.E. and Bettman, J.R. (2003) "You Are What They Eat: The Influence of Reference Groups on Consumer Connections to Brands." *Journal of Consumer Psychology* 13(3): 339–48.

——(2005) "Self-Construal, Reference Groups, and Brand Meaning." *Journal of Consumer Research* 32 (December): 378–89.

——(2009) "Self-Brand Connections: The Role of Reference Groups and Celebrity Endorsers in the Creation of Brand Meaning." In Joseph Priester, Deborah MacInnis, and C.W. Park (eds), *Handbook of Brand Relationships*. Armonk, NY: M.E. Sharpe, Inc., pp. 107–23.

Higgins, E.T. (1987) "Self-Discrepancy: A Theory Relating Self and Affect." *Psychological Review* 94: 319–40.

Higgins, E.T., Bond, R.N., Klein, R., and Strauman, T. (1986) "Self-Discrepancies and Emotional Vulnerability: How Magnitude, Accessibility, and Type of Discrepancy Influence Affect." *Journal of Personality and Social Psychology* 51(1): 5–15.

Hirschman, E.C. (1980) "Commonality and Idiosyncrasy in Popular Culture: An Empirical Examination of the 'Layers of Meaning' Concept." In E.C. Hirschman and M.B. Holbrook (eds), *Symbolic Consumer Behavior: Proceedings of the Conference on Consumer Esthetics and Symbolic Consumption*. Provo, UT: Association for Consumer Research.

Kampmeier, C. and Simon, B. (2001) "Individuality and Group Formation: The Role of Independence and Differentiation." *Journal of Personality and Social Psychology* 81 (September): 448–62.

Kleine, S.S., Kleine, R.E., III, and Allen, C.T. (1995) "How is a Possession 'Me' or 'Not Me'? Characterizing Types and Antecedents of Material Possession Attachment." *Journal of Consumer Research* 22 (December): 327–43.

Levy, S.J. (1959) "Symbols for Sale." *Harvard Business Review* 37 (July–August): 117–24.

McAuley, E., Duncan, T.E., and Russell, D.W. (1992) "Measuring Causal Attributions: The Revised Causal Dimension Scale (CDSII)." *Personality and Social Psychology Bulletin* 18(5): 566–73.

McCracken, G. (1986) "Culture and Consumption: A Theoretical Account of the Structure and Movement of the Cultural Meaning of Consumer Goods." *Journal of Consumer Research* 13 (June): 71–84.

——(1989) "Who is the Celebrity Endorser? Cultural Foundations of the Endorsement Process." *Journal of Consumer Research* 16 (December): 310–21.

Miller, D.T. and Ross, M. (1975) "Self-Serving Biases in Attribution of Causality: Fact or Fiction." *Psychological Bulletin* 82 (March): 213–25.

Richins, M.L. (1994) "Valuing Things: The Public and Private Meanings of Possessions." *Journal of Consumer Research* 21 (December): 504–21.

Ross, L. (1977) "The Intuitive Psychologist and his Shortcomings: Distortions in the Attribution Process." In L. Berkowitz (ed.), *Advances in Experimental Social Psychology*, vol. 10. New York: Academic Press.

Schultz, S.E., Kleine, R.E., III, and Kernan, J.B. (1989) "'These Are a Few of my Favorite Things': Toward an Explication of Attachment as a Consumer Behavior Construct." *Advances in Consumer Research* 16: 359–66.

Sprott, D., Czellar, S., and Spangenberg, E. (2009) "The Importance of a General Measure of Brand Engagement on Market Behavior: Development and Validation of a Scale." *Journal of Marketing Research* 46(1): 92–104.

38

WHEN DOES IDENTITY SALIENCE PRIME APPROACH AND AVOIDANCE?

A balance-congruity model

Justin W. Angle, Mark R. Forehand and Americus Reed, II

Identity salience is defined as the activation of a particular identity dimension within an individual's social self-schema and typically heightens sensitivity to identity-relevant stimuli. For example, being at work (home) might increase the salience of one's organizational (family) identity. In addition, being consciously or non-consciously exposed to symbols, words, pictures, ideas, brands or people can increase the salience of any identity related to these cues. Indeed, identity salience generally follows consumer evaluation of relative similarity or dissimilarity (cf. Eiser *et al.* 2001; Forehand *et al.* 2002). Interestingly, some instances of this self-categorization process may undermine one's basis for identification (e.g. if one's ethnic identity salience is increased by exposure to a threatening stereotype prime). Although such self-categorizations *can* threaten the consumer's identification with a group, the literature shows both approach behaviors, such as seeking high-status products when power identity is threatened (Rucker and Galinsky 2008) and avoidance behaviors, such as shunning gender-associated products after gender identity is threatened (White and Argo 2009; White *et al.* 2012), are possible. Given these mixed findings, the extant literature would greatly benefit from a theoretical exploration of when identity salience is threatening and what factors determine whether such threats prompt approach or avoidance.

To illuminate these issues, we propose a model of identity salience and threat that intentionally defines threats in terms of specific associations. For example, when a *man* hears a statements like "all men are pigs" the association of his gender with positive valence is threatened. On the other hand, when he is told "you are a poor excuse for a man" his association of self with male is challenged without saying anything positive or negative about being a man. As we will show conceptually, analyzing the threat in terms of specific associations enables more refined theoretical predictions for when and why threatening salient identities can produce identity approach or identity avoidance. In addition, the proposed model identifies important mediating mechanisms yet to be examined.

Identity salience precursors and outcomes

Identity salience can be increased by a variety of factors, including stable individual traits, stimulus cues, and social context (Forehand *et al.* 2002). Individuals vary in how strongly they associate themselves with an identity. Stimulus cues and social context also often produce increases in identity salience, albeit more temporarily. Simply seeing a member of a particular group (Marques *et al.* 1988; Torres 2007) or encountering identity-related images or words (Forehand and Deshpandé 2001; Mastin *et al.* 2007; Reed and Aquino 2003) can heighten identity salience. One's social context can also increase identity salience by making one feel more distinctive or unusual (McGuire *et al.* 1978) or by highlighting one's inclusion in the statistical majority (Yip 2005). These triggers can function singularly or interact with other situational variables to produce behaviors that either reinforce an identity or create distance from it.

Identity salience can produce approach

A salient identity shapes the perspective with which consumers view the world and influences the perceived relevance of new information (Maitner *et al.* 2010; Turner 1988). In many cases, heightening awareness of a particular identity leads consumers to think, feel, or behave in an identity-consistent fashion (Reed 2004). For example, those with chronically salient moral identities are more apt to donate to charity (Reed *et al.* 2007). Similarly, individuals who scored higher on global (versus local) identity, preferred products tailored to the global (versus local) marketplace (Zhang and Khare 2009), and bicultural subjects primed with cultural symbols increased their preference for objects associated with the primed culture (Chattaraman *et al.* 2009; LeBoeuf *et al.* 2010; Chattaraman *et al.* 2010; Hong *et al.* 2000; Zou *et al.* 2008). Furthermore, consumers tend to favor products endorsed by spokespeople of shared ethnicity (Forehand and Deshpandé 2001), and minority consumers prefer service encounters in which more customers of the same race are present (Baker *et al.* 2008). In the educational domain, students primed with education-dependent future selves (doctor, lawyer, etc.) were more likely to take on extra credit assignments (Destin and Oyserman 2010).

Identity salience can produce avoidance

It should not be assumed, however, that identity salience uniformly results in enhanced evaluation of identity-related objects (Wheeler and Petty 2001). For example, exposure to Spanish-language advertisements made Hispanic participants less likely to spontaneously acknowledge their ethnicity (Dimofte *et al.* 2003), and minority workers in Southeast Asia placed lower dollar values on their own work after being asked to identify their ethnicity on a demographic questionnaire (Cheung and Hardin 2010). Furthermore, informing consumers that a salient identity is non-diagnostic can turn identity approach into avoidance (Zhang and Khare 2009). In general, consumers tend to avoid a salient identity when that self-association has negative consequences for the self (Steele and Berkowitz 1988) or if the self-association triggers a feeling of loss of freedom to express an identity (Bhattacharjee *et al.* 2011).

Given that these findings indicate that identity salience can produce both approach and avoidance, a comprehensive model that identifies the moderators and key mediators of identity-based consumer behavior would be very useful.

Identity salience and threat

The studies mentioned thus far typically employ stable individual differences, contextual variables, or stimulus primes to make salient a particular identity. These sorts of activations can be either threatening or non-threatening. A self-concept threat is anything that presents potential negative consequences for the self, and simply making a particular identity salient can constitute a threat, as demonstrated by social-distinctiveness theory (McGuire *et al.* 1978; McGuire *et al.* 1979). Steele and Aronson's (1995) seminal work on stereotype threat illustrates this perfectly, as the activation of a stereotyped identity can be threatening enough to impede cognitive function and lead to ironic and unintentional confirmation of the stereotype. Such threats can be overcome by making salient in-group members highly competent in the negatively stereotyped dimension (Marx and Roman 2002).

Self-concept threats, however, are not driven solely by stereotypes. Simply casting a salient group identity in a negative light or manipulating its status is enough to constitute a threat. For instance, high-status group members tend to feel threatened when they perceive group boundaries to be unstable (Scheepers 2009; Grier and Deshpandé 2001). Alternatively, identity is threatened when group membership is challenged, leading highly identified group members to exert greater effort on the group's behalf (Ouwerkerk *et al.* 2000). Such demonstrations are consistent with social identity theory (Tajfel and Turner 1986; Tajfel and Turner 1979).

Threatening salient identities also impacts self-esteem, but it is not clear that the effects are uniformly negative. For example, many studies have demonstrated decreased explicit self-esteem in response to social rejection (for a review, see Leary and Baumeister 2000) or performance feedback (Williams *et al.* 2000), yet increases in implicit self-esteem have been observed in the face of similar threats (Rudman *et al.* 2007). Finally, more recent work shows that messages that restrict the ways in which a consumer can express an identity can sometimes backfire because they threaten the sense of freedom and personal agency in identity expression (Bhattacharjee *et al.* 2011).

Self-threats can also dramatically shape consumer preference, although the mediating mechanisms involved are not well understood. For example, threatening a consumer's salient identity with negative information about that identity leads to avoidance of identity-related products (White and Argo 2009; White *et al.* 2012). Specifically, women confronted with negative information about female intelligence avoided low-intellect female products such as biographies of Britney Spears and Whitney Houston (White and Argo 2009). This avoidance of identity-related products is a form of self-protection. On the other hand, this self-protection strategy can also produce identity approach effects. Challenging the strength of association between the self and a salient identity will lead individuals to take action to restore threatened associations (Tetlock *et al.* 2000; Zhong and Liljenquist 2006). When Gao *et al.* (2009: experiment 2) threatened health identity, their subjects responded by choosing an apple over a pack of M&Ms, most likely in a effort to reaffirm the pressured identity.

Although all of the findings to date are motivated by self-protection, the actual threats involved are fundamentally different. We propose that self-concept threats are best understood in terms of the precise associations they target. Specifically, does the threat target the association of a group with positive valence, or the association of the self with the group? Conceptualizing salient identity threat along associational lines leads to a better understanding of when to expect identity approach or avoidance.

To parsimoniously model when identity threats lead to approach versus avoidance, we present a single theoretical framework that can explain the current findings and offer predictions for consumer behavior in the face of a variety of self-threat situations. Using the unified theory of implicit social cognition (Greenwald *et al.* 2002) as an organizational lens, the proposed framework explains identity salience and threat response in terms of three types of associations: self-valence, self-group, and group-valence. Conceptualizing identity salience and threat in this fashion leads directly into a comprehensive model of threat that provides predictions for both identity approach and avoidance behaviors and the mediating mechanisms that drive them. Furthermore, this framework illuminates key potential moderators of threat response.

The concept of balance is central to the unified theory. The balance-congruity principle states that self-object relationships can develop non-consciously via the formation of balanced triads of associations through a mechanism similar to cognitive consistency theory (Festinger 1957; Heider 1958; Osgood and Tannenbaum 1955; Greenwald *et al.* 2002). A balanced triad consists of the *self*, any *object* (e.g. social group) associated with the self, and a mental conception of *valence*, ranging from positive to negative. Implicit self-esteem is defined as the measured association between self and valence (Farnham *et al.* 1999; Greenwald and Farnham 2000), an attitude is a measured association between a group and valence (Greenwald *et al.* 1998), and an implicit identity is the measured association between a group and the self (Rudman *et al.* 2001). Balanced triads form when any two associations share a common association with a third concept. For example, if self is associated with both male and positive valence, an association of male with positive will develop, completing the triad. A balanced triad can be thought of as an equilibrium state and a threat to any single association in the triad leads to predictable and specific strategies for restoring balance.

Unified theory of threat response: theoretical predictions

Applying the concept of *balance-congruity* to the different operationalizations of self-threat intimates key distinctions in how threats to salient identities operate and the responses they produce. For example, telling an American citizen, "all Americans are bad," may weaken the association between the group and positive valence and thereby throw the triad of associations between the self, the group and valence out of balance. Restoring balance requires either some form of counterargument that will re-establish the association of the group with positive valence, or a weakening of the self-group association (in unusual circumstances, this could also lead to changes in self-valence association, but this final association is comparatively resistant to change). If the threat to group-valence association proves too strong to move via counter-arguing (Eisenstadt *et al.* 2006) or source derogation (Dechesne *et al.* 2000), the self-group association is likely to weaken. As White and Argo (2009) found, one expression of this weakened association is the avoidance of products related to the threatened group. We refer to threats of this sort as *identity valence threats*.

Alternatively, self-group association can be threatened with the statement, "you are un-American." This threat could be met with a variety of responses, including acceptance of the message and the resultant detachment from the American identity, a motivation to restore balance and actively rebuild the self-American association, or a desire to reaffirm the self-concept in an unrelated domain (Shrira and Martin 2005). Gao *et al.* (2009) utilized threats of this type and observed that consumers faced with such threats sought products that would restore the threatened self-group association. We refer to threats of this sort as *identity strength threats*.

Using this framework we can predict approach and avoidance behaviors based on threat type and the expected shifts in *implicit* associations that the threat produces. Implicit, rather than explicit, associations drive this model for two critical reasons. First, they have greater predictive validity of social behavior in sensitive domains (Greenwald *et al.* 2009). Since salient identities and threats to them often involve social categories with the potential for stigmatization, the focus on implicit associations can lead to more meaningful insights. Second, their measurement via the implicit association test offers a straightforward methodological mechanism for observing the associational changes driving threat response.

Identity valence threat mechanism

Identity valence threats pressure the association of a salient social group with positive valence. If there is no opportunity to counter-argue the threat or derogate the source of the threat, a weakening of the group-valence association should be observed. Evidence of this weakening should be detectable by a group-valence implicit association test or other similar implicit measure. When this weakening occurs, the triad becomes unbalanced and the primary path to restoring balance is to dissociate the self from the group, observable through an implicit measure of self-group association. This self-group disassociation should motivate specific consumer behaviors, such as the avoidance of products associated with the threatened group.

Identity strength threat mechanism

Identity strength threats also involve shifts within the balanced triad, but the process focuses solely on the self-group association. For example, a college student's school spirit could be threatened if he learns he is the only one not attending an important school sporting event. If the threat is credible, a weakening of the self-group (university) association is expected. This threat, however, says nothing about the positivity of the group, and therefore the group-valence association remains unchanged. The self-valence association (self-esteem) is also expected to remain unchanged. To restore balance, the only possibility in this instance is for the student to do something that reaffirms the threatened association. Behaviors that exhibit school spirit, such as attending future games, wearing university-branded clothing, or purchasing university-branded products, would be expected expressions of the self-group association. These sorts of approach responses reaffirm the association of the self with the group.

Implicit self-esteem predicts strength of threat response

Investigations of identity salience and self-concept threat have largely ignored the role of implicit self-esteem. Implicit self-esteem is integral to identity salience and self-threat because it may function as a monitoring system that determines which identities within a social self-schema become salient (Reed and Forehand 2012). In addition, implicit self-esteem is a central component of *balance-congruity*, and it should play an important role in moderating threat response. Prediction 1 of the unified theory of implicit social cognition states that the strength of any single association in the balanced triad is a multiplicative function of the strength of the other two associations (Greenwald *et al.* 2002). For example, in a balanced triad of self-gender, self-valence, and gender-valence associations, the strength of the self-gender association can be calculated by multiplying the self-valence (implicit self-esteem) and gender-valence associations. It therefore follows that initial implicit self-esteem can be used to predict strength of response to both identity strength and identity valence threats.

In the case of identity valence threat, the avoidance response operates through a weakening of the group-valence association, which manifests in avoidance of products related to that group. As a consumer's self-esteem increases, his or her motivation to protect the self through this avoidance strategy also increases, resulting in more vigorous response. Implicit self-esteem should similarly predict strength of response to identity strength threats. These threats weaken

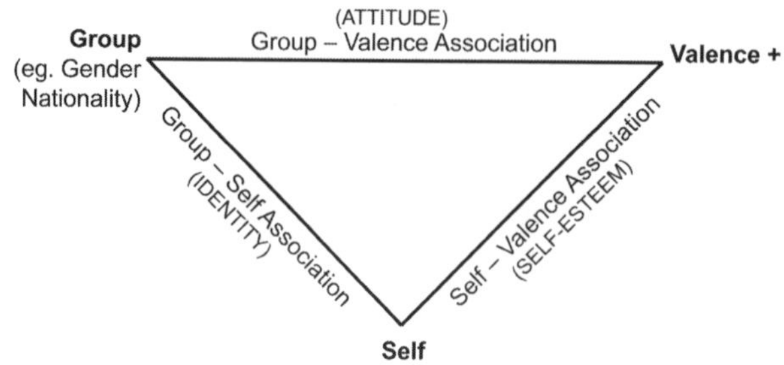

Figure 38.1 Balance triad, adapted from Greenwald *et al.* 2002

the self-group association yet do not affect the group-valence association. In the resultant state of imbalance, higher implicit self-esteem yields stronger threat response because the multiplication of the unchanged group-valence association with a higher self-valence association indicates that a stronger self-group association is required to respite balance. Consumers with high implicit self-esteem will thus engage in more forceful effort to re-associate with the group through group-related product choices.

Conclusions and future directions

This chapter presents a unifying theoretical framework for understanding threats to salient identities. Although other threat taxonomies have been presented (for example, see van Dellen *et al.* 2011; Branscombe *et al.* 1999), they have bucketed threats in terms of situational variables or outcome behaviors. We argue it is more constructive to classify threats according to the specific associations they target as this generates specific predictions for consumer threat response and illuminates mediating mechanisms as well as potential moderators. *Balance-congruity* provides the structure for our conceptualization in a single, parsimonious model. Self-threats can be conceived as attacking one of three associations in a balanced triad: self-group, self-valence, or group–valence. Whichever association is targeted will determine the predicted path to restore balance. These paths, in turn, can inform predictions for consumer behavior. This conceptualization offers a more flexible model and one that can be used to guide research projects aimed at gaining a deeper understanding of the mechanisms involved when a salient identity is threatened.

In addition to illuminating the associational processes involved in both identity valence and identity strength threat, the proposed model opens the door to two particularly interesting and important research areas. First, if identity is defined in terms of component associations, what happens to the self-concept when a brand closely associated with the self is threatened? Is the brand simply an extension of the self? If so, will threats to brands function the same as threats to groups? Preliminary evidence suggests this is indeed the case. Consumers are more responsive to corporate social responsibility campaigns when self-brand identities are made salient (Marin *et al.* 2009). In addition, threats to brands closely linked to the self can produce patterns of approach and avoid response similar to those observed with direct threats to the self (Angle and Forehand 2012). More research is needed to fully understand the processes driving these effects.

Another fruitful area for future research involves the processes by which threats shape identity over time. Repeated exposure to threats may not only reinforce or weaken the salience of an identity, but may also influence the relationship between multiple identities. One way to model these interrelationships using the proposed framework is based on the notion of *pressured concepts*. A pressured concept is any identity object that comes under consistent pressure to associate with two concepts that are bipolar opposed (Greenwald *et al.* 2002). For example, what happens when Nike, a brand often associated with both the self and positive valence, becomes associated with something negative, such as sweatshops? Nike becomes a pressured concept and the consumer's mental representation of the brand could split into two concepts – one piece of Nike associated with the self, and a distinct piece of Nike associated with sweatshops (Greenwald *et al.* 2002). From an attitude standpoint, the consumer would develop two distinct attitudes toward Nike (Cohen and Reed 2006). To date, this process of differentiation has not been empirically observed, but in practice, situations like this come up time and time again. The balanced-congruity perspective provides an excellent starting point for research projects aimed at clarifying this process.

References

Angle, J. W. and Forehand, M.R. (2012) "Implicit Brand Pursuit: The Effects of Self-Brand Association Threats on Choice." Working Paper, Michael G. Foster School of Business.

Baker, T.L., Meyer, T., and Johnson, J.D. (2008) "Individual Differences in Perceptions of Service Failure and Recovery: The Role of Race and Discriminatory Bias." *Journal of the Academy of Marketing Science* 36: 552–64.

Bhattacharjee, A., Berger, J., and Menon, G. (2011) "Escaping the Crosshairs: Reactance to Identity Marketing." Working Paper, The Wharton School of Business.

Branscombe, N.R., Ellemers, N., Spears, R., and Doosje, B. (1999) "The Context and Content of Social Identity Threat." In N. Ellemers, R. Spears, and B. Doosje (eds), *Social Identity: Context, Commitment, Content.* Oxford: Blackwell.

Chattaraman, V., Lennon, S.J., and Rudd, N.A. (2010) "Social Identity Salience: Effects on Identity-based Brand Choices of Hispanic Consumers." *Psychology & Marketing* 27: 263–84.

Chattaraman, V., Rudd, N.A., and Lennon, S.J. (2009) "Identity Salience and Shifts in Product Preferences of Hispanic Consumers: Cultural Relevance of Product Attributes as a Moderator." *Journal of Business Research* 62: 826–33.

Cheung, R.M. and Hardin, C.D. (2010) "Costs and Benefits of Political Ideology: The Case of Economic Self-stereotyping and Stereotype Threat." *Journal of Experimental Social Psychology* 46: 761–6.

Cohen, J.B. and Reed, A., II (2006) "A Multiple Pathway Anchoring and Adjustment (MPAA) Model of Attitude Generation and Recruitment." *Journal of Consumer Research* 33: 1–15.

Dechesne, M., Janssen, J., and van Knippenberg, A. (2000) "Derogation and Distancing as Terror Management Strategies: The Moderating Role of Need for Closure and Permeability of Group Boundaries." *Journal of Personality and Social Psychology* 79: 923–32.

Destin, M. and Oyserman, D. (2010) "Incentivizing Education: Seeing Schoolwork as an Investment, Not a Chore." *Journal of Experimental Social Psychology* 46: 846–49.

Dimofte, C.V., Forehand, M.R., and Deshpandé, R. (2003) "Ad Schema Incongruity as Elicitor of Ethnic Self-Awareness and Differential Advertising Response." *Journal of Advertising* 32: 7–17.

Eisenstadt, D., Hicks, J.L., McIntyre, K., Rivers, J.A., and Cahill, M. (2006) "Two Paths of Defense: Specific Versus Compensatory Reactions to Self-threat." *Self & Identity* 5: 35–50.

Eiser, J.R., Pahl, S., and Prins, Y.R.A. (2001) "Optimism, Pessimism, and the Direction of Self-other Comparisons." *Journal of Experimental Social Psychology* 37: 77–84.

Farnham, S.D., Greenwald, A.G., and Banaji, M.R. (1999) "Implicit Self-esteem." In D. Abrams and M. A. Hogg (eds), *Social Identity and Social Cognition.* Malden, MA: Blackwell Publishers Inc.

Festinger, L. (1957) *A Theory of Cognitive Dissonance.* Palo Alto, CA: Stanford University Press.

Forehand, M.R. and Deshpandé, R. (2001) "What We See Makes Us Who We Are: Priming Ethnic Self-Awareness and Advertising Response." *Journal of Marketing Research* 38: 336–48.

Forehand, M.R., Deshpandé, R., and Reed, A., II (2002) "Identity Salience and the Influence of Differential Activation of the Social Self-Schema on Advertising Response." *Journal of Applied Psychology* 87: 1086–99.

Gao, L., Wheeler, S.C., and Shiv, B. (2009) "The 'Shaken Self': Product Choices as a Means of Restoring Self-View Confidence." *Journal of Consumer Research* 36: 29–38.

Greenwald, A.G., Banaji, M.R., Rudman, L.A., Farnham, S.D., Nosek, B.A., and Mellott, D.S. (2002) "A Unified Theory of Implicit Attitudes, Stereotypes, Self-esteem, and Self-concept." *Psychological Review* 109: 3–25.

Greenwald, A.G. and Farnham, S.D. (2000) "Using the Implicit Association Test to Measure Self-esteem and Self-concept." *Journal of Personality and Social Psychology* 79: 1022–38.

Greenwald, A.G., McGhee, D.E., and Schwartz, J.L.K. (1998) "Measuring Individual Differences in Implicit Cognition: The Implicit Association Test." *Journal of Personality and Social Psychology* 74: 1464–80.

Greenwald, A.G., Poehlman, T.A., Uhlmann, E., and Banaji, M.R. (2009) "Understanding and Using the Implicit Association Test: III. Meta-analysis of Predictive Validity." *Journal of Personality and Social Psychology* 97: 17–41.

Grier, S.A. and Deshpandé, R. (2001) "Social Dimensions of Consumer Distinctiveness: The Influence of Social Status on Group Identity and Advertising Persuasion." *Journal of Marketing Research* 38: 216–24.

Heider, F. (1958) *The Psychology of Interpersonal Relations*. New York: Wiley.

Hong, Y.-y., Morris, M.W., Chiu, C.-y., and Benet-Martinez, V. (2000) "Multicultural Minds: A Dynamic Constructivist Approach to Culture and Cognition." *American Psychologist* 55: 709–20.

Leary, M.R. and Baumeister, R.F. (2000) "The Nature and Function of Self-Esteem: Sociometer Theory." *Advances in Experimental Social Psychology* 32: 2–51.

LeBoeuf, R.A., Shafir, E., and Bayuk, J.B. (2010) "The Conflicting Choices of Alternating Selves." *Organizational Behavior and Human Decision Processes* 111: 48–61.

McGuire, W.J., McGuire, C.V., Child, P., and Fujioka, T. (1978) "Salience of Ethnicity in the Spontaneous Self-concept as a Function of One's Ethnic Distinctiveness in the Social Environment." *Journal of Personality and Social Psychology* 36: 511–20.

McGuire, W.J., McGuire, C.V., and Winton, W. (1979) "Effects of Household Sex Composition on the Salience of One's Gender in the Spontaneous Self-concept." *Journal of Experimental Social Psychology* 15: 77–90.

Maitner, A.T., Mackie, D.M., Claypool, H.M., and Crisp, R.J. (2010) "Identity Salience Moderates Processing of Group-relevant Information." *Journal of Experimental Social Psychology* 46: 441–4.

Marin, L., Ruiz, S., and Rubio, A. (2009) "The Role of Identity Salience in the Effects of Corporate Social Responsibility on Consumer Behavior." *Journal of Business Ethics* 84: 65–78.

Marques, J.M., Yzerbyt, V.Y., and Rijsman, J.B. (1988) "Context Effects on Intergroup Discrimination: In-group Bias as a Function of Experimenter's Provenance." *British Journal of Social Psychology* 27: 301–18.

Marx, D.M. and Roman, J.S. (2002) "Female Role Models: Protecting Women's Math Test Performance." *Personality and Social Psychology Bulletin* 28: 1183–93.

Mastin, T., Andsager, J.L., Choi, J., and Lee, K. (2007) "Health Disparities and Direct-to-consumer Prescription Drug Advertising: A Content Analysis of Targeted Magazine Genres, 1992–2002." *Health Communication* 22: 49–58.

Osgood, C.E. and Tannenbaum, P.H. (1955) "The Principle of Congruity in the Prediction of Attitude Change." *Psychological Review* 62: 42–55.

Ouwerkerk, J.W., de Gilder, D., and de Vries, N.K. (2000) "When the Going Gets Tough, the Tough Get Going: Social Identification and Individual Effort in Intergroup Competition." *Personality and Social Psychology Bulletin* 26: 1550–9.

Reed, A., II (2004) "Activating the Self-importance of Consumer Selves: Exploring Identity Salience Effects on Judgments." *Journal of Consumer Research* 31: 286–95.

Reed, A., II, Aquino, K., and Levy, E. (2007) "Moral Identity and Judgments of Charitable Behaviors." *Journal of Marketing* 71: 178–93.

Reed, A., II and Aquino, K.F. (2003) "Moral Identity and the Expanding Circle of Moral Regard Toward Out-groups." *Journal of Personality and Social Psychology* 84: 1270–86.

Reed, A., II and Forehand, M.R. (2012) "A Return to the Self: A Review of Critical Constructs Processes and an Agenda for Future Research or Social Identity." Wharton Working Paper Series.

Rucker, D.D. and Galinsky, A.D. (2008) "Desire to Acquire: Powerlessness and Compensatory Consumption." *Journal of Consumer Research* 35: 257–67.

Rudman, L.A., Dohn, M.C., and Fairchild, K. (2007) "Implicit Self-esteem Compensation: Automatic Threat Defense." *Journal of Personality and Social Psychology* 93: 798–813.

Rudman, L.A., Greenwald, A.G., and McGhee, D.E. (2001) "Implicit Self-concept and Evaluative Implicit Gender Stereotypes: Self and Ingroup Share Desirable Traits." *Personality and Social Psychology Bulletin* 27: 1164–78.

Scheepers, D. (2009) "Turning Social Identity Threat into Challenge: Status Stability and Cardiovascular Reactivity During Inter-group Competition." *Journal of Experimental Social Psychology* 45: 228–33.

Shrira, I. and Martin, L.L. (2005) "Stereotyping, Self-affirmation, and the Cerebral Hemispheres." *Personality and Social Psychology Bulletin* 31: 846–56.

Steele, C.M. and Aronson, J. (1995) "Stereotype Threat and the Intellectual Test Performance of African Americans." *Journal of Personality and Social Psychology* 69: 797.

Steele, C.M. and Berkowitz, L. (1988) "The Psychology of Self-affirmation: Sustaining the Integrity of the Self." *Advances in Experimental Social Psychology, Vol. 21: Social Psychological Studies of the Self: Perspectives and Programs*. San Diego, CA: Academic Press.

Tajfel, H. and Turner, J.C. (1979) *An Integrative Theory of Intergroup Conflict*. Monterey, CA: Brooks/Cole.

Tajfel, H. and Turner, J.C. (eds) (1986) *The Social Identity Theory of Intergroup Behaviour*. Chicago, IL: Nelson-Hall.

Tetlock, P.E., Kristel, O.V., Elson, S.B., Green, M.C., and Lerner, J.S. (2000) "The Psychology of the Unthinkable: Taboo Trade-offs, Forbidden Base Rates, and Heretical Counterfactuals." *Journal of Personality and Social Psychology* 78: 853–70.

Torres, I.M. (2007) "A Tale of Two Theories: Sympathy or Competition?" *Journal of Business Research* 60: 197–205.

Turner, J.C. (1988) *Rediscovering the Social Group: A Self-categorization Theory*. Oxford: Basil Blackwell.

van Dellen, M., Campbell, W., Hoyle, R., and Bradfield, E. (2011) "Compensating, Resisting, and Breaking: A Meta-Analytic Examination of Reactions to Self-Esteem Threat." *Personality and Social Psychology Review* 15: 51–74.

Wheeler, S.C. and Petty, R.E. (2001) "The Effects of Stereotype Activation on Behavior: A Review of Possible Mechanisms." *Psychological Bulletin* 127: 797–826.

White, K. and Argo, J.J. (2009) "Social Identity Threat and Consumer Preferences." *Journal of Consumer Psychology* 19: 313–25.

White, K., Argo, J.J., and Sengupta, J. (2012) "Associative Versus Dissociative Responses to Social Identity Threat: The Role of Consumer Self-Construal." *Journal of Consumer Research* (December, forthcoming).

Williams, K.D., Cheung, C.K.T., and Choi, W. (2000) "Cyberostracism: Effects of Being Ignored over the Internet." *Journal of Personality and Social Psychology* 79: 748–62.

Yip, T. (2005) "Sources of Situational Variation in Ethnic Identity and Psychological Well-Being: A Palm Pilot Study of Chinese American Students." *Personality and Social Psychology Bulletin* 31: 1603–16.

Zhang, Y. and Khare, A. (2009) "The Impact of Accessible Identities on the Evaluation of Global Versus Local Products." *Journal of Consumer Research* 36: 524–37.

Zhong, C.-B. and Liljenquist, K. (2006) "Washing Away Your Sins: Threatened Morality and Physical Cleansing." *Science* 313: 1451–2.

Zou, X., Morris, M.W., and Benet-Martinez, V. (2008) "Identity Motives and Cultural Priming: Cultural (Dis)identification in Assimilative and Contrastive Responses." *Journal of Experimental Social Psychology* 44: 1151–9.

IV.II

Advertising, media, and self

39

MEDIA IMAGE EFFECTS ON THE SELF

Daniele Mathras, Katherine E. Loveland and Naomi Mandel

This chapter explores some of the inherent complexities of how exposure to media images, such as advertisements using thin, attractive models, affects self-esteem. While conventional wisdom suggests that the prevalent use of thin models makes women feel badly about themselves, this chapter calls this idea into question by exploring how factors such as the extremity of the size of the model and the viewer's own body size can help determine whether such media effects are positive or negative. Media images define consumers' worlds by sketching societal ideals (Lippmann 1922) of physical attractiveness (Wertheim *et al.* 1997) as well as wealth (Shrum *et al.* 2005). Frequent exposure to such images creates unrealistic perceptions about the prevalence of these norms in society. At present, when more than 60% of women in America are considered overweight (26.9%) or obese (33.7%) (US National Center for Health Statistics 2003–6), while the majority of media images project a thin ideal, it is no surprise that 50% of young women report dissatisfaction with their bodies (Bearman *et al.* 2006). The resulting dieting behavior can lead to further lowered self-esteem, weight fluctuations, and eating disorders (Polivy and Herman 1995).

In an effort to combat the negative effects of thin media images on self-esteem, some organizations have taken action to diminish consumers' exposure to these idealized images. For example, Milan and Madrid fashion week organizers recently banned extremely thin models from the catwalk (Tan 2007). Additionally, Dove used average-sized and overweight models in their first "Campaign for Real Beauty" in order to convey the message that ultra-thin is not the only shape that is beautiful. While these efforts have received support from the public, recent research from Smeesters *et al.* (2010) suggests that they may not be serving their intended purpose of helping women's self-esteem, due to the processes of social comparison and selective accessibility (Mussweiler 2003). In the balance of this chapter, we discuss social comparison processes and self-esteem, the selective accessibility model, the state of current research, and directions for future research.

Social comparison processes and self-esteem

Most researchers in this domain utilize social comparison theory (Festinger 1954) to explain the process resulting from exposure to media images. Social comparison is an automatic process by which individuals evaluate their own attributes and abilities in comparison to the attributes and abilities of someone else (i.e. a comparison standard). When they find similarities between their own attributes and those of the comparison standard, their self-evaluation assimilates to the standard, and when they find dissimilarities between their own attributes and those of the comparison standard, their self-evaluation contrasts away from the standard (Mussweiler 2003; Schwarz and Bless 1992). While social comparison theory has been widely supported when used to study how thin images impact self-judgments, the findings have often been contradictory, with some studies finding that exposure to idealized thin images leads to decreased self-esteem and others finding that exposure to idealized thin images leads to increased self-esteem.

The roles of assimilation and contrast in upward and downward social comparisons

Historically, researchers have primarily demonstrated the negative effects of thin media images on appearance self-esteem and body satisfaction (Richins 1991; Grabe *et al.* 2008). An upward (downward) comparison is a comparison to someone who is superior (inferior) to the self on a given dimension. Comparing oneself to a thin model represents an upward social comparison and comparing oneself to a heavy model represents a downward social comparison, because thin people are perceived more positively than heavy people in most modern cultures (Wertheim *et al.* 1997). However, exposure to a thin media image in an advertisement might also serve as an inspiration to some consumers, whereas exposure to a heavy media image might serve as discouragement to others (Stapel and Koomen 2001). Indeed, some recent research (e.g. Mills *et al.* 2002; Smeesters and Mandel 2006) suggests that whether these media image effects are positive or negative may depend on whether the consumer assimilates to or contrasts away from the model or standard of comparison.

Contrast effects

On the one hand, some research has found that exposure to thin models in advertisements leads to contrast effects, lowering women's satisfaction with their own attractiveness (Martin and Gentry 1997). Myers and Biocca (1992) found that exposure to thin media images in both television programming and commercials lowered women's body-image perceptions. A recent meta-analysis also supports the belief that exposure to thin media images is negatively related to appearance self-esteem for women; results from 77 studies and 141 effect sizes indicated that self-esteem and body satisfaction decreased when women viewed thin media images (Grabe *et al.* 2008).

Assimilation effects

On the other hand, other researchers have demonstrated that assimilation processes following exposure to thin media images can lead to self-enhancement (Henderson-King and Henderson-King 1997). Dieters who consider such thin images attainable (Lockwood and Kunda 1997) may enjoy a "thin fantasy," thereby rating both their ideal and current body sizes as smaller and increasing their subsequent food intake (Mills *et al.* 2002). Because weight and shape are personally relevant to dieters, exposure to idealized body images may serve as inspiration, allowing dieters to assimilate toward the thin comparison standards portrayed by the media.

What factors determine whether a consumer will assimilate toward or contrast away from an advertisement depicting a thin or heavy model? In the following sections, we discuss the selective accessibility model (Mussweiler 2003), as well as several moderating variables that can shape these social comparison processes after exposure to a media image.

The selective accessibility model and media effects

To resolve this apparent conflict in the literature, in which exposure to thin media images can lead to either decreased (e.g. Myers and Biocca 1992; Martin and Gentry 1997) or increased (e.g. Henderson-King and Henderson-King 1997; Mills *et al.* 2002) self-evaluations, Smeesters and Mandel (2006) built upon the selective accessibility model (SAM) of social comparison (Mussweiler 2003). This model emphasizes the importance of the type of self-knowledge rendered accessible by a comparison standard to explain when assimilation versus contrast occurs. Specifically, the selective accessibility model proposes a three-step process to explain when an upward (or downward) comparison standard leads to assimilation and when it leads to contrast. In the first step, individuals select a comparison standard, for example a physically fit model in an advertisement for shoes. Smeesters and Mandel (2006) experimentally manipulated this step by providing comparison standards in the form of (extremely or moderately) heavy or thin models. In step two, comparison occurs. At this stage, a quick, automatic assessment of similarity between the self and the comparison standard takes place. If the self and the comparison standard are perceived as similar, which Smeesters and Mandel (2006) proposed is more likely after exposure to a moderately thin or moderately heavy model, then standard-consistent information about the self is more accessible. On the other hand, if the self and the comparison standard are perceived as different, which they proposed is more likely after exposure to an extremely thin or extremely heavy model, then standard-inconsistent information about the self is more accessible. Building on the example above, the individual would be likely to make an assessment of similarity between themselves and the model in the shoe advertisement because while the model is fit, she is not *excessively* thin. This, in turn, activates self-knowledge that is consistent with perceived similarity, such as "my hips curve like the model's" or "my arms are toned like the model's." In the final stage, the individual makes a judgment about her own attributes. The type of information about the self that is activated in the second step determines the type of self-judgment formed. The individual assimilates toward the comparison standard after accessing standard-consistent information, and contrasts away from the comparison standard after accessing standard-inconsistent information. So here, the individual ends by feeling good about herself and her body because she sees how she is similar to the model.

Recent findings are consistent with SAM, even when participants do not explicitly compare themselves with the models (Smeesters and Mandel 2006; Smeesters *et al.* 2010). Smeesters and Mandel (2006) conducted a series of studies in which participants saw several successive images of extremely thin, moderately thin, moderately heavy, or extremely heavy models. The authors reasoned that average-sized participants would view themselves as more similar (and thus assimilate) to the moderately thin or heavy models, compared to the extremely thin or heavy models. As predicted by SAM, participants who formed self-judgments were more likely to assimilate to moderately sized models and contrast away from extremely sized models. Specifically, after exposure to a thin model, which represents an upward comparison standard, participants assimilated toward a moderately thin model, resulting in increased self-esteem, and contrasted away from an extremely thin model, resulting in decreased self-esteem. Similarly, after exposure to a heavy model, which represents a downward comparison standard, participants assimilated toward a moderately heavy model, resulting in decreased self-esteem, and contrasted away from an extremely heavy model, resulting in increased self-esteem.

Smeesters and Mandel (2006) provided further evidence, via lexical decision tasks, that the type of self-knowledge that is accessible drives whether assimilation or contrast occurs. After exposure to moderately thin- or heavy-sized models, participants recognized words more quickly when they were related to standard-consistent self-knowledge (e.g. thoughts about one's own thinness after exposure to a moderately thin model), compared to standard-inconsistent self-knowledge. In contrast, after exposure to extremely thin- or heavy-sized models, they recognized words more quickly when they were related to standard-inconsistent knowledge (e.g. thoughts about one's own heaviness after exposure to an extremely thin model). It is worth noting that work in other domains has also demonstrated the importance of knowledge accessibility on self-assessment. For example, in their seminal work on perceived well-being, Schwarz and Clore (1983) found that when positive thoughts were more accessible, whether through priming or environmental factors such as weather, people were more likely to perceive themselves as generally happier and more satisfied with their lives than when sadder thoughts were more accessible.

In a follow-up study, Smeesters *et al.* (2010) explored how the consumer's size impacts the comparison process. In particular, they compared the responses of underweight (body mass index (BMI) < 18.5), normal weight (BMI between 18.5 and 25), and overweight (BMI > 25) participants after exposure to extremely thin, moderately thin, moderately heavy and extremely heavy models. Not surprisingly, results for participants in the normal BMI range replicated those of Smeesters and Mandel (2006) (where the majority of participants had a normal BMI); however, underweight participants expressed relatively high self-ratings regardless of the size of the models they viewed, and overweight consumers expressed relatively low self-ratings regardless of the size of the models they viewed.

While model size did not appear to have a significant effect on self-ratings for either underweight or overweight consumers, an exploration of process measures revealed that the type of self-knowledge that led to these judgments differed based on model size, and that these differences were based on where the self is anchored relative to others. When individuals themselves represent a more extreme standard, the size of the models toward whom they assimilate and contrast should also shift accordingly (see Figure 39.1). In the case of underweight participants, exposure to both extremely thin and moderately thin models led to increased accessibility of standard consistent information (like the models, I am thin), and exposure to both moderately heavy and extremely heavy models led to standard inconsistent information (unlike the models, I am not heavy), and both of these routes increased self-ratings. In the case of overweight participants, exposure to both extremely thin and moderately thin models led to increased accessibility of standard inconsistent information (unlike the models, I am not thin) and exposure to both moderately heavy and extremely heavy models led to standard consistent information (like the models, I am heavy), and both of these routes decreased self-ratings.

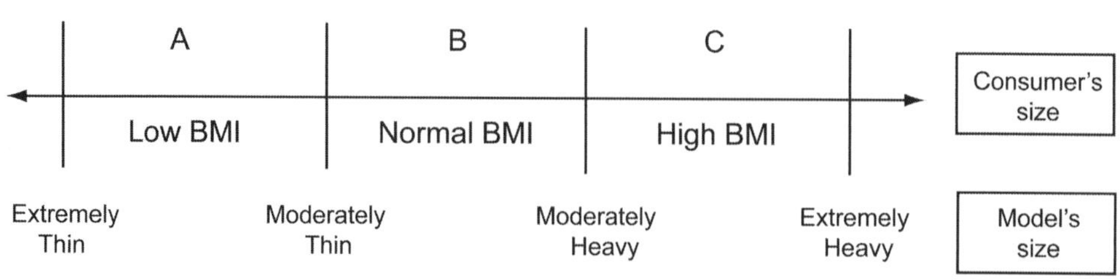

Figure 39.1 The effects of thin and heavy media images on overweight and underweight consumers: social comparison processes vary according to model size and consumer size

Moderating variables

Researchers have identified additional moderators that can lead either to assimilation or contrast effects in social comparison processes. For example, dieting (i.e. restrained eating status) leads to different self-evaluations and behavioral eating differences in response to exposure to idealized media images (Mills *et al.* 2002; Lockwood and Kunda 1997; Strauss *et al.* 1994). Other variables that increase assimilation effects after exposure to normative media images include the self-relevance of the model (Tesser and Campbell 1980), the feasibility of attaining the comparison target's desired characteristics (Lockwood and Kunda 1997), and the degree to which familiarity experiences are triggered by the comparison with the media image (Häfner 2009).

Ongoing controversies and future research in media image effects on the self

While the findings of Smeesters and Mandel (2006) are consistent with the selective accessibility model, when first reported they raised a fair amount of controversy. There have been repeated calls for more realistic, attainable, and inclusive representations of female beauty in the media, particularly in terms of body size (Milkie 1999; Creeden 2010). This call is driven by the underlying assumption that using only thin models makes women feel badly about themselves because these models represent an ideal unattainable for most women, and that using models representing a wide variety of body types would allow women to be more accepting of their own unique beauty. While this is a noble desire, the findings of Smeesters and Mandel (2006) suggest that exposure to heavier, more realistic models does not necessarily increase self-esteem and that even when it does, in the case of extremely heavy models, the positive effect is not due to identification with the model but rather is due to women seeing themselves as different from the heavy models.

Balancing marketability and consumer welfare: future directions

Marketing practitioners should focus on balancing the goals of advertising campaigns (e.g. attractiveness of models, similarity of models to viewership) with the key drivers of self-esteem (e.g. social comparison processes) that result from exposure to media images. One key controversy is the commercial viability of using a more inclusive standard of beauty in the marketplace. For example, *MODE* magazine, the first high-fashion magazine to exclusively feature plus-sized models, folded after just four years, in late 2001. At around the same time, several high-end fashion designers attempted to offer plus-sized lines modeled by plus-sized women, which also failed (e.g. Versace (*GV Versatile Couture*), Valentino (*Carisma*), and *Anne Klein Plus*). Furthermore, while several magazines (e.g. *Vogue*, *Elle*, *Glamour* and *V*) pay lip-service to the idea of presenting a more inclusive image of beauty by creating occasional "shape" and "size" issues (e.g. *Vogue Italia*, June 2011), and a few designers have featured plus-sized models on the runway (e.g. Mark Fast 2010, Chanel 2011, Jean-Paul Gaultier 2006 and 2011, Zac Posen 2010), these fashionable images of larger women are the exception rather than the rule. As such, it is possible that these "special" issues, rather than normalizing heavier models, only serve to further segregate large models from "normal" models, and are used more to create buzz and shock value than to promote positive images of larger women. Moreover, plus-size advertising campaigns that consumers view as inauthentic can backfire. For example, when American Apparel offered a modeling contest for "the next big thing," the top vote-getting contestant openly mocked the contest by submitting ironic photos of herself eating fatty foods (Krupnick 2011).

There are several promising avenues of research on the effect of media images on consumption and consumer welfare. One area that has been underexplored is the behavioral impact of media images on consumption decisions. Given that models are often one element of a persuasion tactic, understanding how model size impacts both attitude toward the advertisement and compliance with the advertisement's message are topics worth exploring. There are many factors that are likely to moderate the relationship between model size and consumer choice. For example, ongoing work by Loveland *et al.* (n.d.) suggests that both perceived similarity to the model and level of self-awareness at the time of message exposure impact health message compliance, in terms of the healthfulness of foods chosen and consumed. Additionally, Loveland and Mandel (n.d.) have found that advertisements with extremely thin models, which do pose a self-threat to consumers, may be more effective for promoting aspirational products (such as diet foods or luxury goods), while more relatable, moderately sized models may be more effective for promoting comforting, quotidian products (such as comfort foods or household goods). Message processing might also determine the effect of media images on persuasion. For example, when consumers use the central route for processing the advertisement, as is more likely for high-involvement goods (Petty *et al.* 1983), moderately sized models with whom the consumer can more easily identify might be more effective. On the other hand, when consumers use the peripheral route for processing the advertisement (Petty *et al.* 1983), extremely thin models might be more effective at improving self-esteem and directing consumption dollars.

Contextual effects represent another avenue for future research. For example, in most studies participants see an image of a single model, or several consecutive images of models of the same body type. Given that the overwhelming majority of models used in the marketplace are extremely thin, showing participants a single heavy model intermixed with several thin models might have a different impacts on self-esteem than showing a single image or a series of images all representing the same body type. One possibility is that a single moderately heavy image intermixed with many extremely thin images (as occurs when consumers see a *Dove* Campaign for Real Beauty advertisement in a fashion magazine) will heighten the negative self-esteem findings of Smeesters and Mandel (2006), since participants will simultaneously feel different from the idealized thin images and similar to the realistic, moderately heavy images. On the other hand, a single extremely thin image intermixed with several moderately sized images might cause the extremely thin model to appear grotesque when the contextual norm is heavier. Another question is how the use of heavy models in high-fashion magazines impacts perceptions of the surrounding advertisements. Given the importance of advertising revenue to magazines, this question has high managerial relevance.

Impact of non-media images

While the focus of this chapter is the impact of media images on the self, it is worth noting that several recent studies have also explored how social comparison between the self and others in the surrounding environment impacts both self-ratings and behavior. For example, Christakis and Fowler (2007) struck a chord with their assertion that obesity spreads through a community as a contagion, leading to the question, "are our friends making us fat?" Additionally, McFerran *et al.*'s (2010) recent findings suggest that individuals are more likely to assimilate their food choices toward those of thin consumers (e.g. choose a larger portion when a thin person has previously chosen a large portion), and use their food choices to distance themselves from heavy consumers (e.g. choose a smaller portion after a heavy person has chosen a large portion). On the other hand, work by Campbell and Mohr (2011) suggests that exposure to heavy individuals activates overweight stereotypes, leading to stereotype-consistent behavior (taking more food), compared to exposure to thin individuals.

Conclusion

While it is easy to accept the conventional wisdom that women would feel better about themselves if a wider range of female beauty were represented in the media, this chapter explores some of the inherent complexities of this issue. There are many factors that impact how models influence self-perceptions, not the least of which are the extremity of the model's size and the relative size of the viewer. In particular, Smeesters and Mandel (2006) demonstrate that moderately thin models can actually make average-sized consumers feel good about themselves, while moderately heavy models can make average-sized consumers feel badly about themselves. Furthermore, Smeesters *et al.* (2010) demonstrate that overweight consumers feel badly about themselves after viewing any advertisements with models, regardless of their size. Given the complexity of the issue, this is a rich area of research with many avenues open to future researchers.

Acknowledgments

The authors would like to thank Dirk Smeesters for his helpful suggestions.

Further reading

Mills, J.S., Polivy, J., Herman, C.P., and Tiggemann, M. (2002) "Effects of Exposure to Thin Media Images: Evidence of Self-enhancement Among Restrained Eaters." *Personality and Social Psychology Bulletin* 28 (December): 1687–99.

Mussweiler, T. (2003) "Comparison Processes in Social Judgment: Mechanisms and Consequences." *Psychological Review* 110 (July): 472–89.

Richins, M. (1991) "Social Comparison and the Idealized Images of Advertising." *Journal of Consumer Research* 19 (June): 71–83.

Smeesters, D. and Mandel, N. (2006) "Positive and Negative Media Image Effects on the Self." *Journal of Consumer Research* 32 (March): 576–82.

Smeesters, D., Mussweiler, T., and Mandel, N. (2010) "The Effects of Thin and Heavy Media Images on Overweight and Underweight Consumers: Social Comparison Processes and Behavioral Implications." *Journal of Consumer Research* 36 (April): 930–49.

References

Bearman, S.K., Presnell, K., and Martinez, E. (2006) "The Skinny on Body Dissatisfaction: A Longitudinal Study of Adolescent Girls and Boys." *Journal of Adolescence* 35 (April): 217–29.

Campbell, M.C. and Mohr, G.S. (2011) "Seeing is Eating: How and When Activation of a Negative Stereotype Increases Stereotype-conducive Behavior." *Journal of Consumer Research* 38(3) (forthcoming).

Christakis, N.A. and Fowler, J.A. (2007) "The Spread of Obesity in a Large Social Network Over 32 Years." *New England Journal of Medicine* 357(4): 370–9.

Creeden, M. (2010) "The Beauty of Health: Resizing the Sample Size." *Vogue.com.* www.vogue.com/vogue-daily/article/vd-the-beauty-of-health- resizing-the-sample-size/ (accessed 1 October 2011).

Festinger, L. (1954) "A Theory of Social Comparison Processes." *Human Relations* 7: 117–40.

Grabe, S.L., Ward, M., and Hyde, J.S. (2008) "The Role of the Media in Body Image Concerns Among Women: A Meta-analysis of Experimental and Correlational Studies." *Psychological Bulletin* 134(3): 460–76.

Häfner, M. (2009) "Knowing You, Knowing Me: Familiarity Moderates Comparison Outcomes to Idealized Media Images." *Social Cognition* 27: 496–508.

Henderson-King, A. and Henderson-King, D. (1997) "Media Effects on Women's Body Esteem: Social and Individual Difference Factors." *Journal of Applied Social Psychology* 27 (March): 399–417.

Krupnick, E. (2011) "Nancy Upton Wins American Apparel Contest, Has It Taken Away By Retailer." *Huffington Post.* www.huffingtonpost.com/2011/09/14/nancy-upton-wins-american_n_962472.html (accessed 14 September 2011).

Lippmann, W.E. (1922) *Public Opinion.* New York: Macmillan.

Lockwood, P. and Kunda, Z. (1997) "Superstars and Me: Predicting the Impact of Role Models on the Self." *Journal of Personality and Social Psychology* 73 (July): 91–103.

Loveland, K.E. and Mandel, N. (n.d.) "Effects of Model Size and Product Type on Message Compliance." Working paper.

Loveland, K.E., Mandel, N., and Miller, E.G. (n.d.) "Seeing Isn't Always Believing: Effects of Self-awareness on Defensive Processing in Response to a Personally Relevant Health Message." Working paper.

McFerran, B., Dahl, D.W., Fitzsimons, G.J., and Morales, A.C. (2010) "I'll Have What She's Having: Effects of Social Influence and Body Type on the Food Choices of Others." *Journal of Consumer Research* 36(6): 915–29.

Martin, M.C. and Gentry, J.W. (1997) "Stuck in the Model Trap: The Effects of Beautiful Models in Ads on Female Pre-adolescents and Adolescents." *Journal of Advertising* 26 (June): 19–33.

Milkie, M.A. (1999) "Social Comparisons, Reflected Appraisals, and Mass Media: The Impact of Pervasive Beauty Images on Black and White Girls' Self-Concepts." *Social Psychology Quarterly* 62(2), Special Issue: Qualitative Contributions to Social Psychology: 190–210.

Mills, J.S., Polivy, J., Herman, C.P., and Tiggemann, M. (2002) "Effects of Exposure to Thin Media Images: Evidence of Self-enhancement Among Restrained Eaters." *Personality and Social Psychology Bulletin* 28 (December): 1687–99.

Mussweiler, T. and Strack, F. (2000) "The 'Relative Self': Informational and Judgmental Consequences of Comparative Self-evaluation." *Journal of Personality and Social Psychology* 79 (July): 23–38.

Myers, P.N. and Biocca, F.A. (1992) "The Elastic Body Image: The Effect of Television Advertising and Programming on Body Image Distortions in Young Women." *Journal of Communication* 42 (September): 108–33.

Petty, R.E., Cacioppo, J.T., and Schumann, D. (1983) "Central and Peripheral Routes to Advertising Effectiveness: The Moderating Role of Involvement." *Journal of Consumer Research* 10 (September): 135–47.

Polivy, J. and Herman, C.P. (1995) "Dieting and its Relation to Eating Disorders." In K.D. Brownell and C.G. Fairburn (eds), *Eating Disorders and Obesity: A Comprehensive Handbook.* New York: Guilford.

Richins, M. (1991) "Social Comparison and the Idealized Images of Advertising." *Journal of Consumer Research* 19 (June): 71–83.

Schwarz, N. and Bless, H. (1992) "Constructing Reality and its Alternatives: Assimilation and Contrast Effects in Social Judgment." In L.L. Martin and A. Tesser (eds), *The Construction of Social Judgments.* Hillsdale, NJ: Erlbaum.

Schwartz, N. and Clore, G.L. (1983) "Mood, Misattribution, and Judgments of Well-being: Informative and Directive Functions of Affective States." *Journal of Personality and Social Psychology* 45(3): 513–23.

Shrum, L.J., Burroughs, J.E., and Rindfleish, A. (2005) "Television's Cultivation of Material Values." *Journal of Consumer Research* 32 (December): 473–9.

Smeesters, D. and Mandel, N. (2006) "Positive and Negative Media Image Effects on the Self." *Journal of Consumer Research* 32 (March): 576–82.

Smeesters, D., Mussweiler, T., and Mandel, N. (2010) "The Effects of Thin and Heavy Media Images on Overweight and Underweight Consumers: Social Comparison Processes and Behavioral Implications." *Journal of Consumer Research* 36 (April): 930–49.

Stapel, D.A. and Koomen, W. (2001) "Let's Not Forget the Past When We Go to the Future: On Our Knowledge of Knowledge Accessibility Effects." In G.B. Moskowitz (ed.), *Cognitive Social Psychology.* Mahwah, NJ: Erlbaum, pp.229–46.

Strauss, J., Doyle, A.E., and Kreipe, R. (1994) "The Paradoxical Effect of Diet Commercials on Reinhibition of Dietary Restraint." *Journal of Abnormal Psychology* 103: 441–4.

Tan, C.L.L. (2007) "Fashion Group Sets Guides to Rein in Ultra-Thin Models." *The Wall Street Journal* 8 (January): B4.

Tesser, A. and Campbell, J. (1980) "Self-definition: The Impact of the Relative Performance and Similarity of Others." *Social Psychology Quarterly* 43: 341–7.

US National Center for Health Statistics (2003–06) *Age-Adjusted Percent Distributions of Body Mass Index (BMI) Among Persons 18 Years Old and Over by Selected Characteristics 2003 to 2006.* www.cdc.gov/nchs/nhanes.htm (accessed 1 September 2011).

Wertheim, E.H., Paxton, S.J., Schutz, H.K., and Muir, S.L. (1997) "Why Do Adolescent Girls Watch Their Weight? An Interview Study Examining Sociocultural Pressures to Be Thin." *Journal of Psychosomatic Research* 42 (April): 345–55.

40

EXPLICIT AND IMPLICIT SEXUAL ORIENTATION

Homoerotic imagery in advertising and health

Patrick T. Vargas and Hillary Greer

Around the turn of the millennium some Americans became concerned about clothing retailer Abercrombie & Fitch's *A&f Quarterly* "magalog." The *Quarterly* was a combination lifestyle *magazine* and clothing *catalog* intended to influence young people to shop at A&f. It was very popular, with peak circulation reaching 1.2 million in the early 2000s. The controversy arose as a result of increasingly sexual content, including an interview with a porn star, sex advice regarding threesomes and oral, and plenty of images of nude and semi-nude models draped atop each other. Much of the imagery was homoerotic; for example, issue 15 of the *Quarterly* featured homoerotic imagery of male models the Carlson twins, then aged 23. At the time quite a bit of A&f advertising featured ambiguously homoerotic imagery. One such advertisement pictured a group of young men in a locker room shower gleefully attempting to pull down the underwear of another young man.

At the time, the general popularity of the A&f clothing brand and the *Quarterly* itself, seemed inconsistent with the prevalence of homophobia, and general attitudes toward homosexuality in America. Even in 2010, a sizeable minority of Americans (one-quarter to one-third, depending on the survey) was opposed to having openly gay soldiers serve in the military. Homophobia is alive and well in the 21st century. As reviewed in greater depth below, homoerotic imagery, especially involving men, is exceedingly rare in mainstream advertising (i.e. advertising not targeted toward lesbian, gay, bisexual, and transgender (LGBT) consumers). "Comedy" based on ostensibly heterosexual men finding themselves in "gay" situations is fairly common in advertising, but genuine homoeroticism between men is not. Yet A&f's use of homoerotic imagery seemed to be quite popular among gay and straight consumers alike.

The combination of homophobia and homoeroticism is a strangely recurring phenomenon. Gayhomophobe.com lists 19 "prominent homophobes" who have been involved in a gay sex scandal since 2004. The list includes religious leaders and politicians who were known to advocate against LGBT equality. Reverend Ted Haggard and Senator Larry Craig are among the most famous, but they are not alone. Wikipedia has a page named, "List of scandals involving evangelical Christians," which includes five additional prominent evangelicals who were not listed on gayhomophobe.com but were also involved in homosexual relationships.

This sort of inconsistency has been studied empirically (Adams *et al.* 1996; Meier *et al.* 2006), with mixed results. In one study homophobic and non-homophobic men were shown videos featuring male-female sex, female-female sex, and male-male sex. Homophobes and non-homophobes alike were physiologically aroused by the male-female and female-female videos, but only homophobes were aroused by the male-male videos (Adams *et al.* 1996). The tentative conclusion was that homophobia seemed to be associated with homosexual arousal; however, anxiety has also been shown to increase sexual arousal (Barlow *et al.* 1983), so the homophobes' physiological response to the male-male sex videos could have been due to either sexual arousal, or anxiety, or some combination of both. Meier *et al.* (2006) did not find any evidence that homophobic participants were attracted to gay sex.

It's not just homophobic evangelicals and conservative politicians engaging in secret homosexual relationships. In the early 2000s a number of newspaper articles and books were published about African-American men who were on the "Down Low," effectively bringing that phenomenon into the mainstream (e.g. Boykin 2004; Denizet-Lewis 2003; King 2004). To be on the Down Low, or DL, is to have secret homosexual relationships while maintaining an outwardly heterosexual identity. Men on the DL typically do not identify as gay, or even bisexual. They place great importance on masculinity and toughness, and often have girlfriends or wives. Although the DL concept tends to be applied only to African-American men, the practice of having secret homosexual relations is certainly not limited to African-Americans (see Humphreys 1970), or men.

The labels "MSM," for "men who have sex with men," and "WSW," for "women who have sex with women," were coined to help distinguish between homosexual behavior and self-identification of heterosexual, homosexual, and bisexual status. Anecdotally, many gay men speak of frequent encounters with "heterosexual" men who are actually gay. For example, a friend of one of the authors shared, "If I had a dollar for every time I've met a guy who had to go home to his wife … " Another friend's status on Facebook was, "What's up with all the gay dudes?" This was followed by comments, "With their wives and children in tow?" and "Yeah, like that's at least half of the gay guys I know … " And women's sexual fluidity has also been well covered. For example, the practice of women leaving men for other women is common enough that CNN has reported on it (Fischer 2009).

All of the preceding suggests that sexual orientation is much more complex than discrete heterosexual, homosexual, and bisexual categories. Perhaps it is even possible that people, at times, do not truly know all aspects of their own sexual orientation! Is it possible that people may have consciously unacknowledged erotic desires for members of the same sex? Certainly it seems possible that people may be unwilling to acknowledge same-sex attraction, even to themselves, but is it also possible that they truly do not know about their own same-sex attraction? We know that people can be unaware of their stereotypes and prejudices (e.g. Lapore and Brown 1997, 2002), and show serious limitations in self-knowledge, more generally (Wilson 2002), so maybe it is possible that people do not know about their own same-sex attraction. Below we describe a program of research that was intended to investigate these questions.

The use of homoerotic imagery in A&f advertising led the first author of this chapter to wonder whether the efficacy of homoerotic imagery in advertising might somehow be related to conscious and non-conscious, or explicit and implicit, sexual preferences. In the remainder of this chapter we briefly review research on advertising and homoerotic imagery, and then describe some new research that explores implicit and explicit sexual preferences, and the relationship between sexual orientation, advertising efficacy, and both physical and psychological health.

LGBT and homoerotic imagery in advertising

The representation of sexual orientation in advertising so far has, at best, been fairly benign albeit overwhelmingly heterosexual. Although advertisers have perpetuated "chic" homoeroticism to promote products, they have generally glossed over realistic portrayals of different sexual orientations; overall, representation of the LGBT demographic in advertising is severely lacking. In early September 2011 *The Huffington Post* ran an article on the lubricant company K-Y portraying a lesbian couple in one of their ads and the lack of visibility lesbians have had in advertising thus far. K-Y released a press statement about the ad stating that "[g]ay male couples have been featured in print advertising since 2008 and now the brand is continuing its tradition of support and visibility with advertising that [is] inclusive of lesbian couples" (Stampler 2011). Other companies such as McDonald's and Levi's have produced ads featuring gay couples; unfortunately, the former only aired in France and the latter only appeared on a channel targeting LGBT viewers, Logo, and both focused on solely male homosexuality rather than female.

The inclusion of any part of the LGBT community in the media other than gay males is clearly inadequate, especially obvious in the lack of lesbian representation. Two notable ads featuring lesbian characters were mentioned in the *Huffington* article but neither is without serious criticism. In 2000 an ad for John Hancock Financial Services portrayed a lesbian couple adopting a child, but was edited after it aired to leave the relationship between the women ambiguous (Stampler 2011). A 2005 Canadian ad for the Toyota Corolla portrayed a young woman's partner picking her up from her home. The young woman discusses her partner with her father, who deems the partner appropriate based on "his" (the partner's) car. In discussing her partner the young woman omits the fact that her new "boyfriend" is actually a woman. The ad ends with a kiss between the two but the father of the woman is left in the dark about his daughter's relationship.[1] Unfortunately, these are some of the only examples of mainstream visibility lesbians have. In fact, in a study of queerness in mainstream advertising (Tsai 2010), 62 ads with LGBT themes were analyzed and only nine contained lesbians and the representation of the "butch" lesbian image was mostly ignored. Other sexuality and identities analyzed, such as male homosexuality, bisexuality, transgender people, all tended to follow a similar path: bisexuality was associated with male fantasy and female promiscuity, the sensationalism of transgender women as artificially hyperfeminine, and gay men portrayed as "guppies" – gay yuppies "defined by high-end tastes and conspicuous consumption" (Tsai 2010: x). Although various orientations have been depicted in the mass media, positive and believable portrayals of the "other" (i.e. any orientation other than heterosexuality) in advertising are clearly lacking.

Sexual orientation is fairly misrepresented in the case of "chic" lesbian images in advertising. Even though "lesbian-eroticism had become a standard device in [fashion] designers' advertising arsenal" (Reichert 2003: 247), a series of ads created for Christian Dior in 2000–1 portrayed overtly lesbian themes, especially compared to earlier ads. Previous ads with lesbian eroticism had only alluded to sexual encounters; Dior's ad showed the two women strongly embracing and they appeared to be very physically aroused. Although moving away from the subdued or implied homosexual themes, women viewing the homoerotic content "did not see [the ads] as advocating lesbianism" (Reichert 2003: 251). In fact, "these sexually charged images are meant to communicate that their brand is chic and at the cutting edge" (Reichert 2003: 251). While the influence of the ads might be "liberating" for some women, it ultimately alienates those who look for representation with which they can relate.

Audiences that are exposed to more non-heterosexual advertising are usually those who seek LGBT content. *The Advocate*, a magazine directed toward gay audiences, does contain more gay-positive ads than would a publication that is directed toward heterosexual audiences or whose demographic is not based upon sexuality. Advertising in *The Advocate*, along with the format and content, has changed since its creation in the 1960s. Early on, while the magazine was actually a newspaper solely about gay civil rights, there was little advertising. Later, advertising consisted of mostly classified ads and "predominantly featured baths, bars, pornography, and bookstores" (Sender 2001: 81). This has changed in the last 20 years and "[t]he 1990s also saw the inclusion of lesbians and gays in the advertising campaigns of a broad range of national corporations" (Sender 2001: 79). Although the existence of ads featuring people of different orientations is proactive, it is still underwhelming in that it does not pervade mainstream advertising. It may reach audiences that are already exposed to and support sexualities other than heterosexual; however, others who do not seek publications like *The Advocate* may have a harder time understanding that heterosexuality is not the only existing construction of sexual identity. An important point to be made is that "the successful construction of a respectable, consuming, homosexual public is precisely what is needed for openly gay people to gain credibility and acceptance" (Sender 2001: 93).

A factor that is vital to the issue of advertising with LGBT themes is how society responds to it. Bhat *et al.* (1996) attempted to find out how participants reacted toward ads with heterosexual themes and contrasted that with the response toward homosexual themes. At the time of the study, only 5.7% of the population reported being homosexual and "39% of the American public found the homosexual lifestyle unacceptable" (Bhat *et al.* 1996: 164). The publication itself even begs the question "[g]iven the generally negative attitudes toward homosexuality in mainstream American society, why would an advertiser risk alienation of a substantial portion of a market to make a differential appeal to a very small segment such as homosexuals?" (Bhat *et al.* 1996: 163). The results showed, unsurprisingly, that those who were tolerant of homosexuality were more likely to respond positively to images of same-sex coupling in advertising. Conversely, those who were intolerant responded quite negatively. However, one interesting find was the negative response of tolerant participants to heterosexual images; they preferred the ads with homosexual images over heterosexual images. Although the article ends with a warning for advertisers about the risks involved with featuring homosexuals and states that "the use of homosexual imagery in advertisements in mainstream media is not a good idea" (Bhat *et al.* 1996: 173), the rights of those in the LGBT community have expanded greatly since this study was conducted. The current political and societal climate could very well cause people to be more accepting of ads featuring varied sexual orientations.

Oakenfull *et al.* (2008) are much more positive about the future of advertisers and the use of homosexual themes. In their research they identify three possible paths for advertisers to take to include more homosexual content in their ads. The first, which they do not recommend, is to continue to place most ads with homosexual themes in content directly focused on homosexuality such as *OUT* and *The Advocate*. Unsurprisingly, this does not reach a large number of people, homosexual or otherwise. Other options are to simply include homosexual themes in mainstream advertising – but as many heterosexuals still respond negatively to these kinds of ads, this is also not recommended – or to capitalize on homosexual subculture (i.e. including content widely known by the LGBT community but mostly foreign to heterosexuals). Oakenfull *et al.* (2008) showed mainstream ads with no homosexual content, ads with explicit homosexual content, and ads that evoke homosexual subculture to both homosexual and heterosexual respondents. In general, they found: 1 no effect of sexual orientation on evaluations of the mainstream ads; 2 homosexuals liked the explicitly homosexual ad more than heterosexuals, and heterosexuals tended to like this ad less than they liked the mainstream ad; and 3 homosexuals also liked the subculture ad more than heterosexuals, but heterosexuals liked the subculture ad just as much as they liked the mainstream ad. One interesting result of the study was the dichotomy between men and women and their responses to homosexuality in ads. Women reacted much more positively to ads with homosexual images than men, leading one to believe that "homosexually-oriented advertising content may be tolerated in cases where the audience is exclusively or primarily female" (Oakenfull *et al.* 2008: 7). Conversely from

Bhat *et al.* (1996), the Oakenfull *et al.* (2008) study promotes, rather than warns about, the use of homosexual imagery in mainstream media.

Another study of responses to homosexual themes in advertising came to similar conclusions (Hester and Gibson 2007) and implores advertisers that include homosexual themes to expand out of media directed solely at homosexuals. In fact, "such a strategy, according to the results of this study, would generate more approval and more positive attitude toward the ad and brand among audience members who are more tolerant of homosexuality" (Hester and Gibson 2007). However, more recent studies have found that "the more easily that people are able to identify the models used in the advertisements as being gay or lesbian, the more they dislike the advertisements and do not plan to purchase the products" (Hooten *et al.* 2009: 1236). Further research including more participants over a wider geographical area, as well as a collection and analysis of all the empirical studies on the topic so far, would be more indicative of Americans' view of homosexuality in mainstream advertising. Unfortunately, this is beyond the scope of the present chapter. The current uncertainty of the effects of homosexuality in advertisements does not give advertisers a conclusive answer as to how or if they should include homosexual imagery in their content.

Implicit and explicit sexual orientation

The work by Oakenfull *et al.* (2008) is the only work that we know of examining effects of sexual orientation on perceptions of advertising using homosexual imagery. In their work participants are self-identified as homosexual or heterosexual. Measuring sexual preferences is a notoriously difficult – and controversial – task (Sell 1997). Sexual orientation is generally not considered dichotomous (i.e. heterosexual vs. homosexual), but more of a continuum. Alfred Kinsey *et al.*'s (1948) original measure of sexual orientation was a seven-point scale anchored by "exclusively heterosexual" and "exclusively homosexual," with a midpoint labeled, "equally heterosexual and homosexual." Even defining sexual orientation has been a challenge, with one summary concluding that, "Sexual orientation is most often described as including behavioral, affective (i.e. desire or attraction) and cognitive (i.e. identity) that occur along continua" (Dolan 2005: 14). That summary sounds very much like the tripartite model of attitudes (see Breckler 1984). If we think of sexual orientation as an attitude, we may be able to apply other aspects of attitude research to the study of sexual orientation.

In the past 13 years the study, and use, of implicit attitude measures has expanded our understanding of the attitude construct. We now know, for example, that conflicting implicit and explicit attitudes can co-exist (e.g. Karpinski and Hilton 2001), and we know that implicit and explicit attitudes can predict different types of behaviors (Gawronski and Bodenhausen 2006). The research presented here was intended to examine implicit and explicit measures of sexual attraction, in order to: 1 learn whether implicit and explicit sexual attraction could be independent of one another; and 2 examine whether implicit and/or explicit measures of sexual attraction could predict liking for advertisements featuring gay, lesbian, and heterosexual couples. As well, if implicit and explicit measures of sexual attraction could be independent, we wanted to examine the effects of such independence on respondents' well-being. Why would divergent implicit and explicit measures of sexual attraction be related to well-being? To answer the question we must review some basic attitude research.

Attitudes serve a number of important functions (Katz 1960): they help us to navigate the world, seek out rewards, avoid punishment, etc. Having strong, easily accessible attitudes actually contributes to physiological health (Fazio and Powell 1997). However, attitudes can also be quite complex: individuals who hold evaluatively inconsistent beliefs toward a single object are said to be ambivalent. For example, one may believe that abortion is both necessary and morally wrong. If strong, accessible attitudes promote health, it follows that attitudinal ambivalence might undermine health, or daily functioning. Indeed, individuals who are ambivalent regarding certain personality traits (e.g. high extraversion, low need for affiliation) experience more disrupted marriage, more intimacy low points, and more relationship dissatisfaction (Winter *et al.* 1998). One area in which attitude ambivalence might be particularly important is sexual preference. Individuals who have a clear, strong, easily accessible sexual identity ought to be generally healthier than those who do not. In a related vein, individuals who show ambivalence regarding gender identity experience less positive, and more negative affect (Zucker and Bradley 1995). Psychologists formerly referred to sexually ambivalent individuals as "ego-dystonic homosexuals," and counted them among those who may require clinical treatment.

One obvious difficulty with assessing sexual preference is that homosexuality is often considered socially undesirable, and individuals may be unwilling and/or unable to admit their homosexuality to others or themselves – "closeted," or "repressed" homosexuals, respectively, in the vernacular. Recent advances in research on attitude measurement have uncovered techniques for obviating "willing and able" problems in assessing attitudes toward socially undesirable topics (e.g. racial prejudice; Fazio *et al.* 1995). These new measures are called implicit attitude measures (Greenwald *et al.* 1998), in contrast to traditional explicit (self-report) attitude measures. The present research aims to assess sexual preference using both explicit and implicit measures, and to use implicit and explicit measures of sexual preference to predict responses to advertising, as well as a variety of health-related outcomes (e.g. positive and negative effect, health complaints, visits to health center, school performance, etc.).

In four studies, participants (n = 78, 177, 79, 86) completed explicit and implicit measures of sexual attraction. The explicit measure was a simple 10-point scale; in all studies approximately 90% of respondents indicated that they were exclusively heterosexual. Hereafter, *all data involve only those respondents who explicitly identified themselves as exclusively heterosexual.* Two implicit measures were administered: the IAT (implicit association test) (Greenwald *et al.* 1998) and a priming-based measure (Wittenbrink 2007).

The IAT and priming measures are both response time-based measures of implicit (or non-conscious) attitudes. The measures differ in their specifics, but both rely on the idea that items with similar valences (e.g. a picture of a flower and the word "beautiful"; a picture of a cockroach and the word "ugly") can be processed more quickly than items with different valences (e.g. a picture of a cockroach and the word "beautiful"). If participants see an attractive face, they should be quicker to identify a positive word than a negative word; if they see an unattractive face, they should be quicker to identify a negative word than a positive word. Over the course of dozens of trials like this, average response times can be calculated. The speed with which these identifications occur serves as a measure of participants' implicit attitudes toward the stimuli. It is extremely difficult for people to intentionally manipulate their response times, so these measures are thought to be particularly useful when people are either unwilling or unable to self-report their attitudes. More specific details about these measures are beyond the scope of this chapter, but interested readers may consult Greenwald *et al.* (2009) for the IAT, and Wittenbrink (2007) for priming.

The implicit measures varied across studies. The IAT and priming measures always featured images of normatively attractive males and females, along with good and bad words. The exact types of good and bad words were systematically varied across studies in hopes of triangulating on sexual attraction.

In study one, participants categorized good and bad words (e.g. caress, rainbow; abuse, disaster). In study two participants categorized approach/avoid words that are more distinctly sexual (e.g.

kiss, passion; avoid, escape). In study three participants categorized attractive/unattractive words (e.g. attractive, beautiful; unattractive, homely). In study four participants categorized sexy/neutral words (e.g. lust, orgasm; walk, normal). In general, implicit preference for females would be indicated by faster response times when female images were accompanied with positive words (compared to negative words), and when male images were accompanied with negative words (compared to positive words). Implicit preference for males would be indicated by faster response times when male images were accompanied with positive words (compared to negative words), and when female images were accompanied with negative words (compared to positive words).

Participants also evaluated a series of advertisements featuring: 1 solo male models; 2 solo female models; 3 female couples; 4 male couples; and 5 male/female couples. They used seven-point scales to respond to the following questions: How much do you like this ad? How effective is this ad? How much would this ad influence you to purchase this product? How much would this ad influence a consumer to purchase? How would you evaluate this ad, overall?

Finally, participants completed a questionnaire assessing the extent to which they suffered from somatic symptoms (e.g. coughing or sore throat, nausea or upset stomach), a set of measures of psychological well-being (Ryff 1989), the positive and negative affect scale (PANAS) (Watson *et al.* 1988), and a measure of subjective well-being (Diener *et al.* 1999).

In short, implicit and explicit measures of sexual attraction did not reliably predict evaluations of the advertisements. Research on this topic continues.

Across four studies the priming and IAT measures were unrelated to each other (average correlation = 0.02). Further, there were no correlations among implicit measures of sexual attraction and sex of (exclusively heterosexual) respondents! Across four studies, the average correlation between sex of respondent and priming measure was 0.12; the average correlation between sex of respondent and the IAT was -0.03. Thus, 422 self-reported exclusively heterosexual respondents were almost as likely to show an implicit preference for same-sex images as they were for opposite-sex images. Approximately half of these exclusively heterosexual participants showed an implicit preference for images of attractive members of the same sex. These data are remarkably consistent with the Winter *et al.* (1998) study of extraversion (explicit trait measure) and the need for affiliation (implicit motive measure), described above.

Also consistent with Winter *et al.* (1998), participants in the present research who showed implicit-explicit ambivalence (i.e. heterosexual males who were implicitly attracted to males and heterosexual females who were implicitly attracted to females) scored lower on some measures of psychological well-being, reported more somatic symptoms, reported lower subjective well-being, and more negative effect. A sample of significant findings is presented in Figures 40.1–40.4.

These studies mark the beginning of a program of research, and any findings must be considered tentative. It remains uncertain that the implicit measures are, in fact, assessing sexual attraction. It is possible the implicit measures are tapping respondents' belief that the models are attractive to others, or some type of actual-ideal self-concept discrepancy (Higgins 1987). Future work will attempt to distinguish among alternative interpretations of the implicit measures by including body esteem measures, sexual esteem measures, and the like.

However, if the measures are tapping sexual attraction, these data suggest that human sexuality may be much more fluid than previously believed, and they reinforce the notion that repressing sexual attraction is detrimental to well-being (Newman *et al.* 1997; Miranda and Storms 1989).

A series of four preliminary studies suggests that implicit and explicit measures of sexual orientation are uncorrelated, and that individuals who show the highest levels of implicit-explicit conflict (i.e. explicit preference for opposite-sex stimuli, but implicit preference for same-sex stimuli, or vice-versa) tend to report suffering more somatic symptoms, and tend to score lower

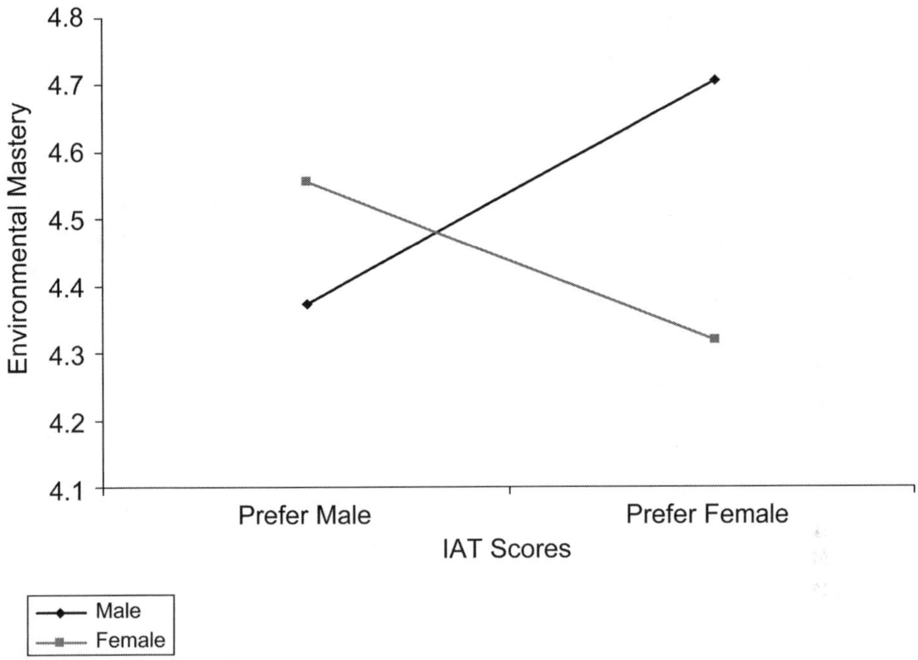

Figure 40.1 From study one, men and women who show an implicit preference for same-sex erotic images score lower on environmental mastery

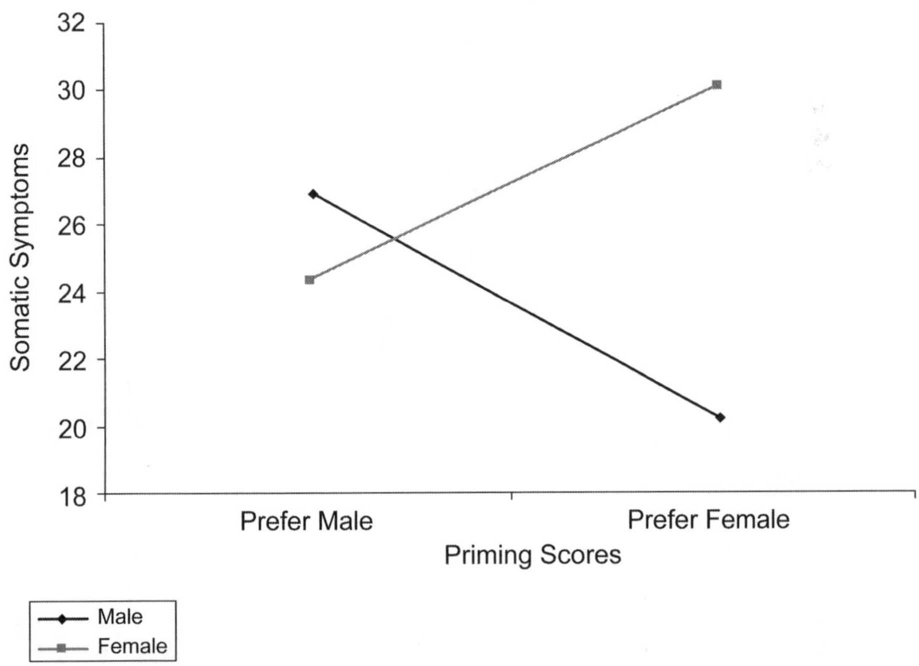

Figure 40.2 From study two, men and women who show an implicit preference for same-sex erotic images report more somatic symptoms

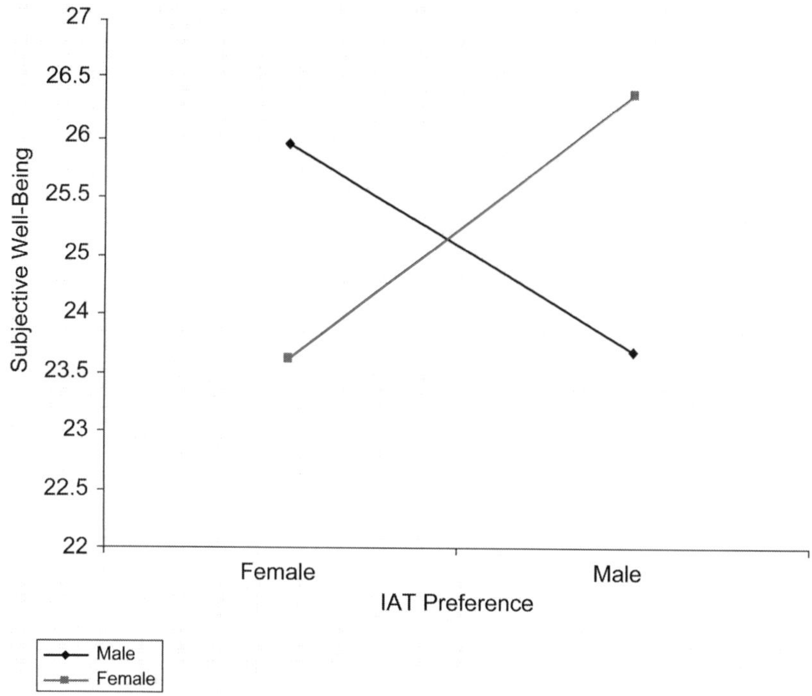

Figure 40.3 From study three, men and women who show an implicit preference for same-sex erotic images score lower on subjective well-being

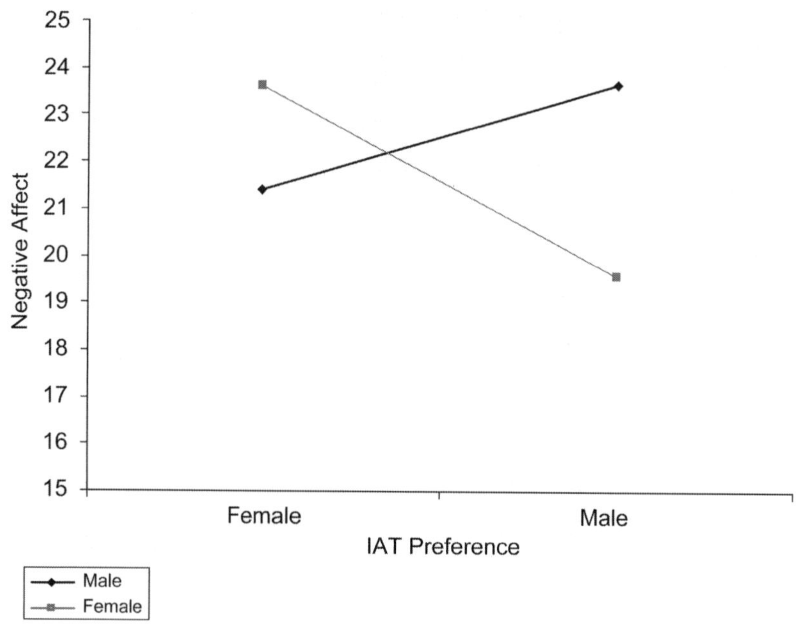

Figure 40.4 From study four, men and women who show an implicit preference for same-sex erotic images report more negative effect

on a number of measures of psychological well-being (Ryff and Keyes 1995). Unfortunately, neither implicit nor explicit measures (nor the interaction thereof) seem to predict liking for advertisements depicting a variety of heterosexual and homosexual themes.

This line of research has the potential to enhance our understanding of sexual preference, implicit and explicit attitudes, attitude ambivalence, responses to advertising, and, not least, to identify potentially at-risk individuals.

Note

1 To watch the advertisement, visit: www.commercialcloset.org/common/adlibrary/video_large.cfm?AdDetail.video=799toyota-corollaBIG.flv& clientID=11064.

References

Adams, A.E., Wright, L.W., Jr, and Lohr, B.A. (1996) "Is Homophobia Associated With Homosexual Arousal?" *Journal of Abnormal Psychology* 105(3): 440–5.

Barlow, D.H., Sackheim, D.K., and Beck, J.G. (1983) "Anxiety Increases Sexual Arousal." *Journal of Abnormal Psychology* 92: 49–54.

Bhat, S., Leigh, T.W., and Wardlow, D.L. (1996) "The Effect of Homosexual Imagery in Advertising on Attitude Toward the Ad." *Journal of Homosexuality* 31(1/2): 161–76.

Boykin, K. (2004) *Beyond the Down Low: Sex, Lies, and Denial in Black America.* New York: Carroll & Graf.

Breckler, S. (1984) "Empirical Validation of Affect, Behavior, and Cognition as Distinct Components of Attitude." *Journal of Personality and Social Psychology* 47: 1191–205.

Denziet-Lewis, B (2003) "Double Lives on the Down Low." *The New York Times*, 3 August. www.nytimes.com/2003/08/03/magazine/double-lives-on-the-down-low.html?pagewanted=all&src=pm (accessed 21 September 2011).

Diener, E., Suh, E.M., Lucas, R.E., and Smith, H.E. (1999) "Subjective Well-being: Three Decades of Progress." *Psychological Bulletin* 125: 276–302.

Dolan, K.A. (2005) *Lesbian Women and Sexual Health: The Social Construction of Risk and Susceptibility.* New York: The Haworth Press.

Fazio, R.H., Jackson, J.R., Dunton, B.C., and Williams, C.J. (1995) "Variability in Automatic Activation as an Unobtrusive Measure of Racial Attitudes: A Bona Fide Pipeline?" *Journal of Personality and Social Psychology* 69: 1013–27.

Fazio, R.H. and Powell, M.C. (1997) "On the Value of Knowing One's Likes and Dislikes: Attitude Accessibility, Stress, and Health in College." *Psychological Science* 8: 430–6.

Fisher, M.A. (2009) "Why Women are Leaving Men for Other Women." CNN. articles.cnn.com/2009-04-23/living/o.women.leave.menfor.women_1_sexual-women-danny-mozes?_s=PM:LIVING (accessed 22 September 2011).

Gawronski, B. and Bodenhausen, G.V. (2006) "Associative and Propositional Processes in Evaluation: An Integrative Review of Implicit and Explicit Attitude Change." *Psychological Bulletin* 132: 692–731.

Greenwald, A.G., McGhee, D.E., and Schwartz, J.L. (1998) "Measuring Individual Differences in Implicit Cognition: The Implicit Association Test." *Journal of Personality and Social Psychology* 74: 1464–80.

Greenwald, A.G., Poehlman, T.A., Uhlmann, E.L., and Banaji, M.R. (2009) "Understanding and Using the Implicit Association Test: III. Meta-analysis of Predictive Validity." *Journal of Personality and Social Psychology* 97(1): 17–41.

Hester, J.B. and Gibson, R. (2007) "Consumer Responses to Gay-Themed Imagery in Advertising." *Advertising Educational Foundation.* muse.jhu.edu/journals/advertising_and_society_review/toc/asr8.2.html (accessed 21 September 2011).

Higgins, E.T. (1987) "Self-discrepancy: A Theory Relating Self and Affect." *Psychological Review* 94: 319–40.

Hooten, M., Noeva, K., and Hammonds, F. (2009) "The Effects of Homosexual Imagery in Advertisements on Brand Perception and Purchase Intention." *Social Behavior & Personality: An International Journal* 37(9): 1231.

Humphreys, L. (1970) *Tearoom Trade: Impersonal Sex in Public Places.* Chicago, IL: Aldine.

Karpinski, A. and Hilton, J. (2001) Attitudes and the Implicit Association Test. *Journal of Personality and Social Psychology* 81: 774–88.

Katz, D. (1960) The Functional Approach to the Study of Attitudes. *Public Opinion Quarterly* 24: 163–204.

King, J.L (2004) *On the Down Low: A Journey Into the Lives of "Straight" Black Men Who Sleep with Men.* New York: Broadway.

Kinsey, Alfred C. *et al.* (1948) *Sexual Behavior in the Human Male.* Philadelphia, PA: W.B. Saunders.

Lapore, L. and Brown, R. (1997) "Category and Stereotype Activation: Is Prejudice Inevitable?" *Journal of Personality and Social Psychology* 72: 275–87.

——(2002) "The Role of Awareness: Divergent Automatic Stereotype Activation and Implicit Judgment Correction." *Social Cognition* 20: 321–51.

Meier, B.P., Robinson, M.D., Gaither, G.A., and Heinert, N.J. (2006) "A Secret Attraction or Defensive Loathing? Homophobia, Defense, and Implicit Cognition." *Journal of Research in Personality* 40: 377–94.

Miranda, J. and Storms, M. (1989) "Psychological Adjustment of Lesbians and Gay Men." *Journal of Counseling and Development* 68: 41–5.

Newman, L.S., Duff, K.J., and Baumeister, R.F. (1997) "A New Look at Defensive Projection: Thought Suppression, Accessibility, and Biased Person Perception." *Journal of Personality and Social Psychology* 72: 980–1001.

Oakenfull, G.K., McCarthy, M.S., and Greenlee, T.B. (2008) "Targeting a Minority without Alienating the Majority: Advertising to Gays and Lesbians in Mainstream Media." *Journal of Advertising Research* 48: 191–8.

Reichert, T. (2003) *The Erotic History of Advertising.* Amherst, MA: Prometheus.

Ryff, C.D. (1989) "Happiness is Everything, Or Is It? Explorations on the Meaning of Psychological Well-being." *Journal of Personality and Social Psychology* 57: 1069–81.

Ryff, C.D., and Keyes, C.L.M. (1995) "The Structure of Psychological Well-being Revisited." *Journal of Personality and Social Psychology* 69: 719–27.

Sell, R.L. (1997) "Defining and Measuring Sexual Orientation: A Review." *Archives of Sexual Behavior* 26 (6): 643–58.

Sender, K. (2001) "Gay Readers, Consumers, and a Dominant Gay Habitus: 25 Years of the *Advocate* Magazine." *Journal of Communication* 51(1): 73–99.

Stampler, L. (2011) "K-Y To Air its First Commercial Featuring Lesbian Couple." *The Huffington Post.* www.huffingtonpost.com/laura-stampler/k-y-first-lesbian-commercial_b_946865.html (accessed 24 September 2011).

Tsai, W.H.S. (2010) "Assimilating the Queers: Representations of Lesbians, Gay Men, Bisexual, and Transgender People in Mainstream Advertising." *Advertising & Society Review.* muse.jhu.edu (accessed 22 September 2011).

Watson, D., Clark, L.A., and Tellegen, A. (1988) "Development and Validation of Brief Measures of Positive and Negative Affect: The PANAS Scale." *Journal of Personality and Social Psychology* 54: 1063–70.

Wilson, T.D. (2002) *Strangers to Ourselves: Discovering the Adaptive Unconscious.* Cambridge, MA: Belknap of Harvard University Press.

Winter, D., John, O., Stewart, A., Klohnen, A., and Duncan, L. (1998) "Traits and Motives: Toward an Integration of Two Traditions in Personality Research." *Psychological Bulletin* 105: 230–50.

Wittenbrink, B. (2007) "Measuring Attitudes Through Priming." In B. Wittenbrink and N. Schwarz (eds), *Implicit Measures of Attitudes.* New York: Guilford Press, pp. 17–58.

Zucker, K. and Bradley, J. (1995) *Gender Identity Disorder and Psychosexual Problems in Children and Adolescents.* New York: Guilford Press.

INDEX

Italic page numbers indicate tables; bold indicate figures.